Client/Server Database
Design with SYBASE

Other McGraw-Hill Books of Interest

ALLEN/BAMBARA/BAMBARA • *Informix: Client/Server Application Development*, 0-07-913056-9

BAMBARA/ALLEN • *PowerBuilder: A Guide for Developing Client/Server Applications*, 0-07-005413-4

BERSON • *Client/Server Architecture, 2E*, 0-07-005664-1

BERSON/ANDERSON • *Sybase and Client/Server Computing, Feature System II, 2E* 0-07-006080-0

CLIFFORD • *Sybase Replication Server Primer*, 0-07-011515-X

CLIFFORD • *Mastering Sybase SQL Server II*, 0-07-011662-8

GREEN/BROWN • *PowerBuilder 5: Object-Oriented Design & Development*, 0-07-024469-3

JONES • *Developing Client/Server Applications with Microsoft Access*, 0-07-912982-X

JONES • *Ready-Made PowerBuilder Applications*, 0-07-912062-8

NEMZOW • *Visual Basic Developer's Toolkit*, 0-07-912309-0

ROSEEN • *InfoMaker 5: A Guide to Developing Client/Server Applications*, 0-07-053999-5

RIBAR • *The PowerBuilder Construction Kit*, 0-07-882079-0

SANDERS • *Developer's Guide to DB2 for Common Servers*, 0-07-057725-0

In order to receive additional information on these or any other McGraw-Hill titles, in the United States please call 1-800-822-8158. In other countries, contact your local McGraw-Hill representative.

Client/Server Database Design with SYBASE

A High-Performance and Fine-Tuning Guide

George W. Anderson

McGraw-Hill

New York San Francisco Washington, D.C. Auckland Bogotá
Caracas Lisbon London Madrid Mexico City Milan
Montreal New Delhi San Juan Singapore
Sydney Tokyo Toronto

Library of Congress Cataloging-in-Publication Data

Anderson, George W.
     Client/server database design with SYBASE : a high performance and
fine-tuning guide / George W. Anderson.
          p.   cm.
     Includes bibliographical references and index.
     ISBN 0-07-001697-6
     1. Client/server computing.   2. Database design.   3. Sybase.
I. Title.
     QA76.9.C55A53   1997
     005.75′8—dc20   96-24082
                                                                                  CIP

McGraw-Hill

A Division of The McGraw-Hill Companies

ISBN 0-07-001697-6

*The sponsoring editor for this book was John Wyzalek, the
editing supervisor was Scott Amerman, and the production supervisor
was Suzanne Rapcavage. It was set in Century Schoolbook by
McGraw-Hill's Professional Book Group composition unit.*

Printed and bound by R. R. Donnelley & Sons Company.

McGraw-Hill books are available at special quantity discounts to use
as premiums and sales promotions, or for use in corporate training programs. For more information, please write to the Director of Special
Sales, McGraw-Hill, 11 West 19th Street, New York, NY 10011. Or contact your local bookstore.

Trademarks

The following trademarks are listed in alphabetical order, not in the order in which they appear in the book:

AIX, AS/400, APPC/LU6.2, APPN, CICS, DB2, DISOSS, DRDA, ESA, IMS/VS, IMS/DC, LAN Server, Micro Channel Architecture, MCA, MVS, NCP, NetView, OS/400, PS/2, RS/6000, SAA, SNA, SQL/I)S, VM, VSAM, and VTAM are trademarks of International Business Machine Corporation.

Apollo, Network Computing system, and NCS are trademarks of Apollo Computer, Inc.

AppleTalk and Macintosh are trademarks of Apple Computers, Inc.

AViiON is a trademark of Data General.

Banyan Vines is a trademark of Banyan Systems, Inc.

Berkeley Software Distribution and BSD are trademarks of the University of California at Berkeley.

DEC, DECforms, DECnet, DECtp, DECwindows, DNA, ULTRIX, VAX, and VMS are trademarks of Digital Equipment Corporation.

Display PostScript is a trademark of Adobe Systems, Inc.

EDA/SQL is a trademark of Information Builders, Inc.

Encina and Transarc are trademarks of Transarc Corporation.

Excel, MS Windows, LAN Manager, Windows/NT, Windows 95, and Xenix are trademarks of Microsoft Corporation.

GemStone is a trademark of Servio Corporation.

Gupta, SQLBase, and SQL Windows are trademarks of Gupta Technologies, Inc.

HP, HP-UX, NewWave, PRISM, and OpenView are trademarks of Hewlett-Packard Corporation.

IDMS is a trademark of Computer Associates International, Inc.

Informix, Informix OnLine, and Informix-Star are trademarks of Informix, Inc.

Ingres, Ingres 4GL, and Ingres-Star are trademarks of Ingres Corporation.

Intel is a trademark of Intel Corporation.

InterBase is a trademark of Borland International, Inc.

LightShip is a trademark of Pilot Software.

Lotus and Lotus 1-2-3 are trademarks of Lotus Development Corporation.

Mips is a trademark of Mips Computers, Inc.

MS DOS is a registered trademark of Microsoft Corporation.

Motorola is a trademark of Motorola, Inc.

MultiMate is a trademark of MultiMate, Inc.

NCA, Open Look, Network File System, NFS, NEWS, NEWS Development Environment, NDE, Solaris, SunOS, SUN SPARC, SunView, and XView are trademarks of Sun Microsystems, Inc.

NCR and Top End are trademarks of NCR Corporation.

NetWare and Tuxedo are trademarks of Novell Corporation.

NeXT is a trademark of NeXT, Inc.

NFS is a registered trademark of Sun Microsystems, Inc.

Objectivity/DB is a trademark of Objectivity.

ObjectStore is a trademark of Object Design, Inc.

ONC and UI are trademarks of Unix International, Inc.

Oracle, Oracle*CASE, Oracle SQL*FORMS, and Oracle*Tookit are trademarks of Oracle Corporation.

OSF, OSFII, DCE, DME, and Motif are trademarks of Open Software Foundation.

PowerBuilder is a trademark of PowerSoft.

Pyramid is a trademark of Pyramid Technologies, Inc.

Rhapsody, StarServer E, and STARLAN are trademarks of AT&T.

SCO is a Trademark of Santa Cruz Operations, Inc.

SYBASE, the Sybase logo, Data Workbench, and VQL are registered trademarks of Sybase, Inc. SYBASE SQL Server, SYBASE SQL Toolset, Transact-SQL, DB-Library, Net-Library, APT Workbench, APT Library, APT-SQL, APT-Build, APT-Execute, APT-Edit, Report Workbench, Report-Execute, SYBASE Embedded SQL, Hyper DB-

Library, PC-APT Execute, PC DB-Library, PC Net-Library, Open Client, SYBASE Developer's Workbench, SYBASE User Workbench, Replication Server, Open Server, Client/Server Interfaces, SYBASE Server-Library, SYBASE Open Gateway, Tabular Data Stream, SQL Server/DBM, SQL Server/CFIF, SYBASE Secure SQL Server, Sybase Synergy Program, Adaptable Windowing Environment, and SYBASE Virtual Server Architecture are trademarks of Sybase, Inc.

Symmetry 2000 is a trademark of Sequent Computers, Inc.

UniSQL is a trademark of UniSQL, Inc.

WordPerfect is a trademark of WordPerfect, Inc.

XCOM6.2 is a trademark of Spectrum Concepts, Inc.

Xerox is a trademark of Xerox Corporation.

X/Open is a trademark of X/Open Corporation.

XVT is a trademark of XVT, Inc.

X Window System, XII, and Kerberos are trademarks of the Massachusetts Institute of Technology.

3COM, 3 + Share, 3 + Mail, 3 + Route, 3 + Route, 3 + Remote, and 3 + NetConnect are trademarks of 3COM Corporation.

*To Elvira Ranieri Anderson and
our nephew, Joshua Fisher*

"*Nothing in the world can take the place of
persistence. Talent will not; nothing is more
common than unsuccessful people with
talent. Genius will not; unrewarded genius is
almost a proverb. Education will not; the
world is full of educated derelicts. Persistence
and determination alone are omnipotent. The
slogan 'press on' has solved and always will
solve the problems of the human race.*"
—CALVIN COOLIDGE

"*If you resist change, you die. If you adapt to
it, you survive. If you cause it, you lead.
Of course, if you cause change you can die too
but it is a more exciting death.*"
—RAY NOORDA, NOVELL, INC.

Contents

Foreword

For the past several years, Sybase and its user community have enjoyed the benefits of George Anderson's careful testing and keen analysis of our products, from beta test through production. As an active participant in beta testing and early access partner programs, George has materially aided our efforts to deliver quality products that contain the features our customers need. As a systems integrator, George has further put Sybase products to the test in some very demanding client/server applications for some of our largest customers.

It is therefore a pleasure for me to introduce this book, in which George again displays his value to the Sybase community as an articulate commentator. This book pays particular attention to Sybase SQL Server 11 and our System 11 family of products, detailing how SQL Server 11's improvements in performance, scalability, and quality can help designers of complex client/server applications. Even better, the book puts our products in context by providing an overview of the current state of database technology and client/server products.

Our customers need a book like this—one that is broad in scope but grounded in practical experience. This book is both a comprehensive study of implementing client/server applications and a step-by-step description of how Sybase products work under real-world conditions. Since it details the differences between SQL Server 10 and SQL Server 11, the book can also help customers migrate their existing client/server applications to SQL Server 11.

We at Sybase, as well as our customers, can always use good advice from an outside expert. We hope that George Anderson will continue to be both a strong advocate and a vigilant analyst of Sybase technology.

Dennis L. McEvoy
President, Enterprise Business Group

Preface

This book has been written as a result of my experiences participating in several large-scale system integration projects implementing SYBASE client/server architecture in open systems environments.

Being a long-time user of SYBASE technology, I have tried to write this book from a practical viewpoint. The book will provide the reader with a point of view based on the successful implementation of SYBASE software on several large projects. The bulk of material is intended for SYBASE system architects and administrators, database administrators, and developers but will also be invaluable to technical management.

In discussing the architecture, advantages, and benefits of the SYBASE client/server computing model, I met with many DP managers, system integrators and administrators, database and data communication specialists, and system programmers working with CICS and other transaction management systems, all of whom may be potential readers of this book.

This book can be used as a guide for system architects, integrators, designers of distributed systems, database administrators considering the issues of distributed databases and DBMSs for open systems, and systems administrators and network specialists looking for theoretical or practical knowledge of distributed cooperative processing and client/server database architecture.

Client/server implementations specific to SYBASE, as described in the book, can help DP managers, system administrators, SYBASE DBAs, network and communications specialists, and application developers to make informed decisions when selecting platforms and products to implement client/server environments. The innovations that became available with System 11, especially performance-related enhancements, are discussed at such a level of detail that the book should be an invaluable tool to any professional developing distributed client/server applications, struggling with problems related to application and database performance, and, in general, solving a whole spectrum of issues and concerns related to client/server implementations. In fact, this book is a must for any system professional who deals with open systems and standards, client/server architecture, and distributed cooperative transaction processing.

Finally, those readers who are looking into such advanced topics as high-performance commercial computing using massively parallel processors will find the implications of client/server computing for their favorite technologies.

Prerequisites. Readers with any data processing experience can understand this book. Those who deal with only COBOL batch programs will find this book useful. Those with CICS, SQL, DB2, or any other database expertise, including DBA experience, will benefit. Unix, Windows/NT, OS/2, Netware, and MS DOS-Windows application developers, system and network administrators, and LAN specialists should not have any problems reading this book. I assume the reader has little or no previous knowlege of SYBASE client/server architecture. The book has been structured as a self-teaching guide, with the introduction to SYBASE client/server architecture and general related issues placed in Part 1 of the book, and the rest of the book dedicated to SYBASE implementation, design, and applications development. Given the level of attention Sybase is getting from users and the stock market alike, the book emphasizes the latest SYBASE technology—System 11.

Style used. This book includes a fair number of diagrams, figures, examples, and illustrations in an attempt to present a lot of rather complicated material in as simple a form as possible. Client/server architecture is a complex, involved, and often misunderstood subject, so that, whenever possible, theoretical issues are explained through practical examples. The same is true about SYBASE in general—its architecture is very advanced and complex, especially when it concerns the System 11 SQL Server and its internals. Therefore, I made a serious effort to illustrate SYBASE's client/server architecture on the theoretical foundation of client/server computing presented in Part 1. For those readers interested in the theory, the book provides a sufficient theoretical overview of the client/server architecture and today's client/server technology. In fact, this book is a comprehensive guide to the client/server theory and architecture, as well as to popular SYBASE client/server implementations.

This book is about a very dynamic subject. All material included in the book is current at the time the book is written. But I realize that as the client/server computing model continues to evolve, as vendors like Sybase continue to improve and expand on their product quality and functionality, changes will be necessary. I intend to revise the book if a significant development in Sybase's suite of products or in the client/server arena makes it necessary to add, delete, or change parts of the text.

What is included. Part 1 begins with an introduction to current trends in the development and implementation of distributed database environments. As an introduction, this part describes in detail such components of database architecture as multithreading, buffer management, disk file management, multiprocessor servers, and loosely coupled multiprocessing. Where added value is provided, contrasts to Oracle and Informix are drawn. Discussions of controversial design issues such as locking strategies and scalable architecture are also provided. This part of the book includes a description of high-performance hardware and techniques such as RISC, SMP, LCMP, MPP, RAID, hardware caching, and solid-state disk drives. The book also describes several performance issues and gives explanations of how the major database vendors (Sybase, Informix, IBM, and Oracle) address these issues.

Part 2 provides a detailed look at several factors that influence database server performance as well as a discussion of tuning long-running jobs and tuning in the client/server environment. Chapter 8 describes several aspects of server monitoring, including SQL Server activity, user activity, and lock activity. SQL Server Monitor is used in this chapter as well as several SQL Server commands and procedures. Memory allocation, I/O techniques, CPU utilization, design, and indexing techniques are discussed in great detail. Features new to System 11, such as the buffer manager, cache analysis tool, and private log cache, are described in great detail.

Part 3 provides a complete discussion of transaction management. Locking and concurrency issues are discussed in great detail. SYBASE locking strategies are compared with those of Oracle, Informix, and DB2/6000. Topics such as isolation levels, transaction termination and constraints, and distributed transaction management are included. Transaction monitors such as IBM's CICS, Encina from Transarc, and Novell's Tuxedo are described. SYBASE XA compliance is also described.

Part 4 deals with issues of application development using Sybase's Transact-SQL. A general discussion of SQL Server error handling and coding techniques is included. This part of the book is expecially invaluable for SYBASE DBAs, system administrators, and developers. Practical rules, hints, and guidelines are presented to readers, together with essential utilities and commands. Issues such as referential integrity, enforcement of business rules, and housekeeping tasks are also covered.

The conclusion of the book describes future directions for client/server databases in general as well as Sybase product directions in particular. SYBASE System 11 and follow-on products are discussed in this part.

George W. Anderson

Acknowledgments

First and foremost, I thank my wife (and best friend) Elvira for having extraordinary patience with me while this book was being written. Without her understanding and support, this project would not have been possible. I must also thank Elvira for her help in designing and producing the many illustrations required for the book.

I must thank Alex Berson for his friendship, tutelage, consistent hard work, and encouragement. Alex, I look forward to many more successful joint ventures! Special thanks to my many friends at Merrill Lynch, Chase Manhattan, Bankers Trust, Goldman Sachs, and Scudder, Stevens, and Clark for providing a creative and challenging atmosphere and for giving me the opportunity to learn and work in a very stimulating environment. Specifically, I would like to thank Jim Heinz, Larry Caminiti, Ed Gallagher, John Ginelli, Vince Pelly, and Paul Yaron.

Needless to say, SYBASE provided invaluable assistance and I am deeply grateful to Mike Yeager, Bridget Piraino, Bill Trapani, Stacey Cooper, Ed Van Beilen, Margaret Bloom, Danielle Scherer, Dianne Peakos, Karen O'Keefe, and Lola Brewton. I would also like to thank my numerous friends at Informix, Forté, Microsoft, Platinum Technology, and Sun Microsystems, especially Dave Huber, Brendan McAdams, Jerry Bolger, and Anthony Freglette.

I would like to thank my friends and colleagues at Enterprise Engineering, Inc., including Dan Quin, Harry Mosca, and Diane Pescatore. Special thanks to Frank Orkin, who provided technical review of this manuscript. Thanks to my father, Domenico Ranieri, and to my uncle, Peter Perri, for having confidence in our company.

Thanks to several friends who provided detailed technical review of the manuscript, including George Smith, Barry Obut, Joseph Bambara, and Tim Jones. Special thanks to Paul Allen, who was dedicated enough to review this manuscript while on vacation in Florida; thanks also to Martha Allen for tolerating this behavior! Finally, thanks to Mike Hayes and Scott Amerman at McGraw-Hill for their hard work and for making this book a reality.

Lastly, because SYBASE is a complex and continually evolving product, it is possible that there are low-level discrepancies between the text and the product as it exists. The text has been reviewed and repeatedly checked by technical personnel at SYBASE and several user organizations, so hopefully any inaccuracies will be minor.

George W. Anderson

SYBASE System 11 Overview and Architecture

Part 1 of the book begins with an introduction to current trends in the development and implementation of distributed database environments. As an introduction, this part is used to describe in detail such components of database architecture as multithreading, buffer management, disk file management, multiprocessor servers, and loosely coupled multiprocessing. To add value, comparisons to Oracle and Informix will be drawn. Discussions of controversial design issues such as locking strategies and scalable architecture are also provided. This part of the book provides a necessary introduction and overview of the SYBASE SQL Server engine and the SYBASE family of products. Also included is a description of high-performance hardware and techniques such as RISC, SMP, LCMP, MPP, RAID, hardware caching, and solid-state disk drives. The book describes several performance issues and explains how the major database vendors (Sybase, Informix, Oracle) address these issues.

It may be important for the reader to note that this book is the product of an independent opinion. I have attempted to present not only the strengths of SYBASE but also areas where the product might be improved. The book will provide the reader with a point of view based on the successful implementation of SYBASE software on several large projects. The primary goal is to provide practical information that can be used to help improve the reader's job performance.

I would like to take this opportunity to thank Alex Berson for his support and assistance with Part 1 of this book.

1

Introduction

Sybase, Inc.'s latest release of the SQL Server database engine (System 11) is primarily a performance release. With the release of System 11, Sybase is attempting to address scalability and performance questions raised by customers, industry analysts, and competitors. System 11 is designed to make better use of hardware and hardware cycles by maximizing the use of idle time and multiprocessor environments. The company will be providing incremental releases to enable faster shipment of features to users and to provide easier migration. Another primary goal is the ability to use new features without modifying applications. The key points of System 11 are

- The ability to support mixed workloads—on-line transaction processing (OLTP) and decision support systems (DSSs)
- Support for very large databases (VLDBs) from 500 Gbytes to 1 Tbyte
- Support for hundreds, and even thousands, of concurrent users provided by an architectural enhancement called multiple network engines (MNEs)
- Very high transaction volumes
- Performance with scalability and parallelism

The previous version of SQL Server (System 10) brought several new functionality enhancements, including

- The simultaneous release of a *family* of products including Replication Server, OmniSQL Server, and SYBASE Navigation Server (now called SYBASE MPP)
- Improved backup and restore functionality and performance

- Several major architectural changes to support new functionality and to provide improved performance
- Declarative referential integrity
- Complete compliance with C2-level security for secure databases (with an optional B1 level of security)
- Automatic server-based generation of sequential values using a new IDENTITY column
- Support for several new data types including decimal and numeric

Frequently when the functionality of a product is increased, there is a corresponding decrease in performance. Vendors (like everyone else) have a finite amount of resources that must be allocated to complete the work at hand. System 10 has been the target of much criticism regarding support for large databases and server scalability on large SMP machines. Sybase's stock value and revenues were flattened by the combined effects of a soft quarter of growth in server license revenues and concerns about product performance and scalability. Sybase has also experienced some loss of market share to competitors Oracle and Informix.

When building System 11, Sybase used SQL Server Monitor and other tools to analyze and reduce contention points in the server. Some of the contention points that were identified in the System 10 kernel include

- *Append log semaphore.*   Basically, an SQL Server client asks the log manager for a slot to write to the transaction log. The append log semaphore is single-threaded and was identified as a bottleneck.
- *Network I/O.*   Network I/O is not symmetric. In the System 10 SQL Server all network I/O is performed by a single operating system process. This places an upper bound on the number of users that can be supported by the server.
- *Disk I/O.*   Several disk I/O bottlenecks were identified.
- *Buffer manager.*   Contention was identified in the buffer manager area due to the use of a single buffer cache.

These contention points and others will be discussed and explained in detail in subsequent parts of the book. One purpose of this book is to explain database performance issues and how SYBASE System 11 addresses those issues. The book will also explain how to implement System 11 technology and use it to solve real-world performance problems. Some of the key architectural changes made to System 11 include

- *Data partitioning.*   This permits parallel loads and multiple concurrent inserts.

- *Symmetric kernel.*   Introduction of symmetric networking and parallel lock management improves the server's ability to balance loads and support greater numbers of user connections.

- *Named memory caches.*   The ability to configure any number of memory caches per server can be used to fully optimize database resources. It allows for the partitioning and optimization of large memory.

- *Tunable block I/O sizes.*   This allows for faster bulk loading and the use of implicit prefetch.

- *Configuration tuning.*   It permits a high degree of system and application optimization through fine-grained configuration tuning.

- *Subquery processing changes.*   The System 10 SQL Server included a number of changes to subquery processing, mostly to correct a number of problems in 4.x versions of the server. There are also several known problems in System 10 having to do with NULLs, empty tables, and duplicates. These issues (performance and correctness problems) are now resolved while compatibility with existing views and procedures is maintained.

ISO 9000 certification.   Concerns about System 10's quality prompted Sybase to seek the International Standards Organization (ISO) 9000 quality certification for System 11. To keep the ISO certification, Sybase must follow requirements defined by the ISO. Among the requirements that must be met, before going GA (generally available to the public), Sybase must run internal applications for a minimum of one week with no priority 1 (serious) bugs reported. In addition, the stress tester must be run continuously for 72 h without failure. There cannot be any priority 1 bugs reported within two weeks of the final release date. ISO audits the certification process, ensuring that all quality objectives are met. The ISO 9000 process probably resulted in a delayed ship date for the final release of System 11; however, the quality of System 11 is evident. Sybase is the first database vendor to obtain the ISO 9000 certification.

Why tuning?   Because System 11 is a performance release, much of the information provided in this book can be used for performance and tuning. Database performance issues can range from the extremely simple to the extremely complex. Some common reasons for tuning include the following:

- "I've been waiting over 15 minutes for a response to my query—what is the system doing?"

- "The system administrator says that our system is I/O-bound. What can we do?"

- "This application ran fine in the development environment, but in production, response time is terrible. Why?"

Responsibilities.   Most database performance issues are not solved by a single person. Typically, application development projects are completed by a collaboration of people including a systems architect, operating system administrator, SYBASE system administrator, database administrator, replication system administrator, and a team of application developers. Performance issues are commonly identified and resolved by some combination of these resources. The following loose definitions are provided for the reader's benefit.

Systems architect.   This person designs the systems architecture including technology selection and infrastructure from planning to production. In reality, the architecture may be designed by a group of people. The systems architect may need to get involved with distributed performance issues involving use of a global catalog, replication software, and/or other types of middleware. Typically, the SYBASE system administrator will inherit responsibility for distributed tuning issues. The systems architect may call on other resources including network services and communications consultants.

SYBASE system administrator.   The job of the SYBASE administrator (SA) typically encompasses many functions, some of which may overlap with those of the operating system administrator. In smaller installations, the SYBASE administrator often doubles as the O/S system administrator. In fact, a good system administrator is one part UNIX (or Windows NT) systems administrator and one part database administrator (DBA). Some of the SA's responsibilities are

- Software installation and support
- Diagnosing system problems
- Installation of emergency bug fixes (EBFs) and new versions of the SYBASE software
- Database backup and recovery
- Disk space allocation, creation of database devices, and database segments
- Fine-tuning and monitoring of SQL Server to achieve the best performance
- Granting roles and permissions to SQL Server users

- Managing and monitoring the use of available disk space, memory, connections, error logs, state-of-transaction logs, device problems, portmapper problems, etc.

- Database design and analysis, creation of user databases, and granting of ownership of them

- Transfer of bulk data between SQL Server and other software programs

- SQL review prior to production

- Management of development and production databases; coordination of migration from development to production.

Database administrator. The database administrator is usually involved in the design of the database(s) and takes responsibility for ongoing database maintenance, once the system is in production. Some of the DBA's tasks include physical design issues, such as to

- Maintain the Data Dictionary and catalogs.

- Ensure data type consistency across tables in the database.

- Determine data types for individual columns.

- Maintain primary and foreign key relationships.

- Suggest index definitions and types.

- Enforce standards and naming conventions.

- Write stored procedures, triggers, rules, and referential integrity enforcement. These functions may overlap with the work of application designers.

There may be overlap between tasks performed by the SA and tasks performed by the DBA. Additionally, the SA and DBA may be one and the same.

Replication system administrator. The Replication Server system administrator (RSA) is involved with distributed application design issues and selecting replicated data strategies. The RSA must plan and implement data designs and evaluate options for processing distributed transactions. The RSA may perform the following tasks:

- Create replication definitions and subscriptions

- Create routes to replicated databases

- Materialize and bulk-load data into replicated databases

- Manage distributed data recovery

- Monitor the status of all replication system components

Developer/Programmer. This person develops the application and tunes specific programs for performance. Developers may write programs using C language, PowerBuilder, Visual Basic, or newer application partitioning tools such as Forte from Forte Software. Additionally, developers may write stored procedures and triggers that are passed on to the DBA or SA for review and performance analysis.

To ensure the success of a project, the *project manager* must facilitate communication between the systems architect, system administrator(s), database administrator(s), and application developers. Frequent communication facilitates discussion and the free exchange of ideas. This typically results in

1. The early discovery of problems and issues that need to be addressed.

2. Solutions to these same problems and issues.

3. The identification of bottlenecks (to the project schedule) and milestones. This is even more important today due to the increased complexity of client/server systems and the System 11 family of products.

Some methods that have been proved to work in my experience are the use of work group sessions and/or developers' conferences. These conferences can be held on a weekly basis and should be driven by a good agenda and moderated by the project manager. They should not be long sessions but more of a forum for communication among the attendees. For example, the moderator may ask about specific problems or situations encountered during the past week. These sessions can also be a good forum for vendor presentations. The project manager may want to arrange presentations with SYBASE technical representatives to discuss implementation issues and new products or upgrades.

What causes performance problems? Performance problems can be caused by an almost infinite number of factors. The largest performance gains to be realized will come from proper table design and index selection. Even the most powerful *database management system* (DBMS) will suffer from the effects of poor database design.

Some common database design mistakes include these:

- Database designer did not consider performance when setting up the physical data model, or when translating the logical data model to a physical model.

- Application programs were not appropriate for a relational database.
- Hot spots have been designed into the database application.

Typical application programming mistakes:

- Programmers' SQL statements that do not make efficient use of the query optimizer
- The use of functions in WHERE clauses
- The mathematical manipulation of SEARCH arguments (SARGs) in WHERE clauses
- Failure to recognize the amount of network traffic generated by various application design approaches

Database configuration mistakes:

- Failure by the DBA to use the machine's resources effectively
- Incorrect load balancing across available disks

Systems problems:

- Other server-based applications affecting SYBASE
- An untuned operating system (e.g., improper configuration of shared memory)
- Inadequate system resources to support SYBASE

While the largest performance gains will be realized by proper database design, the reader should be aware of how system components interact and affect overall system performance. The basic system components are

1. Memory
2. Disk I/O
3. Central processing unit (CPU)
4. Network

Memory. Memory bottlenecks occur when there isn't enough memory to accommodate the needs of the server. Memory bottlenecks can cause excessive paging and swapping, resulting in severely I/O-bound systems.

Disk I/O. Disk bottlenecks occur when one or more disks or a disk controller begins to exceed the maximum I/O rate.

CPU.   CPU bottlenecks occur when the operating system or user programs are making excessive demands on the CPU. This is often caused by excessive paging and memory swapping (which may be the result of insufficient memory in the system).

Network.   Network bottlenecks occur when the amount of traffic on the network is too high or when network collisions occur.

Keep in mind that the basic system components are interdependent. For example, reducing memory in a system can cause excessive paging in the system which can also cause CPU and/or disk bottlenecks. Conversely, increasing memory can relieve disk I/O or CPU I/O bottlenecks.

Note that one bottleneck may be masking another. There is frequently a second bottleneck hiding behind the first. When the first bottleneck has been alleviated, a second may rise to the surface depending on how the first one was removed.

1.1   Implementation Trends and Features

The remainder of this chapter is intended to discuss some practical, technical relational database management system (RDBMS) implementation trends and features that client/server RDBMS designers and users alike should be aware of. This discussion will be referred to throughout the rest of the book, when we describe various SYBASE products and features.

Distributed relational database systems make special demands on the database logical and physical design, and on the database management system architecture and functionality as well. At the very least, a distributed RDBMS must

- Maintain data integrity by providing local and global locking mechanisms and by supporting database commit/rollback transaction integrity

- Automatically detect deadlocks and perform transaction and database recovery

- Be intelligent enough to optimize data access for a wide variety of application requests

- Have an architecture that is capable of taking advantage of the high-powered platforms it runs on

- Overcome the traditional DBMS bottleneck—input/output (I/O)—by tuning the DBMS engine and I/O subsystem to achieve high data throughput and high I/O rates

- Provide support for optimum space management, which is especially important if the underlying platform is a resource-constrained microcomputer

- Support database security and administration facilities for distributed data/application locations, preferably from a single, centralized location

And all this must be done by a distributed RDBMS reliably and within acceptable performance and throughput parameters, especially in a multiuser distributed on-line transaction processing (OLTP) and on-line complex processing (OLCP) environments.

Therefore, even if every distributed DBMS implementation is designed to support some of or all C.J. Date's 12 distributed database rules (see App. I), the users must take a close look at the actual technology of a given product. It is important to see how each particular rule is implemented regardless of the hardware platform. At the same time, it is as important to understand how a DBMS can take advantage of a particular hardware/software platform and what advanced features (if any) a given DBMS product offers to satisfy and possibly exceed customer expectations. In this respect, especially in an OLCP environment, it is important to understand how a selected RDBMS is engineered for the one or more of the increasingly popular hardware architectures:

- Symmetric multiprocessors (SMPs), for example, Sun SPARCServer 1000 and 2000

- Massively parallel processors (MPPs), for example, AT&T GIS, IBM SP/2

- Loosely coupled multiprocessing (LCMP) systems, often called *clusters,* for example, Sun Clusters, DEC Alpha

This is not an insignificant consideration. Granted, these emerging high-performance computing solutions appear more expensive than traditional uniprocessors. But in return, they promise an unprecedented scalability for higher performance and throughput. And that scalability is extremely important today, when client/server applications are pushing the capacity and performance of network servers to their engineered limits.

System performance can be measured by the following yardsticks:

- *Response time*—the amount of time required to process a user query

- *Throughput*—the number of transactions that can be processed by the system in a given time period

A scalable system will be able to get higher throughput when increasing the number of users by adding hardware while still maintaining acceptable response times.

So let's examine some key requirements for a database server architecture that have to be considered for the implementation of complex mission-critical distributed systems.

1.1.1 Relational DBMS architecture
for scalability

In a distributed multiuser client/server environment, a database management system resides at the database server and should be designed as a server component of the client/server computing model. As such, the DBMS server should be designed to receive and process a variable number of concurrent database requests from multiple remote users.

Scalability.   The server RDBMS should process client requests efficiently, and the performance and throughput characteristics of the RDBMS should not change as the number of concurrent users, database size, etc., grows. To maintain these characteristics, additional computing resources (for example, CPU, memory, disks) may have to be added to the system at a relatively small incremental cost, with the *predictable* effect on the system and *without changing the application or administrative practices*. This property of the system is often referred to as system's *scalability*.

Users are constantly searching for better database performance in both speed and scalability. *Speed-up* means that the same request takes less time on the same amount of data. *Scale-up* means that the user gets comparable performance on a request as the size of the database increases.[1]

There are two approaches to achieve scalability:

1. The *external* approach increases the number of servers in the environment and lets multiple server systems run concurrently to share the workload. Loosely coupled systems running distributed databases support external scalability. Often this approach requires additional administrative support.

2. *Internal* (in-system) scalability implies a single system that can be scaled up by adding a computing resource such as faster CPU, or more CPUs, or more memory, etc., to the existing server platform. This approach should not require additional software components

---

[1]Judith R. Davis, "Parallel Execution of Database Operations," *Open Information Systems,* vol. 10, no. 4, April 1995.

as scale goes up and, therefore should not require a change in administrative practices.

Both types of scalability dictate that an RDBMS should be able to effectively use all available computing resources, thus supporting an incremental approach to capacity planning. In effect, from a capacity planning perspective, a truly scalable RDBMS is equivalent to a *free hardware upgrade*.

The internal scalability is the focus of this discussion, since today it is achievable on multiprocessor machines—SMP and MPP. These multiprocessor platforms allow the addition of processors without changing the applications or the administrative process.

To provide scalability, a server RDBMS architecture should support

- *Extensibility.* The DBMS should not be specialized for a particular system configuration (e.g., a certain number of processors) and should automatically take advantage of the new configuration, without the need for reinstallation. This can be achieved by a sophisticated task-scheduling algorithm that can assign new tasks to additional resources in a load-balanced, predictable fashion, by breaking large tasks (e.g., complex database queries) into a set of small subtasks that can be performed in *parallel.* By definition, a parallel scalable RDBMS provides predictable extensibility. The principles of a parallel scalable DBMS are discussed later in this chapter.

- *Limitation-free architecture.* If a DBMS has built-in architectural limitations (limits on the number and size of supported tables, number of concurrent connections, etc.), it will not scale (beyond the built-in limit) regardless of how well it can parallelize tasks and operations.

- *Application transparency.* An application should not be aware of the platform architecture, configuration, and changes to the platform implemented to achieve the next level of performance and throughput; ideally, migrating from one platform to another (e.g., from an SMP to an MPP) should not require application changes, even though the DBMS itself may have to adopt to a new processing model (in this case, from the shared-memory model to a distributed-memory model).

Multithreading. Operating in a limited-resource environment (the server system) under the control of an operating system, the DBMS designers can follow different strategies to achieve server efficiency.

One strategy is to create an operating system server process for every DBMS client, which typically results in, among other things, additional operating system overhead (e.g., context switching) and

Client 1

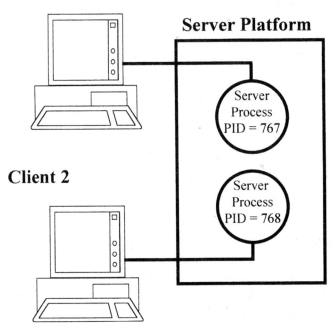

Figure 1.1 Single-threaded architecture.

additional CPU and memory requirements (see Fig. 1.1). A unit of context management under the control of a single process is called a *thread* (sometimes called a *lightweight process,* or LWP). A thread can be implemented either within the server process or via operating system services. The latter is considerably more expensive for process creation, destruction, and context switching. We will call this a *single-threaded architecture.*

A considerably more efficient approach is to launch a separate thread for each separate task (such as a client connection supported by a server). Such a "lightweight" task can be controlled by the DBMS server rather than the operating system (see Fig. 1.2). In principle, threads can clone themselves and thus perform concurrent tasks.

Threads do not incur operating system overhead after being launched. A true multithreaded architecture provides a high degree of resource sharing (e.g., threads can share memory space with other threads) and tends to make system performance more stable with respect to the number of users and additional server functionality. In general, a multithreaded DBMS server architecture is preferable to a single-threaded one. A multithreaded database server can manage all the resources required by the RDBMS itself (including buffers, disk

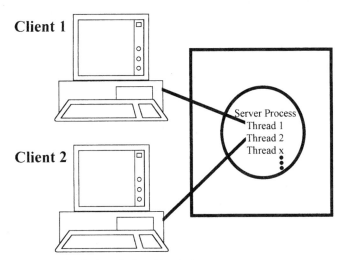

Figure 1.2   Multithreaded architecture.

I/O, locking, and logging), which essentially makes it a special-purpose operating system (OS) dedicated to DBMS operations by scheduling thread execution.

The multithreaded scheduler can be either *preemptive* or *nonpreemptive*. Nonpreemptive threads execute until they give up control of the CPU or until a specified time interval (time slice) has expired, and therefore an "unfriendly" thread can block every other one from running. This approach imposes some requirements on the OS and DBMS design as well as some limitations on the system scalability.

Preemptive threads can be interrupted by a scheduler when another thread requires the processor and satisfies some requirements (e.g., new thread's priority, thread class, the state of the current thread) imposed by the scheduler to initiate the switchover. Preemptive thread scheduling is effective for database servers that must share resources between a DBMS application and a non-DBMS application. Preemptive threads are usually implemented by the operating system.

Among UNIX-based RDBMS server implementations, Sybase's SQL Server is one example of a multithreaded server architecture. Sybase's latest release of the SQL Server extends the concept of the multithreaded architecture to Symmetric MultiProcessing (SMP) hardware platforms. The SQL Server kernel is nonpreemptive.

Memory.   Hardware trends toward larger memories using 64-bit addresses and more computing power provided by SMP boxes provide new opportunities for high performance database systems. The move to 64-bit addresses will allow for the support of huge memory spaces which users will want to partition in the same manner as disk drives are partitioned today. This large memory space can be used to make database tables, indexes, or even databases *sticky,* which is to say that the system administrator will be able to designate these objects as memory-resident. To support this capability, RDBMS vendors will need to provide new memory management features in their RDBMS engines. To that end Oracle is providing Oracle 7 64-bit very large memory (VLM), Informix offers INFORMIX-OnLine Dynamic Server, and Sybase offers SYBASE System 11.

This movement will be championed by most major UNIX vendors because UNIX can run native in 64-bit environments, whereas Microsoft Windows NT cannot. A few of the vendors already in the picture are DEC with the Alpha chip and OSF/1, Sun Microsystems with the UltraSparc running Solaris, and Hewlett-Packard with the PA-RISC.

Figure 1.3 illustrates how SYBASE System 11's buffer management system (with its multiple data caches) can be used to partition very large memory. The System 11 Buffer Manager is discussed in Chaps. 7 and 9.

1.1.2   DBMS performance and efficiency features

Relational DBMS server performance is usually measured by using standard benchmarks as well as some proprietary application transaction mix. Because many external factors affect RDBMS performance (operating system environment, hardware platform, etc.), benchmarks usually demonstrate some particular small aspect of the performance picture as a whole, and they can be unreliable as a predictor for any specific environment or configuration.

Clearly, a well-designed database server should be able to manage appropriate resources transparently from the application, and use these resources efficiently. For example, the way the database server allocates and manages the system and shared memory, and the lock-

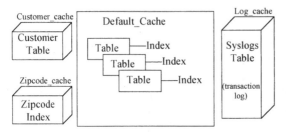

Figure 1.3   Partitioned memory.

ing strategy in effect, determines some overall performance characteristics of the RDBMS. There are certain relational DBMS design features that quite definitely affect its performance. Some of these features are applicable to the performance of the individual database engines, while others, such as global optimization, affect the performance of the entire distributed database system.

Server-enforced integrity and security. Data integrity and data security are critical requirements for database management systems. Integrity features, such as referential and domain integrity, ensure the accuracy and consistency of data, while database *security* refers to authorization and control of data access. Integrity and security can be implemented in several different ways. For example, referential integrity constraints and security procedures can be included in every application. In the client/server computing model, it may mean duplication of the relevant code on every client running these applications. However, the more efficient approach would call for the implementation of the integrity and security features centrally, directly at the DBMS server level. Such DBMS server architecture will provide for higher application reliability, reduced development and maintenance costs, and increased database security.

Global optimization. The performance of a relational DBMS is largely determined by the capabilities of the query optimizer. C.J. Date's seventh distributed database rule specifies that in a truly distributed database system, the optimizer must take into account not only local, but also global factors, including distributed nodes and network characteristics.

Typical cost-based optimization selects the access path for a given query based on the estimated cost of the query processing. Usually, the optimizer calculates the cost in such units as the number of I/O operations and/or CPU cycles, and it takes into account the number of rows needed to satisfy the query, availability of indexes, and various statistical information about data organization. These statistics are accumulated and maintained by the RDBMS in its internal system catalog. Optimization becomes even more critical in distributed query processing. Consider an application that attempts to join two database tables that are distributed to two different locations.

The size of each node's databases and relevant tables, the network speed, and the processing and I/O power of each node are among the major factors that affect the performance of a distributed query. The distributed (global) query optimization requires access to a global database directory or catalog in order to obtain necessary node characteristics and statistical information about the remote databases.

Without global query optimization, a distributed relational DBMS may perform extremely inefficiently. Such a system may send all the records of the bigger table to another, remote location, for selection and join, and then send the results back. As the complexity of the queries exceeds the two table join requirements, each additional table and/or database increases the number of choices for, and the complexity of, the optimizer.

Therefore, an efficient implementation of global query optimization is a rather difficult task that only a handful of RDBMS vendors attempt. Products such as INFORMIX and Ingres support global optimization with certain limitations, and even then the quality of optimization decreases with the complexity of the query.

Parallel relational DBMS processing. A special case of global query optimization is the query optimization in distributed-memory parallel systems (clusters and MPPs). Often, it is referred to as *parallel query processing.* Generally speaking, parallel RDBMS processing offers a solution to the traditional problem of poor RDBMS performance for complex queries and very large databases. Intuitively, it is quite clear that accessing and processing portions of the database by individual threads in parallel (instead of a monolithic, sequential access of the entire large database) can greatly improve the performance of the query. This is especially important for large decision support systems (DSSs) and batch processing. Let's consider a typical query against a relational database. Such a query may consist of three distinct steps—table scan, two-table join, and sort of the result set (e.g., to eliminate duplicates, or to satisfy an ORDER BY clause). In a traditional nonparallel DBMS environment, these steps are performed by a RDBMS sequentially (see Fig. 1.4, case 1).

This long sequential process can be shortened in several different ways:

Data partitioning. If the entire database is partitioned into a number of smaller segments, each located on its own (logical) device, then the total query can be decomposed into the equal number of subqueries, all running in parallel against a corresponding partition of the database (horizontal parallelism). The resulting execution time is significantly reduced in comparison with a sequential query (Fig. 1.4, case 2). Obviously, this approach requires a multiprocessor server (SMP or MPP). However, as illustrated in Fig. 1.5, processor-based parallelism does not reduce a traditional DBMS bottleneck—I/O. It is only logical, then, that the multiprocessor server and a parallel RDBMS should benefit from a server architecture that supports parallel I/O. As illustrated in Fig. 1.6, additional performance improvements can be achieved by placing data partitions on separate physical devices

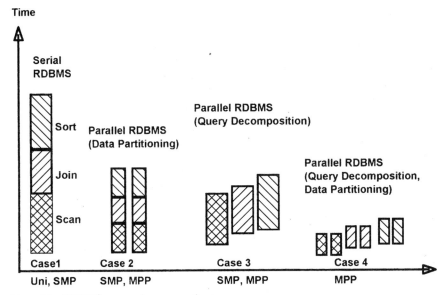

Figure 1.4   RDBMS processing comparison.

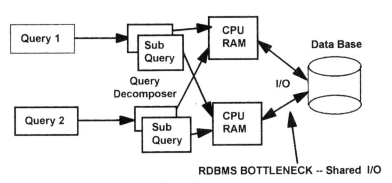

Figure 1.5   Shared I/O bottleneck.

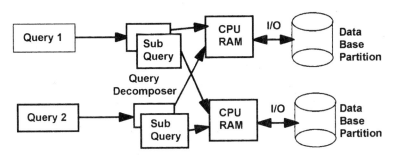

Figure 1.6   Parallel scalable RDBMS, MPP, and parallel I/O.

(preferably, connected via separate I/O buses). The optimizer can partition the query based on the data partitioning rules (e.g., key ranges, hash algorithms).

Query decomposition. This approach requires a much higher level of sophistication from the RDBMS engine. It assumes that the RDBMS engine can decompose the query based on its functional components (in our example, scan, join, and sort). Once decomposed, the query components can start executing in parallel, with a minimum delay between the execution steps (vertical parallelism). Ideally, as database records are processed by one step (e.g., scan), they are *immediately* given to the next step (e.g., join), thus eliminating the wait time inherited in the sequential query processing. In this case (Fig. 1.4, case 3), the query decomposer and the optimizer can allocate different query components to available processors from the processor pool. As in the previous approach, an SMP or MPP server is required.

Hybrid approach. Finally, a parallel scalable RDBMS can employ a combination approach, where the query decomposer and the optimizer can partition the query both horizontally (based on the data partitioning algorithm) and vertically (based on the functional composition of the query). The hybrid approach can result in the highest utilization of computing resources available in an MPP database server, and it will provide for the best scalability, performance, and throughput of the DBMS (see Fig. 1.4, case 4).

The ability to decompose and process large queries in parallel is applicable to on-line transaction processing as well. In the OLTP and especially OLCP environments, parallel query processing can supplement an overall multithreaded approach where individual threads can be executed on separate processors. In other words, to take full advantage of the SMP and MPP architectures and to achieve high performance of complex queries in a very large database environment, a relational RDBMS should be able to balance the workload of individual threads across multiple processors and to decompose a complex query into multiple subqueries that can be executed in parallel.

In addition to parallel query processing, traditional RDBMS utilities such as sort, index build, database load, and backup should be parallelized to take full advantage of SMP and MPP server specialization for a true parallel, scalable relational DBMS.

Several major DBMS vendors offer various degrees of availability of parallel query processing, frequently coupled with a particular platform on which the query decomposer was developed. Most prominent among them are Oracle 7 with the Parallel Query Option (PQO), INFORMIX Dynamic Scaleable Architecture (DSA), and SYBASE MPP (formerly Navigation Server).

Lock granularity. Locking preserves data integrity by preventing multiple updates to the same records simultaneously. Some servers permit manual locking, but in reality, automatic locking in a database management system is imperative. The importance of locking becomes especially clear in a parallel RDBMS environment, where multiple users execute various steps of complex queries across multiple data partitions.

Users or processes that are locked out from access must wait until the required data are freed (locks are released). When this happens, the user's response time, and thus a perception of DBMS performance, suffers. For instance, table level update locks, as a rule, result in poor performance. Although locking, in itself, preserves data from corruption, it could limit the number of users simultaneously accessing the RDBMS.

If a DBMS locks an entire database for each user, then the DBMS becomes, in effect, a single-user DBMS. Therefore, the size of locks that the RDBMS can impose on a database, or the *locking granularity,* becomes very important.

Ideally, the RDBMS should lock only those rows that are being updated. The smallest level of granularity in commercial databases is the *row* level. Row-level locking implies that the database can use a lock granularity of a single row. This means that multiple users can simultaneously update different rows on the same page. Each user locks only the row on which the operation is performed and does not interfere with other users in the same page. Row-level locking permits the highest degree of concurrency by allowing users not to lock each other out. The disadvantage of the row-level locking is its significant overhead. For example, the Oracle and Informix RDBMSs both support row-level locking. However, since each lock requires a certain amount of memory and/or disk space, the number of locks imposed on a database (and therefore, the number of users) may be limited by the amount of available space. Some RDBMS servers can *escalate* locks from one level (e.g., row) to a higher level (e.g., data page or table), and release lower-level locks when their number exceeds a user-defined limit. For example, IBM's DB2 and SYBASE System 11 both support lock escalation.

The next level of locking granularity is at the *page* level. Thus, when one user updates a row, the entire page is locked and other users are blocked from updating, and sometimes even reading, rows in that page. Page-level locking introduces moderate overhead at the cost of reduced concurrency.

Table-level locking means that the database can lock an entire table at a time. This level is useful for locking a table for batch updates, locking out users for maintenance or reporting, etc.

Finally, *database*-level locking means that the entire database can be locked with a single command. Obviously, this level of locking practically eliminates concurrency and is typically used only for database maintenance.

Deadlock detection. Locking is associated with another performance problem—deadlocks. A deadlock occurs when process A locks a record that process B needs and process B locks the record that process A needs. Each program must wait until the other completes, which is impossible. Thus, a *deadlock* (also known as a *deadly embrace*) has occurred. The DBMS server should automatically detect deadlocks and use appropriate algorithms to resolve them. As with global optimization, deadlock detection becomes much more complicated in a distributed environment. The time criterion might not be sufficient, since network delays and slow response time may be confused with a lock at a remote site. A truly distributed RDBMS server should be capable of resolving "distributed" deadlocks, even though the majority of the available DBMS implementations use some simple, timeout-based rules to resolve deadlocks.

Dirty reads. Some RDBMS products support a fast read mode without data integrity where the database system can scan the data as they currently exist on disk or in memory, regardless of whether the data have been committed. Even though dirty reads offer measurable performance advantages, their use has to be balanced against the potential exposure to inaccurate data.

Asynchronous I/O. RDBMS input/output is potentially a source of a performance bottleneck. Properly designed database management systems should minimize the number of actual physical disk I/Os and spread the cost of I/O operations across many users. One technique that facilitates reduction in the number of disk accesses is asynchronous I/O.

This technique involves overlapping I/O operations with other work that the RDBMS server needs to perform. In this case, the server does not wait for the completion of an I/O request. Such an overlapping can be improved even further when the data are updated in shared buffers and the data writes are forced to disk only when the data buffers are full or by a database checkpoint. The consistency of data in this case is guaranteed by write-ahead logging to a shared transaction log. In IBM system environments, asynchronous I/O is frequently implemented on an operating system level, as well as by a DBMS itself (for example, DB2). UNIX-based databases, however, must be designed to implement asynchronous I/O. Oracle, Ingres, Sybase, and Informix all offer asynchronous I/O capabilities in UNIX environments.

Stored procedures. Stored procedures are collections of SQL statements and control-of-flow directives (e.g., IF, THEN, ELSE) that are parsed, verified, compiled, bound, and stored at the DBMS server. Stored procedures support the use of input and output parameters, user-defined variables, and conditional execution. Stored procedures can call other procedures and can be executed on remote relational DBMS servers. Stored procedures not only enhance the efficiency and flexibility of SQL, but also dramatically improve RDBMS performance. Due to the nonnavigational nature of SQL, the access path selection is performed by the relational DBMS optimizer when an SQL statement is bound (parsed, verified, etc.). This process is resource-intensive—the corresponding instruction path length may be measured in several thousands of machine instructions. If it has to be performed every time an SQL statement is executed, the resulting performance will be greatly decreased (this type of SQL access is called *dynamic* SQL).

The SQL statements are *static* when they are parsed, verified, compiled, bound, and stored in the RDBMS server before they are executed, or the first time they are executed. If SQL statements are static, the consecutive executions will be done at much smaller expense and, therefore, more rapidly. Some RDBMS systems (for example, DB2) implement static SQL in such a way that the SQL statements are parsed and compiled before execution during the program preparation process. The resulting objects are stored in appropriate RDBMS libraries (Database Request Modules and DB2 Plans), from which they can be recalled. Other products (say, SYBASE) parse and compile SQL statements the first time they are executed, and may store the results in memory (usually, in a shared-procedure cache). Of course, even though there is no need to recall procedures from the libraries, one drawback of the latter technique is the possibility of the compiled stored procedure being paged out in a very active environment. Regardless of the implementation technique, stored procedures improve the performance of SQL statements by eliminating costly preprocessing overhead. They also reduce network traffic by eliminating the need to send lengthy SQL statements from applications to RDBMS servers. In a typical UNIX-based client/server environment, e.g., a stored procedure can be processed in a fraction of the time it takes to process a single embedded SQL command.

Cursor support. Cursors are programming constructs that allow applications to process the returned result set one row at a time. The result set can be derived from executing a single SQL query or multiple SQL queries in a single database connection. This row-at-a-time processing is typical of, and required by, OLTP systems. All RDBMS cursor implementations permit at least a unidirectional (forward) access of the result set. Some RDBMS products also allow backward scrolling, which is useful for many retrieval applications.

Mixed workload.   With the widespread use of powerful SMP machines, it is becoming possible to run larger and more varied workloads on client/server systems. DSS workloads are characterized by long, complex queries, for example, *n*-way joins. DSS queries typically cannot be predicted in advance and usually affect large amounts of data, thus exhibiting slower response times. OLTP workloads consist of small atomic updates, inserts, and selects that affect small amounts of data and exhibit very fast response times.

For simplicity's sake, a mixed-workload environment may be defined as support for decision support systems and on-line transaction processing applications running on the same database server. From a cost standpoint, an RDBMS that can support a mixed workload would be extremely advantageous. System 11 has several new features designed to support mixed-workload environments including SYBASE IQ (query accelerator), improved load balancing and query optimization, a new buffer management scheme, and variable block I/O sizes.

1.1.3   DBMS connectivity

Heterogeneous data access.   An advanced RDBMS implementation should be able to support the distribution of applications and data over networks and, as such, should be able to interconnect with like (homogeneous) and unlike (heterogeneous) systems and databases. Homogeneous connectivity is often built into the relational database system itself. Some distributed RDBMS products offer distributed data consistency by supporting two-phase commit protocols.

Heterogeneous databases are much more difficult to interconnect— data structure, access, and language can all be different, dissimilar. The traditional approach to heterogeneous DBMS connectivity is to build gateways that allow foreign database management systems to look like the native DBMS from an application's perspective. Sometimes, gateways allow third-party software vendors' programming tools and foreign databases to access data in the selected DBMS. However, because of the differences in heterogeneous DBMS architectures and supporting environments (e.g., SYBASE on a UNIX server and DB2 on IBM MVS mainframes), gateways do not provide for seamless data access. Gateways may involve connection between different networks (i.e., Ethernet and SNA), different communication protocols (that is, TCP/IP and APPC), different data representation

(ASCII and EBCDIC), etc. Therefore, gateways are rarely used to support database transactions that span multiple heterogeneous environments, where all data consistency is guaranteed by a distributed heterogeneous two-phase commit protocol. Such implementations will require a cross-platform transaction manager that can interface with all participating heterogeneous databases. Such transaction processing (TP) managers are being designed within the guidelines of open systems. For example, the X/Open DTP model is a DTP system specified by the X/Open Company in the *XA Interface Specification*. X/Open has proposed XA interfaces for open systems TP managers, and OSF's Distributed Computing Environment, among other products, has selected these interfaces for its TP manager.

Nevertheless, today gateways solve a critical need to interconnect new and existing RDBMSs. Gateways play an important role by providing access to heterogeneous systems, especially when critical business data and legacy applications all reside on an organization's mainframes. Almost all gateways available today offer access to IBM's DB2. Better gateway implementations use Advanced Program-to-Program Communications (APPC/LU6.2) to provide real-time read-write access to mainframe data. Some gateways, such as Net/Gateway from Sybase, are DBMS-extensible and allow UNIX- and Windows NT-based RDBMS to interactively access mainframe data available via CICS/VS (IBM's transaction monitor for IBM mainframes). The SYBASE MDI Gateway is a low-cost gateway suitable for small-scale solutions.

Remote procedure calls. If gateways represent one of the most popular ways to access heterogeneous data from one hardware/software platform to another, server-to-server and client-to-server RDBMS connectivity is best supported via the mechanism of remote procedure calls (RPCs). Remote procedure calls represent a connectionless mechanism by which one process can execute another process residing on a different, usually remote, system, possibly running a different operating system. Any parameters needed by a subroutine are passed between the calling and called processes. A database RPC is a clearly defined request for a service or data issued over a network to a RDBMS server by a client or another server. Unlike traditional remote procedure calls, database RPCs (e.g., SYBASE RPC) can call stored procedures and allow the DBMS server to return multiple rows in response to a single request. Since database RPCs eliminate the need for a client to send lengthy SQL statements and to receive individual records separately, they greatly reduce network traffic. In addition, RPCs can help implement heterogeneous DBMS connectivity by solving the language incompatibility problems. One system can call a remote procedure on another system without concern for the remote system's language syntax.

1.1.4   Advanced RDBMS features

Database triggers and rules.   Advanced relational DBMS implementations should provide users with the ability to initiate (trigger) certain user-defined actions based on a particular data-related event. Triggers, which can be viewed as a special type of stored procedure, are often used to implement referential integrity constraints. For example, a user may attempt to insert data into or update a table column which represents a foreign key. The appropriate trigger can be designed to check the new column value against the values of the primary key. Similarly, delete actions can be controlled (e.g., prevented or cascaded) by using user-developed delete triggers. In general, triggers can call other triggers or stored procedures, and they are powerful tools for application development. Centrally located on the server (in SYBASE and Ingres, e.g.), triggers can improve RDBMS performance, although they require programming efforts, especially when referential integrity is implemented.

Therefore, dictionary-based declarative referential integrity implementations may be preferable to those using triggers. Declarative referential integrity provides better documentation and clarity by using standard nonprocedural SQL statements to define referential integrity constraints. SYBASE, DB2, and DB2/6000 all support declarative referential integrity. If triggers are often used to support referential integrity, RDBMS rules are used to implement user-defined domain constraints. For example, a database rule may say that the state code must be one of the approved two-character codes—NY, NJ, and CT.

Products that support database-resident rules facilitate the development of applications by implementing many business rules centrally as RDBMS rules. Ingres and SYBASE are just two examples that implement RDBMS-resident rules.

Image support.   Today, business requirements often include the need to support several media, in particular, image applications. Ideally, a RDBMS selected for a client/server distributed environment should also support special IMAGE data types—BLOBs. A BLOB is a *b*inary *l*arge *ob*ject, and it can represent very large (up to several gigabytes) fields that are used to store images, graphics, long text documents, and even voice recordings. Ideally, the RDBMS should be capable of not only storing and retrieving BLOBs, but also making BLOB fields available through the use of standard SQL, as any other data element. Several RDBMSs available today (e.g., Informix, Ingres,

SYBASE) provide BLOB support. In addition, some RDBMS vendors and standards groups such as SQL Access Group are working on SQL extensions that would allow BLOB manipulations from the SQL statements. Alternatively, object-oriented DBMSs (OODBMSs) are probably even better suited to handle this type of data.

Products such as Illustra from Illustra Technologies, Inc. (recently acquired by Informix Corp.) are very well suited to managing complex data in the multimedia, entertainment, Internet, earth sciences, and other markets. It should be interesting to see how Informix can leverage the Illustra technology and integrate it into Informix-OnLine (its core parallel database technology). The combination of Illustra and Informix should result in a powerful database engine well suited for Web applications which require high-performance and dynamic content management capabilities. The Web will spawn a large and dynamic new market for information management technology. Web applications require the user to interact with three-dimensional graphics, audio, video, HyperText Markup Language (HTML), spatial data, and other complex data types. Traditional RDBMS offerings designed for static and fixed data types are not well suited for this purpose.

Graphical front-end development tools. Users of distributed RDBMSs all demand an advanced graphical suite of application development tools. Today, users can see two trends in the front-end tools for DBMS application development. Some RDBMS products (such as by Ingres, Informix, Gupta, and Oracle, to name just a few) provide graphical application development tools as an integrated solution. Oracle even offers computer-aided software engineering (CASE) tools to facilitate application development. Other RDBMS vendors rely on third-party front-end tool vendors to supply application development tools that can be used to construct applications efficiently for a given RDBMS. Examples of such tools are JYACC, Uniface, and Neuron Data. Intimate knowledge of the underlying database system often results in better application performance when integrated front-end/DBMS solutions are used. On the other hand, independent front-end tool vendors often offer better and more open graphical user interfaces (GUIs), and allow users to be more flexible about choosing the best database management system. Whatever the case, front-end tools must be considered in the selection of an RDBMS.

In the traditional two-tier client/server model, application developers and designers separate processing logic into two layers. For example, the client uses a traditional front-end tool (e.g., PowerBuilder), and the database server uses stored procedures and triggers. The front-end application program typically encompasses a large amount of functionality. We will refer to this client application as a *fat client*

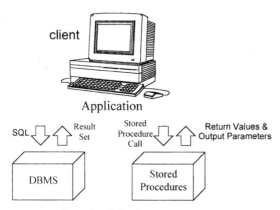

Figure 1.7   Two-tiered database server-centric model.

or application model, as illustrated in Fig. 1.7. This model is very popular, even commonplace in the corporate environment today; however, there are scaling and reliability problems that will not allow this model to support many mission-critical systems.

Using a three-tier model, developers can distribute application processing using application servers, in addition to the front-end and the database server. This type of application can be referred to as a *skinny client* or application model.

Several methods have been used for application partitioning, including

- Development of customized application servers using tools such as SYBASE Open Server, Novell's AppWare, and Novell Netware's Value Added Server (VAS) Application Programming Interface (API) calls

- Remote procedure calls

User application architecture is continuing to evolve with the introduction of application partitioning tools such as INFORMIX-NewEra from Informix Software, Forte from Forte Software, Inc., and Dynasty from Dynasty Technologies, Inc. These relatively new tools divide an application into separate pieces that execute on different platforms accessible via a network. (See Fig. 1.8.) The benefits of application partitioning with these tools include

- The ability to develop scalable, partitioned applications that can be easily modified and redistributed as business needs change.

- Design and deploy applications in a team environment.

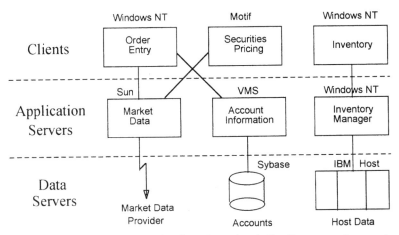

Figure 1.8 Application partitioning in a three-tiered client/server environment.

- Distribution of an application over several platforms (e.g., Sun Solaris, IBM AIX, Microsoft Windows NT) as well as relocation application processing, without affecting the functionality or changing code. Forte provides a drag-and-drop application partitioning tool that can be used to repartition applications. Forte also provides a performance monitor that can be used to tune distributed applications.

- Support for event-driven programming.

- Integration with client/server TP monitors including Transarc's Encina and Novell's Tuxedo. Forte can also use its own proprietary transaction processing monitor to manage transactions.

- The ability to reroute application processing automatically to replicated platforms when a server fails.

Multidimensional analysis (MDA). Often, system designers and users like to differentiate operational databases, designed for OLTP applications, from decision support systems. Aside from purely operational considerations (availability, multiuser support, etc.), databases designed for DSSs should easily lend themselves to support ad hoc analytical queries that appear to exceed the two dimensions (rows and columns) of the classical relational data model.

A multidimensional DBMS allows users to

- View data from many different viewpoints

- Easily switch between many different viewpoints

- Drill down into the data with a parent-child relationship between the data points

For example, a user (i.e., product manager for a package goods company) may look for a sales report of actual sales numbers for several manufacturing products (each is a *dimension*) by quarter (a dimension) across geographical regions (a dimension), demographic areas (a dimension), distance from a certain location (a dimension), weather conditions (a dimension), social status of buyers (a dimension), etc. The result set may look like a multidimensional spreadsheet (thus, the name), and typically, an analyst may drill down into these data to see, e.g., how an individual salesperson's performance affects quarterly sales numbers. Conversely, the drill-down procedure may help discover certain patterns in sales of a given product. This discovery can force another set of questions of similar or greater complexity. Technically, these questions can be answered by a large number of rather complex queries against a set of detail and presummarized data views. In practice, however, even if the analyst could quickly and accurately formulate SQL statements of this complexity, a typical RDBMS may take a long time to process such a request. One solution to this problem could be a parallel scalable DBMS running on a high-performance MPP system. Since not every business can justify this level of hardware investment, other, PC and server-based solutions are now available for multidimensional analysis applications. Examples include Essbase from Arbor Software, LightShip from Pilot Software, and NDR from New Dominion Resources. While not a common requirement for DSS, MDA functionality may be a necessary feature for some client/server DSS applications. It is, therefore, critical that an MDA product selected for its multidimensionality be capable of operating in a client/server environment.

Object-oriented DBMS.   The object-oriented approach continues to grow in acceptance. Object-oriented analysis and design and object-oriented programming are becoming a desired and preferred way of developing applications rapidly and efficiently due to the ability to reuse application code and entire business objects. The need for and the benefits of object-oriented database management systems (OODBMSs) are the driving forces that result in the development of a new database system model—OODBMS. Therefore, while OODBMS discussions are beyond the scope of this book, a few comments should be made for the sake of completeness. The development of the new OODBMS follows two major approaches—extending the relational model to accommodate object concepts and building radically different, nonrelational database systems.

The first approach is pursued by many vendors (including traditional RDBMS vendors) and is facilitated by the ANSI SQL committee and SQL Access Group (SAG) working toward the object-oriented extensions to SQL (SQL3).

The second approach is promoted by OODBMS vendors who believe that the relational data model is not suited for the object-oriented approach. These vendors have developed a common set of standards for OODBMS, a set that is quite different from the one being developed by ANSI.

It is a fair assumption that both approaches will eventually result in a OODBMS model that will incorporate the best features of both worlds. Some OODBMS products on the market today, such as GemStone from Servio Corporation and ObjectStore (Object Design Inc.), are examples of the new generation of object-oriented database management systems that provide access to objects through applications written in C++ and SmallTalk. Others, such as Matisse (ADB Inc.), Objectivity/DB (Objectivity), and UniSQL (UniSQL Inc.), support object databases through the standard SQL interfaces, including Open DataBase Connectivity (ODBC).

1.2   DBMS Reliability and Availability

The key factors affecting DBMS availability are

- *Robustness*—the ability to reduce the effects of any particular failure, coupled with the ability to recover from failures automatically

- *Manageability*—the ability to administer a DBMS on line, often from a remote site

Although availability is critical to any DBMS model (relational, non-relational, object), the discussion below will focus on how these factors affect the design of relational database systems.

1.2.1   Robustness, transactions, recovery, and consistency

A database transaction treats one or more SQL statements as a single unit of work, which is the atomic unit of database recovery and consistency. Consistency in RDBMS prevents simultaneous queries and data modification requests from interfering with each other and prevents access to partially changed and not yet committed data.

An RDBMS should provide for automatic database consistency by implementing the proper levels of locking, validating logical and physical database consistency, and supporting two-phase commit protocols.

Consistency checking should be performed automatically during transaction and database recovery. There are two major types of recovery—transaction recovery from a system or application failure and system recovery from a media failure.

Transaction recovery means that in case of system or application failure, all committed changes must be made permanent—committed data must be written to a database device (disk). At the same time, all data affected by this transaction but not yet committed are recovered (rolled back) to the pretransaction state completely and automatically. The direction of the recovery process is backward—from the point of failure to the last point of consistency.

In the case of media failure (i.e., disk crash), an RDBMS must be designed to perform point-in-time recovery, which includes restoration of the lost data using the most current backup, and forward recovery of data from the point of the latest backup to the point immediately before the media failure. Transaction logs are usually used to store changes to the database and perform recovery procedures—before-change image (for backward recovery) and after-change image (for forward recovery). Often, an RDBMS uses an automatic checkpoint mechanism to maintain the currency of the transaction log. The majority of the database products available today support various degrees of database consistency and recovery.

Shared log files.   Technically speaking, the mechanism a DBMS employs to ensure the integrity of database transactions is database *logging*. DBMS logging requires that every change to the database be automatically written to the database log file. These change records can be used by the DBMS to recover from an in-flight transaction failure (ROLLBACK) and for point-in-time forward recovery. Advanced RDBMS implementations allow one physical write to the log file to contain the COMMIT and ROLLBACK information for several transactions. The resulting reduction in log I/O improves RDBMS update performance, allows for the efficient use of resources, and facilitates multiuser support. SYBASE System 11 supports this technique by using a private log cache (PLC) which will be discussed in greater detail later in this book.

Dynamic configuration.   An RDBMS must have dynamic configuration to provide high availability and to support 24 × 7 continuous operations. This means that it should be possible for the system administrator to configure (without stopping and restarting) such parameters as

- Total server memory
- Number of supported user connections
- Number of locks supported by the server
- Size of memory pools and procedure caches
- Disk I/O parameters

If these options cannot be dynamically configured, the server must be stopped and restarted which obviously impacts system availability.

On-line backup and recovery. The database backup and recovery mechanisms should be able to operate dynamically, on line, while the RDBMS server continues to operate. Indeed, in a multiuser, multi-database environment, a backup of one database should not prevent users from accessing other databases, even on the same physical system. That is especially true when many organizations authorize database owners to be responsible for backing up their databases and corresponding transaction logs. On-line recovery should allow a database to recover automatically from an application or transaction failure (i.e., perform automatic rollback), and support a forward recovery procedure. On-line backup and recovery should be a mandatory feature for RDBMS products selected for real-time, OLTP environments (e.g., banking, brokerage, ticket reservation, air traffic control).

Fault tolerance. While backup and recovery are important availability features, database management systems also employ hardware and software measures typically found in fault-tolerant systems. In fact, INFORMIX-OnLine provides the ability to maintain a single read-only replicate of a primary database. Hardware fault tolerance requires a physical system implementation where all (or the majority) of the components are duplicated, so that when one component fails, the "hot" standby takes over immediately. Among the fault-tolerant measures found in DBMSs are the ability to work with RAID (redundant array of inexpensive disks) devices, disk mirroring, and disk duplexing. In addition to protecting from disk failures, these measures often help optimize I/O performance.

Disk mirroring. Several vendors supply hardware fault-tolerant solutions (e.g., Tandem and Stratus computers). Unfortunately, these solutions are rather expensive and lock RDBMS developers and users into a particular vendor or product. Several RDBMS vendors offer software-based fault tolerance by providing disk mirroring for transaction logs and/or databases. For example, SYBASE supports disk mirroring for either the transaction log or the database itself.

Mirroring a transaction log protects against the loss of any committed transaction (see Fig. 1.9), while mirroring a database guarantees continuous operation in the event of media failure. Mirroring a database means nonstop recovery (see Fig. 1.10).

Disk mirroring requires availability of a separate physical disk drive device on an RDBMS server, and it actually duplicates all writes to the primary device on the mirror. Disk mirroring has an

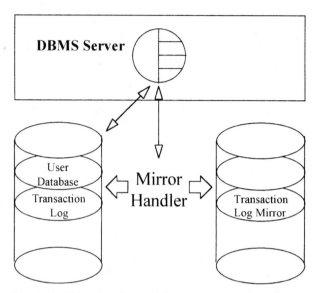

Figure 1.9   Disk mirroring—minimum guaranteed configuration.

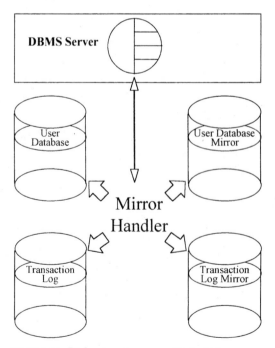

Figure 1.10   Disk mirroring on multiple disks.

added advantage that both disks—the primary and the mirror—are available for read operations. Some RDBMS products take advantage of this fact by routing read requests to the disk drive that provides better response time. SYBASE SQL Server will queue reads up against both sides of the mirrored device. SQL Server will use the data from the side (of the mirror) that responds first and ignore the result of the second read.

Chapter

2

Client/Server RDBMS Solutions

Although this book is focused on the SYBASE database management system, added value is provided by comparing SYBASE to the architectural and implementation background of the other market leaders in this technology.

Database management systems are the information backbone of today's organizations. Current technology and business requirements make it increasingly clear that distributed systems are playing a major role in the advanced computing environments of today and of the future. Client/server computing, network computing, and peer-to-peer computing are just several examples of such environments. As these environments assume mission-critical roles in the enterprise, several trends affecting the DBMS technology are becoming evident. One of these trends forces the DBMS technology to enable the development and support of distributed environments, while another trend is driving the complexity and the sheer volume of the data toward the next generation of DSS and OLTP applications—on-line complex processing (OLCP). A clear indication of this trend can be found in the advancements in the area of commercial high-performance computing, in the amount of data that organizations are trying to process on the emerging client/server platforms, and in the general high level of expectations that developers and users alike have of the client/server distributed DBMS. These new OLCP-capable database management systems can provide businesses with a quantum leap in the ability to *understand,* and not just process, huge amounts of data. This understanding will allow organizations to manage the business more efficiently, to recognize trends, to avoid mistakes and bad business decisions, and to provide customers with answers and value added information directly, in a common, integrated platform.

Up to this point in the book, the emphasis has been on the general theoretical criteria of an ideal distributed relational DBMS. Today, evaluating and choosing a database management system are steadily becoming one of the first system decisions MIS managers must make. And, with OLCP requirements steadily pushing the limits of the traditional RDBMS technology, the task of selecting an "appropriate" DBMS becomes even more critical.

There are several DBMS products designed to work in client/server environments based on various hardware and operating system platforms. SYBASE is the focus of much of this book; however, contrasts to Oracle and Informix will be made. To make the picture complete, to demonstrate how the architectural and design features discussed above apply to the major RDBMS products, and to show how Sybase's competition stacks up, the discussion below focuses on some of these products—UNIX-based DB2/6000, Oracle, and Informix-OnLine. Database vendors tend to get a reputation for being good at providing certain features, or for supporting a certain type of application. In that vein, the database vendors might be classified as follows:

- *SYBASE.*   Known for strong OLTP performance and wide front-end support; very popular in financial markets. Sybase is also recognized for its cross-DBMS interoperability and gateway solutions.

- *Informix-OnLine.*   Superior architecture for data warehousing, large database support, parallelization, and scalability. The Informix database is embedded in several third-party vertical market products.

- *Oracle.*   Recognized for wide platform support, large database support, and the ability to run on the mainframe. Oracle has a large installed base and was the first vendor to introduce parallel database support.

- *IBM DB2/6000.*   Starting with Version 2, DB2/6000 is one of the most function-rich DBMSs available. Known for DB2 compatibility and interoperability, support of the CICS/6000 transaction manager. A popular choice in IBM shops.

2.1   IBM DATABASE 2 AIX/6000

Advances in client/server architecture and distributed computing, the emergence of open-system standards, and wide acceptance by users of open-system goals continue to change the directions and trends of the computing environment, information systems market.

One of the most noticeable changes in the computer industry today is that the market for traditional mainframe and even mini computers continues to contract, while the market for microprocessor-based solutions and local-area networks is expanding. These market changes and customer demands for the availability of distributed, open, client/server products have led IBM to accept and embrace the client/server computing architecture and ideas of interoperability and support for open systems. As a result, IBM extended the range of available services by providing connectivity, network management, distributed database, shared files, presentation services, mail exchange, and common languages not only among its operating environments (MVS, OS/2, and AIX) but also interoperability among multiuser multivendor systems. In the context of distributed data management, however, this chapter will briefly discuss DB2/6000 for AIX (Advanced Interactive eXecutive operating system—IBM's version of UNIX). DB2/6000 is IBM's RDBMS answer to such established RDBMS industry leaders as Oracle, Informix, and Sybase.

Access to host data.   One of the clear advantages of IBM DB2/6000 is its transparent access to distributed corporate data. This connectivity is based on IBM's Distributed Relational Database Architecture (DRDA). DB2/6000 uses Distributed Database Connection Services/6000 (DDCS/6000)—an implementation of the DRDA Application Requester (AR) for the AIX platform. Using Distributed Database Connection Services/6000, DB2/6000 can directly participate in the remote unit of work with any DRDA-compliant RDBMS including DB2/MVS, SQL/DS (VM and VSE), and Database Manager for OS/400.

In addition to providing direct connections to these RDBMSs, DDCS/6000 can act as a gateway for remote database clients, including DOS, MS Windows, AIX, and OS/2 clients using TCP/IP and SNA APPC/LU6.2 protocols.

Transaction management.   DB2/6000 provides full transactional support in compliance with X/Open's XA transactional interfaces. As an XA-compliant resource manager, DB2/6000 can participate in the CICS-controlled two-phase commit. In addition, since CICS/MVS APIs are supported by CICS/6000, a mainframe COBOL/CICS/DB2 application can be easily ported to the AIX platform running CICS/6000 and DB2/6000. DB2/6000 can support other XA-compliant transaction managers, including Transarc's Encina.

Administration.   DB2/6000 administration and management are facilitated by the database system monitor, which allows the user to gather real-time statistical information for the entire DBMS, individual databases, tables, and application. Other administration tools provide graphical support for database configuration, directory management, recovery, user, and user group security.

DB2/6000 Backup and Recovery is an integrated facility that supports on-line backup operations. Database restore and forward recovery procedures are also supported. Remote backup to MVS and VM systems is supported via the Adstar Distributed Storage Manager (ADSM).

Finally, DB2/6000 supports a directory functionality that allows a DBA to define databases and specify their locations. Once the location directory is complete, access to the database is transparent to users and applications, regardless of the database location.

Application development. DB2/6000 supports application development by providing a rich set of application programming interfaces (APIs) and supporting static and dynamic SQL, referential integrity, call-level interface (CLI), SQL precompiler, and embedded SQL from C, FORTRAN, and COBOL programs. Microsoft's ODBC support is provided by DB2 Client Enabler/DOS component. The ANSI-standard SQL support is extended to include a subset of the ISO/ANSI SQL3 standard—compound SQL statements and the VALUE scalar function. The compound SQL allows application developers to group several SQL statements into a single executable block. The VALUE function returns the first nonzero result from a series of expressions.

Query by image content (QBIC). QBIC for DB2/6000 is used to query image data in a DB2/6000 database. QBIC can be used to locate a range of records based on shape, color, or texture. This technology can be used for faster data access for applications including multimedia.

Performance. Many RDBMS performance enhancement features are incorporated into the DB2/6000 design. Among them are row-level locking, highly advanced cost-based query optimizer and buffer manager, and DB2/6000 stored procedures, which are implemented via the database application remote interface (DARI).

The DB2/6000's performance features allow it to support database sizes up to 64 Gbytes, with the maximum table size of 512 Mbytes. Other Version 2 enhancements include

- Support for *user-defined data types* (UDTs).

- Support for *user-defined functions* (UDFs). Support for UDFs enables the creation of function libraries which can be developed by third-party vendors or by customers and then integrated directly into the database.

- *Large objects* (LOBs). LOBs allow users to store very large (multi-gigabyte) binary or text objects in a DB2/6000 database. Binary large objects (BLOBs) can be used to store multimedia objects such as voice recordings, images, or video.

- *Constraints and triggers.* These enable database designers to implement complex referential integrity rules to enforce the correctness of a database.

- *Recursive SQL queries.* The query optimizer has been enhanced to allow DB2/6000 databases to support the classic bill-of-materials queries, as well as recursive queries such as path expression queries.

- *Database partitioning using tablespaces.* Version 2 allows DBAs to partition a database into parts called *tablespaces.* Tablespaces allow index and LOB structures to be stored separately from the rest of the table data.

- *Extended SQL capabilities.* They provide support for SQL92 entry-level standards.

- *Higher availability.* This comes about through improvements in backup/restore capabilities including parallel backup/recovery, backup/recovery of database partitions (tablespaces), and online backup/recovery.

Note that IBM has been very late to market with several of these features including stored procedures and triggers.

Finally, DB2/6000 is designed to take advantage of distributed-memory systems (MPP). By incorporating parallel query processing into DB2/6000, IBM can achieve significant performance levels running on the IBM MPP system—SP2. In fact, DB2/6000 is designed to be almost linearly scalable in the SP2's parallel environment (there is a nearly linear improvement in speed-up with the addition of new processors to the system). The IBM RS/6000 SP2 is profiled in Chap. 6.

2.2   Oracle

Oracle is one of the largest RDBMS vendors. The Oracle RDBMS is available on practically every hardware platform and every operating system. Starting with Version 7, Oracle provides parallel query processing capabilities, and as such, it is the first commercial RDBMS that is available on several SMP and MPP platforms. Oracle offers not just a relational database management system, but an entire suite of integrated software tools, including an integrated computer-aided software engineering (I-CASE) tool set. Some of the strongest features of Oracle are

- Hardware and system software portability

- Wide communication protocol support

- Distributed processing capabilities

- Parallel query processing

- Active Data Dictionary

- Enhanced SQL support including Procedural (PL/SQL), SQL pre-compiler support, ANSI SQL support, and extended SQL support (SQL*Plus)

Oracle front-end tools include SQL*FORMS, Developer/2000 (graphical tools for application development), SQL*ReportWriter, and SQL*Menu products.

Oracle offers a standard SQL implementation with several useful extensions and two programming interfaces—low-level Oracle call interface and embedded SQL with SQL precompilers. Oracle offers sophisticated concurrency control, row-level locking, contention-free queries, event-related triggers, and asynchronous I/O. In addition, Oracle supports shared databases via its global cache system, where multiple Oracle instances residing on multiple systems can share the same database located on a shared disk.

Beginning with Version 7, the Oracle RDBMS supports cost-based optimization, clustered indexes, stored procedures, database triggers, disk mirroring, server-enforced integrity constraints, BLOB data types, on-line backup/recovery, and on-line, remote database administration.

The Oracle distributed RDBMS implementation is facilitated by the SQL*Net and SQL*Connect products. These components allow Oracle to support distributed queries and updates, data location transparency, site autonomy, heterogeneous DBMS access, and network independence. Oracle's SQL*Net is a heterogeneous network interface and supports DECnet, TCP/IP, SNA LU0, LU2 and APPC/LU6.2, Novell's IPX/SPX, Named Pipes, X.25, OSI, and Banyan Vines, to name just a few. Oracle SQL*Connect heterogeneous DBMS connectivity facility supports access to DB2, SQL/DS, and VAX RMS.

One of the most important components of the Oracle RDBMS is its active Data Dictionary, which is a set of read-only tables containing information about the database and database objects (tables, views, indexes, synonyms, sequences, and clusters). The Data Dictionary provides information about user names, user privileges, table constraints, column default values, primary and foreign keys, object space allocation, audit data; and it is, in fact, a database reference guide for all database users.

As was mentioned earlier, Oracle was the first commercial RDBMS that successfully ventured into the high-performance scalable commercial computing arena with the support of very large databases. To that end Oracle's architecture supports two configurations:

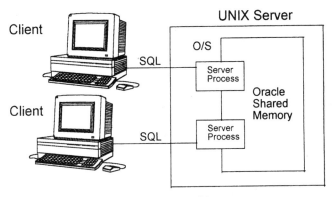

Figure 2.1 Oracle 7 dedicated server architecture.

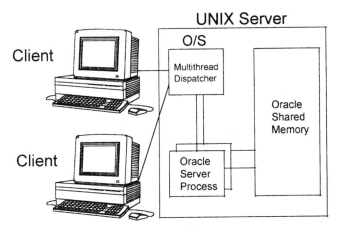

Figure 2.2 Oracle 7 shared server architecture.

- Oracle 7 dedicated server architecture uses simulated multithreading, with one server process for each concurrently executing user request, as shown in Fig. 2.1.

- Oracle 7 shared server architecture allows users to share a set of processes, as shown in Fig. 2.2. Oracle automatically balances the number of shared server and dispatcher processes, governed by the length of an internal request queue. The database administrator can control this balancing by setting configuration parameters for the server in the INIT.ORA file. The DBA can also manually override the number of servers and dispatcher process numbers by means of an ALTER SYSTEM command. Dedicated server processes can be allocated to particular user processes, thus avoiding the use of the dispatcher and shared server. This can be advantageous for critical user processes with large data loads.

It may be obvious from looking at Fig. 2.1 that there is a large amount of overhead required by the dedicated server architecture. Because each user request requires a dedicated server process, each user connection can use between 300 and 500 kbytes of server memory. In the Oracle 7 shared server architecture, incoming processes are dispatched to a server process assigned from the process pool, with the number of both servers and dispatchers tunable by the database administrator. One drawback of this approach is that the entire process (and not a lightweight thread) can be blocked waiting for I/O, memory, or other system resources. The shareability of the server processes can result in what Oracle calls *artificial deadlocks*. These occur when a server process acquires an exclusive lock needed by other servers, but then is released from the current user and is used by another user. If no other server is available to process SQL statements holding the lock, Oracle will attempt to start another server from the limited pool. If the maximum number of servers is reached, a DBA must intervene to resolve the conflict.

Oracle's Parallel Server Option.   Despite these drawbacks, Oracle uses process switching to facilitate its port to an SMP or MPP architecture. Oracle offers two options for parallel processing applications. The first is the parallel server option (PSO) for loosely coupled clusters or massively parallel processing systems. The second is the Oracle parallel query option (PQO) for tightly coupled SMP systems. Both the parallel query option and the parallel server option are necessary for distributed-memory MPP systems. PSO and PQO are designed to take advantage of SMP and MPP architectures by allowing separate instances of Oracle to run on individual processors, while sharing access to database files. Oracle solves the critical issue of memory and cache management in multiprocessor environments by implementing a Global Lock Manager and the GigaCache system, which provide for cache coherency and in-cache data integrity.

The Oracle implementation uses several different operating system processes including a query coordinator and a pool of query servers. The individual operating system processes are single-threaded by design. The query coordinator intelligently breaks down a query into subqueries which are then passed to the corresponding pool of query server processes. This is similar to the SYBASE MPP product where the Data Administrator parses requests and sends stored procedures and SQL to data servers. For example, the PQO can break a scan-join-sort sequence of the two-table join into two-table scan operations running in parallel, join, and sort, all running on individual processors, as in case 3, Fig. 1.4. The server processes work in parallel, and the Oracle coordinator is also responsible for receiving results from the query servers, postquery processing, and returning results to the requesting client. The query coordinator encompasses the functionality of the SYBASE MPP Control Server and Data Administrator. Oracle PQO can parallelize most SQL operations (SELECT, DELETE, UPDATE), including joins, scans, sorts, aggregates, and groupings. In addition, Oracle can parallelize the creation of indexes, database load, backup, and recovery. Oracle currently has no internal data partitioning mechanism so performance gains will be limited since data partitioning is necessary for a linear increase in performance.

The Oracle Server dynamically starts and kills query servers to adjust for system load. During peak loads the Oracle Server may spin off additional query servers to process subtasks. Conversely, during light loads the Server will kill query servers to reduce process overhead on the server. The minimum and maximum number of query servers can be specified by the database administrator prior to server initialization.

2.3 INFORMIX-OnLine

INFORMIX-OnLine Dynamic Server (available starting with Release 6) is a completely reengineered RDBMS product based on the Informix dynamic scalable architecture (DSA). INFORMIX-OnLine Dynamic Server offers a number of fully integrated, no-extra-cost advanced features. Among them are

- True multithreaded architecture
- Distributed DBMS capabilities
- Symmetric MultiProcessing (SMP)
- Parallel disk I/O and utilities
- Hot standby support—the ability to maintain a single read-only replicate of a primary database
- Multiprotocol network support

In addition, Release 7 of the INFORMIX-OnLine Dynamic Server offers

- Parallel query processing
- Table partitioning
- Partition-level backup and restore

■ Support for very large databases

INFORMIX dynamic scalable architecture supports multiple concurrent threads, which are scheduled on the basis of resource availability independent of the mechanism used by the platform's operating system. The scheduler itself is nonpreemptive and assigns tasks from the multiple, different-priority *ready queues* on a first-in, first-out (FIFO) basis. The architecture supports two additional queue types—wait queue (where threads waiting for an event such as resource availability are placed) and sleep queue (inactive threads).

INFORMIX-OnLine Dynamic Server SMP support is provided via true multithreading features of the DSA. In essence, although it looks like a single server to the user, the DSA schedules multiple virtual processors, each of which is running multiple threads by context switching. A virtual processor is assigned to a particular CPU and belongs to one of the processor classes. The number of virtual processors can be altered dynamically by users for some classes and automatically by the system for other classes.

Parallel disk I/O, parallel utilities, and parallel query processing features are integrated into the DSA, which divides each atomic database operation into multiple concurrent threads. In addition, each database operation is data-flow-driven and begins its processing as soon as input data are available. In turn, the output of each database operation is fed to the next operation for processing. This approach allows concurrent threads to be assigned in parallel to sort, merge, scan, join, selection, and projection operations (see case 3 in Fig. 1.4)—vertical parallelism. Similarly, this architecture allows different tasks to run in parallel—horizontal parallelism (as in case 4, Fig. 1.4). The latter can benefit from data partitioning supported by the DSA in three modes—index key partitioning, hash partitioning, and expression partitioning (partitions are established based on an SQL expression).

Other INFORMIX-OnLine features include software disk mirroring, on-line backup and recovery, asynchronous parallel I/O, flexible monitoring facilities for the configuration information and DBMS activity, and cost-based optimization. INFORMIX-OnLine supports binary large objects (BLOBs) for image, graphics, voice, and large text objects. In fact, INFORMIX is so efficient in multimedia applications that it is often chosen as the underlying DBMS for commercial imaging systems. INFORMIX distributed database support is provided by Informix Star and includes distributed cost-based optimization, data location transparency, and distributed queries. For heterogeneous DBMS connectivity, Informix uses third-party software vendors to implement its mainframe gateway strategy.

INFORMIX-OnLine Extended Parallel Server (OnLine XPS) version 8.0.
Designed for the UNIX and Windows NT operating systems, OnLine
XPS extends DSA to loosely coupled or shared-nothing computing
architectures, including clusters of symmetric multiprocessor (SMP)
and massively parallel processor (MPP) systems.

OnLine XPS is targeted at data warehousing, decision support, and
other very large database (VLDB) applications. OnLine XPS provides
a set of features including enhanced parallel SQL operations, high-
availability capabilities, and a suite of systems management tools
based on the Tivoli Management Environment (TME). The TME-
based tools allow database administrators to manage multiple database platforms as a "single-system image."

Overall, INFORMIX-OnLine offers an innovative server architecture, relatively few hardware and software requirements, impressive
software development tools (Informix/4GL and Informix New-Era),
and excellent performance. Figure 2.3 depicts the INFORMIX-OnLine
XPS architecture.

Informix console.   DB/Cockpit is a Tivoli-based graphical tool designed
for INFORMIX-OnLine Dynamic Server administration tasks.
DB/Cockpit allows the administrator to monitor INFORMIX-OnLine
system parameters reported by other utilities.

2.4   SYBASE MPP

SYBASE MPP (formerly Navigation Server) is a component of
SYBASE System 11 designed to provide scalable performance and
high availability on parallel computing platforms. By partitioning the

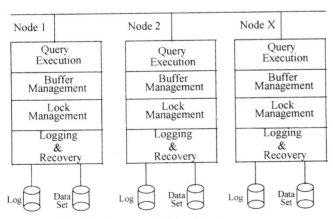

Figure 2.3   INFORMIX-OnLine XPS architecture.

data across multiple SYBASE SQL Servers, SYBASE MPP provides high-speed access to very large databases (20 + Gbytes to Tbytes). SYBASE MPP is also designed to support thousands of users, thousands of concurrent queries, and very high transaction rates for both decision support and transaction processing applications. SYBASE MPP parallel features include index access, insert, load, update, delete, and backup and restore.

Data partitioning.   In the context of this book, a *node* is defined as a single UNIX server known to other nodes by a single entry in their */etc/hosts* file; a *partition* as a portion of a table's data allocated on a set of disks and accessed by a single database server; and a *home* as a collection of processing nodes within the system in which all the partitions of a table reside. If the entire database is partitioned into a number of smaller segments, each located on its own (logical) device, then the total query can be decomposed into the equal number of subqueries, all running in parallel against a corresponding partition of the database (horizontal parallelism). The resulting execution time is significantly reduced in comparison with a sequential query. Clearly, for maximum speed-up, both the multiprocessor server and a parallel RDBMS should be able to support parallel I/O. By placing data partitions on separate physical devices (preferably connected via separate I/O buses), the relational DBMS optimizer can parse the query based on data partitioning rules (e.g., key ranges, hash algorithms). SYBASE MPP supports three data partitioning methods, all of which can be applied at the table level.

- *Range partitioning.*   This type of partitioning locates rows based on the value of one or more columns in the row (usually the primary key). Figure 2.4 shows a large customer account table partitioned across five different disk drives and/or nodes in the system.

- *Schema partitioning.*   This is a simple strategy whereby tables in an application schema are distributed across multiple disk drives and/or nodes in the network, as shown in Fig. 2.5.

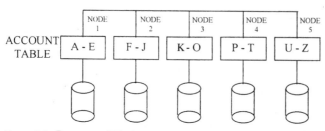

Figure 2.4   Range partitioning.

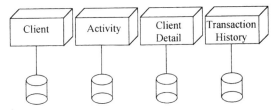

Figure 2.5 Schema partitioning.

Account Table

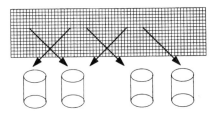

Figure 2.6 Hash partitioning.

■ *Hash partitioning.* SYBASE MPP calculates a hash value for each row, which determines the node or partition on which the data are stored, as illustrated in Fig. 2.6.

Future partitioning choices for SYBASE MPP will include the following:

■ Replicated small tables to boost join performance. Small tables will be replicated across *all nodes* in the parallel query system. This saves time when a table is needed by a particular node to satisfy a join request.

■ Vertical (column set) partitioning for mixed data types. This will allow binary large objects, images, graphics, and text to be stored separately from the rest of the data table.

■ Time-related—mixed data storage media. As data age and the probability of access decreases, the data can be moved to different types of storage media. For example, a brokerage firm might keep trading activity on disk for 6 months. After 6 months activity data can be migrated to a CD-ROM, and after 18 months data can be migrated to a tape archive.

SYBASE MPP architecture. Architecturally, SYBASE MPP is a collection of servers built on SYBASE SQL Server, SYBASE Open Server,

SYBASE Open Client, and the SYBASE Tabular Data Stream (TDS) messaging protocol. SYBASE MPP incorporates the following components:

- *Control Server*—front-end processor for the SYBASE MPP system.
- *DBA Server*—the brain of the SYBASE MPP system, comprised of a DBA Server process and a Schema Server.
- *Schema Server*—a SYBASE SQL Server used to control the Global Directory.
- *Data Server*—the smallest unit of parallelization within SYBASE MPP. A Data Server is comprised of a Split Server and an SQL Server.
- *Split Server*—an Open Server application used primarily to process join requests in the parallel system.

Control Server. In the traditional SYBASE client/server environment, application programs log into the SQL Server directly. In the SYBASE MPP environment, Open Client applications log into an Open Server application called the *Control Server.* The Control Server uses Open Client (CT-Library calls) to connect to and communicate with the DBA Server to parse and optimize client requests, and/or Data Servers to process the requests. The Control Server also merges results received from the SQL Servers to be sent back to the requesting client. So the Control Server acts as both a server and a client within SYBASE MPP.

The Control Server also monitors and initiates recovery for the Data Server and initiates recovery for the Data Server as a unit by sending the appropriate BEGIN, COMMIT, and ROLLBACK directives to the Data Server.

There can be a many-to-many relationship between Control Servers and Data Servers, enabling SYBASE MPP to handle a large number of concurrent users. The architecture can also be reversed (few Control Servers acting as front end for many Data Servers) when there are a few users accessing large amounts of data (see Fig. 2.7).

Data Server. A *Data Server* is not to be confused with a *dataserver,* which is the SYBASE SQL Server process. A Data Server consists of a Split Server and an SQL Server (the *dataserver* process). It is the smallest unit of parallelization within SYBASE MPP. The Split Server and SQL Server work together as a unit. The SQL Server executes the parallel SQL requests generated by the SYBASE MPP system. SQL Server is the workhorse of the SYBASE MPP system.

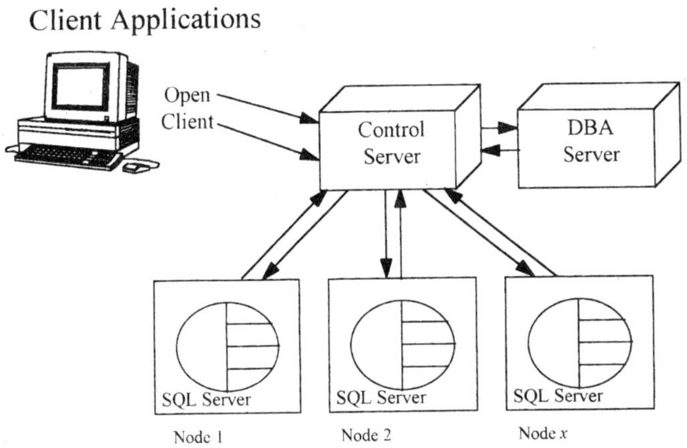

Client Applications

Figure 2.7   Control Server architecture.

Split Server.   The *Split Server* is used primarily to redistribute tables to satisfy join requests. The Split Server is an Open Server application built with the Server Library, C/S Library, and CT-Library APIs. The role of the Split Server and its relationship to the Control Server are discussed further in the section titled "Join Strategies."

Schema Server.   The *Schema Server* is a SYBASE SQL Server used to control the Global Directory. It is located on the same node as the DBA Server. The Global Directory is the data dictionary used by SYBASE MPP to resolve user requests.

DBA Server.   The *DBA Server* is basically a Control Server with additional functionality. It is the "brains" of the system and contains the Parallel SQL (PSQL) compiler and DDL interpreter. As such, it is mirrored on an alternate node for fault tolerance. DBA Server is an Open Server application that in addition to handling the compilation process provides Global Directory Services, implements DDL statements, verifies security, and monitors Control Servers for recovery purposes. For example, the DBA Server will restart a Control Server and relocate it to another node if necessary (due to component failure). It also initiates backup and restore operations in concert with the Administration Server.

The DBA Server also contains a *Recovery Manager* that is responsible for global deadlock detection, monitoring of nodes, and all the servers in the system. The recovery manager provides restart of any failed component in the system. Figure 2.8 represents the SYBASE MPP components and their relationships.

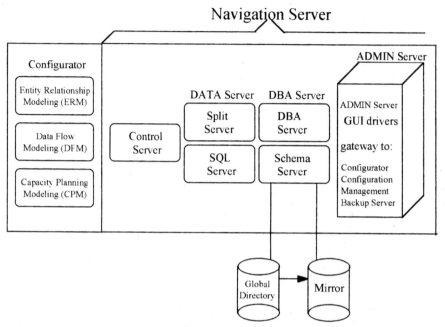

Figure 2.8 System software components.

System administration.   The Administration Server (Admin Server) handles the tasks necessary to administer the SYBASE MPP environment. This is a special process that initiates administrative and configuration utility interfaces. It provides access to Sybase tools such as the Backup Server for database backup and restore and the *Configurator.*

The Admin Server reduces the complexities of managing the system by hiding the operating system interfaces and parallel features from the system administrators. The interface facility, known as *MPP Manager,* supports graphical interfaces for backup and restore, configuration management (monitoring system activities), configuration modeling (logical database design, data flow modeling, and capacity planning), stored procedures (access to SYBASE MPP system schema), design installer (a set of services used to export new and modified database designs), and SYBASE MPP Log Management facilities (support for debug, diagnostic, and statistics options).

Backup and recovery.   The SYBASE MPP backup and recovery procedures are built on the SYBASE backup capabilities. MPP Manager provides the administrator with a single view of the database and logs (see Fig. 2.9). MPP Manager supports partition-level recovery. Database dumps can be automatic (event-driven) or time-specified. The database must be quiesced to perform a restore.

Figure 2.9 SYBASE MPP Manager.

Log Management. The Log Management system is used for collection, storage, and manipulation of error, trace, and statistics data. Data are logged by the various SYBASE MPP components using a log management API. There is a logging thread in each server which manages I/O to the log files. The system administrator can access the logs, set various levels of error reporting, and clear SYBASE MPP logs.

Configuration Management. The Configuration Management facility is a graphical application used to monitor the system's database hardware and software configuration. This tool can be used to determine if any part of the system is overloaded or improperly configured.

Global Directory.   The Global Directory is a private SQL Server database used by SYBASE MPP to run the system. The Global Directory is maintained by the Schema Server. It is used to maintain configuration data and partitioning information generated by the Configurator's Capacity Planning Modeling (CPM) module. All Schema Server data are mirrored and accessible from two nodes (primary and alternate) to guarantee high availability of Global Directory data.

Control Servers and Split Servers read select information from the Global Directory to local cache. The Recovery Manager keeps cached data consistent across the servers for configuration management and interserver communication.

The Global Directory is accessed and manipulated via MPP Manager by using SYBASE system procedures and SYBASE MPP system procedures. Global Directory data can also be transferred to the Configurator where administrative reports can be generated.

The Configurator.   The Configurator is a tool used for up-front planning and ongoing management of the SYBASE MPP configuration. Since the location of data in a parallel database processing environment is the key to performance of the system, the Configurator is designed to recommend partitioning choices based on available hardware, database design, transaction characteristics, and performance and capacity requirements.

The Configurator combines entity relationship modeling, data flow modeling, capacity planning, and workload simulation to determine the optimal system configuration.

After SYBASE MPP is installed, the Configurator is used to monitor actual performance and recommend changes to optimize system performance. It uses statistics information gathered by the Log Management system for this purpose.

Entity Relationship Modeling (ERM) module.   ERM is a GUI-based tool that can be used for Logical Data Modeling of tables and indexes in the database. It can also be used to provide table capacity estimates.

Data Flow Modeling (DFM) module.   DFM is a GUI-based tool used to define transactions and queries. The DBA can work with the GUI tool or with Transact-SQL. Extensions are available to analyze the number of sources for data, throughput requirements, response time requirements, and transaction rates for specified time intervals.

Capacity Planning Modeling (CPM).   CPM is a tool used to generate hardware, software, and data partitioning configurations based upon data provided by the ERM and DFM modules. The CPM tool can ana-

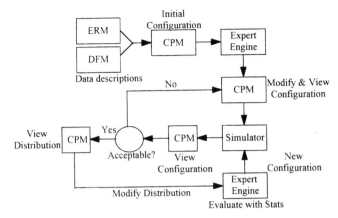

Figure 2.10 Configurator flow.

lyze and/or simulate the workload and may recommend new data partitioning based on the existing workload. CPM provides performance reports and graphics based on statistics gathered by the Log Management system.

· Figure 2.10 illustrates the work flow of the Configurator.

- The CPM creates an initial configuration based on output from the ERM and DFM.

- The initial configuration is analyzed and refined by the Configurator's expert engine.

- At this point, the configuration can be modified by the database administrator before it is sent to the workload simulator.

- After workload simulation is completed, the configuration and results can be analyzed and modified. This is an iterative process that can be repeated until an acceptable configuration is achieved.

Parallel SQL engine. At this point, Sybase has not built parallelization into the SQL Server process. Instead, it opted to build the parallel SQL (PSQL) compiler into a separate Open Server process (the DBA Server). The SQL is parallelized by the DBA Server, and the execution plans are sent to individual SQL Servers in each partition. This means that multiple *dataserver* processes are required to run on the multiprocessor system, a minimum of one on each processing node.

Query processing. Figure 2.11 illustrates the flow of query processing within SYBASE MPP.

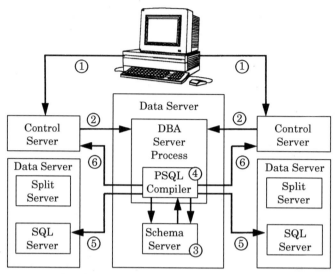

Figure 2.11   Parallel SQL compilation.

1. Client applications log into the Control Server and send data requests using Open Client APIs.

2. The requests are passed to the DBA Server by the Control Server using an Open Client connection.

3. The DBA Server works with the Schema Server to parse the client requests.

4. The parallel SQL compiler compiles and optimizes the SQL.

5. Stored procedures are sent from the PSQL compiler to the participating SQL Servers.

6. PSQL plans are loaded into memory for execution and initiated by the Control Server.

Table scan.   When SYBASE MPP performs a table scan on a partitioned table, the Control Server issues nonblocking stored procedure or SQL requests to the SQL Servers that control all partitions of the table (the table's home). The Control Server receives result sets from each partition and merges the results. Result sets are ordered if there was a GROUP BY or ORDER BY request. Rows are returned to the client application using standard TDS protocol. Figure 2.12 illustrates the run-time flow of a table scan.

Join strategies.   The Split Server is responsible for redistributing tables to resolve join requests when tables are not partitioned in the

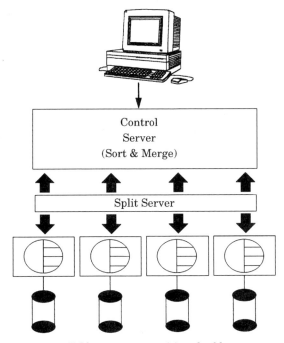

Figure 2.12 Table scan on a partitioned table.

same way. There are two methods used by the Split Server to process joins: *Redecluster* and *Replicate*.

- *Redecluster 1.*   A subset of one table is moved (on its joining column) into the *home* of another table. This method is appropriate for equi-joins when one of the tables is not declustered on its joining column.

- *Redecluster 2.*   Subsets of both tables are moved (on their joining columns) to a new *home*. This is appropriate for equi-joins when neither table is declustered on its joining column.

- *Replicate 1.*   A subset of one table is replicated onto each partition of the other tables' *home*. This method is usually required for non-equi-joins and small tables.

All redistribution strategies require sufficient working space for the temporary tables to service the requests. Working space is taken from the *tempdb* database of the individual SQL Server. The Configurator will provide recommendations for temporary table requirements based on workload simulations.

Run-time flow. SYBASE MPP joins are executed in two basic forms:

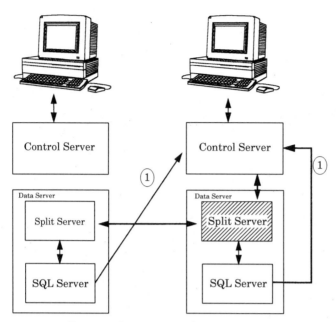

Figure 2.13   Run-time flow—join.

- *'IN-PLACE' join.*   The columns in the join match the columns in which both tables have been declustered. The flow for this type of join is similar to a table scan, except join requests are sent to the SQL Servers.
- When any other type of join occurs, Split Servers are utilized. The Control Server initiates a request to one Split Server which then becomes the *master* Split Server. The *master* communicates with other Split Servers in the system to redistribute data in the form of temporary tables (in a collection of *tempdb* databases). After the temporary tables are created, an in-place join can take place. Sufficient workspace must be available.

Figure 2.13 illustrates the execution path that occurs prior to an 'in-place' join. In the final step (indicated by the circled 1), the individual SQL Servers pass results directly back to the Control Server.

Hardware.   SYBASE MPP is designed to take advantage of multiprocessing systems—SMP (processing nodes are connected via shared memory), shared-nothing systems (MPP) or clustered systems connected via a fast LAN, also supporting configurations where each node has its own data storage subsystem. Initial releases of SYBASE

MPP will require homogeneous nodes that share the same type of interconnect.

SYBASE MPP will run on AT&T Global Information Systems (GIS) massively parallel systems and the 3450 and 3550 models (both SMP machines). Other supported platforms include the IBM SP-2 MPP platform, SUN SPARC 1000 and 2000 SMP machines, and the Sun SPARC cluster. In addition, Sybase has announced support for the Hewlett-Packard Enterprise Server system—T-500 (an SMP system).

3

SQL Server Introduction

This chapter is used to lay some necessary groundwork for the remaining parts of the book. We will introduce the SYBASE product line and discuss SQL Server architecture and SQL Server features. Also covered in this chapter are the SYBASE systems management tools SQL Server Manager and Enterprise SQL Server Manager.

Style. As a convention, commands such as ISQL, BCP, and DBCC are printed here in uppercase to make the text more readable. *SYBASE* refers to the products (the technology) of Sybase, Inc. *Sybase* refers to the company. Sybase, Inc. is traded on the NASDAQ National Market System under the symbol *SYBS*.

The SYBASE family of products. The latest release of the Sybase product line is called System 11. System 11 does not refer to just the SQL Server but to an entire family of products. The System 11 family of products currently includes

- *SQL Server.* This is the Sybase DBMS engine that is the focus of much of this book. It is bundled with Backup Server.

- *SQL Anywhere.* Formerly the Watcom SQL engine, it is available in single-user and multiuser versions. SQL Anywhere will offer Transact-SQL compatibility and will focus on the mass deployment marketplace. Replication Server will be able to replicate data to SQL Anywhere databases.

- *Sybase IQ.* This advanced indexing technology is focused on data warehousing solutions on SMP and MPP platforms.

- *Open Server.* This is a set of tools and interfaces used to build custom server applications. Open Server is the foundation for many other Sybase products.

- *Open Client.*   It provides client access to SQL Server and other Sybase products.

- *OmniSQL Gateway.*   This is an Open Server application designed to provide a Transact-SQL interface to heterogeneous distributed data.

- *SQL Server Monitor.*   It is a graphical tool used to monitor SQL Server performance.

- *SQL Server Manager.*   This is a Microsoft Windows–based systems management tool for SQL Server administrators.

- Enterprise SQL Server Manager (*ESSM*).   This database administration tool was developed for single-screen control of distributed SQL Server databases. It is based on the Tivoli TME architecture.

- *SQL Debug.*   It is a source-level debugger for Transact-SQL code.

- *Embedded SQL.*   This is a precompiler for in-line SQL commands.

- *Replication Server.*   Distributed database technology is designed to provide reliable data distribution. Sybase Replication Server was the groundbreaker for an important technology market—database replication.

- *SYBASE MPP* (formerly Navigation Server).   This system software is designed to provide scalable performance and high availability on high-end parallel computing platforms. SYBASE MPP is a data warehousing solution.

- *Configurator.*   On this SYBASE MPP product, system software is used for entity relationship modeling, data flow modeling, and capacity planning.

The following depicts the SYBASE System 11 products and the categories that they fit into.

SYBASE icons.   Sybase uses a standard set of icons to represent the different SYBASE components. These icons will be used in illustrations throughout the book.

3.1   SQL Server Architecture

At the heart of the SYBASE System 11 product line is the relational database management system (RDBMS) that Sybase calls SQL Server. This chapter will begin discussion on the Sybase RDBMS implementation by taking a close look at the SQL Server architecture. The chapter describes the functionality and architecture of the database engine and focuses on some of the features that have made Sybase so successful. These discussions are based on the foundation built in Chap. 1.

Enterprise	SYBASE MPP SYBASE IQ OMNI SQL Enterprise SQL Server Manager Replication Server
Department	SQL Server SYBASE IQ OMNI SQL SQL Server Manager Replication Server
Workgroup	Workgroup SQL Server (Windows NT) SQL Server SQL Server Manager
Mass Deployment Desktop	SQL Anywhere

SYBASE System 11 Products.

SYBASE Icons.

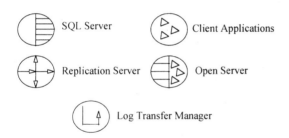

SQL Server

Client Applications

Replication Server

Open Server

Log Transfer Manager

One reason for the success of Sybase is its unique, highly efficient, multithreaded architecture (a thread is basically a lightweight process). For a relatively long time, it has been one of the most advanced architectures available for relational database management. The following sections will analyze SQL Server features based on the requirements for a robust high-performance database server discussed in Chap. 1. Let's start by taking a closer look at how the SYBASE SQL Server is designed.

Multithreaded design. The SQL Server engine has a multithreaded architecture as opposed to a multiprocess (or process per user) architecture. By comparison, Oracle 6 has a process-per-user architecture, while Oracle 7 can function as a process-per-user system or as a hybrid multiprocess multithreaded system (as described in Chaps. 1 and 2). SQL Server's multithreaded architecture allows for a low server memory requirement per user (approximately 50-kbytes per user connection for System 10 and 60 kbytes for System 11).

Figure 3.1 provides a high-level view of SQL Server's multithreaded architecture running on a uniprocessor machine. An instance of SQL Server may be a single operating system process (see Fig. 3.1) or, in a multiprocessor environment, a set of tightly coupled processes. The SQL Server process (called the *dataserver*) creates a thread for each user connection to the SQL Server, a thread for each logical database device, and a thread for the SQL Server error log. SYBASE multiprocessor design is described further in Chap. 11.

Asynchronous I/O.   The SQL Server engine uses asynchronous device I/O on platforms that support it. SQL Server allows the user to partition a physical device into several logical devices. Within the dataserver process each logical database device uses a separate thread, providing asynchronous I/O capabilities even within one physical device.

Because a separate thread is used for each logical device, the SQL Server can write concurrently to different database devices. The asynchronous I/O capability also allows for nonserial writes within mir-

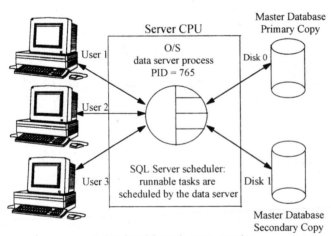

* One thread for each user connection
* One thread for each logical database device
(enables asynchronous disk I/O within one physical device)

Figure 3.1   Multithreaded architecture running on a uniprocessor machine.

rored devices. This means that the system can queue up writes immediately to both sides of mirrored devices. Without asynchronous I/O the system would have to wait for each write to finish before starting another.

In addition to asynchronous I/O, the I/O performance and reliability of UNIX systems can be improved by using *raw device I/O*. RDBMS products like SYBASE use raw devices to bypass the UNIX file system buffering schema and often offer much higher performance and recoverability than those of the UNIX file systems and buffer managers.

As illustrated in the following log fragment, the SQL Server error log indicates that asynchronous I/O is being used on a database device.

```
00:96/04/21 14:38:43.11 kernel Initializing virtual device 0,
  '\SYBASE\DATA\MASTER.DAT'
00:96/04/21 14:38:43.55 kernel Virtual device 0 started using
  asynchronous i/o.
00:96/04/21 14:38:46.48 server Opening Master Database ...
```

UNIX raw partitions.   A raw partition on a UNIX system is a part of the disk where there is no file system. That is, the disk has not been prepared for use by an operating system format utility. SYBASE formats the disk during an initialization process (the DISK INIT command) and accesses it directly with no operating system intervention. Raw partition installations are recommended for production databases because of their recovery capabilities and increased I/O performance.

UNIX file systems.   In the UNIX environment, development databases are typically installed on operating system files. This is done when up-to-the-minute database recoverability is not an issue. When the development database stabilizes and storage requirements are well known, the database is migrated to a raw disk partition. Operating system files are recommended only for testing and fine-tuning databases.

UNIX: Raw partitions versus file systems.   Although SQL Server can use UNIX operating system files for database devices, all production databases should be stored on raw partitions. Sybase strongly recommends the use of raw partitions.

Most UNIX systems use a buffer cache for disk input/output. Writes to the disk are stored in the buffer and may not be written to disk immediately. If the SQL Server completes a transaction and sends the results to an operating system file, the transaction is considered complete even though the UNIX buffer cache may not have been written to the disk. If the system crashes before the buffer cache is written,

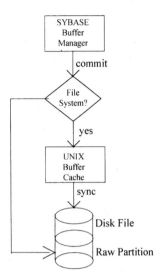

Figure 3.2   SYBASE disk I/O.

the transaction will be lost. SQL Server has no way of knowing that the write to disk ultimately failed, so the transaction cannot be rolled back.

By using raw partitions for database devices, SQL Server will process its own I/O requests. The SQL Server does not need to pass through the UNIX buffering scheme. By writing directly to the disk, SQL Server knows exactly what portions of a transaction completed or failed in the event of a system crash. Figure 3.2 illustrates the disk write path, using UNIX files and raw disk partitions.

System 10 and earlier versions of SQL Server read and write data to physical disk using a 2-kbyte page size. Each read or write of a 2-kbyte page is recognized as a disk transaction. A good high-performance SCSI-2 disk drive might be able to handle 100 or more transactions per second. This means that disk transfer is limited to 200-kbytes/s (2-kbyte pages × 100 transactions per second) which does not approach the transfer rate limit of the SCSI-2 disk drive.

The System 11 SQL Server can read and write data using larger I/O block sizes. The smallest size is 2-kbytes, and the largest is currently 16 kbytes. Actually, the (11.0) server can use 2-, 4-, 8-, and 16-kbytes I/O sizes. The 16-kbyte limitation has something to do with the way that the server performs space allocations using extents. I would expect future versions of the SQL Server to read and write I/O block sizes of up to 512 kbytes.

Client-side asynchronous I/O. Client applications can benefit greatly from the use of asynchronous programming capabilities. Asynchronous applications are designed to make efficient use of time by performing other work while waiting for server operations to complete.

SYBASE users who have worked with DB-Library programs (as a user or programmer) on Microsoft Windows-based personal computers (PCs) have probably been frustrated by synchronous database calls. How many times have you sent a query to the SQL Server and waited (watching the little hourglass) for the results to come back? If these applications were designed to operate asynchronously, the user would be able to perform other work while the SQL Server was processing the query.

Open Client Client-Library (CT-Library), introduced with System 10, provides programmers with a set of routines for asynchronous programming. These asynchronous I/O capabilities allow client applications to use a single connection for multiple actions. The SYBASE Open Client software is discussed in Chap. 14.

Query optimization. Optimization is used to ensure that SQL query results are returned in the shortest possible time with the fewest accesses against the database tables. Different RDBMS products offer different optimization techniques, which can be divided into two major classes:

- Rule-based optimization, also known as *syntax-based* optimization
- Cost-based optimization

C.J. Date's seventh rule deals with the performance issues of the distributed database system. To fully understand these issues, let's look at how a query is processed in a nondistributed centralized relational database (in a nonrelational DBMS, the performance of the query depends on the DBMS access path selected by a user or a program). Remember that nonrelational DBMSs are navigational. That is, the access is directed by the user, and the DBMS itself follows the user's directives.

A relational DBMS provides for nonnavigational data access where users request *what* data they need, and not *how* to access them. Generally speaking, a RDBMS contains a navigational brain—an optimizer—that is "intelligent" enough to select the best access path for a given query, totally transparent to the users and applications.

Rule-based optimizers select an access path based on certain rules that the optimizers follow. For example, when a query to be processed is a join of two tables, the rule-based optimizer may decide that the table coded first (from left to right) in the SQL statement should be searched before the second table is read. The drawback of such an approach can be demonstrated in the following example. Suppose that XYZ Financial's central office (server S1) maintains a table of all company employees and a table of managers. The query in question should look up all employees who are managers whose education level is MBA. Such a query could look like this:

```
SELECT * FROM xyzDatabase.dbo.employee A, xyzDatabase.dbo.manager B
WHERE A.employeeID = B.managerID
AND A.education = "MBA"
AND B.education = "MBA"
```

It is safe to assume that there will be more employees than managers. Following that statement, let's assume that the *employee* table contains 100,000 rows and the *managers* table contains 1000 rows. If the rule-based optimizer processes the leftmost referenced table first, the RDBMS will search 100,000 rows of the *employee* table to select all those with the education level of MBA and then compare them with the 1000 rows of the *managers* table. Obviously, such an approach would not be very efficient. Rule-based optimization is an art form that requires the services of skilled programmers who can generate SQL that is well formed. The advantage of syntax-based optimization is low overhead on the server.

With cost-based optimization, the function of the optimizer is to choose, for each query that it processes, an optimal access strategy. The optimizer selects the access path for a given query based on the estimated cost of the query processing. Typically, the optimizer calculates the cost in such units as the number of I/O operations and/or CPU cycles. To assist the optimizer, statistics are kept on the database tables; these statistics must be updated as frequently as necessary to ensure that they provide an accurate depiction of the database content, i.e., the number of rows in a table, type of data in a column, index availability, key distribution, etc. The optimizer makes use of the data to determine the best plan for execution of a particular query. Cost-based optimization helps to transfer the expertise for determining an efficient way to execute a query from the programmer to the database optimizer.

When a cost-based optimizer processes the query described above, it attempts to calculate the least expensive access path based on the database statistics. Therefore, the query processing should start from a smaller table (*managers*) and compare the selected managers to the list of employees whose education level is equal to MBA. SYBASE SQL Server supports both syntax-based and cost-based optimization. Informix and Oracle both provide cost-based optimization. Sybase has supported cost-based optimization since Version 4.x; while Oracle introduced cost-based optimization with Oracle 7, Oracle 6 uses rule-based optimization.

Global optimization. Performance becomes a major issue in *distributed* query processing. Imagine that the *employee* table and the *managers* table are distributed to two different locations. The size of each node's databases and relevant tables, the network speed, the processing, and the I/O power of each node are then among the major factors that affect the performance of a distributed query. In the client/server architecture, the distributed DBMS (DDBMS) should maintain the list and processing characteristics of every available server.

To find the proper data location and obtain all necessary node characteristics and statistical information about remote databases, distributed query optimization requires access to a *global* database dictionary or catalog. A global dictionary can be implemented by replicating all local dictionaries or catalogs on all nodes (database servers) where the query is performed. To perform cost-based optimization based on real-time statistics, a truly distributed DBMS must maintain all dictionary replicas current.

In distributed query processing, one DBMS server must provide the coordination of optimization and synchronization efforts between all participating databases. Such a coordinator is usually called a *distributed data manager (DDM)*. It is elected dynamically by the DDBMS based on various criteria. In the client/server architecture, the DBMS server that receives the query first can be elected to be the DDM.

Date's seventh rule (see App. I) specifies that in a truly distributed database system, the optimization must take into account both local and global factors, including distributed nodes and network characteristics. Let's consider an example that illustrates the issues of distributed query optimization and the role of the DDM.

Let's assume that XYZ Financial's central office (server S1) maintains a table of all employees, while the processing center (server S2) holds a separate table of managers. The query in question should look up all employees who are managers whose education level is MBA. Here's how such a query can be processed in a truly distributed database system:

- The server that first receives the query is elected to become the DDM (in our example, it is server S1).

- The DDM knows that the tables in question reside at different locations (S1 and S2) and modifies the original query (see above) accordingly.

```
SELECT * FROM server_s1.xyzDatabase.dbo.employee A,
 server_s2.xyzDatabase.dbo.managers B
  WHERE A.employeeID = B.managerID
  AND A.education = "MBA"
  AND B.education = "MBA"
```

- The DDM accesses its own system catalog to assign costs to the local join component (*employee* table).

- The DDM connects to the remote server (S2) and accesses the system catalog to assign costs to the remote components of the join (see Fig. 3.3).

- Based on the estimated costs and server characteristics, the DDM decides where the join is to be performed and which table is to be joined to the other.

- The DDM selects server S1 as the site for the join execution, because it is a more powerful server and less data must be moved. The DDM decides that the smaller table (*managers*) will be joined to the *employee* table, since it requires fewer I/O operations and less network data movement between servers.

- The DDM initiates the selection of the proper rows from the smaller table and sends the filtered records (managers with the MBA degree) across the network to server S1.

Without distributed query optimization, the DDBMS may choose an extremely inefficient alternative—sending all 100,000 employee records to remote server S2 for selection and join, then sending the results back to S1. Clearly, joining data between two tables is the simplest possible case. Each additional table and/or database increases both the number of choices for the optimizer and the complexity of the DDM. Therefore, a complete implementation of the distributed query optimization is a rather difficult task that only a handful of DBMS vendors attempt.

Products such as SYBASE, Oracle, INFORMIX, and Ingres support

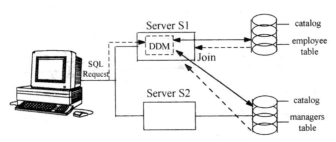

Figure 3.3 Distributed query processing.

Date's seventh rule with certain limitations, and even then the quality of optimization decreases as the complexity of the query grows.

Multiple network engines. Multiple network engines (MNEs) extend network I/O capability to all SQL Server engines in the SMP environment. This improves server performance, scalability, and load balancing by distributing network I/O operations to each server engine on a per-connection basis. SQL Server engines prior to System 11 perform all network I/O using engine 0. Using server *trace flags,* the system administrator can force engine 0 to be exclusively used for network and disk I/O. There is also a trace flag to prevent engine 0 from running nonaffinitied tasks (tasks other than network and disk I/O). These server trace flags are typically used in tandem.

MNEs also increase the number of connections that SQL Server can support. Typically, the number of connections supported by an operating system process is limited by the operating system itself. By routing all network I/O to engine 0, the total number of simultaneous user connections is limited (say, to 4096). By making networking symmetric, each engine can handle the maximum number of connections. For example, a four-engine system could handle over 16,000 simultaneous connections (4 engine processes $\times$ 4096 connections per engine).

Primary platform and porting sequence. The original version of the SQL Server was developed from 1984 to 1986 on Sun hardware. Today the SYBASE SQL Server runs on many platforms including SPARC, RISC, and Intel. Although SYBASE runs on multiple hardware and software platforms, new versions of the product are not available on all platforms simultaneously. Also, not all products are available on all platforms.

It is important to note the attention and new strategic direction for Microsoft's Windows NT. In the past, Windows NT had been a secondary platform. NT has been receiving priority attention from all the database vendors including Sybase, Informix, and Oracle. When selecting a hardware platform for SQL Server, users should consider the importance of new Sybase features and when they will be available for a given platform. Here is a list of some of the hardware platforms supported by Sybase:
UNIX, first tier (primary platforms):

- Sun SPARC running SunOS and Solaris
- IBM RS/6000 and PowerPC running AIX
- DEC Alpha running OSF/1
- DEC VAX and MicroVAX running VMS, UNIX, ULTRIX

- HP running HP/UX
- NCR running UNIX V.4

UNIX, second tier (secondary platforms):

- Data General AViiON running DG/UX
- Groupe Bull
- ICL
- Motorola
- NEC running SVR4 (Unix System V Release 4)
- Pyramid ES running C062
- Sequent running PTX
- Silicon Graphics Incorporated running IRIX
- Stratus FTX running FTX

Non-UNIX platforms:

- Intel hardware (and DEC Alpha) running Microsoft Windows NT
- Intel hardware running Novell's NetWare
- Intel hardware running IBM's OS/2

3.2   SQL Server Product Line and Features

The SQL Server is the core of the Sybase product line. The previous sections illustrated a number of technical innovations incorporated into the architecture of SQL Server. This section briefly describes some features of SQL Server and explains how they are used in the enterprise client/server environment. The focus of this section is on some of the features that have made Sybase so successful.

3.2.1   SYBASE System 11 feature set (technical summary)

SQL Server has earned a reputation for reliability and high performance, making it the relational database management system of choice for on-line transaction processing (OLTP) applications. SQL Server, developed in 1986, was the first intelligent, programmable database server designed for on-line transaction processing. For completeness, this discussion covers SYBASE Versions 4.9, System 10, and the newest release SYBASE System 11. Note that the majority of Version 4.9 and System 10 features are included in System 11.

Some particular strengths of SYBASE and SQL Server are as follows:

- A 32-bit multiprocess multithreaded architecture, 64-bit versions of SYBASE, is available for DEC Alpha, Sun UltraSPARC, and other hardware platforms.
- Dynamic (on-line) backup and continuous operations.
- Database triggers.
- Scalability and flexibility.
- Enforcement of business rules and referential integrity.
- Support for user-defined data types.
- Third-party front-end support.
- Product maturity and breadth of product line.
- Cross-DBMS interoperability, gateway, and middleware solutions.

3.2.2   Structured Query Language (SQL) support

Structured Query Language (SQL) is the de facto standard of database languages. The ANSI Standards for SQL specify two levels of compatibility: ANSI SQL Level 1 and ANSI SQL Level 2, which is a superset of Level 1. There is also an integrity enhancement addendum. The best compatibility claim that a vendor can make for its product is ANSI SQL Level 2 with the Integrity Enhancement addendum. SQL Server Versions 4.2 and 4.9 are ANSI SQL Level 1 compliant. SYBASE System 10 and System 11 are compliant with ANSI/SQL-89, FIPS 127-1, and entry-level ANSI/ISO SQL-92.

Vendors can also provide enhanced versions of standard SQL that support extensions such as stored procedures and triggers. SYBASE Transact-SQL and Oracle PL/SQL are examples of enhanced SQL dialects.

Transact-SQL.   SYBASE Transact-SQL has been enhanced to minimize the necessity to resort to a programming language to accomplish a desired task. Transact-SQL goes beyond many commercial versions of SQL by adding several advanced features such as *control-of-flow language, triggers, stored procedures, rules,* and *defaults.*

Control-of-flow language can be used as part of any SQL statement or batch. Some available constructs are: BEGIN . . . END, BREAK, CONTINUE, DECLARE, GOTO, IF-ELSE, RETURN, and WHILE. Also special error handling techniques are available to the Transact-SQL programmer. The RAISERROR and PRINT statements, in combination with control-of-flow language, can direct error messages to the users of Transact-SQL applications. Programmers can also capture return values from stored procedures, pass parameters from a procedure to its caller, and get status information from global variables such as @@error.

SYBASE is both a compiled system and an interpreted system designed to work as a server in a client/server environment. SQL Server is capable of accepting SQL language statements that are passed to it from a client; these language statements are interpreted by the server. It can also store precompiled batches of SQL and control-of-flow statements (Transact-SQL stored procedures) as well as remote procedure calls (RPCs).

Stored procedures. Stored procedures are precompiled SQL statements that are stored on the SQL database server. Stored procedures offer several benefits:

- *Improved execution performance.* Because the SQL statements are already optimized and compiled, most of the query processing work has already been done when the stored procedure is executed.

- *Reduced network traffic.* A client can send two words across the network (i.e., "execute procedure_name") rather than sending the hundreds of words that may be in the procedure.

- *Single point of code maintenance.* Stored procedures provide a single point of code maintenance (at the server, not the client workstations or application programs).

- *Security.* The authority to execute a stored procedure is independent of any permissions required to execute the specific statements that the procedure performs (e.g., UPDATE, INSERT, DELETE).

Frequently executed queries are likely candidates for stored procedures. Stored procedures can accept command line arguments and can also return values to the calling program.

Triggers. As explained in Chap. 1, triggers are similar to stored procedures and are associated with a particular table. Triggers are invoked automatically by the dataserver whenever the table is the target of an INSERT, UPDATE, or DELETE statement. For example, a stockbroker may want to delete an account due to inactivity over several months. An SQL statement is issued to delete the account (DELETE account WHERE account_number = '185123456'), but a trigger is tied to the DELETE statement. The trigger will check to see if the account has a position in any security. If there is no position, the account is deleted; otherwise, an error message is displayed. Triggers can also call local and remote stored procedures and other triggers. They can be used to implement cascading deletes; in this instance if the stockbroker requests that an account be deleted, all associated position (child) rows will be deleted. These are both examples of referential integrity (RI), which is discussed in greater detail in Sec. 3.2.3. Enforcement of RI is a major—but not the only—use of triggers.

Sybase was the first database vendor to implement database triggers; IBM introduced trigger support with Version 2 of DB2/6000. Oracle 6 does not support triggers; Oracle Version 7 provides trigger support.

Rules and defaults. *Rules* and *defaults* are provided to help maintain *entity integrity* and *domain integrity*. Entity integrity is used to ensure that a value is entered for all columns that require a value; domain integrity makes sure that each value in a column belongs to a set of legal values for that column. Defaults and rules define integrity constraints during the entry and modification of data.

A *default* is a value linked to a column or data type which is inserted when no value is provided during data entry. Rules are user-defined integrity constraints also linked to a column or data type and enforced at data entry time.

3.2.3 Referential integrity

Let's use a brief example to explain referential integrity. In our example, a stockbroker maintains positions for an account by executing trades on behalf of a client. In this scenario, the account table is related to the position table. Since there can be multiple positions for an account, the relationship is said to be *one-to-many*. When these tables are joined, the account table is the parent and the position table is the child. If a parent row is deleted and the related child rows are not, the child rows are said to be *orphaned*. Referential integrity means that no orphans are permitted in any table. File/server databases expect the programmer to include logic to enforce RI. Most client/server SQL databases including Sybase, Oracle, DB2/6000, and Informix provide referential integrity features.

SYBASE System 10 and System 11 provide support for two types of referential integrity: declarative referential integrity and procedural referential integrity. Sybase Version 4.9 supports referential integrity through the use of triggers (procedural referential integrity). Oracle 6 offers no support for referential integrity.

Declarative referential integrity. *Declarative RI* is supported by SYBASE System 10 and System 11. Declarative RI is implemented through keys that are stored within the database tables themselves.

Parent tables contain primary keys that are composed of foreign keys found within each of the child tables. This method follows the ANSI Level 2 Integrity Enhancement addendum.

ISQL is an interactive and batch SQL interface to the SQL Server. It can be used as an interactive tool or as a batch SQL interface to the server. When starting ISQL, the user is presented with a numbered prompt (1>) symbol for all input lines.

The following example illustrates how SYBASE Transact-SQL is used to implement a declarative referential integrity constraint. In the example, the ACCOUNT table is created with a constraint on the *balance* column. The constraint is used to guarantee that a negative value cannot be inserted into the balance column. Here is the SQL used to create the SQL Server table:

```
ISQL Session:

1> CREATE TABLE tbaccount(
       acct#            smallint          not null,
       owner            char(30)          not null,
       balance          float             not null,
       constraint       positive_balancecheck(balance > 0))
2> go
```

The *sp_helpconstraint* system procedure is used to display information about constraints that are defined on a specific table. For example,

```
1> sp_helpconstraint tbaccount       /* Display table constraints */
2> go
name                        defn
----------------            -------------------------------------------
positive_balance            CONSTRAINT positive_balance CHECK (balance>0)

(1 row affected, return status = 0)
```

Now, let's bind a message to the table that will be displayed whenever the integrity constraint is violated. Two SYBASE system stored procedures (*sp_addmessage* and *sp_bindmsg*) are used to do this. The *sp_addmessage* procedure is used to add a user-defined message to the SQL Server catalog. The *sp_bindmessage* procedure is used to bind the user-defined message to the constraint.

```
1> sp_addmessage 20020, "An account cannot have a negative balance"
2> go
An account cannot have a negative balance
The message has been inserted.
(return status = 0)

1> sp_bindmsg positive_balance, 20020 /* bind message to the constraint */
2> go
Message bound to constraint.
(return status = 0)
```

Now, let's illustrate what happens when the constraint is violated using an ISQL session.

```
1> INSERT tbaccount(acct#, owner, balance) VALUES( 10, 'DAN MARINO', 1000000
)
2> go
(1 row affected)

1>INSERT tbaccount(acct#, owner, balance) VALUES( 20,'BOOMER ESIASON', -1000000)
2> go
Msg 20020, Level 16, State 1:
Server 'cougar', Line 1:
An account cannot have a negative balance
Command has been aborted.
```

Procedural referential integrity. Procedural RI is implemented through the use of triggers. Triggers ensure RI by automatically executing SQL statements that enforce business rules whenever an INSERT, UPDATE, or DELETE command is performed on a table. For example, whenever a parent row is deleted, either all the child rows are deleted (cascading deletes) or an error condition is reported and the deletion is disallowed. Procedural RI is used by SYBASE engines prior to System 10.

Let's see how to use a trigger to implement a procedural integrity constraint on the *balance* column. First, use Transact-SQL to create the base table.

```
CREATE TABLE tbaccount(
      acct#           smallint         not null,
      owner           char(30)        ·not null,
      balance         float            not null)
```

Now create an INSERT trigger to enforce referential integrity on the *balance* column:

```
CREATE TRIGGER tiaccount ON tbaccount FOR INSERT
AS
        /***********************
        DECLARE LOCAL VARIABLES
        ***************************/

        DECLARE     @status         int,
                    @tableName      varchar(30),
                    @triggerName    varchar(30)

        DECLARE     @acct           smallint,
                    @owner          char(30),
                    @balance        float

        SELECT @status = 0, @tableName = 'tbaccount', @triggerName =
        'tiaccount'

        /**************************************************
```

```
      USE A CURSOR TO HANDLE MULTIROW TRANSACTIONS
      ***********************************************/

  DECLARE insertCursor CURSOR FOR SELECT
   acct#,
   owner,
   balance
  FROM inserted

  OPEN insertCursor

  /***********************************************
    LOOP THROUGH ROW(S) IN THE inserted TABLE
    ***********************************************/
  WHILE ( @status = 0 )
  BEGIN
          FETCH insertCursor INTO
           @acct,
           @owner,
           @balance

          SELECT @status = @@sqlstatus

          /******************
            CHECK @@sqlstatus
            ******************/

          IF ( @status = 1 )
          BEGIN
                  /************
                    CURSOR ERROR
                    ************/
                  CLOSE insertCursor
                  DEALLOCATE CURSOR insertCursor
                  ROLLBACK TRAN
                  RAISERROR 120510, @status, @triggerName
                  RETURN
          END

          IF ( @status = 0 )
          BEGIN
                  IF ( @balance < 0 )
                  BEGIN
                          CLOSE insertCursor
                          DEALLOCATE CURSOR insertCursor
                          ROLLBACK TRAN
                          RAISERROR 20020
                          RETURN
                  END
          END
  END

  /************************************
    CLOSE & DEALLOCATE THE CURSOR
    ********************************/

  CLOSE insertCursor
  DEALLOCATE CURSOR insertCursor
  RETURN
```

Now, let's duplicate the earlier attempt at inserting data into the

table and illustrate what happens when the trigger constraint is violated.

```
1> insert tbaccount(acct#, owner, balance) VALUES( 10,'DAN MARINO', 1000000 )
2> go
(1 row affected)

1> insert tbaccount(acct#, owner, balance) VALUES( 20, 'BOOMER ESIASON',
-1000000 )
2> go
Msg 20020, Level 16, State 1:
Server 'cougar', Procedure 'tiaccount', Line 69:
An account cannot have a negative balance
```

3.2.4 Data integrity

A *database transaction* can be defined as a sequence of one or more
data manipulation statements that together form an atomic, logical
unit of work. Either all statements in the transaction will execute
successfully, or none of the statements will be executed. Formally, a
database transaction should possess the ACID properties, defined
as *a*tomicity (an entire transaction is either completed or aborted),
*c*onsistency (a transaction takes databases from one consistent state
to another), *i*solation (a transactions effect is transparent to other
transactions, applications, and end users until the transaction is committed), and *d*urability (changes to recoverable resources made by a
committed transaction are permanent).

In general, a transaction, or logical unit of work, is said to be committed when it completes all processing successfully. A database
transaction is committed when all data manipulation statements
have been executed successfully. In this case, all changes made by the
transaction to recoverable data become permanent. Transactions can
be committed implicitly, by successfully terminating, or explicitly, by
issuing special commitment statements. If any of the data manipulation statements fails, the entire database transaction fails, and all
partial changes to the database made before the data manipulation
statement failure (if any) must be rolled back in order to bring the
database to its before-transaction consistent state. In a relational
database management system like SYBASE SQL Server, a database
transaction that consists of one or more SQL statements is committed
when all SQL statements are completed successfully, and it is aborted
if one of the SQL statements fails.

When the transaction processing environment is localized (not distributed) and the only recoverable resource in question is the database,
then SQL Server itself can handle database transaction processing. The
picture changes drastically as the environment becomes distributed,
and additional resources (e.g., databases, files) come into play. Then the

transaction manager becomes necessary to control global transactions. Section 16.3 discusses the X/Open Distributed Transaction Processing (DTP) model and Sybase's compliance with that model.

Transaction management is critical to maintaining and ensuring data integrity. When the request for data modification (database transaction) is committed, it is written to disk from cache memory. SQL databases maintain a transaction log that records information about all modifications that have been requested to a database. SYBASE SQL Server uses transaction logs for transaction rollback (the ability to reverse committed transactions and restore a database to its previous state).

Point-in-time recovery.   Unfortunately, databases can and do fail. A database failure can be the result of many problems including hardware failures, software failures, power failures, and application errors. The SYBASE SQL Server provides a roll-forward capability. This allows for change requests to be applied to an instance backup of a database. For example, a database backup is taken at 1:00 p.m., and a hardware failure occurs at 2:00 p.m. The database administrator (DBA) can restore the 1:00 database backup and use the database transaction log to *roll forward* all changes that occurred between 1:00 and the time of the hardware failure. This procedure is known as *forward recovery*. In short, this is a procedure that requires a backup to be successful. This is in contrast with transaction *rollback*.

Transaction rollback is used in user-defined transactions with the BEGIN TRANSACTION, COMMIT TRANSACTION and ROLLBACK TRANSACTION commands. For example, a client issues a BEGIN TRANSACTION command to SQL Server. In the middle of the transaction the client workstation fails. The SQL Server will detect the lost connection and automatically roll back the transaction. There is no backup required, and no data modifications have actually been *committed*.

The current release of SQL Server does not provide true *point-in-time* recovery. True point-in-time recovery would allow the system administrator to use the database transaction log to roll forward all changes that have been committed up to a certain time. Let's apply this to the earlier example where a database backup is taken at 1:00 p.m. and a hardware failure occurs at 2:00 p.m. Using true point-in-time recovery, the database administrator can restore the 1:00 database backup and use the database transaction log to roll forward all changes that occurred between 1:00 and 1:30 (not the actual time of the hardware failure).

Private log cache.   As mentioned in Chap. 1 (pre-System 11) SYBASE systems often experience I/O bottlenecks in the area of transaction logging. The private log cache (PLC) is designed to improve the scalability of SQL Server by reducing contention on the transaction log semaphore and the *syslogs* table.

Pre-System 11 SQL Servers use a single *append log semaphore* for all user processes. Basically, each client asks the log manager (via the log semaphore) for a slot to write to the transaction log. This requires synchronous writes to the transaction log (e.g., BEGIN, INSERT, UPDATE, INSERT, COMMIT). This requires several trips through the append log semaphore. It is easy to see that significant contention could exist as multiple database processes write log records to the *syslogs* table. Furthermore, prior to each write, the database process must acquire *exclusive* access to the log semaphore. The System 10 SQL Server writes log records to the stack prior to writing them to the *syslogs* table.

3.2.5   Applications development

SYBASE SQL Server incorporates a number of features that ease the task of application development. This section discusses several database features from the ease-of-use category.

Database cursors.   As described in Chap. 1, a database cursor is a mechanism for accessing the results of an SQL SELECT statement one row at a time. Using a cursor mechanism, applications can process each row individually rather than being forced to process the entire set of rows returned by the SELECT.

Scrollable cursors are essential to the development of graphical applications (all list boxes in database applications are likely to use cursors). If the database does not provide backward and forward scrollable cursors, the programmer must write code to emulate a scrollable cursor. SYBASE System 10 and System 11 provide a cursor interface that was introduced with System 10; SYBASE versions prior to System 10 do not support cursors. The SYBASE Embedded SQL precompilers prior to System 10 simulate cursors at the front end.

The System 10 or System 11 SQL Server supports all fundamental cursor operations defined in the SQL-89 standard (DECLARE, OPEN, FETCH, positioned UPDATE/DELETE, and CLOSE). Sybase has added some significant extensions, such as these:

- Cursors can be declared as read-only or updatable (as specified by SQL-92).

- An array interface can be used to reduce network traffic by retrieving multiple rows with a single FETCH statement and buffer them at the client. This is implemented by using a SET command to adjust the number of rows to fetch.

- Cursors can remain open across transactions.

Cursors are supported in the server and are callable from stored procedures, SQL precompilers, and CT-Library.

Domain integrity.   *Domain integrity* support includes the ability to define new data types and the ability to enforce domain integrity at the server.

SYBASE allows the user to add new data types to the server. For example, a user may want to create a data type called *ssn* that will be used to store social security numbers or a data type called *row_id* that will be used as a sequence number in database tables. This feature promotes the notion of having consistent data types in the database tables that are easy to identify.

SQL Server also allows the user to define a range of acceptable values (the domain) for a column or for any column of a user-defined data type. Sybase calls these definitions *rules*. After creation, these rules are enforced at the server. In conjunction with rules Sybase allows the creation of default values. A default is a value linked to a column or data type which is inserted when no value is provided during data entry. So if a value is provided, it will be checked against a rule; and if no value is provided, a default value can be used.

3.2.6   Disk file management

Disk file management has significant implications on I/O performance and availability. SYBASE provides a number of features to maximize both server performance and data availability.

Mirroring.   Mirroring is the capability to maintain a replicate of all data stored on a database device. SYBASE mirroring provides a form of redundancy to protect against hardware failures and to provide a degree of fault tolerance. Note that SQL Server mirrors *logical devices,* not physical devices or databases.

SQL Server supports mirroring of any logical device which means that the SQL Server can mirror a database table (using database segments), any part of a database, the whole database, the transaction log, or any combination of these. If a hard-disk crash occurs, the damaged copy is automatically taken off line and all reads and writes are directed to the remaining undamaged copy. In the event of a media failure, the mirror can take over, typically without any downtime. When the damaged device is repaired or replaced, it is synchronized with the undamaged copy by a process called *on-line remirroring.* Mirroring can be disabled and reenabled without bringing down the database. Remember that SYBASE mirroring is done on a device basis and that a database may reside on several database devices. Therefore, to mirror a database, every device that is allocated to the database must be mirrored. Because database devices can be shared by multiple databases, this can have the side effect of mirroring portions of other databases that share the device.

Database transaction logs are ideal candidates for mirroring. Production databases should have the transaction log stored on a separate device to provide recoverability and improved performance. When a log device is lost, up-to-the-minute database recoverability is lost as well. So log devices should be mirrored whenever possible.

If data fault tolerance is essential, then the system administrator should mirror the database devices as well as the transaction logs. This can benefit read performance, but it will slow the write performance. When SYBASE performs a read on mirrored devices, the read is issued against both sides of the mirror. The result that is returned first is used, and the second read is ignored. Write performance is degraded because the write must be performed against both sides of the mirror. Device mirroring supports the option of specifying serial or nonserial writes. With serial writes, the system will wait for the first write to finish before the second write takes place. Nonserial writes occur in parallel and are not as reliable as serial writes. Serial writes are generally slower than nonserial writes.

Obviously, a certain amount of additional hardware (i.e., multiple disk drives, disk controllers, etc.) is required to see the real advantages of device mirroring. It does not make much sense to mirror a database device on the same disk drive. Disk I/O will become a bottleneck, and performance will be adversely affected. There is also a strong possibility that if the disk has problems, both devices will be affected, so the mirroring will not buy much.

A general rule is that if the database application warrants disk mirroring, it justifies the cost of additional hardware. Therefore, when you are planning hardware purchases, allocate additional funds for extra disk drives and controllers. Disk drives and controllers can be used to split I/O and to balance the additional load imposed by disk mirroring, which can also be used as a justification for additional costs.

Mirroring alternatives.   There are alternatives to SYBASE mirroring that should be investigated. The first is the use of RAID (*r*edundant *a*rray of *i*nexpensive *d*isks) devices, which, depending on the level of RAID supported, provide various degrees of data integrity, availability, and performance.

Second, several operating systems provide mirroring capabilities including IBM's AIX, Novell's NetWare, and Microsoft Windows NT Advanced Server. SunOS and Sun Solaris provide mirroring using a product called On-Line Disk Suite. If the selected operating system provides mirroring, it has to be evaluated on its features and performance, and then compared with the functionality provided by SQL Server.

Disk allocation.   SQL Server will also allow the transaction log to be stored on a separate device. This enables the Database Administrator to split I/O across multiple disks or disk channels. SQL Server allows the database and transaction log to *span* multiple disks. In addition, the database and transaction log can be striped. *Striping* is an interleaving technique for distributing I/O across multiple disk drives. Disk I/O techniques are discussed in Chap. 10.

3.2.7   Backup and recovery

SQL Server System 10 and System 11 are bundled with a separate server product called the Backup Server. Backup Server software runs as a separate operating system process and is used for database backup and restore.

With Backup Server, SYBASE is able to do high-speed database backups of multigigabyte databases, thus adding capacity to the local SQL Server. In pre-System 10 databases, the SQL Server process (dataserver) handled backups and data loads as ordinary tasks to be interleaved with on-line user requests. Backup Server offloads backup tasks from the SQL Server engine. In SMP systems Backup Server can run on its own CPU.

Other capabilities of the backup process include

- The ability to centrally manage the backup procedures for multiple servers across the network

- The ability to schedule and perform backup tasks without operator intervention

- The ability to automatically back up data based on user-configurable thresholds (a function of the Threshold Manager)

Variables in the form of parameters passed to stored procedures can be used with the DUMP and LOAD commands. This allows a single stored procedure to be used for all database and transaction log backups. This ensures that all database dumps are performed in a consistent manner. Backup Server is a first step toward an automated operations environment and a further extension of its ability to manage very large databases.

In addition to Backup Server, Sybase has added several features to System 10 and System 11 for VLDB support. Some other features are reduced granularity of some database consistency checks, e.g., the ability to check allocations on a single table or index using the data-

Node 1

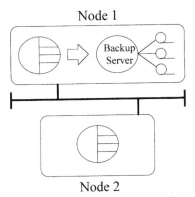

Node 2

Figure 3.4 Backup server architecture.

base consistency checker (DBCC); speed enhancements to DBCC; and the CREATE DATABASE FOR LOAD feature. The FOR LOAD extension to CREATE DATABASE bypasses the overhead of initializing the database pages on a CREATE (when it will be immediately loaded from a database dump).

Figure 3.4 shows two UNIX nodes attached to a network. One node runs an SQL Server and a Backup Server; the second node runs only an SQL Server process. The Backup Server process running on the first node can be used to back up SQL Server databases on either node.

Threshold Manager. The *Threshold Manager* is a feature that was introduced in System 10. Thresholds monitor the amount of free space available on a particular database segment. A threshold always has a stored procedure associated with it. When the amount of free space falls below a user-defined threshold, the SQL Server will automatically execute the stored procedure that has been associated with the threshold. Threshold events are designed to allow for easier automation of system administration. For example, the Threshold Manager can be used to

- Monitor the space available to a database transaction log and run a stored procedure when space runs low. The stored procedure can work with the Backup Server to enable automated transaction log dumps.

- Monitor the space available for the data segments of a database. When space runs low, messages in the error log warn the system administrator before space runs out. A threshold procedure can be written and associated with the threshold to automatically allocate more space to the affected data segment.

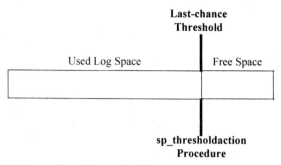

Figure 3.5   Last-chance threshold.

When data and logs are stored on separate segments, SQL Server installs a *last-chance threshold* (*LCT*) on the log segment (as illustrated in Fig. 3.5). The threshold value is an estimate of the number of free log pages required to dump the transaction log. The amount of free log pages is calculated by SQL Server and cannot be changed by a user. The LCT helps ensure that there is always enough space to dump the transaction log. By default, the LCT calls a user-written stored procedure named *sp_thresholdaction*. The *sp_modifythreshold* system procedure can be used to call a different stored procedure. Prior to System 10, database administrators had to dump the transaction log at specified time intervals (whether it needed it or not), or they had to write their own procedures to emulate the functionality of Threshold Manager.

3.2.8   Security and auditing

SQL Server System 10 and System 11 are designed for compliance with the C2 level for secure databases. A B1 level of security is optional. The B1-level security is provided by a version of SQL Server called Secure SQL Server and is beyond the scope of this book.

Audit Server.   Auditing capabilities are a critical part of any production-quality DBMS. The System 10 SQL Server includes a flexible auditing system that can be dynamically configured to record server-level events, the actions of individual users, and access to database objects. Audit Server sits between clients and an SQL Server, analyzing information requests and capturing audit data from the results streams. In addition to providing C2-level security the Audit Server offers an entire security environment for a wide variety of system requirements. By examining the audit trail, system security officers can view patterns of access and attempted misuse of the system. All audit records can be attributed to specific users of the system.

The audit system.   The audit system consists of four components:

- The *sybsecurity* system database.   It contains the audit system for the System 10 SQL Server. The *sysaudits* table contains the audit trail; a row is inserted into *sysaudits* for every auditable event. The *sysauditoptions* table contains rows describing the Audit Server audit options.

- *System stored procedures.*   A set of system procedures is used to set the various auditing options.

- *Audit queue.*   This is an in-memory holding area where audit records are held before they are written to the audit trail (the *sysaudits* table).

- *Audit process.*   It is responsible for writing data from the audit queue to the *sybsecurity.dbo.sysaudits* table.

The auditing system can be installed during the initial installation of the SQL Server or at a later time. No auditing actually occurs until the audit system is enabled with the *sp_auditoption* system procedure.

Figure 3.6 illustrates the flow of audited events from the client to the *sysaudits* table located in the *sybsecurity* database.

3.3   SYBASE Systems Management

Sybase realizes there is a need for tools that can be used to administer departmental and enterprisewide SQL Servers. Sybase offers several management tools that are introduced here:

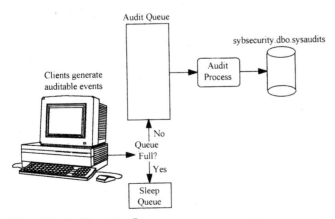

Figure 3.6   Audit system flow.

- *SYBASE SQL Server Manager.*   SQL Server Manager is a Microsoft Windows program and is the successor to the SYBASE SA Companion product.

- *SYBASE Enterprise SQL Server Manager.*   This is a graphical tool designed for administering multiple SQL Servers distributed across an enterprise.

- *SYBASE SQL Server SNMP (Simple Network Management Protocol) Subagent.*   This agent allows network management tools to monitor the characteristics of SYBASE SQL Server and Open Server applications.

3.3.1   SYBASE SQL Server Manager

SQL Server Manager is an easy-to-use systems management tool for SYBASE SQL Server administrators. It provides the operational capabilities necessary to administer both local and remote servers in development and production environments. SQL Server Manager is a Microsoft Windows-based application and is designed to support SYBASE Environments (Version 10.0 and greater, excluding Microsoft SQL Server for Windows NT).

These are some of the tasks that the SQL Server Manager is designed to perform:

- Carry out options using a Windows-based drag-and-drop interface.
- Manage local and remote SYBASE SQL Servers.
- Connect to, disconnect from, configure, and stop servers.
- Display and terminate SQL Server processes.
- Generate and run server data definition language (DDL) scripts.
- Allocate and manage storage resources.
- Administer log-ins, users, and user access permissions for database users and groups.
- Manage SQL Server configuration options.
- Execute backup and recovery operations.
- Manage database objects including tables, views, indexes, stored procedures, triggers, and rules.
- Manage data caches by creating user-defined data caches, defining buffer pools, and binding databases and objects to a cache.
- Generate database DDL.

The following section provides a brief description of selected features of SQL Server Manager. The SQL Server Manager window is shown in Fig. 3.7.

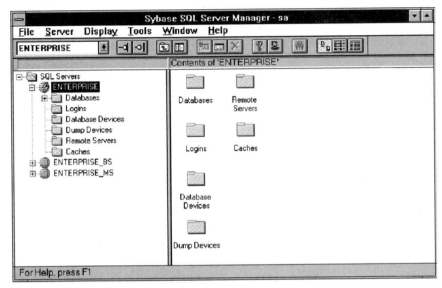

Figure 3.7 SQL Server Manager.

Managing stored procedures. As described earlier, a stored procedure is a named collection of precompiled SQL statements and control-of-flow statements. After a procedure has been created, the owner of the procedure can modify the permission to access it. By using SQL Server Manager it is also possible to display the procedure's dependencies and navigate to them. SQL Server Manager can be used to perform the following actions:

- Create a procedure.
- Display procedure properties.
- Navigate to objects with dependencies on a procedure.
- Update user and group permissions on a procedure
- Navigate to users and groups.

The SQL Server Manager stored procedure window is shown in Fig. 3.8.

Transaction log space. SQL Server Manager allows the database administrator to graphically view transaction log space available in all databases on an SQL Server (see Fig. 3.9).

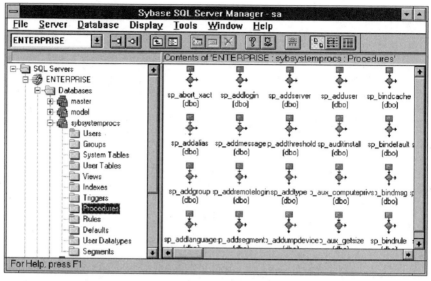

Figure 3.8   SQL Server Manager—stored procedure maintenance.

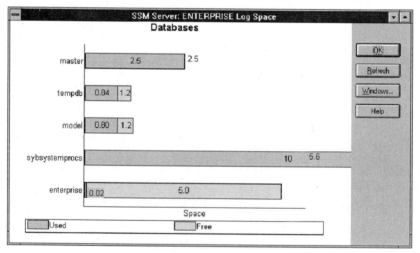

Figure 3.9   SQL Server Manager—transaction log space.

3.3.2   SYBASE Enterprise SQL
Server Manager

Recently, the author was asked how to administer a widely distributed network of SYBASE SQL Servers. The answer was far from simple and straightforward. Sybase is attempting to provide a straightforward answer to this question with the Enterprise SQL Server Manager.

Enterprise SQL Server Manager (ESSM) is the industry's first database administration tool developed for single-screen control of unlimited numbers of distributed SQL Servers regardless of host operating system or hardware platform. It is based on the Tivoli TME architecture so that it can be easily integrated with third-party systems management tools for faster resolution of system problems.

From a Motif-based graphical user interface, Enterprise SQL Server Manager allows the user to configure, start, and stop SQL Servers; monitor server status and performance; manage space utilization; set up database security; create and manage database objects; and schedule and perform backup and recovery operations. Unlike current administration tools, ESSM allows the SA to manage groups of servers with simple drag-and-drop operations.

For example, the SA can create a logical collection of SQL Server databases under the title of SALES. After the individual SQL Servers have been associated with the collection, a log-in account can be added to the group of servers (label SALES) instead of individually to each server in the group. The SA is saved from repetitive and monotonous tasks by using ESSM to control large numbers of servers consistently.

Enterprise SQL Server Manager can also be used to consolidate the error logs from multiple SQL Servers into a single management console. From this console, the SA can filter the information to view only messages of interest (e.g., warning messages and error messages). The TME Desktop is shown in Fig. 3.10.

3.3.3   SQL Server SNMP Subagent

The SQL Server SNMP (Simple Network Management Protocol) Subagent is an application that allows network management tools to monitor the characteristics of SYBASE SQL Server and Open Server applications. Open Server applications include Replication Server, Log Transfer Manager, OmniCONNECT, and user-written Open Server applications. In addition, the subagent also acts as an event monitoring tool that automatically notifies the network manager when an event occurs.

To communicate with the subagent, network managers use the Simple Network Management Protocol. The SYBASE Subagent supports Version 1 and Version 2 of SNMP. This section describes the SQL Server and Open Server characteristics that can be monitored with the subagent and describes how network managers communicate with the subagent.

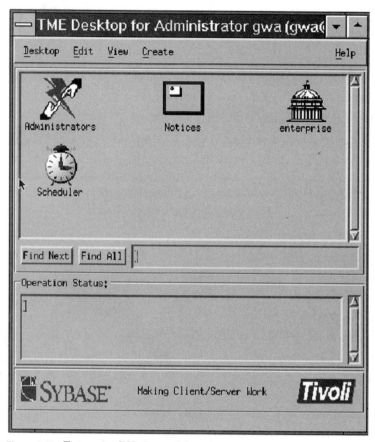

Figure 3.10   Enterprise SQL Server Manager.

Monitoring SQL Servers.   The SNMP Subagent monitors the following SQL Server characteristics:

- Status of SQL Server.
- For System 10 and System 11, the full name of the SQL Server contact person. For SQL Server Release 4.9.x, the subagent will provide the server log-in name of the contact.
- Number of active connections and total number of attempted inbound connections.
- Date and time when a change in the number of inbound connections occurred.
- Date and time that the most recent connection occurred.
- Maximum number of configured connections.

- Number of transactions completed; this characteristic is not available from SQL Server Release 4.9.x.

- Total number of database reads and database writes.

- Number of network packets received and network packets sent.

- Maximum number of concurrent users.

- Current configuration parameters.

- SQL Server device names, device space allocated, and device space available.

- Maximum amount of device space used and number of times the maximum amount of device space has been reached.

- State of database access and status of database options.

- Date and time the database was made active.

- Database contact person (database owner). For SQL Server Release 4.9.x, the subagent provides the server log-in name of the contact; it cannot provide the full name of the contact.

- Server that created or last restructured the database.

- Date of the last transaction log dump.

- Database size and database segments.

- For System 10 and System 11 SQL Servers, the maximum size of database segments.

- Current utilization of each database segment.

- Maximum usage of each segment.

- Number of times the system attempted to exceed allocated space.

Monitoring Open Servers. The SYBASE SNMP Subagent can monitor the following Open Server characteristics:

- Server status (active, hung, suspect). The server can be a Replication Server, Log Transfer Manager, OmniCONNECT Server, or other user-written Open Server application.

- Number of inbound connections.

- Date and time when the number of inbound connections changed.

Notifying network managers of SQL Server events. Another feature of the SNMP Subagent is automatic event notification. This feature enables the subagent to notify a network manager when the following events occur:

- The subagent starts.
- A database status is not *active* or *available*.
- A database segment becomes full.

Accessing Server information.   The following components are required to access SQL Server or Open Server information using SNMP:

- *Network manager.*   The network manager requests information from objects in the network. Network managers can also modify the values of some objects. The network manager uses the user datagram protocol (UDP) to send requests and listen for responses to requests, and for event traps generated by the subagent. To request information and to modify values, network managers use protocol data units (PDUs).

- *Master agent.*   The master agent listens to UDP port 161 and routes the requests to the appropriate subagent. The master agent returns responses from subagents to the network manager, using port 162. As part of the Subagent distribution, Sybase provides the master agent EMANATE.

- *SQL Server SNMP Subagent.*   The SNMP Subagent monitors characteristics of the SQL Servers and Open Servers and stores this information in an internal cache. When the subagent receives a request from EMANATE, it accesses the internal cache and returns the requested information. The subagent also detects events and reports these events as SNMP traps.

Figure 3.11 illustrates how a network manager accesses SQL Server information.

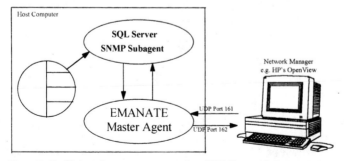

Figure 3.11   Network manager accessing SQL Server information.

Management information bases. A *management information base* (*MIB*) is a virtual information store that allows access to a set of managed objects. Before a network manager can access objects in the network, it must import a set of MIBs to know what objects are available. There are three MIBs that the SYBASE SNMP Subagent supports that allow network managers to access server information using SNMP:

- *Relational Database Management System* (*RDBMS*) *MIB.* This is an Internet standard for supplying information about installed servers, databases, and the relation of servers and databases. A network manager reads a compiled version of the RDBMS MIB so that it knows what types of information it can access about a server or database. The RDBMS MIB is also known as Request for Comment (RFC) 1697.

- *Network Services MIB.* This is an Internet standard for supplying information on network service applications. The SNMP Subagent supports the application table (*applTable*) of this MIB. The application table contains an entry for each SQL Server or Open Server that the SNMP Subagent is monitoring. A network manager reads a compiled version of the Network Services MIB so that it knows which servers are available. The Network Services MIB is also known as Request For Comment 1565.

- *Sybase MIB.* This SYBASE-specific MIB identifies current values of polling intervals and log-in information used by the SNMP Subagent to monitor servers. A network manager reads a compiled version of this MIB so that it can read and modify polling intervals, log-in information, and servers to monitor.

4

The SQL Server Catalog

To properly administer SQL Server, the user must understand the SYBASE SQL Server catalog, system stored procedures, and system databases. The SQL Server catalog contains information about various objects that are used by the system itself. Examples of these objects are databases, tables, indexes, views, and permissions.

System stored procedures are used to access and update the SQL Server catalog. These are a special class of stored procedures and have names that begin with *sp_*. They are used to administer the SQL Server and save the user from accessing the system tables directly.

A database consists of a collection of tables, views, indexes, data, and other objects. SQL Server uses several system databases to manage the system and user-created databases. The system databases are the subject of Sec. 4.3.

In addition to these topics, this chapter discusses special users of the database and introduces a concept introduced with SYBASE System 10—database roles.

4.1 The Catalog

The *master* database contains system tables (the system catalog) that keep track of SQL Server's operation as a whole. All SYBASE-supplied tables in the *master* database are system tables. A subset of the system tables that are present in the *master* database exists in every SQL Server user database. These tables are used to track information that is specific to that user database. The system tables are automatically created with the CREATE DATABASE command.

The names of all system tables begin with *sys*. For example, *sysobjects* resides in all SQL Server databases and contains one row for each

SQL Server object (table, view, stored procedure, trigger, rule, check constraint, etc.). The *syslogins* table exists only in the *master* database and contains one row for each SQL Server user account. The *sysprocesses* table is a special kind of table that resides only in the *master* database. And *sysprocesses* is a dynamic table built by the SQL Server engine when it is queried by a user. The SQL Server system tables are listed in App. C.

4.1.1   Database object identifiers

Identifiers are used to name database objects including databases, tables, views, stored procedures, columns, indexes, triggers, defaults, rules, and cursors.

SQL Server identifiers can be a maximum of 30 characters long. The first character of an identifier can be as follows:

- The symbol @ as the first character of an identifier defines a local variable.

- The pound sign # as the first character of an identifier indicates a temporary database table. SQL Server performs special operations on temporary tables created by using this convention. (Refer to Sec. 4.3.3 for more information on temporary tables and naming conventions.)

- Any alphabetic character defined in the SQL Server character set can be used.

- The underscore _ symbol can be used.

Object uniqueness within a database is identified by the owner of the object and the object name. Object names do not need to be unique within a database. Database names must be unique on each SQL Server. SQL Server naming conventions are

```
[[database.]owner.]table_name
```

For example,

```
production.gwa.mytable
```

The default value for *database* is the current database, and the default value for *owner* is the current user. A *fully qualified* object name uses the form *database.owner.objectName*. The system function *valid_name* is used to determine whether an identifier that has been created is valid to SQL Server. The system stored procedure *sp_rename* can be used to rename user objects; the *sp_renamedb* procedure is used to rename databases.

4.1.2   Querying the catalog

The SQL Server system catalogs can be queried just as any user-defined table can. The following example shows a stored procedure used to query the catalog and display the object ID, owner name, and table name of all user-defined tables in a database:

```
CREATE PROCEDURE sp_usertables
AS
    SELECT id, sysusers.name AS owner,sysobjects.name
    FROM sysusers, sysobjects
    WHERE sysobjects.uid = sysusers.uid AND sysobjects.type = 'U'
GO
```

The output from *sp_usertables:*

```
1> sp_usertables
2> go
id              owner           name
-----------     -----------     ------------------
5575058         andersog        tbaccount
860450098       andersog        tbdetail
910626287       dbo             tbactivity
1330103779      andersog        tblogging
1605580758      dbo             tbposition
1680009016      andersog        tbsupport
(6 rows affected, return status = 0)
```

SQL Server provides several system stored procedures that are used to query the system catalogs. Some of the system procedures are listed in Table 4.1.

4.1.3   Updating the catalog

The system tables contain information that is critical to the normal operation of the SQL Server engine. Data modifications (INSERTs, UPDATEs, DELETEs) to the system catalogs are performed using SQL Server commands such as CREATE DATABASE and DROP DATABASE. While it is possible to perform direct updates to the system tables, it should only be done when required by SYBASE documentation or Sybase technical support staff.

If it should become necessary to update the system tables, the system administrator must use the *sp_configure* system procedure to enable the *allow updates* option. The *sp_configure* system procedure is used to display or change engine configuration variables. The *allow updates* configuration variable allows system tables to be updated directly.

The following guidelines should be followed when system tables are updated:

■ Updates to system tables should be performed inside a transaction. The user should *always* issue a BEGIN TRANSACTION statement

TABLE 4.1   Sybase-Supplied System Stored Procedures

System procedure name	Description	System tables accessed
sp_helpdevice	Displays information about SQL Server database and dump devices	*master.dbo.spt_values,* *master.dbo.sysdevices*
sp_helpdb	Displays information about SQL Server databases	*master.dbo.spt_values,* *master.dbo.sysdatabases,* *master.dbo.sysdevices,* *master.dbo.syslogins,* *master.dbo.sysusages*
sp_configure	Displays or changes SQL Server configuration variables	*master.dbo.sysconfigures,* *master.dbo.syscurconfigs,* *master.dbo.syslogins,* *master.dbo.syslanguages,* *spt_values*
sp_lock	Displays information about active SQL Server locks	*master.dbo.spt_values,* *master.dbo.syslocks,* *master.dbo.sysprocesses*
sp_logiosize	Changes the log I/O size of current database	*master.dbo.sysattributes*
sp_monitor	Reports information about SQL Server activity	*master.dbo.spt_monitor*
sp_who	Reports information about active SQL Server users and process	*master.dbo.sysprocesses*
sp_help	Displays information about database objects and SQL Server supplied or user-defined data types	*syscolumns, sysindexes,* *syssegments, systypes,* *master.dbo.spt_values*
sp_helplog	Reports name of database device that contains first page of transaction log	*sysindexes,* *master.dbo.sysdevices*
sp_helpgroup	Displays information about user groups in current database	*sysusers*
sp_spaceused	Displays information about space used by a table or by all tables in current database	*sysindexes, sysobjects,* *master.dbo.sysusages*
sp_helpuser	Displays information about user(s) in current database	*sysalternates, sysusers,* *master.dbo.syslogins*
sp_helpprotect	Reports on permissions for database objects, users, or groups	*syscolumns, sysobjects,* *sysprotects, sysusers,* *master.dbo.spt_values*

before performing any modifications. This provides the capability to verify (and optionally roll back) the changes prior to committing the work.

- Some system tables should *never* be updated. For example, some tables (such as *sysprocesses*) are built dynamically when a command is issued. Modifying certain system tables can scramble permissions, terminate the database connection, and corrupt the SQL Server configuration.

- The *sp_configure* system procedure should be used to disable the *allow updates* option immediately after the updates are performed. When this option is enabled, any SQL Server user with permissions can modify the system tables. For this reason, the administrator may want to start the SQL Server engine in single-user mode prior to allowing updates to the system tables.

4.2   System Procedures

The names of system stored procedures begin with *sp_*. Sybase-supplied system procedures are located in the *sybsystemprocs* (SYBASE system procedures) database and can be run from any database. With the exception of procedures that update only system tables in the *master* database, the system procedure is executed in the current database. For example, if the database owner of the user database *inventory* executes the *sp_adduser* stored procedure, an entry is created in the *inventory.dbo.sysusers* system table.

Permissions on system procedures must be set from within the *sybsystemprocs* database. Certain system procedures can be run only by users possessing special *database roles*. Security-related system procedures can be run only by users possessing a *system security role*; others can be run only by system administrators (*SA role*); still others can be run by *database owners* (such as *sp_adduser*). Finally, other system procedures can be run by any user granted EXECUTE permission to the procedure.

4.2.1   Using system procedures

Most system procedures accept one or more parameters. Parameters that are SQL Server reserved words or contain punctuation characters must be enclosed in double quotes ("reserved word") or single quotes ('reserved word'). Also, if the parameter is a fully qualified object name (e.g., "master.dbo.sysobjects") it must be in double or single quotes.

System procedures can be invoked by sessions using chained or unchained transaction modes. These are described in Sec. 17.2.4. The default mode for SQL Server is Transact-SQL mode, or *unchained* mode. Transact-SQL mode requires explicit BEGIN TRANSACTION statements paired with COMMIT TRANSACTION or ROLLBACK TRANSACTION statements to complete transactions. *Chained mode* or ANSI-compatible mode implicitly begins a transaction before any data retrieval or modification statement. System stored procedures cannot be invoked from a transaction using *isolation level 3. Isolation level 3* provides ANSI compliance with the *chained* transaction mode. Isolation levels were introduced to SYBASE in the System 10 SQL Server. Isolation levels are described in Sec. 17.2.5.

Following is a simple illustration of Transact-SQL mode versus ANSI-compatible transactions.

Transact-SQL mode	ANSI-compatible
1> BEGIN TRANSACTION	1> SET CHAINED ON
2> GO	2> GO
1> UPDATE BANKBOOK	1> UPDATE BANKBOOK
2> SET address = '1000 ANY STREET'	2> SET address = '1000 ANY STREET'
3> WHERE account = 1001	3> WHERE account = 1001
4> GO	4> GO
1> COMMIT TRANSACTION	1> COMMIT TRANSACTION
2> GO	2> GO

Note that with ANSI-compatible mode, the BEGIN TRANSACTION statement is *implied* and does not need to be explicitly typed. Also note that the application must provide a COMMIT TRANSACTION or ROLLBACK TRANSACTION directive to avoid long-running transactions. Because the BEGIN TRANSACTION is implied, a COMMMIT or ROLLBACK must *always* be provided.

If no transaction is active when a system procedure is executed, SQL Server turns off chained mode and sets transaction isolation level 1 (the default) for the duration of the procedure. Before returning to the caller, the original chained mode and isolation level are reset. All system stored procedures return a status (typically 0 for success). The following is a Transact-SQL code fragment used by system procedures.

```
if @@trancount = 0          /* No transactions are active */
begin
      set transaction isolation level 1
      set chained off
end
```

Some system procedures use *system procedure tables* that are located
in the *master* database. These system procedure tables (prefixed with
*spt_*) are used to convert internal system values (such as status bits
on the *sysdevices* table) to readable format. For example, a hexadeci-
mal value of 0x200 in the *sysdevices.status* column means that the
mirror device is enabled for a particular device. The *spt_values* table
is used by the *sp_configure, sp_helpdb, sp_dboption,* and *sp_depends*
system procedures. The *spt_values* table is never updated. The following code fragment provides an example of how a system procedure
uses the *spt_values* table:

```
/*
** Look for the "settable options" mask in spt_values
*/
select @statopt = number From master.dbo.spt_values
  where type = "D" and name = "ALL SETTABLE OPTIONS"
select @stat2opt = number from master.dbo.spt_values
  where type = "D2" and name = "ALL SETTABLE OPTIONS"
/*
** Use @optname and try to find the right option.
** If there isn't just one, print appropriate diagnostics and return.
*/
select @optcount = count(*) from master.dbo.spt_values
  where name like "%" + @optname + "%"
  and ((type = "D" and number & @statopt = number)
  or (type = "D2" and number & @stat2opt = number))
```

Other system procedure tables are *spt_monitor* and *spt_committab*.
Many of the system stored procedures create and drop temporary
tables.

4.3   System Databases

Prior to System 10, the SYBASE SQL Server maintains three *system
databases* when the product is installed:

- The *master* database
- The *model* database
- The temporary database (*tempdb*)

The System 10 SQL Server introduced a new system database called
sybsystemprocs which is used to maintain and store the system procedures. Prior to System 10, the system stored procedures were maintained in the *master* database.

   In addition to these mandatory system databases, there are three
optional databases, two of which were introduced with SYBASE
System 10. The *pubs2* database is a sample database used to illustrate SQL Server features. The *pubs2* database is common to System

10 and System 11 and earlier versions of the SQL Server. The other optional databases are *sybsecurity,* which is the audit database, and *sybsyntax,* which contains the syntax of SQL Server commands and language libraries.

4.3.1   The *master* database

The *master* database contains the system catalogs. All tables in the *master* database are system tables. A subset of these tables also exists in user databases and is automatically created by the CREATE DATABASE command. There are several tables that exist exclusively in *master*; some examples are *sysdatabases* (there is one entry in *sysdatabases* for each database in the SQL Server) and *syslogins,* which has one entry for each SQL Server log-in account. The master database is created at SQL Server installation using the *installmaster* script. An SQL Server script is an operating system file that holds batch Transact-SQL commands.

The *master* database controls all user databases and is crucial to the operation and maintenance of the SQL Server engine. The *master* database maintains

- User accounts in the *syslogins* table
- SQL Server engines on-line [Virtual Server Architecture (VSA) implementations]
- Information about SQL Server processes
- Information about user-settable configuration variables
- Entries for SQL Server databases
- Disk allocation information for SQL Server databases
- SQL Server devices including tape dump devices and disk dump devices
- Devices used for database storage and partition information for databases
- System errors and warning messages
- Information about active locks
- Remote user accounts used for remote procedure calls
- Remote servers for intraserver communications
- System defined roles assigned to server log-ins

The *master* database should not be used to store any user-defined database objects. The reader may wish to note that some third-party products such as Microsoft Access break this rule by creating objects in the *master* database. As a rule, the *master* database will change infrequently and should be backed up with the DUMP DATABASE command after any modification.

4.3.2   The *model* database

The *model* database is the "model" or template for all other SQL Server databases. When the user creates a database using the SQL Server CREATE DATABASE command, the SQL Server copies the *model* database and expands it to the requested size. The *model* database is created during SQL Server installation using the *installmodel* script.

Because the *model* database is used to create all new databases, it can be modified to include standard user-defined data types, stored procedures, and even default users. Typically, most users are not granted permission to modify the *model* database. The *model* database should be backed up by using the DUMP DATABASE command after all modifications.

4.3.3   The *tempdb* database

The temporary database is used as a storage area for temporary tables and working storage needs such as intermediate results generated by sorts and the GROUP BY clause. Every time SQL Server is started, a process called *automatic recovery* occurs. The *tempdb* database is created during automatic recovery by copying the *model* database and initializing it to the required size. The *tempdb* database is a copy of *model:* therefore any user-defined data types, stored procedures, and other objects that may exist in *model* will also exist in *tempdb*.

There are two kinds of temporary tables: shareable and nonshareable. Nonshareable temporary tables are creating by prefixing the table name in the CREATE TABLE statement with a pound sign #. Shareable temporary tables are created by prefixing the table name with '*tempdb*..' (for example, 'tempdb..mytable') in the CREATE TABLE statement.

Temporary tables that are created with a pound sign are accessible by the current SQL Server session only. SQL Server assigns these temporary tables a 17-byte numeric suffix; therefore if the table name (including the pound sign) exceeds 13 bytes, SQL Server will truncate the name before appending the numeric suffix. If the table name is less than 13 characters (including the pound sign), SQL Server will pad the table name with underscore characters. The first 13 bytes of the table name must be unique. These nonshareable tables are destroyed when the current session ends. See Sec. 4.1.1, Database Object Identifiers, for more information on naming conventions.

Shareable temporary tables do not have these naming restrictions; table names can be 30 characters, as in any other SQL Server table. These temporary tables can be shared between different SQL Server connections. Temporary tables created by this method remain in existence until the SQL Server is rebooted or until the owner explicitly drops the table, using the DROP TABLE statement.

The following example illustrates the creation and naming of SQL Server temporary tables. The table named *temporary_table* is a shareable temporary table; *#temp* is only accessible to the current SQL Server session.

```
1> use tempdb
2> go
1> create table #temp(id# numeric(5,2) not null, description char(30)
not null)
2> go
1> create table tempdb..temporary_table(id# numeric(5,2) not null,
2> description char(30) not null)
3> go
1> sp_usertables
2> go
id               owner          name
_____    _____     _____

400004456        dbo            #temp_____00000010017301590
432004570        dbo            temporary_table

(2 rows affected, return status = 0)
1>
```

The default size of the temporary database is 2 Mbytes. And *tempdb* is created on the master device by the SQL Server installation process. The size of *tempdb* can be increased by using the ALTER DATABASE command. The amount of space required by *tempdb* will be affected by

- The size of the largest table being sorted with an ORDER BY clause

- Simultaneous sorts or subqueries and aggregates using the GROUP BY clause

- Heavy activity in *tempdb* which can fill up the transaction log—*syslogs* table

- Large or numerous temporary tables

Guidelines for temporary tables. Whenever possible, temporary tables should be created by prefixing a pound sign to the table name. Shareable tables must be explicitly dropped, or else they remain in *tempdb* until the server is rebooted. If an application abnormally ends, it can leave tables in *tempdb* occupying space and causing *tempdb* to fill up. Also, for consistency's sake, temporary tables should be explicitly dropped regardless of how they are created. The following Transact-SQL illustrates temporary table usage.

```
/*
* CREATE TEMPORARY TABLE TO BUILD DATABASE DESCRIPTIONS
*/
CREATE TABLE #databases(
     dbid smallint null,
     dbdesc varchar(102) null
     )

/* INITIALIZE #databases FROM sysdatabases */

INSERT INTO #databases(dbid)
     SELECT dbid FROM master..sysdatabases WHERE name LIKE 'db_%'
.
.
.
/*
* DROP THE TEMPORARY TABLE
*/
DROP TABLE #databases
```

Automatic recovery. Each time SQL Server is restarted, a process called *automatic recovery* performs a set of recovery procedures on each database. The automatic recovery process ensures that transactions succeed or fail as a unit.

During the recovery process, each database is compared to its transaction log. If the transaction log holds more recent information than the corresponding data page in the database, the change is reapplied to the database from the transaction log (*forward recovery*). If any transactions were occurring at the time of the SQL Server shutdown (or failure), the recovery process reverses their effects (*transaction rollback*).

During an SQL Server boot, databases are recovered in the following order:

- The *master* database
- The *sybsecurity* database
- The *model* database
- The *tempdb* database, created by copying the *model* database and initializing it to the required size
- The *sybsystemprocs* database
- User databases recovered in order of the *dbid* (database id) column in the *master.dbo.sysdatabases* table

Normally, after user databases are recovered, a checkpoint record is added to the database. The checkpoint ensures that the recovery process will not be unnecessarily rerun; this checkpoint record is not written if the no-checkpoint-on-recovery option is set in the user database.

SQL Server will accept user connections as soon as the system databases are recovered; however, access to user databases is suspended while they are being recovered.

4.3.4   The *sybsystemprocs* database

The *sybsystemprocs* or system procedures database was introduced with System 10. It is used to store the SYBASE system procedures. When a user in any database attempts to execute a system stored procedure (a procedure that begins with the characters *sp_*), SQL Server will look for the procedure first in the *sysobjects* table of the *sybsystemprocs* database. If the procedure is not found in *sybsystemprocs,* the *master* database is searched.

System procedures will reside in the *master* database when a 4.9.x SQL Server is upgraded to System 10 or to System 11. Some SYBASE and third-party products will create stored procedures in the *master* database. For instance, the SYBASE SQL Server Monitor product installs stored procedures in the *master* database. This is done for compatibility, because SQL Server Monitor can be used with 4.9.x and System 10 and System 11 SQL Servers.

If changes are required to permissions on system procedures, the changes must be made in the *sybsystemprocs* database. System administrators should create their own system stored procedures in the *sybsystemprocs* database, using an *sp_* prefix. The *sybsystemprocs* database should be backed up whenever changes are made.

4.3.5   Optional databases

The optional System 10 and System 11 SQL Server databases are *sybsecurity, sybsyntax,* and *pubs2.* The *sybsecurity* database is created by the SYBASE SQL Server installation program *sybinit.* The *sybsyntax* and *pubs2* databases are created by running SQL scripts with the SYBASE ISQL utility.

The *sybsecurity* database.   The *sybsecurity* database contains the audit system for the System 10 and System 11 SQL Servers. It contains all the default system tables in the *model* database, the *sysaudits* table, and the *sysauditoptions* table. The *sysaudits* table contains the audit trail; a row is inserted into *sysaudits* for every auditable event. The *sysauditoptions* table contains rows describing the Audit Server audit options.

The *sybsyntax* database. The *sybsyntax* database is used to store the syntax of SQL Server commands, Transact SQL commands, and language libraries for Sybase products. SQL Server engines prior to System 10 used the *syman* utility (SYBASE manual pages) to obtain on-line help text. The *syman* utility is similar to the UNIX MAN command which is used to display pages from the UNIX system manuals.

The System 10 and 11 SQL Servers use the *sp_syntax* stored procedure to retrieve help text. Unfortunately, it is necessary to use a utility such as ISQL with an open database connection to retrieve help. Help is not available from a UNIX command line.

The *pubs2* database. The *pubs2* is the sample database and is provided as a learning tool. Many of the examples in the SQL Server documentation are based on the *pubs2* database. The *pubs2* database is installed using the SYBASE ISQL utility and the *installpubs2* SQL script.

4.4   Understanding Database Roles

The concept of database roles was introduced with the System 10 SQL Server. The special roles in SQL Server are

- The System Administrator—*sa_role*
- The System Security Officer—*sso_role*
- The Operator—*oper_role*
- The Database Owner—*dbo*
- The Database Object Owner—*dboo*
- *Navigator,* for System 10 Navigation Server (SYBASE MPP in System 11)
- *Replication,* for System 10 and System 11 Replication Server

Prior to System 10, SQL Server uses an *sa* log-in in place of the SA role. If an installation has several administrators and the *sa* log-in is shared (the norm rather than the exception in larger installations), there is no way to attribute actions taken by the *sa* log-in to an individual. So the problem with the *sa* account was accountability. By implementing *sa_role* that drawback is eliminated in System 10 and System 11.

The system administrator, system security officer, and operator obtain their special status by using the *sp_role* system procedure. The *sp_role* procedure grants or revokes roles to an SQL Server log-in account.

When the System 10 or 11 SQL Server is installed, the user can log into the SQL Server as *sa* with a NULL password. At this point, the installer should create additional SQL Server log-ins and give them *sa* status by assigning them *sa_role*. After this has been done, the *sa* log-in can be locked by using the *sp_locklogin* procedure (also introduced with System 10). The installer must assign *sa_role* to another SQL Server user prior to locking the *sa* account.

The *dbo* and *dboo* concepts are used by all versions of SQL Server, including System 10 and System 11. An SQL Server log-in account obtains *dbo* or *dboo* status by owning a database or database objects.

Discussion of the replication and navigator roles is beyond the scope of this book.

4.4.1   Roles required for SA tasks

Many of the commands and procedures pertaining to system administration require the system administrator, system security officer, and/or operator roles. These special SQL Server roles are discussed in detail in the following subsection. System administrators operate outside the normal SQL Server object and command permission system; SQL Server does no permission checking. The System 10 and System 11 SQL Servers provide an audit system that can be used to log the use of privileged commands requiring one of the roles for execution.

Other sections of this chapter discuss information relevant to database owners. A *dbo*'s name within the database is *dbo*. A user cannot log into SQL Server as *dbo*; the SQL Server engine *aliases* a log-in account to *dbo*. In certain situations where there may be more than one person acting as a database owner, the *sp_addalias* system procedure can be used. The *sp_addalias* procedure maps one user to another in a database (in this case to *dbo*).

4.4.2   SQL Server roles

This subsection provides a brief overview of the special SQL Server roles: the SA role, the SSO role, and the OPER role. These roles are given to an SQL Server log-in account using the *sp_role* system stored procedure.

Figure 4.1 displays the different SQL Server roles and the privileged commands of each. Some of the privileged commands can be transferred to other SQL Server users. For example, a system administrator can grant CREATE DATABASE to any SQL Server user. In addition to the commands displayed, all SQL Server accounts can run the *public* system procedures. The *public* system procedures are those procedures that have execute permission to the group *public*.

System administrator.   SQL Server system administrators perform tasks that are often unrelated to specific database applications. The

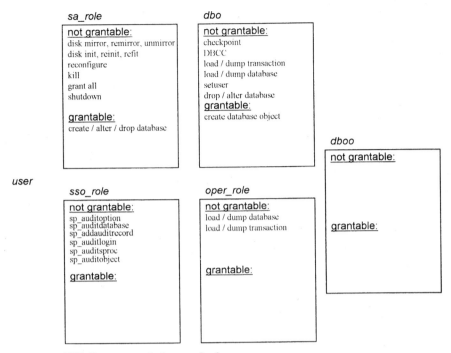

Figure 4.1   SQL Server permissions and roles.

system administrator may not be one individual; in fact in large organizations, the role may be carried out by a group of people. It is, however, imperative that the system administrators' functions be performed through a controlled administration point. System administration tasks were described in Chap. 1. A system administrator account automatically assumes the identity of *dbo* in any database that is entered with a USE DATABASE command. This is done by assuming user ID 1, which is the ID of the database owner.

There are several SQL Server commands that can only be executed by a system administrator. Permissions for these commands cannot be granted to other users.

Larger installations and sites with multiple administrators will want to use the *sp_role* system procedure to grant SA permissions to SQL Server log-in accounts. The SYBASE *sa* account can be locked as long as one or more SQL Server accounts possess the SA role. SQL Server will not allow the last SA role to be locked.

System security officer.   The system security officer (SSO) role was created to perform security-sensitive tasks such as

- Creating SQL Server log-in accounts

- Changing account passwords
- Setting the password expiration interval
- Granting and revoking the SSO and operator roles
- Managing the audit system

The system security officer is not given any special permissions on database objects. There are several security-specific system procedures that can only be run by a system security officer. Permissions on these procedures cannot be granted to other SQL Server users.

The following set of system procedures can be run only by a system security officer:

sp_auditoption	sp_auditsproc
sp_auditdatabase	sp_auditlogin
sp_auditobject	sp_addauditrecord

Operator account. An operator account — oper — is given permission to use the SQL Server DUMP DATABASE, LOAD DATABASE, DUMP TRANSACTION, and LOAD TRANSACTION commands. The operator account can be used to dump and load databases on a serverwide basis. These operations can also be performed on a serverwide basis by system administrators and on a single database by the database owner. The following special commands can be run on a serverwide basis by an operator:

DUMP DATABASE

LOAD DATABASE

DUMP TRANSACTION

LOAD TRANSACTION

4.4.3   The database owner

The database owner is the creator of a database (or group of databases) or someone to whom database ownership has been transferred. SQL Server log-in accounts are granted permission to use the CREATE DATABASE command by the system administrator.

Database owners log into an SQL Server, using a log-in name and password. When the user is in a database that he or she owns, the SQL Server recognizes the user as *dbo*. In other databases the user is known to the SQL Server engine by her or his regular log-in name.

Database owners may perform the following tasks:

- Use the *sp_adduser* system procedure to give other SQL Server users access to the database.

- Use the GRANT command to assign permissions to create objects and execute commands within the database.

- Use the DUMP DATABASE, LOAD DATABASE, DUMP TRANSACTION, and LOAD TRANSACTION commands to back up and restore a database.

- Use the SETUSER command to impersonate another user in the database. The SETUSER command is used to adopt the identity of another user in order to access his or her database objects, to grant permission on an object, or for some other reason.

Here are some simple guidelines for database owners to follow when managing production databases:

- Database modifications (creating tables, views, stored procedures, etc.) should be performed through a controlled administration point, the designated database administrator(s), or database owner.

- All objects in production databases, excluding application-specific requirements, should be owned by the database owner.

- Logical groups of databases should be owned by a specific database owner.

These privileged commands can be run by a database owner:

CHECKPOINT	DBCC
GRANT/REVOKE	SETUSER
LOAD DATABASE	DUMP DATABASE
LOAD TRANSACTION	DUMP TRANSACTION

4.4.4   The database object owner

Database objects are tables, views, indexes, defaults, triggers, rules, stored procedures, and user-defined data types. Permission to create objects can be granted to SQL Server users by a system administrator or by the database owner.

Any user who creates a database object is its owner. The database owner or system administrator must first grant the user permission to create a particular type of object. A database object owner (DBOO) first creates an object with a CREATE statement and then uses the GRANT command to assign permission to other users.

The following example is used to represent two parallel ISQL sessions. The first connection belongs to the system administrator or DBO, the second belongs to the SQL Server user 'testaverde'. The example illustrates the steps required for a user to create and own database objects. The GRANT statement on the user side is required to allow other SQL Server users to access the table.

```
SA/DBO session                              SQL Server user
1> USE mydatabase                           1> USE mydatabase
2> GO                                       2> GO
1> GRANT CREATE TABLE TO testaverde         1> CREATE TABLE football(
2> GO                                       2> pk int not null,
                                            3> name char(30) not null )
                                            4> GO
                                            1> GRANT SELECT ON football TO moon
                                            2> GO
                                            1> INSERT football( pk, name)
                                            2> VALUES(1, "TERRY BRADSHAW")
                                            2> GO
                                            1> SELECT * FROM football
                                            2> GO
1> SELECT id, sysusers.name AS owner,
2> sysobjects.name FROM sysusers, sysobjects
3> WHERE sysobjects.uid = sysusers.uid AND
4> sysobjects.type = 'U'
5> GO
```

Objects in a database that are not owned by the database owner must be accessed with the object owner's ID. For example, if *testaverde* (not a DBO) owns a table and grants SELECT permission on that table to another log-in ID, it must be accessed as follows:

```
1> select * from testaverde.football
2> go
```

If the table is owned by *dbo,* it can be accessed without the *owner* qualifier:

```
1> select * from football
2> go
```

As mentioned earlier, SQL Server stores object information in the system table *sysobjects*. Objects are uniquely identified by a compound key made up of object name plus SQL Server user ID. The following piece of SQL code is used to query the *sysobjects* system table for the existence of a stored procedure. The Transact-SQL *object_id* function is used to uniquely identify the procedure.

```
IF EXISTS(SELECT * FROM sysobjects WHERE id =
object_id('testaverde.procedureName'))
BEGIN
        PRINT "PROCEDURE EXISTS"
END
```

These are privileged commands of a database object owner: GRANT/REVOKE, DROP OBJECT.

5

SQL Server Storage Structure

This chapter describes the various SQL Server storage structures and components. It also discusses the impact of data manipulation (DML statements) including the SQL Server INSERT, UPDATE, and DELETE operations.

The system administrator is required to understand SQL Server's storage structure to properly interpret the output from DBCC commands (the SYBASE Database Consistency Checker) and to deal with messages and errors reported by the SQL Server and by DBCC commands.

It is important for application developers and database designers to understand how SQL Server stores data and index pages. The performance implications of certain design decisions will not be fully grasped without this knowledge. The information presented in this section will help the reader answer such questions such these:

- Should there be a clustered index on this table?

- This column will be updated frequently by the application. Should it allow NULLs? Should it be a variable-length column?

- This table will see significant UPDATE activity in production. Are there too many indexes on the table?

5.1 Storage Hierarchy

This section describes the SQL Server storage hierarchy and the relationships between the various storage objects. SYBASE allocates disk space to an SQL Server. This allocation is accomplished using *database devices*. Figure 5.1 is a logical representation of the SQL Server storage hierarchy. SQL Server databases and transaction logs are

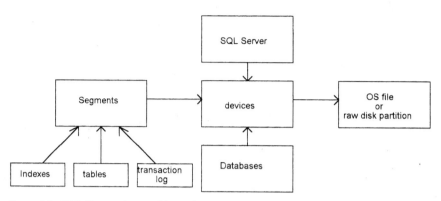

Figure 5.1   SQL Server storage hierarchy.

stored on database devices. Database devices are logical devices (created with the DISK INIT command) that are mapped to a raw disk partition or an operating system file. There can be a one-to-one or one-to-many relationship between a database and database devices.

When a database device is initialized using the DISK INIT command, SYBASE divides the storage space into *allocation units* of 256 2K data pages or 0.5 Mbyte. The smallest unit of allocation for a database device is the size of the *model* database or the configuration value *database size,* whichever is larger.

The default size of the model database is 2 Mbytes or 1024 2K data pages for a total of four allocation units. The database size configuration variable is set with the *sp_configure* system procedure (the default run value is also 2 Mbytes). A database device that will be used to store a transaction log or for small tables or indexes on a *segment* can be as small as 1 Mbyte.

Database devices are allocated to a database or transaction log. When a portion of space on a device is allocated to a database, the portion is called a *device fragment.* Device fragments are tracked by SQL Server using the *sysusages* table which resides in the *master* database.

Database segments.   Database devices are logically divided into database *segments* to allow for specific object placement. Segments are labels that point to one or more database devices and are used to subdivide the device. Segments provide the ability to place an object on one device or to split its storage across several devices. The database device can be thought of as one floor in an apartment building and the segments as the actual apartments on that floor.

Database *segments* are named subsets of a database device (or device fragment) available to an SQL Server database. Segments are used in CREATE TABLE and CREATE INDEX commands to place tables and indexes on specific database devices. Database segments can be used to increase SQL Server performance. A more detailed discussion of database segments is provided in Chap. 10.

5.2 System Tables

There are a total of five system tables that track storage information on databases, tables, and indexes. The first two (*sysusages* and *sysdevices*) are located in the *master* database, and three more (*syssegments, sysindexes,* and *sysattributes*) reside in all SQL Server databases. Figure 5.2 illustrates the relationships between the system tables used for storage information.

The *sysdevices* table. The *sysdevices* table is located in the *master* database and is used to track information about database devices and dump devices. Dump devices can be tape, disk, or an operating system file. There is one row in *sysdevices* for each database device or dump device.

Database devices are added to the *sysdevices* table with the DISK INIT command, and dump devices are added with the *sp_addumpdevice* system stored procedure. Database dump devices allow the sys-

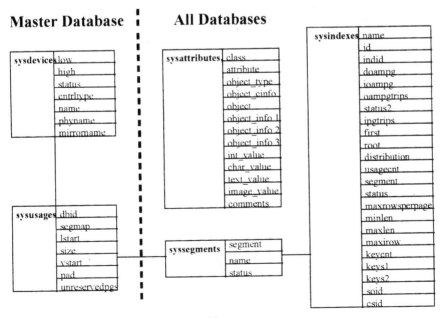

Figure 5.2 SQL Server system storage tables.

tem administrator to assign a logical device name to a physical back-up (or dump) device.

The *sysdevices* table maintains the mapping between physical device names and logical device names. A *logical device name* is used in SQL Server storage management commands. The logical name is typically a user-friendly name used to indicate the purpose of the device (e.g., database_1, log_1, or 5gb_tapedrive).

The *physical device name* is the operating system name of the device. It is only necessary to create the database or dump device; after the device has been created, all SQL Server commands use the logical name.

The *sysusages* table.   The *sysusages* table is also located in the *master* database. It is used to keep track of all space that is assigned to SQL Server databases. The *sysusages* table contains one row for each *fragment* or allocation piece assigned to a database.

When a database is created or expanded with the CREATE DATA-BASE or ALTER DATABASE command, a row is added to the *sysusages* table. When a portion of the space on a physical device is allocated to a database, that portion is called a *fragment*.

The *sysusages* table also maps a *fragment* to its possible segment assignments. The system procedures *sp_addsegment, sp_extendsegment,* and *sp_dropsegment* modify rows in the *sysusages* table.

The *syssegments* table.   The *syssegments* table is present in all data-bases. It contains one row for each database *segment*. A *segment* is a collection of disk pieces available to a particular database.

Tables and indexes can be assigned to a particular segment. A segment can be extended over several database devices, allowing a particular database object to span several physical disks.

The CREATE DATABASE command makes default entries in *syssegments*. Further discussion of the default entries is provided in Chap. 10. The system procedures *sp_addsegment* and *sp_dropsegment* add and remove entries from the *syssegments* table.

The *sysindexes* table.   The *sysindexes* table is present in all databases and contains

- One row for each clustered index
- One row for each nonclustered index
- One row for each table that has no clustered index
- One row for each table that contains *text* or *image* columns

The *sysindexes* table also maintains the page number for the object allocation map (OAM), a pointer to the first data or leaf page, other pointer information, minimum and maximum row sizes, maximum number of rows per page, and the number of the segment in which the object resides.

A row is created in *sysindexes* by the CREATE TABLE and CREATE INDEX commands.

The *sysdatabases* table.   The *sysdatabases* table resides in the *master* database only. There is one row in *sysdatabases* for each SQL Server database. The CREATE DATABASE command inserts rows into the *sysdatabases* table. The *sysdatabases* table is used to maintain database-specific information including

- The server user ID (SUID) of the database owner
- Database-specific options such as *select into/bulkcopy* and *trunc log on chkpt*
- Database creation date
- Default audit settings
- Date of the last transaction log dump

The *sysattributes* table.   The *sysattributes* table is present in all SQL Server databases. System attributes define the properties of objects such as databases, tables, indexes, procedures, users, and log-ins. There is one row in *sysattributes* for each one of an object's attribute definitions configured by various system stored procedures.

5.3   Storage Summary

Let's summarize some key points about SQL Server storage:

1. Database devices belong to an SQL Server.
2. A portion of a device that is allocated to a database is called a *fragment*.
3. A database device maps to an operating system file (e.g., */sybase/master.device*) or a raw disk partition (e.g., SunOS—*/dev/rsd0a*, Solaris—*/dev/rdsk/c1t0d0s0*, AIX—*/dev/rmaster00*).
4. Databases and transaction logs reside on database devices.
5. An SQL Server database can be logically divided into 192 segments.
6. There can be a one-to-one or one-to-many relationship between a database and database devices. A database can be created and/or expanded across many database devices. A database device can be used to store multiple databases.

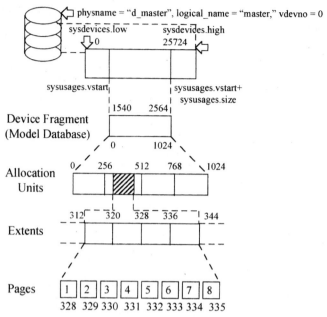

Figure 5.3   SQL Server storage hierarchy.

7. Database objects such as tables and indexes can be created on a specific segment or split across several database segments. This means that storage for a table can be split across many disks.

Figure 5.3 illustrates the physical storage hierarchy within SQL Server. Extents and pages are the subject of Sec. 5.4.

5.4   Page and Object Allocation

When a database device is initialized using the DISK INIT command, SYBASE divides the storage space into *allocation units* of 256 2K data pages (data pages are 4K on Stratus machines). This conversation will focus on 2K data pages which are typical to most versions of the SQL Server. The first page of each allocation unit is called an *allocation page*. The allocation page is used to track the use of all pages in the allocation unit. Each allocation unit is broken up into groups of 8 pages called *extents*. An extent is associated with a specific database object.

Allocation page.   Allocation pages store information about each *extent* contained in the allocation unit. All allocation pages contain a 32-byte page header that is used to record the logical page number and data-

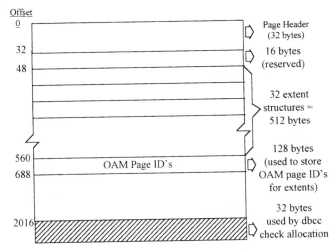

Offset

0	Page Header (32 bytes)
32	16 bytes (reserved)
48	
	32 extent structures = 512 bytes
560	OAM Page ID's
	128 bytes (used to store OAM page ID's for extents)
688	
2016	32 bytes used by dbcc check allocation

Figure 5.4   Allocation page layout.

base ID of allocation. The database ID is the value found in the *dbid* column of the *master.dbo.sysdatabases* table.

The basic layout of an allocation page is illustrated in Fig. 5.4. Allocation pages (like all pages), have a header portion and a body portion. The body portion starts at offset 32. A series of 32 extent structures on the allocation page are used to control page allocation. Each *extent* controls 8 pages, and each *allocation page* controls 32 extents (for a total of 256 pages or one *allocation unit*). The extent structures are 16 bytes in length and occupy 512 bytes on the *allocation page*. An extent structure can be represented as follows:

```
typedef struct {
    smallint    nextExtentID;       /* Pointer to next extent in list */
    smallint    previousExtentID;   /* Pointer to previous extent in list */
    int         objectID;           /* as found in sysobjects.id */
    char        allocationMap;      /* bitmap of allocation pages in this
                                       extent */
    char        deallocationMap;    /* bitmap of pages marked for dealloca-
                                       tion */
    int         indexID;            /* ID of the index that allocated this
                                       extent */
                                    /* Pointer to sysindexes.indid */
    smallint    status;             /* internal system status info (sort
                                       bit/reference bit)*/
} extent;
```

- *nextExtentID* and *previousExtentID:*   They point to the next and previous extents in the chain. This is a linked list of pointers to the next extent in the chain and the previous extent in the chain. 0 is used to indicate the end of the chain.

- *objectID:*   It identifies the object that this extent is allocated to and maps to the *id* column in the *sysobjects* table.

- *allocationMap:*   This element is a 1-byte field with each bit setting representing the status of an allocation page in the extent. If the bit is on, the page is already allocated to the object. If the bit is off, the page is reserved for use by the object but is not currently allocated.

- *deallocationMap:*   This element is a 1-byte field with each bit serving as a flag for page deallocation. If a row is deleted (within a transaction) and the object has shrunk off the page, the bit flag will be set on. The page deallocation will be written to the allocation page when the transaction is committed. If the object has shrunk off the extent, the extent will be deallocated when the transaction is committed.

- *indexID:*   The value in the *indexID* column points to the ID of the index that allocated the extent. Here *indexID* is used to map back to the *indid* column in the *sysindexes* table. A value of 0 refers to the table itself; a value of 1 refers to a clustered index; values greater than 1 refer to nonclustered indexes on the table.

- *status:*   This is internal system status information. It maintains sort and reference bits.

The System 11 SQL Server uses 128 bytes immediately following the extent structures to store OAM page IDs for extents. Extent OAM page IDs are used to directly access the OAM page entry for the allocation page without incurring the additional overhead of an OAM page scan during page allocation and deallocation. Each OAM page ID is 4 bytes, so 32 extents require 128 bytes of storage (4 × 32 extents = 128).

Figure 5.5 illustrates how data pages are set up within extents and allocation units in SQL Server databases.

Extents.   Whenever a table or index requires space, SQL Server allocates an extent to the object (8 × 2K pages). All the pages in an extent must belong to the same database object (table or index). Pages in an extent that is allocated to a table or index but not yet used for storage are known as *reserved pages*. As stated previously, every SQL Server allocation unit contains 32 extents. SQL Server uses extents to allocate and deallocate space to tables and indexes. Things to remember:

- SQL Server allocates an extent to a table or index when a CREATE TABLE or CREATE INDEX statement is executed.

- When inserting rows into an existing table, SQL Server will allocate another data page if all existing pages are full. If there are no

Allocation Page

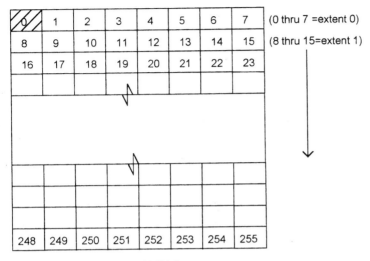

1 allocation unit = 256 2K data pages

Figure 5.5 Allocation page structure.

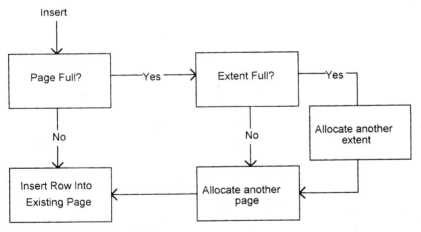

Figure 5.6 INSERT algorithm.

more pages available in existing extents, SQL Server will allocate another extent to the table. Figure 5.6 illustrates this algorithm.

- When a table or index is dropped with a DROP TABLE or DROP INDEX command, SQL Server deallocates all extents allocated to the object.

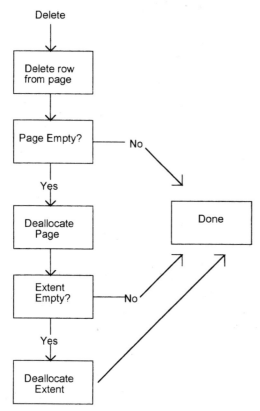

Figure 5.7 DELETE algorithm.

- If rows are deleted from a table or index, causing it to shrink off a page, SQL Server will deallocate the page. Similarly, if the object shrinks off an extent, SQL Server will deallocate the extent. Figure 5.7 illustrates the delete algorithm.

- Whenever space is allocated or deallocated on an extent, SQL Server records the action on the allocation page that tracks the extents for that object.

The Global Allocation Map. Every SQL Server database maintains a bit map called the Global Allocation Map (GAM) for the allocation units in that database. There is a minimum of one GAM page per database. SQL Server allocates and initializes the GAM page(s) when it creates a database. The GAM pages are adjusted if the database is altered with an ALTER DATABASE command. SQL Server uses the GAM page to determine whether there is space in a given 256-page allocation unit. GAM page bit maps have 16,128 bits representing the same number of allocation units in a database.

```
((page_size - sizeof(header))) * 8) = bits
        (2048 - 32) * 8 = 16,128
```

This means that a single GAM page can maintain allocation information for databases up to 8 Gbytes. Platforms that use a 4K page size can obviously store more information.

```
(4096 - 32) * 8 = 32,512 bits
```

Figure 5.8 portrays the structure of the GAM page. Note that when a GAM bit is set to 1, there are no free extents in the corresponding allocation unit.

Every GAM page has a 32-byte page header which can be described by the following data structure:

```
typedef struct {
    int    pageno;    /* Logical Page Number of this GAM page */
    int    nextpg;    /* Next page number in the sysgams page chain, or 0 */
    int    prevpg;    /* Previous page number in the sysgams page chain, or 0 */
    int    objectID;  /* Object ID for sysgams, which is 14 */
} pageHeader;
```

Some things to know about the Global Allocation Map include these:

- GAM bits are set to 1 if SQL Server searches an allocation page and finds no free extents.

- GAM bits are set to 0 initially and when an extent is deallocated.

- SQL Server scans GAM pages when it needs a free extent. The GAM page makes it unnecessary to scan each allocation page to find a free extent, which results in performance improvements especially for large databases.

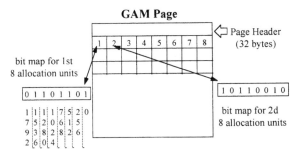

Figure 5.8 Global Allocation Map.

- The *sysgams* table in each database contains the Global Allocation Map. The *sysindexes* entry for the *sysgams* table maintains a pointer to the first page in the *sysgams* page chain (*sysindexes.first*), a pointer to the last page in the page chain (*sysindexes.root*), and the object ID for *sysgams* (which is 14).

- Note also that GAM pages do not have an Object Allocation Map (OAM) page.

The Object Allocation Map.   Every table and every index on a table have an *Object Allocation Map* (OAM). The OAM is stored on pages allocated to the table or index and is checked when a new page is needed for the index or table.

The OAM page holds pointers to each allocation unit on which the object uses space. In turn, the allocation page holds pointers to the extents used within an allocation unit. The allocation page also holds information about the pages used on each extent. So the allocation page maintains information about extents, and the allocation unit maintains information about pages. A generic OAM page is displayed in Fig. 5.9.

Note that the OAM structure on the first OAM page contains summary information about the object. This summary information (object statistics) includes number of rows, total used and unused pages, etc., and is maintained by using the UPDATE STATISTICS command. These statistics are used by the SYBASE query optimizer. There is one OAM entry for each allocation unit that has extents allocated to that database object.

The *sysindexes* table maintains pointers to the Object Allocation Map for database objects. Also *sysindexes* maintains a pointer to the first and last data pages for database tables and a pointer to the first leaf page, root page, and distribution page (index statistics page) if the object is an index.

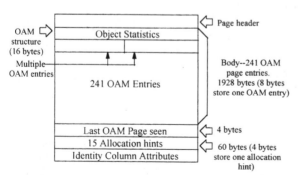

Figure 5.9   Generic OAM page.

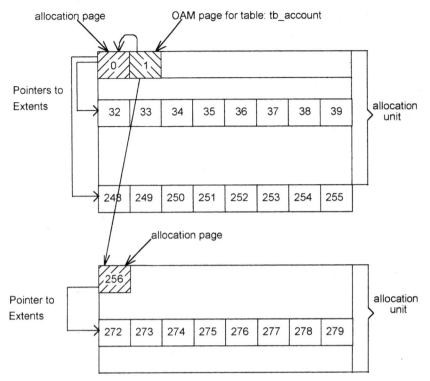

Figure 5.10 Object Allocation Map.

Figure 5.10 shows how the OAM page is used to track allocation for a database object, in this case a table named *tb_account*.

- The *sysindexes* table holds a pointer to the OAM page for the *tb_account* table.

- The *allocation page* maintains *extent structures* for the *allocation unit*. The extent structures keep track of pages within the extent.

- The OAM holds pointers to allocation units on which the object uses space. Page numbers for allocation units start at 0 and include all pages that are divisible by 256 (0, 256, 512, 768, 1024,. . .).

- The OAM for table *tb_account* is stored in page 1 of the first allocation unit. As the reader can see, the OAM points to allocation pages 0 and 256, so our table uses space within those two allocation units.

- Within those allocation units, allocation page 0 tells us that the object uses space on extent 4 (pages 32 through 39) and extent 31 (pages 248 through 255) and allocation page 256 tells us that the object uses space on extent 2 (pages 272 through 279).

Allocation hints.   System 11 maintains *allocation hints* which tell SQL Server where to look first for an unused page. Allocation hints are stored on the first OAM page (see Fig. 5.9). When an object is created, space for allocation hints is automatically created on the first allocation page. Note that only the first OAM page stores 241 OAM entries; subsequent OAM pages have space for 250 OAM entries. SQL Server uses space near the end of the first OAM page to store up to 15 hints. In reality, hints are page numbers and therefore require 4 bytes of storage. The page number of the last OAM page scanned is also maintained on the first OAM page. By storing the last OAM page scanned, SQL Server can begin its next scan at this page. The server is more likely to find an unused page from this point forward.

Data pages.   Data rows are stored in data pages which are chained in a double-linked list. Every data page has a 32-byte page header that can be described by the following data structure:

```
typedef struct {
   int          virtualPage;   /* Virtual Page Number */
   int          pageno;        /* Logical Page Number */
   int          nextpg;        /* Page number of the next page */
   int          prevpg;        /* Page number of the previous page */
   int          objectID;      /* ID of the object that owns the page */
   time         timestamp;     /* Time stamp */
   char         nextrno;       /* Next available row number in page */
   int          level;         /* Index Level */
   int          indid;         /* Index ID */
   smallint     freeoff;       /* Offset of free space in page */
   smallint     minlen;        /* Minimum row length */
   smallint     status;        /* Page status bits */
   } pageHeader;
```

- *virtualPage:*   The virtual page number on the database device.

- *pageno:*   The logical page number of this data page.

- *nextpg:*   The logical page number of the next page.

- *prevpg:*   The logical page number of the previous page.

- *objectID:*   The identifier of the object that owns this data page. *objectID* maps to the *id* column of the *sysobjects* table.

- *nextrno:*   Next available row number in the data page. Each data row stored on the page is assigned a row number (known as *row_id*). The row number is a 1-byte field which restricts the number of rows in a data page to 256.

- *level:*   Used if *indid* is not equal to zero. *level* indicates the level of the B-tree (see Fig. 5.11).

- *indid:*   A value of 0 indicates the data table, 1 indicates a clustered index, and nonclustered indexes start with a value of 2.

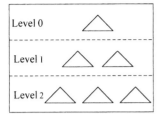

Figure 5.11 B-tree index levels.

- *freeoff:* Byte location of free space on the data page. This space is available for row storage and is always at the end of the data page.
- *minlen:* If fixed-length rows are stored on the data page, this is the minimum amount of space required to store a data row.

Logical page numbers versus physical page numbers. The pages in each database are assigned sequential ID numbers beginning with 0 and ending with the last page of the database. These ID numbers are referred to as *logical page numbers*. SQL Server translates the logical page numbers in a database into an offset on the appropriate database device. By structuring all the database devices owned by an SQL Server into a virtual address space, each page in a database device is assigned a *virtual page number.*

Data rows. The page header is followed by the actual *data rows*. Data rows cannot be split across data pages, so the number of fixed-length data rows that can be stored on a page is calculated as

$$\frac{(\ \mathtt{sizeof(\ datapage)\ -\ sizeof(\ pageheader\ )\ )}}{(\ \mathtt{sizeof(\ datarow\ )\ +\ 4\text{-}byte\ overhead\ )}}$$

The maximum amount of space available on a data page for row storage is 2016 bytes, which is the size of a data page minus the size of the page header. The maximum size of an individual data row is 1962 bytes. Actually, the CREATE TABLE statement will not allow the user to create a data row larger than 1960 bytes. The difference between the two numbers (2016 and 1962) is overhead that SYBASE needs when logging modifications to the data row in the *syslogs* table. The overhead for each row in the transaction log is 54 bytes.

Figure 5.12 shows the format of fixed-length data rows. Note the 2-byte overhead for the number of variable-length columns and *row number*. SYBASE maintains an offset table at the end of the data page. The offset table grows inward from the end of the data page and

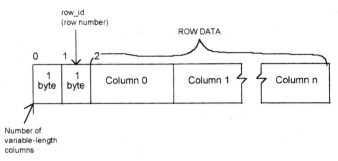

Figure 5.12 Layout of fixed-length data row.

is used to store the byte location of data rows stored within the page. If the data rows are of fixed length, SYBASE calculates the location of the data row, using the algorithm

```
sizeof( pageheader ) + ( ( sizeof( datarow ) + 2-byte overhead ) *
row_number )
```

For example,

```
32 + ( ( 34 + 2 ) * 4 ) = 176
```

So row number 4 is located at offset 176.

Now, let's look at an example:

```
create table football(
  pk int not null,
  name char(30) not null
  )
```

This table will require 38 bytes to store a data row which is described in Table 5.1. Using the established formula helps determine that 53 rows can be stored on a data page.

$$\frac{(\ \text{sizeof}(\ \text{datapage})\ -\ \text{sizeof}(\ \text{pageheader}\ )\ )}{(\ \text{sizeof}(\ \text{datarow}\ )\ +\ 4\ \text{byte overhead}\ )}$$

TABLE 5.1 Storage Requirements for *football*

Data type	Description	Storage requirements, bytes
smallint	Overhead associated with offset table	2
char	Number of variable-length columns	1
char	Row number of this data row	1
int	Data column *pk* (primary key)	4
char	Data column *name*	30
		38

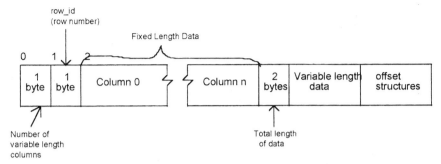

Figure 5.13   Layout of variable-length data row.

$$\frac{(2048 - 32)}{(34 + 4)}$$

$$\frac{2016}{38} = 53$$

Obviously, variable-length data rows have different storage requirements. The offset structures pictured in Fig. 5.13 are used to maintain the size of the variable-length data so that they can be parsed into columns after retrieval from the data page.

Log rows.   Log rows are obviously different from data rows; however, the page format is the same. Some of the information contained in a log record includes

- *row_number:*   It is used to indicate the row that the log record occupies on the page.

- *transaction_ID:*   The transaction ID is a unique number made up of the logical page number and the row number of the record at the start of this transaction. Every log record belonging to a particular transaction is identified with the same transaction ID.

- *record_type:*   Each log record is identified with a record type. A description of log record types is given in App. L.

- *variable information:*   Additional information; varies depending on log record type.

Parameter *fillfactor.*   The *fillfactor* parameter (to the CREATE INDEX statement) is used to set the percentage to which index and clustered data pages are filled during initial creation and loading. The *fillfactor* percentage is relevant only at the time the index is created. As the data changes, the pages are not maintained at any particular level of fullness. The *fillfactor* parameter is discussed in detail in Chap. 12.

Maximum number of rows per page. Maximum rows per page allows the user to specify the maximum number of rows that can be stored on a data page or the leaf page of a nonclustered index. If maximum rows per page is set for the clustered index, it affects data pages only. This is similar to the *fillfactor* option, with the caveat that the specified number of rows is continuously maintained by the server.

Although it has other uses, the *max_rows_per_page* feature is somewhat of a kludge put in place to make up for the absence of row-level locking. Consider an application that performs frequent updates to a narrow table. For argument's sake, let's use the *football* table described earlier in this section. We have determined that the *football* table can store 53 rows on a data page. Assume that the *football* table is small, say, 100 rows and requires 2 data pages of storage. Now if multiple users are updating the *name* column, there may be a significant amount of contention, because a user cannot update a data page without acquiring an exclusive lock on that data page. Therefore, whenever an update is performed, approximately half of the table is locked! Given this scenario, it may be useful to store a smaller number of rows on the data page. This can be used to simulate row-level locking by setting *max_rows_per_page* equal to 1. The value of *max_rows_per_page* is stored in a new column in the *sysindexes* table called *maxrowsperpage*.

Other benefits of *max_rows_per_page* include an increased probability for direct updates on variable-length columns. Don't worry too much about this yet; we cover this in Sec. 5.6. The drawbacks include a potentially large amount of wasted space and the increased possibility of *page splits*. The *max_rows_per_page* feature is discussed in greater detail in Chap. 12.

Page splits. Page splitting occurs when the server attempts to insert a row and there is not enough room on the data page for that row. Figure 5.14 shows a simple 50:50 page split. Page splits impose a severe performance overhead when data are loaded into a table with a clustered index. The System 10 page split algorithm looks like this:

1. Allocate a new data page.

2. Split the target page in half, and move the rows in the second half of the page to the new data page.

3. Flush the new page to disk to provide a point of recoverability.

Keep in mind that every time a page is split, each nonclustered index entry that points to that data page must be updated. One exception to the 50:50 page split is the case where the new entry belongs at the end of the page. In this case the page does not split.

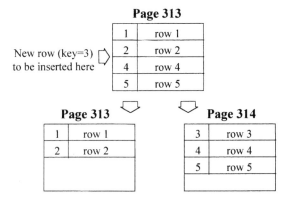

Figure 5.14   Page split—50:50.

The System 11 page split algorithm is slightly different:

1. Allocate new data page.
2. If rows are moving from the current page to the new data page, the server will move the rows without logging the movement and will flush the new page to disk. If rows are not being moved to the new page, the server will allocate the new page and will log the page allocation. The row is then inserted on the appropriate page, and the insertion is logged.

Page allocations.   SQL Server allocates pages to an object when the following operations or events occur:

- A table or index is created.
- A data or index page splits.
- An *overflow* page is created.
- A *distribution* (index statistics) page is created. Index statistics pages are described in the next section.
- The transaction log (*syslogs* table) grows.
- A bulk copy or sorting is performed.

An *overflow* page is created for duplicate key inserts into a nonunique clustered index at the end of a full page. An overflow data page is maintained in a separate page chain from other data pages. When many duplicate keys are added, the overflow chain can be more than a single data page. The performance implications of overflow chains are considerable because the overflow chain must be scanned anytime a duplicate value is specified. The best way to avoid this extra I/O is to avoid using a nonunique clustered index.

Page linkage. SYBASE maintains a double-linked list for pages that are allocated to a table or index. The page linkage is used for fast sequential access to data pages. Each page has a header that can be described as follows:

```
typedef struct {
    int         pageno;       /* Logical page number of this page */
    int         previousPage; /* Page number of the previous page */
    int         nextPage;     /* Page number of the next page */
} pageLinkage;
```

When a page is allocated to a table or index, the page must be linked with the other pages being used by the object.

```
previousPage->nextPage    = pageno;        /* reset link on first page */
pageno->previousPage      = previousPage;  /* set links on middle page */
pageno->nextPage          = nextPage;
nextPage->previousPage    = pageno;        /* reset link on last page */
```

Similarly, when a page is deallocated, the links for the previous and next pages must be reset. The DBCC PGLINKAGE command (see App. G) is used to traverse the page chain for a table or index. The output from DBCC PGLINKAGE looks like this:

```
1> dbcc pglinkage(9,361,6,2,369,1)
2> go
Object ID for pages in this chain = 16003088
Page : 361
Page : 362
Page : 363
Page : 364
Page : 365
Page : 366
End of chain reached
6 pages scanned. Object ID = 16003088. Last page in scan = 366.
```

Text and image page chains. The text and image data types support the storage of large quantities of character or binary data. Text and image data are stored in a separate page chain from the actual data page. A 16-byte pointer to the page chain is stored in the data page with the corresponding row. Each page in the text and image chain can store approximately 1800 bytes of text or image data. A pointer to the next page in the chain is maintained in each page, as illustrated in Fig. 5.15.

5.5   Indexes

SYBASE uses B-tree structures to index SQL Server tables. A B-tree index is a multilevel, tree-structured index that is extremely efficient. The SYBASE B-tree implementation provides uniform, predictable performance with very fast data retrieval.

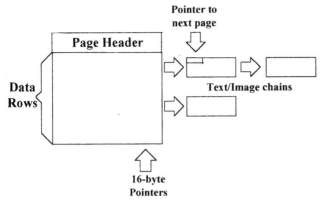

Figure 5.15   Text and image page chain.

A B-tree index consists of a root page, zero or more levels of intermediate pages, and leaf pages. The leaf pages contain index key values and pointers to data pages. All leaf pages are equidistant from the root pages; this means that all leaf pages are located in the same *level* of the tree. Technically, the B-trees used by SYBASE are called B + trees. A B-tree maintains pointers to data pages in its intermediate nodes as well as the leaf nodes. B+ trees maintain pointers to data only at the leaf level.

Figure 5.16 illustrates the layout of a small B-tree index. A few comments about Fig. 5.16 are in order:

- A pointer to the root page of the index is maintained in the *sysindexes* table (*sysindexes.root*).

- The root page holds pointers to intermediate pages; there can be several levels of intermediate pages.

- Intermediate pages hold pointers to the next level of intermediate pages or pointers to leaf pages. The bottom level of intermediate pages holds pointers to leaf pages.

- The leaf pages hold pointers to data pages.

- Index leaf pages are linked together in index key sequence for fast sequential access.

There are two types of indexes: *clustered* and *nonclustered*. A table can have at most one clustered index.

Clustered index.   With a clustered index, rows are stored in the data pages in the same order as the index values. In a SYBASE clustered index, only the first row in a data page has an index entry. Because

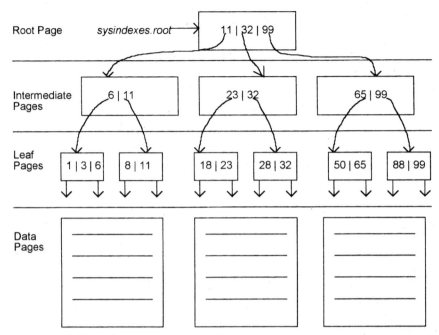

Figure 5.16 B-tree index structure.

there is not an index entry for each data row, a clustered index is also known as a *sparse* index. For clustered indexes the index page entry consists of the index key value of the first row on the corresponding data page.

It is the author's recommendation that every base table have a primary key. It is also a recommendation that every table have a clustered index. While the clustered index may not always be the same as the primary key, the primary key is often a good candidate for being the clustered index.

Nonclustered index.   In a nonclustered index, each row in the data pages has an entry in the index pages. For this reason nonclustered indexes are also known as *dense* indexes. For nonclustered indexes, the index page entry consists of the index key value, the page number, and the row number of the corresponding data row.

Index pages.   Index pages also have a 32-byte header. The header on an index page can be depicted by the following data structure:

```
typedef struct {
  int            virtualPage;   /* Virtual Page Number */
  int            pageno;        /* Logical Page Number */
  int            nextpg;        /* Page number of the next page */
  int            prevpg;        /* Page number of the previous page */
  int            objectID;      /* ID of the object that owns the page */
  time           timestamp;     /* Time stamp */
  char           nextrno;       /* Not used */
  char           level;         /* Index Level */
  char           indid;         /* Index ID */
  smallint       freeoff;       /* Offset of free space in page */
  smallint       minlen;        /* Minimum row length */
  char           status;        /* Page status bits */
} indexHeader;
```

- *virtualPage:* The virtual page number on the database device.

- *pageno:* The logical page number of this index page.

- *nextpg:* The logical page number of the next page.

- *prevpg:* The logical page number of the previous page.

- *objectID:* The identifier of the table that owns this index. *objectID* maps to the *id* column in the *sysobjects* table.

- *nextrno:* Index pages do not use row numbers.

- *level:* Index level.

- *indid:* The identifier of the index that this page belongs to.

- *freeoff:* Byte location of free space on the index page. This space is available for index row storage.

- *minlen:* The size of the index rows.

The pages of each index are chained together in index key sequence for fast sequential access (see previous "Page Linkage" section). Index rows are stored after the index header on the index pages. The index rows consist of key values and pointer combinations.

Data access—Nonclustered index. For nonclustered indexes, pointers are built by combining the values of *data page number* and *row number.* (Please refer to the discussion on data pages earlier in this section.)
Let's use a structure to illustrate data retrieval via *row_id.*

```
typedef struct {
  int pageNumber;
  int rowNumber;
} row_id;
```

When retrieving data rows using a nonclustered index, SYBASE uses two algorithms. First, the algorithm for retrieving fixed-length data rows using a nonclustered index is as follows:

- Use *row_id->pageNumber* to access the data page.
- Use *row_id->rowNumber* to calculate the offset of the data row.

```
sizeof( pageHeader ) + ( ( sizeof( dataRow ) + 2-byte overhead ) *
rowNumber )
```

- Retrieve the data row from the data page, using the calculated offset.

Variable-length data rows are retrieved by using a different algorithm:

- Use *row_id->pageNumber* to access the data page.
- Use *row_id->rowNumber* to retrieve the offset of the data row from the offset table at the end of the data page.
- Retrieve the data row from the data page, using the offset obtained from the offset table.

Figure 5.17 illustrates how SYBASE uses *row_id* to retrieve variable-length data rows.

Data access—Clustered index.   Data access using a clustered index is obviously very different from that with a nonclustered index. When a clustered index is used, there is no index entry for every data row; also, there is no *row_id* to locate the record with. To locate a row using a clustered index:

- Search the index level to find the index entry for the data page in which the row is found.
- Read the data page sequentially to find the row.

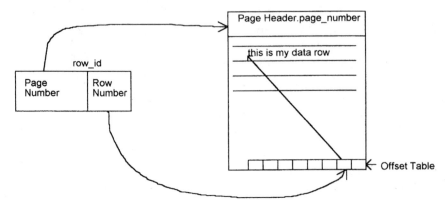

Figure 5.17   Accessing variable-length data using *row_id*.

Index statistics pages. Index statistics pages are used to maintain up-to-date information on table indexes for the query optimizer. The statistics page has a 32-byte header (for compatibility with allocation pages), followed by index field key values. The index field key values are obtained by reading the value of the index key at each nth position in the table. Each sampled row is referred to as a *step*. Index statistics pages are maintained by running the UPDATE STATISTICS command; they are not dynamically updated by SQL Server.

Information maintained on the index statistics page is used to estimate the number of rows in a table. This information is used by the *rowcnt* system function and the *sp_spaceused* system stored procedure. Index statistics pages are also known as *distribution pages*.

5.6   Deletes and Updates

This section provides an overview of SQL Server 11 DELETE and UPDATE processing.

Deletes

The SYBASE DELETE operation can be processed by the server in two ways:

1. Direct delete, single phase
2. Deferred delete, two phases

We will use the following tables and data to illustrate direct and deferred deletes.

```
create table team(
  team                    int                not null,
  name                    char(30)           not null,
  constraint              team_key           primary key(team)
  ) on 'default'
insert team(1, 'DOLPHINS')
insert team(2, 'STEELERS')
insert team(3, 'VIKINGS')
insert team(4, 'GIANTS')
insert team(5, 'COWBOYS')

create table player(
  player                  numeric(8,0)       identity,
  name                    char(30)           not null,
  team                    int                not null,
  constraint              team_name          foreign key(team)
                          references         team(team)
  ) on 'default'
create unique clustered index x0player on player(player)

insert player values('MARINO', 1)
insert player values('GREENE', 2)
```

```
insert player values('MOON', 3)
insert player values('TAYLOR', 4)
insert player values('AIKMAN', 5)
insert player values('SMITH', 5)
```

Let's take a look at the deferred-delete method first. Consider the following Transact-SQL statement:

```
delete player from player, team
  where team.name = 'VIKINGS' and player.team = team.team
```

The server will process this SQL statement, using the algorithm for deferred deletes:

- In the first phase, the server will fetch the qualifying rows and pages and write them to the transaction log.

- In the second phase, the server will scan the transaction log for the qualified rows and pages and refetch the data pages.

- Deletes are then written to the transaction log for the index and data pages.

- In the final step the data pages are modified.

- The transaction log page(s) is (are) flushed to disk when the transaction commits.

It is important to note that a deferred delete creates two log records for every data row that is deleted. The data page is accessed twice for each row that is deleted: once for the scan and a second time for the delete.

The following SQL statement will be processed using the algorithm for direct deletes:

```
delete player where name = 'MARINO'
```

The server uses a simpler algorithm for direct deletes:

- All index entries for the row are logged and deleted.

- The row is deleted from the data page. Note that a single log record is written for every row that is deleted.

- The transaction log page(s) is (are) flushed to disk when the transaction commits.

SQL Server will use the direct mode whenever possible, as it generates less overhead and fewer log records than the deferred mode. This applies to both updates and deletes. DELETE operations are performed in direct mode unless the DELETE statement includes a join or columns used for referential integrity. For example, because of the *team_key* constraint on the *team* table, the following SQL statement will use deferred-delete mode:

```
delete team where team = 3
```

Updates

At the simplest level, SYBASE UPDATE operations can be handled by the SQL Server in two ways:

1. Direct update, single phase
2. Deferred update, two phases

Update operations are complicated by the fact that data rows can be updated *in place* or *not in place*.

- An *in-place* update occurs when a data row is updated without being shuffled from its current position.

- A *not-in-place* update is an UPDATE that is actioned as a physical DELETE followed by a physical INSERT.

Figure 5.18 should help clarify the situation.

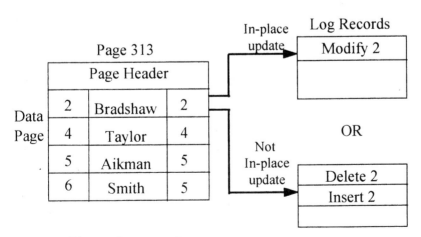

Figure 5.18   Direct-update processing.

In some cases, the SYBASE UPDATE will cause the row to move. That is, the row will not have the same row ID after the update. The row ID is composed of the logical page number and the row number within the data page. An *expensive* update is one that causes a data row to move to a different page. A *cheap* update occurs when no data row changes its row ID.

Let's use the *team* and *player* tables to illustrate direct and deferred updates. The first example will perform a *direct* update.

```
update player set name = 'BRADSHAW' where player = 2
```

The direct-update algorithm goes like this:

- The data page is accessed once for each updated data and index row.

- A single log record is written for an in-place UPDATE versus two log records for a not-in-place UPDATE. If an UPDATE trigger exists on the table or the table is replicated (using Replication Server), then UPDATEs are not in place.

- Any unsafe indexes are updated, and the changes are logged. An index is said to be *safe* if no part of the key is being modified.

- The transaction log page(s) is (are) flushed to disk when the transaction commits.

The deferred-update algorithm is somewhat more complex:

- The server will fetch the qualifying rows and pages and write them to the transaction log.

- Next the server will scan the log for the qualified rows and pages. The server will perform the deletes on the data pages and delete affected index rows.

- Reread the transaction log and make all inserts on the data and index pages.

- The transaction log page(s) is (are) flushed to disk when the transaction commits.

A large amount of overhead is required for deferred-update processing. For each updated row, the data page is accessed three times (once to determine the qualifying rows, once to refetch the data pages and write changes to the log, and once to modify the data pages). This creates four log records for each updated row and two log records for each updated index. Obviously deferred updates can lead to a high level of contention and increased probability of deadlocks.

Because of the *team_name* constraint that is present on the *player* table, the scrver will use the deferred-update mode for this statement.

```
update player set team = 4 where player = 2
```

To summarize the performance characteristics of direct- and deferred-update operations:

- *In-place direct update* is the least expensive type of update. It occurs when there is no row movement.

- *Cheap direct update* occurs when there is data movement within the page but no data row changes its row ID. It is logged as a DELETE followed by an INSERT, which means that it can be used on replicated tables or tables having UPDATE triggers.

- *Expensive direct update* occurs when the update causes a data row to move to a different page and all indexes must be updated. No index is considered safe. It is allowed when only one row is updated (determined by the optimizer at run time).

- *Deferred update* is the most expensive type of update.

Update-in-place design. As previously mentioned, an *in-place update* occurs when a row is updated without being shuffled from the current data page. The SYBASE direct, in-place update is much faster than the alternative update (physical DELETE followed by a physical INSERT). Implementing an update in-place design can result in

- Decreased lock contention
- Decreased chance of deadlock
- Improved response time and throughput

Performance gains realized by in-place update operations are dependent on several factors, including the number of indexes on the table being updated. Remember that if the row moves, all index entries must be updated. SYBASE claims substantial performance gains with in-place update operations.

The user must pay close attention to physical design to get SYBASE to perform an in-place update on database tables. Current rules for in-place direct update processing include these:

- Replication Server disables direct in-place update operations for replicated tables. For performance reasons, transaction logging is minimized for in-place operations. The Log Transfer Manager requires full logging of SQL Server UPDATE operations in order to scan data modifications and distribute them to replicate sites. Note that a cheap direct update can occur on a replicated table.

- There cannot be an UPDATE trigger on the table being updated. The *inserted* and *deleted* tables used in triggers get their data from the transaction log (the *deleted* table from the "before" image, the *inserted* table from the "after" image). Note that a cheap direct update can occur on a table with an UPDATE trigger.

- The modified row must be the same length as the original row. Note that with System 11, variable-length columns can be modified.

- The clustered index must be safe.

Deferred updates will occur under the following conditions:

- Deferred updates will be used when the UPDATE statement includes a join. For example,

```
update player set name = 'swann' from player,team
 where player.team = team.team and player.player = 2
```

- Deferred updates will occur if the affected columns are used for referential integrity.

- Deferred updates occur when data rows must move to another page due to an unsafe clustered index or when there is not enough room on the data page to fit the modified row.

The *sp_sysmon* procedure.   The *sp_sysmon* system procedure is a system stored procedure used to monitor the internals of SQL Server performance. It is based on an undocumented DBCC interface into the server monitor counters. The index management section reports information about SQL Server index maintenance. The output is shown here:

```
=========================================================
Index Management
----------------

Nonclustered Maintenance   per sec   per xact   count        % of total
------------------------   -------   --------   -----   -------
Ins/Upd Requiring Maint      0.0       0.0        0             n/a
  # of NC Ndx Maint          0.0       0.0        0             n/a

Deletes Requiring Maint      0.0       0.0        0             n/a
  # of NC Ndx Maint          0.0       0.0        0             n/a

RID Upd from Clust Split     0.0       0.0        0             n/a
  # of NC Ndx Maint          0.0       0.0        0             n/a

Page Splits                  0.0       0.0        0             n/a

Page Shrinks                 0.0       0.0        0             n/a
=========================================================
```

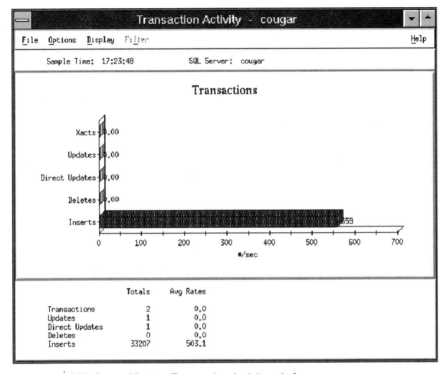

Figure 5.19 SQL Server Monitor Transaction Activity window.

SQL Server Monitor. The SQL Server Monitor Transaction Activity window (shown in Fig. 5.19) is used to monitor transactions processed by SQL Server. The display contains the number of updates to database tables as well as the number of *direct updates,* inserts, and deletes.

The Transaction Activity window can be used in a controlled environment to determine which stored procedures and other Transact-SQL statements are using direct updates. The best way to determine whether a particular piece of code is using direct updates is to examine the query plans, using the methods described in Chap. 12. There is also an excellent discussion on understanding query plans in the *SQL Server Performance and Tuning Guide.*

6

Hardware

The discussion of the high-performance aspects of server platform specialization will concentrate on the specialization and advances in server hardware architecture. This analysis of server hardware architecture trends is intended to clarify often misused and misunderstood technological jargon used by some hardware vendors, at the same time giving readers a reference point that can be used when a server purchasing decision is to be made. The bulk of the discussion concerns three popular server architecture features: *reduced instruction set computer* (RISC), *symmetric multiprocessing* (SMP), and *Massively Parallel Processor* (MPP) architectures.

System considerations. The basic principles of computer design describe, among other things, the factors that affect computer performance. In general, these factors include CPU architecture, the size and implementation methods of the instruction set, the ability of compilers to optimize for performance, computer chip technology, and the operating system. From the application's point of view, the CPU architecture, technology, and instruction set are the resources that the compilers and operating systems should be capable of exploiting to achieve the highest possible performance. Ideally, a system's hardware architecture, operating systems, and enabling software (i.e., compilers) are all balanced and tuned according to the nature of the application, in order to achieve the highest possible performance and throughput. For example, applications that tend to be easily vectorized can benefit from running on a computer equipped with a vector facility (e.g., a supercomputer like the Cray Y-MP). Many applications, on the other hand, are not vectorizable, and can best operate on systems with scalar performance. These applications may take advantage of a superscalar CPU design (i.e., IBM POWER and POWER 2 RISC chips). Other architectures include distributed-memory massively parallel systems and clustered systems. In either case, to fully utilize often-expensive hardware solutions, operating systems should be aware of hardware configurations, and the compilers should be able to produce machine code optimized for these platforms.

Thus, the underlying instruction set becomes one of the critical performance factors. Computer performance can be described by the following symbolic formula:

$$\text{Performance} = \frac{1}{\text{cycle time} \times \text{path length} \times \text{cycles/instruction}}$$

The *cycle time* is the opposite of the system clock rate, and is mostly limited by the underlying chip technology. Most of today's personal computers and workstations can operate at speeds from 66 to greater than 120 MHz, although some high-end workstations offer commercial CPUs with speeds of 150, 167, and 200 MHz. Faster clock speed may require new, higher-density chip technologies. The shorter the cycle time, the higher the performance.

The *path length* describes the number of machine instructions necessary to execute one command. The shorter the path length, the higher the resulting performance. CPU architecture, underlying instruction set, and optimizing compilers are the factors that can reduce the path length. The *cycles per instruction* factor describes how many computer cycles are necessary to execute one instruction. This number can vary from less than 1 (in RISC architectures) to greater than 1 in traditional CISC architectures. If the number is less than 1, then more than one instruction can be executed in one CPU cycle. Thus, performance is better. Computer designers continuously introduce innovative solutions to improve the cycles/instruction ratio. Superscalar design and superpipelining are the two best-known approaches to this problem.

Other factors affecting computer performance include memory access times, external storage characteristics and I/O data transfer rates, and, in a networking environment, communications and networks.

Some systems can be optimized best for commercial environments, which are generally characterized by integer processing, transaction processing, file and disk subsystem manipulation, and a significant number of attached low- to medium-function terminals and workstations. Other systems may be best suited to scientific environments, which are generally characterized by very-high floating-point performance requirements, and few high-function graphical workstations attached to the central server via very high-speed interconnections. Still other systems may be designed to achieve a careful balance between integer and floating-point performance, thus extending the system's applicability to both commercial and scientific end users.

In any event, when system designers wish to address the performance issue, they may concentrate their efforts on one of the following:

- Shortening the instruction path length
- Improving the cycles/instructions ratio
- Speeding up the system clock

The designers may attempt to achieve the desired performance for the mix of integer and floating-point instructions, thus creating a universal high-performance architecture.

6.1   RISC Architectures

In the early 1980s, some system designers argued that the then-current chip architectures could yield higher performance if new architectures would adopt the same principles as some of the best optimizing compilers.

That is, optimizing compilers could produce code almost as good as the best programmers could write in Assembler language. Analyzing the compiled code, David Patterson of the University of California at Berkeley found that compilers used the simplest instructions of an available instruction set. These simple instructions could be used more efficiently than the complex instructions if the system hardware was optimized for this task. Unfortunately, the opposite was true. Traditional computer architectures were optimized for more complex instructions. The instructions in these architectures were decoded by the microcode which was placed in the microprocessor hardware. Patterson proposed the *reduced instruction set computer* (RISC), as opposed to the traditional *complex instruction set computer* (CISC). In RISC architectures instructions are decoded directly by the hardware, thus increasing the speed of the processing.

Originally, a RISC processor contained only the simplest instructions extracted from a CISC architecture, and the hardware was optimized for these instructions. Not only did the RISC design contain the simplest instructions, but also the number of available instructions was significantly lower than that for a comparable CISC design. Beginning in 1980, Patterson's group undertook the task of implementing RISC prototype processors, called RISC I and RISC II. RISC I contained 44,000 transistors, was completed in 19 months, and outperformed a DEC VAX 11/780 by the ratio of 2:1.

An interesting historical fact is that the first RISC machine (though not identified by that name) was the IBM 801 System—a result of a research project conducted by IBM from 1975 to 1979. The development of the 801 led to the subsequent appearance of two widely recognized architectures: the RT-based PC and the more powerful and successful RS/6000 platform (also known as the POWER architecture). Note that, besides the performance, the apparent simplicity of the RISC architecture provides another advantage—a designer can realize the RISC design in silicon chips faster. Therefore, time to market can be reduced, and the latest in technology can be used in a current design more quickly than in a comparable CISC design.

The simplicity of RISC architecture is relative. Second generation RISC designs introduced more complex instruction sets and increased the number of instructions (sometimes comparable to CISC design). Therefore, the real performance leverage in the second generation RISC design is achieved by an optimized definition of the instruction set, machine organization, and processor logic design.

An important RISC feature is that each instruction is simple enough to be executed in one CPU cycle. In a "simple" RISC architecture, this may be true for a simple integer addition, but a floating-point addition may be simulated by several single-cycle instructions. To alleviate this and other similar problems, second-generation RISC architecture may be improved by a *superscalar* implementation (IBM's RS/6000, PowerPC, and DEC Alpha are examples of the superscalar RISC implementation). Superscalar design splits the processor into separate units so that the processor can sustain execution of two or more instructions per clock cycle. For example, the branch processor decodes instructions and assigns them to the other two units—integer processor and floating-point processor. Figure 6.1 illustrates the logical view of IBM's RS/6000 superscalar POWER RISC implementation.

Each of the three units can perform several instructions simultaneously. Integer and floating-point units contain multiple buffers to handle new operations before old ones are completed; the branch can initiate multiple instructions. The resulting instruction "pipeline" in effect breaks instruction processing into a series of stages (e.g., instruction fetch, decode, and execution) connected as stations in an assembly line. In the RS/6000 example, the five-stage pipelining and superscalar design allows up to four instructions (one fixed point, one floating-point, one branch, and one condition) or five simultaneous operations per cycle (three integer operations—fixed-point, branch and condition, and two floating-point operations that constitute one floating-point instruction—multiply and add). That's why a superscalar RISC machine performs well in commercial, high-performance integer processing environments and in scientific, floating-point intensive applica-

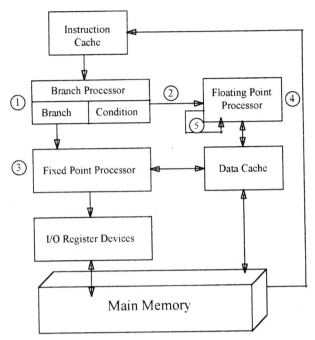

Figure 6.1 Superscalar RS/6000 RISC architecture.

tions. Multiple vendors continuously work on the innovations in super-scalar design, which results in frequent leapfrogging in performance among the vendors. For example, the coming generation of 64-bit processors will bring supercomputer-level performance to the desktop.

The PowerPC chip is the result of a partnership among IBM, Motorola, and Apple. The PowerPC chip is based on the IBM POWER architecture which is used in IBM's RS/6000 line of workstations. The relatively new PowerPC chips offer new levels of price/performance with a relatively low cost and low power consumption.

Pipelining. Another fundamental implementation technique used in RISC architectures is *pipelining*. As was described above, pipelining is a technique that allows more than one instruction to be processed at the same time. A typical pipelined CPU uses several execution steps, or stages, to execute one cycle-long instruction. As an instruction goes through each stage of the pipeline, the next instruction follows it without waiting for it to completely finish (see Fig. 6.2). Pipelining achieves high performance through the parallelism of processing several instructions at once, each in a different pipeline stage. To optimize the performance and increase the throughput of the

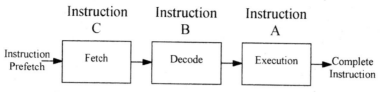

Figure 6.2 Pipelining instructions.

pipeline, designers increase clock rates and introduce higher granularity of stages—*superpipelining*. For example, the Mips R4000 uses
eight stages of pipelining, and the DEC Alpha uses parallel pipelines
with different numbers of stages—10 for floating-point and 7 for integer and load and store instructions.

   In a well-designed pipeline, all stages contain logic with approximately the same execution times. A careful balance between the number of instructions, clock speed, and number of pipeline stages in
superscalar RISC implementations will result in even higher performance levels of microcomputers, and workstations capable of hundreds of SPECint92 and SPECfp92 [Standard Performance
Evaluation Corporation (SPEC) benchmarks for the integer and floating-point performance] will be available in the near future at the cost
of a regular PC. The performance advantage of the RISC architecture
has to be leveraged by optimizing compilers and operating systems.
To date, many UNIX-based operating systems and Microsoft's
Windows/NT are capable of supporting RISC architecture.

6.1.1 64-bit systems

As mentioned in Chap. 1, the movement to 64-bit environments will
be led by the major UNIX vendors. These vendors will have a significant competitive advantage because UNIX can run native in these 64-
bit environments, whereas Microsoft Windows NT cannot. Obviously,
DEC has led the pack with the early introduction of the Alpha chip
running OSF/1. Some of the other vendors entering the market are
Sun Microsystems with the UltraSPARC, Hewlett-Packard with the
PA-8000, and Mips with the R10000.

   The computing power and large memory capacities of these systems
represent new opportunities for high-performance database systems.
The potential of next-generation computing platforms and relational
database management system (RDBMS) products is clearly a level of
magnitude beyond what is being supported today. In addition, these
new hardware platforms will raise the limits of applications that can
be supported for data warehousing, DSS, OLAP, and MPP.

   What follows is a brief description of the DEC and Sun offerings.

DEC Alpha. Digital Equipment Corp. offers several high-end UNIX-based Alpha systems. One system, the Alpha TurboLaser is ideal for the requirements of very large memory database applications. DEC offers two symmetric multiprocessing systems: the AlphaServer 8200 and 8400. Oracle, Informix, and Sybase have all announced database products optimized for the TurboLaser.

Sun UltraSPARC. The new 64-bit UltraSPARC microprocessors from Sun provide new levels of processing speed, price/performance, and computing innovations. Processing speeds of 143 and 167 MHz are supported initially, with future versions to 250 MHz and higher. The UltraSPARC chip demonstrates the scalability of the SPARC architecture, combining high processor speeds with an efficient four-way superscalar design. It uses a nine-stage pipeline to issue up to four instructions per cycle.

The new processor takes advantage of a high-performance, packet-switched interconnect of the type usually found in supercomputers. Sun calls this the UltraSPARC Port Architecture, or UPA. UPA is capable of multiple simultaneous data transfers to provide higher performance than traditional bus-based architectures. What this means is that data transfers between the processor, memory, I/O, networking, and graphics are much faster. The UPA is derived from technology used in Sun's high-end SPARCServer 1000 and SPARCCenter 2000 servers.

The UltraSPARC uses an integrated Visual Instruction Set (VIS) to provide an array of on-chip multimedia, graphics, and imaging technologies. The VIS enables two- and three-dimensional graphics, video, and image processing including real-time video compression.

In summary, the introduction of the UltraSPARC microprocessor places the SPARC line at the top of the competitive field of RISC microprocessors—at least for the moment.

6.2 Multiprocessor Systems (Symmetric Multiprocessor Systems)

Multiprocessing is becoming an indispensable tool for improving the performance of computer systems struggling to support ever more complex and demanding applications. Generally, adding processors creates the possibility of performing several computing tasks in parallel, thus speeding up the overall execution of the program. As CPU costs are decreasing, users find that adding processors to their existing multiprocessor hardware is significantly more economical than either adding computer systems or replacing existing systems with more powerful uniprocessor systems. Conversely, adding entire computers to increase throughput has its drawbacks:

- Adding processors usually requires the addition of expensive peripheral devices.

- Stand-alone uniprocessors cannot share memory, unless they are networked at an additional expense. To speed up the applications operating environment, appropriate load-balancing software must be in place to distribute and synchronize applications, usually at additional cost and complexity.

- Adding faster uniprocessors is more expensive than obtaining the same performance by increasing the number of processors.

Therefore, designers are focusing on computing architectures where the processing units are physically close and are often integrated by a single operating system. In such a system, the processing units (PUs) speed up a single computational task by executing it jointly (in parallel). These *parallel* systems have high-performance computing as their objective, but also add such objectives as synchronicity, reliability, resource sharing, and extensibility.

Multiprocessor systems can be classified by the following:

- Degree of coupling that measures how strongly the PUs are connected by evaluating the ratio of the amount of data exchanged among PUs to the amount of local processing performed by PUs in executing a task

- Interconnection structure that determines the network topology— bus, star, ring, tree, etc.

- Component independence that determines the level of dependence between PUs

Multiprocessor parallel systems have either *shared* or *distributed* memory. While in general the topology of a distributed system can change due to communication link failure, for instance, interprocess communications in distributed-memory parallel systems are more reliable and predictable.

6.2.1 SMP design

A *shared-memory* multiprocessor (typically, a symmetric *multiprocessor*, or SMP) incorporates a number of processors, called *processing units,* that share common memory, common I/O, and various other common system resources. Such an SMP machine coordinates interprocess communication (IPC) through global memory that all PUs share. A typical shared-memory multiprocessor consists of a relatively small number (4 to 30 on average) of processors. Processors (PUs) select tasks to be executed from a common task pool, and they are

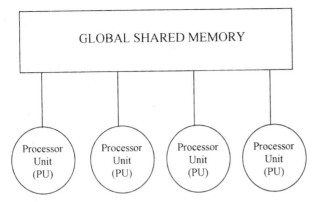

Figure 6.3 Symmetric shared-memory multiprocessor.

interconnected via a high-speed common system bus, thereby providing extremely efficient interprocessor communication. See Fig. 6.3.

A shared-memory multiprocessing system ensures that any processor completing one task is immediately put to work on another, next-available task. All PUs execute a single copy of an operating system, and each PU executes a task selected from a common task pool. Typically, to reduce the volume of shared-memory traffic, each PU has one or more memory caches. One or more memory controllers may be included in this architecture to support the high memory access requirements of multiple PUs.

A system where all PUs in a shared-memory multiprocessor have equal capabilities and can perform the same functions is called a symmetric multiprocessor, or SMP. Each PU in an SMP system can run user applications as well as any portion of the operating system, including such operations as I/O interrupts, operating system kernel functions, and I/O drivers.

In addition, any task can be executed on any PU and can migrate from PU to PU as the system load characteristics change.

SMP implementations have a significant positive effect on scalability. Clearly, if a system designates one PU to perform a particular task (e.g., service I/O interrupts), this PU will become overloaded as the number of I/O requests increases, and overall system performance will degrade.

SMP architecture provides two high-level features:

- *Seamless execution* is the ability of an SMP system to seamlessly, transparently to the user, support existing applications. In truly seamless implementations, all applications originally written for a uniprocessor will be able to run on the SMP system unmodified. By taking full advantage of multiprocessing, applications can achieve significant performance gains. This is especially important for servers running DBMSs and supporting transaction processing.

- *Limited scalable performance* encompasses two components: computational growth and I/O growth. Computational growth can be achieved by adding processing elements, while I/O growth can be a result of adding peripherals and/or I/O buses. It is important to note that the addition of a PU increases the overall system performance up to a limit. The per-PU increase is not equal to the performance of the individual PU, but rather corresponds to a fraction of this PU performance. As the number of PUs grows, factors such as system bus and memory subsystem design, cache sizes, and the need to keep all caches synchronized affect the resultant performance increase.

If one was asked to name the two most important SMP characteristics, they could be the following:

- The most significant benefit is the use of a familiar, traditional programming paradigm. As the result, today's SMP machines support standards-based operating systems and application enablers (compilers, tools, database management systems, etc.).

- The most significant drawback is related to the limited scalability—the throughput of an SMP system does not demonstrate a linear growth in direct proportion to the number of PUs. Depending on the PU and system bus speed, the SMP throughput does not increase (and can even decrease, due to the local cache coherency problem) when the number of PUs exceeds some (machine-specific) value, typically less than 30.

Within their scalability limitations, SMP-based systems provide the ability to increase performance incrementally. This allows for future upgradability and represents a cost-effective solution for such applications as DBMS, gateways, and transaction processing. Typically, these applications are composed of smaller, relatively independent tasks, which can be assigned to multiple processors. Applications like these are ideally suited to be run on servers in a client/server environment.

Providing symmetry in shared-memory systems has an impact on both hardware and software architectures. Software features supporting scalable SMP performance include capabilities to execute the operating system kernel, I/O interrupts, and I/O drivers on all PUs.

Operating system design becomes more complex on an SMP system. For example, the Open Software Foundation's OSF/1 operating system supports SMP by implementing an IEEE POSIX 1003.4 *P-Threads* standard-compliant thread. A *thread,* which is defined by POSIX as a single sequential flow of control within a process, allows developers to write cooperative routines, all sharing access to the same data in memory. Programs employing multiple threads can automatically make use of multiple processors on an SMP system.

The operating system locking strategy is designed to prevent simultaneous updates to data structures and codes in SMP common shared memory. The locking strategy represents an important requirement for a scalable software architecture.

Dynamic load balancing is another critical requirement of an SMP software architecture. Indeed, if a PU has been added to an SMP system, the operating system and application software should be able to take advantage of the additional PU by dynamically redistributing the load among all available PUs.

Scalable software architectures are designed not only to take advantage of the SMP hardware architecture transparently and seamlessly but also to provide for an easy entry into parallel computing, where multiple applications can run simultaneously. There are several techniques for developing parallel applications capable of achieving maximum performance in a multiprocessing system. Among them are problem partitioning (dividing a problem into several smaller, independent parts) and data decomposition for load balancing.

6.2.2   SMP implementations

High-performance SMP systems offer comparable performance or higher performance than traditional uniprocessors, while promising an impressive incremental performance scalability within the design limits. Properly designed SMP systems allow for seamless execution and the ability of existing applications to execute transparently without modifications. That is why several SMP systems available today are used as DBMS servers, communication gateways, and transaction processing platforms.

Some popular shared-memory systems include products such as Pyramid Technology high-end machines, which combine SMP implementation with RISC technology, Sequent Computers Symmetry series, Sun SPARCCenter 1000 and 2000, and HP's Enterprise Server—T-500. Even such a well-known supercomputer maker as Cray Research is serious about SMP architecture, as demonstrated by its CRAY SUPERSERVER 6400 (Sun SuperSPARC-based, 4 to 64 PUs SMP offering running Solaris 2.x).

Today's SMP servers are quite powerful, and they often exceed performance ratings traditionally attributed to high-end mainframes and supercomputers. Consider the T-500 SMP offerings from Hewlett-Packard (HP), a well-known and reliable UNIX server vendor. This system combines HP's advanced PA-RISC processor architecture with symmetric multiprocessing software and a balanced high-end memory and I/O bus. The HP Corporate Business Server T-500 uses up to 12 state-of-the-art RISC-based processors, each equipped with a large, high-speed cache memory (1 Mbyte per CPU for instructions and data each).

It is designed to be independent of the semiconductor and implementation technologies. Therefore, the T-500 can take advantage of leading-edge technologies as they develop. For example, the use of CMOS VLSI technology enables the entire CPU to be integrated into a single-circuit-board module. The resulting reduction in complexity reduces system cost while increasing performance and reliability. It is designed for growth by incorporating a 64-bit virtual address capability with the total addressing range of 256 Tbytes.

The T-500 offers a high-speed processor memory bus capable of accessing main memory at the bandwidth of 1 Gbyte/s. This bus is designed to minimize bus contention. Special hardware features ensure processor cache coherency—a well-known problem in SMP designs. To satisfy commercial customers running large databases, T-500 supports eight I/O channels with an aggregate I/O throughput of 256 Mbytes/s. Its HP-UX operating system support is standards-based and is compliant with POSIX 1003.1 and 1003.2, FIPS 151-1, and X/Open Portability Guide Issue 4 (XPG4).

6.3 Clustering

A *cluster* is a group of high-performance workstations typically connected via a high-speed network. Clearly, the distributed-memory *multiple-instruction multiple-data* (MIMD) architecture maps well onto a collection of loosely coupled workstations connected by local-area networks. While appearing to be easy to implement, clustered workstations are even more sensitive to communications, data sharing, and synchronization requirements than MPP systems, since the communication in clusters is over a standard communication network and typically is based on standard communications protocols (usually TCP/IP), although systems using FDDI, ATM, HiPPI, and FCS (Fiber Channel Standard) are capable of supporting an extremely high bandwidth. While the major cost element of the MPP system is the high-speed internal interconnection network, workstation clusters shift the cost to the large number of software licenses that result from the need to install operating system software on each of the workstations.

It is quite possible that, with improvements in systems management capabilities and networking on the workstation level, organizations will attempt to establish clusters of workstations to perform resource-intensive tasks, either as a dedicated environment or as a part-time solution available to the users during the off hours.

Probably, one of the best justifications for server specialization is the price/performance characteristics of the latest in server designs. Traditionally, system performance is measured in millions of instructions per second (MIPS) or a little more meaningful transactions per second (TPS). The cost of each TPS rating is quite high for a high-end mainframe. The price/performance characteristics of specialized server systems compare very favorably with those of a mainframe-class machine. In fact, it is not unusual to achieve an order-of-magnitude improvement in price/performance when a specialized high-end server is used. And as technology continues to advance, the price/performance value of the specialized servers is getting even better, thus justifying architectural specialization for a server platform.

6.4 MPP

As was described above, SMP machines have an inherent architectural limitation on scalability. One solution that avoids this limitation is a nontrivial approach employed by distributed-memory Massively Parallel Processors. A *distributed-memory* machine interconnects PUs and their local memory units via an interconnection network (see Fig. 6.4). An interconnection network can be a high-speed *external* local-area network (LAN), high-speed *internal* switch, a connection tree, a hypercube, a star, a mesh, etc. Some of these solutions are proprietary innovative designs, but the standardization efforts continue into this area as well: There is an interconnection system called the Scalable Coherent Interconnect (SCI), which is an IEEE standard.

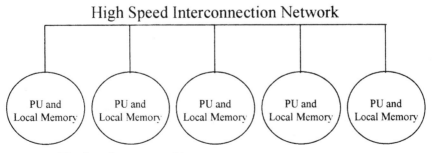

Figure 6.4 Distributed-memory architecture.

In a distributed-memory machine, PUs communicate by passing messages. One obvious drawback in such an architecture is its requirement for a "new" distributed programming paradigm. The result is a need for a new operating system design, new compilers, new languages, etc.

The distributed-memory machines were originally designed to solve numeric-intensive Grand Challenge problems, and they were once limited to specialized communities focused around a handful of centralized and extremely expensive computing facilities. Now these technologies are known to a large number of researchers, engineers, and software developers; are accessible from a desktop; and are beginning to become commercially available. These machines can be classified by their interconnect architectures or by the way the messages are passed and synchronized. Parallel architectures can be divided into contemporary *multiple-instruction multiple-data* (MIMD) and older *single-instruction multiple-data* (SIMD) machines. In MIMD systems (such as the Intel Paragon XP/S) multiple processors can simultaneously execute different instructions on different data. Therefore, MIMD systems are inherently asynchronous computers that can synchronize processes either by accessing control data (semaphores, switches, etc.) in shared memory or by passing synchronization messages in distributed-memory systems. MIMD systems are best suited to *large-grain* parallelism (on a subroutine and task level).

SIMD machines (such as the Thinking Machine Corporation's CM-2 and MasPar's MP-1 and MP-2) are by design synchronous parallel computers in which all PUs execute the same instruction at the same time (or remain idle). SIMD machines are typically controlled by a central control unit that broadcasts a single instruction to all PUs, at which time PUs execute that instruction in synchronous fashion on their local data. *Fine-grained* (instruction-level) parallelism is best suited for SIMD machines.

In general, MPP systems promise a tremendous increase in scalable performance and throughput. Arguably MPP systems are the result of the shift in the computing paradigm, discussed in Chaps. 1 and 2, and could become a dominant enterprise server architecture for mission-critical applications of today and tomorrow.

Research issues. Since MPP architecture uses a different computing and programming paradigm, its emergence in the commercial marketplace is surrounded by a number of active theoretical and practical issues. The bulk of the issues are related to what is known as the *paradigm integration* caused by the advent of high-power MPP machines and low-latency high-bandwidth intercommunication networks. Paradigm integration means that a new MPP-compliant program should combine both task and data parallelism with a single application. The need for the paradigm integration is driven by the code reuse requirement in parallel-architecture, heterogeneous models that combine multidisciplines of the numeric-intensive tasks, data visualization, and commercial computing. The latter deserves special interest due to its often contradictory on-line transaction processing (OLTP) and decision support system (DSS) requirements. Another important demand of commercial high-performance computing is its requirement for and the design complexity of parallel database management systems capable of very complex query and very large database processing. These parallel RDBMSs were the subject of Chap. 2.

Some of the current MPP research issues are listed below:

- Traditional performance measurements (MIPS, Mflops) have to be redefined for MPP and SMP systems, since they do not reflect real performance characteristics.

- There is the scalability issue. How is MPP system performance affected by the problem size, or by the number of PUs?

- Operating systems for distributed and parallel processing are in their infancy. Operating system design and construction are an open problem, especially given the state of accepted standards in the area of microkernels, interprocess communications, object-oriented operating systems, load balancing, etc.

- Task scheduling is a rather complex issue that has led so far to a number of heuristic solutions, each of which may or may not work under different circumstances.

- Innovative programming methods are an issue. Traditional sequential shared-memory programming methods may not work or may not be able to take advantage of the MPP architecture. Issues such as MIMD-based programming, data-parallel programming, functional programming, and tuple-space programming are just a few areas researchers are working on.

- Compilers and optimization work mostly focus on two directions. The *implicit* approach modifies existing languages or introduces new ones that help conceal the underlying system from the programmer (the preferred way for commercial computing). Obviously, this approach shifts a burden of parallel complexity to the compiler-developer. Currently, there is a shortage of good parallel compilers. The *explicit* approach extends existing languages, or introduces new languages to express parallelism directly. This approach has a serious impact on the skill sets required for existing programmers.

- Database systems are an issue. Many vendors and researchers in a scientific community are working diligently to develop truly parallel database management systems. Oracle, Sybase, and Informix already have *limited-functionality* versions of their products targeted for a *specific* MPP environment (there is a production version of Oracle 7—Parallel Query Option—for several MPP systems). Full-function parallel DBMS (PDBMS) development is facing the same issues of reliability, scalability, performance, etc., that the rest of the MPP community is forced to deal with.

- Heterogeneous processing, reliability, and code portability are "traditional" distributed systems issues that are becoming even more pressing with the advent of MPP, especially in the commercial arena.

The advent of the revolutionary MPP architectures is a clear indication of the necessity and benefits of server specialization. Indeed, specialization would not go that far if the set of business problems facing the server did not require extraordinary measures.

6.4.1 IBM RS/6000 SP2

At the high end of the IBM RS/6000 line stands the scalable POWERparallel Systems SP2. The SP2 provides the scalability and unequaled performance of parallel computing. The RS/6000 and SP2 systems support AIX Version 3.2.5 and AIX Version 4, which is the latest version of IBM's UNIX operating system. Parallel processing on the SP2 links together between 2 and 512 IBM RS/6000 processors. A wide range of IBM and third-party software is available to support general computing needs such as relational database, transaction processing, and network management.

To that end IBM offers POWERquery, which is a large-scale decision support solution for commercial use built on IBM's parallel relational database, DATABASE 2 Parallel Edition for AIX. IBM also offers the CICS/6000 transaction management system, and Netview for AIX for network management. IBM Load Leveler and Job Scheduler/6000 software are available for job scheduling and workload balancing. In addition, there is high-availability software for the RS/6000 and SP2. The high-availability solution, which is called AIX High Availability Cluster Multi-Processing/6000 (long enough name for you?), allows the system administrator to configure up to eight SP2 nodes into a single high-availability cluster. In addition, a single SP2 system may support multiple independent eight-node clusters. These clusters, called *HACMP clusters,* can be configured to eliminate any single point of failure. This level of reliability is required for mission-critical OLTP applications such as trading systems and banking.

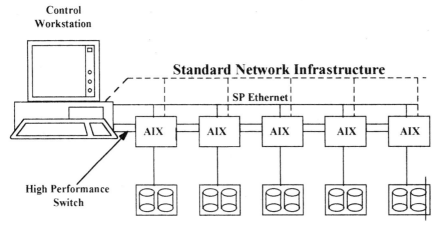

Figure 6.5   IBM RS/6000 SP2.

IBM also markets software and hardware solutions designed to provide interoperability and high-speed data transfer between IBM or IBM-compatible mainframes and the SP2, as well as associated UNIX workstations.

Figure 6.5 depicts the architecture of the IBM RS/6000 SP2.

6.5   Redundant Array of Inexpensive Disks (RAID)

RAID devices, depending on the level of RAID supported, provide various degrees of data integrity, availability, and performance. Many RAID implementations utilize a *hot-spare* feature which reserves a drive (or pool of drives) to automatically take the place of a drive that fails, thus increasing array availability.

The different levels of RAID are actually different techniques for data protection. Six levels of RAID (numbered 0 through 5) were described by researchers at the University of California at Berkeley (UCB) in 1988 and 1989. Sometimes called Berkeley RAID, these levels are recognized by the RAID Advisory Board (a 55-member trade organization). The six levels of RAID are defined as follows:

- *Level 0:*   disk striping. Data is written data across multiple physical disks. It has fast read-write performance and low cost but is not fault-tolerant. The I/O transfer speed is increased by this architecture; however, a single drive element failure can result in unrecoverable data loss.

- *Level 1:* disk mirroring. Data is mirrored (or shadowed) between at least two drives. It has fast read and slow write performance, using twice the amount of storage. Level 1 may be a good choice for small systems and offers high fault tolerance. It is often implemented in server operating systems such as Novell's Netware.

- *Level 0 + 1:* striping plus shadowing. Again, write performance is degraded by this architecture because both drives in the mirror set need to be written.

- *Level 2:* disk striping across mirrored disks, including bit and parity data checking. This introduces the possibility of data recovery without complete duplication of data; however, it does require several check disks. It offers no speed benefits, and its high cost does not buy greatly improved reliability.

- *Level 3:* data striping across drives in the array. Level 3 requires a single, dedicated parity drive to accomplish redundancy. Level 3 RAIDs can handle only one write at a time. This is because level 3 requires that all disks in a group be accessed, even for small transfers, and wait for the slowest drive to finish before the transfer is complete. Typically, the drive spindles are synchronized. It is oriented toward sites handling large blocks of data, such as video-on-demand or imaging servers. Because of problems with spindle synchronization, it's hard to create level 3 systems with drives from different manufacturers.

- *Level 4:* disk striping at the data block level. Level 4 also requires a dedicated parity drive. It offers fast read performance, but slow write operations will degrade overall system performance. The parity check disk usually becomes a throughput bottleneck.

- *Level 5:* disk striping of both data and parity. Unlike in level 4, parity information is striped across all data drives which eliminates the problem of the parity disk bottleneck. Level 5 offers better performance with a lower initial cost. It can handle concurrent read and write operations, but writes are slower than they are with RAID level 0. It is configured to meet the needs of relational or on-line database storage.

Some vendors have developed and are marketing their own "interpretations" of RAID 5, sometimes labeling them a new RAID level. Some of these, such as Storage Computer, Incorporated's RAID 7, represent real advances in the technology. Some of these RAID levels include

- *Level 6:* striped data and parity with two parity drives. Level 6 offers superior availability with excellent read performance.

- *Level 7:* asynchronous I/O with an embedded operating system. The level 7 architecture provides for complete I/O independence and asynchrony. This is accomplished by giving each I/O device a separate device cache as well as independent control and data paths. Each device interface is connected to a high-speed data bus which has a central cache capable of supporting multiple host I/O paths. A real-time operating system is embedded into the disk array architecture.

6.6   Hardware Cache

One of the problems constantly plaguing chip designers is slow physical memory accesses. Modern microprocessors can execute instructions at a far faster pace than the system can provide them or any associated data. One way of solving the problem of slow memory access is the implementation of *cache memory.*

By using cache memory, instructions and/or data can be stored locally in very fast memory. The first access for machine instructions or data goes to main memory and is considerably slower than cache access. After the first access, a copy is stored in the fast cache memory. Any subsequent access to this memory location is now made to cache, which results in faster access and improved performance.

Hardware vendors can provide different *levels* of caches: level 1 and level 2. The level 1 cache normally built into the CPU chip is extremely fast. Level 2 caches are also known as *secondary caches.* Secondary caches are external caches used to provide the best possible memory bandwidth and overall system performance. Level 2 caches are slower than level 1 caches; however, level 2 cache is still faster than main memory. There are several factors associated with cache implementations which can affect performance. The most obvious factor is cache size and organization. The larger the memory cache, the more instructions and/or data are stored, thus resulting in higher cache hit rates.

The System 11 SQL Server is designed (and can be tuned) to maintain hardware cache locality. For optimal performance, a task that sleeps should be scheduled to run on the same engine it was most recently using. Remember that the memory cache contains the latest hits that the dataserver did on a particular CPU. For most systems, this will result in a higher hardware cache hit ratio and increased performance of the system. When tasks are switched too often from CPU to CPU, the memory cache is invalidated, resulting in data being migrated back and forth. This forces a higher number of accesses to physical memory. When data is migrated, it is migrated through the bus, which slows down the system. By doing this, the server is using processing cycles to manage the memory caches instead of using the cycles for transaction processing.

6.7   Solid-State Disk

We learned in Chap. 1 that the traditional DBMS bottleneck is input/output. In many SQL Server environments that support a large number of users, transaction logging and *tempdb* database performance can suffer from major disk I/O bottlenecks.

A solid-state disk (SSD) emulator uses battery-backed memory to provide low access latency and high I/O bandwidth. In fact, some SSDs are capable of delivering I/O rates that are hundreds of times faster than those of conventional disk devices. An SSD performs both reads and writes at memory speed, reaching up to 1000 I/Os per second for small block I/Os.

SSD emulators can be used with SQL Server to provide faster decision support response time, reduced batch job run time, and reduced table load times. Vendors offering solid-state disk devices include Database Excelleration Systems, Inc. and Imperial Technology, Inc.

2

Performance Tuning

Part 2 of the book provides a detailed look at several factors that influence database server performance as well as a discussion of tuning long-running jobs and tuning in the client/server environment. Chapter 8 describes several aspects of server monitoring including SQL Server activity, user activity, and lock activity. SQL Server Monitor is used in this chapter as are several SQL Server commands and procedures. Memory allocation, I/O techniques, CPU utilization, design, and indexing techniques are discussed in great detail. Features new to System 11 such as the buffer manager, cache analysis tool, and private log cache are also described in great detail.

7

Memory Utilization and Server Configuration

This chapter covers SQL Server memory utilization and provides an introduction to the buffer manager, SQL Server configuration, and multiple network engines. The first section gives an overview of how SQL Server uses available memory. This material provides the groundwork for an in-depth discussion of SQL Server configuration. Section 7.2 introduces the new buffer management capabilities of System 11 including multiple-user caches, sequential prefetch, and integration of these features with a completely rewritten query optimizer. As described in Chap. 3, another important architectural improvement to SQL Server is the changes in network architecture provided by multiple network engines (MNEs). The chapter closes with a discussion of the implementation of MNEs.

7.1 Memory Utilization

This section gives a high-level overview of how the System 11 SQL Server uses available memory. Figure 7.1 shows how SQL Server allocates memory at run time.

Total server memory. The total amount of memory available to SQL Server is controlled by the system administrator using the *sp_config-ure* system procedure. The amount of memory is specified as the number of 2K pages to be allocated. When the dataserver boots, it will ask the operating system for this amount of memory and set aside a portion for its kernel. At this point the dataserver will begin to allocate memory for internal catalog structures such as lock structures, user connections, database structures, and device structures. After memo-

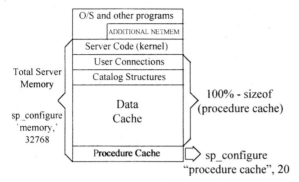

Figure 7.1 SQL Server memory allocation.

ry has been allocated for the catalog structures, the amount of memory that is left over is split between the data and procedure caches.

Server code. This is memory used by the SQL Server kernel. The size of the kernel will vary for different operating systems.

User connections. Static memory is allocated for user connections at run time. This means that the number of available user connections is not dynamic. User connections support things such as DB-Library and CT-Library programs, user-defined thresholds, output to the SQL Server error log, and connections to the Backup Server.

Device usage. Static memory for database devices is also allocated at run time (which means that the maximum number of devices is not dynamically configurable). The maximum value that can be used in a DISK INIT command is 1 less than the maximum number of devices.

Catalog structures. Catalog structures include object structures (used to manage open objects such as tables), lock structures (used to manage active locks), and database structures (used to manage open databases). Most of these structures are allocated at run time and cannot be changed without restarting SQL Server.

Procedure cache. The memory allocated to the data and procedure caches is the number of pages left over after static memory requirements (server code, user connections, devices, catalog structures, etc.) have been allocated by SQL Server at run time. This leftover memory is actually split between the procedure cache and the data cache. The split ratio can be controlled by the system administrator using the *sp_configure* system procedure.

Data cache.   The data cache is used to store data pages and index pages in memory. SQL Server will try to locate data and index pages in cache (logical read) before reading them from disk (physical read). The size of the data cache may affect checkpoint time.

SQL Server memory utilization can be determined by using the DBCC MEMUSAGE command. Information is displayed about total server memory, actual size of the SQL Server code, number of page buffers, and procedure buffers available. Also listed are the top 20 users of procedure cache and buffer cache. This output is similar to that of the UNIX *top* command. The following is a partial listing of output from DBCC MEMUSAGE:

```
1> dbcc traceon(3604) /* direct output to the user terminal */
2> go
1> dbcc memusage
2> go
DBCC execution completed. If DBCC printed error messages, contact a
  user with System Administrator (SA) role.
Memory Usage:
                        Meg.         2K Blks         Bytes

  Configured Memory:    32.0000      16384           33554432

  Code size:            3.5123       1799            3682936
  Kernel Structures:    2.3540       1206            2468381
  Server Structures:    3.8224       1958            4008118
  Cache Memory:         17.6406      9032            18497536
  Proc Buffers:         0.1637       84              171684
  Proc Headers:         4.5039       2306            4722688

Buffer Cache Memory, Top 20:

Cache    Buf Pool    DB Id    Object Id    Index Id    Meg.

default data cache    4         5             0         0.5059
          2K          4         5             0         0.5059
default data cache    5         5             0         0.0840
          2K          5         5             0         0.0840
.
.
.

Procedure Cache, Top 19:

Database Id: 4
Object Id: 1648008902
Object Name: sp_recompile
Version: 1
Uid: 1
Type: stored procedure
Number of trees: 0
Size of trees: 0.000000 Mb, 0.000000 bytes, 0 pages
Number of plans: 1
Size of plans: 0.020826 Mb, 21838.000000 bytes, 11 pages
---
Database Id: 5
```

```
Object Id: 838294046
Object Name: sp_get_address_list
Version: 1
Uid: 1
Type: stored procedure
Number of trees: 0
Size of trees: 0.000000 Mb, 0.000000 bytes, 0 pages
Number of plans: 1
Size of plans: 0.012478 Mb, 13084.000000 bytes, 7 pages
---
Database Id: 5
Object Id: 144771623
Object Name: vladdress
Version: 0
Uid: 1
Type: view
Number of trees: 1
Size of trees: 0.007498 Mb, 7862.000000 bytes, 4 pages
Number of plans: 0
Size of plans: 0.000000 Mb, 0.000000 bytes, 0 pages
---
  .
  .
  .
---
DBCC execution completed. If DBCC printed error messages, contact a
  user with System Administrator (SA) role.
```

At the top of the DBCC MEMUSAGE output there is a section labeled *Memory Usage* (in boldface type). The size of the executable code (*code size*) will vary between versions and operating systems. The *kernel structures* and *server structures* represent a combination of static and user-configurable overhead, as described earlier. A *proc buffer* is a data structure used to manage compiled objects (e.g., a stored procedure, trigger, rule, default, or view) in the procedure cache. There are a total of 21 proc buffers on a 2K page. The number of proc buffers represents the maximum number of compiled objects that can reside in the procedure cache at one time. *Cache memory,* also known as *page cache,* corresponds to the data cache. The size of cache memory can be changed by increasing or decreasing the *procedure cache* server configuration variable. *Proc headers* are used to indicate the number of pages dedicated to the procedure cache.

7.2 Buffer Manager Overview

One of the most notable features of System 11 is the introduction of new buffer management capabilities including multiple-user caches, sequential prefetch (using large block I/O sizes), and integration of these features with a completely rewritten query optimizer. The buffer manager is key to increasing OLTP performance and gives SQL Server the ability to support mixed-workload environments.

As mentioned in Chap. 1, hardware trends are moving toward larger memories using 64-bit addressing and operating systems. As users implement new hardware, they will want to partition memory in the same manner as disk drives are partitioned today. Furthermore, the widespread implementation of large SMP machines will necessitate this partitioning to decrease the scaling bottlenecks incurred by multiple-server processes competing for resources such as shared memory, page, and procedure caches.

Memory management in SQL Server is handled by the *buffer manager*. The buffer manager is used to manage the page cache with the goal of minimizing the number of physical I/Os necessary to service all logical I/Os in the system. Typically, the cost of a query may be measured by using a combination of logical and physical I/Os. The cost of a query will vary depending on the number and type of indexes available, the number of data pages in cache, and the number of index pages in cache. The query optimizer may determine that one access path has a high number of logical I/Os while another access path has fewer logical I/Os but more physical I/Os.

The effectiveness of the buffer manager is measured by the *cache hit ratio,* which is the percentage of pages requested that were found in cache. So it is expressed as the number of logical I/Os versus the number of physical I/Os. Another measure of effectiveness is *access contention,* which affects server scalability and is a key architectural weakness of System 10. Because the buffer manager is a shared resource, access control is coordinated by a spinlock. In System 10, access to the page cache by multiple-server engines on SMP platforms is single-threaded, as illustrated in Fig. 7.2.

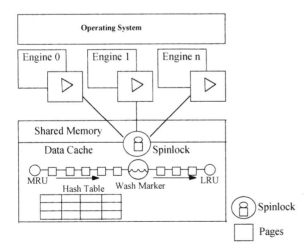

Figure 7.2   Pre-System 11 Buffer Manager architecture.

The page cache is an MRU/LRU (most recently used/least recently used) chain and is a circular, doubly linked list. The *MRU side* of the chain is the set of MRU buffers that are currently not in use, but were used in the past, and may or may not be *clean* (data exists in the buffer). The *LRU side* of the chain is the set of buffers that are available to the buffer manager. The buffer manager will grab buffers from the LRU side to perform disk I/O. The *hash table* contains the list of buffers that currently reside in cache. SQL Server uses the hash table to quickly determine whether a page is in cache or whether the buffer manager must perform physical I/O to read the page into cache. Using a hash table is faster than searching the MRU/LRU chain. The *wash marker* is located in the MRU/LRU chain and ensures that buffers on the LRU side of the chain are either clean or in the process of being written to disk.

SQL Server Release 11 provides the ability to create multiple data caches, meaning that available memory can be partitioned into multiple *named caches* by the system administrator (see Fig. 7.3). Each named cache can be reserved for use with specific application objects (e.g., databases or database objects including tables and indexes). The administrator can tune the characteristics of each named cache, including

- Size of the cache
- Size of block I/O—a particular named cache can be configured for multiple I/O sizes
- Location of the wash marker in the MRU/LRU chain

This level of tuning allows the system administrator to configure a named cache in a manner that will be optimal for all applications. All I/O for an object or group of objects *bound* to a named cache (using a system stored procedure) will then be isolated to that named cache. Obviously, if there is only a single cache configured (e.g., the default cache), there will still be a single point of contention for the spinlock, as illustrated in Fig. 7.2.

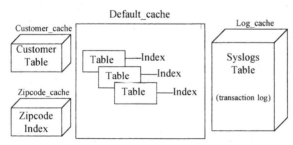

Figure 7.3 Named cache configuration.

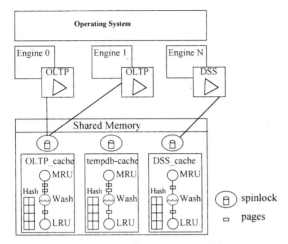

Figure 7.4   System 11 buffer manager architecture.

As shown in Fig. 7.4, two applications (for example, OLTP order entry trading system and a DSS reporting system) that are bound to separate named caches will not compete with each other for memory or spinlock synchronization. Scalability and the ability to support mixed workloads are therefore dramatically improved.

System 11 allows the system administrator to change cache assignments and tune named caches dynamically, meaning it is possible to change the cache binding for a database object without restarting the server. For example, during normal operations a table containing sales order information is bound to a default data cache. Once a day, feeds arrive from other systems that must be processed and loaded into the sales order table. Using system stored procedures, the administrator can transparently bind the sales order table to another named cache (possibly using a larger I/O size than the default cache), load the feeds into the table using BCP (the Sybase Bulk Copy Program), and bind the table back to the default data cache. In summary, this ability to dynamically modify cache assignments gives the administrator a powerful capability that can be used to reallocate memory resources and to adjust for changing workloads. The query optimizer has been designed to detect any changes in cache assignments and to recompile any affected query plans.

Well, by now most readers are saying, "Hey, this is great...but how much memory will I need to take advantage of these features?" Adding more memory to any RDBMS server will usually increase the overall performance of the system. Server platforms designed to take advantage of the System 11 buffer manager will have plenty of memory, with plenty being defined as 512 Mbytes to 3 Gbytes and beyond.

Fetch-and-discard replacement strategy. Usually, buffers in a buffer pool are subject to a FIFO (first in, first out) buffer replacement strategy based on the MRU/LRU scheme. When the FIFO replacement strategy is used, all buffers take the same number of hops (down the MRU/LRU chain) before being replaced. What this means is that pages that will not be reused must still move to the LRU side of the buffer chain before being replaced. This potentially creates a situation where pages that are not reused waste data cache resources and interfere with other user queries (scans).

System 11 uses a new fetch-and-discard (MRU) replacement strategy to help control cache hit ratios and contention in mixed-workload environments. When this strategy is used, the query optimizer designates buffers that are likely to be reused as *hot* and buffers not likely to be reused as *cold*. The buffer manager will flush the pages that are cold while holding the pages that are hot in cache.

DSS queries typically use this buffer replacement strategy to avoid forcing buffers used by OLTP systems out of cache. This prevents DSS applications from interfering with mission-critical revenue-generating OLTP applications. The query optimizer generates this buffer replacement strategy automatically.

The syntax of the Transact-SQL SELECT, UPDATE, and DELETE statements has been modified so that the programmer can specify the buffer replacement strategy to be used by SQL Server. The caller can specify *lru* to force the optimizer to read the table into cache on the MRU/LRU chain. The *mru* option is used to discard the buffer from cache and replace it with the next buffer for the table (fetch-and-discard replacement strategy). For example,

```
1> select a.name, b.name
    from player a (index x0player mru), team b (index team_key mru)
    where a.team = b.team
2> go
```

In summary, SQL Server 11 provides a very high level of user control in configuring multiple data caches. There is also a background process that will utilize CPU idle time in order to offload processing overhead (and performance degradation) from OLTP applications. This process, called the *housekeeper,* is described in Chap. 20. The buffer manager is discussed in greater detail in Chap. 9.

7.3 SQL Server Configuration

As stated in Chap. 1, for a database to be highly available, it must support dynamic configuration of parameters such as total server memory, size of internal memory pools and procedure caches, and number of available lock structures. If the RDBMS does not support dynamic configuration, the system administrator must schedule downtime to restart the server and set new parameters. In distributed environments, especially those using Replication Server, this can be extremely difficult.

From a software engineering perspective, dynamic configuration requires the software to be capable of allocating, deallocating, and/or reallocating server memory for internal data structures. Let's consider an example. Assume that the dataserver process is busier than usual; there are several batch jobs running (e.g., month-end processing in an accounting system), while several users are processing on-line transactions, and still others are requesting reports. Now, let's say that the number of available server lock structures is exhausted and the server is incapable of granting additional requests for locks. Obviously, this would not be a convenient time to reconfigure and restart the dataserver. Ideally, the RDBMS would allow the system administrator to adjust the number of available locks "on the fly" to correct this condition.

Consider the following fictional lock structure:

```
typedef struct {
    int         pageID;        /* Page number to be locked */
    int         objectID;      /* ID of object to be locked */
    int         databaseID;    /* ID of database */
    int         xactID;        /* Transaction ID */
    int         suid;          /* Server User ID owning the lock */
} lock;
```

The software requirements would look something like this: When the server boots, it allocates memory for a number of lock structures designated by preset server configuration variables.

```
lock *locks;
locks = (lock *)malloc(maxLocks*sizeof(lock));
```

Now, the server runs out of available lock structures, and the system administrator changes the configuration variable controlling server locks. At this point the server should be able to reallocate the amount of memory assigned to server lock structures. Clearly, several questions need to be answered including, Where does the memory for the additional locks come from? There are several options, including

- The memory can be taken from other memory pools in SQL Server such as the procedure cache or data cache. However, this may not be what the system administrator intended, and it can affect other aspects of SQL Server operation.

- SQL Server can request additional memory from the operating system. Memory may or may not be available. If memory is available, the allocation may starve other server-based processes (including the operating system) which are sharing memory on the server platform. Again, this may not be what the system administrator intended.

Clearly, dynamic server configuration is not a trivial task. Now let's take a detailed look at SYBASE SQL Server configuration.

The configuration block. The SYBASE *configuration block* resides on the *master* device and is used to store engine configuration information (the configuration block is actually the first 2K page of the *master* device). SYBASE hard-codes the information necessary to boot SQL Server in the configuration block.

The *sp_configure* system procedure is used to modify the values of SQL Server configuration options. Much of the information listed by the *sp_configure* procedure is written to the configuration block, including

- Recovery interval
- Number of user connections
- Total server memory
- Number of locks
- Number of open objects
- Size of procedure cache
- Default fill factor

The BUILDMASTER command. The BUILDMASTER utility is used to build the master device and to create the *master, model,* and *tempdb* databases on the device. It is used to build the master device during installation or to rebuild the device after the *master* database has been damaged. The *sybinit* installation program runs BUILDMASTER to build the initial *master* database on the device specified in answer to the installation prompts.

At the user's option, just configuration information can be written to the *master* device. This option resets SQL Server configuration variables to their default values. Also at the user's option, BUILDMASTER can rewrite only the *master* database or *model* database without changing the configuration of SQL Server. This option should be used when the *master* or *model* database is corrupted but the other databases on the *master* device are undamaged.

The syntax for BUILDMASTER is

```
buildmaster [-v] [-d disk] [-c controller] [-s size] [-m] [-r] [-x]
```

Table 7.1 describes the various BUILDMASTER parameters.

TABLE 7.1   BUILDMASTER Parameters

Parameter	Parameter description
-v	Used to display the version of the BUILDMASTER utility
-d	The physical name of the raw disk partition or operating system file where the *master* device resides
-c	Controller number for the *master* device. The default value is 0 and should not be changed unless instructed to by Sybase technical support
-s	The size of the *master* device in 2K blocks
-m	Rewrites only the *master* database
-r	Rewrites the configuration block
-x	Rewrites only the *model* database.

Be sure to shutdown the SQL Server before attempting to run the BUILDMASTER command.

Configuration interface. Before the release of SYBASE System 11, SQL Server configuration was something akin to black magic. The majority of SQL Server configuration information and parameters were undocumented. In addition, server configuration was accomplished by using a mixture of *sp_configure,* mostly undocumented BUILDMASTER commands, undocumented DBCC commands (see App. G), and undocumented server trace flags (see App. J).

Sybase has been a very "closed" company, guarding this information as if it were the crown jewels. Over the years, I have seen quite a bit of information regarding undocumented configuration techniques. It never fails to amaze me when I call Sybase technical support with a question about an undocumented "feature." "How did you get this information? Are you sure you really want to use that? That command is unsupported!" My response? I am glad I pay Sybase for technical support.

With System 11, Sybase decided to build a new *configuration interface* for SQL Server. The configuration interface introduces a number of new configuration parameters and publicizes many previously undocumented configuration parameters. The System 11 SQL Server provides over 100 configuration parameters as opposed to 40 in System 10. These additional parameters provide the system administrator with increased flexibility; however, they also provide more opportunities for error.

Some of the more obvious changes to SQL Server configuration include these:

- SQL Server configuration information is stored in an operating system file named *$SYBASE / <servername>.cfg.*

- The SQL Server RECONFIGURE command is now reduced to a *no-op,* which means that the command can still be executed but it has no effect.

- It is no longer necessary for the system administrator to use obscure BUILDMASTER and DBCC commands.

- *Configuration levels* are introduced which can be used to restrict the amount of configuration data a user is permitted to view.

With System 11, when SQL Server is booted, it uses values from a specified configuration file (via a new *dataserver* command line parameter). If the specified configuration file does not exist, then a default file is created and default values are used. A fringe benefit of the new configuration file is the ability to store multiple configurations or versions of the configuration file. Versions of the configuration file can be created and optimized for bulk-loading data into the server, OLTP, and DSS processing. It is also possible to optimize a particular configuration and distribute it to other servers in the enterprise by using software distribution techniques.

Configuration groups.   Now that there are over 100 server configuration parameters, Sybase has taken the time to organize configuration parameters into groups and subgroups, as shown in Fig. 7.5. There

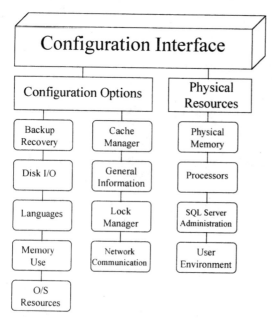

Figure 7.5 Configuration interface.

are two major groups in the configuration interface: configuration options and physical resources. The other configuration "subgroups" fall under one of these categories.

Configuration information. SQL Server uses two tables located in the *master* database to maintain user-settable configuration data:

- The *sysconfigures* table contains one row for each user-settable configuration option. The values in this table may not reflect the values currently being used by SQL Server.

- The *syscurconfigs* table contains the values currently being used by SQL Server.

The *sp_configure* system procedure is used to maintain these system tables.

Configuration levels. The new configuration interface defines three display levels that are used to restrict the amount of configuration information that a user can display:

- Level U1 restricts the display of information to *basic* parameters.

- Level U5 restricts the display of information to *intermediate*-level parameters.

- Level U10 has no restriction. It allows the user to view *comprehensive* parameters.

The *sp_displaylevel* system stored procedure is used to modify and display configuration levels for an SQL Server log-in.

System stored procedures. A set of system stored procedures is used to manage the System 11 configuration interface. Specifically, the system procedures are *sp_configure* and *sp_displaylevel.*

The *sp_displaylevel* procedure. The *sp_displaylevel* system procedure is used to set or display the user display level. The syntax is

```
sp_displaylevel [login_name [, level]]
```

for example,

```
sp_displaylevel gwa, 'comprehensive'
```

The *login_name* parameter is the name of the SQL Server log-in. Unless the caller possesses the *sa_role,* the caller is restricted to setting his or her own display level. The *level* parameter can be basic, intermediate, or comprehensive. When called with no parameters, *sp_displaylevel* reports the current level for the caller. Information regarding the current user display level is maintained in the *sysattributes* system table. It might be a good idea for Sybase to modify this procedure so that only the administrator can assign a higher display level to a user log-in.

Resetting configuration variables.   The *sp_configure* system procedure is used to display or change SQL Server configuration variables. This section covers some of the configuration variables that are commonly changed by using *sp_configure*. The syntax of *sp_configure* is

```
sp_configure [config_name [, config_value]]
```

The *config_name* parameter is the name of the configuration variable. The *sp_configure* system procedure can be run with no arguments to get a list of all configuration variables. The complete *config_name* is not necessary; the caller can specify just enough to uniquely identify it. For example,

```
sp_configure 'proc', 15
```

is equivalent to

```
sp_configure 'procedure cache', 15
```

The *config_value* parameter is used to assign a new value to the configuration variable.

SQL Server generates a new operating system configuration file every time *sp_configure* is executed to change a value. The existing configuration file will be renamed to *<servername>*.001, and the new one will be named *<servername>*.cfg. This can be somewhat annoying when a batch of configuration commands is executed from an SQL script. If the script contains five calls to *sp_configure*, SQL Server will create five operating system configuration files.

There is also an extended syntax used with *sp_configure* for System 11:

```
sp_configure
"configuration file", 0, {"write" | "read" | "verify" | "restore"},
"file_name"
```

The *configuration file* parameter tells the server that the caller wants to perform an operation on a configuration file. The second parameter, 0, is used as a place holder. The third parameter is used to specify the type of operation: *read* and *write* are self-explanatory, *verify* is used to do a sanity check on the values contained in *file_name,* and *restore* creates *file_name* by using the values contained in *sysconfigures.* The *file_name* parameter is used to specify the name of a configuration file. If the file already exists (and the operation is *write* or *restore*), the existing file is renamed by using the naming convention *filename.001, filename.002,* etc.

The following is a partial listing of a System 11 configuration file:

```
####################################################################
#
#          Configuration File for the Sybase SQL Server
#
#          Please read the System Administration Guide (SAG)
#          before changing any of the values in this file.
#
####################################################################

[Configuration Options]

[General Information]

[Backup/Recovery]
        recovery interval in minutes = 10
        print recovery information = 1
        tape retention in days = DEFAULT

[Cache Manager]
        number of oam trips = DEFAULT
        number of index trips = DEFAULT
        procedure cache percent = DEFAULT
        memory alignment boundary = DEFAULT

[Named Cache:default data cache]
        cache size = DEFAULT
        cache status = default data cache

[Disk I/O]
        allow sql server async i/o = DEFAULT
        disk i/o structures = DEFAULT
        page utilization percent = DEFAULT
        number of devices = 16
    .
    .
    .
[Lock Manager]
        number of locks = 12000
        deadlock checking period = DEFAULT
        freelock transfer block size = DEFAULT
        max engine freelocks = DEFAULT
        address lock spinlock ratio = DEFAULT
        page lock spinlock ratio = DEFAULT
        table lock spinlock ratio = DEFAULT
```

Certain engine configuration parameters can be displayed only by a system administrator or a system security officer. The following listing shows partial output from the *sp_configure* procedure when it is called with no arguments:

```
1> sp_configure
2> go
Group: Configuration Options

Group: Cache Manager
```

Parameter Name	Default	Memory Used	Config Value	Run Value
procedure cache percent	20	0	20	20
total data cache size	0	0	1104	1104
number of oam trips	0	0	0	0
number of index trips	0	0	0	0
memory alignment boundary	2048	0	2048	2048

```
Group: Lock Manager
```

Parameter Name	Default	Memory Used	Config Value	Run Value
number of locks	5000	0	12000	12000
deadlock checking period	500	0	500	500
freelock transfer block size	30	0	30	30
max engine freelocks	10	0	10	10
address lock spinlock ratio	100	0	100	100
page lock spinlock ratio	100	0	100	100
table lock spinlock ratio	20	0	20	20

```
Group: Physical Memory
```

Parameter Name	Default	Memory Used	Config Value	Run Value
total memory	7500	0	16384	16384
additional network memory	0	0	1536000	1536000
lock shared memory	0	0	0	0

```
Group: Processors
```

Parameter Name	Default	Memory Used	Config Value	Run Value
max online engines	1	0	1	1
min online engines	1	0	1	1
engine adjust interval	0	0	0	0
current number online engines	1	0	1	1

```
        .
        .
        .
(return status = 0)
```

The system administrator will commonly use the *sp_configure* procedure to modify the total amount of memory available to SQL Server, the number of concurrent user connections, and the maximum number of SQL Server devices. Normally, these changes are made immediately following the initial SQL Server installation. After the initial modifications, the configuration will usually remain static with changes being made when applications are added and during the tuning phase. Changes to hardware configuration such as additional memory, disk drives, and/or tape devices may affect server configuration, as will additional users or connections required by application programs.

When a parameter is changed on a pre-System 11 SQL Server using *sp_configure,* the administrator must use the RECONFIGURE command to set the configuration variables. We will discuss the RECONFIGURE command in greater detail shortly. Because many of the configuration options affect run-time memory allocations, it may be necessary to restart SQL Server to make the new configuration active. This can make it difficult to reconfigure 24×7 production systems. The *allow updates, default language,* and *recovery interval* parameters are dynamic, meaning that they can be changed and made active without restarting the SQL Server.

7.4 Group: Configuration Options

The configuration options group contains the bulk of SQL Server configuration parameters. The various configuration options are profiled in this section. Some of the more important parameters are described in greater detail in other sections of the book.

7.4.1 Backup and recovery

recovery interval. As users make changes to data in SQL Server databases, only the transaction log is written to disk immediately. The transaction log must be written to disk immediately to ensure recoverability. *Dirty* data and index pages are kept in cache and written to disk at a later time.

The *recovery interval* controls the frequency of an SQL Server checkpoint. A checkpoint flushes all completed transactions to disk (*dirty* data) and writes out the last page of the transaction log. Follow these guidelines when setting this option:

- A low number results in faster retrieval and slower updates because of the increased number of checkpoints and the associated overhead of I/O.

- A high number results in slower retrieval but faster updates because of the decrease in the number of checkpoints. Automatic recovery may take a substantial amount of time during server boot-up.

The default for *recovery interval* is 5 minutes.

tape retention. Dump files created by the SYBASE Backup Server are ANSI-labeled. The server configuration variable *tape retention* is used to specify the number of days that backup tapes are protected from being overwritten. By default, the value of *tape retention* is 0, which means that tapes can be overwritten immediately.

print recovery information. This flag is used to determine what information is written to the SQL Server error log (and the console) during automatic recovery. The default value is zero, which tells SQL Server to display only the database name and a message stating that recovery is in process. If the value is 1, SQL Server will display the names of individual transactions that are rolled forward or rolled back during recovery. The information provided can be quite voluminous.

7.4.2 Cache manager

procedure cache percent. As described earlier, the amount of memory allocated to the *procedure cache* is what is left over after static memory (user connections, catalog structures, etc.) requirements have been allocated by SQL Server at run time. The leftover memory is split between the procedure cache and the data cache.

However, the percentage allocated to the procedure cache is configurable. The default value is 20 percent. The procedure cache holds internal structures for rules, stored procedures, triggers, and views, i.e., for anything that is compiled. The larger the procedure cache, the less chance the server will have to reread from disk any procedures, rules, and so on. The procedure cache typically must be higher during the development process because of the high level of compilation that occurs.

The *data cache* is used to store data pages and index pages in memory. SQL Server will try to locate data and index pages in cache before reading them from disk. The size of the data cache affects checkpoint time. Generally, a heavy update system with a large data cache will require more time to align completed transactions to disk.

total data cache size. This is a read-only configuration parameter which is calculated by SQL Server during start-up. This is the total number of data pages allocated to the data cache.

number of oam trips. This parameter specifies the number of times that an aged OAM page recycles itself onto the MRU chain. As this parameter is increased, the longer aged OAM pages will remain in cache. The default value is 0. This parameter is discussed in greater detail in Sec. 13.4, Tuning BCPs.

number of index trips. This value specifies the number of times an aged index page recycles itself onto the MRU chain. As this parameter is increased, the longer index pages will remain in cache. The default value is 0.

memory alignment boundary. This parameter determines on which boundary data caches are aligned to disk. This value will vary between operating systems and is typically set to the native block I/O size of the host operating system. For example, Sun Solaris and Windows NT both use 2K I/O while IBM's AIX uses 4K I/O. This allows Sybase to align page I/Os up with the operating system for greater efficiency. Do not modify this variable without input from Sybase technical support.

7.4.3   Disk I/O

number of devices. The *devices* configuration variable controls the maximum number of database devices that SQL Server can use. This number does not include database dump devices. The default value for devices is 10. The maximum value that can be specified for *vdevno* in a DISK INIT command is 1 less than the value of *devices*. Device number 0 is always the *master* device.

Every database device that gets created requires 512 bytes of SQL Server memory. Devices created with Open Server require 64K of server memory.

allow sql server async i/o. This parameter is implemented as a trace flag (T1603) prior to System 11. The default value is 1, which means that SQL Server will use asynchronous I/O. A value of 0 forces the server to use standard UNIX calls for disk I/O. Asynchronous disk I/O is faster than synchronous disk I/O because SQL Server does not have to wait for a response before issuing further I/Os.

disk i/o structures. A user process requires a disk I/O control block before SQL Server can perform an I/O request on behalf of the process. This parameter controls the initial number of disk I/O structures allocated by SQL Server at start-up. The memory for disk I/O structures is allocated at run time and cannot be changed dynamically. The default value is 256, which is sufficient for most installations.

page utilization percent. This option is new to Release 11 and is used to control when SQL Server will scan the Object Allocation Map (OAM) to find unused pages. If this variable is set to 100, SQL Server will scan all OAM pages allocated to the object before allocating a new extent.

When this value is lower than 100, SQL Server will compare the ratio of *used* to *unused* pages allocated to the table before performing an OAM scan. This can result in higher performance for large tables but will also result in more unused pages (and wasted space). The default run value is 95.

7.4.4 General information

configuration file. This indicates the name of the configuration file that the server is currently using.

7.4.5 Languages

default sortorder id. This is a read-only variable used to indicate the current default sort order on this SQL Server. This variable is set during SQL Server installation and can be changed with the *sybinit* program.

default language id. The number of the default language used to display system messages. SQL Server client applications can override the default language programmatically.

number of languages in cache. This value indicates the maximum number of languages that can be held in cache simultaneously. The default value is 3.

default character set id. The number of the default character set used by SQL Server.

7.4.6 Lock manager

The parameters in this group are used to configure various locking characteristics within SQL Server. Some of these parameters are described in greater detail in Chap. 12. The reader may also wish to refer to the SYBASE *SQL Server System Administration Guide* for more information.

locks. The maximum number of locks available to SQL Server can be set with the *locks* parameter. This is the total number of locks available (serverwide) in the *global freelock list,* as illustrated in Fig. 7.6. The SQL Server requires approximately 80 bytes of static memory for each configured lock. The default value is 5000.

max engine freelocks. This is the percentage of locks (in the global freelock list) that will be made available to each server engine in the SMP environment. The range of values is from 1 to 50 percent; the default value is 10. This is a dynamic configuration variable.

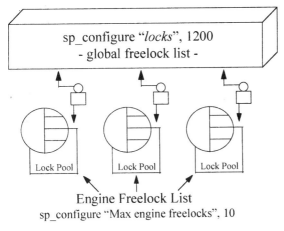

sp_configure "*locks*", 1200
- global freelock list -

Lock Pool   Lock Pool   Lock Pool

Engine Freelock List
sp_configure "Max engine freelocks", 10

- Freelock transfer block size
  sp_configure "*freelock transfer*", 30

Figure 7.6   SQL Server lock pools.

freelock transfer block size.   This variable pertains to SMP systems only. If a particular engine runs out of locks in its local lock pool, lock structures will be taken from the global freelock list and transferred to the engine. As locks are released by processes serviced by that engine, the lock structures will be migrated back to the global freelock list. The default value is 30.

deadlock checking period.   This parameter is used to specify the minimum amount of time in milliseconds before SQL Server initiates a deadlock check for a process waiting on a lock to be released. This is a dynamic configuration variable; the default value is 500.

address lock spinlock ratio.   This variable only pertains to SMP systems. This variable sets the ratio of spinlocks used to protect the address lock hash table. The address lock hash table has 1031 rows (also known as *hash buckets*). The configuration ratio is based on the number of rows protected by each spinlock. So if the address lock spinlock ratio is set to 100, the first 10 spinlocks will protect 100 rows and the 11th spinlock will protect the remaining 31 rows. Uniprocessor servers require only one spinlock. Lock hash tables are described in greater detail in Chap. 15. The default value is 100.

page lock spinlock ratio.   Like the address lock spinlock ratio, the page lock spinlock ratio is used to set the ratio of spinlocks used to protect the page lock hash table. The default value is 100.

table lock spinlock ratio.   Like the address and page lock spinlock ratios, the table lock spinlock ratio is used to set the ratio of spinlocks used to protect the internal table lock hash table. The default value is 20.

7.4.7   Memory use

executable code size.   This read-only variable indicates the size of the server code, as shown in Fig. 7.1.

7.4.8   Network communication

allow remote access.   It indicates whether users from remote servers are permitted to access this SQL Server. To support communication with the Backup Server, the default for System 10 and 11 servers is 1; the default for pre-System 10 servers is 0.

number of remote logins.   It controls the number of active user connections from this site to remote servers. The default value is 20.

number of remote sites.   This is the number of simultaneous remote sites permitted to access this SQL Server. The default is 10.

number of remote connections.   It is the limit on active connections initiated to and from this server. The default is 20.

remote server preread packets.   This parameter is the maximum number of data packets the site handler will preread for any user process. In most cases, the default value of 3 should not be changed because higher values can use too much memory.

default network packet size.   It sets the default size of network packets for all users on SQL Server. It is possible to set the packet size for an individual ISQL or BCP session by using the -A command line parameter. The packet size must be between 512 and the value of *max network packet size* and must be a multiple of 512. The default is 512 bytes.

max network packet size.   On occasion, using a larger packet size can improve performance. This is especially useful for large bulk-copy operations or other operations which are I/O-intensive. The default is 2048 bytes, and the maximum network packet size must be a multiple of 512.

max number network listeners.   This variable specifies the maximum number of network listeners allowed by SQL Server at one time. As discussed in Chap. 13, each master port has one network listener. Normally there is no need for multiple master ports unless SQL Server will be communicating over more than one network. The default value is 15.

tcp no delay. Some environments may benefit from disabling TCP packet batching. Packet batching is a technique used by TCP/IP to batch small packets into one larger physical packet. Packets will be briefly delayed in an effort to fill the physical network frames with as much data as possible. Applications sending very small result sets or statuses from stored procedures will usually benefit. This makes SQL Server open all connections with a no-delay option, forcing packets to be sent regardless of size. Pre-System 11 servers can disable packet batching by starting SQL Server with the 1610 Trace Flag (see App. J). The default is 0, which means that packet batching is enabled.

7.4.9 O/S resources

o/s file descriptors. This is the number of operating system file descriptors. The default is 1024; this is a read-only parameter.

o/s asynch i/o enabled. This flag is used to toggle the setting for operating system asynchronous I/O. The default is 0, which means that asynchronous I/O is enabled.

max async i/os per engine. This is the maximum number of asynchronous disk I/Os that each SQL Server engine may have outstanding at any time. SQL Server keeps a count of outstanding asynchronous I/Os per engine and per server. If the number of outstanding I/Os per engine exceeds the value of *max async i/os,* the server will delay I/Os and print messages to the SQL Server error log.

max async i/os per server. This parameter specifies the maximum number of asynchronous disk I/O requests that can be outstanding for SQL Server at one time. The default value is 200. Large bulk-copy jobs may force the administrator to increase this value. When running on uniprocessor platforms, only *max async i/os per server* is supported.

7.5 Group: Physical Resources

The physical resources group contains parameters that pertain to physical memory, number of processors, SQL Server administration, and control of the user environment. The various configuration options are profiled in this section. Some of the more important parameters are described in greater detail in other areas of the book.

7.5.1 Physical memory

total memory. This variable sets the size of total server memory (in 2K pages) that SQL Server allocates from the operating system during start-up. The administrator should set memory as high as possible, depending on the other requirements of the system. Memory is allocated to SQL Server in 2K pages. The minimum value varies between platforms. This is a good rule of thumb for memory allocation:

Dedicated database server	75 to 80 percent of RAM
Nondedicated database server	50 to 60 percent of RAM

Be careful not to set the *total memory* parameter too high, or else SQL Server will not boot. Some platforms require the amount of shared memory configured in the operating system to be changed along with this parameter. If this applies to the platform, the amount of memory configured for SQL Server using the *total memory* parameter cannot exceed the amount of shared memory configured in the operating system. To increase SQL Server memory, the administrator may have to change the shared-memory size in the operating system. If the *total memory* parameter is changed and SQL Server will not boot, memory has probably been set too high.

When total server memory is configured, keep in mind that memory is required for user-configurable parameters such as user connections, database devices, open databases, open objects, and locks.

additional network memory. It allocates additional memory for clients who request packet sizes that are larger than the default packet size for the server (see Fig. 7.1). The default is 0.

lock shared memory. Lock shared memory into physical memory on platforms that support it. This disallows swapping of SQL Server pages to disk. Supported platforms include HP, NCR, Data General, SGI, and SCO UNIX. Check with Sybase technical support before changing this value.

7.5.2 Processors

max online engines. The *max online engines* variable is used to control the number of *dataserver* processes running concurrently in the SMP environment. This variable cannot be set higher than the number of available CPUs.

min online engines.   This variable is not currently used.

engine adjust interval.   This variable is not currently used.

current number online engines.   This is the number of engines currently running in this SQL Server. This variable is maintained by the
SQL Server.

7.5.3   SQL Server administration

allow updates.   When the *allow updates* flag is enabled, any user with
permission can update system tables directly. The default for this
variable is off (disabled), and there are a very few reasons for it to be
enabled. There are two reasons to enable the *allow updates* variable:

- To create a system stored procedure that will update system tables
- Because Sybase technical support requires it

open databases.   The maximum number of databases that can be
open at one time is configured with the *open databases* parameter.
The server requires approximately 644 bytes of memory per open
database. The default run value is 12.

open objects.   The maximum number of database objects that can be
open at one time is configured with the *open objects* parameter.
Approximately 315 bytes of memory is required for each open database object. The default for open objects is 500.

fillfactor.   The *fillfactor* parameter sets the percentage to which index
and clustered data pages are filled during initial creation and loading.
A *fillfactor* can be used to specify the percentage that an index page
should be filled to allow for future expansion. When fillfactor is 100
percent, index pages are completely filled. This is optimal for quick-
retrieval purposes but is not optimal for UPDATEs because of page
splits. A value of 50 to 60 percent is preferred for tables that are updated because of a lower occurrence of page splits (improves concurrency
and minimizes deadlocks), but it makes for slower retrieval time.
    The user is able to override the *fillfactor* parameter by providing
another value, using a CREATE INDEX statement.

```
CREATE UNIQUE CLUSTERED INDEX x0account ON tbaccount(acct#)
WITH fillfactor = 60
```

Please refer to Chap. 12 for more information on *fillfactor.*

time slice. The *time slice* variable sets the number of milliseconds that the SQL Server scheduler allows a user process to run. The default value is 100.

The SQL Server kernel is not preemptive. The kernel does not control time spent on a process; the process controls the time spent in the CPU and schedules itself out. However, if the process does not give itself up (i.e., exceeds the *time slice* configuration), the kernel will terminate the process because it assumes that the program is in a hard loop. If *time slice* is set too low, the system may slow down due to overhead caused by the system thrashing; i.e., the programs are frequently scheduling themselves in and out of the CPU. If *time slice* is set too high, it may cause long response time when one process fails to schedule itself out of the CPU for a long time.

default database size. The database size configuration variable is used to control the default number of megabytes allocated to a new user database with the CREATE DATABASE command. The default value is 2 Mbytes.

allow nested triggers. When this option is enabled, data modifications caused by triggers can cause other triggers to fire. The default is 1 (enabled).

upgrade version. This variable contains the revision level of this SQL Server. The upgrade version is changed by the UPGRADE program provided with new releases. The upgrade version includes the version number, hardware development platform, O/S development platform, and date of creation.

cpu accounting flush and i/o accounting flush. The *cpu flush* and *i/o flush* variables were introduced to SQL Server with System 10. They are used with the chargeback accounting facility. *cpu flush* specifies how many machine clock ticks to accumulate before adding the CPU usage data to the *master.dbo.syslogins* table; and *i/o flush* specifies how many disk I/Os to accumulate before flushing the data to *syslogins*.

audit queue size. The *audit queue size* variable controls the number of records that the audit queue can hold. The default value is 100. Size this variable carefully:

- If the number is too small and the audit queue fills up, user connections will be put in the sleep queue until space becomes available. This will have an adverse effect on system performance.

- The audit queue is an in-memory storage area. In the event of a system crash, records held in the audit queue will be permanently lost.

number of extent i/o buffers.   It allocates the specified number of extents for use by the CREATE INDEX command. Do not set this variable to more than 100. SQL Server uses large buffers for BCP, CREATE DATABASE, and CREATE INDEX statements. The default value is 0, the recommended value is 10.

identity burning set factor.   This value specifies the percentage of potential *identity* column values that is made available in each block. If this value is set too high and the server crashes due to power failure, hardware failure, etc., the pool of numbers is permanently lost. This causes gaps in *identity* column values, which in some cases is unacceptable (e.g., in check numbers or invoice numbers). The default value is 5000.

size of auto identity column.   This parameter sets the precision of *identity* columns automatically created with the *sp_dboption 'auto identity'* option. When the auto identity database option is true, an *identity* column is defined in each new table that is created without a primary key, unique constraint, or explicitly defined *identity* column. The default value is 10, which means that the *identity* column will be 10 digits.

identity grab size.   It allows each SQL Server process to reserve a block of *identity* column values for INSERTs into tables that have an *identity* column. The default value is 1.

print deadlock information.   This variable prints out (to the error log) deadlock chains and victims in simple language. Because the server will incur extra overhead when this option is enabled, it should be used for troubleshooting purposes only. Pre-System 11 servers can achieve the same results by using the 1204 and 1205 server trace flags.

number of mailboxes.   It specifies the number of *mailbox* structures that SQL Server allocates during start-up. Mailboxes are used for process-to-process communication and synchronization. The default value is 30.

number of messages.   This specifies the number of *message* structures that SQL Server allocates during start-up. Message structures are used in conjunction with mailboxes to support process-to-process communication and synchronization. The default value is 64.

number of alarms. It specifies the number of *alarms* allocated by SQL Server. Alarms are used with the SQL Server WAITFOR command (e.g., WAITFOR MIRROREXIT). The default value is 40.

number of preallocated extents. It specifies the number of extent buffers allocated in a single trip to the page manager. A higher value may increase the performance of large bulk-load operations. The default value is 2.

event buffers per engine. The *event buffers per engine* parameter specifies the maximum number of events to be buffered (per engine). The default event buffer size is 100, a number which most users will want to increase when using SQL Server Monitor. Tradeoffs are involved in selecting an optimal buffer size, since a low number forces more frequent scans by the Monitor Server, while a large buffer size reduces the amount of memory available for other uses, such as procedure cache. A size of 2000 is generally large enough to avoid event buffer overruns.

sql server clock tick length. This parameter specifies the duration of the server's clock tick in microseconds. Please refer to Sec. 11.4 for more information about the SQL Server clock tick length.

runnable process search count. It specifies the number of times an engine will loop looking for work in the run queue before relinquishing control of the CPU. This is used in an attempt to avoid relinquishing control of the CPU and to maintain hardware cache locality.

i/o polling process count. It specifies the number of tasks the engine will run before checking for disk and/or network I/O completions. The default value is 10.

deadlock retries. This specifies the number of times the server will retry a lock before declaring a deadlock and terminating one of the offending processes. It works in conjunction with the deadlock checking period. The default value is 5.

cpu grace time. This is the maximum time in microseconds that a user process can run without yielding the CPU before SQL Server infects it. SQL Server normally prints a stack trace to the error log when a task is infected.

number of sort buffers. It specifies the number of buffers used to hold pages read from input tables. Increasing the value of number of *sort* *buffers* can improve performance when indexes on large tables are created. The recommended value can be derived from this simple formula:

$$\max\left(100,\ \sqrt{n}\,\right)$$

where n is the number of data pages in the largest table.

sort page count. It specifies the maximum amount of memory (in pages) that a SORT operation can use. This parameter is no longer used by System 11.

partition spinlock ratio. This variable is the number of partition caches that each spinlock protects. A partition spinlock is used to ensure that only one process has access to a partition cache at any given time. The default value is 32 (meaning 1 partition spinlock is used for 32 partition caches), and it should be sufficient for most installations. The suggested number of available spinlocks is 10 percent of the total number of partitions in use at any given time.

partition groups. It specifies the number of partition groups to allocate for the server. SQL Server uses partition groups to control access to the individual partitions of a table. Please refer to Chap. 10 for more information on partition groups.

housekeeper free write percent. This parameter specifies the maximum percentage by which the housekeeper task can increase database writes. The *housekeeper* process is described in Chap. 20. The default value is 20 percent.

lock promotion LWM. This parameter specifies the number of page locks allowed during a single scan of a table or index before SQL Server attempts to promote page-level locks to a table lock. The default value is 200.

lock promotion HWM. This is the lock promotion high water mark; it sets the number of page locks allowed before SQL Server escalates the page locks to a table-level lock. This feature is new to System 11. The default value is 200.

The System 11 SQL Server behaves as System 10 does when the lock promotion LWM and HWM parameters are left at the default values. System 10 escalates page locks to table locks when the number of page locks exceeds 200.

lock promotion PCT. The *lock promotion PCT* parameter is used with the *lock promotion HWM* and *lock promotion LWM* parameters. This parameter sets the percentage of page locks permitted by a Transact-SQL command (if the number of locks is between *lock promotion LWM* and *lock promotion HWM*) before the server attempts to escalate the page locks to a table-level lock. The default is 100 percent.

7.5.4 User environment

user connections. The number of *user connections* must be high enough to cover all simultaneous connections to the SQL Server. Each user connection requires approximately 50K (23,552 bytes + *stack size + stack guard size*) of server memory as overhead. Static memory for user connections is allocated at run time (hence, the inability to dynamically change the number of user connections). To estimate the number of user connections required at the server, use the following guidelines:

- One connection per master network listener (a *master* network listener is defined by a *master* line in the *interfaces* file entry for that SQL Server).
- One (per engine) for standard output.
- One (per engine) for the SQL Server *errorlog* file.
- One (per engine) for configuration purposes.
- One (per engine) for the *interfaces* file.
- One (per engine) for internal use.
- One user connection per defined threshold.
- One user connection for each defined database device.
- One connection for the Backup Server. More connections may be required if there will be concurrent dumps of multiple databases.
- One connection is required per *dbopen()* or *ct_connect()* call in a DB-Library or CT-Library program. Most applications require between one and three concurrent connections.

The number of user connections required at the SQL Server can be calculated by multiplying the average number of *dbopen()* or *ct_connect()* calls required for each application by the number of simultaneous application users. This requires a fairly good amount of application knowledge and/or testing. For example, for a uniprocessor SQL Server:

3 *dbopen()* calls for application *a* × 50 users	150
3 *ct_connect()* calls for application *b* × 10 users	30
6 *dbopen()* calls for application *c* × 5 users	30
+ connection for *master* network listener	1
+ connection for stdout (standard out)	1
+ connection for SQL Server errorlog	1
+ connection for SQL Server configuration	1
+ connection for *interfaces* file	1
+ connection for internal use	1
+ connection for defined thresholds	10
+ connections for configured devices	10
+ connection for the Backup Server	1
Total user connections	237

Additional user connections may be required for other SQL Server processes, such as remote procedure calls or maintenance jobs that monitor database consistency and perform database backups.

Also, if other SYBASE products such as SQL Server Monitor or Replication Server are being used, these products can demand several connections each. When these products are used or their installation is planned, try to determine how many additional user connections will be required.

The maximum number of user connections that can be made to SQL Server in this computer environment (hardware-OS combination) is stored in the global variable @@*max_connections*.

```
1> select @@max_connections
2> go
 ----------
2042
```

stack size. This is the size of the SQL Server execution stack. The default is 30,720 bytes. Some third-party software tools, such as SQL BackTrack from Datatools, Inc., require the system administrator to increase the stack size.

password expiration interval. The *password expiration interval* variable sets the number of days that passwords remain in effect after they are changed. The default is 0, which means that passwords do not expire.

permission cache entries. This option determines the number of cache protectors per task. Information on user permissions is held in the permission cache. When SQL Server needs to check permissions, it first checks the permission cache before accessing the *sysprotects* system table. Each cache protector takes 28 bytes of memory. The default is 15.

stack guard size. This parameter is used to set the size of the stack guard area. This is an overflow stack which is tacked onto the end of each stack. SQL Server allocates one stack for each user connection during start-up. The default is 4096 bytes.

user log cache size. This is the size of each private log cache (PLC); the default size of the PLC is 2048 bytes. The minimum value is 2048 bytes, and the maximum value is 2,147,483,657 bytes. The private log cache size does not have to be a multiple of 2K.

user log cache spinlock ratio. This is the number of PLCs per PLC spinlock. Spinlocks are used to control the PLC semaphores. The default is 20, which should be optimal for most applications. In uniprocessor environments, this value is ignored, and there is only one spinlock.

7.5.5 Summary

SMP server configuration is a constant learning and tuning process. The administrator should test several different configurations while monitoring all aspects of the server including CPU utilization, cache hit ratios, and context switches. Not every application will benefit from a single "standard" configuration. Test each configuration in a controlled environment, using a set of well-defined test scripts. Record the performance results after each iteration. Avoid changing several unrelated parameters between tests, as it will be difficult to determine which parameter had the greatest impact.

7.6 The RECONFIGURE Command

The RECONFIGURE command is used by pre-System 11 dataservers to set configuration variables that are controlled by the *sp_configure* system procedure. With System 11, the command can still be called, but it is reduced to a *no-op,* meaning that it does nothing and returns to the caller. The user must have SA equivalence by possessing an *sa_role* or by using the SA log-in. Permission to use RECONFIGURE is not transferable. The syntax of RECONFIGURE is

```
RECONFIGURE [WITH OVERRIDE]
```

The optional **WITH OVERRIDE** clause is required to set the *allow updates* option with *sp_configure*. It is also required when SQL Server thinks that a value is suspect, i.e., that the new value is not reasonable and may result in less than optimal performance.

```
1> sp_configure 'allow updates', 1
2> go
Configuration option changed. Run the RECONFIGURE command to install.
(return status = 0)
1> reconfigure with override
2> go
```

The RECONFIGURE command is obsolete in System 11!

7.7 Multiple-Network Engines

As described in Chap. 3, an important architectural improvement to Release 11 SQL Server is the changes in network architecture provided by multiple-network engines (MNEs). MNEs provide symmetric network I/O capabilities to SQL Server in the SMP environment. This improves server performance, scalability, and load balancing by distributing network I/O operations to each server engine on a per-connection basis.

Configuring multiple-network engines. A multiple-network engine is automatically enabled by starting SQL Server with additional server engines. As discussed in Sec. 7.5.2, additional engines are started by using *sp_configure* to adjust the *max online engines* configuration variable and restarting the server.

```
sp_configure 'max online engines', 12
```

Remember that this variable cannot be set higher than the number of available CPUs.

SQL Server 11 has a few "undocumented hooks" that can be used with MNE for testing and debugging purposes. The first is a server trace flag (Trace Flag 7810) that can be used to disable MNE when the server boots. See App. J for more information on server trace flags.

There are also some new DBCC hooks provided with SQL Server 11 to support MNE. The first is used to turn MNE on or off at run time.

Note that turning MNE *off* at run time will not change the network affinity of any currently connected SQL Server users. When MNE is off, all network I/O will be performed by engine 0 (System 10 behavior). The syntax used to toggle MNE functionality is

```
dbcc engine( net, migrateon | migrateoff )
```

Additionally, the following DBCC command can be used to display task affinity information about MNE. The output includes the status of MNE (enabled or disabled), details about particular tasks that are affinitied to each engine, and the total number of tasks that are affinitied to each engine. The syntax is

```
dbcc engine( net, {showall | show}, [engine_number] )
```

For example,

```
1> dbcc traceon(3604) /* Direct output to this terminal */
1> go
1> dbcc engine(net, showall, 0)
2> go

Network affinity migration is enabled.

Tasks that are network affinitied to Engine 0:
      kpid          vsn      psn      status
      ----------    ----     ----     ----------------------------
      78644         1        15       sleeping(0xe9181160) setdataok
      1150156838    2        16       running(engine 0) setdataok

Total number of tasks that are currently affinitied to engine 0 is 2
```

SQL Server Monitor. At the time of this writing, there are no hooks available for SQL Server Monitor to monitor MNE. The administrator will need to be able to determine the total networking load of applications and the distribution of that load across server engines. At a minimum, I would expect Sybase to include the following capabilities in a future release of SQL Server Monitor:

- Total number of network write operations
- Pending network I/O contention for each engine
- Total number of TDS packets received and sent for each engine
- Total number of bytes received and sent for each server engine

8

Monitoring SQL Server

This chapter is used to describe several aspects of server monitoring including SQL Server activity, user activity, and lock activity. The SYBASE SQL Server Monitor is a graphical tool designed for performance tuning and management. SQL Server Monitor is used in this chapter as well as several SQL Server commands and procedures.

The chapter concludes with a discussion about a new system table called the *syslogshold* table. This table is designed to improve the usability and reliability of SQL Server by providing information about long-running transactions.

8.1 SYBASE SQL Server Monitor

The SYBASE SQL Server Monitor is a graphical tool designed for performance tuning and management. SQL Server Monitor allows the system administrator to quickly isolate problems, manage system resources, and fine-tune SQL Server engines. Like so many of the Sybase products, SQL Server Monitor is built on Open Client and Open Server technology. SQL Server Monitor is a client/server application that runs in the OSF/Motif and Microsoft Windows graphical environments.

8.1.1 Feature set

SQL Server Monitor provides the database administrator with constant access to data including

- *Database locking status.* This is information on the level of lock contention in SQL Server. The SQL Server Monitor client can display information on the lock activity for each lock type.

- *Cache statistics.* The amount of memory allocated to the data and procedure caches within SQL Server can be controlled by the database administrator. SQL Server Monitor displays information about the number of requests for data and stored procedure plans that are serviced from the cache. This type of information is used to determine if available memory is being properly utilized. If a large number of stored procedure plans are being read and reread from disk, the administrator may want to change the size of the procedure cache.

- *Cache analysis tool.* The cache analysis tool (CAT) is a monitor server application that performs internal workload sampling. It is used to calculate cache hit ratios and proximity page requests and to determine the optimum size for data caches and I/O buffer pools.

- *Device I/O.* The number of device I/Os and the hit rate for each configured database device can be displayed. This type of information can help determine the requirements that the SQL Server is placing on its devices and how well the I/O load is distributed.

- *Memory allocation.* SQL Server Monitor can optionally show the percentage of SQL Server memory currently allocated to the kernel, to the server executable, and to the data and procedure caches. Memory allocated to the SQL Server kernel is used for static overhead, user connections, open databases, database devices, and SQL Server locks.

- *Network traffic.* The number of client/server reads and writes performed by the SQL Server can be displayed. This gives the administrator an indication of the load placed on the network by its clients' activities.

- *User processes.* SQL Server Monitor can display information for specific user processes, including the display of CPU utilization and page I/O for single processes or for all processes executing on an SQL Server.

- *Server transactions.* SQL Server Monitor can provide information about server transactions and DML operations including INSERT, UPDATE, and DELETE activity. The DBA can use SQL Server Monitor to obtain information about UPDATE activities including traditional UPDATEs versus direct UPDATEs.

8.1.2 SQL Server Monitor architecture

SQL Server Monitor consists of four components:

- *SQL Server Monitor Server*—an Open Server application which collects statistics and counter information from the SQL Server.

- *SQL Server Monitor Historical Server*—an Open Server application that connects to SQL Server and SQL Server Monitor Server and records performance data to a file.

- *SQL Server Monitor Client*—a client application that connects to SQL Server Monitor Server and SQL Server to read and display real-time performance data using a graphical user interface.

- *SQL Server Monitor Client Library*—an application programming interface that enables developers to write client applications that connect to SQL Servers, SQL Server Monitor Servers, and SQL Server Monitor Historical Servers to gather performance data.

The architecture of SQL Server Monitor Server is described in Fig. 8.1. The SQL Server Monitor Server is an Open Server application that accesses SQL Server shared memory to capture performance data. By utilizing shared memory, SQL Server Monitor is unobtrusive; i.e., it does not place any overhead on the SQL Server by obtaining its performance data through the use of SQL queries. This is an advantage that SYBASE has over competing monitoring tools.

The SQL Server Monitor Client is an Open Client application that connects to the SQL Server Monitor Server and SQL Server and displays performance data in a graphical user interface. The SQL Server Monitor Client can be an MS Windows or OSF/Motif application. SQL Server saves performance data in a shared-memory area (*server-*

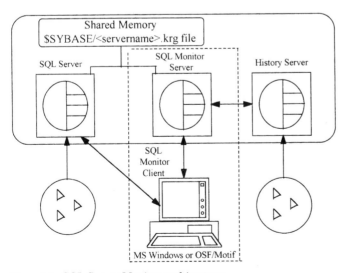

Figure 8.1 SQL Server Monitor architecture.

name.krg); the performance data is updated as the server runs. The SQL Server Monitor Server obtains its information from this shared-memory file and sends it to the SQL Server Monitor Client on request. Obtaining the performance data in this manner has a minimal impact on the performance of the SQL Server.

For some performance data, the SQL Server Monitor client connects directly to the SQL Server. Memory allocation information is received directly from the SQL Server in this manner. The SQL Server Monitor Client uses the DBCC MEMUSAGE command to retrieve memory allocation information from SQL Server. It may be important to note that the SQL Server process is frozen when DBCC MEMUSAGE is executing. During this time, other user connections will appear to be hung and the server will not accept additional user connections.

The SQL Server Monitor main window is shown in Fig. 8.2. Available options include data cache, device I/O, performance summary, performance trends, process activity, process detail, process list, and transaction activity.

SQL Server Monitor API.   The SQL Server Monitor Client Library functions enable corporate developers and independent software vendors (ISVs) to write applications that collect SQL Server performance data.

After an SQL Server Monitor connection is created, the SQL Server Monitor Client Library application defines the performance data to be

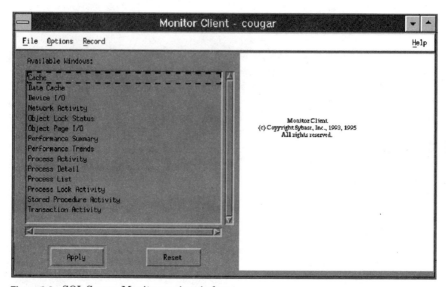

Figure 8.2   SQL Server Monitor main window.

collected, using that connection. An application can have any number of monitor connections, therefore having any number of related data groupings. Related data is data obtained from one monitor connection and updated at exactly the same time.

An SQL Server Monitor Client Library application defines views that specify what performance data is to be collected. Each view contains data items. Each data item consists of a data item name and a statistical type.

Some of the capabilities offered by SQL Server Monitor Client Library include

- Full access to performance data

- Flexibility in the definition of the performance data

- A single consistent interface, independent of the type or version of the server

- User-defined filters on performance data

- User-defined alarms on performance data

8.1.3 Implementation

The SQL Server Monitor is available for the IBM RS/6000, HP 9000/800/700, SunOS, and Sun Solaris as well as several other platforms. The SQL Server Monitor Client is available for AIX, Sun's SunOS and Solaris, and Microsoft Windows.

8.2 Monitoring SQL Server

Prior to the release of System 11, Sybase did not provide much help with monitoring the SQL Server engine. Sybase now provides SQL Server Monitor free of charge with System 11. Another welcome addition is the introduction of the *sp_sysmon* system stored procedure which is used to display performance data. Other monitoring tools consist of several system stored procedures which will be described in this section. Specifically, the system stored procedures are

```
sp_monitor
sp_who
sp_lock
sp_spaceused
sp_reportstats
```

There are also some DBCC commands that can be used for monitoring purposes. A DBCC command summary is presented in App. G. The DBCC commands are

```
DBCC LOCK
DBCC MEMUSAGE
```

SQL Server Monitor is a graphical tool designed for performance tuning and management. It is an invaluable tool for database administrators, helping to quickly isolate problems, manage system resources, and fine-tune SQL Server engines. SQL Server Monitor is a client/server application that runs in the OSF/Motif and Microsoft Windows graphical environments.

8.2.1   SQL Server activity

SQL Server uses a series of predefined global variables to keep track of dataserver activity. Global variables are distinguished from local variables by two @ signs preceding their names. Some of the SQL Server global variables are listed in Table 8.1.

The global variables can be queried directly by using ISQL or some other front-end query tool. To query the global variables:

```
1> select @@cpu_busy, @@io_busy
2> go

------      ------
  45           0
(1 row affected)
```

TABLE 8.1   Global Variables and Their Meanings

Global variable	Meaning
@@cpu_busy	The number of seconds in CPU time that SQL Server's CPU was doing SQL Server work
@@error	Contains the latest error number generated by the system
@@io_busy	The number of seconds in CPU time that SQL Server has spent doing input and output operations
@@idle	The number of seconds in CPU time that SQL Server has been idle
@@packets_received	The number of input packets read by SQL Server
@@packets_sent	The number of output packets written by SQL Server
@@packet_errors	The number of errors detected by SQL Server while reading and writing packets
@@procid	Contains the ID of the currently executing stored procedure
@@rowcount	The number of rows affected by the last command
@@servername	The name of this SQL Server (set by using the *sp_addserver* system procedure)
@@trancount	The number of currently active transactions for the current user
@@version	The version string of SQL Server

The *sp_monitor* system procedure displays the current values of some of the global variables, and how much they have changed since the system procedure was last run. A system procedure table called *spt_monitor* is used to store results from the most recent execution.

The *sp_monitor* procedure accepts no parameters. Only a system administrator has permission to run *sp_monitor*. The following output is from the *sp_monitor* system procedure:

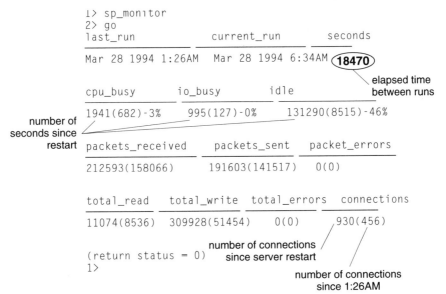

```
1> sp_monitor
2> go
last_run                current_run             seconds

Mar 28 1994 1:26AM   Mar 28 1994 6:34AM    18470
                                                        elapsed time
                                                        between runs
cpu_busy          io_busy          idle

1941(682)-3%      995(127)-0%      131290(8515)-46%
                                                        number of
                                                        seconds since
                                                        restart
packets_received      packets_sent      packet_errors

212593(158066)        191603(141517)    0(0)


total_read      total_write    total_errors   connections

11074(8536)     309928(51454)    0(0)         930(456)

                        number of connections
(return status = 0)     since server restart
1>
                                      number of connections
                                      since 1:26AM
```

- each column is printed in the form *number(number)-number%*
the first number refers to the number of seconds (or total number) since SQL Server was restarted
the second number (the number in parentheses) refers to the number of seconds (or total number) since sp_monitor was last run
the last number is the percent of time since sp_monitor was last run

Each column is printed in the form *number(number)-number%*. The first number refers to the number of seconds, or total number, since SQL Server was started. The second number, the number in parentheses, refers to the number of seconds or total number since *sp_monitor* was last run. The percentage (*number%*) is the percentage of time since *sp_monitor* was last run.

8.2.2 Determining who is logged into a server

The system procedure *sp_who* is used to report information on current users and processes on the SQL Server. The syntax is

```
sp_who [loginName | 'spid']
```

for example,

```
sp_who '18'
```

The *loginName* parameter is the server user's log-in name. The *spid* argument is used to provide the number of a specific SQL Server process. Both parameters are optional.

If no parameters are specified, the procedure will report on all active SQL Server processes. When a log-in name is provided, *sp_who* will report information on all active processes being run by the specified user. Here is an example of the output generated by *sp_who:*

```
1> sp_who
2> go
spid  status     loginame  hostname blk dbname   cmd
----  --------   --------  ----------- ------ -------  ------------
1     running    gwa       enterprise  0      master   SELECT
2     sleeping   NULL                  0      master   NETWORK HANDLER
3     sleeping   NULL                  0      master   DEADLOCK TUNE
4     sleeping   NULL                  0      master   MIRROR HANDLER
5     sleeping   NULL                  0      master   HOUSEKEEPER
6     sleeping   NULL                  0      master   SHUTDOWN HANDLER
7     sleeping   NULL                  0      master   CHECKPOINT SLEEP
8     sleeping   NULL                  0      master   AUDIT PROCESS
9     running    era       starship    0      pubs2    SELECT
10    lock sleep jf        lego        9      pubs2    SELECT
```

For each process being run, *sp_who* reports the *server process identifier* (SPID), its status (running, sleeping), the log-in name of the process user, the name of the host computer, the server process ID of any process that's blocking this one (0 if none), the current database, and the command being run. A blocking process is one that is holding server resources that another process needs. The procedure obtains information by querying the *master.dbo.sysprocesses* table.

If a server user's command is being blocked by locks held by another process (see SPID 10 in the preceding example), the following conditions are true:

- The *status* column shows "lock sleep."

- The *blk* column shows the server process ID of the process that is holding the lock or locks. In the example, SPID 9 is the blocking process.

Common values for the *status* column are presented in Table 8.2.

TABLE 8.2 **Process Status and Description**

Process status	Description
running	The server process is running.
runnable	The task can run, but there is no engine available to run the task. The task is waiting in the runnable task queue.
sleeping	The task is waiting for a resource to post network or disk I/O.
recv sleep	The task is sleeping, waiting on a network read.
send sleep	The task is sleeping, waiting on a network send.
alarm sleep	The task is sleeping, waiting on an alarm, such as WAITFOR TIME 22:00.
lock sleep	The task is sleeping, waiting on a lock acquisition.
log sleep	Task is waiting for space in the transaction log; the process has been placed in a sleep state because the transaction log is full.
background	Task is executing as a background task; tasks initiated when a threshold is crossed are executed as background tasks.
bad status	The task is not reporting a valid status.
infected	The task is in the process of printing a stack trace and terminating.

SQL Server uses special kernel processes for internal tasks. Those processes are visible in the output from *sp_who:*

- AUDIT PROCESS. This is used if SQL Server auditing is installed and enabled.
- CHECKPOINT SLEEP. It is responsible for database checkpoint commands.
- DEADLOCK TUNE. The DEADLOCK TUNE service task is used to handle changes made to the *deadlock checking period* server configuration variable. This service task provides a context to set or modify alarms. If deadlock checking is deferred, it is initiated by an *alarm handler routine.*
- HOUSEKEEPER. This is the housekeeper service task.
- MIRROR HANDLER. It is used if disk mirroring is active.
- NETWORK HANDLER. This is responsible for SQL Server network I/O.
- SHUTDOWN HANDLER, It is used to initiate an SQL Server SHUTDOWN.
- SITE HANDLER. It is used if SQL Server remote procedure calls are enabled.

The *checkpoint* process is a special SQL Server process that "wakes up" approximately once a minute. It checks each database on the server to see how may rows have been written to the transaction log since the last checkpoint. Using this information, the checkpoint handler can estimate the time required to recover these transactions. If this time estimate is greater than the database's recovery interval (set with the *sp_configure* stored procedure), SQL Server issues a checkpoint.

8.2.3 SQL Server lock activity

Monitoring lock activity and resource contention in a database management system (DBMS) is always a concern for the system administrator. The *sp_lock* system procedure reports information on all processes that currently hold locks. The syntax of *sp_lock* is

```
sp_lock [spid1 [, spid2]]
```

for example,

```
sp_lock 12, 15
```

The *spid1* parameter is an optional parameter used to indicate an SQL Server process ID number. The SPID is found in *master.dbo.sysprocesses* and can be found by using the *sp_who* procedure. If the parameter is not supplied, information on all locks will be displayed. The *spid2* parameter is another SQL Server process to be checked for lock activity.

If *sp_lock* is called with no parameters, it will display information on all locks currently held by SQL Server. Here is a sample report created by *sp_lock:*

```
1> sp_lock
2> go
spid  locktype       table_id     page   dbname  class

1     Ex_intent      1308713927   0      master  Non cursor lock
1     Ex_page        1308713927   932    master  Non cursor lock
5     Ex_page        144008374    1440   prism   Non cursor lock
5     Sh_page        144008374    1440   prism   Non cursor lock
5     Sh_table       144008374    0      prism   Non cursor lock
5     Update_page    144008374    1440   prism   Non cursor lock
12    Ex_table       240012931    0      testdb  Non cursor lock
12    Sh_intent      112003284    0      testdb  Non cursor lock
12    Ex_intent-blk  124103284    352    testdb  Cursor Id 123912
15    Ex_table       312312931    0      testdb  Non cursor lock
15    Sh_intent      124103284    0      testdb  my_cursor
15    Ex_intent-blk  124103284    0      testdb  Non cursor lock
```

The *class* column will display:

- the name of the cursor for locks associated with a cursor
- the cursor id for a lock on a cursor owned by another user
- otherwise 'Non cursor lock'

The *locktype* column is used to provide information about the lock. A shared lock has an *Sh_* prefix while an exclusive lock has an *Ex_* prefix. The *locktype* column also identifies an *update* lock and whether it is held on a table (*table* or *intent*) or on a *page*. There is no row-level locking in SQL Server; any attempt to lock a row will lock the page that the row is in. An *intent* lock indicates the intention to acquire a shared or exclusive lock on a data page. In the example above, process 12 is waiting to acquire a lock on the table identified by object ID 112003284; the name of the object can be found by using the *object_name()* function. An intent lock blocks other users from acquiring an exclusive lock on the table that contains that page.

A *-blk* suffix indicates that this process is blocking another process which needs to acquire a lock. When this process completes, the other blocked process or processes will be added to the runnable task queue and will move forward. It is easy to find the process that is being blocked by running the *sp_who* system procedure.

A *-demand* suffix indicates that this process will acquire an exclusive lock when all shared locks are released. A *demand* lock prevents any more shared locks from being issued. Demand locks are necessary because shared locks can overlap, allowing read transactions to block a write transaction indefinitely. After it waits on several different read transactions, a write transaction is given a demand lock. As soon as the existing read transactions finish, the write transaction is allowed to proceed. All new read transactions will have to wait for the write transaction to complete.

Generally, read operations acquire shared locks, and write operations acquire exclusive locks. *Update* locks are created at the page level (SQL Server does not support row-level locking) and are acquired at the start of an UPDATE operation when the pages are being read. Later in the transaction, if the pages are changed, update locks are promoted to exclusive locks.

To summarize the lock types:

- *Shared* and *exclusive* locks can be acquired at the table and/or row level, on a data page, or on an index page.

- *Update* locks are created at the page level and are acquired by an UPDATE operation when pages are being read.

- *Intent* locks indicate the intention to acquire a shared or exclusive lock on a data page.

- *Extent* locks are held on a group of eight database pages while they are being allocated or deallocated. Extent locks are typically acquired by a CREATE or DROP command (e.g., CREATE TABLE/INDEX) or while an INSERT operation requires new data or index pages.

- *Demand* locks prevent any more shared locks from being set so that a write transaction can proceed.

SQL Server Monitor. The SQL Server Monitor Object Lock Status screen is shown in Fig. 8.3. Information provided includes the database name, object name, lock type, server process ID (SPID), and server log-in name of the lock owner.

DBCC. The DBCC LOCK keyword is used to display information about active SQL Server locks. DBCC LOCK displays more information about active locks than the *sp_lock* system procedure. The form of the statement is

```
DBCC LOCK
```

Here is a simulated example and a comparison to *sp_lock:*

```
1> use tempdb
2> go
1> create table #junk(pk int not null, name char(30) not null)
2> go
1> insert #junk values(1,'george')
2> go
(1 row affected)
1> insert #junk values(2,'patrick')
2> go
(1 row affected)
1> begin tran
2> go
1> select * from #junk holdlock where pk=1
2> go
pk    name

      1 george

(1 row affected)
1> sp_lock
2> go
```
The class column will display the cursor name for locks associated with a cursor for the current user and the cursor id for other users.
```
spid  locktype     table_id    page    dbname      class

  9   Sh_intent    384004399    0 master      Non Cursor lock
  9   Ex_table     384004399    0 tempdb      Non Cursor lock

(2 rows affected, return status = 0)
1>

1> dbcc lock
2> go
```

LOCKS: lock is on database id 2 (tempdb)
TABLE LOCKS   lock has been granted

```
dbe10094 Objid 383004399, dbid 2 (2)  ucket 74)
dbe106ec  swatatus=(), swskipped=0, swsemaphore=0xdbe10094
dbe117fc   lrspid=(9) ype=(ex_tab) emawait=0xdbe106ec, lrstatus=(granted), lrsuffclass=0
PAGE LOCKS
ADDRESS LOCKS                        lock type us 'exclusive table'
SEMAPHORES              SYBASE process ID (as seen with sp_who)
```

DBCC execution completed. If DBCC printed error messages, contact a user with System Administrator (SA) role.
```
1>
```

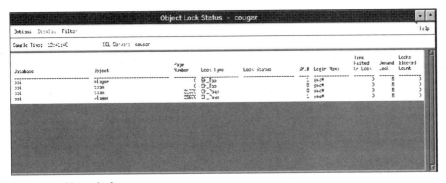

Figure 8.3 Object lock status.

8.2.4 System activity reports

One of the features of the System 10 and System 11 SQL Server is the ability to track CPU and I/O usage for each server user. Prior to the release of System 10, this facility was only available with the VMS implementation of SYBASE. Sybase calls this feature *charge-back accounting*.

When a user logs into the SQL Server, the server begins to accumulate information about CPU and I/O usage. Information for each server user is maintained in the *master.dbo.syslogins* table. Statistics information is accumulated in memory, and two configuration variables are responsible for controlling the frequency of table updates. The configuration variables are *cpu flush* and *i/o flush*. See Sec. 7.5.3 for more information.

Usage statistics are not maintained for any process with a server user ID of 1. This includes all SA accounts as well as the special kernel processes (e.g., CHECKPOINT, NETWORK, MIRROR) discussed in the previous section. Two system procedures are available to manipulate usage statistics:

```
sp_reportstats
sp_clearstats
```

The *sp_reportstats* system procedure is used to display statistics on system usage. The form of *sp_reportstats* is

```
sp_reportstats [userName]
```

The *username* parameter is optional. If the user name is not provided, statistics will be displayed for all server users. Here is the output from *sp_reportstats:*

```
1> sp_reportstats
2> go
Name            Since        CPU     Percent    CPU I/O   Percent I/O
------------    ---------    ------   -------    -------   -------
sa              Jan 1 1900   0        0.0000%    0         0.0000%
probe           Feb 23 1995  0        0.0000%    0         0.0000%
gwa             Feb 23 1995  0        0.0000%    0         0.0000%
elvee           Mar 1 1995   269      1.0942%    853       5.0194%
rssd_user       Apr 29 1995  24199    98.4379%   12509     73.6083%
prism_maint     Apr 29 1995  115      0.4678%    3632      21.3722%

(6 rows affected)
 Total CPU    Total I/O
 ---------    -----------
   24583         16994

(1 row affected, return status = 0)
```

The *sp_clearstats* procedure is used to initiate a new accounting period (i.e., to clear the statistics for a user or all users). The form of *sp_clearstats* is

```
sp_clearstats [userName]
```

Again, the *userName* parameter is optional. If a user name is not provided, *sp_clearstats* will clear the statistics for all server users.

8.2.5 SQL Server Monitor

The SYBASE SQL Server Monitor is an excellent tool used for server monitoring. SQL Server Monitor provides performance data including

- Memory allocation
- Data and procedure cache effectiveness
- Database device activity
- Transaction activity
- Lock activity and contention
- Network traffic
- User processes

Lock activity and contention. The SQL Server Monitor Performance Trends window can be used to display information about SQL Server lock activity including

- *Lock request rate.* This is the rate at which SQL Server received lock requests, independent of lock type.
- *Lock hit rate.* This is the ratio of lock requests granted to total lock requests. The lock hit rate is used to indicate contention.

Figure 8.4 illustrates the SQL Server Monitor Performance Trends window.

The Performance Summary window can be used to illustrate locks requested and granted, by type. The lock types reported are

- *sh_page:*   shared page lock
- *sh_int:*   shared intent; intention to acquire a shared lock
- *sh_tab:*   shared table lock
- *up_page:*   update page; UPDATE operation wants to lock a page

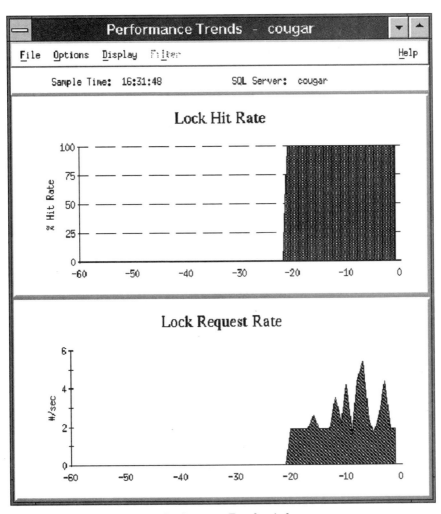

Figure 8.4   SQL Server Monitor Performance Trends window.

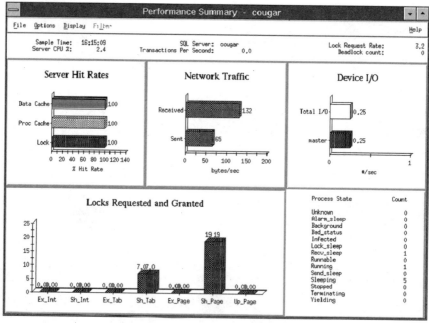

Figure 8.5   SQL Server Monitor Performance Summary window.

- *ex_page:*   exclusive page lock
- *ex_int:*   exclusive intent; intent to acquire an exclusive lock
- *ex_tab:*   exclusive table lock

The Performance Summary window also includes information on server hit rates, network traffic, device I/O, lock requests, and network traffic. The Performance Summary window is shown in Fig. 8.5.

The Process Lock Activity window is used to report the number of lock requests made by each server user. See Fig. 8.6.

User connections.   SQL Server Monitor provides three windows that are used to display information about active SQL Server user connections:

1. Process List
2. Process Detail
3. Process Activity

The Process List window lists all currently active SQL Server processes. This is like a real-time, graphical *sp_who* with information being obtained from the *master.dbo.sysprocesses* table. The Process

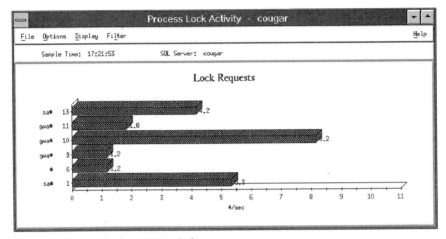

Figure 8.6   Process Lock Activity window.

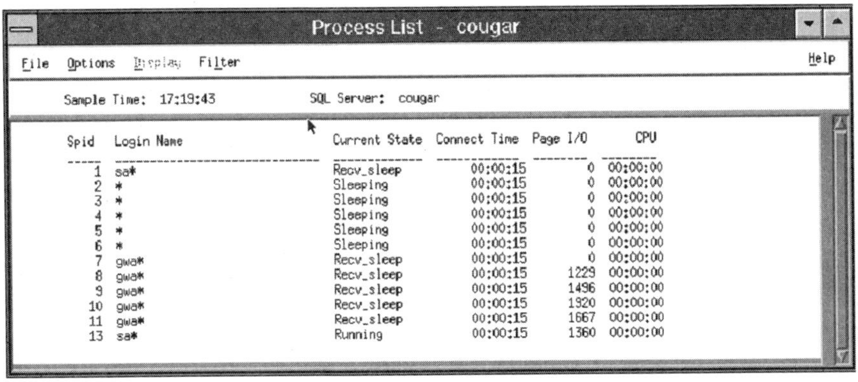

Figure 8.7   Process List window.

List window (see Fig. 8.7) can be used to provide a quick overview of SQL Server process activity.

The Process Detail window (see Fig. 8.8) is used to display information about a specific SQL Server connection. Detailed information is displayed for one process at a time. Process details include

- The name and SQL Server process ID (SPID) of the selected process

- The connect time or time elapsed since the process connected to the SQL Server

- The current state of the process (e.g., running, sleeping).

- The number of the engine on which the process was running as of the most recent sample interval (This is provided for SMP environments; uniprocessor servers will only have engine 0.)

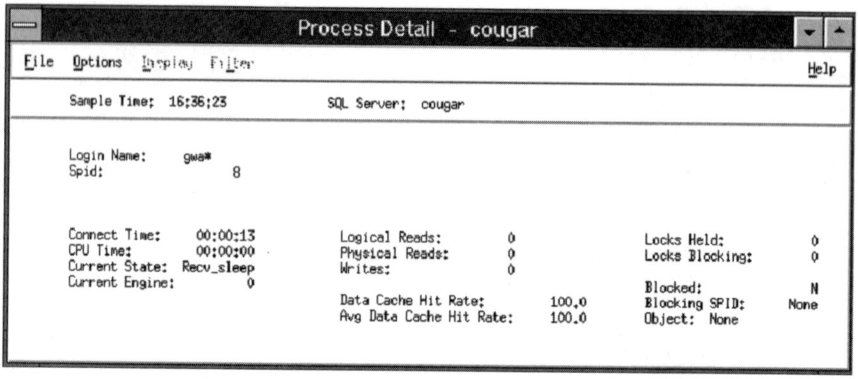

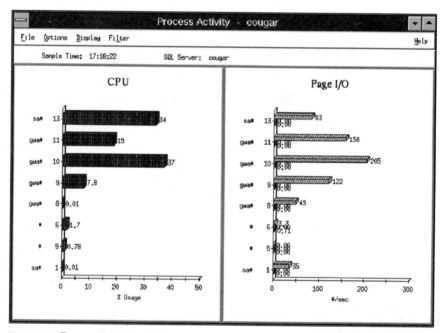

Figure 8.8 Process Detail window.

Figure 8.9 Process Activity window.

- The amount of SQL Server CPU ticks the process used since the window was opened
- Page I/O—logical reads, physical reads, and writes for the process accumulated since the Process Detail window was opened

The Process Activity window (see Fig. 8.9) consists of graphs displaying CPU rate and page I/O rate for as many as 20 user processes.

SQL Server Monitor selects the processes to monitor by using user-specified filtering criteria. This window allows the administrator to visually compare the way processes are using SQL Server resources. Processes can be selected by name and rate of activity in a specific performance indicator, or with a rate of activity equal to or greater than a specific threshold.

8.2.6   Killing SQL Server processes

It is sometimes necessary to terminate a user process being serviced by the SQL Server. The most common reasons for this are that

- The process is blocking another process which needs to acquire a lock.
- The process is delaying a SHUTDOWN command issued by the system administrator.

A user process is terminated with the KILL statement. The form of the KILL statement is

```
KILL spid
```

The *spid* parameter is the server process ID of a process to be killed. Parameter *spid* must be a constant; it cannot be a parameter passed to a stored procedure or a local variable.

The server process ID can be identified by running the *sp_who* system procedure. Generally, the SA can kill most of the SQL Server user processes. However, the KILL statement may not always succeed, as illustrated below.

```
1> sp_who '21'
2> go

spid    status    loginame    hostname blk    dbname    cmd
----    -------   --------    -----------    ----    -------  --------
  21    sleeping  elvee       searay         0       forty    WAITFOR
1> kill 21
2> go

Msg 6108, Level 16, State 0:
Server 'enterprise', Line 1:
Process '21' is not sleeping under a valid KILL condition, and therefore
cannot
be KILLed.
1>
```

8.3   The *syslogshold* Table

Here's a new feature that many SQL Server administrators will appreciate! The *syslogshold* table is designed to improve the usability and reliability of SQL Server by providing information about long-running transactions. A single long-running transaction can cripple even the most reliable database system. The system may utilize the most expensive RAID systems, mirrored database devices, and high-availability hardware, but database activity can be stopped by issuing one simple command:

```
1> begin tran
2> go
go to lunch...
```

This prevents the transaction log from being truncated with the DUMP TRANSACTION command. The transaction log will continue to grow because SQL Server cannot dump the inactive portion of the transaction log. Not even the *truncate log on checkpoint* database option can help this situation.

Long-running transactions are usually the result of application errors or poor programming practices but can also be caused by network, operating system, or SQL Server problems. The administrator must detect the presence of these transactions before they become problematic.

If the long-running transaction is caused by a runaway query or by user interaction within a query (as represented by the preceding simple example), the KILL command can be used to terminate the process. If the transaction cannot be identified or if the KILL command cannot stop the process, long-running transactions can be cleared by recycling SQL Server. This causes the automatic recovery process to detect the BEGIN TRANSACTION with no matching COMMIT TRANSACTION, so the outstanding transaction will be rolled back.

When one is monitoring a System 10 or earlier SQL Server, there is no easy way to identify the oldest outstanding transaction (and its owner) in a database. There are actually some undocumented DBCC commands that can be used to find the information, but these commands are not supported by Sybase.

The *syslogshold* table is a "fake table" (similar to the *sysprocesses* table) built by the SQL Server engine in the *master* database when it is queried by the user. The *syslogshold* table can be queried to identify which process owns the oldest outstanding transaction.

```
1> select * from master.dbo.syslogshold
2> go
dbid    reserved      spid    page     xactid          masterxactid
----    --------      ----    ----     -----------     ----------------
        starttime                      name
        --------------------           ------------
9        0             7      115805   0x0001c45d000e  0x0002ea060010
        Nov 4 1995 6:40AM             $ins
5        0             7      190982   0x0002ea060010  0x000000000000
        Nov 4 1995 6:40AM             $user_transaction
(2 rows affected)
```

A row is kept in the *syslogshold* table for the oldest active transaction in each database. An *active* transaction is defined as a transaction that has written at least one record to the database's transaction log and has not yet completed. Given this definition, there will not be an entry for a transaction that has only log records in the private log cache (PLC). A given database will have zero, one, or two rows. If the database is being replicated, there may be a row for the Replication Server truncation point in the transaction log. A database will have one row for an active transaction or replication and two rows if both are active. This allows the administrator to determine what is holding the transaction log: Replication Server or an active transaction. The *syslogshold* table can be monitored by a DBA or system administrator, or possibly in a last-chance threshold stored procedure. Table 8.3 describes the *syslogshold* table.

System-supplied transaction names (and possible values for *syslogshold.name*) for SQL Server Release 11.0 and Replication Server are represented in Table 8.4. All system-generated transaction names start with the $ sign.

The following query can be used to obtain information about the application and transaction name for a process blocking log truncation.

TABLE 8.3   Columns in *syslogshold* Table and Their Meanings

Column name	Data type (size in bytes)	Meaning for outstanding transaction	Meaning for Replication Server
dbid	smallint	Database ID of transaction—unused	Database ID
reserved	int	Unused	Unused
spid	smallint	Server process ID (SPID) of user owning transaction	0
page	int	Starting page number of active portion of transaction log (*syslog*)	Log Transfer Manager (LTM) truncation page in transaction log (*syslog*)
xactid	binary(6)	Transaction ID	0
masterxactid	binary(6)	ID of master transaction if this is a multidatabase transaction; otherwise, 0	0
starttime	datetime	Time transaction started	Time transaction point set
name	char(67)	Name of transaction	$replication_truncation point

TABLE 8.4   **System-Supplied Transaction Names**

User command	Transaction name	Transaction name generated by Replication Server
BEGIN TRAN	$user_transaction	user_transaction
BEGIN TRAN name	name	name
INSERT ... with no BEGIN TRAN	$ins	ins

```
1> select p.hostname, p.hostprocess, p.program_name, h.name, h.starttime
   from master..sysprocesses p, master..syslogshold h
   where p.spid = h.spid
   and h.dbid = db_id()      /* db_id() returns ID of current database */
   and h.spid != 0
2> go
hostname    hostprocess    program_name    name    starttime
---------   ------------   --------------   ------  ----------------
elvee       416            isql             gwa     Dec 24 1995 2:07PM
```

9

Memory

The total amount of system memory and its efficient use by the operating system and by SYBASE contribute dramatically to the overall performance and throughput of the server platform. It is important to understand the implications of memory allocations and how much memory is used by the various SQL Server data structures.

This chapter provides an overview of virtual memory implementation and how to monitor virtual memory utilization on systems based on UNIX and Windows NT. Additionally, information is provided on SQL Server memory and the data and procedure caches. Section 9.4 covers named cache implementation, usage, and monitoring. SQL Server Monitor, the cache analysis tool, system stored procedures, and DBCC commands are discussed.

9.1 Virtual Memory

Most UNIX operating systems, Microsoft Windows, and Microsoft Windows NT use what is known as *virtual memory*. Virtual memory gives a user program the illusion that the entire range of memory that the CPU can address belongs to that program. This means that a program is not restricted by the amount of physical memory that is installed in the host machine. The UNIX operating system implements virtual memory using user-configurable *swap* space, while Windows NT uses a *paging file.*

Physical memory is treated somewhat as a database *cache* and contains frequently used or recently used blocks of memory. The hardware will detect an attempt to access a page that is not in memory, find the corresponding disk block for the data, read it into memory, and allow the user program to continue with its access. The user program contin-

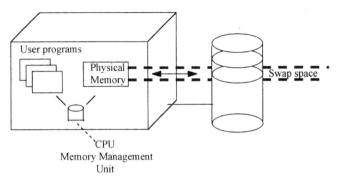

Figure 9.1 Virtual memory management.

ues to run as if nothing happened (albeit slower due to the disk access-es). The hardware performs translations on the *virtual addresses* speci-fied by the program and maps them into the addresses of real physical memory. Most modern CPUs rely on a memory management unit (MMU) to perform memory address translations and to signal the processor when a translation fails due to an illegal reference. Figure 9.1 depicts virtual memory management on a UNIX-based system.

Paging and swapping. Physical memory is usually organized in terms of fixed-size *pages* so that it can be easily manipulated. For example, Sun's Solaris operating system manages memory using 2K pages while IBM's AIX uses 4K pages, and the page size for Intel-based Windows NT systems is 4K (8K for DEC Alpha processors). The virtu-al memory processing in the kernel consists of managing physical memory as a collection of pages. The kernel will hold as much of a user process in memory as possible, then the kernel will attempt to store some pages out to disk until those pages are needed again. As men-tioned earlier, this is done by using swap space or a paging file. After swapping has become necessary, the kernel will keep most recently used pages in memory. *Paging* involves moving parts of an application or process out to secondary storage (swap space). *Swapping* occurs when entire processes are copied from memory to secondary storage.

Memory inside most UNIX kernels is known as *kernel* memory and is "nailed down," meaning that it cannot be swapped out of physical memory. User memory can be swapped to disk at any time (based on kernel algorithms) so that the pages can be reused for another task or process. As discussed in Chap. 7, SQL Server provides a configuration option that can be used to lock shared memory into physical memory on platforms that support it. This disallows swapping of SQL Server pages to disk.

The job of the SYBASE system administrator is to ensure that memory structures used by SYBASE can fit into real memory. Swap space utilization is typically monitored by operating-system-dependent utilities. For example, the swap command can be used to monitor the system swap areas used by the memory manager in a Solaris system. The following is output from the Solaris *swap* command:

```
% swap -s
total: 41604k bytes allocated + 4880k reserved = 46484k used, 33796k
available
```

The *-s* parameter is used to print summary information about total swap space usage and availability.

Windows NT.   Microsoft Windows NT provides several tools to monitor memory activity and paging. The first is the Windows NT diagnostics facility. This facility is used to view information about physical memory and paging-file space, as shown in Fig. 9.2. The *memory load index* for the system at this point is 86 percent. The reader should also note that approximately 20 Mbytes of paging space is currently in use and that there are only 4 Mbytes of physical memory available. It is easy to see that this system would benefit from the installation of additional memory.

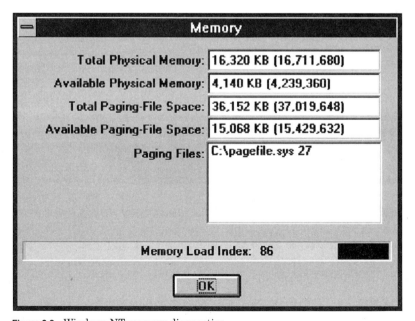

Figure 9.2 Windows NT memory diagnostics.

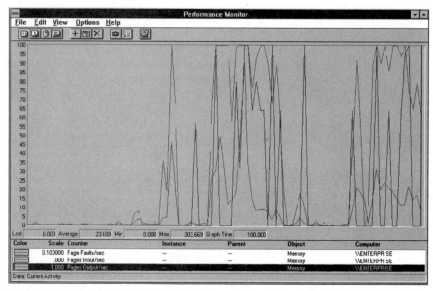

Figure 9.3   Windows NT Performance Monitor.

The second tool provided by Windows NT is the *Performance Monitor.* The Performance Monitor can be used to monitor activity such as cache, logical disk, memory, network, paging file, physical disk, and several other types of object activity. Each category (e.g., memory) has several subcategories or *counters* which can be added to the display. For example, the display in Fig. 9.3 contains page faults per second, pages input per second, and pages output per second. Again, it is easy to see that this system would benefit from the installation of additional physical memory. The Windows NT Performance Monitor can also be used to view paging-file activity including % Usage and % Usage Peak. The graph in Fig. 9.4 shows a system with high paging activity, indicated by % Usage of approximately 60 to 70.

Virtual memory statistics—UNIX.   The *vmstat* command is commonly used to display information about virtual memory activity in a UNIX system. Command syntax varies between host operating systems, so check the UNIX *man* page for command options. On a Sun Solaris system, when *vmstat* is called with no options, it displays a one-line summary of virtual memory activity since the system was booted.

```
% vmstat
procs memory            page           disk      faults      cpu
 r b w  swap   free  re mf pi po fr de sr f0 s3 -- --  in  sy  cs us sy id
 0 0 0  32968   860   0  0  0  0  0  0  0  0  0 --  0  49 238  96  0  0 99
```

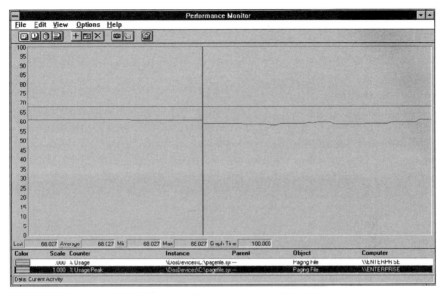

Figure 9.4 Windows NT Performance Monitor—paging-file activity.

The -*S* option is used to report on swapping rather than paging activity. Note that the *re* (page reclaims) and *mf* (minor faults) fields shown above have been replaced by *si* (swap-ins) and *so* (swap-outs).

```
% vmstat -S
procs memory           page            disk       faults      cpu
 r b w   swap   free  si so pi po fr de sr f0 s3 -- --  in  sy   cs us sy id
 0 0 0  32968   860   0  0  0  0  0  0  0  0  0 --  0  49 238   96  0  0 99
```

The *r, b,* and *w* fields indicate the number of processes in the run queue, number of processes blocked for resources, and the number runnable but swapped. The *pi* (kilobytes paged-in) and *po* (kilobytes paged-out) fields indicate that virtual memory activity in this system is nil.

The Solaris *perfmeter* can also be used to monitor system activity including system load, CPU, disk, paging, swap, packets, network collisions, and several other categories of activity.

Page faults. In simple terms, a *page fault* is a reference to data that is not presently in memory. A page fault occurs when a program tries to reference a memory address and the translation step performed by the memory management unit indicates an error. When this happens, the CPU is interrupted in the middle of the instruction (because it cannot access the memory address). This generally happens because there is no valid page in memory to reference. It then becomes the responsibility of the operating system kernel to decide whether the referenced page is valid (i.e., the page exists on disk somewhere) or is an illegal reference. If the memory address is valid, the kernel must read the page from disk into memory and let the offending instruction run again. If it is an illegal reference, the operating system will normally kill the program.

The administrator should never allow the SQL Server to page-fault. It is better to configure SQL Server with less memory and do more physical database I/Os than to allow the dataserver to page-fault. Operating system page faults are synchronous and stop the dataserver engine until the page fault completes. Because database I/Os are asynchronous, other user tasks can continue to run when the dataserver is performing physical I/Os.

9.2   More on SQL Server Memory

Proper memory configuration can be the single most important factor affecting SQL Server performance. For example, I was asked to troubleshoot an SQL Server 10 installation because of significant performance problems. The customer had recently upgraded from SQL Server Version 4.9.2 to System 10 and was experiencing poor performance. It turned out that the problem was very simple. The installer had never reconfigured the total memory available to SQL Server. The host UNIX platform had 128 Mbytes of RAM, but SQL Server was only using 7500 pages!

When tuning memory and ensuring that there is sufficient memory available in the machine, keep in mind that memory is required for user-configurable parameters, as shown in Table 9.1.

The worksheet listed in Table 9.2 can be used to determine the approximate amount of memory required for a particular configuration.

The bottom line? The more memory that is available, the more resources SQL Server has for its internal catalog structures, page, and procedure caches. Obviously, this reduces the necessity to perform physical disk I/Os to read data or compile procedure plans from disk and results in improved overall performance.

9.3   Data and Procedure Cache

As discussed in Chap. 7, the memory that remains after SQL Server allocates memory for internal structures and the server code is split between the procedure cache and the data cache. The procedure cache is used for query plans, stored procedures, triggers, and views. The data or page cache is used for data, index, and log pages.

TABLE 9.1 Configuration Variables that Use Significant Memory

Object	Default value	Bytes per resource (approximate)	Memory required (kbytes—approximate)
User connections	25	23,552 + stack size*	1325
Database devices	10	45,056	440
Open databases	12	644 bytes	8
Open objects	500	315 bytes	154
Locks	5000	32 bytes	156
Audit queue size		424 bytes?	
Default network packet size	512	3 times number of user connections times default network packet size	38
Extent I/O buffers	0	8 pages (16K on most platforms)	0
Procedure cache	20	Percentage of leftover memory	—

*The stack size is configurable, as discussed in Chap. 7; the default is 30,720 bytes.

TABLE 9.2 Memory Worksheet for System 11 Running on Solaris 2.5.*

Category of memory use	Value (approximate)
SQL Server executable size:[†]	3.51 + Mbytes
Static overhead	1 + Mbytes
User connections:[‡]	
Stack size @ 30,720 bytes × user connections	768,000 bytes
Stack guard area @ 4096 bytes × user connections	102,400 bytes
(Default network packet size × 3) × user connections	38,400 bytes
Number of open databases	7,728 bytes
Number of locks	160,000 bytes
Number of devices	450,560 bytes
Size of procedure cache	4,842 kbytes
Size of data cache	16,314 kbytes
Size of buffers used for extent I/O buffers	0
Additional network memory	0
Total memory:	

*Total configured server memory is 32 Mbytes.

[†]SQL Server executable size can be determined with the DBCC MEMUSAGE command, as illustrated in Sec. 7.1. This example is based on a System 11 dataserver running on Solaris 2.x.

[‡]*User connections* are based on the default value of 25. The default value of 512 is used for *default network packet size*.

Procedure cache. The procedure cache holds internal structures for rules, stored procedures, and triggers, i.e., anything that is compiled. The larger the procedure cache, the less chance the server will have to reread from disk any triggers, rules, and so on.

The procedure cache is an MRU/LRU (most recently used/least recently used) chain and is a circular, double-linked list. SQL Server also maintains an MRU/LRU chain of stored procedure query plans. As users execute stored procedures, the dataserver looks for a query plan in the procedure cache. If a query plan is available, it is placed on the *MRU side* of the chain, and execution begins.

If a plan is not available or all plans are currently in use, the server must read the query tree for the procedure from the *sysprocedures* table. The query tree is then optimized and placed on the MRU side of the chain, and execution begins. Plans at the LRU side of the page chain that are not in use are aged out of the procedure cache and discarded.

It is important to note that stored procedure code is not reentrant. What this means is that if several users are executing a single stored procedure, there may be several plans for that same stored procedure in the procedure cache at any given time. The stored procedure plan cannot be shared.

Data cache. When SQL Server is first installed, it has a single data cache (the *default data cache*) which is used by all SQL Server processes and objects for data, index, and log pages. Named data caches are used to increase SQL Server performance by dividing the data cache into multiple named caches. Section 9.4, "Named Data Caches," describes the process of creating and configuring named caches, and how to bind objects to these named caches.

The data cache is an MRU/LRU chain and is a circular, double-linked list. Objects typically found in the data cache include

- The system tables for each database including *sysobjects* and *sysindexes*
- Frequently accessed tables
- The higher levels (and portions of the lower levels) of frequently accessed indexes
- Hot or active log pages for each database

As pages in the cache are aged, they enter the wash area where dirty pages are flushed to disk. There are some exceptions to the MRU/LRU strategy:

- *Index pages and OAM pages.* Index and OAM pages are aged out more slowly than data pages. These pages are accessed frequently, so keeping them in cache reduces the necessity of physical reads. This behavior can be tuned by the system administrator using the *number of oam trips* and *number of index trips* configuration variables. These variables are used to specify the number of times that an aged index or OAM page recycles itself onto the MRU chain.

- *Checkpoint process and housekeeper task.* If the checkpoint process determines that the number of changes to a database will take longer to recover than the value of *recovery interval* (configuration parameter), dirty pages will be flushed to disk. Also, the housekeeper task may flush dirty pages to disk when idle time is available between user processes.

- *Fetch-and-discard strategy.* For queries that scan heap tables or tables with a clustered index, the query optimizer may use a cache replacement strategy that does not flush other pages out of the data cache. This prevents decision support type of queries from destroying the contents of the data cache.

The effects of time on the data cache should be fairly obvious. When the server is booted, the data cache will initially be empty. If the cache is empty, the first SELECT statement is guaranteed to generate physical disk I/O. As users execute more queries, the dataserver will try to locate data and index pages in cache before reading them from disk. As more queries are executed, the page cache is being filled, increasing the probability that page requests can be satisfied from cache. This process can be referred to as *warming up* the cache. Eventually, the page cache should reach a *steady state,* at which time there is a fixed probability of finding a page in cache from that point forward. Figure 9.5 illustrates the effects of time on the cache hit ratio.

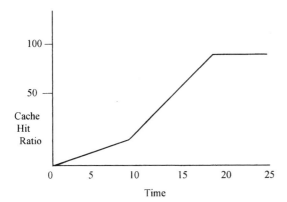

Figure 9.5 Effects of time on the cache hit ratio.

If the cache is smaller than the total number of used database pages, some queries will force the server to perform physical disk I/O. In summary, the data cache does not decrease the maximum run time for a particular query; it does, however, decrease the probability that a user will incur the maximum run time for that query.

The behavior of the data cache is complicated by update transactions. As pages in the cache are updated, there is a point at which the dataserver must begin to flush dirty pages to disk. Physical writes may be caused by the checkpoint process, the housekeeper task, or by the lack of clean pages on the LRU side of the MRU/LRU chain. In an OLTP environment, the mix of physical reads and writes will begin to stabilize over time. At this point the server has reached another steady state, with each transaction having a given probability of incurring physical writes and another probability of incurring physical reads.

SQL Server Monitor.   The effectiveness of the procedure and data caches is measured by a *cache hit ratio*. The cache hit ratio is expressed as the percentage of times the server finds a page or plan in cache. A cache hit ratio of 100 percent is optimal; however, this indicates that the data cache is as large as or larger than the data being accessed. A low percentage indicates that insufficient memory is allocated to SQL Server. Very large tables or heap tables with random access usually have a low cache hit ratio. The SQL Server Monitor Performance Trends window is used to monitor the effectiveness of the procedure and data caches, as shown in Fig. 9.6.

The *sp_sysmon* procedure.   The sp_sysmon system procedure can be used to display information about data and procedure cache management. The output is shown here:

```
= = = = = = = = = = = = = = = = = = = = = = = = = = = = = = = = = = = = = = = = =
Data Cache Management
---------------------

  Cache Statistics Summary (All Caches)
  ------- ----------------------------
    Cache Search Summary
      Total Cache Hits            0.5        30.0        30        100.0 %
      Total Cache Misses          0.0         0.0         0          0.0 %
    ------------------        ---------
      Total Cache Searches        0.5        30.0        30

    Cache Turnover
      Buffers Grabbed             0.0         0.0         0         n/a

    Cache Strategy Summary
      Cached (LRU) Buffers                                           %
      Discarded (MRU) Buffers                              %
```

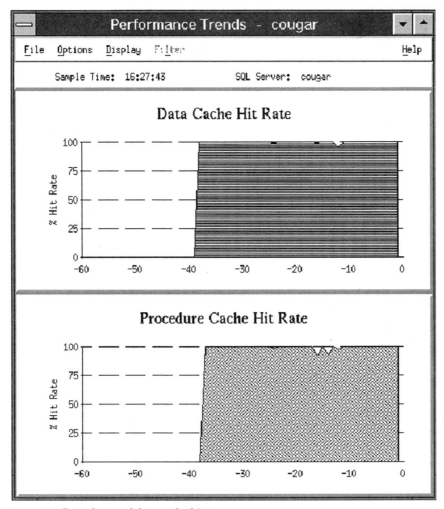

Figure 9.6   Procedure and data cache hit rates.

Large I/O Usage				
	0.0	0.0	0	n/a
Large I/O Effectiveness				
Pages by Lrg I/O Cached	0.0	0.0	0	n/a
Dirty Read Behavior				
Page Requests	0.0	0.0	0	n/a

default data cache	per sec	per xact	count %	of total
Utilization	n/a	n/a	n/a	100.0 %
Spinlock Contention	Sorry, Not Available Yet!			

```
Cache Searches
  Cache Hits                0.5        30.0       30      100.0 %
    Found in Wash           0.0         0.0        0        0.0 %
  Cache Misses              0.0         0.0        0        0.0 %
-----------------------    --------   --------   ------
  Total Cache Searches      0.5        30.0       30

Pool Turnover               0.0         0.0        0       n/a
-----------------------    --------   --------   ------
  Total Cache Turnover      0.0         0.0        0

Buffer Wash Behavior
  Statistics Not Available - No Buffers Entered Wash Section Yet!

Cache Strategy
  Cached (LRU) Buffers                                             %
  Discarded (MRU) Buffers                             %

Large I/O Usage             0.0         0.0        0       n/a

Large I/O Detail
  No Large Pool(s) In This Cache
= = = = = = = = = = = = = = = = = = = = = = = = = = = = = = = = = = = =
Procedure Cache Management  per sec    per xact   count %  of total
------------------------   --------   ---------   ---------  --------
Procedure Requests          0.0         0.0         0       n/a

= = = = = = = = = = = = = = = = = = = = = = = = = = = = = = = = = = = =
```

9.4   Named Data Caches

The *data cache* (also known as *page cache*) holds data, index, and log pages that are currently in use or have recently been used by SQL Server. As discussed in Sec. 7.2, the System 10 SQL Server uses a single data cache. When System 11 is installed, it, too, uses a single data cache. However, System 11 allows the administrator to divide the page cache by creating multiple *named data caches*. These named caches can be further divided into *pools,* which can be used to perform variable-sized I/O. The system administrator can then bind a database, table, index, text, or image object to a named data cache.

Effects on performance.   The performance potential of named caches is huge. For example, named caches give the system administrator the following capabilities:

■ Named caches can be configured to hold critical tables and indexes. This prevents other server-based activity from competing for data cache space.

■ Hot tables can be separated from their indexes to improve concurrency.

■ Index pages that are frequently accessed can be bound to a separate named cache.

- For OLTP applications, the *syslogs* table can be bound to its own cache, typically using 4K I/O.

- An entire database can be bound to a named cache. The *tempdb* database is typically assigned to its own cache.

- Named caches reduce the spinlock contention encountered when a single cache is used in an SMP environment.

- Multiple caches are also helpful on uniprocessor systems. For example, the text and image data associated with a table can be bound to another named cache. This prevents data and index pages from being replaced (aged out) in memory. Also, the named cache being used for text and image pages can be configured to use larger I/O sizes. When a single cache is used, text and image data can destroy the contents of the page cache, forcing frequently used pages to be aged out of the cache. This results in increased physical I/O in the system.

Named caches can be used to tune applications for improved performance and to improve concurrency. Note that this type of tuning is very difficult and is not a substitute for proper database design and indexing. It is easy to starve the default data cache by allocating too much memory to user-defined named caches. In fact, it is possible to *decrease* performance by splitting the default data cache into smaller caches. There is a risk that a query running well before partitioning will run poorly after partitioning, because the table no longer fits into cache (as shown in Fig. 9.7). It is also possible that owing to the growth of tables over time, a table no longer fits into the cache, creating the situation illustrated in Fig. 9.7. For this reason, it is the administrator's responsibility to monitor data cache performance on a regular and frequent basis.

Large I/Os and sequential prefetch.   The query optimizer is designed to make intelligent decisions regarding choice of I/O size. The query optimizer can also decide to use sequential prefetch for queries that

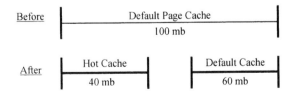

Query 1: T1 is the inner table requiring 85-mb
Query 2: T2 is the inner table requiring 70-mb

Figure 9.7 Named cache behavior.

scan large amounts of data. The System 11 optimizer can perform I/O for the same object, using different block sizes. For example, data records for a table may be retrieved using 4K I/Os while text and image data for the same table may be performed using 16K I/Os. This allows the buffer manager to make very efficient use of memory. This strategy can also be used to prevent text and image data or DSS data from displacing more critical OLTP data from cache memory.

To perform large I/Os on a table, a buffer pool must be configured for large I/Os and the table must be bound to that cache, as described later in this section. The principle behind large I/Os is simple: Large I/Os reduce the number of physical I/Os required by obtaining more data per physical I/O. A 16K pool consists of several 16K buffers that form a separate LRU/MRU chain with separate wash size configuration. Large I/Os are not suitable for all operations because pages in the buffer move together, and therefore age out of the cache at the same time. The most significant performance gains are seen in DSS, BCP, and text and image handling. Figure 9.8 illustrates the relationship of the optimizer to the buffer manager.

The default data cache and any named caches that have been created can be used for large I/Os by splitting the cache into multiple buffer pools. The default I/O size for the server is 2K (a single data page). For certain types of queries, where pages are stored sequentially, the server can read up to 8 data pages in a single I/O. This may not seem like a lot of data, and it isn't; future versions of the SQL Server should be much more aggressive with read-ahead strategies. Large I/Os can significantly reduce disk access time and increase performance for the following types of operations:

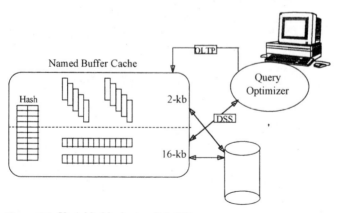

Figure 9.8 Variable block size disk I/O.

- Queries that use text or image data
- Queries that perform table scans including those that perform multi-table joins
- Queries that allocate several pages, such as SELECT INTO or INSERT INTO
- Queries that scan the leaf level of a nonclustered index
- Bulk-copy operations into or out of heap tables
- The UPDATE STATISTICS command

Buffer pools. Every named data cache contains a 2K buffer pool. The 2K buffer pool is used for internal utilities and commands such as CREATE DATABASE, CREATE INDEX, DISK INIT, DBCC, and DROP TABLE. Also, database recovery uses only the 2K memory pool. The buffer pool can be resized; however, the administrator should keep the 2K buffer pool at a reasonable size to avoid performance degradation. To better understand buffer pools and named caches, the following definitions are provided:

- *Kept chain*—the list of buffers currently in use. Any buffers present in the kept chain are not available for replacement.
- *Page*—a page of data read from disk.
- *Buffer*—composed of a buffer header and a page.
- *Buffer header*—a small header that contains information about the buffer, such as the state of the buffer, whether it is on the kept chain, and where it belongs on the MRU/LRU chain. A buffer header is linked with a page at boot time. The linking of the page and the buffer header is fixed until the SQL Server is rebooted.
- *Buffer pool*—a circular, double-linked list of 2K pages.
- *Pool size*—the total amount of memory allocated to the buffer pool.
- *Hash table*—table containing the list of buffers currently in cache. The hash table is used instead of searching the MRU/LRU chains.
- *Wash marker*—marker located in the MRU/LRU chain and used to ensure that buffers on the LRU side of the chain are either clean or in the process of being written to disk.
- *Named cache*—an instance of a buffer cache with the following characteristics: a unique name, a user-defined cache size, a user-configured buffer pool size, and cache type (e.g., *log, data,* or *mixed*). Each cache contains a hash table, a minimum of one MRU/LRU chain of 2K buffers, and the kept chain.
- *Buffer pools*—a minimum of one default 2K buffer pool per cache. There may be more than one buffer pool in a cache.

table_cache

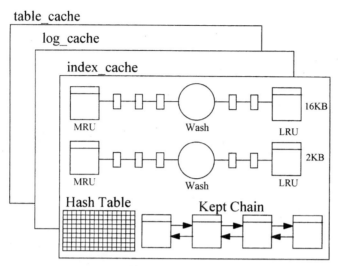

Figure 9.9   SQL Server 11.0 buffer pools.

- *Mass size*—a group of individual buffers which are treated as a single unit and used for large I/Os.

Now let's put it all together, using the diagram in Fig. 9.9. Multiple buffer pool sizes are used to achieve large I/Os. Multiple buffer pools are useful for operations that perform a large number of allocations (e.g., BCP), reading sequentially clustered data and writing data to the transaction log. There (currently) is a maximum of four buffer pools per data cache, and the available buffer pool sizes are 2K, 4K, 8K, and 16K. The current limit of 16K is due to an architectural limitation of the page manager and should be remedied in the future.

Mixing buffer pool sizes.   The administrator should mix large and small I/O sizes with caution. Note that if a requested page is already in memory, it cannot change buffer size. After the page has been flushed, the next read from disk can use a different buffer size. Let's use an example to clarify the situation. Consider Fig. 9.10. User 1 performs a SELECT, using 4K I/O. As a result, the table is resident in the 4K buffer pool. User 2 then performs a SELECT, using 16K I/O. Because the pages are already in memory, user 2 reverts from the 16K to the 4K buffer pool, and the 16K prefetch is ignored.

The default cache.   When SQL Server is booted, there is always a default data cache called the *default cache*. It is not necessary to add user-defined caches. In fact, the administrator should beware of creat-

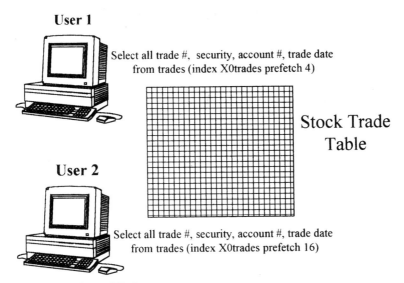

User 1

Select all trade #, security, account #, trade date
from trades (index X0trades prefetch 4)

Stock Trade
Table

User 2

Select all trade #, security, account #, trade date
from trades (index X0trades prefetch 16)

Figure 9.10   Mixing I/O sizes.

ing named caches unnecessarily due to overhead associated with the
internal structures required to support multiple data caches. The
default cache is used when no named caches have been specified for
objects and for database recovery using the LOAD DATABASE and
LOAD TRANSACTION commands.

SQL Server 11 supports three types of named caches:

- *Default.*   The *default data cache* is present on all SQL Server
  installations and is a *mixed* cache.

- *Mixed.*   A mixed data cache can be used for data, index, and log
  pages.

- *Log-only.*   A log-only cache contains only log pages; the *default
  data cache* cannot be changed to log-only. The SQL Server housekeeper task does not do any buffer washing in caches with a type of
  log-only. We will learn more about this in Chap. 20.

The default cache is created when SQL Server is booted and is a
mixed data cache. The size of the default data cache can be modified;
however, it cannot be deleted. The default data cache is the only cache
available for database recovery when SQL Server is rebooted. For this
reason, the smaller the default data cache, the more time it may take
for automatic recovery to run. For high-transaction-rate environments, the system administrator should ensure that the default cache
size is large enough for recovery to occur in a reasonable time.

Keep in mind that cache configuration and buffer pool management are a delicate balancing act. This is definitely a "take from Peter to pay Paul" situation. When a named cache is created, memory is taken away from the default data cache. When a buffer pool is created or enlarged, it is done at the expense of another buffer pool. Always remember that memory has to come from somewhere!

9.4.1 Implementation

This section describes the system stored procedures that are used to manage named data caches and object assignments. The discussion covers named cache creation, modification, deletion, and configuration.

System stored procedures.   Several system stored procedures are used to manage named caches. Specifically, the system procedures are listed in Table 9.3. The *sp_cacheconfig* stored procedure is used to create, configure, and drop named data caches. Creating data caches divides SQL Server's default data cache into smaller named caches. After a data cache has been created, it can be divided into memory pools (using *sp_poolconfig*), each with a different I/O size. These pools are created to allow SQL Server to perform large I/Os. The administrator can bind tables, indexes, databases, text, or image data to a specified cache by using the *sp_bindcache* system procedure. It is important to remember that memory for a new cache is taken from the *default data cache*. Don't starve the default data cache!

TABLE 9.3   System Procedures Used to Manage Named Caches

System procedure	Description
sp_bindcache	Binds a database, table, index, text or image chain to a named data cache
sp_cacheconfig	Used to create, configure, drop, and display information about named data caches
sp_cachestrategy	Used to enable or disable large I/Os and MRU cache replacement strategy for a table, index, text, or image chain
sp_helpcache	Used to display information about objects bound to a data cache, or the amount of overhead required to create a cache of a specified size
sp_logiosize	Changes the log I/O size used by SQL Server for the current database
sp_poolconfig	Creates, drops, resizes, and reports information about memory pools within named data caches
sp_unbindcache	Used to reverse the effects of *sp_bindcache*
sp_unbindcache_all	Used to unbind all objects from the specified data cache

sp_cacheconfig.   The syntax for *sp_cacheconfig* is

```
sp_cacheconfig [cachename [, "cache_size[P|K|M|G}"] [, logonly | mixed]
```

for example,

```
sp_cacheconfig 'tempdb data cache', "50M"
```

The *cachename* parameter is used to specify the name of the data cache; the cache name must be unique. The *cache_size* can be specified in pages (P), kilobytes (K), megabytes (M), or gigabytes (G). A cache size of zero will force SQL Server to remove the cache when the server is rebooted. If the caller attempts to drop a cache that has objects bound to it, a warning message will be generated. The object bindings will be marked invalid when SQL Server is restarted, and the object will be assigned to the default data cache. A recommendation is to unbind objects using *sp_unbindcache_all* before the named cache is deleted. The minimum cache size that can be specified is 512K.

The *logonly* and *mixed* parameters are mutually exclusive. The default cache type is *mixed*. The caller must possess the *sa_role* to successfully execute this procedure.

SQL Server must be rebooted to have cache creation or deletion take effect. As discussed in Chap. 1, a RDBMS must have dynamic configuration to provide high availability and to support continuous operations. So SYBASE should make it a point to make cache configuration more dynamic in the future.

When the System 11 dataserver is installed, all the memory in the page cache is assigned to the default data cache. Information about data caches can be displayed by executing *sp_cacheconfig* with no parameters as follows:

```
1> sp_cacheconfig
2> go
Cache Name                    Status   Type     Config Value   Run Value
------------------------       -------  -------  -------------  ----------
default data cache            Active   Default       0.00 Mb    16.72 Mb
                                                 -----------    ---------
                                       Total         0.00 Mb    16.72 Mb
= = = = = = = = = = = = = = = = = = = = = = = = = = = = = = = = = = = = = =
Cache: default data cache,   Status: Active,   Type: Default
        Config Size: 0.00 Mb,     Run Size: 16.72 Mb

IO Size   Wash Size   Config Size    Run Size
-------   ----------  ------------   ---------
  2 Kb      512 Kb         0.00 Mb    16.72 Mb

(return status = 0)
```

The above example is from a new SQL Server installation. The reader can see that there are approximately 17 Mbytes of total memory in the data cache. By default, memory pool allocation for named caches is 2K buffers. The cache *Status* column can be one of the following:

- *Active.*   This cache is currently active.

- *Pend/Act.*   This means pending/active; this cache was created since the last restart of SQL Server. The cache status will be changed to *active* the next time SQL Server is restarted.

- *Act/Del.*   This means active/delete; the cache is currently active but has been marked for deletion with the *sp_cacheconfig* system procedure. The cache will be deleted when SQL Server is restarted.

Named caches can be modified for several reasons, including

- To change the cache size
- To alter the type of the cache
- To add buffer pools to achieve better performance
- To delete buffer pools when designated memory can be used more efficiently elsewhere or to experiment with different cache configurations

The *sp_cacheconfig* procedure is used to modify named caches. For example,

```
sp_cacheconfig 'eei log cache', logonly
```

changes the cache type to log-only,

```
sp_cacheconfig 'mycache', 0
```

causes SQL Server to drop 'mycache' at the next start of SQL Server, and

```
sp_cacheconfig 'eei log cache'
```

reports the current configuration of 'eei log cache.'

There are a few important details to remember about modifying named caches. First, the *default cache* cannot be changed to *logonly*. A cache cannot be changed to *logonly* if there are objects (other than the *syslogs* table) currently bound to that cache.

sp_helpcache.   The *sp_helpcache* system procedure is used to display information about a specific cache or to determine the overhead required to create a cache of a specified size. The syntax is

```
sp_helpcache {cache_name | "cache_size[P|K|M|G]"}
```

for example,

```
sp_helpcache 'default data cache'
```

A data cache requires a small amount of overhead for data structures that are used to manage the cache. The *sp_helpcache* system procedure is used to determine what that overhead actually is:

```
1> sp_helpcache '100M'
2> go
5.19Mb of overhead memory will be needed to manage a cache of size 100M
(return status = 0)
```

sp_logiosize. The transaction log I/O size for a database can be changed by using the *sp_logiosize* system procedure. This changes the I/O size used by SQL Server to a different memory pool for the current database. The syntax is

```
sp_logiosize ["default" | "2|4|8|16"]
```

for example,

```
sp_logiosize '8'
sp_logiosize 'default'
```

The *default* keyword sets the I/O size for the current database to the default value of 4K, if a 4K memory pool is available in the cache being used by the database's transaction log. If a 4K pool does not exist, SQL Server sets the log I/O size to 2K. The size must be enclosed in quotes; valid values (at present) are 2, 4, 8, and 16. Any value that is specified for *sp_logsize* must correspond to an existing memory pool for the cache used by the database's transaction log.

The log I/O size for each database is recorded in the SQL Server error log each time the server is started. The following is a fragment of an SQL Server error log.

```
00:95/12/26 13:18:58.45 server Opening Master Database ...
00:95/12/26 13:18:59.57 server Loading SQL Server's default  sort
  order and character set
00:95/12/26 13:19:00.58 server Recovering database 'master'
00:95/12/26 13:19:00.74 server Recovery dbid 1 ckpt (1876,15)
00:95/12/26 13:19:00.77 server Recovery no active transactions before
  ckpt.
00:95/12/26 13:19:01.23 server Database 'master' is now online.
00:95/12/26 13:19:01.33 server The transaction log in the data base
  'master' will use I/O size of 4 Kb.
00:95/12/26 13:19:01.67 serverserver is unnamed
00:95/12/26 13:19:01.83 server Activating disk 'sysprocsdev'.
00:95/12/26 13:19:01.83 kernel Initializing virtual device 1, 'C:\system
  10\data\sybprocs.dat'
00:95/12/26 13:19:01.86 kernel Virtual device 1 started using asyn
  chronous i/o.
```

```
00:95/12/26 13:19:02.92 server Recovering database 'model'.
00:95/12/26 13:19:02.93 server Recovery dbid 3 ckpt (436,24)
00:95/12/26 13:19:02.93 server Recovery no active transactions before
  ckpt.
00:95/12/26 13:19:03.03 server The transaction log in the database
  'model' will use I/O size of 4 Kb.
00:95/12/26 13:19:03.06 server Database 'model' is now online.
00:95/12/26 13:19:03.10 server Clearing temp db
00:95/12/26 13:19:07.31 server Recovering database 'sybsystemprocs'.
00:95/12/26 13:19:07.34 server Recovery dbid 4 ckpt (6668,22)
00:95/12/26 13:19:07.34 server Recovery no active transactions before
  ckpt.
00:95/12/26 13:19:08.06 server The transaction log in the database
  'sybsystemprocs' will use I/O size of 4 Kb.
00:95/12/26 13:19:08.08 server Database 'sybsystemprocs' is now online.
00:95/12/26 13:19:08.08 server Recovery complete.
```

The log I/O size for a database can also be reported by executing
sp_logiosize with no parameters.

```
1> sp_logiosize
2> go
Log I/O is set to 4 Kbytes.
The transaction log for database 'eei' will use I/O size of 4 Kbytes.
```

sp_poolconfig. The *sp_poolconfig* system procedure is used to configure and display information about memory pools within named data
caches. Memory pools are created, dropped, and resized by using
sp_poolconfig. The *sp_poolconfig* procedure is used to move memory
around between buffer pools and to change wash sizes within a
named cache. And *sp_poolconfig* is a dynamic command, which means
that the server does not have to be restarted for the command to take
effect. The syntax has two forms. The first is used to create or change
the size of a memory pool in an existing cache. The form of the statement is

```
sp_poolconfig cache_name [, "mem_size[P|K|M|G]",
"config_poolK" [, "affected_poolK"]]
```

for example,

```
sp_poolconfig 'default data cache', '5M', '16K', '2K'
```

The *cache_name* is the name of an existing data cache. The
mem_size is the size of the memory pool to be created, or the new size
for an existing pool. Size can be specified in pages (P), kilobytes (K),
megabytes (M), or gigabytes (G). The *config_pool* parameter is used to
specify the I/O size performed in the memory pool where the memory
is to be allocated or removed. Currently, valid I/O sizes are 2K, 4K,
8K, and 16K. The *affected_pool* is the size of I/O performed in the
memory pool where the memory is to be deallocated. If this parameter

is not supplied, the memory is taken from the default 2K buffer pool. Let's look at a simple example:

```
1> sp_poolconfig 'default data cache', '5M','16K'
2> go
(return status = 0)
1> sp_cacheconfig
2> go
Cache Name                       Status    Type     Config Value   Run Value
------------------------         -------   -------  ------------   ---------
default data cache               Active    Default      0.00 Mb     96.72 Mb
                                                     ------------   ---------
                                           Total        0.00 Mb     96.72 Mb
= = = = = = = = = = = = = = = = = = = = = = = = = = = = = = = = = = = = = =
Cache: default data cache,     Status: Active,    Type: Default
        Config Size: 0.00 Mb,     Run Size: 96.72 Mb

IO Size   Wash Size    Config Size    Run Size
-------   ----------   ------------   ---------
  2 Kb      512 Kb        0.00 Mb     96.72 Mb
 16 Kb      608 Kb        5.00 Mb      5.00 Mb
```

In the above example, *sp_poolconfig* is used to create a 16K buffer pool in the *default data cache*. Memory is taken from the default 2K buffer pool to satisfy the request for the new 16K buffer pool.

The second syntax of *sp_poolconfig* is used to configure the wash size for a specified buffer pool. The wash size is the point in the LRU/MRU chain at which SQL Server writes dirty pages to disk. The default value for the wash size is either 256 buffers (masses) or 20 percent of the buffer pool, if the number of configured buffers in the pool is less than 512. A buffer is a grouping of pages equal to the I/O size of the pool. All pages in a buffer are read from disk, written to disk, or flushed from the page cache simultaneously. The syntax is as follows:

```
sp_poolconfig cache_name, "io_size", "wash = size[P|K|M|G]"
```

for example,

```
sp_poolconfig 'default data cache', '16K', 'wash = 1536K'
```

Common reasons to modify a buffer pool include:

- The wash size is incorrect.
- The buffer pool is too large, and memory can be better used elsewhere.
- The buffer pool is too small, forcing queries to use different buffer pool sizes.
- Buffer pools can be created and tuned to support varying workloads. For example, a batch application that ran overnight can

reconfigure the buffer pools to support traditional OLTP applications during the regular business day.

Configuring buffer wash size. The wash area is configurable for each pool in a data cache. When dirty pages move into the wash area, SQL Server performs asynchronous writes on these pages. The wash area must be large enough that pages are written to disk before they reach the LRU side of the page chain. If the wash area is too small, SQL Server tasks may be forced to wait for I/O, resulting in performance degradation. If the wash area is too large, SQL Server may be performing unnecessary writes.

In general, the default wash buffer size should be optimal for high performance. For very large caches with high update rates, be sure that wash size is high enough. The wash size must be large enough for all writes to complete, or else tasks will be placed in the sleep queue, waiting for clean buffers. A large wash area makes the fetch-and-discard strategy more lenient by allowing more time for a buffer to be reused. The housekeeper task (Chap. 20) washes buffers during CPU idle cycles.

sp_bindcache. In Chap. 1, we talked about partitioning large memory and using large memory space to make tables, indexes, or even databases *sticky.* The *sp_bindcache* procedure is used to bind a database, table, index, text, or image chain to a data cache. If no objects are bound to a named cache, the cache memory is wasted! When the cache binding for an object is changed by using the *sp_bindcache, sp_unbindcache,* or *sp_unbindcacheall* procedure, all the stored procedures that reference the object are recompiled the next time they are executed.

It is recommended to change object bindings when database activity is light. The *sp_bindcache* and *sp_unbindcache* procedures need to acquire an exclusive table lock when binding or unbinding a table or its indexes to a cache.

The syntax of *sp_bindcache* is

```
sp_bindcache cachename, dbname [,[owner.]table[.index] [, text]]
```

for example,

```
sp_bindcache 'tempdb', tempdb
sp_bindcache 'eei log cache', eei, syslogs
sp_bindcache 'eei data cache', eei, tbaccount
sp_bindcache 'eei index cache', eei, 'tbaccount.x1account'
sp_bindcache 'eei data cache', eei, tbaccount, text
```

The *cachename* parameter is the name of an existing data cache. The *dbname* parameter is the name of the database to bind to the cache, or the database containing the object bound to the cache. The *owner* parameter is optional and is the name of the table's owner. The *table* parameter is the name of the table to bind to the cache, or the name of a table whose index, text, or image chain is to be bound to the cache. *Index* is the name of the index to be bound to the cache. The *text* parameter is used to bind text or image objects to a cache.

A few things to know about *sp_bindcache:*

- If a database is bound to a cache, objects are also bound to that cache, not to the default cache.
- The database must be in single-user mode to bind a system table (e.g., *syslogs*) to a cache. This is done with the *sp_dboption* system procedure.
- The *master* database cannot be bound to a cache.
- Only the *syslogs* table can be bound to a *logonly* cache.
- The caller must invoke *sp_bindcache* from the *master* database to bind or unbind a database.
- The *sp_bindcache* procedure can be used to *cool down* a cache. When an object is bound to a cache, any of the object's pages that are already in memory are removed from cache, and dirty pages are flushed to disk. So by binding an object to a cache (or rebinding it to the same cache), the cache can be cooled down. This can also be used as a checkpoint at the object level.
- Cache bindings and I/O sizes are integral to the query plan for triggers and stored procedures. Therefore, when cache bindings are changed for an object, all stored procedures that reference the object are recompiled the next time they are executed.

sp_unbindcache. The *sp_unbindcache* procedure is used to reverse the effects of *sp_bindcache.* The syntax of *sp_unbindcache* is

```
sp_unbindcache cachename, dbname [,[owner.]table[.index] [, text]]
```

for example,

```
sp_unbindcache 'tempdb', tempdb
sp_unbindcache 'eei index cache', eei, 'tbaccount.x1account'
```

The *cachename* parameter is the name of an existing data cache. The *dbname* parameter is the name of the database that is bound to the cache, or the database containing the object (table, index, text, or image chain) bound to the cache. The *owner* parameter is optional and is the name of the table's owner. The *table* parameter is the name of the table bound to the cache, or the name of a table whose index, text, or image chain is bound to the cache. *Index* is the name of the index that is bound to the cache. The *text* parameter is used to unbind text or image objects.

sp_unbindcache_all.   The *sp_unbindcacheall* system procedure is used to unbind all objects from a named cache. The syntax is

```
sp_unbindcacheall cache_name
```

The *cachename* parameter is the name of an existing data cache.

Determining object bindings.   Object bindings are determined with the *sp_helpcache* or *sp_help* system procedure. Database bindings can be determined by using the *sp_helpcache* or *sp_helpdb* system procedures. For example,

```
1> sp_helpcache 'eei data cache'
2> go
```

Cache Name	Config Size	Run Size	Overhead
eei data cache	4.00 Mb	4.00 Mb	0.25 Mb

```
---------------Cache Binding Information: -----------------
```

Cache Name	Entity Name	Type	Index Name
eei data cache	eei.dbo.team	table	
eei data cache	eei.dbo.player	table	

```
(return status = 0)

1> sp_help player
2> go
```

Name	Owner	Type
player	dbo	user table

Data_located_on_segment	When_created
default	Jul 14 1995 2:34PM

Column_name	Type	Length	Prec	Scale	Nulls	Default_name	Rule_ name	Identity
playerID	int	4	NULL	NULL	0	NULL	NULL	0
playerName	char	30	NULL	NULL	0	NULL	NULL	0
teamID	int	4	NULL	NULL	0	NULL	NULL	0

attribute_class	attribute	int_value	char_value	comments
buffer manager	cache binding	1	eei data cache	
NULL				

```
index_name    index_description    index_keys    index_max_rows_per_page
------------  -------------------  -----------   -----------------------
x0player      clustered, unique located on default    playerID 58
No defined keys for this object.
Object is not partitioned.

(1 row affected, return status = 0)

1> sp_helpdb tempdb
2> go

name          db_size     owner     dbid   created      status
------------  ---------   --------  ------  -----------  -------------
tempdb            2.0 MB sa            2 Jan 03, 1996  select into/bulkcopy

name     attribute_class     attribute     int_value  char_value    comments
-------  ------------------  ------------  ---------  -----------  --------
tempdb  buffer manager     cache binding      1 tempdb cache    NULL

device_fragments     size          usage          free kbytes
-----------------  -----------   ------------   --------
master              2.0 MB        data and log      1200

device             segment
---------          ----------------------------------------------
master             default
master             logsegment
master             system
(return status = 0)
```

sp_cachestrategy. The *sp_cachestrategy* system procedure is used to enable or disable large I/Os and MRU cache replacement strategy for a table, index, text, or image object. The syntax is

```
sp_cachestrategy dbname, objname [, strategy, "on|off"]
```

for example,

```
sp_cachestrategy eei, tbaccount
sp_cachestrategy eei, tbaccount, prefetch, 'off'
sp_cachestrategy eei, 'tbaccount.x0account', mru, 'off'
```

The *dbname* parameter is the name of the database in which the database object resides. The *objname* is the name of the table, index, text, or image column. The *strategy* parameter is *prefetch* or *mru* and specifies which option to change. The *on* or *off* parameter specifies the setting.

9.4.2 Usage guidelines and tuning

This section provides some valuable tips and can serve as a starting point for named cache configuration and usage. Ideally, named caches are used to distribute buffer operations across named caches and to bind objects to those named caches. The net result should be distributed logical I/O, resulting in lower spinlock contention, and lower physical I/O, resulting in better performance.

Here is the best starting point that I can offer: *Do not change the SQL Server defaults unless there is a known problem.*

Every SQL Server installation will start with a single cache (the default data cache). SQL Server supports an unlimited number of caches, but the administrator should use common sense when configuring caches.The following guidelines can be used as a starting point:

- Assign the *tempdb* database to its own named cache. Configure the cache for 4K I/O for the *syslogs* table and 16K I/O for use by SELECT INTO queries.

- Create 4K and 16K buffer pools in the default data cache, using the *sp_poolconfig* system procedure. The 4K buffer pool can be used by the transaction logs of any databases that are not bound to another cache, and the 16K buffer pool can be used for large I/Os. If the 4K pool is not created, the transaction log of any database that is not explicitly bound to another cache will use 2K I/Os.

- Assign the *syslogs* table to its own *logonly* cache for very active databases. Configure buffer pools in this cache to match the log I/O size set using the *sp_logiosize* system procedure.

- Sybase recommends that a 4K pool be configured for the transaction log. It is suggested that most of the space in a *logonly* cache be configured for 4K I/O.

- Most caches should have at least a small 16K buffer pool. The 16K I/Os are used for fast BCP, table scans, and some DBCC checks. The optimizer will also use large I/Os on some range selects on clustered indexes, and covered queries on nonclustered indexes.

- In OLTP environments, the *sysindexes* table is a *hot* SYBASE object. Assign it to a named cache other than the default. If applications include ad hoc queries, a performance gain may be seen by binding the *sysobjects, syscolumns,* and *sysprotects* system tables to cache.

- Assign small lookup tables and indexes to their own data caches if they need to be memory-resident. The benefits are obvious for applications that may populate data windows using these lookup tables.

- Lock other hot tables into memory to reduce physical I/O. SQL Server Monitor can be used to identify hot objects, as shown later in this chapter.

- Clustered indexes are typically smaller than nonclustered indexes. For large tables, bind clustered indexes to a designated named cache.

- Assign hot nonclustered indexes to a separate cache from data.

- Leave the remaining database objects in the default data cache.

- If spinlock contention on a particular cache is greater than 10 percent, split the cache into multiple caches. This can be determined by using the SQL Server Monitor Data Cache window.

Remember not to starve the default data cache. The default data cache is critical during automatic recovery, and all unbound database objects will use the default data cache. Because certain types of operations (e.g., DISK INIT, some DBCCs, DROP TABLE) always use 2K I/O, it is the administrator's responsibility not to starve the 2K buffer pool in any cache.

On SMP systems, it is a good idea to spread hot objects (tables and indexes) over multiple named caches to reduce spinlock contention. The administrator may want to consider changing buffer pool configurations to match changing workloads. Changes to buffer pools take effect immediately; however, named caches require a server restart to take effect. An example is off-hours DSS reporting. It may be advantageous to move memory from 2K buffer pools to the 16K buffer pool. When DSS reporting has been completed, memory can be shifted back to the 2K buffer pools for OLTP.

Binding system tables.   System tables can also be bound to a named data cache. Candidates include the *sysobjects, sysindexes,* and *syscolumns* tables. The database must be placed in single-user mode by using the *sp_dboption* system procedure to bind system tables. This includes binding the transaction log (*syslogs*) for a database. An example follows:

```
1> use master
2> go
1> sp_dboption eei, 'single user', true
2> go
1> use eei
2> go
1> checkpoint
2> go
1> sp_bindcache 'eei data cache', eei, sysindexes
2> go
1> use master
2> go
1> sp_dboption eei,'single user',false
2> go
1> use eei
2> go
1> checkpoint
2> go
```

Transaction logs.   The administrator should assign the *syslogs* table to its own *logonly* cache for very active databases. Configure buffer pools in this cache to match the log I/O size set, using the *sp_logiosize* system procedure. The default value for log I/O is 4K, so any cache used for log I/O should have a 4K memory pool. If it does not have a 4K pool, the 2K pool will be used, thus forcing the SQL Server to use 2K log I/O.

Try to size the log's cache so that all stored procedure rollbacks can find their needed log pages in cache. Other user processes that need to access log pages are triggers that read the *inserted* and *deleted* tables and deferred updates.

```
1> use master
2> go
1> sp_dboption eei,'single user',true
2> go
1> use eei
2> go
1> checkpoint
2> go
1> sp_cacheconfig 'eei log cache','10M','logonly'
2> go
1> sp_poolconfig 'eei log cache','8M','4K'
2> go
1> sp_bindcache 'eei log cache',eei,syslogs
2> go
1> sp_logiosize '4'
2> go
1> use master
2> go
1> sp_dboption eei,'single user',false
2> go
1> use eei
2> go
1> checkpoint
2> go
```

Assign *tempdb* to its own cache. It may be a good idea to assign the *tempdb* database to its own named cache. Configure the cache for 4K I/O for the *syslogs* table and 16K I/O for use by SELECT INTO queries. To determine the size of the named cache, use the *sp_helpdb* and *sp_spaceused* system procedures to determine the size of the database. Next, determine the amount of overhead required for a named cache of that size. Add these two numbers, and create a named cache of that size. Use the SQL Server Monitor Object Page I/O screen to determine whether any work table is performing physical I/O (see Fig. 9.12). If work tables are performing physical I/O, the administrator may want to increase the size of the cache assigned to *tempdb*.

```
1> sp_cacheconfig 'tempdb','100M'
2> go
1> shutdown
2> go

1> sp_bindcache tempdb,tempdb
```

```
2> go
1> sp_poolconfig tempdb,'4M','4K'
2> go
1> sp_poolconfig tempdb,'4M','16K'
2> go
```

Locking in memory for the default cache. It may be a good idea to lock in a portion of memory for the default data cache. This will guarantee that the size of the default data cache cannot be reduced beyond a specified amount of memory. When SQL Server is installed, the default data cache does not have a configured size, as shown in the following output:

```
1> sp_cacheconfig
2> go

Cache Name              Status     Type       Config Value Run Value
----------------  ----------  -----  ------------  ----------
default data cache    Active     Default   0.00 Mb      8.44 Mb
eei data cache        Active     Mixed     4.00 Mb      4.00 Mb
tempdb cache          Active     Mixed     2.00 Mb      2.00 Mb
                                           --------  --------
                      Total                 6.00 Mb    14.44 Mb
= = = = = = = = = = = = = = = = = = = = = = = = = = = = = = = = = = = = = =
Cache: default data cache, Status: Active, Type: Default
    Config Size: 0.00 Mb, Run Size: 8.44 Mb
IO Size  Wash Size  Config Size  Run Size
-------  -----  ----------  -----------
   2 Kb      512 Kb     0.00 Mb     1.44 Mb
   4 Kb     1024 Kb     3.00 Mb     3.00 Mb
  16 Kb      816 Kb     4.00 Mb     4.00 Mb
= = = = = = = = = = = = = = = = = = = = = = = = = = = = = = = = = = = = = =
Cache: eei data cache,  Status: Active,  Type: Mixed
    Config Size: 4.00 Mb,  Run Size: 4.00 Mb

IO Size  Wash Size  Config Size  Run Size
-------  -----  ----------  -----------
   2 Kb      512 Kb     0.00 Mb     4.00 Mb
= = = = = = = = = = = = = = = = = = = = = = = = = = = = = = = = = = = = = =
Cache: tempdb cache,  Status: Active, Type: Mixed
    Config Size: 2.00 Mb, Run Size: 2.00 Mb

IO Size  Wash Size  Config Size  Run Size
-------  -----  ----------  -----------
   2 Kb      512 Kb     0.00 Mb     2.00 Mb

(return status = 0)
```

Use the *sp_cacheconfig* stored procedure to explicitly configure the default data cache as follows:

```
1> sp_cacheconfig 'default data cache', '50M'
2> go
The change is completed. The SQL Server must be rebooted for the
change to take effect.
(return status = 0)
```

Random-access queries.   Typically, the number of logical I/Os on indexes is 3 to 4 times that of data pages. The leaf and nonleaf pages of a clustered index can be bound to different named data caches. It is a good idea to separate index pages from the data pages because index pages are accessed more frequently than data pages.

Range queries.   Range queries generally access data pages more frequently than index pages. For range queries, there is less motivation to place nonleaf index pages in a separate named cache.

SQL Server Monitor.   It is the administrator's responsibility to monitor I/O patterns and tune the buffer manager on an ongoing basis. I would expect Sybase to build more "intelligence" into SQL Server Monitor for tuning and monitoring.

SQL Server Monitor can be used to display data cache page I/O and effectiveness, as shown in Fig. 9.11. Keep an eye on the *Spinlock Wait Pct* value; if it is greater than 10 percent, it may be a good idea to split the data cache into separate named caches. Any data cache showing a high number of physical reads is a candidate for additional memory.

Identifying hot objects.   SQL Server Monitor can be used to provide information on a per-object basis. The Object Page I/O screen is shown in Fig. 9.12. The number of logical reads, physical reads, and

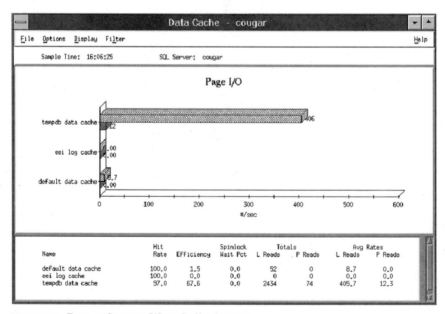

Figure 9.11   Data cache page I/O and effectiveness.

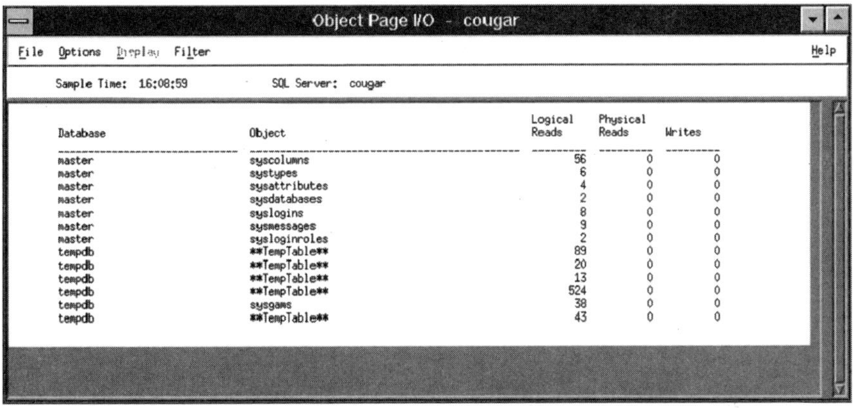

Database	Object	Logical Reads	Physical Reads	Writes
master	syscolumns	56	0	0
master	systypes	6	0	0
master	sysattributes	4	0	0
master	sysdatabases	2	0	0
master	syslogins	8	0	0
master	sysmessages	9	0	0
master	sysloginroles	2	0	0
tempdb	**TempTable**	89	0	0
tempdb	**TempTable**	20	0	0
tempdb	**TempTable**	13	0	0
tempdb	**TempTable**	524	0	0
tempdb	sysgams	38	0	0
tempdb	**TempTable**	43	0	0

Figure 9.12 Object page I/O.

writes is provided for each database object. This information can be used to determine particularly "hot" database objects that may benefit from new cache assignments.

9.5 Cache Analysis Tool

Sybase recognizes the fact that the buffer manager can be very difficult to tune. The cache analysis tool (CAT) is a monitor server application that performs internal workload sampling. The cache analysis tool is used to calculate cache hit ratios and proximity page requests. It then statistically determines the optimal buffer cache size and I/O size for a particular application.

Information can be presented at the object level similar to the following:

DBID	indid	objid	Optimal Cache Size	I/O Size
8	0	160033088	100-KB	2-KB
8	1	48003202	28-KB	2-KB
.				
.				

Currently, the cache analysis tool is an internally developed Sybase tool. Let's hope that Sybase can deliver this product to its customers!

9.6 DBCC Commands

In addition to the system procedures discussed in this chapter, there are a number of DBCC commands that can be used with the buffer manager, including

```
DBCC CHECKOBJCACHE
DBCC SHOWCACHE
```

The DBCC *checkobjcache* keyword is used to display the current cache bindings for a table or index. The syntax follows:

```
dbcc checkobjcache( dbid, objid, indid )
```

for example,

```
dbcc checkobjcache( 8, 160033088, 0 )
```

The *dbid* parameter is the ID of the database in which the object resides (as found in *master.dbo.sysdatabases*). The *objid* is the object ID of the table as found in *master.dbo.sysobjects*. The database ID can be determined by using the *db_id()* system function, and the object ID can be found by using the *object_id()* system function. The *indid* parameter identifies the index to be displayed; 0 indicates the table, 1 is used for a clustered index, and values greater than 1 are used for nonclustered indexes.

Use the DBCC *traceon* keyword to direct I/O to the user terminal before executing *checkobjcache*. For example,

```
1> dbcc traceon( 3604 )
2> go
1> dbcc checkobjcache( 5, 16003088, 0 )
2> go
Index 0 for object 16003088 in database 5 bound to cache default data
cache (id 0)
```

The DBCC *showcache* keyword is used to display the number of buffers on the LRU/MRU, the number of buffers in the wash section, and the pool prefetch size. The syntax is

```
dbcc showcache( "cache_name" )
```

The *cache_name* parameter specifies the name of the data cache. For example,

```
1> dbcc traceon( 3604 )
2> go
1> dbcc showcache( 'default data cache' )
2> go
Cache information for named cache default data cache id 0
```

POOL	IN MRU	IN WASH	KEPT	HASHED	TW	REDIRTY
2k	161	5328	0	479	51	11
4k	1	763	4	7	15	0
16k	0	192	0	0	0	0

Table-level DBCCs.   The *DBCC tune* keyword can be used to set the value for *indextrips* for a table's indexes or *oamtrips* for a table's OAM pages. The syntax is

```
dbcc tune( {indextrips|oamtrips}, value, table_name )
```

for example,

```
dbcc tune( indextrips, 3, player )
dbcc tune( oamtrips, 5, player )
```

The *indextrips* keyword is used to set the value for the named table's indexes. The *oamtrips* keyword is used to set the *oamtrips* value for a table's OAM pages. The *value* parameter is an unsigned short data type used to specify the number of index and OAM trips. The *table_name* is the name of the affected table. The command must be run for the named table in the current database.

If the table's *indextrips* value has not been set via DBCC, or if it has been set to 0 by using DBCC, then its index pages will use the global *indextrips* value from the configuration interface (as described in Sec. 7.4.2). Similarly if the table's *oamtrips* value has not been set or has been set to 0, then its OAM pages will use the global *oamtrips* value from the configuration interface.

Chapter

10

Input/Output

I/O is one of the most important aspects of RDBMS performance. There are many aspects to consider in a discussion of I/O. First, there is the I/O subsystem itself. Typically, for database applications a larger number of small, fast disks will perform better than a smaller number of large disks. This is because I/O can be distributed across many disks and I/O channels.

Second, there is the object placement. If all the objects (tables, indexes, logs) for a particular database are stored on a single disk in the I/O subsystem, database performance will suffer. Ideally, database object storage will be spread out over all available disks. Nonclustered indexes will be separated from their base tables (known as *table and index splitting*), and transaction logs will be separated from other database objects.

SQL Server allows the database and transaction log to *span* multiple disks. In addition, the database and transaction log can be *striped*. Striping is an interleaving technique for distributing I/O across multiple disk drives. Striping can occur at the hardware level as provided by RAID subsystems or at the software level.

System 11 supports *data partitioning* to provide a higher level of concurrency when multiple inserts into a heap table are performed. Data partitions improve performance by providing multiple concurrent insert points to minimize lock contention. Data partitions are ideal for heap objects such as transaction logs (*syslogs* table), history, and audit tables.

In this chapter we will discuss several I/O strategies including the use of table and index segments, table and index splitting, and table and index striping. Section 10.6 provides a complete discussion of SQL Server log I/O using System 11. Section 10.8 describes the new variable block I/O size features and offers some valuable pointers. Finally, the chapter concludes with a discussion of typical database *hot spots,* what to do about them, and how to avoid them.

10.1   Table and Index Segments

Database devices are logically divided into database *segments* to allow for specific object placement. A database may contain as many as 128 devices, which limits the size of a database to 256 Gbytes on most systems (several operating systems support a maximum database device size of 2 Gbytes). A database device can have as many as 192 segments. A segment can use storage on up to 255 logical devices. Tables and indexes can be assigned to a particular segment by using the CREATE TABLE and CREATE INDEX statements.

Segments will usually contain multiple database tables, although it is possible to dedicate a segment (and therefore a physical device) to a single table. The clustered index for a table must be stored on the same segment as the table itself, because the table is an integral part of the clustered index. The CREATE CLUSTERED INDEX statement can be used to move a table from one segment to another.

The *syssegments* table is present in all databases and contains one row for each database *segment.* The CREATE DATABASE command makes the following default entries in *syssegments:*

- *system.*   The system tables for the database are stored on the *system* segment.
- *default.*   Tables and indexes are created on the *default* segment unless the name of another segment is explicitly provided.
- *log.*   The database transaction log is stored on the *log* segment.

The principal purpose of database segments is to level out disk activity on each database device. To do this, the database administrator must control the placement of database objects on specific devices. For example, the segment allocation for a database named *production* is shown in Fig. 10.1. Without DBA intervention, as user objects are created, they will be stored on the *default* segment of the *database_1* device. When the *database_1* device fills up, objects will be stored on the *default* segment on *database_2.* Database devices are used in order of appearance in *sysdevices* (e.g., alphabetically).

10.1.1   System procedures

Database segments and object placement are controlled by a set of system stored procedures. Specifically, the system procedures are

```
1>create database production on database_1=40, database_2=40 log on tranlog_1=20
2>go
```

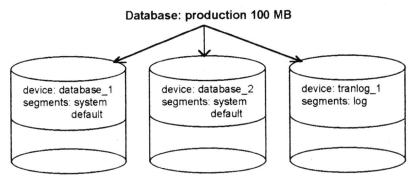

Figure 10.1   Segment allocation for database *production*.

sp_addsegment

sp_dropsegment

sp_extendsegment

sp_helpsegment

sp_placeobject

sp_addsegment.   Database segments are created with the *sp_addsegment* system procedure. The form of the statement is

```
sp_addsegment segname, dbname, devname
```

for example,

```
sp_addsegment indexSegment, production, database_2
```

The *segname* parameter is the name of the segment to be created. Segment names are unique in each database. One entry is created in the *syssegments* table for each new segment. The *dbname* parameter is the name of the database where the new segment is to be defined. The *devname* parameter is the name of the database device on which the segment is to be placed. A database device can have more than one segment associated with it.

sp_dropsegment.   Segments are removed from the system with the *sp_dropsegment* procedure. The form of *sp_dropsegment* is

```
sp_dropsegment segname, dbname [, devname]
```

for example,

```
sp_dropsegment system, production, database_2
```

The *segname* parameter is the name of the segment to be removed; *sp_dropsegment* will remove entries from the *syssegments* system table. The *dbname* parameter is the name of the database where the segment is located. The *devname* parameter is optional unless the segment to be removed is a system segment (*system, default,* or *log*). This is the name of the database device that the segment should no longer use.

sp_extendsegment.   The *sp_extendsegment* procedure is used to expand an existing segment onto another database device. The form of *sp_extendsegment* is

```
sp_extendsegment segname, dbname, devname
```

for example,

```
sp_extendsegment indexSegment, production, database_3
```

The *segname* parameter is the name of the database segment to be expanded. The *dbname* parameter is the name of the database where the segment is located, and *devname* is the name of the database device to be added to the segment's domain.

sp_helpsegment.   The *sp_helpsegment* procedure is used to display information about an existing database segment or all segments in the current database. The form of the command is

```
sp_helpsegment [segname]
```

for example,

```
1> sp_helpsegment
2> go
segment      name               status
-------      ----------------   ------
      0      system                  0
      1      default                 1
      2      logsegment              0
      4      customer_1              0
      5      customer_2              0
      6      orders                  0
      7      inventory               0
      9      idx                     0

(return status = 0)
```

The *segname* parameter is the name of the database segment; *segname* is optional. If no argument is provided, *sp_helpsegment* will display information for all segments in the current database.

In the output from *sp_helpsegment,* the *status* column is used to indicate that the segment is a default segment. It should be obvious from the example that if *status* is 1, the segment is a default segment.

sp_placeobject.   The *sp_placeobject* system stored procedure is used to move future space allocations for a table or index onto a particular segment. It does not affect the placement of existing table or index data. The procedure cannot be used with system tables. The form of *sp_placeobject* is

```
sp_placeobject segname, objname
```

for example,

```
sp_placeobject idx, 'trade.x1trade'
```

The *segname* parameter is the name of the segment on which the table or index should be placed. The *objname* parameter is used to specify the name of the table or index to be affected.

The *sp_placeobject* procedure is often used to split a table or index across multiple disk fragments. To split a 100,000-row table across two disk fragments, the administrator follows these steps:

1. Use the CREATE TABLE...ON SEGMENT_NAME command to create the base table on the first segment.

2. Use the SYBASE bulk-copy program (BCP) to load the first 50,000 records into the table.

3. Use the *sp_placeobject* procedure to move future storage allocations onto another segment.

4. Use the bulk-copy program to load the remaining rows into the base table.

5. Create a database segment, and then extend it by using *sp_extendsegment* so that it labels both devices. Use *sp_placeobject* to place the table on the segment that spans both devices.

The procedure is outlined in the following steps. The first step is to create the base table on the first database segment, which in this example is named *segment_1.*

```
create table inventory(
      partno          int                 not null,
      description     char(30)            not null
      ) on segment_1

create unique clustered index x0inventory on
   inventory(partno) on segment_1
```

The BCP program is then used to load the first half of the rows into the table.

```
% bcp db_inventory.dbo.inventory in inventory.data1 -Ugwa -Selvee -
b50000 -c
password:
```

The administrator should then use the *sp_placeobject* system procedure to place future allocations for the table on the second database device, in this case, *segment_2.*

```
sp_placeobject inventory, segment_2
```

The BCP program is then used to load the second half of the rows into the table.

```
% bcp db_inventory.dbo.inventory in inventory.data2 -Ugwa -Snike -
b50000 -c
password:
```

Last, the object is placed on a database segment that spans both disk devices.

```
sp_addsegment segment_both, db_inventory, mydisk_1
sp_extendsegment segment_both, db_inventory, mydisk_2
sp_placeobject inventory, segment_both
```

10.1.2   Segment summary

Following is a short summary of segment information:

- A database device can have as many as 192 segments.
- There is currently a limit of 32 segments per database.
- A database device may have more than one segment associated with it.
- A segment can be extended over several database devices.
- After a segment has been defined, it can be used in CREATE TABLE and CREATE INDEX statements to place objects on the segment.
- A table can be stored on many database segments. A table and its associated indexes can be in separate segments. (A table and its

clustered index must reside on the same segment; if the clustered index is moved, the table's data will be moved with it.)

- When the *logsegment* is extended, SQL Server recalculates its last-chance threshold (LCT). See Sec. 3.2.7 for more information on the LCT.

- A segment may be dropped if it is not being referenced by a database object.

- When a given segment needs to be extended, storage can be acquired from any logical SQL Server device.

10.2 Table and Index Splitting

The first general rule that should be applied to object placement is to split the nonclustered indexes from their tables. This is accomplished by creating separate database segments for table data and index data. The *system* segment is used to store the database catalog tables and should not be used to store any user objects.

Whenever possible, the index segments and the data segments should be created on separate disks. Database objects are placed on a specific segment with the CREATE TABLE and CREATE INDEX statements. The logic behind this is obvious: to divide the reads and writes for the object across multiple I/O paths. Reads and writes will happen faster because one disk is maintaining the index while a second disk is maintaining the table data. If the table and index data were on the same disk, the disk would need to reposition itself for the index data and the table data. This would result in a dramatic decrease in I/O throughput in the system.

In addition to splitting tables and nonclustered indexes on separate disks, I/O throughput can be increased by storing certain tables on separate disks. For instance, if two tables are going to be accessed and/or updated at the same time (i.e., read access using a database view that contains a join operation), it will improve performance to store each of these tables on different disks. This can also be applied to indexes. For example, when database rows are being updated, certain update operations will cause the row to move. In this instance, the nonclustered index rows will also need to be updated. Performance will be increased when these indexes and the table data itself are stored on different disks.

To summarize this discussion, the way that the data in a database is to be used must be understood to form a comprehensive data placement strategy. Database objects that will be accessed frequently should be split over several separate disks (database segments) to minimize the potential for a disk I/O bottleneck.

10.3 Table and Index Disk Striping

In the previous section, we assume that the database administrator will control placement for all database objects. This does not take into account the reality of multiple users accessing different data at the same time. In this case, the system may start running into I/O contention because of the *number* of users on the system as opposed to contention caused by hardware limitations. I/O contention occurs when a particular hardware resource (e.g., disk drive or I/O channel) begins to exceed its maximum throughput rate. The end result is that user processes are waiting for other user processes to complete so that they can use the resource.

Given the performance limitations of a single disk drive, it is sometimes desirable to combine several disk drives into a single logical drive. As mentioned earlier, this process is called *disk striping*. The disks that are participating in the logical drive are commonly referred to as a *stripe set*.

When a database object is large, it may be beneficial to place the object on multiple disks in a stripe set. Prior to System 11, disk striping is accomplished by estimating the size of the table and loading the table incrementally into different segments, as shown in Sec. 10.1.1. This process is less than ideal and assumes that the table data already exists. Disk striping allows the data from a single object (e.g., database table) to be stored on multiple disks, making it possible to simultaneously access different data from the object on different disks.

Database systems commonly rely on RAID 5 disk subsystems for disk striping. As described in Chap. 6, the level 5 RAID implementation provides disk striping of both data and parity. Parity information is striped across all data drives. RAID 5 can handle concurrent read/write operations and is configured to meet the needs of relational or on-line database storage.

10.4 Disk Controllers

Disk controllers are I/O devices that control the actions of one or more disk drives. These controllers can also create a bottleneck in the I/O subsystem. Most disk controllers include cache memory to store recently used data. A caching disk controller can significantly improve performance for reading data from disk drives.

Some disk controllers also cache writes of data. These controllers retrieve data from main memory and store it in the write-ahead cache instead of immediately writing the data to the disk drive. At this point, the controller notifies the CPU that the data has been written to disk. This means that the program which wrote the data believes that the write has been successful, when in fact it has not yet been written to disk. The controller will flush data from its write-ahead cache to disk when it is advantageous to perform the I/O. Such a write-ahead controller can improve overall I/O throughput by optimizing read/write requests to minimize the number of disk transactions. This type of controller can affect transaction recoverability in the same manner as I/O to a UNIX file system (as described in Sec. 3.1).

When considering object placement, the administrator should be aware of which disk drives are connected to which disk controllers. A controller can control the I/O for more than one disk drive, so requests made to two disks attached to the same controller can result in decreased performance. In addition to storing objects on separate disks being utilized at the same time, make sure that those disks are serviced by different controllers. Ideally, a table and its clustered index would reside on a disk attached to disk controller A, while the nonclustered indexes for the table would reside on a separate disk attached to controller B. This is illustrated in Fig. 10.2.

When SYBASE or operating system mirroring is used, always try to split the primary copy and secondary copy across separate disk controllers. Obviously, a certain amount of additional hardware (i.e., multiple disk drives, disk controllers, etc.) is required to see the real advantages of device mirroring. It does not make much sense to mirror a database device on the same disk drive. Disk I/O is sure to be a bottleneck, and if the drive has problems, both devices (copies of the data) are likely to be affected, so the mirroring will not buy much.

A general rule is that if the database application warrants disk mirroring and high performance, it justifies the cost of additional hardware. Therefore, when hardware purchases are planned, allocate additional funds for extra disk drives and controllers.

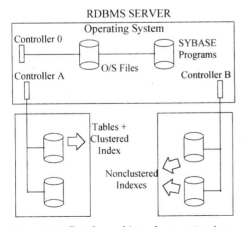

Figure 10.2 Database object placement using multiple controllers.

Whenever possible, try to distribute I/O evenly over available disk controllers and disk drives. Also remember that even in a dedicated RDBMS environment, the operating system needs access to disk drives and controllers. Try to separate the operating system and SYBASE programs from the databases and transaction logs.

10.5   The *tempdb* Database

SYBASE systems (pre-System 11) will often experience I/O bottlenecks in two key areas: (1) the creation of temporary data in the *tempdb* database and (2) transaction logging. In this section we discuss the first potential bottleneck, which is the *tempdb* database.

We discuss two possible methods for improving I/O performance in *tempdb*. These solutions are not for everybody; the pros and cons of each solution must be considered for each application. The first solution involves storing *tempdb* on a conventional UNIX file system (using buffered I/O), while the second solution uses solid-state disk (SSD) technology. The SSD solution is much more expensive, considering that the UNIX file system is free! Keep in mind that when System 11 is used, the ideal solution (and the one that the author recommends) may be to purchase more conventional RAM for the server platform and binding *tempdb* to its own named cache. The reader may wish to note that careful use of the System 11 buffer manager can help reduce any perceived performance gains of using file system files for database devices.

UNIX file systems.   The device that *tempdb* is stored on can be either a UNIX file system or a raw partition. In general, SYBASE recommends the use of raw partitions for database devices. Because *tempdb* is replaced by the automatic recovery process during an SQL Server reboot, *tempdb* may be an exception. When properly managed, the UNIX file system can provide better performance than a raw partition device. This is because most UNIX systems use a buffer cache for disk I/O. Writes to the disk are stored in the buffer and may not be written to disk immediately. When raw partitions are used, SYBASE writes directly to the disk, which may result in decreased performance. This may be highly dependent on the host platform (hardware and operating system) and the number of concurrent users.

Solid-state disk.   As described in Chap. 6, a solid-state disk emulator uses battery-backed memory to provide low-access latency and high I/O bandwidth. Solid-state disk devices are essentially expensive RAM disks capable of reaching 1000 I/Os per second for small block

I/Os. Superior I/O performance for *tempdb* can be achieved by storing the *tempdb* database on a solid-state disk.

Moving *tempdb*. When SQL Server is installed, the *tempdb* database resides on the *master* device. The default size of the temporary database is 2 Mbytes, and the size of *tempdb* can be increased by using the ALTER DATABASE command. If the *master* device is mirrored (as it should be), the first 2 Mbytes of *tempdb* will also be mirrored. This will have an adverse impact on overall server performance when *tempdb* is very active because I/O on the *master* device and its mirror will be high. Moving *tempdb* to its own device will usually increase performance. If *tempdb* is very large, it may be a good idea to spread *tempdb* across several database devices. The overall I/O rate will be improved due to the increased number of I/O channels.

It is important to consider disk placement when the *tempdb* database is expanded. Ideally, *tempdb* should be placed on its own device which does not share disk with any other I/O-intensive device (such as transaction logs). The system administrator is always at the mercy of available hardware, but if resources are available, they definitely should be used.

The following steps can be taken to move *tempdb* from the *master* device to its own dedicated device.

1. Dump the *tempdb* database to a disk file, using the DUMP DATABASE command (i.e., dump database *tempdb* to "/dump/foo.dump")

2. Use the DISK INIT command to initialize a new device for *tempdb* (i.e., disk init name=tempdb, physname='/tempdb/tempdb.device', size=51200, vdevno=3).

3. Create a temporary database on *tempdb*'s new device (i.e., create database *foo* on *tempdb*=2). The segment mapping for the new database must match the segment mapping of the existing *tempdb*.

4. Load the dump of *tempdb* into the new database (i.e., load database *foo* from "/dump/foo.dump").

5. Boot the SQL Server in single-user mode (using the -*m* parameter to *startserver*).

6. Run the following SQL statements against the SQL Server.

```
1> begin tran
2> go
1> delete master..sysusages where dbid=2
2> delete master..sysdatabases where dbid=2
3> go
(1 row affected)
(1 row affected)
1> update sysusages set dbid=2 where dbid=db_id('foo')
2> update sysdatabases set dbid=2,name='tempdb'
```

```
3> where dbid=db_id('foo')
4> go
(1 row affected)
(1 row affected)
1> commit tran
2> go
1> sp_dboption tempdb,'select into',true
2> go
```

7. Shutdown and restart the SQL Server in multiuser mode. Dump the *master* database to establish a point of recoverability.

The SYBASE *SQL Server Troubleshooting Guide* contains a complete discussion of the issues of managing *tempdb*.

10.6 Transaction Logs

Most SQL Server processing is logged in the transaction log table *syslogs*. Every database, including the system databases *model, master,* and *tempdb,* and *sybsystemprocs* has its own transaction log. The transaction log continues to grow until it is truncated with a DUMP TRANSACTION command or automatically via the *trunc log on chkpt* database option.

Several factors influence the size of the transaction log for a database. The actual size of the transaction log depends on information including

- Frequency of insert, update, and delete transactions
- The amount of data modified per transaction
- The effects of long-running transactions
- The value of the *recovery interval* configuration parameter
- Whether the transaction log is being kept for media recovery (*trunc log on chkpt* database option is false)
- The use of Replication Server

Large transactions will also affect the amount of data in the SQL Server transaction logs. Consider the effects of large multirow updates, deleting a table (as opposed to truncating a table), inserts based on subqueries, and bulk-copying data into an SQL Server database.

Large multirow updates can generate a large amount of log data. Let's examine this simple SQL statement:

```
update abigtable set price = price*1.10
```

Since many UPDATE statements require logging of both the before and after images of a row, applications that require mass updates or a

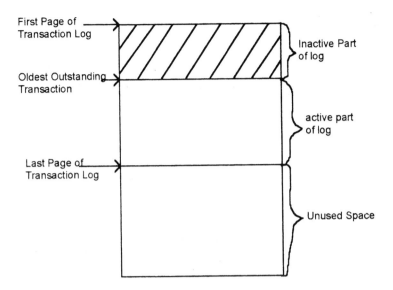

- DUMP TRANSACTION will truncate the log to the point of the oldest outstanding transaction

Figure 10.3   Log truncation points.

large number of updates should plan transaction log space according-ly. Also, there will be logging associated with any indexes that may be on the table. Start with a number at least twice as large as the largest table requiring mass updates.

The best way to determine the size of the transaction log is by run-ning a test in a simulated production environment. For example, load the database to its anticipated capacity, and run the applications with the same number of users expected in production. As a general rule, to start, create a transaction log that is approximately 10 to 25 per-cent of the actual database size. Obvious factors will impact this rule; for example, if a 5-Gbyte database is mostly read-only, there will not be a need for a 1-Gbyte transaction log. Figure 10.3 illustrates man-agement of the SYBASE transaction log.

10.6.1   Replication Server—secondary log truncation point

The Replication Server log transfer manager maintains a secondary log truncation point. This secondary truncation point is used by the Replication Server as a marker for replicated data (e.g., all data in the transaction log is replicated up to this point). As transactions in the log are replicated, this secondary truncation point is moved for-

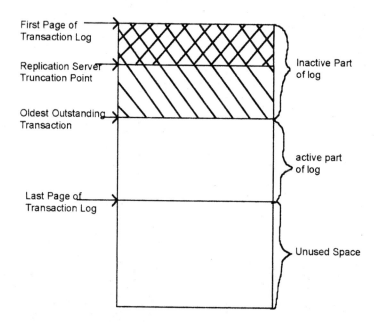

First Page of
Transaction Log

Replication Server
Truncation Point

Oldest Outstanding
Transaction

Last Page of
Transaction Log

Inactive Part
of log

active part
of log

Unused Space

- DUMP TRANSACTION will truncate the log to the point of the Replication Server truncation point
NOT the oldest outstanding transaction. If any part of the replication system is down, the replication
server truncation point cannot be moved. The transaction log must have enough space available to
sustain a possibly long failure period.

Figure 10.4 Log truncation points with Replication Server.

ward in the log. The DUMP TRANSACTION command cannot truncate the log after this point, or else data will be lost. Figure 10.4
shows the effect of Replication Server on the SYBASE transaction log.
The DUMP TRANSACTION command will truncate the transaction
log to the point of the Replication Server truncation point, *not* the oldest outstanding transaction. If any part of the replication system is
down, the Replication Server truncation point cannot be moved. The
transaction log must have enough space available to sustain a possible lengthy failure period.

If the database is to be used in a Replication Server environment,
the transaction log must be large enough to withstand a network failure or failure of a Replication Server component. Remember, the
database transaction log cannot be truncated until the transactions
are replicated by the log transfer manager. The secondary transaction
marker can be overridden, but this will create a problem with syn-
chronizing the remote site when it comes back on line.

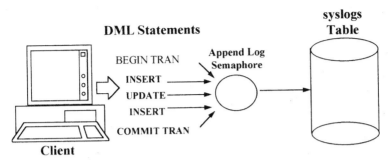

Figure 10.5   Pre-System 11 transaction logging.

10.6.2   Private log cache

Here's another System 11 feature that SYBASE DBAs everywhere will appreciate! As mentioned earlier, (pre-System 11) SYBASE systems often experience I/O bottlenecks in the area of transaction logging. The private log cache (PLC) is designed to improve the scalability of SQL Server by reducing contention on the transaction log semaphore and the *syslogs* table.

To illustrate the benefits of the private log cache (also known as the *user log cache*), let's look at how a pre-System 11 SQL Server handles transaction log I/O. Figure 10.5 illustrates the process of transaction logging. The pre-System 11 SQL Server uses a single *append log semaphore* for all user processes. The *append log semaphore* is a lock manager semaphore used to enforce the single-threaded addition of log records to the *syslogs* table. Basically, each client asks the log manager (via the log semaphore) for a slot to write to the transaction log. This requires synchronous writes to the transaction log (e.g., BEGIN, INSERT, UPDATE, INSERT, and COMMIT in Fig. 10.5). This requires several trips through the append log semaphore. It is easy to see that significant contention could exist as multiple database processes write log records to the *syslogs* table. Furthermore, prior to each write, the database process must acquire *exclusive* access to the log semaphore. The System 10 SQL Server writes log records to the stack prior to writing them to the *syslogs* table.

10.6.3   PLC architecture

With System 11, each user task has its own memory area where log records for the user's transactions are cached. There is one PLC per SQL Server process. The private log cache is actually a 2K (by default) buffer maintained by the System 11 SQL Server for each Open Client connection. The contents of the PLC are flushed through the *append log semaphore* when the transaction commits or when the buffer is

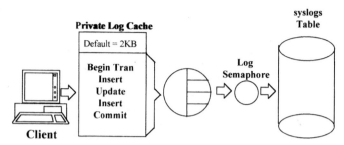

Figure 10.6   System 11 transaction logging.

full. The PLC can also be flushed when the transaction modifies an object in a different database or before a trigger is run by SQL Server.

Writes to the transaction log are performed in batch mode with the contents of the user log cache written to the transaction log (as opposed to individual DML, statements as illustrated in Fig. 10.5). This means that the frequency of access by the Open Client process to both the transaction log and the append log semaphore is reduced.

This architecture reduces contention for multiple transactions in a given database, thus improving scalability. Less contention for the *append log semaphore* also results in a lower schedule-out rate (user process being moved to the disk I/O sleep queue). Figure 10.6 describes the architecture of the private log cache. Two server configuration parameters affect the operation of the private log cache:

- *User log cache size.* This is the size of each private log cache; the default size of the PLC is 2048 bytes. The maximum size of the PLC is 2,147,483,647 bytes. The PLC should not be larger than the largest single transaction. It is not a good idea to configure the PLC for long-running transactions.

- *User log cache spinlock ratio.* This is the number of PLCs per PLC spinlock. Spinlocks are used to control the PLC semaphores. The default is 20, which should be optimal for most applications. In uniprocessor environments, this value is ignored, and there is only one spinlock.

The SQL Server 11.0 transaction logging subsystem is responsible for implementing the PLC and the *syslogshold* table (described in Chap. 8). The transaction logging subsystem is also known by the acronym *XLS*.

PLC and chained transaction mode.   Chained mode or ANSI-compatible mode implicitly begins a transaction before any data retrieval or modification statement. This can be problematic for a pre-System 11 SQL

Server because of network and application errors. Chained-mode transactions introduce the possibility of user interaction within the transaction. Some front-end tools (e.g., PowerBuilder with *autocommit* = false) issue a BEGIN TRAN statement when they connect to the SQL Server. With a System 10 server, this will establish a point beyond which the transaction log cannot be truncated (a long-running transaction).

With System 11, chained-mode transactions are handled by the PLC. The BEGIN TRANSACTION statement is written to the PLC, and *not* directly to the SQL Server transaction log. Nothing will be written to the transaction log until there is at least one changed record requiring logging. This increases the reliability of SQL Server by reducing the possibility of a long-running, chained-mode transaction holding up the transaction log.

10.6.4   System procedures

The following system stored procedures are used to modify the transaction logging system of SQL Server:

sp_logiosize

sp_logdevice

The *sp_logiosize* system procedure was described in Sec. 9.4.1, and *sp_logdevice* is explained here.

sp_logdevice.   The *sp_logdevice* system procedure is used to move the transaction log of a database with log and data on the same device to a separate database device. The syntax follows:

```
sp_logdevice dbname, devname
```

for example,

```
sp_logdevice db_swaps, log_device1
```

The *dbname* parameter is the name of the database whose transaction log is to be placed on the separate database device. The *devname* argument is the name of the database device which will be used to hold the transaction log.

The reader should note that this procedure only affects future allocations of space for the transaction log. The preferred method of placing the transaction log on its own device is with the CREATE DATABASE ... LOG ON ... command, which places the entire transaction log on the specified device.

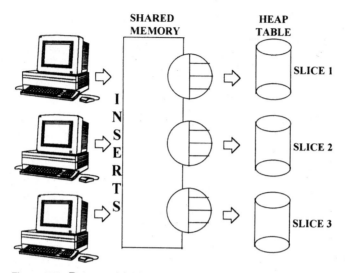

Figure 10.7   Data partitioning using SYBASE.

10.7   Data Partitioning

Data partitioning is critical to RDBMS scalability. As mentioned in Chap. 1, if the entire database can be partitioned into a number of smaller segments, then a database query can be decomposed into the equal number of subqueries running in parallel against these smaller segments. The resulting execution time (on an SMP or MPP server) will be significantly reduced in comparison to that of a sequential query. SYBASE MPP uses multiple SQL Server instances running on several nodes to achieve parallelism. See Fig. 10.7.

To carry the conversation to the next level, it is obvious that a parallel RDBMS should benefit from a server architecture that supports parallel I/O. Additional performance improvements will be achieved by placing data partitions on separate physical devices. Ultimately, database partitioning can be used to support parallel loads and parallel scans.

10.7.1   The SYBASE implementation

The primary goal of SYBASE data partitioning is to improve performance when doing multiple inserts to a table by creating multiple page chains for that table. As we learned in Chap. 5, all inserts into a nonpartitioned heap table go to the last page with locking contention possible (even likely) on that last page. A *heap* table is a table that does not have a clustered index. SYBASE data partitioning reduces contention by providing multiple last pages (by using multiple page chains). In this section we will learn how to use SYBASE data partitioning and see how partitioning affects the storage structure of a SYBASE table.

The SYBASE implementation uses table partitions to provide high concurrency when data is inserted into heap tables. A classic example is inserts into a history table as required by the TPC-A benchmark tests. In the case of TPC-A, performance using a partitioned table for history should be better than or equal to that using multiple history tables.

SYBASE also refers to table partitions as *slices*. SYBASE data partitioning provides concurrent insert points to heap tables in order to minimize lock contention. Slices can be assigned to database segments to minimize hardware contention. A table can be sliced into x partitions, with each partition being stored on a different storage device.

Slices are ideal for heap objects such as transaction logs, history, and audit tables. Unfortunately, due to technical limitations (at the time of this writing), SYBASE cannot partition the *syslogs* table. This has something to do with the fact that log records must be serialized chronologically. That is, during recovery SYBASE must apply transactions to the database (forward recovery) in chronological order or risk data corruption. Hopefully this problem will be solved in a future release of SYBASE.

When data is inserted into a partitioned table, SYBASE groups inserts by transaction. So all inserts for a single transaction will go into the same slice or partition. SYBASE uses a random-number scheme to determine which slice is the target for a particular transaction. For this reason, a partitioned table may not be ideal for large transactions performing a large number of inserts. Chapter 13 includes some pointers on bulk-loading data (using BCP) into a partitioned table.

Page stealing.   Page stealing is a strategy used when a slice for a partitioned table runs out of space. For example, assume that we have a heap table that already contains data. If we partition this table, all the existing data will be part of the first page chain. Obviously, then, the first partition will run out of space before the other partitions. So what happens is this: When the first partition runs out of space, it will *steal* pages from another partition. The page allocation algorithm allocates a page from a device or extent other than the set of devices or extents which are assigned to the data partition requesting the page allocation.

If page stealing were not allowed, then filling a single partition would result in an "unable to allocate space" error message, and ultimately failure to insert more rows. Page stealing can occur for a number of reasons including unequal sizes of the object's partitions, uneven distribution of data due to large insert transactions, or assignment of other objects to the same device. Page stealing is undesirable because it destroys the physical contiguity of the logical page chains of a partition. Partitioned tables may require periodic maintenance, as described in Chap. 20.

Limitations.   The SYBASE data-partitioning model currently has several limitations, including these:

- The table to be partitioned cannot have a clustered index. This limits application to heap tables. Note that this will be fixed in a future release of SQL Server.

- If the partitioned table contains text or image data, the text and/or image page chains are not partitioned.

- Any indexes defined on the table are not partitioned.

- Several SQL statements cannot be used on a partitioned table, including TRUNCATE TABLE, DROP TABLE, CREATE CLUSTERED INDEX, and *sp_placeobject*.

- Data partitioning cannot be used to slice the transaction log. For a heap table prior to System 11, it was guaranteed that pages were in inserted order. With a partitioned heap table, that is no longer the case.

- All inserts for a given transaction are performed in the same partition. If the table is the target of large insert transactions, the result may be uneven distribution of data in the table's slices. This can lead to page stealing if one of the partitions runs out of free space.

- If the table contains data before it is partitioned, all existing data will be stored in the first page chain. This results in uneven distribution of data in the partitioned table.

10.7.2   Addendum to Chap. 5—Effects of data partitioning on storage structure

Let's see what data partitioning does to the internal storage structure of a heap table.

The *sysindexes* table.   We learned in Chap. 5 that a row in *sysindexes* with *indid* equal to 0 points to a table. We also learned that *sysindexes.first* is the page number of the first page in the heap, and *sysindexes.root* is the page number of the last page in the heap.

Well, here comes the curveball. Data partitioning changes all that. When a table is partitioned, rows are inserted into a new system table named *syspartitions,* and *sysindexes.root* and *sysindexes.first* are ignored.

The *syspartitions* table.   When a table is partitioned, one row is inserted into *syspartitions* for each partition. The *syspartitions* table looks like this:

```
CREATE TABLE syspartitions(
     state          smallint     not null,
     id             int          not null,
     partitionid    int          not null,
     firstpage      int          not null,
     controlpage    int          not null,
     spare          binary(32)   not null,
     )
```

The columns are used as follows:

- Column *state*—internal information about the state of the partition.

- Column *id*—the object ID of the partitioned table (as found in *sysobjects*).

- Column *partitionid*—the partition number; from 1 to *n*.

- Column *firstpage*—the page number of the first page in this partition's page chain.

- Column *controlpage*—the page number of the *control page* for the partition's chain. For a partitioned heap table, there are multiple last pages (one for each partition). The *last page* information is contained on the control page for each partition. The control page also maintains information about which database devices are contained within this partition.

- Column *spare*—reserved for future use.

Figure 10.8 illustrates the relationship of entries in the *syspartitions* table to their associated page chains.

To determine whether an object is partitioned, use the *sp_helpartition* system procedure, or check to see if there are rows in *syspartitions,* using the following query:

```
1> select count(*) from syspartitions where id = object_id('mytable')
2> go
--------
       0

(1 row affected)
```

If the query returns 0, the table is not partitioned.

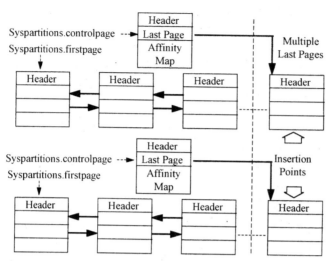

Figure 10.8 The *syspartitions* structure.

The *sysusages* table.   The *sysusages* table can also be used to monitor space for a given partition. The *unreservedpgs* column lists pages in extents that are not yet allocated. This can be used to monitor the space available to a given fragment to see if it is filling up.

10.7.3 Basic implementation

In this section we discuss the general steps followed to partition a heap table. We will learn how to use the SQL Server commands and stored procedures that are applied to table partitions. In general, data partitioning is a three-step process:

1. Optionally establish a database segment for the partitioned table.

2. Optionally place the table on the segment.

3. Specify that partitioning is desired with the ALTER TABLE...PARTITION command.

By default, tables are stored on the *default* data segment. A table can be partitioned on the *default* segment or on a segment that has been created for this table. Tables that already contain rows can be partitioned; however, it makes more sense to unload the table, partition it, and reload the table by using BCP. If the table contains data before it is partitioned, all existing data will be stored in the first page chain. This results in uneven distribution of data in the partitioned table. Please refer to Sec. 13.4, "Using the Bulk Copy Program," for more information.

SQL Server commands. The SQL Server ALTER TABLE command has been enhanced to work with partitioned tables. The command syntax is

```
alter table tableName [partition number_of_partitions | unpartition]
```

for example,

```
alter table tbaccount partition 5
alter table tbaccount unpartition
```

The *partition* keyword is used to create multiple-database page chains for the specified table. SQL Server can perform concurrent insert operations into the last page of each chain. The *number_of_partitions* must be an integer number greater than or equal to 2. As described in the previous section, each partition or slice requires a control page.

The *unpartition* keyword performs the following actions:

1. The different page chains of the partitioned table are concatenated.
2. If a partition (other than the first) has only one page and that page contains no rows, the page is freed.
3. The control page for each partition is freed.
4. The *sysindexes.root* and *sysindexes.first* entries for the table are updated.
5. All rows for the table are deleted from *syspartitions*.

The ALTER TABLE...PARTITION and ALTER TABLE...UNPARTITION commands cannot be used within a transaction. To use the TRUNCATE TABLE or DROP TABLE command (or to create a clustered index on a table), the table first must be unpartitioned by using the ALTER TABLE...UNPARTITION command.

System stored procedures. The system stored procedures that have been added (or affected) by the addition of data partitioning are

sp_helpartition

sp_help

The *sp_helpartition* stored procedure is used to display information about partitioned tables. It is used to display the first page and the control page for each partition of a partitioned table. The syntax is

```
sp_helpartition table_name
```

for example,

```
1> sp_helpartition football
2> go
partitionid firstpage   controlpage
---------- ----------   -----------
         1        417        44960
         2      44968        44969
         3      44976        44977
         4      44984        44985
         5      44992        44993

(5 rows affected, return status = 0)
```

The *sp_help* stored procedure is used to report information about any database object listed in the *sysobjects* table, and about SQL Server-supplied or user-defined data types. The procedure has been altered to call *sp_helpartition* for partitioned tables. The syntax is

```
sp_help [object_name]
```

DBCC commands. The DBCC *page* keyword is used to view the contents of a data page within a database. Page and header information can be displayed, as well as page data in row format or in raw format. The page offset table can be displayed. The different parts of the SQL Server data page are described in Chap. 5. The form of DBCC *page* is

```
dbcc page( cache_name, database_id, page_number, format )
```

The *cache_name* parameter is the name of the buffer cache, or *default data cache*. The *database_id* is the database ID number as found in the *master.dbo.sysdatabases* system table. The database ID can be found with the *sp_helpdb* system stored procedure. The *page_number* is the page number to be displayed. In the example that follows, we display the control page for the first partition. The *format* argument is used to specify formatting options, as shown in Table 10.1. For example,

TABLE 10.1 Formatting Options for DBCC *page*

Option	Description
0	Display page and buffer header only (this is the default)
1	Display header information, data in row format, and page offset table
2	Display header information, unformatted (raw) data, and page offset table
3	Used to format the control page

```
1> sp_helpartition tbaccount
2> go
partitionid firstpage      controlpage
----------- ---------      -----------
          1       417            44960
          2     44968           44969
          3     44976           44977
          4     44984           44985
          5     44992           44993

(5 rows affected, return status = 0)

1> dbcc page('default data cache',9,44960,3)
2> go

PAGE:
Page found in cache.

BUFFER:
Buffer header for buffer 0xe96875c0
   page=0xe9687800 bdnew=0x0 bdold=0x0 bhash=0x0 bmass_next=0x0
   bmass_prev=0x0 bvirtpg=0 bdbid=0 bkeep=0
     bmass_stat=0x0800 bbuf_stat=0x0000 bpageno=44960
     bxls_pin=0x00000000 bxls_next=0x00000000b
     bxls_flushseq 0 bxls_pinseq 0

PAGE HEADER:
Page header for page 0xe9687800
pageno=44960 nextpg=0 prevpg=0 objid=2028534260 timestamp=0001
0031f8e7
nextrno=0 level=0 indid=0 freeoff=32 minlen=60
page status bits: 0x1,

Control Page Data:
lastpage=44844
slicenum=1
alloccount=4483
device affinity map count=1
lstart=0
size=76800
DBCC execution completed. If DBCC printed error messages, contact a user
   with System Administrator (SA) role.
```

Partition groups. The *partition groups* configuration parameter is used to specify the number of partition groups to allocate for the server. Partition groups are internal data structures that SQL Server uses to control access to the individual partitions of a table.

Partition groups are used to store information about a single partition. A partition group is composed of 16 partition caches. All caches in a partition group are used to maintain information about the same partitioned table. Thus if a table has less than 16 partitions, the other partition caches in the partition group are wasted. If a table has more than 16 partitions, it requires multiple partition groups.

The default value of partition groups is 64. This allows for a maximum of 64 open partitioned tables and 1024 open partitions. The *partition groups* configuration option is not dynamic, so the server must be restarted for the new value to take effect. If there are insufficient partition groups available, access to the partitioned table will fail.

An example. Let's take a look at a simple example of how to use data partitioning on a SYBASE table. The procedure is described here.

The first step is to create a database segment for the partitioned table. This step is optional; however, it makes sense to partition the table across several physical storage devices.

```
sp_addsegment partition_segment, myDatabase, device_1
sp_extendsegment partition_segment, myDatabase, device_2
sp_extendsegment partition_segment, myDatabase, device_3
```

Remember, it is possible to have multiple segments assigned to a given device for a database.

The next step is to create the heap table on the database segment, which in this example is named *partition_segment*.

```
create table tbaccount_audit(
     acct#          int          not null,
     description    char(30)     not null,
     suser_name     char(30)     not null,
     timestamp      datetime     not null
) on partition_segment

create index x1account_audit on
  tbaccount_audit(acct#) on index_segment
```

Finally, use the ALTER TABLE command to partition the heap table.

```
alter table tbaccount_audit partition 6
```

Tips. The following pointers are provided for implementing data partitioning.

- Use data partitions for a table with heavy insert activity and a noticeable hot spot.

- Don't partition for the sake of partitioning. If there is no contention for the last page in the table and the table is partitioned, there may actually be a *decrease* in performance. The decrease in performance can come from overhead associated with maintaining the control pages.

- Look for consistent blocking locks on a specific table. If the table shows up regularly, it may be a candidate for partitioning.

- Try to avoid single large-insert transactions. All rows in the transaction will be inserted into one slice, resulting in partitions of unequal sizes and decreased performance benefits. All rows inserted into the table in a given transaction will be inserted into the same partition.

- When an existing table that already contains data is partitioned, (1) unload the data, (2) recreate the table, (3) partition the table, and (4) bulk-copy the data back into the table, using a reasonable batch size.

- Don't hesitate to establish 30 to 60 partitions for a large history table with heavy insert activity.

- Establish regular maintenance procedures for partitioned tables as described in Chap. 20.

10.8   I/O Strategies

Most modern disk drives are capable of reading 16K data blocks with the same overhead as 2K data pages. Given that fact, it follows that for certain types of queries it makes sense for a state-of-the-art RDBMS to perform larger I/Os instead of 2K I/Os. This would certainly apply to many queries common to DSS environments. In the case of the SYBASE environment, this would allow SQL Server to read and write entire *extents* (8×2K pages) for the same cost as a single 2K page. This can dramatically reduce the overall number of physical reads required to complete a query.

The buffer management system in System 11 allows the system administrator to tune the I/O block size. A particular named cache can have a mixture of sizes. This capability helps the server support mixed-workload environments. For example, some random-access applications might be running while other applications are performing decision support aggregation. The system can be tuned to mix and match these applications using a single buffer cache. Each individual buffer can have a mixture of sizes.

Any named buffer cache can have its own I/O size. The smallest size is 2K and the largest is currently 16K. Actually, the server can use 2K, 4K, 8K, and 16K I/O sizes. The 16K limitation has something to do with the way that the server performs space allocations using extents. There is no limit on the number of caches that can be configured.

Large I/Os and sequential prefetch.   The query optimizer is designed to make intelligent decisions regarding the choice of I/O size. The query optimizer can also decide to use sequential prefetch for queries that scan large amounts of data. The System 11 query optimizer can perform I/O for the same object using different block sizes. For example, data records for a table may be retrieved using 4K I/Os while text and image data for the same table may be performed using 16K I/Os.

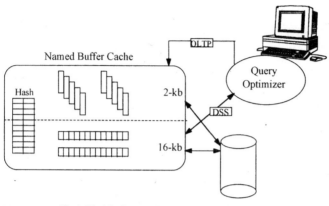

Figure 10.9   Variable block size disk I/O.

This allows the buffer manager to make very efficient use of memory. This strategy can also be used to prevent text and image data or DSS data from displacing more critical OLTP data from cache memory.

To perform large I/Os on a table, a buffer pool must be configured for large I/Os and the table must be bound to that cache, as described in Chap. 9. A 16K pool consists of several 16K buffers that form a separate LRU/MRU chain with separate wash size configuration. Large I/Os are not suitable for all operations because pages in the buffer move together, and therefore age out of the cache at the same time. The most significant performance gains are seen in DSS, BCP, and text and image handling. Figure 10.9 illustrates the relationship of the optimizer to the buffer manager.

10.9   Hot Spots

If there is one point that should be made in this chapter, it is this: *Distribute I/O as evenly as possible across as many disks and disk controllers as possible.* To achieve this goal requires a good knowledge of how applications will be using the data. The time spent at the beginning to develop a strategy for object placement will be time well spent. The largest performance gains to be realized will come from proper table design, index selection, and object placement. Even the most powerful DBMS will suffer from the effects of poor database design and object placement.

With the exception of history tables and audit tables, all tables should have a unique clustered index defined. A table with no clustered index is treated as a heap structure. Without a clustered index, INSERTs and out-of-place UPDATEs will occur in the last data page. This increases the possibility of contention, as all processes are competing for one 2K data page in the table. This last page in a heap table can become a *hot spot,* because of the contention present in that page. Heap tables are often good candidates for data partitioning.

Monotonic data is defined as data with a sequentially increasing key (1, 2, 4, 6, 7, 8, . . .). Hot spots can be created by insert operations on clustered indexes that use a monotonically increasing key. A clustered index on monotonic data can result in high contention for the last data page in the table similar to that found in a heap structure. Try to pick a clustered index that offers a high degree of randomness. A table's primary key may not always be the best candidate for a clustered index. Also, try to keep index keys as small as possible. This results in faster index scans and b-tree traversals (and less disk space utilization—especially with nonclustered indexes). Unique indexes should be defined as unique to assist the query optimizer.

```
1> create unique clustered index x0_account on tb_account( accountNumber )
2> go
```

10.10   Monitoring I/O

This section provides an overview of how to monitor disk I/O utilization on systems based on UNIX and Windows NT.

UNIX.   The *iostat* and *sar* commands are commonly used to display information about I/O activity in a UNIX system. Command syntax varies among host operating systems, so check the UNIX *man* page for command options. On a Sun Solaris system, when *iostat* is called with no options, it displays a one-line summary of terminal and disk I/O activity since the system was booted.

```
elvee:/opt/sybase:{sybase}\: iostat
     tty            fd0          sd3           cpu
 tin tout Kps tps serv Kps tps serv us sy wt id
  0   2    0   0    0   2   0   43  0  1  0  99
```

The -*x* option is used to report extended disk statistics for each disk present in the system.

```
sun3:/opt/sybase:{sybase}\: iostat -x
                   extended disk statistics
disk      r/s  w/s   Kr/s   Kw/s wait  actv   svc_t   %w   %b
sd0       0.3  0.4   1.3    2.0  0.0   0.0    32.8    0    1
sd1       0.1  0.1   2.0    2.1  0.0   0.0    27.0    0    0
sd2       0.0  0.3   0.1    1.2  0.0   0.0    22.1    0    0
sd3       0.0  0.1   0.3    2.1  0.0   0.0    41.0    0    0
sd31      2.5  1.9   9.8    6.5  0.0   0.1    19.4    0    3
sd32      1.1  1.9   5.9    9.7  0.0   0.1    18.8    0    3
sd50      0.2  1.8   0.6    3.6  0.0   0.0    14.2    0    2
sd51      2.0  2.0   15.2   16.6 0.0   0.1    31.0    0    4
```

The *sar* command is the UNIX *system activity reporter.* The *sar* utility can be used to report on several areas of system activity including
buffer activity (transfer activity using block and raw devices), cache hit
ratios, system calls, paging activity, kernel memory allocation (KMA)
information, average run queue length, CPU utilization, system swapping activity, TTY device activity, and a wide range of other information. The *sar* utility has the ability to collect data to a file so that it can
be reviewed at a later time.

The *-g* option to *sar* is used to report paging activities. Included in
the output is page-out requests, pages paged out, pages placed on the
free list by the UNIX page-stealing demon, and the percentage of UNIX
file system (UFS) inodes taken off the free list.

```
elvee:/home/gwa:{gwa}\: sar -g 2 2

SunOS elmo 5.4 Generic_101945-13 sun4m 12/26/95

14:58:09 pgout/s ppgout/s pgfree/s pgscan/s %ufs_ipf
14:58:11   60.00   12.00     0.00     0.00     0.00
14:58:13   77.00   15.20     0.00     0.00     0.00

Average     0.00    0.00     0.00     0.00     0.00
```

Windows NT. The Windows NT Performance Monitor can be used to
monitor disk I/O activity, as shown in Fig. 10.10. The subcategories
displayed in Fig. 10.10 include average disk bytes per read (average
number of bytes transferred from the disk during read operations),
average disk bytes per write (average number of bytes transferred
from the disk during write operations), and disk queue length (number of requests outstanding on the disk at the time the performance
data is collected).

SQL Server Monitor. SQL Server Monitor provides several ways of
monitoring device- and object-level I/O activity. The Device I/O window shown in Fig. 10.11 is used to display I/O requests at the database device level. In this instance, the SYBASE engine has only two
devices, the *master* device and *sysprocsdev.*

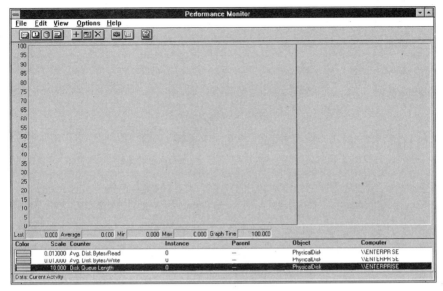

Figure 10.10   Windows NT Performance Monitor—disk I/O.

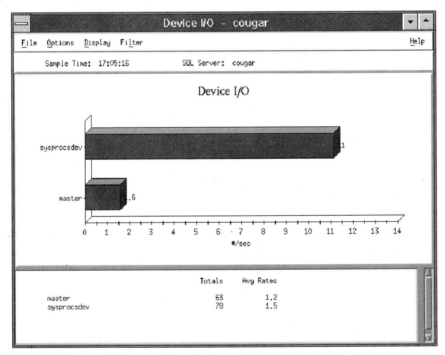

Figure 10.11   SQL Server Monitor—Device I/O.

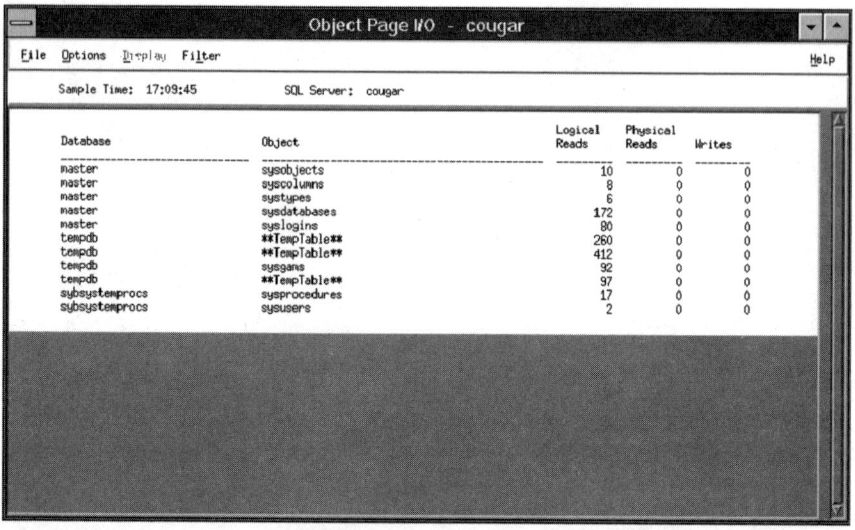

Database	Object	Logical Reads	Physical Reads	Writes
master	sysobjects	10	0	0
master	syscolumns	8	0	0
master	systypes	6	0	0
master	sysdatabases	172	0	0
master	syslogins	80	0	0
tempdb	**TempTable**	260	0	0
tempdb	**TempTable**	412	0	0
tempdb	sysgams	92	0	0
tempdb	**TempTable**	97	0	0
sybsystemprocs	sysprocedures	17	0	0
sybsystemprocs	sysusers	2	0	0

Figure 10.12 SQL Server Monitor—Object Page I/O window.

The Object Page I/O window (shown in Fig. 10.12) is used to display I/O information about SQL Server objects. The report includes database and object names, logical reads, physical reads, and number of writes.

Central Processing Unit

The processing potential of any RDBMS is influenced by the host computer's CPU. Factors such as speed, architecture (CISC, RISC, 32-bit, 64-bit), and number of CPUs all come under consideration. CPU bottlenecks occur when the operating system or user programs are making excessive demands on the CPU. This is often caused by excessive paging and memory swapping (which may be the result of insufficient memory in the system).

The past several years have seen dramatic advances in CPU power and architecture. Sybase, along with the other database vendors, has come to realize that the software it develops and markets has not made very good use of the hardware cycles available in state-of-the-art server platforms. The discussions of Chaps. 1 and 2 describe some of the ways that vendors have improved and continue to improve their products to make better use of hardware cycles.

One of the first suggested solutions to every performance problem may be, Can we throw more hardware at it? More hardware is usually better. However, how does the performance team determine what hardware will deliver the most for the money? Will the system benefit from additional memory, disks, and/or CPU? Keep in mind that the traditional RDBMS bottleneck is I/O and not CPU. Also, CPU bottlenecks are often caused by insufficient memory in the system or by improper I/O strategies.

For example, consider the difference in the performance and throughput potential of a dedicated four-CPU SPARC 1000 and an eight-CPU SPARC 1000 running SYBASE System 10. The performance difference is probably less than 10 percent. In most cases the cost of the additional processors cannot be justified by the 10 percent increase in performance. Because of the scalability improvements

Sybase has made to System 11, these same server platforms running System 11 would change the price/performance picture dramatically.

Several factors need to be assessed to determine how much work a CPU will be required to do.

- Is the server platform a dedicated database server, or is it being shared by other applications such as batch processes, management tools, job scheduling, Replication Server, and transaction monitors?
- CPU utilization during periods of peak activity.
- CPU utilization during periods of low activity. This is a good time to utilize CPU idle time for backup and maintenance jobs.
- CPU requirements to support SYBASE.
- The balance of CPU time dedicated to user and system services.

In this chapter, we will discuss SYBASE architecture for SMP, managing the CPU, assessing the load on the CPU, and ways to tune SQL Server engines and the scheduler.

11.1 Uniprocessor

Performance issues are obviously very different for uniprocessor and SMP systems. Uniprocessor systems do not experience any of the synchronization issues found in SMP systems. The operating system kernel does not need to worry about protecting critical data structures and memory areas from simultaneous access. Similarly, the database kernel does not need to use spinlocks to guarantee the integrity of data caches and catalog structures. This results in lower overhead because there is no contention for caches and data structures.

11.2 Symmetric Multiprocessors

To briefly recap the discussions of Chap. 6, computer vendors continue to expand and develop new-generation computers utilizing multiple processors. At the most basic level, there are two ways to build a machine with multiple processors:

- Shared-memory symmetric multiprocessors
- Shared-nothing massively parallel systems

The symmetric multiprocessor (SMP) architecture involves multiple CPUs utilizing shared memory and disks. The operating system runs concurrently and provides scheduling so that tasks execute on all CPUs in a symmetric fashion. Each processor runs tasks from a common execution or task queue. Modern SMP systems can have up to 64 processors; the Sun SPARCServer 1000 can have up to 8 CPUs, while the SPARCServer 2000 can have up to 20 CPUs.

The SMP environment is complicated by many different tasks running concurrently and competing for the same data and resources. Operating system kernels use facilities such as kernel locks (spinlocks), atomic instructions (operations guaranteed by the hardware to be uninterruptable), mutual-exclusion structures, and semaphores to coordinate these tasks.

SYBASE has its own kernel which is responsible for coordinating internal threads that may be running on several CPUs and competing for the same data. In previous chapters, we have seen that SYBASE uses spinlocks to coordinate access to internal data structures and data caches. We have also established that the chief architectural advantage of the System 11 buffer manager is reduced spinlock contention.

Multiprocessor servers. SYBASE multiprocessor design is based on Sybase's Virtual Server Architecture (VSA) which allows it to utilize parallel processing features on SMP systems.

SQL Server can be run as a single operating system process which does not utilize SMP (described in Chap. 3) or as multiple cooperating processes, as illustrated in Fig. 11.1. Depending on the number of CPUs available and the demands placed on the server, good practice

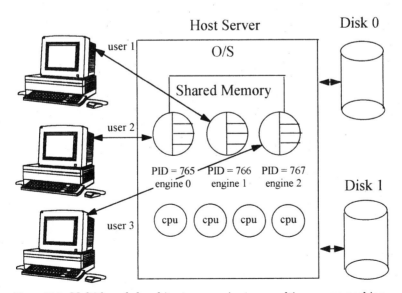

Figure 11.1 Multithreaded architecture running on a multiprocessor machine.

is to run a maximum of one SQL Server engine per available CPU. The VSA implementation will not allow the server to be started with more CPUs than are available.

The minimum and maximum number of engines can be controlled by the system administrator using server configuration variables. It is possible to start the SQL Server with a single engine (server process) and dynamically put on line more engines by using a DBCC command. It is not, however, possible to put server engines off line after they have been started. SYBASE would benefit from the ability to dynamically start and stop server engines while the server is running, to adjust for differing workloads. SYBASE MPP would benefit from this capability, as it would be able to start and stop DBA servers to adjust for system load. During peak loads SYBASE MPP could start additional DBA servers on a central node. Conversely, during light loads SYBASE MPP would kill DBA servers to reduce process overhead on the server.

Before we proceed further, let's define several terms used to describe the SYBASE Virtual Server Architecture. Whenever possible, I will attempt to use the Sybase definitions for SYBASE-specific features.

- *Virtual Server Architecture*—Consists of two or more SQL Server processes running in parallel. Virtual SQL Server starts and coordinates these parallel SQL Server processes to present a single virtual SQL Server interface and functionality.

- *Process*—an execution environment scheduled onto physical CPUs by the operating system.

- *Engine*—a process running an SQL Server that communicates with the other SQL Server processes via shared memory. An engine can be thought of as one CPU's worth of processing power. It does not represent a particular CPU.

- *Task*—an execution environment within the SQL Server scheduled onto engines by the SQL Server. Tasks are also referred to as *server processes* and *server threads*.

- *Affinity*—describes a process in which a certain SQL Server task runs only on a certain engine, or in which a certain engine runs only on a certain CPU.

- *Network affinity migration*—describes the process of transferring network I/O from one engine to another. SMP systems which support this migration allow SQL Server to distribute the network I/O load among all their engines.

The SYBASE SMP product is intended for machines with the following capabilities:

- A symmetric multiprocessing operating system (e.g., Sun's Solaris 2.x)
- Shared memory over a common bus
- From 1 to 32 processors
- No master processor (equality between processors)
- Very high throughput

SQL Server consists of one or more cooperating processes or engines, running the server program in parallel. The first engine, engine 0, serves as the network listener and accepts client connections. After engine 0 accepts the client connection, it may pass the connection off to another SQL Server engine. This process is performed in a round-robin fashion, which is to say that client connections will be load-balanced across currently running server processes (if the SMP system supports *network affinity migration*). For example, if there were four users in a four-engine system, each user would connect to a different engine. Connections are migrated by passing a *process slot structure* (PSS) from engine 0 to the receiving engine (engine *n*) by using a *channel* (see Fig. 11.2). All engines are peers and communicate via shared memory. Server resources (e.g., disks, memory, internal data structures) are shared among engines.

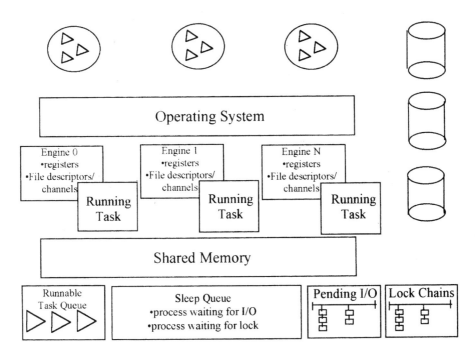

Figure 11.2 SQL Server task management.

Access to shared data structures is synchronized through a mechanism called a *spinlock*. Basically, a spinlock is a mutual-exclusion (mutex) semaphore and is single-threaded by design. If a spinlock is locked, other engines attempting to access it *spin,* repetitively testing the lock until it becomes available.

Server engines are instances of the SQL Server (the *dataserver* executable); they are multithreaded and perform all database operations including updates and transaction logging. SQL Server dynamically schedules client tasks onto available engines. When an engine becomes available, SQL Server runs the next runnable task. Note that there is no dispatcher; each available engine is looking for work in the *runnable* task queue. Currently, there is a single runnable task queue used by VSA. This can be a point of contention because available engines are constantly polling the run queue, *competing* for runnable tasks. Look for this to change in subsequent versions of the SQL Server.

The operating system schedules the engine processes onto physical CPUs. Any available CPU is used for any engine. There is no affinity between engines and CPUs. The processing is called symmetric because the lack of affinity between processes and CPUs creates a symmetrically balanced load. Some UNIX operating systems (e.g., Sequent's Dynix and Sun's Solaris) allow the system administrator to *bind* a particular operating system process to a processor. In this case, server processes will have an affinity to a particular CPU.

SQL task management for SMP.   Figure 11.2 illustrates SQL Server task management in SMP environments. Here is a brief description of the process:

- The client application makes a log-in request (e.g., by using the appropriate Open Client API calls). In response, the SQL Server creates a user task for the client. The user task will go to the *sleep queue* until the client requests work from the SQL Server engine.

- The client sends Transact-SQL commands to the SQL Server via TDS packet.

- SQL Server places the user task into the runnable task queue, where the engines will compete for the task.

- An engine will pull the task from the run queue, parse, normalize, compile, and finally execute the Transact-SQL commands. During these steps the Transact-SQL code is converted to low-level tasks such as requests for disk I/O.

- The engine will execute each step until the task completes, blocks on locks, is blocked waiting for disk I/O, or exceeds its *time slice.* If the task is blocked (waiting for I/O or locks), it will be removed from the run queue and placed in the sleep queue.

- When the block is resolved (i.e., the disk I/O is complete or the lock is granted), the user task will again be added to the runnable task queue.

- When the task blocks for the last time, it will continue to execute to completion. At this point, the user task will be placed in the sleep queue and yield the server engine to another task.

To summarize, SQL Server consists of one or more cooperating processes, or *engines,* running the server program in parallel. The first engine, engine 0, serves as the network listener and accepts client connections. All engines are peers and utilize common data structures in shared memory.

Server engines are instances of the *dataserver* executable and perform all database operations including updates and transaction logging. SYBASE dynamically schedules client tasks onto available engines. When an engine becomes available, it runs the next runnable task.

The effectiveness of VSA is highly dependent on the host operating system. The operating system schedules the engine processes onto physical CPUs. Any available CPU is used for any engine. The host operating system may have features to establish an affinity or *binding* of a dataserver process to a particular CPU. This can reduce the overhead involved in switching process information between CPUs.

Upon start-up, SQL Server will start one *dataserver* process (engine 0). SQL Server will then complete its initialization, including the recovery of all system and user databases. The final task during server boot-up is to fork additional *dataservers* (based on the *max online engines* configuration variable). For example, if *max online engines* is 3, engine 0 will fork two additional dataserver processes.

Depending on the number of CPUs available and the demands placed on the server, the administrator will want to run a maximum of one SQL Server engine per available CPU. There should only be as many engines as there are *usable* CPUs. Don't forget about the processing requirements of other processes (Replication Server, system services, batch jobs) which share the server platform. Keep in mind that the operating system also needs CPU time. Generally, it is a good practice to start with a few dataserver processes and monitor dataserver activity. The dataserver engines should be kept busy; one busy dataserver process may run better than three lightly utilized dataservers. Remember, VSA was created for large multiuser systems.

Keep the dataserver processes busy. If the dataserver has nothing to do, it will yield the CPU. Increase the priority of the dataserver processes if the host operating system supports it. Also, take advantage of process affinitying (binding) if the host operating system supports it. For example, Sun's Solaris operating system provides a utility call *pbind* that is used to control and query bindings of processes to processors.This can reduce the overhead involved with switching process information (context) between available CPUs. When binding is being used, most SMP operating systems will schedule other tasks onto other CPUs, leaving more CPU time for the dataserver process. Avoid the following:

- Binding dataserver processes to processors that are used by the operating system
- Binding more than one dataserver process to a single processor

Also, beware of operating systems which externalize their asynchronous I/O drivers. Early versions of Solaris 2.x do this, causing asynchronous I/O tasks to be scheduled as any user task would be.

11.3   Assessing whether CPU Is Busy

One of the steps required in the overall tuning process is to analyze the amount of work the server CPU(s) is (are) being asked to do. In this section we look at how to determine CPU requirements based on these factors:

1. Determine CPU utilization during periods of peak activity.
2. Determine CPU utilization during periods of light activity.
3. Assess the CPU requirements for SYBASE.
4. Assess the amount of CPU time required for user processes and system services.

11.3.1   Accessing whether CPU is busy

This section discusses how to determine the optimum number of SQL Server engines for a particular workload and system configuration. To do this, it is necessary to monitor system and SQL Server CPU utilization.

The reader should note that processor activity and bottlenecks depend on when they are monitored. Obviously, for applications that have a batch processing window, CPU activity will be higher during that window. Trading applications typically see peak activities during normal business hours, but may also see a high level of activity when receiving feeds from other systems or during normal maintenance.

Trading applications also need to contend with those high-volume *triple witching*[1] Fridays.

Assessing whether CPU is busy—Unix. The *sar* command is commonly used to display information about processor activity in a UNIX system. The command syntax varies among host operating systems, so check the UNIX *man* page for command options. On a Sun Solaris system, when *sar* is called with no options, it displays CPU utilization including the portion of time spent running in user mode, system mode, idle with some process waiting for block I/O, and otherwise idle.

```
starship:/home/gwa:{gwa}\: sar 2 5

SunOS starship 5.4 Generic_101945-13 sun4m 12/26/95

14:54:58   %usr  %sys  %wio  %idle
14:55:00    25    75     0     0
14:55:02    29    71     0     0
14:55:04    30    70     0     0
14:55:06    34    66     0     0
14:55:08    28    72 ·   0     0


Average     29    71     0     0
```

The Solaris *mpstat* command is used to report per-processor statistics in tabular form. Each row in the output represents the activity of one processor. Included in the output are minor and major faults, interrupts, context switches, thread migrations, spins on mutual exclusions, spins on read/write locks, system calls, and user percentage, system wait, and idle time.

```
starship:/opt/sybase:{sybase}\: mpstat 2 2
CPU minf mjf xcal intr ithr csw icsw migr smtx srw syscl usr sys wt idl
  0    0   0    0  142   42  25    0   10   19   0    38   2   2 10  87
  1    0   0    0   38   37  25    0   10   11   0   114   2   3  9  85
  2    0   0    0    2    0  24    0    9   11   0   137   3   4  9  84
  3    0   0    0   37   36  28    0   11   10   0   121   3   4  9  84
  4    0   0    0   37   35  30    0   12   11   0   135   3   4  9  84
  5    0   0    0    2    0  37    1   10   15   0   192   5   5  8  82
  6    0   0    0    2    0  35    1    9   16   0   224   6   6  7  81
  7    0   0    0   10    0  35   10    7   19   0    42  20  21  5  54
```

The *ps* command can be used to report information about active processes. On a Solaris system when called with the *-c* option, *ps* displays the process ID (PID), priority of the process (PRI), and cumulative execution time for the process (TIME). Higher numbers in the PRI column mean higher priority.

---

[1]In each year, there are four maturing S&P 500 futures contracts. On these Fridays, the expiration of S&P index options plus options on some individual stocks all occur simultaneously. Thus, these dates have been dubbed "triple witching hour."

```
starship:/opt/sybase:{sybase}\: ps -c
PID   CLS   PRI    TTY    TIME      COMD
345   IA    32    pts/2   0:00     RUN_coug
346   IA    59    pts/2   3:19     dataserv
316   IA    59    pts/2   0:00     csh
351   IA    59    pts/2   0:08     dataserv
903   IA    48    pts/2   0:00     ps
```

The *time* command is used to time a command. After the command is completed, *time* displays the elapsed time during the command, time spent in the system, and the time spent in execution of the command (user mode).

```
starship:/opt/sybase:{sybase}\: time monitor.csh
Results saved in filename monitor.121795
55.0u 92.0s 17:52 16% 0 + 0k 0 + 0io 0pf + ow
```

This command can be useful to determine the amount of user, system, and real time resources used over a complete testing run.

Assessing whether CPU is busy—Windows NT. The Windows NT Performance Monitor can be used to chart processor performance, as shown in Fig. 11.3. Included in the chart are processor interrupts per second (the number of device interrupts the processor is experiencing), percentage of user time (the percentage of processor time spent in user mode in nonidle threads), percentage of processor time (per-

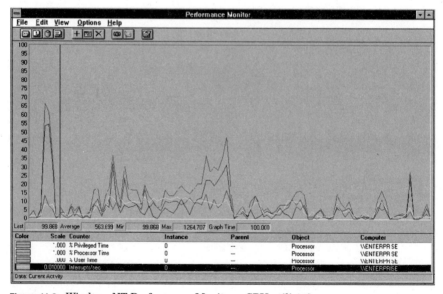

Figure 11.3 Windows NT Performance Monitor—CPU utilization.

centage of the elapsed time that a processor is busy executing a non-idle thread), and percentage of privileged time (percentage of processor time spent in privileged mode in nonidle threads).

The Windows NT service layer, the Executive routines, and the Windows NT kernel execute in privileged mode. Device drivers for most devices other than graphics adapters and printers also execute in privileged mode.

Comments.   Note that operating system monitors should not be relied upon to measure the availability of idle CPU time in the SQL Server. The SQL Server will often fall into a *busy wait* loop in an effort to improve system response time. The System 11 SQL Server will use the busy-wait loop as an attempt to maintain hardware cache locality (rather than relinquishing the CPU to the operating system). When an engine is in a busy-wait loop, it is polling the run queue, looking for work to do. While the engine is polling the run queue, it is consuming CPU time but is not accomplishing any useful work. For this reason, SQL Server can appear very busy to the operating system even though it is not performing work on behalf of a client.

11.3.2   CPU requirements for SYBASE

As discussed in Chap. 8, the output from the *sp_monitor* system procedure includes the amount of time SQL Server uses the CPU during an elapsed time interval. It is important to know that there is no relationship between operating system reports on CPU usage and SQL Server's internal CPU-busy counters. SQL Server may display very high CPU utilization while performing an I/O-bound task. This is because (under certain conditions) SQL Server enters a low-priority busy-wait loop while waiting for asynchronous disk I/O. Before CPU utilization is measured, it is a good idea to disable the housekeeper task to eliminate its effect on CPU measurement. This is done by setting the *housekeeper free write percent* parameter to 0, using the *sp_configure* system procedure as follows:

```
sp_configure 'housekeeper free write percent', 0
```

On uniprocessor servers, if SQL Server CPU utilization is above 85 percent for extended periods, it may be time to consider an SMP-based server platform or offloading processing to another SQL Server.

For multiprocessor implementations, measure the CPU usage for SQL Server using operating system utilities. If CPU usage is high (over 85 percent) for extended periods, consider adding more CPUs to the server platform.

Effects of housekeeper task on CPU utilization. The housekeeper is an internal SQL Server process whose sole function is to wash buffers. The housekeeper process is designed to improve CPU utilization by taking advantage of SQL Server idle cycles to wash buffers. The housekeeper uses CPU effectively by walking through all active buffer pools in all configured named caches.

Monitoring kernel utilization. The *sp_sysmon* procedure can be used to gauge CPU utilization of the SQL Server. The output is shown here:

```
= = = = = = = = = = = = = = = = = = = = = = = = = = = = = = = = = = = = = = = =
CPU Availability
----------------
  Engine 0           99.4 %
= = = = = = = = = = = = = = = = = = = = = = = = = = = = = = = = = = = = = = = =
Kernel Utilization
------------------
Engine Busy Utilization:
  Engine 0           0.0 %

CPU Yields by Engine      per sec    per xact    count %   of total
----------------------    -------    --------    -------   --------
                            0.0        0.0          0        n/a

Network Checks
  Non-Blocking              285.9    17257.0      17257     93.6 %
  Blocking                   19.6     1183.0       1183      6.4 %
-----------------------    -------    --------    ------    -------
Total Network I/O Checks:   305.5    18440.0      18440
Avg Net I/Os per Check      n/a        n/a      0.00043      n/a

Disk I/O Checks
  Total Disk I/O Checks     305.5    18440.0      18440       n/a
  Checks Returning I/O        0.0        0.0          0      0.0 %
= = = = = = = = = = = = = = = = = = = = = = = = = = = = = = = = = = = = = = = =
Task Management           per sec    per xact    count %   of total
--------------------      -------    --------    -------   --------
Connections Opened          0.0        2.0          2        n/a

Task Context Switches by Engine
  Engine 0                  0.4       26.0         26      100.0 %

Task Context Switches Due To:
  Voluntary Yields          0.0        1.0          1        3.8 %
  Cache Search Misses       0.0        0.0          0        0.0 %
  Logical Lock Contention   0.0        0.0          0        0.0 %
  Address Lock Contention                                        %
  Log Semaphore Contention  0.0        0.0          0        0.0 %
  Group Commit Sleeps       0.0        0.0          0        0.0 %
  Last Log Page Writes      0.0        0.0          0        0.0 %
  I/O Device Contention     0.0        0.0          0        0.0 %
  Network Packet Received   0.1        6.0          6       23.1 %
  Network Packet Sent       0.0        2.0          2        7.7 %
  SYSINDEXES Lookup         0.0        0.0          0        0.0 %
  Other Causes                                                   %
= = = = = = = = = = = = = = = = = = = = = = = = = = = = = = = = = = = = = = = =
```

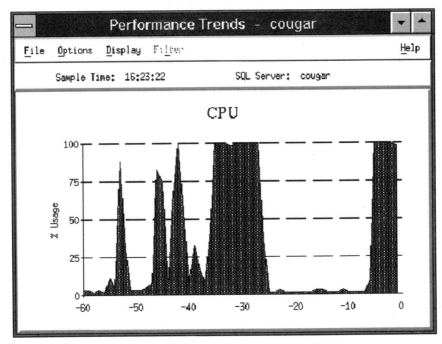

Figure 11.4 SQL Server Monitor Performance Trends—CPU utilization.

SQL Server Monitor. SQL Server Monitor can be used to monitor SQL Server CPU utilization over time, as shown in Fig. 11.4. As described in Chap. 8, the Process Detail window is used to display the amount of SQL Server CPU used and page I/O performed by a specific SQL Server connection. The Process Activity window consists of graphs displaying CPU rate and page I/O rate for as many as 20 user processes. Processes can be selected by name, by rate of activity in a specific performance indicator, or by a rate of activity equal to or greater than a specific threshold.

11.4 Tuning SQL Server Engines

This section gives a brief summary of tuning SQL Server engines. The *sp_configure* system procedure is used to change the *max online engines* parameter, which controls the number of dataserver engines running concurrently. When SQL Server is started, it will start one dataserver process (engine 0). SQL Server will then complete its initialization including the recovery of all system and user databases.

The final task during server boot-up is to fork additional dataservers. Each dataserver process accesses common data structures using shared memory.

A few words of advice before we go on:

1. There is seldom any reason to attempt to tune the scheduler.
2. Talk to Sybase technical support before you change any of these values.
3. Do not experiment with these parameters in a production environment.

Tuning the scheduler. The following configuration parameters can be used to tune the SQL Server kernel:

- *sql server clock tick length*
- *i/o polling process count*
- *time slice*
- *cpu grace time*
- *runnable process search count*

The SQL Server *clock tick length* (known as *cclkrate* in the configuration block) is used to control the number of milliseconds in an SQL Server *tick*. At each tick, the operating system interrupts the dataserver kernel by using a mechanism such as a signal. This serves as an inexpensive way of timing task execution. Among other things, SQL Server may perform routine checking at every clock tick for the following purposes:

- Check the sleep queue for incoming tasks (e.g., a command for a connection).
- Check the pending I/O queue to see if a task's I/O has been completed. There are pending I/O queues for both disk and network I/O. The *io polling process count* configuration variable controls the number of tasks the engine will run before checking the pending I/O queues.

The SQL Server *clock tick length* can be changed by using the *sp_configure* system procedure. Certain CPU-intensive environments may see a small performance benefit when a few queries monopolize an engine, because they fail to sleep voluntarily. If *sp_sysmon* indicates a high percentage of *task switches by voluntary yield,* it may warrant testing lower values for *clock tick length*. A lower value of *cclkrate* is used to force a smaller *time slice* to encourage multiuser throughput.

The *cpu grace time* parameter must be increased by the same factor as *sql server clock tick length* is decreased by (and vice versa).

The *cpu grace time* configuration variable specifies the maximum amount of time, in microseconds, that a user process can run without yielding the CPU before SQL Server infects it.

The SQL Server kernel is not preemptive. The *time slice* configuration variable is used to set the number of milliseconds that the SQL Server scheduler allows a user process to run. The kernel does not control time spent on a process; the process controls the time spent in the CPU and "schedules itself out." However, if the process does not give itself up (i.e., exceeds the *time slice* configuration), the kernel will terminate the process because it assumes that the program is in a hard loop. If the *time slice* variable is set too low, the system may slow down due to overhead caused by the system thrashing; i.e., the programs are frequently scheduling themselves in and out of the CPU. If *time slice* is set too high, it may cause long response time when one process fails to schedule itself out of the CPU for a long time.

Large batch jobs that may benefit from more CPU time may benefit from experimentation with higher values for *time slice*.

The *i/o polling process count* configuration variable (known as *cmaxscheds* in the configuration block) is used to specify the number of tasks each engine will run before checking the pending I/O queues for disk and/or network I/O completions. To perform disk and network I/O checks more often, use a lower value for *i/o polling process count*. Higher values may increase system throughput while lower values may lower response time. Applications that generate a large amount of disk and network activity may experience tradeoffs between system throughput and task response time.

The *runnable process search count* configuration variable (known as *cschedspins* in the configuration block) is used to determine the number of times an engine will loop while looking for work in the run queue before relinquishing control of the CPU. When tasks are switched too often from CPU to CPU, the hardware cache is invalidated and data is migrated back and forth. This forces a higher number of accesses to physical memory. When data is migrated, it is migrated through the bus, which slows down the system. By doing this, the server is using processing cycles to manage the caches back and forth instead of using the cycles for transaction processing. A higher value for *runnable process search count* can be used to avoid relinquishing control of the CPU.

12

Design and Indexing

The bulk of the performance and tuning process begins after a proper database design has been implemented. There is no point in devoting a significant amount of time to performance and tuning with a bad database design. Good database performance is the result of a combination of factors including database design, hardware selection, and tuning.

12.1 Database Design

The largest performance gains to be realized will come from proper table design and index selection. Even the most powerful RDBMS will suffer from the effects of poor database design. Design has two components: logical and physical. Logical design is data planning and results in a normalized entity relationship model. Physical design is data implementation and results in performance.

Based on the database design process and entity relationship modeling, physical database design involves the following tasks:

- Definition of tables
- Definition of indexes
- Placement of tables and indexes on physical devices
- Definition of primary and foreign keys
- Definition of database devices and segments
- Denormalization as a result of a performance problem
- Partitioning of heap tables where appropriate
- Implementation of procedural and declarative referential integrity

Normalized data. Always start with a normalized database, which eliminates repeating groups, nonkey attributes, and facts about nonkey attributes. A normalized database results in accelerated searching, sorting, and index creation because tables tend to be narrower. Narrower tables mean that more rows can fit on a page. The benefit of this is less logical and physical I/O because more rows fit on a page and more rows fit into cache. The downside is that because SYBASE uses page-level locking, it can lead to increased contention and concurrency problems.

The increased number of tables found in a normalized database results in more joins, more clustered indexes, and fewer indexes per table. Joins are generally very fast provided that proper indexes are available. SQL Server can be optimized to keep higher levels of the index in cache, which minimizes the number of physical I/Os required for many queries. This also provides more flexibility in tuning queries, since there are more tables. Minimizing the number of indexes per table has the effect of reducing contention for index pages. This results in improved UPDATE, INSERT, and DELETE performance which is especially important in SMP environments. There is a tradeoff here since indexes decrease the performance of INSERTs, UPDATEs, and DELETEs and increase the performance of SELECTs and joins.

Due to the increased number of tables, normalized data allows for better use of database segments to control the placement of tables. It also reduces the presence of redundant data which accelerates trigger execution by minimizing the job of maintaining redundant data.

Denormalization. Denormalization is an important technique in physical database design. It can help to reduce join operations, reduce the number of foreign keys requiring maintenance, and accelerate data retrieval. Denormalization should be an optimization taken as the result of a performance problem.

Denormalize when

- Many queries require access to the full set of joined data.
- A large number of applications scan database tables when performing joins.
- A table is used only for retrieval.
- The complexity of derived columns requires storage for SELECT statements.

Note that denormalization usually benefits read-only or low-update applications at the expense of OLTP performance.

Denormalization techniques. The following are commonly used denormalization techniques:

1. Collapsing tables
2. Adding redundant columns
3. Adding derived columns

Collapsing tables. To collapse tables is to combine two or more tables into a single table. The DBA may wish to collapse tables when the application must frequently access data in multiple tables in a single query and acceptable response time is not met.

Subtype tables are often a good candidate for collapsing into the supertype. The key columns are often the same, and while rows in the supertype that do not pertain to the subtype will contain columns without applicable data, little space will be wasted if the cardinality of the subtype is close to that of the supertype, or if the subtype table is relatively narrow.

When tables are collapsed in a parent-child relationship, the columns from the parent record must be repeated for each child record. The new table will contain one row for each parent-child row combination. Remember that this will affect the way that referential integrity and redundant data are maintained.

The first order of business is to identify transactions that require a significant amount of data from more than one table, especially those with one-to-one relationships. The second step is to create the new table containing the columns from each individual table.

The disadvantages of collapsing tables include the overhead associated with maintaining redundant copies of parent data for each corresponding child row. An UPDATE trigger should be created on the new table to maintain the redundant data, which can result in decreased performance for UPDATE transactions. Storage requirements for the new table will be increased due to the necessity of storing redundant data.

Adding redundant columns. Redundant columns can be added to a table to reduce the number of joins required by critical transactions, or transactions that are not delivering acceptable performance. Tables that are in the join path of critical transactions may be good candidates for this type of denormalization.

Again, this type of denormalization may be a tradeoff. Transactions that require access to the redundant data will see improved performance; however, transactions that maintain the replicated data will see slower performance.

The disadvantages of maintaining redundant columns include these:

- Excessive overhead may be imposed on UPDATE transactions because triggers are required to maintain the replicated data.

- The row width of the modified table is increased due to the addition of redundant columns. Transactions that do not benefit from the elimination of the join may also see a reduction in performance.

Let's take a look at how redundant columns might be used. This is a normalized version of an inventory and an inventory location table. The *inventory* table is used to store high-level information about items including part number, name, and inventory type. The *location* table is used to identify different locations at which the inventory may be available. The *inventory_location* table is used to identify the availability of a particular item at one or more locations.

```
create table inventory(
        partNumber      char(10)        not null,
        partName        char(40)        not null,
        type            char(1)         not null
        )
create unique clustered index x0inventory on inventory(partNumber)

create table location(
        location        char(6)         not null,
        locationName    char(30)        not null
        )
create unique clustered index x0location on location(location)

create table inventory_location(
        partNumber      char(10)        not null,
        location        char(6)         not null,
        qtyOnHand       int             not null,
        baseprice       float           not null
        )
create unique clustered index x0inventory_location(partNumber,location)
```

Now, assume that we need to get a report that includes part number, part name, and quantity on hand by location. This request can be satisfied by using the following query:

```
select a.partNumber,a.partName,b.location,b.qtyOnHand
  from inventory a, inventory_location b
 where a.partNumber = b.partNumber
```

If this report is run very often, we can eliminate the join by adding the *partName* column to the *inventory_location* table as follows.

```
create table inventory_location(
        partNumber      char(10)        not null,
        location        char(6)         not null,
        partName        char(40)        not null,
        qtyOnHand       int             not null,
        baseprice       float           not null
        )
create unique clustered index x0inventory_location(partNumber,location)
```

```
select partNumber, partName, location, qtyOnHand
from inventory_location
```

Keep in mind that it is now necessary to add an update trigger to the *inventory* table to maintain the redundant data in the *inventory_location* table. We have also increased the width of the *inventory_location* table by 40 bytes.

```
if update(partName)
begin
        update inventory_location set partName = inventory.partName
        where partNumber = x
end
```

Adding derived columns. A *derived value* is a value created as the result of a calculation involving values found in other columns. Adding columns for derived data to a table can be useful for queries that require access to the derived data for selecting. Applications that do reporting and decision support type of queries are usually benefactors of this type of denormalization.

Whenever possible, avoid the use of functions in WHERE clauses. If it is absolutely necessary, consider the use of an extra column of the transformed data type where a function is required. Also try to avoid mathematical manipulation of *select* arguments (SARGs). Let's take a look at how derived columns might be used.

In this case, XYZ Corp. maintains an inventory record for each product that it sells. There is also a transaction table which holds transaction details for each inventory item. In this case, the *inventory* table is the parent, and the *invtran* table is the child (or detail) table.

```
create table inventory(
        partNumber      char(10)        not null,
        partName        char(40)        not null,
        type            char(1)         not null
        baseprice       float           not null
        )
create unique clustered index x0inventory on inventory(partNumber)

create table invtran(
        partNumber      char(10)        not null,
        date            datetime        not null,
        quantity        int             not null,
        price           float           not null
        )
create nonclustered index x1invtran on invtran(partNumber, tranType, date)
```

The following SQL statement can be used to determine the number of items in inventory (quantity on hand) for a particular part number from the normalized schema:

```
select sum(quantity) from invtran
where partNumber = x
```

Obviously depending on the amount of activity over time, this query might be very intrusive. An example of a denormalized version of an *inventory* and *invtran* table that stores a derived value is

```
create table inventory(
        partNumber       char(10)          not null,
        partName         char(40)          not null,
        type             char(1)           not null,
        qtyOnHand        int               not null,
        baseprice        float             not null
        )
create unique clustered index x0inventory on inventory(partNumber)

create table invtran(
        partNumber       char(10)          not null,
        date             datetime          not null,
        quantity         int               not null,
        price            float             not null
        )
create nonclustered index x1invtran on invtran(partNumber, tranType, date)
```

To obtain the quantity on hand for a part number with the denormalized schema, the following SQL statement can be used:

```
select qtyOnHand from inventory
 where partNumber = x
```

One disadvantage of storing the derived column is that a trigger is required on the *invtran* table to automatically update the *inventory* table.

Now, let's assume that the marketing department needs to know the total number of any item sold on a year-to-date basis. This can be done in a number of ways including the following query:

```
select sum(quantity) from invtran
 where quantity < 0 and partNumber = x   /* Less than zero means that */
                                         /* the item was removed */
                                         /* from inventory */
```

If the marketing department is going to run this query on a regular basis, it may make sense to add a column to the *inventory* table for the derived data. With this solution, it will not be necessary to access the inventory transaction detail for an item to obtain the required information.

```
create table inventory(
        partNumber       char(10)          not null,
        partName         char(40)          not null,
        type             char(1)           not null,
        qtyOnHand        int               not null,
        ytdSales         int               not null,
        baseprice        float             not null
        )
create unique clustered index x0inventory on inventory(partNumber)
```

The derived column can be maintained by the trigger on the *invtran* table or (if the business requirements allow) by using a month-end processing program. At this point the marketing department can satisfy the request for information by using the following query, which will be very fast since it only requires access to the *inventory* table using the clustered index:

```
select ytdSales from inventory
 where partNumber = x
```

Some of the disadvantages of storing derived data include these:

- The storage requirements of the parent table will grow in size due to the addition of derived data.
- The performance of queries that do not benefit from the presence of the derived columns may decrease because of the increased table size.
- The development team will need to write triggers and/or maintenance programs to maintain the data in the parent tables. This can lead to slower response times for applications affected by the triggers, especially if the derived column is the target of frequent updates.

An advantage of storing derived data:

- There may be a reduction in I/O as well as reduced demand on the CPU because join operations are no longer required with the detail table.

12.2 Types of Indexes

Indexes usually represent separate data structures (e.g., various B-tree structures) that contain record keys and pointers to the corresponding records. Indexes can be used to access records directly by the key values, and they can guarantee uniqueness of the keys (if the keys are defined as unique). Indexes should be constantly maintained—kept in synchronism with the key values of the records when the data is updated, added, or deleted. Even though index maintenance can negatively affect the RDBMS performance, lack of indexes could result in serious performance degradation in direct (by full or partial key) data access. In this respect, clustered indexes are most important.

Clustered indexes. Clustered indexes are usually built on a primary (as opposed to foreign) key, require the data to be sorted in ascending or descending key order, and are also sorted in the same order as the

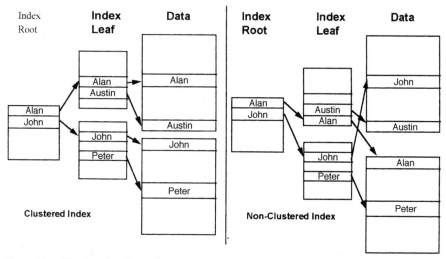

Figure 12.1 Clustered and nonclustered indexes.

data (see Fig. 12.1). Thus, clustered indexes can significantly improve record search and sequential retrieval in key order by reducing the required number of input/output operations (I/Os). For example, if we wanted to retrieve 100 rows from a table with no clustered index, it could easily result in 100 I/Os. When a clustered index is used, it is possible for the server to retrieve the first row with only a few I/Os, and then to locate the remaining rows on the same data page (depending on the row width).

Note that some RDBMS products (e.g., Ingres, Gupta) reduce or completely eliminate index I/O by supporting *hash indexes,* where records can be found by a key stored at locations calculated by a special algorithm. Hash indexes facilitate direct access and can coexist with indexes in the same RDBMS.

In addition to clustered indexes, some RDBMS products support *clustered tables.* Tables are said to be clustered when they are stored close to each other on disk based on a commonly used join key. Clustered tables help speed up the data access if two tables are always accessed by the same join key.

A relational database management system's optimizer can improve the access path by automatically determining whether an index should be used for a given query. That is because index I/Os also consume resources and affect performance. Advanced optimizers, such as the one found in DB2, maintain index statistics and can actually determine whether a clustered index is still clustered after heavy insert and delete activity, before the decision is made to use the index.

Index selection.   As a general rule, all tables should have a unique clustered index. The index should be defined as unique because duplicate key values in a clustered index will cause the creation of overflow data pages. Without a clustered index, all INSERTs and out-of-place UPDATEs will go to the last page in the table (unless the nonclustered table is partitioned). *Monotonic data* is defined as data with a sequentially increasing key (1, 2, 4, 6, 7, 8, . . .). This is also true for INSERTs into a clustered table using a monotonically increasing key. This causes increased lock contention in high-transaction environments, which can be very costly. Obviously, there will be exceptions to this rule such as audit tables and tables used for some types of batch processing.

High-INSERT environments should always cluster using a key which provides some degree of randomness that is usable in many queries. This is frequently not the primary key for the table. This is done to minimize lock contention and prevent INSERTs from competing for the same page in the table (e.g., the last page).

Some prime candidates for a clustered index include

- Columns that are accessed by a range (used to specify ranges in the WHERE clause)
- Columns that are used in ORDER BY, GROUP BY, or join operations

Prime candidates for nonclustered indexes include

- Columns used to join one or more tables (often primary and foreign keys)
- Columns likely to be used as search arguments (SARGs)
- Columns used in aggregate functions
- Columns used in queries requiring index coverage (discussed in detail in Sec. 12.2)
- Columns used to access less than 20 percent of the total number of rows in the table

Perhaps most importantly, try to minimize the number of indexes defined on a table. The increased number of tables found in a normalized database usually results in fewer indexes per table. As a general rule, it is good practice to allow a maximum of two or three indexes on any table exposed to high update activity. Minimizing the number of indexes per table has the effect of reducing contention for index pages, which results in improved UPDATE, INSERT, and DELETE performance and is especially important in SMP environments. Remember that indexes often need to be maintained when their tables are updated. Therefore, if there are a lot of indexes for a table, UPDATEs, INSERTs, and DELETEs may be slow.

Clustered versus nonclustered indexes. The key question here is, What is more important, retrieval or UPDATE, INSERT, and DELETE performance? With a clustered index, the rows are sequenced and the index data is sequenced. With a nonclustered index, only the data of the index is clustered. Thus a clustered index provides faster sequential retrieval. Less space is used because one level of the index tree is omitted. However, UPDATE performance may be slower because of the overhead associated with the sequencing of rows.

Distributing index I/O. If several disks are available, it is generally a good idea to distribute indexes for *hot* tables across the available disks. As discussed in Sec. 10.2, the first general rule is to split the nonclustered indexes from their tables. This is accomplished by creating separate database segments for table data and index data.

Whenever possible, the index segments and the data segments should be created on separate disks. Database objects are placed on a specific segment with the CREATE TABLE and CREATE INDEX statements. The logic behind this is obvious: to divide the reads and writes for the object across multiple I/O paths. Reads and writes will be done faster because one disk is maintaining the index while a second disk is maintaining the table data.

fillfactor. The *fillfactor* parameter is used to set the percentage to which index and clustered data pages are filled during initial creation and loading. The *fillfactor* percentage is only used at index creation and is not maintained by SQL Server. As the data changes, the pages are not maintained at any particular level of fullness. The range of values is from 0 to 100 with the default being 0.

A *fillfactor* of 0 means that clustered indexes are created with completely full-leaf (data) pages. A reasonable amount of space (approximately 80 percent) is left on intermediate levels within the B-tree in both cases.

The user is able to override the *fillfactor* parameter by specifying another value in a CREATE INDEX statement.

```
CREATE UNIQUE CLUSTERED INDEX x0account ON tbaccount(acct#)
    WITH fillfactor = 75
```

When the server attempts to add a new entry to a full page, the page will split into two pages, each approximately 50 percent full. The SQL Server may make exceptions to the 50-50 page-split rule:

- Overflow pages are left 100 percent full.

- When the last page of a table having a clustered index is split (because a row is inserted into the end of the table), SQL Server will leave the last page 100 percent full and will continue on the next page.

As mentioned in Chap. 5, page splitting can cause significant transaction overhead that can be minimized by allocating an initial amount of free space to the index pages by specifying a *fillfactor* value. The percentage used with *fillfactor* is application-dependent but can be guided by a few simple rules:

1. There is seldom reason to change the default value for *fillfactor.*

2. A *fillfactor* value of 100 percent would only be used for read-only tables with zero anticipated growth. When *fillfactor* is 100 percent, index pages are completely filled. This is optimal for quick retrieval purposes but is not optimal for updates because of page splits.

3. Unless there is a very heavy insert rate on the table, start with a *fillfactor* value of 75 percent. A range of 50 to 60 percent is preferred for tables that are frequently updated because of a decreased occurrence of page splits and/or shrinks, but it makes for slower retrieval time.

Setting *max_rows_per_ page*. Maximum rows per page allows the user to specify the maximum number of rows that can be stored on a data page or leaf page of a nonclustered index. If *max_rows_ per_ page* is set for the clustered index, it affects data pages only. This is similar to the *fillfactor* option, with the caveat that the specified number of rows is continuously maintained by the server.

For tables and indexes that experience a high level of contention, it may be a good idea to limit the number of rows on data and index pages. As described in Chap. 8, the SQL Server Monitor Object Lock Status screen can be used to monitor lock contention at the object level. One drawback of *max_rows_per_page* is the amount of wasted space on the data pages caused by limiting the number of rows.

To support *max_rows_ per_ page,* Sybase modified the CREATE TABLE, CREATE INDEX, and ALTER TABLE statements. The complete syntax of these commands is beyond the scope of this book; however, for the sake of clarity, a brief example is provided.

```
create table team(
      team              int              not null,
      name              char(30)         not null,
      constraint        team_key         primary key(team)
      ) with max_rows_per_page = 10 on 'default'

create table player(
      player            numeric(8,0)     identity,
      name              char(30)         not null,
```

```
        team             int                not null,
        constraint       team_name          foreign key(team)
                         references         team(team)
    ) on 'default'
create unique clustered index x0player on player(player)
with max_rows_per_page = 20
```

It is probably not a good idea to use *max_rows_per_page* under the following conditions:

- On read-only tables (there is no need to waste space for read-only transactions).

- On tables that will be the target of table scans. Because of the increased number of pages required to store the table, the pages may flood the data cache and force more valuable pages out of cache. Similarly, it may not be a good idea when multiple rows must be accessed.

- On large tables and indexes. Disk space requirements may become a factor for large tables. Similarly for large indexes, it may increase the number of levels for the index (because of the reduced number of values at the leaf level).

- On insert- and delete-intensive tables and indexes. A high number of INSERTS and DELETES will increase the probability of pages splits and/or shrinks.

The *sp_chgattribute* procedure.   The *sp_chgattribute* system procedure is a new stored procedure used to change the *max_rows_per_page* value for future page allocations. The syntax is

```
sp_chgattribute objname, optname, optvalue
```

for example,

```
sp_chgattribute player, 'max_rows_per_page', 15
```

The *objname* parameter is the name of the table or index to be modified. Currently, the only valid value for *optname* is 'max_rows_per_page'. Now *max_rows_per_page* is a Transact-SQL reserved word. The *optvalue* parameter is used to provide a new value for *max_rows_per_page*. A value of 0 instructs SQL Server to behave as if *max_rows_per_page* did not exist. The range of acceptable values for tables and clustered indexes is between 0 and 256. The following SQL statement can be used to calculate the maximum value for a nonclustered index:

```
select (select @@pagesize-32) /
  (select minlen from sysindexes where name = 'indexname')
```

As discussed in Chap. 5, a new column in the *sysindexes* table called *maxrowsperpage* (this column is called *rowpage* in pre-System 11 *dataservers*) is used to store the value for a table or index. The value for a table or index can be displayed with the *sp_help* system procedure.

Note that existing page allocations remain unaffected by changes in *max_rows_per_page* made with the *sp_chgattribute* procedure.

General tips. As stated earlier, all tables should have a unique clustered index defined. A table with no clustered index is treated as a heap structure. Without a clustered index, INSERTs and out-of-place UPDATEs will occur in the last data page (unless the nonclustered table is partitioned). This increases the possibility of contention because all processes are competing for one 2K data page in the table.

Beware of INSERT operations on clustered indexes that use a monotonically increasing key. A clustered index on monotonic data can result in high contention for the last data page in the table similar to that found in a heap structure. Try to pick a clustered index that offers a high degree of cardinality and randomness. A table's primary key may not always be the best candidate for a clustered index—although it will always have the high cardinality, it may not have the necessary degree of randomness.

It is a considered good practice to keep the size of the index key as small as possible. This results in faster index scans and B-tree traversals (and less disk space utilization—especially with nonclustered indexes). To that end, use small data types when possible.

By keeping the index key small, SQL Server can maintain more index key information in the distribution page. It may also be important to note that statistics data is only kept for the first column in a composite index.

Unique indexes should be defined as UNIQUE to help the query optimizer.

```
1> create UNIQUE clustered index x0player on tbplayer(player#)
2> go
```

12.3 Queries

This section presents some tips for using stored procedures and Transact-SQL queries. Also covered are query processing options that affect the optimizer's choice of cache strategy, I/O size, join order, and index selection. It is important for developers to understand these optimization techniques and their impact on performance.

SQL Server's cost-based optimizer is quite advanced and normally produces plans that are suitable for most applications. There are, however, times when it may be necessary to "tinker" with the query plans generated by the optimizer. Do this with care, as the wrong decision can have a very negative effect on query performance.

Some of the optimization choices that can be controlled by the programmer include

- Index selection
- Cache strategy (MRU/LRU)
- I/O size
- Join order
- The number of tables considered by the optimizer during join selection

12.3.1 Types of queries

The following types of queries are explained in this subsection: range queries, covered queries, and path expression queries.

Covered queries. Index covering occurs when SQL Server uses only a nonclustered index to return data for a query. A covered query does not need to read the actual data rows, therefore requiring a small percentage of the page I/O needed for a table scan. The following example shows a nonclustered index being used for index coverage.

```
create table tranhist(
        partNumber      char(10)          not null,
        location        char(6)not null,
        date            datetime          not null,
        type            char(1)not null,
        doc#            int               not null,
        quantity        int               not null,
        cost            float             not null,
        sale            float             not null
        )
create nonclustered index x1tranhist
 on tranhist(partNumber,location,quantity)

1> select partNumber,location,quantity from tranhist
2> go
        /* Index contains all columns needed, base table will not be read */

1> select * from tranhist
2> go
        /* Table scan */
```

Developers should look for opportunities to cover queries using a nonclustered index. Benefits include these:

- The server should be able to maintain higher cache hit ratios.
- It can result in fewer physical and logical I/O operations due to the larger number of rows maintained in the index page.

Range queries. Range queries are best served by clustered indexes and covering indexes. Range queries that use the keys of noncovering clustered indexes use the index for ranges that return a limited number of rows. As the number of rows (specified by the range) increases, the nonclustered index path can be more expensive than a table scan.

Path expression queries. Object-oriented systems typically support *path expressions* instead of *join*. Such expressions are the object-oriented equivalent of a relational expression.

12.3.2 Stored procedures

Stored procedures are generally faster than ad hoc queries because their execution plans are stored in the procedure cache, thus requiring less I/O. However, stored procedures can be slower when a search value cannot be determined until run time; i.e., a parameter is being passed to the stored procedure. This is due to the fact that the plan stored with the procedure may not be optimal for the search value(s) being passed to the procedure. Stored procedures are the subject of Chap. 17.

12.3.3 Joins

SQL statements should not involve more than four tables wherever possible. On joins of four or more tables, the optimizer will cost plans four tables at a time in the order listed in the FROM clause. This may not be very efficient, because not all permutations will be evaluated. System 11 supports configurable join order optimization. A new SET command is used to configure the number of tables in the join order search space. The *set table count* option can be used to increase the number of tables that are evaluated at the same time. The syntax is

```
set table count int_value
```

for example,

```
set table count 8
```

Currently, the maximum value that can be specified for *int_value* is 8. Keep in mind that the number of tables considered by SQL Server during *join* optimization will affect the time it takes to optimize a query.

The programmer can influence the optimizer on large joins by the order of the tables in the FROM clause. To force SQL Server to access tables using the order in the FROM clause use

```
set forceplan [on|off]
```

for example,

```
create procedure pr_forceplan
as
      set forceplan on
      select a.name, b.name from player a, team b
      where a.team = b.team
go
```

SQL statements may be written with redundant joins to help the query optimizer choose the best index for a query. For example, tables *a*, *b*, and *c* all have a column called ID#. Usually a programmer will write the SQL as

```
select ... from a, b, c where a.id# = b.id# and b.id# = c.id#
```

Adding the clause

```
and a.id# = c.id#
```

is redundant but may improve the performance of the optimizer (this is called *transitive closure* in DB2).

There is also the case of *associative closure:*

```
select ... from a, b
 where a.col1 = 18 and b.col1 = 18
```

It may improve performance to modify the SQL as follows:

```
select ... from a, b
 where a.col1 = 18 and b.col1 = a.col1
```

which implies that *b.col1* is also 18.

12.3.4   Cache strategy and I/O size

During optimization, SQL Server evaluates each query and decides if prefetching will improve performance. The programmer can disable prefetching by using a *set* command:

```
set prefetch [on|off]
```

If prefetching for an object has been disabled by using the *sp_cache-strategy* system procedure, the *set* command has no effect. The *set prefetch* command cannot be overridden by specifying a prefetch size in a SELECT, UPDATE, or DELETE statement.

Cache strategy and prefetching. To perform prefetching on the data pages of a table, provide the name of the clustered index or the table itself, e.g.,

```
create table inventory(
        partNumber      char(10)            not null,
        partName        char(40)            not null,
        type            char(1)             not null,
        qtyOnHand       int                 not null,
        baseprice       float               not null
        )
create unique clustered index x0inventory on inventory(partNumber)

1> select partNumber, partName, qtyOnHand*baseprice as value
        from inventory_location(index x0inventory_location prefetch 16)
        where partNumber = x
2> go
        /* Using Clustered Index. Index: x0inventory_location */
        /* Using I/O Size 16 Kybtes */
        /* With LRU Buffer Replacement Strategy. */
```

As described in Chap. 9, the *sp_cachestrategy* system procedure is used to enable or disable large I/Os and MRU cache replacement strategy for a table, index, text, or image object. To override the default (LRU) cache strategy and perform the same query using a fetch-and-discard replacement strategy, add the *MRU* keyword as follows:

```
1> select partNumber, partName, qtyOnHand*baseprice as value
        from inventory_location(index x0inventory_location prefetch 16 MRU)
        where partNumber = x
2> go
        /* Using Clustered Index. Index: x0inventory_location */
        /* Using I/O Size 16 Kybtes */
        /* With MRU Buffer Replacement Strategy. */
```

The following example is used to perform prefetching on the leaf-level pages of a nonclustered index using 16K I/Os:

```
create table tranhist(
        partNumber      char(10)            not null,
        location        char(6)             not null,
        date            datetime            not null,
        type            char(1)             not null,
        doc#            int                 not null,
        quantity        int                 not null,
        cost            float               not null,
        sale            float               not null
        )
create nonclustered index x1tranhist
 on tranhist(partNumber,location,quantity)
1> select partNumber,location,quantity
    from tranhist(index x1tranhist prefetch 16)
2> go
        /* Index contains all needed columns, base table will not be read */
        /* Using I/O Size 16 Kbytes */
```

12.3.5 Index selection

System 11 supports a new clause for SELECT, UPDATE, and
DELETE statements which allows the programmer to specify an
index to be used for a query. The ability to force an index can be helpful when the optimizer is not choosing an optimal query plan. This
option should be used with care, as the optimizer may generate different query plans depending on the search values provided. For example, the optimizer may generate a different plan if more than 20 percent of the rows in a table are being selected in a range query.

Be sure to test any query with various *search* arguments before
deciding to implement this option. The new syntax is illustrated here:

```
select name from team(index team_key)
 where team = x

update team set name = 'STEELERS'
 from team(index team_key)
 where team = x

delete from team(index team_key)
 where team = x
```

12.3.6 SELECT arguments

Whenever possible, avoid the use of functions in WHERE clauses. As
discussed in Sec. 12.1, consider the use of an extra column of the
transformed data type where a function is needed. Also try to avoid
mathematical manipulation of SELECT arguments (SARGs), such as

```
SELECT itemkey, description, onhand FROM inventory
 WHERE avgcost*1.05 < 999
```

Try not to use incompatible data types between a column and its
SELECT argument (e.g., *float* and *int, char* and *varchar, binary* and
varbinary).

The Transact-SQL *set* command is used to set query processing
options for the duration of a user's work session. The *set rowcount* keyword causes the SQL Server to stop processing a query after the specified number of rows is affected. When SELECT statements potentially
select a very large amount of data, restriction of the number of rows
returned to the client should be considered to limit the overhead on the
network. For example, A *set rowcount* 1000 could be submitted to the
server prior to submitting the SQL SELECT statement. Applications
should raise a corresponding warning message to the user.

As discussed in the conclusion of this book, (Chap. 21), I expect
SYBASE to provide some type of *query governor* in a future version of
SQL Server. The query governor might restrict queries by size of

result set (eliminating the need for SET ROWCOUNT) or by SQL Server CPU time. Restrictions could be placed on individual server users or on user groups.

12.3.7 Summary

Note that when the options in this section are used, the query plans should be monitored and maintained on a regular basis. Over time, changes to the database including index degradation, changes in table size, and validity of distribution statistics may invalidate plans that were once optimal.

12.4 Monitoring Query Plans

SQL Server provides a group of *set* commands that can be used to monitor the execution of Transact-SQL queries for optimization. The *set* commands that we discuss in this section include the following:

set showplan on	*set noexec on*
set statistics io on	*set statistics time on*
set statistics subquery cache on	

The best tool for this type of query monitoring is ISQL. If the output for a particular query is too long, use ISQL to capture output in an operating system file. For System 11, Sybase has improved the usability of the *showplan* interface.

The *showplan* option.   The *showplan* option can be used to generate a description of the processing plan for the query and immediately process it. This option can give the user an indication of whether an index is being used by a SELECT statement. The *set showplan* option is often used in conjunction with the *set noexec* option. In this case, issue a *noexec after* the *showplan,* or else the *set showplan* command will not execute. Do not use *showplan* inside a stored procedure or trigger; set *showplan* on and then execute the stored procedure or command that fires the trigger. For example,

```
1> set showplan on
2> go
1> exec sp_testproc
2> go
```

For more information, the SQL Server *Performance and Tuning Guide* contains a complete discussion of *showplan* output.

The *noexec* option.   The *noexec* option is often used with *showplan*. It tells the SQL Server to compile each query but not execute it. When *noexec* is turned on, no subsequent commands will be executed until it is turned off.

The *statistics io* option. The *statistics io* option is used to display the number of scans, logical reads (pages accessed), and physical reads (pages not found in the data cache) for each table referenced in the statement. For each command, it displays the number of pages written.

```
1> set statistics io on
2>
1> select * from authors a, titleauthor t
2> where a.au_id = t.au_id and state = 'IN'
3>
    au_id             au_lname              au_fname
    phone
    address    city                                    state
    country            postalcode   au_id    title_id  au_ord royaltyper

    ----------- ---------------------------- -------------------------
    ------ ---------------------------------- ---------------------- ----
    --------- -------- ---------- ---------- -----------

722-51-5454 DeFrance                                    Michel
219
547-9982 3 Balding Pl.                        Gary              IN
USA
46403       722-51-5454 MC3021        1        75
Table: authors scan count 1, logical reads: 1, physical reads: 0
Table: titleauthor scan count 1, logical reads: 1, physical reads: 0
Total writes for this command: 0
(1 row affected)
```

The *statistics time* option. This option displays the amount of time it took to parse and compile each command. For each step in the command, it displays the time it took to execute. Times are reported in SQL Server time ticks.

```
1> set statistics time on
2>
1> select * from authors a, titleauthor t where a.au-id = t.au-id and
state = 'INI 2>

Parse and Compile Time 2.
SQL Server cpu time: 200 ms.
    au_id au_lname au_fname
    phone
    address city state
    country     postalcode      au_id  title_id   au_ord royaltyper

    ----------- ---------------------------- -------------------------
    ------ ---------------------------------- ---------------------- ----
    --------- -------- ----------- ---------- -----------

722-51-5454 DeFrance                                    Michel
219
547-9982 3 Balding Pl.                        Gary              IN
USA
```

```
46403     722-51-5454 MC3021           1          75
Table: authors scan count 1, logical reads: 1, physical reads: 0
Table: titleauthor scan count 1, logical reads: 1, physical reads: 0
Total writes for this command: 0

Execution Time 0.
SQL Server cpu time: 0 ms. SQL Server elapsed time: 13 ms.
(1 row affected)
```

The *statistics subquerycache* option.   This option was introduced with System 11 and is used to display the number of cache hits and misses and the number of rows in cache for each subquery.

```
1> set statistics subquerycache on
2>
1> select title, price from titles where price =
2> (select price from titles where title = 'Straight Talk About
Computers')
3>
Parse and Compile Time 1.
SQL Server cpu time: 100 ms.

title                                             price
----------- ------------------------------        ------
The Busy Executive's Database Guide               19.99
Straight Talk About Computers                     19.99
Silicon Valley Gastronomic Treats                 19.99
Prolonged Data Deprivation: Four Case Studies     19.99

Table: titles   scan count 1,   logical reads: 3,   physical reads: 0
Table: titles   scan count 1,   logical reads: 3,   physical reads: 0
Execution Time 0.
SQL Server cpu time: 0 ms. SQL Server elapsed time: 3 ms.
(4 rows affected)
```

DBCC.   The DBCC *traceon(3604,302,310)* command will display each alternative plan evaluated (and discarded) by the optimizer. This output can help the DBA or programmer understand why the optimizer won't use the plan that is expected.

```
1> dbcc traceon(3604,302,310)
2>
DBCC execution completed. If DBCC printed error messages, contact a user
with System Administrator (SA) role.

1> select * from authors a, titleauthor t
2> where a.au-id=t.au-id and state='IN'
3>
Entering q_score_index() for table 'authors' (objectid 16003088, varno=0).
The table has 23 rows and 1 pages.
Scoring the SEARCH CLAUSE:
  state EQ
Base cost: indid: 0 rows: 23 pages: 1 prefetch: N I/O size: 2 cacheid: 0
replace: LRU

Cheapest index is index 0, costing 1 page and generating 2 rows per scan,
using no data prefetch (size 2) on dcacheid 0 with LRU replacement
Search argument selectivity is 0.100000.
```

Entering q_score_index() for table 'authors' (objectid 16003088, varno=0).
The table has 23 rows and 1 page.
Scoring the JOIN CLAUSE:
  au_id EQ au_id

Base cost: indid: 0 rows: 23 pages: 1 prefetch: N I/O size: 2 cacheid: 0
replace: LRU
Relop bits are: 5
Estimate: indid 1, selectivity 0.043478, rows 1 pages 2 index height 1
Unique clustered index found--return rows 1 pages 2

Cheapest index is index 1, costing 2 pages and generating 1 row per scan,
using no data prefetch (size 2) on dcacheid 0 with LRU replacement
Join selectivity is 23.000000.

Entering q_score_index() for table titleauthor (objectid 176003658,
varno=1).

The table has 25 rows and 1 page.
Scoring the JOIN CLAUSE:
au_id EQ au_id

Base cost: indid: 0 rows: 25 pages: 1 prefetch: N I/O size: 2
cacheid: 0 replace: LRU
Relop bits are: 5
Estimate: indid 1, selectivity 0.043478, rows 1 pages 2 index height 1
Relop bits are: 5
Estimate: indid 2, selectivity 0.043478, rows 1 pages 2 index height 1

Cheapest index is index 1, costing 2 pages and generating 1 row per scan,
using no data prefetch (size 2) on dcacheid 0 with LRU replacement
Join selectivity is 23.000000.
QUERY IS CONNECTED

0 - 1 -
NEW PLAN (total cost = 43):

varno=0 (authors) indexid=0 ()
path=0xecb7d928 pathtype=sclause method=NESTED ITERATION outerrows=1
rows=2
joinsel=1.000000 cpages=1 prefetch=N iosize=2 replace=LRU lp=1 pp=1
corder=1

varno=1 (titleauthor) indexid=0 ()
path=oxecb7db9o pathtype=sclause method=NESTED ITERATION outerrows=2
rows=3
joinsel=23.000000 cpages=1 prefetch=N iosize=2 replace=LRU lp=2 pp
=1 corder=1

1 - 0 -

TOTAL PERMUTATIONS: 2

TOTAL PLANS CONSIDERED: 6

CACHE USED BY THIS PLAN:
CacheID = 0: (2K) 2 (4K) 0 (8K) 0 (16K) 0
FINAL PLAN (total cost = 43):
varno=o (authors) indexid=O ()
path 0xecb7d928 pathtype=sclause method=NESTED ITERATION outerrows=1
rows=2
joinsel=1.000000 cpages=1 prefetch=N iosize=2 replace=LRU lp=1 pp=1
corder=1

TABLE 12.1   DBCC Trace Flags

Trace flag	Description
200	Display before image of query tree
201	Display after image of query tree
302	Information on index selection
310	Information on join selection
317	Complete (voluminous) information on join selection
3604	Redirect output to screen
3605	Redirect output to error log

```
varno=1 (titleauthor) indexid=0 ()
path=0xecb7db90 pathtype=sclause method=NESTED ITERATION outerrows=2
rows=3
joinsel=23.000000 cpages=1 prefetch=N iosize=2 replace=LRU lp=2 pp=1
corder=1
        au_id            au_lname            au_fname
        phone
        address    city                                   state
     country               postalcode au_id     title_id au_ord royaltyper

    -----------  -----------------------------  -----------------------
    ------  -----------------------------  ----------------------  ----
    ---------  --------  ----------  ----------  ------------

722-51-5454 DeFrance                           Michel
219
547-9982 3 Balding Pl.                   Gary                    IN
USA
46403        722-51-5454 MC3021     1       75
(i row affected)
```

Other DBCC trace flags that may be of interest are listed in Table 12.1.

12.5   Update in Place

When possible, promote update-in-place design. The SYBASE update in place is much faster than the alternative UPDATE (physical DELETE followed by a physical INSERT). Out-of-place UPDATEs can result in increased contention for the last page in the table, increased possibility of deadlock, and decreased response time. See Chap. 5 for a complete discussion of update-in-place design.

set showplan on.   The *set showplan on* command can be used to evaluate update methods on a query-by-query basis. For example,

```
1> set showplan on
2> go
1> update tranhist set date-getdate() where partNumber = '1'
2> go
QUERY PLAN FOR STATEMENT 1 (at line 1).
```

```
STEP 1
   The type of query is UPDATE.
   The update mode is direct.
```

Monitoring UPDATES.   The *sp_sysmon* system procedure can be used to view UPDATE activity at the system level.

```
1> sp_sysmon
2> go
= = = = = = = = = = = = = = = = = = = = = = = = = = = = = = = = = = = = = =
Transaction Profile
--------------------
```

Transaction Summary	per sec	per xact	count	% of total
Committed Xacts	0.4	n/a	88	108.6 %
Rolled Back Xacts	-0.0	n/a	-7	-8.6 %
Total # of Xacts	0.4	n/a	81	
Multi-Database Xacts	0.0	n/a	0	0.0 %

Transaction Detail	per sec	per xact	count	% of total
Inserts				
Heap Table	30.7	74.4	6544	97.6 %
Clustered Table	0.8	1.8	161	, 2.4 %
Total Rows Inserted	31.5	76.2	6705	98.4 %
Updates				
Deferred	0.0	0.0	0	0.0 %
Direct In-Place	0.0	0.0	3	100.0 %
Direct Cheap	0.0	0.0	0	0.0 %
Direct Expensive	0.0	0.0	0	0.0 %
Total Rows Updated	0.0	0.0	3	0.0 %
Deletes				
Deferred	0.4	1.0	86	78.9 %
Direct	0.1	0.3	23	21.1 %
Total Rows Deleted	0.5	1.2	109	1.6 %

```
= = = = = = = = = = = = = = = = = = = = = = = = = = = = = = = = = = = = = = =
```

12.6   Referential Integrity

As described in Chaps. 1 and 3, referential integrity is a method of guaranteeing the correctness of data within an RDBMS. Sybase supports both procedural referential integrity and declarative referential integrity (DRI). To that end Sybase provides the following facilities:

- Triggers
- Rules and defaults
- Views with a check option

- Declarative referential integrity—primary and unique key definitions, foreign keys, defaults, check constraints, and null or not null.

Triggers are the subject of Chap. 18.

12.6.1 Rules and defaults

Rules and *defaults* are provided to help maintain *entity integrity* and
domain integrity. Entity integrity is used to ensure that a value is
entered for all columns that require a value; domain integrity ensures
that each value in a column belongs to a set of legal values for that
column. Defaults and rules define integrity constraints during the
entry and modification of data.

Rules have been made somewhat obsolete by check constraints.
Defaults have also been made obsolete by the new CREATE TABLE
syntax. System 10 and System 11 users will probably want to use the
integrity constraints offered by the enhanced Transact-SQL CREATE
TABLE and ALTER TABLE syntax.

Rules.   Rules are user-defined integrity constraints that are linked to
a column or data type and are enforced at data entry time. Rules are
created with the CREATE RULE statement; the syntax is

```
CREATE RULE [owner.]ruleName as condition_expression
```

for example,

```
CREATE RULE ru_priceLimit as @price < 1000
CREATE RULE ru_validzipCodes as @zip in ( '11580', '11581', '11560' )
```

After a rule has been created, it is bound to a column or user-defined
data type with the *sp_bindrule* system procedure. The syntax of
sp_bindrule is

```
sp_bindrule ruleName, objectName
```

for example,

```
exec sp_bindrule ru_priceLimit, tb_inventory.retailPrice
exec sp_bindrule ru_validzipCodes, zipcode
```

The *sp_unbindrule* system procedure is used to unbind a rule. A
rule must be dropped with the DROP RULE statement before it can
be recreated. The DBA (or rule owner) must unbind a rule before it
can be dropped. The syntax is

```
sp_unbindrule objectName
```

for example,

```
sp_unbindrule tb_inventory.retailPrice
```

Defaults.   A default is a value linked to a column or datatype which is inserted when no value is provided during data entry. The syntax used to create a default is

```
CREATE DEFAULT [owner.]defaultName as constant_Expression
```

for example,

```
CREATE DEFAULT df_int as 0
CREATE DEFAULT df_float as 0.00
```

After a default has been created, it is bound to a column or data type with the *sp_bindefault* system procedure. The syntax is

```
sp_bindefault defaultName, objectName
```

for example,

```
sp_bindefault df_int, int
sp_bindefault df_float, float
```

As with rules, the DBA must unbind defaults before they can be dropped. Defaults are dropped with the DROP DEFAULT statement, and the *sp_unbindefault* procedure is used to unbind a default. The syntax is

```
sp_unbindefault objname
```

for example,

```
sp_unbindefault df_int
sp_unbindefault 'activity.date'
```

12.6.2   Views

Views are virtual tables consisting of a subset, union, or join of the columns in one or more tables. In addition to providing a level of isolation from restructuring in the database and changes in naming conventions, views can be used to enhance security by restricting the visible data from the underlying tables. A user can be granted permissions on a view even if he or she has no permissions on the tables that the view references.

Views can be used to hide data from a user or group of users. By accessing data via a view, a user can query and modify only the data that is visible through the view. The rest of the database is not accessible to the user. Views can be used to restrict access to both column (or vertical) subsets and row (horizontal) subsets of a base table. Views allow users to access only that subset of data required to perform the job function.

It is possible to write to the data within a view, but only if one table is updated at a time. A drawback to performing modifications through a view is that SQL Server does not require the new or updated row to satisfy the definition of view. For example, consider access to the following base table:

```
CREATE TABLE player(
        player          numeric(8,0)      identity,
        name            char(30)          not null,
        team            int               not null,
        id_owner        smallint          not null
        ) on 'default'

insert player values( 'BOOMER', 1, suser_id() )
```

When a record is inserted into the *player* table, the *id_owner* column is set to the server user ID of the user inserting the row (as shown in the INSERT statement). This is done to establish "ownership" of the inserted rows. The following view can be used to restrict a user's access to only those records having her or his server user ID:

```
create view v2_player as select player, name from player
 where id_owner = suser_id()
grant insert on v2_player to public
```

However, even if the view is restricted by the clause *id_owner = suser_id()*, it is still possible to insert a row with *id_owner = xx*. This requirement can be imposed by using the *check* option, which validates data modifications against the view selection criteria. In the following view definition, the *check* option is used to ensure that a user cannot falsify information in the *id_owner* column.

```
create view v2_player as select player, name from player
 where id_owner = suser_id()
 with check option
grant insert on v2_player to public
```

12.6.3 Declarative referential integrity

Declarative referential integrity (RI) is supported by SYBASE System 10 and System 11. Declarative RI is implemented through keys that are stored within the database tables themselves. Parent tables contain primary keys that are composed of foreign keys found within each of the child tables.

Syntax modifications to the Transact-SQL CREATE TABLE and ALTER TABLE statements allow the user to specify integrity constraints, including

- Unique and primary key constraints to ensure unique values in a column. Primary key and unique constraints are implemented as unique indexes by SQL Server.

- Check constraints used to limit the values that can be inserted into a table (implemented with *rules* prior to System 10).

- Referential integrity constraints to guarantee that a primary key exists in another table when data is inserted or updated data in a foreign key table (enforced with triggers prior to System 10). Referential integrity is enforced at the end of the statement.

- Defaults to specify default values for columns in a table (implemented with the CREATE DEFAULT statement prior to System 10).

In most cases, DRI offers better performance than triggers. This can be significant when a large number of RI constraints are needed. This is because triggers must scan the *inserted* and *deleted* tables, a process which is inherently slow. The *inserted* and *deleted* tables can be thought of as a view on the *syslogs* table which is not indexed.

Complex applications will probably guarantee integrity by using a mix of declarative RI and trigger-based RI. Declarative referential integrity is applied by SQL Server when a violation occurs, thus aborting the statement causing the violation. Any triggers that will be fired as a result of the statement are fired after all DRI conditions have been satisfied.

Some strengths of procedural RI (triggers) include the following:

- Triggers are fired after processing the affected rows.

- Triggers give the programmer the ability to perform several RI checks in a single trigger. They also offer tremendous flexibility in the actions that can be taken when RI rules are violated.

- Triggers give the programmer the ability to code cascading DELETEs and UPDATEs.

- Transact-SQL statements are available to roll back the effects of the trigger or the entire transaction. These statements are ROLLBACK TRIGGER and ROLLBACK TRANSACTION.

The SYBASE implementation.   DRI was introduced by Sybase with System 10. A constraint is added to a database by coding the primary key in the parent table and one or more foreign keys in the child tables. Constraints can be manipulated by using the Transact-SQL CREATE TABLE and ALTER TABLE statements.

When DRI is implemented between a parent and a child table, the following actions are required:

1. A primary key must be identified on the parent table.

```
create table team(
        team            int             not null,
        name            char(30)        not null,
        constraint      team_key        primary key(team)
        ) on 'seg1'
```

SQL Server automatically creates a unique clustered index (named *team_key*) for the primary key when the primary key constraint is specified. In this example, the unique index is created on the *team* column.

2. A foreign key which references the parent table must be identified in the CREATE TABLE or ALTER TABLE statement.

```
create table player(
        player          numeric(8,0)    identity,
        name            char(30)        not null,
        team            int             not null,
        constraint      team_name       foreign key(team)
                        references      team(team)
        ) on 'seg2'
create unique clustered index x0player on player(player)
```

3. Although SQL Server does not enforce it, an index should be defined on the foreign key for performance reasons.

```
create nonclustered index x1player on player(team)
```

4. User-defined messages can be attached to declarative RI constraints by using the *sp_addmessage* and *sp_bindmsg* system procedures. This is done to provide a display and an understandable message to the user. For example, when the *team_name* constraint is violated on the *team* table, the following message is displayed:

```
1> delete team
2> go
Msg 547, Level 16, State 1:
Server 'elvee', Line 1:
Dependent foreign key constraint violation in a referential
integrity constraint.
 dbname = 'eei', table name = 'team'., constraint name = 'team_name'
```

To provide a more usable error message:

```
1> sp_addmessage 20020,
      'Attempt to delete a team that has players assigned to it.'
2> go
1> sp_bindmsg team_name, 20020
2> go               /* Bind the message to the team_name constraint */
```

Note that user-defined messages are always assigned a message number greater than 19,999 because SYBASE reserves the first 19,999 message numbers for internal use. Now when the constraint is violated, our message and error number is displayed.

```
1> delete team
2> go
Msg 20020, Level 16, State 1:
Server 'elvee', Line 1:
Attempt to delete a team that has players assigned to it.
```

The *sp_addmessage* and *sp_bindmsg* procedures are discussed in greater detail in Chap. 17.

CREATE SCHEMA. The CREATE SCHEMA statement can be used to create several objects and grant permissions on those objects in a single statement. If any statements within a CREATE SCHEMA statement fail, the entire command is rolled back as a unit of work. This can be useful when one is implementing declarative RI. The syntax of CREATE SCHEMA is

```
create schema authorization userName
  create object statement
  [ create object statement... ]
  [ permission statement... ]
```

The *userName* must be the name of the current user in the database. The *create object statement* is a standard CREATE TABLE/view statement. The *permission statement* is a standard grant or revoke command.

Permissions granted or revoked in a schema can be changed with standard grant or revoke commands outside the schema creation. There is no corresponding DROP SCHEMA statement; objects are dropped with the appropriate DROP TABLE/view statements. The following is an example of a CREATE SCHEMA statement:

```
create schema authorization dbo
    create table team(
        team            int             not null,
        name            char(30)        not null,
        constraint      team_key        primary key(team)
        ) on 'seg1'
    create table player(
        player          numeric(8,0)    identity,
        name            char(30)        not null,
        team            int             not null,
        constraint      team_name       foreign key(team)
                        references      team(team)
        ) on 'seg2'
    grant select on team to public
    grant select on player to public
```

The *sp_helpconstraint* procedure. Information about constraints currently defined for a table can be displayed with the *sp_helpconstraint* system procedure. The syntax is

```
sp_helpconstraint table_name
```

for example,

```
1> sp_helpconstraint player
2> go
name          defn
----------    --------------------------------------------------------
team_name     player FOREIGN KEY (team) REFERENCES team(team)
```

12.7   Naming Standards

There are significant benefits to be realized by adopting a standardized naming convention for user-defined objects. The SQL Server supports object names that are up to 30 characters in length, so there is no major need to use codes and abbreviations in object names. Table 12.2 shows suggested naming conventions.

TABLE 12.2   Naming Conventions

Database object	Abbreviation
Tables	tb_<tableName>, e.g., tb_player
Indexes	clustered index: x0_<tableName>, e.g., x0_player
	nonclustered index: xn_<tableName>, where n is the index ID; e.g., x1_player, x2_player
Base views	vw_<baseTable>, e.g., vw_player
Other views	vn_<innerTable>, e.g., v1_player, v2_player
User-written stored procedures	pr_<procedureName>, e.g., pr_getPlayer

Triggers	tr_<tableName>, e.g., tr_player
	For multiple triggers on a single table:
	  td_<tableName> = DELETE trigger
	  ti_<tableName> = INSERT trigger
	  tu_<tableName> = UPDATE trigger

Rules	ru_<columnName | data typeName>, e.g., ru_accountNumber, ru_accountCode
Defaults	df_<columnName | data typeName>, e.g., df_accountNumber, df_accountCode
System stored procedures	sp_<procedureName>, e.g., sp_showdisks

Transact-SQL scripts. To improve the readability of Transact-SQL scripts, developers may wish to follow these guidelines:

- Use uppercase letters for built-in functions and keywords and lowercase letters elsewhere.

- Restrict the length of each line to a maximum of 80 characters.

- Make comments C like (e.g., /* comment here */).

- Use BEGIN and END to delimit all SQL statements, even if only for one statement.

- Declare all variables together in one DECLARE statement at the beginning of each procedure.

- Use DECLARE on an as-needed basis.

- Make sure that error messages are clear, indicate their source, and return a meaningful message.

13

Tuning Long-Running Jobs

Organizations frequently spend an inordinate amount of time and money tuning interactive jobs while spending a minimal amount of time tuning or scheduling long-running jobs. Carefully tuning the response time of preplanned queries from 1.5 s down to 1.0 s will not make much difference if the long-running jobs are exceeding their allocated time window and affecting OLTP users. Unlike on-line transactions and queries, batch processes are customarily scheduled during off-peak hours in order to minimize their impact on other activities supported by the SQL Server. Some examples of long-running jobs include

- Indexing data
- Reorganizing fragmented tables
- Backing up databases and transaction logs
- Checking database consistency
- Bulk-loading data received from an external source
- Archiving data and creating extract files

Most organizations have some type of long-running process that takes too long to run, sometimes for many hours. All too often, performance tuning focuses on short interactive jobs, ignoring the monster batch jobs that often run overnight. The suggestions given in this chapter supplement those found in the rest of the book. Keep in mind that most tuning, i.e., the tuning of SQL statements, is the same for batch and interactive jobs. Before you implement any of these tuning suggestions, verify that the database and SQL statements have been tuned as described in other chapters.

The tuning of long-running jobs requires the participation of the O/S system administrator and the DBA. Although several of the recommendations found in this chapter involve only the DBA, a number of jobs will need to be coordinated with the system administrator.

For the purpose of this conversation, the terms *long-running jobs, batch processing,* and *batch jobs* are used interchangeably.

13.1 Improving Sort Performance

In Sec. 10.5, the *tempdb* database was identified as a potential bottleneck in SYBASE systems. In Chap. 9, we discussed the steps necessary to *assign* tempdb to its own named cache. Chapter 10 also offered several possible solutions to improve *tempdb* performance. In this section we discuss one possible implication of poor *tempdb* performance, which is suboptimal *sort* performance.

Because large batch jobs frequently sort thousands of records, the tuning of sorting areas is critical. One of the largest factors affecting sort performance is placement and optimization of the *tempdb* database. If sorting is slow, users may not understand why queries are taking a long time to run or are providing inconsistent performance.

In Chaps. 8 and 10, we learned how to monitor database objects to observe memory and disk activity and to determine how much activity is in memory (logical I/Os) and how much involves much slower disk accesses (physical I/Os).

If it becomes obvious that sorting is slowing down processing in the system, start with these tuning steps:

- Ask the basic question, Is this sort really necessary? Are we overlooking an index? Can the SQL statement be rewritten to eliminate the sort?

- Use more memory. For pre-System 11 SQL Servers, the configuration parameter *sort page count* is used to control the maximum amount of memory (in pages) that a *sort* operation can use.

- For System 11, the *number of sort buffers* configuration parameter controls the number of buffers used to hold pages read from input tables. Increasing the value of *sort buffers* can improve performance when indexes are created on large tables. See Chap. 7 for more information.

13.2 Temporary Tables

Long-running jobs frequently use temporary tables to hold intermediate results. This section provides some pointers for optimizing a system using temporary tables. The discussion encompasses several topics including

- Sizing *tempdb*
- Logging in *tempdb*
- Caching *tempdb*
- Contention on system tables in *tempdb*
- Optimization techniques
- Creating overnight extract tables

Sizing *tempdb*. To briefly recap the discussions in Chap. 10, when SQL Server is installed, the *tempdb* database resides on the *master* device. The size of the temporary database is 2 Mbytes; the size is increased with the ALTER DATABASE command. This is typically the first database that the system administrator needs to alter. The more users on the server, the larger it needs to be. The *tempdb* database needs to be large enough to handle the following processes for all concurrent SQL Server users:

- Temporary tables (those created with # as the first character of their names)
- Indexes on temporary tables
- User tables created in *tempdb*
- Procedures built by dynamic SQL
- Internal sorts
- Other internal work tables that are created for DISTINCT, GROUP BY, and ORDER BY, for reformatting and for the OR strategy

The following information is required to estimate the optimum size for *tempdb:*

- Maximum number of concurrent user processes
- Size of temporary tables and indexes (obtainable by using the *set statistics io on* command)
- Number of temporary tables and indexes created per stored procedure
- Size of sorts, as reported by the *set statistics io on* command—for queries with ORDER BY clauses not supported by an index
- Size of worktables, as reported by the *set statistics io on* command—for reformatting, GROUP BY, DISTINCT, and the OR strategy
- Number of steps in the query plans for reformatting, GROUP BY, and so on, which indicates the total number of temporary tables created

TABLE 13.1   Total for Normal Processing

Requirement	Formula	Example
Sorts	users * sort_size (pages)	100 * 15 pages = 1500
Other	users * worktable_size (pages)	100 * 8 pages = 800
Subtotal		2300 pages
* 3 steps	Subtotal * 3	6900 pages

TABLE 13.2   Space Required for Temporary Tables and Indexes

Requirement	Formula	Example
Temporary tables	procedures * table_size (pages) * number_of_tables	50 * 8 * 5 = 2000
Index space	procedures * index_size * number_of_indexes	50 * 2 * 2 = 200
Total		2200 pages

TABLE 13.3   Completing the Space Estimate

Requirement	Space required
Total for normal processing	6,900 pages
Total for temporary tables and index space	2,200 pages
Subtotal	9,100 pages
Plus 25 percent padding	2,275 pages
Total	11,375 pages
	= 23.3 Mbytes

- Total number of local and remote stored procedures and/or user sessions that create temporary tables and indexes

Table 13.1 illustrates the calculations used to estimate the space required for normal *tempdb* processing. Table 13.2 is used to estimate the space required for temporary tables and indexes. And Table 13.3 is used to complete the space estimate for *tempdb*. Sybase recommends 25 percent padding of the calculations to cover undocumented server uses of *tempdb* and potential errors in the estimates.

Logging in *tempdb*. Although the *trunc log on checkpoint* database option is enabled in *tempdb*, modifications to *tempdb* are still written to the transaction log. Transaction logging in the *tempdb* database can be reduced by using a few simple techniques:

- Use SELECT INTO to populate temporary tables instead of INSERT INTO.

- Minimize volume by selecting only the columns necessary for the temporary tables.

For example,

```
1> select au_id, au_lname, phone into #temp
2> from pubs2..authors where state = 'IN'
3>
(1 row affected)
```

Caching *tempdb*. The *sp_bindcache* system procedure is used to bind a database to a named data cache. An excellent starting point for investigating *tempdb* performance problems is to assign the *tempdb* database to its own named data cache. Configure the cache for 4K I/O for the *syslogs* table and 16K I/O for use by SELECT INTO queries. Refer to Sec. 9.4 for a complete discussion of how to use named data caches.

Contention on system tables in *tempdb*. The creation and dropping of temporary tables cause frequent updates to system tables in the *tempdb* database. For applications that have a large number of concurrent users, it may be a good idea to bind system tables to a named cache other than the default. In OLTP environments, the *sysindexes* table is a *hot* object. If the application includes ad hoc queries, performance gains may be seen by binding the *sysobjects, syscolumns,* and *sysprotects* system tables to cache. Use the SQL Server Monitor Object Page I/O window (see Sec. 10.10) to identify the hot system tables. Refer to Sec. 9.4 for a complete discussion of how to use named data caches.

Systems that have an extreme amount of contention for system tables in *tempdb* may benefit from the creation of scratch databases. These scratch databases can be used in the same way as *tempdb* is used. One proven technique is to create these scratch databases on a UNIX file system. Also, the following database options should be enabled: *trunc log on chkpt, select into/bulkcopy*. These databases can also be bound to named data caches.

Optimization techniques. The following basic techniques can be used to improve temporary-table optimization:

- Create indexes on temporary tables.

- Split complex uses of temporary tables into multiple procedures or SQL batches to provide better run-time information to the query optimizer.

In many cases, indexes created on temporary tables can be used to improve the performance of queries that access *tempdb*. The optimizer uses these indexes to create an optimal access strategy for each query. Obviously, the index must exist prior to execution of the query it is designed to help. Remember that if the index is created on an empty table, SQL Server does not create the index statistics page. Because SQL Server does not maintain real-time statistics on tables, when data is inserted into the table, the optimizer will have no statistics. The optimizer may choose a suboptimal plan if rows have been added or deleted since the index was created or since UPDATE STATISTICS was run.

Providing an index for the optimizer can greatly increase the performance of complex queries that create and manipulate temporary tables.

Another optimization strategy involves splitting the creation and indexing of temporary tables from the logic used to access the temporary tables. When a temporary table is created inside the same stored procedure or batch where it is used, the query optimizer cannot obtain statistics information (row count, index availability, etc.) about the table. This is because the work of creating the temporary table has not been performed before the query is optimized. Due to the lack of available data, the SYBASE optimizer assumes that any such table has 10 data pages and 100 rows. This can cause the optimizer to choose a suboptimal plan for tables that are very large.

Creating overnight extract tables.   Many organizations run large reports against fully normalized databases. For systems running reports involving multitable joins and large table scans, the system may become extremely overburdened when these reports are running.

Frequently, these reporting jobs may benefit from the creation of denormalized extract tables. Reports are then run against the extract files; this eliminates the need to repeatedly run the same data retrieval operations against the normalized database. By using this technique, complex, multitable joins only need to be performed once (to create the extract tables). Performance can be further improved by creating indexes on the extract tables. As discussed earlier, be sure to create the indexes after the extract tables are populated.

13.3   Enlarging the Buffer Cache

Often when batch jobs are running, there will be a limited number of user processes logged into the system. This provides the system administrator with an opportunity to allocate additional memory to buffer pools used by batch processing. For example, batch jobs may benefit from having additional memory allocated to the 16K buffer pool. The *sp_poolconfig* system procedure is used to move memory around between buffer pools and to change wash sizes within a named cache. Because *sp_poolconfig* is a dynamic command, the server does not have to be restarted for the command to take effect.

Batch processing jobs may be able to increase performance by reconfiguring buffer pools prior to starting. When batch processing is complete, the buffer pools can be reconfigured to support the OLTP applications typical of the regular business day.

13.4   Using the Bulk-Copy Program

BCP is the SYBASE Bulk-Copy Program. It is used to copy a database table to an operating system file in a user-specified format. It can also be used to load the contents of an operating system file into a database table.

The BCP program uses *format files* to store responses from a previous use of BCP on the same table. Format files contain information about the columns in the table, such as the data type and column width. Other stored information includes prefix length (data-type-dependent) and field terminator. Prefix length is a 1-, 2-, and 4-byte integer that is used to represent the length of each data value in bytes. A prefix length immediately precedes the data value in the host file. Common field terminators are a tab (\t), a new-line character (\n) and a return (\r).

If the name of a format file is not provided when BCP is started, the user will be prompted for information about each column in the database table. After values have been entered for each column in the table, BCP will allow the user to save the information to a format file.

The BCP program is optimized to load data into tables that do not have triggers or indexes on them. It loads data into tables without indexes or triggers with a minimum of logging. Only page allocations are logged; the actual insertion of rows is not. This is called *fast BCP.* The *select into/bulkcopy* database option must be set to use *fast* BCP. If this option is not set and a user attempts to copy data into a table without indexes, an error is generated. There is no need to set this option to copy data out of a database table, or to copy data into a table that has indexes or triggers.

Standard BCP (a slower version of BCP) is automatically used when data is copied into a table that has one or more indexes or triggers. This includes indexes implicitly created by using the UNIQUE integrity constraint with a CREATE TABLE statement. BCP does not enforce other integrity constraints (rules or triggers) defined for a table; however, BCP observes any defaults defined for columns and user-defined data types. The slow version of BCP logs all row inserts and page allocations.

Upon completion, the BCP program provides information about the number of rows copied and the number of rows rejected. Performance statistics are also provided, including the number of rows copied per second and the average time it took to copy one row.

13.4.1 Command line options

BCP command line options are used to

- Specify source and destination information.

- Specify the direction of the copy (in or out).

- Set the maximum number of errors permitted before BCP aborts the copy. Rows that cannot be built are optionally placed in an error file and counted as an error.

- Specify a format file. If a format file is not provided, BCP will ask the user for format information interactively.

- Specify an error file where BCP will store any rows that it was unable to transfer from the file to the database table. Error messages from the BCP program appear on the terminal.

- Provide the number of the first and last rows to copy. This is useful in processing host files that contain header and trailer information, or for loading large host files in chunks.

- Specify the number of rows per batch of data copied. Batching applies only for bulk-copying into a database table.

- Specify a default field terminator and a default row terminator. A user can also tell BCP to perform the copy operation with the *char* data type as the default.

- Provide the name of an *interfaces* file to search when connecting to SQL Server.

- Specify a network packet size to use for the BCP session. A larger packet size can improve performance of large BCP operations.

- Initiate client-side password encryption.

13.4.2 Loading data (copy in)

When copying in from an operating system file to a database table, BCP appends data to an existing database table. Input rows that fail a uniqueness check will be ignored or rejected depending on the uniqueness constraint.

To perform a Fast BCP, the *select into / bulkcopy* database option must be set. This is done with the *sp_dboption* system procedure. Because a transaction log dump cannot be used to recover unlogged operations, the DUMP TRANSACTION command is disabled when the *select into / bulkcopy* option is set. When nonlogged operations are completed, the database administrator should issue a DUMP DATA-BASE command and turn off the *select into/bulkcopy* database option.

After bulk-loading data, the table owner should run stored procedures or queries to check whether any of the newly loaded data violates rules.

Handling NULLs. Because BCP considers any data column that can contain null values to be of variable length, a length prefix or terminator should be used to denote the length of each row of data. If there is a null field in a data file, BCP will load the default value instead during the copy.

13.4.3 Unloading data (copy out)

When copying from a database table to an operating system file, BCP overwrites any previous contents of the file. When transferring data to a host file from a database table, BCP allows very specific output file formats to be specified.

13.4.4 Bulk-copy library

The CT-Library/C bulk-copy special library is a collection of functions that provide bulk-copy functionality to CT-Library/C applications. A CT-Library/C application can use the bulk-copy library to exchange data with a nondatabase application, load data into a new database, or move data from one database to another.

There are CT-Library/C functions available to copy data into or out of a database. Data can be copied into a database from program variables or from a host file. Bulk copy does not support the transfer of data from a database into program variables. See Table 13.4.

13.4.5 BCP tips

- When you are using slow BCP, the transaction log can grow very large. The log can be truncated with the DUMP TRANSACTION .. WITH TRUNCATE_ONLY command after the bulk copy completes. Do this after the database was backed up with DUMP DATABASE command.

- Dump the database before turning off the *select into/bulkcopy* flag. If unlogged data is inserted into the database and a DUMP TRANS-ACTION is performed prior to a DUMP DATABASE command, the data will not be recoverable.

- By default, the *select into/bulkcopy* option is off in newly created databases. To change this situation, turn on the *select into / bulk-copy* flag in the *model* database.

TABLE 13.4   BCP Library Routines

Library call	Function supported
bcp_batch	Save any preceding rows in SQL Server
bcp_bind	Bind data from program variable to SQL Server table
bcp_colfmt	Specify format of host file for bulk-copy purposes
bcp_colfmt_ps	Same as bcp_colfmt, with precision and scale support for numeric and decimal columns
bcp_collen	Set program variable-*length* for current copy in
bcp_colptr	Set program variable *data address* for current copy in
bcp_columns	Set total number of columns found in host file
bcp_control	Change various control parameter default settings
bcp_done	End *bulkcopy* from program variables into SQL Server
bcp_exec	Execute *bulkcopy* of data between database table and host file
bcp_getl	Determine if LOGINREC has been set for *bulkcopy* operations
bcp_init	Initialize *bulkcopy*
bcp_moretext	Send part of text or image value to SQL Server
bcp_readfmt	Read data file format definition from host file
bcp_sendrow	Send row of data from program variables to SQL Server
bcp_setl	Set LOGINREC for bulk-copy "copy in" operations
bcp_setxlate	Specify character set translations to use when retrieving data from or inserting data into SQL Server
bcp_writefmt	Write data file format definition to host file

- A good practice is to enable the *dbo use only* option when you are performing bulk copies into a database. This is preferable to the *single user* option because the database owner can use multiple connections to bulk-copy data into the database.

- While the *trunc. log on chkpt.* option is on, the transaction log is truncated every time the checking process occurs (through the checkpoint handler). It may be useful to turn this option on when you are performing BCPs, to prevent the log from growing. The slow version of BCP logs all row inserts and may cause the transaction log to fill up on large bulk copies.

- The performance penalty for copying data into a table with indexes can be severe. When large BCPs are performed, it can be faster to drop the indexes, set the *select into* database option, use Fast BCP to load the data, recreate the indexes, and then dump the database. Remember, large copies with slow BCP can fill up the transaction log. Also remember to allocate disk space for recreating the indexes. If the indexes are dropped prior to loading, the CREATE INDEX statement will require workspace equal to approximately 2.2 times the amount of disk space required for the data.

■ Be careful when copying data in native format from different versions of the SQL Server. Not all SQL Servers have the same data types.

■ Use native format to preserve the precision of SQL Server data. The *datetime* and *float* values preserve all their precision when native format is used. When *money* values are converted to character format, their character format values are recorded to the nearest two decimal places.

■ Specify a batch size when you copy into a database (for example, -*b 1000*). The -*b* command line option forces a checkpoint every *x* rows. The checkpoint will clear out the log and will give the system an intermediate point of recovery. Remember, because fast BCPs are not logged, they are not recoverable.

13.4.6   Tuning performance

Several server configuration parameters can be tuned to influence the performance of bulk-copy and CREATE INDEX operations, including

■ *default network packet size*

■ *max network packet size*

■ *extent i/o buffers*

■ *number of oam trips*

■ *number of index trips*

■ *number of preallocated extents*

■ *additional network memory*

These parameters are discussed briefly in this section; more information is available in Chap. 7.

default network packet size.   It is used to set the default size of network packets for all users on the SQL Server. It is possible to set the packet size for an individual ISQL or BCP session by using the -*A* command line parameter. The packet size must be between 512 and the value of *max network packet size* and must be a multiple of 512.

max network packet size.   On occasion, using a larger packet size can improve BCP performance. This is especially useful when you are running large BCPs or queries that send large result sets to the requesting client. The recommended value is 2048 bytes; however, experimentation is encouraged.

extent i/o buffers.   This parameter allocates a specified number of extents for use by the CREATE INDEX command. This variable should not be set to more than 100. SQL Server uses large buffers for BCP, CREATE DATABASE, and CREATE INDEX statements. The default value is 0; the recommended value is 10.

Fast BCP uses extent I/O buffers to perform I/O using 16K units as opposed to 2K units; slow BCP does not use extent I/O buffers.

number of preallocated extents.   This is used to specify the number of extent buffers allocated in a single trip to the page manager. A higher value may increase the performance of large bulk loads. The default value is 2.

number of oam trips.   This parameter specifies the number of times that an aged Object Allocation Map (OAM) page recycles itself onto the MRU chain. As this parameter is increased, the longer aged OAM pages will remain in cache. This eliminates physical I/O for page allocation. The default is 0; the recommended value is 100.

number of index trips.   This value specifies the number of times an aged index page recycles itself onto the MRU chain. The more this parameter increases, the longer index pages will remain in cache. The default value is 0; the recommended value is 10. For tables that have nonclustered indexes, the best solution is to create a named data cache large enough to hold all the nonclustered index pages.

additional network memory.   This parameter allocates additional memory for clients which request packet sizes that are larger than the *default* packet size for the server. The default is 0; increasing this parameter can provide large bulk-copy jobs that request larger packet sizes with significant performance gains.

tcp no delay.   Some environments may benefit from disabling TCP packet batching. Packet batching is a technique used by TCP/IP to batch small packets into one larger physical packet. Packets will be briefly delayed in an effort to fill the physical network frames with as much data as possible. Applications sending very small result sets or status reports from stored procedures will usually see a benefit. Pre-System 11 servers can disable packet batching by starting SQL Server with the 1610 Trace Flag. The default is 0, which means that packet batching is enabled.

Batch size.   The *batch size* is the number of rows BCP will insert into a table per transaction. The recommendation is to provide a batch size when data is copied into a database. This forces BCP to check-point every x rows. As mentioned earlier, the checkpoint will clear out the log and will give the database an intermediate point of recovery. As a general rule, a batch size of 1000 rows generally provides opti-mal performance.

Housekeeper configuration.   The *housekeeper free write percent* config-uration parameter is used to specify the maximum percentage by which the housekeeper task can increase database writes. The default value is 20 percent, which should provide optimal performance for most sites. This parameter can be used to limit the activities of the housekeeper task. More information is given in Chap. 20.

13.4.7   The DBCC *tune* interface

Several configuration parameters in the SQL Server can only be changed by using the DBCC *tune* keyword. The generalized syntax for DBCC *tune* follows:

```
dbcc tune( parameter_name, parameter_value [, table/index_name] )
```

Serverwide parameters.   The *maxwritedes* parameter is used to control the number of asynchronous I/O operations used by the checkpoint process. Large values cause checkpoints to be more aggressive, at the expense of other tasks running on the server. The default value is 10, which is optimal for most sites.

```
dbcc tune( maxwritedes, asynchIO )
```

for example,

```
dbcc tune( maxwritedes, 20 )
```

The *doneinproc* parameter is used to determine whether SQL Server sends debugging information to clients for each statement that is executed. The default is 1, which is required for debugging tools such as SQL Debug. A value of 0 can improve performance. The syn-tax follows:

```
dbcc tune( doneinproc, 0|1 )
```

Table- and index-level parameters.   The DBCC *tune* keyword can be used to set the value for *indextrips* for a table's indexes or *oamtrips* for a table's OAM pages. The syntax is

```
dbcc tune( {indextrips|oamtrips}, value, table_name )
```

for example,

```
dbcc tune( indextrips, 3, player )
dbcc tune( oamtrips, 5, player )
```

The *indextrips* keyword is used to set the value for the named table's indexes. The *oamtrips* keyword is used to set the *oamtrips* value for a table's OAM pages. The *value* parameter is an unsigned short data type used to specify the number of index/OAM trips. The *table_name* is the name of the affected table. The command must be run for the named table in the current database.

If the tables *indextrips* value has not been set via DBCC, or if it has been set to 0 using DBCC, then its index pages will use the global *index trips* value from the configuration interface. Similarly if the tables *oam trips* value has not been set, or has been set to zero, then its OAM pages will use the global *oamtrips* value from the configuration interface.

The *ascinserts* keyword is used to optimize INSERT performance on tables having a composite clustered index for inserts. The default value is 0, a value of 1 may improve performance. The syntax is

```
dbcc tune( ascinserts, 0|1, table_name )
```

Sybase expects to eliminate the DBCC *tune* interface in a future release of SQL Server.

13.5   Running Jobs in Parallel

Batch jobs are often run serially. That is, one phase of the batch process must complete successfully before the next phase can start to run. This design approach may be necessary for some parts of the batch process. For example, it may be necessary to load a number of feed files received from external sources before calculating overall inventory positions. Further, it may be necessary to run database and transaction log backups before starting a long-running report process. However, often many processes can be run in parallel. Taking advantage of these opportunities may considerably improve the overall performance of the batch process.

The number of jobs that the system is able to parallelize will vary according to several factors. In general, running jobs in parallel improves *overall* performance. However, if too many jobs or conflicting jobs (jobs that are competing for the same resources) are submitted simultaneously, the overall elapsed run time may be greater than that for running the same jobs serially. Also, CPU- and I/O-intensive jobs will also affect the outcome if they are competing for the same resources (hardware and software).

As a general rule, it is recommended that a maximum of four jobs (unless they perform insignificant processing) be submitted in parallel. Use server monitoring tools to observe the run times of these jobs to optimize batch processing in the server. Analyze the individual jobs so that they can be run effectively in parallel. Things to look for include demands on I/O, CPU, and database object dependencies.

Creating indexes. It is possible to create indexes on tables concurrently, with the single exception being that creating a clustered index requires an exclusive table lock. Parallelization of index builds can significantly reduce the elapsed time required to index a database. Some other factors that can affect index creation include the following:

For System 11, the *number of sort buffers* configuration parameter is used to control the number of buffers used to hold pages read from input tables. Increasing the value of *sort buffers* can improve performance when indexes are created on large tables.

The *number of extent i/o buffers* configuration parameter allocates a specified number of extents for use by the CREATE INDEX command. SQL Server also uses large buffers for BCP and CREATE DATABASE statements. The default value is 0; the recommended value is 10.

The CREATE INDEX .. *with sorted_data* keyword can be used to accelerate index creation when the data in the table is already in sorted order, e.g., when the BCP utility has been used to load sorted data into an empty table. The speed increase becomes very significant on large tables with increases several times faster for tables larger than 1 Gbyte. This option can be used in conjunction with any other CREATE INDEX options with no effect on their operation. Beware, if *sorted_data* is specified and the data is not in sorted order, an error message is displayed and the CREATE INDEX command will fail.

This option speeds indexing for clustered indexes or unique nonclustered indexes. Creating a nonunique nonclustered index succeeds unless there are rows with duplicate keys. If there are rows with duplicate keys, an error message is displayed and the CREATE INDEX command is aborted.

DBCC. DBCC is the SYBASE Database Consistency Checker. It is a Transact-SQL language extension and is used to verify the logical and physical consistency of a database. Database administrators typically use DBCC when database damage or corruption is suspected.

It is the responsibility of the database administrator to establish a preventive maintenance program where DBCC is used regularly to ensure database integrity. In addition to checking database integrity, DBCC can be used to fix system problems such as table and index storage allocation errors.

Some DBCC commands can be parallelized for large databases by using some of the lower-granularity commands. For example, instead of running a single *checkdb* command to check the consistency of the entire database, individual *checktable* commands can be run concurrently against multiple tables in the same database. Use common sense when you experiment with this technique. For example, it is probably not a good idea to simultaneously fire DBCC *checktable* commands against every table in the database. The maintenance window for large databases can be significantly reduced by using this technique.

BCP. It is probably not a good idea to attempt to perform concurrent loads (using BCP) into a single table. BCP needs to acquire exclusive locks on all pages touched by each batch copied in. Typically, the absence of concurrent operations on the same table will result in the BCP process being granted an exclusive table lock. In most cases, if multiple BCPs are attempted into a single table, the first BCP process will have its page locks escalated to table locks. The end result will be that the other BCP process will block, waiting for the first BCP to complete, resulting in single-threaded loading.

It may, however, be beneficial to overall performance to run concurrent bulk copies into multiple tables in the same server, and possibly even the same database. The recommendation is to test various combinations to come up with the best possible results.

Bulk copying of data from a database to an operating system file can be performed concurrently. The bulk copying of data out of a table requires shared page locks which roll through the database as the pages are accessed.

Database backup. The SYBASE Backup Server is an Open Server application which places the backup and restore capabilities into a separate server process. The Open Server architecture prevents backup and restore tasks from interfering with user processes. Backup Server supports up to 32 concurrent dumps from one server, uses multidump volumes, and performs multivolume dumps. The server can also read multiple database devices and write to multiple backup devices in parallel.

13.6 Third-Party Tools

Sybase and the UNIX operating system provide the administrator and system designers with a very good starting point. There are, however, some third-party tools available to make life a little easier and to improve system throughput and performance. Specifically, the tools described in this section are

- SyncSort—a sort/merge/copy utility

- Image Analyzer—a tool used to browse through objects and actual data pages in archived databases and transaction logs

13.6.1 SyncSort

SyncSort is a full-function sort/merge/copy utility. It can sort all data formats and record types, provides general-purpose record-level processing for file and data conversion, and minimizes sorting time for large volumes of data. SyncSort reduces sort execution times while improving overall system throughput. Proprietary sorting algorithms, I/O optimization, and dynamic environmental monitoring techniques result in significantly reduced CPU time, elapsed time, and disk I/O activity.

How sorting affects the relational database system. Many client/server applications today are being developed around a relational database, such as Oracle, SYBASE, or Informix. High-performance sorting becomes an issue when any of the following utility functions are performed:

- Data is loaded into the database through inserts and updates.

- Tables are reorganized to increase efficiency and eliminate fragmentation.

- Data is extracted for export, for reports, or for archiving.

As the amount of data in the RDBMS grows, performance will become an increasing concern. Initially, development and QA environments handle data volumes and applications with tens of thousands of records or less. However, performance may be quite different when the insert/update volume increases to hundreds of thousands of records and beyond. With many relational database management systems, update and load times can be reduced dramatically when data is sorted and aggregated before the update/load process begins.

As the database grows larger and business issues change, tables will invariably require reorganization to increase efficiency and keep query response time within acceptable limits. A table reorganization is frequently done by unloading the table, sorting the data, and reloading it. When the table is large (e.g., millions of rows), sort performance becomes critical.

Report programs involving large amounts of data are often processed more efficiently outside the database with a high-performance sort and a report writing tool or shell program.

Figure 13.1 illustrates typical sorting tasks encountered in a DBMS environment.

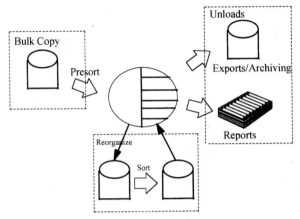

Figure 13.1 Sorting tasks in a DBMS environment.

Reducing RDBMS table load time. A large telecommunications company decided to move a critical transaction-based data analysis application from its MVS mainframe to an RDBMS on Hewlett-Packard computers.

Each day, network switches generate millions of transaction records in both character and binary format, and these records must be loaded into database tables. The loads were projected to take several hours per table because the company was unable to use SYBASE BCP.

BCP required that the data be aggregated to eliminate duplicate records. When BCP encountered a duplicate record, it would abort the load, and the load would have to be restarted from the first record. Further, to achieve acceptable performance, the BCP utility needed to receive sorted data. The UNIX system sort was useless because it does not sort binary data and cannot aggregate data.

When SyncSort was installed and used to sort and aggregate the switching data, the volume of load data was reduced and the load time per table was significantly reduced.

Some of the capabilities of SyncSort are described here.

Input and output

- Performs a sort, merge, or copy
- Processes sequential files, records passed from an input procedure or user exit, records passed in a table in memory, or records passed in from standard input
- Processes fixed-length, variable-length, VFC, and stream format records
- Generates one or more sequential files or an ADDROUT file

- Returns records one at a time to an output procedure, returns records in a table in memory, or returns records to standard output

Record selection and grouping. SyncSort can include or omit records on the basis of comparisons between field contents and constants, on the basis of text scanning for embedded strings of characters, or on the basis of the file from which the records came. Records can be grouped for different sort key processing and reformatting based on selection criteria. SyncSort can process or skip a specified number of records, and it eliminates blank records.

Record reformatting and summarization. SyncSort can insert, remove, and reorder fields within records. It also provides the user with the ability to define new fields and convert data in fields from one format to another. SyncSort can consolidate records with equivalent keys into single records, totaling the values in specified fields.

Sort key processing. SyncSort can sort on an unlimited number of key fields with the following data formats: character, unsigned decimal, signed decimal, edited numeric, packed decimal, signed integer, unsigned integer, and floating point.

13.6.2   Platinum Technologies' Image Analyzer

SYBASE SQL Server uses dump devices to back up a database. The file created when backing up a database is a snapshot image of the database. The Platinum Image Analyzer provides the system administrator with the ability to perform two critical functions:

1. Verify the integrity of the database at the time it was backed up without adversely affecting the performance of the production SQL Server
2. Recover data that has been lost or corrupted at the individual table level

Image Analyzer also allows the administrator to browse through the objects and actual data pages in archived databases and transaction logs.

Features and benefits of Image Analyzer. Image Analyzer for SQL Server is an Open Client program that reads both table data pages and transaction log pages in archived databases. It bypasses the normal SQL access methods to read pages directly, including their contents and status, and presents the information in an easy-to-read format. Some capabilities of Image Analyzer for SQL Server are listed here:

- Image Analyzer can be used to quickly check the integrity of off-line (archived) databases without loading the dump into a development or production SQL Server.

- It provides the capability to browse archived dump files to recover data from individual tables.

- It regenerates data manipulation language (DML) statements from the transaction log for the purpose of (1) replicating UPDATE, INSERT, and DELETE statements; (2) reversing erroneous UPDATE, INSERT, and DELETE statements; (3) creating an audit report from the archived dump file. The audit report can be used to maintain a trail of data modification statements.

How it works.   The SQL Server backup process creates a database dump, which contains an image of all important pages in the source database. Image Analyzer for SQL Server scans the file and builds a map of offsets into the file to page numbers in the database. It then reads pages from the file much as SQL Server reads pages from database devices. The following information is decoded from the page header:

- Page type (data page or transaction log page)
- Page pointers (page linkage)
- Page status
- Database object owning the page

The user enters manufacturer (Sybase or Microsoft), SQL Server version, host platform (UNIX, Windows NT, etc.), and file name into a graphical panel. At this point, the user has the ability to browse table data and transaction log data in an easy-to-read format. Image Analyzer scans all the pages and displays the amount of space used. Information regarding the structure of data pages is retrieved from the system tables found in the dump file itself.

When data is recovered from the log or from data pages, data can be saved to files on the client-side machine in several formats:

- SQL scripts
- Bulk-copy input files
- Lotus or Excel data files
- Audit reports

To restore or load the data into an SQL Server, the administrator must use the bulk-copy program for BCP input files, or the interactive SQL utility for SQL scripts.

Database integrity. Using DBCC can be a lengthy process which dramatically slows production transaction processing applications. Image Analyzer can be used in the background to verify the internal consistency of a database off line. It reads backups and verifies that they are both readable and consistent.

Image Analyzer can be used to verify allocations and page linkage in a dump file. While this takes a significant amount of time, the process does not affect the production environment. If problems are found in the dump file, the administrator can use the appropriate DBCC commands to fix the production database.

13.7 Creating Indexes after Inserts

In some cases it may be a good idea to drop indexes on a table prior to inserting a large number of rows in that table. Performance will be considerably faster than that achieved by inserting into a table with all its indexes in place. When batch loads are run, this approach is particularly beneficial. As a general rule, if the insert will increase the number of rows by over 10 percent, consider dropping the indexes for the load/insert operation. Keep in mind that there is a tradeoff between the overhead of loading data with indexes in place and rebuilding indexes after the load completes.

Sorted data and clustered index. When data is loaded into an empty table, it is always better to create the indexes on the table after the data is loaded. One exception to this rule occurs when sorted data is being loaded into a table having a clustered index. In this case, the recommendation is to

- Load the data into the table in sorted order with the clustered index defined. Use large I/Os on data and the transaction log.
- Create any required nonclustered indexes, using the techniques discussed earlier in this chapter.

Nonsorted data and clustered index. When nonsorted data is loaded into a table by the clustered index, the recommendation is to

- Create the table and load the data by using fast BCP.
- Create the clustered index by using the techniques provided earlier in this chapter.
- Create any required nonclustered indexes by using the techniques discussed earlier.

14

Tuning in the Client/Server Environment

This chapter will cover several client/server-related performance issues. The first part of the chapter includes a complete overview of the SYBASE Open Client software including the Open Client Libraries and Embedded SQL. Other subjects include the difficulties of tuning client/server environments, and the specific ways in which the client/server environment can be tuned to deliver optimal performance.

Many large organizations are still discovering the cost savings that can be realized by migrating to client/server configurations. Over the next few years we will see the demands on network throughput and performance increase dramatically. The sophistication of application development tools, specifically three-tier application development, will continue to push larger applications into the client/server environment.

Internet demands will also require very high network throughput as more and more users discover the benefits of Internet access and demand tools on their desktops. The network requirements of global corporations will continue to increase as wide-area network (WAN) access becomes a critical business requirement.

14.1 SYBASE Open Client

In the client/server architecture, Sybase's solution for client access to SQL Server is called Open Client. Open Client is Sybase's front-end API. Sybase has always had a front-end API known as Database-Library, or DB-Library. Prior to the release of Sybase's System 10, Open Client consisted of DB-Library and Net-Library. DB-Library is a call-level interface (CLI) that provides function calls for application programs to use to communicate with a SYBASE SQL Server or Open Server. In this instance Open Server can be defined as the Sybase Open Server product or another Sybase product built using the Open Server tool kit (such as the OmniCONNECT Gateway or Replication Server). Requests can be database remote procedure calls, Transact-SQL language statements, or command strings in any language.

Net-Library is the network transport layer. Net-Library works in conjunction with networking software to provide applications with access to data managed by SQL Servers. Net-Library is a software layer that consists of two interfaces: one with the network, the other with the application (see Fig. 14.1). It supports several network protocols such as Novell LAN Workplace, IPX, and Named Pipes, and it provides protocol independence. The Net-Library API is made available to some Sybase business partners for development of new Net-Libraries. Currently, the only messaging protocol supported by Net-Library is Sybase's own Tabular Data Stream (TDS).

The System 11 Open Client covers a family of interfaces consisting of

- Database-Library, or DB-Library
- Embedded SQL precompilers
- Microsoft ODBC (Open DataBase Connectivity)
- Client-Library or CT-Library

Sybase built Client-Library by extending Database-Library to take advantage of cursors, ANSI SQL syntax, and the ability of a client to use one database connection for multiple actions (asynchronous I/O) as well as additional APIs. Essentially, Client-Library is Database-Library plus support for all other APIs. The System 10 or System 11 Embedded SQL

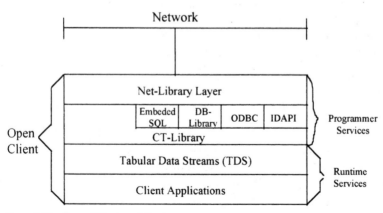

Figure 14.1 Open Client architecture.

and ODBC products resolve themselves down to Client-Library calls. Database-Library calls are passed directly to the SQL Server by Client-Library. This maintains compatibility with the Sybase 4.x database engines. This architecture gives Sybase immense front-end flexibility.

Open Client runs on a wide variety of UNIX platforms: MS-DOS, MS-Windows, Windows NT, IBM OS/2, Apple Macintosh, SunOS, Solaris, VAX/OpenVMS, HP MPE, IBM MVS/CICS, and Digital Alpha/OpenVMS.

The Sybase Open Client and Open Server are used to build the Sybase mainframe products and non-Sybase data gateways such as OmniCONNECT Gateway. Open Client for CICS allows a CICS user on a 3270 terminal to access any Open Server application on the network. This allows 3270 users to access data that has been moved to UNIX in downsizing and right-sizing efforts.

ODBC. ODBC is commonly used with personal computer applications that require communication with many different database servers. ODBC provides an open, vendor-neutral way of accessing data stored in a variety of personal computer, minicomputer, and mainframe databases. Most ODBC drivers translate the standard ODBC calls to those of the native interface of the database system being accessed (e.g., SYBASE Client-Library). This alleviates the need for independent software vendors (ISVs) and corporate developers to learn multiple application programming interfaces. There are several ODBC drivers available for SYBASE that translate ODBC calls into Client-Library calls. This translation introduces a certain amount of overhead, resulting in slower performance than when Client-Library is used directly.

14.1.1 Open Client libraries

Three libraries make up the Open Client programming interface:

- *Database-Library*—a call-level interface used to write client applications. DB-Library includes a bulk-copy library and a special two-phase commit library. DB-Library was the only library available in earlier versions of Open Client and is carried over from earlier SYBASE versions (pre-System 10).

- *Client-Library*—a call-level interface also used to write client applications. Client-Library was introduced with System 10 and is designed to accommodate cursors and other advanced features in the System 10 and System 11 product line. Advanced programming features such as asynchronous programming and callback events are supported. Connection processing and error and message handling have all been improved. Client-Library is designed to be easier to use than DB-Library.

- *CS-Library*—a library of routines useful to both client and server applications. All Client-Library applications include at least one call to CS-Library. Client-Library routines use a structure which is located in CS-Library. CS-Library is included with both the Open Client and Open Server products.

The Client-Library includes routines that send commands to a server and process the results of those commands. Other functions are available to process messages, handle error conditions, and provide information about client interaction with the server.

Call-level approach versus SYBASE Embedded SQL. Applications can be built by using the SYBASE Open Client libraries or the SYBASE Embedded SQL precompiler. The SYBASE Embedded SQL program includes in-line SQL commands. The host language precompiler resolves the in-line SQL down to CT-Library calls. The System 10 and System 11 precompilers use the normal Open Client run-time libraries.

Embedded SQL programs are generally easier to write than library applications. There is also a shorter learning curve for an Embedded SQL programmer. Library applications, however, can take better advantage of the database functionality by utilizing the flexibility of the library routines.

A CT-Library program. Most CT-Library programs will include the following steps:

1. Initialize the Client-Library programming environment.
2. Define error- and message-handling routines. Most applications will install a callback routine to process Client-Library error and informational messages. It is also possible for applications to handle messages in-line.
3. Connect to a server with *ct_connect()*. The server can be an SQL Server or an Open Server application.
4. Send a command or set of commands to the server, using the *ct_command()* and *ct_send()* library routines.
5. Process the results of commands. This is done with the *ct_results()* library routine.
6. Close the client/server connection and terminate the program.

The following example program illustrates the basic framework of a Client-Library application. The program creates a client/server connection with an SQL Server and sends a simple query to the database engine.

```
#include <stdio.h>
#include <ctpublic.h>

/*
 * GLOBAL's
 */

CS_CONTEXT *context;

/* CALLBACK ROUTINES */

CS_RETCODE clientMessageHandler();
CS_RETCODE serverMessageHandler();

int main( argc, argv )
int argc;
char **argv;
{
      CS_CONNECTION *connection = NULL; /* CONNECTION STRUCTURE */
      CS_COMMAND    *command;            /* COMMAND STRUCTURE */

      CS_INT resultType;
      CS_RETCODE retCode;

      /* CHECK COMMAND LINE */

      if ( argc != 4 ) {
          printf( "\nSyntax: ctlib <username> <password>
              <servername>\n" );
          exit( 1 );
          }

      /* GET A CONTEXT STRUCTURE TO USE */
      cs_ctx_alloc( CS_VERSION_100, &context );

      /* INITIALIZE OPEN CLIENT */

      ct_init( context, CS_VERSION_100 );

      /* INSTALL MESSAGE HANDLERS */

      ct_callback( context,\
        NULL, CS_SET, CS_CLIENTMSG_CB, clientMessageHandler );

      ct_callback( context,\
        NULL, CS_SET, CS_SERVERMSG_CB, serverMessageHandler );

      /*
       * ALLOCATE A CONNECTION STRUCTURE,
       * SET USER NAME & PASSWORD
       */

      ct_con_alloc( context, &connection );
      ct_con_props( connection,\
        CS_SET, CS_USERNAME, argv[1], CS_NULLTERM, NULL );
      ct_conprops( connection,\
        CS_SET, CS_PASSWORD, argv[2], CS_NULLTERM, NULL );

      /* CREATE THE C/S CONNECTION */

      ct_connect( connection, argv[3], CS_NULLTERM );

      /* SEND A LANGUAGE COMMAND TO THE SERVER */
```

```
       ct_command( command, CS_LANG_CMD,\
         "USE master", CS_NULLTERM, CS_UNUSED );

       ct_send( command );

       /* PROCESS RESULTS FROM COMMAND */

       while ( retCode = \
            ct_results( command, &resultType ) = = CS_SUCCEED ) {
            switch( resultType ) {
                 case CS_CMD_SUCCEED:
                 case CS_CMD_DONE:
                 case CS_COMPUTE_RESULT:
                      break;

                 case CS_CMD_FAIL:
                      terror( "Error processing result set\n" );
                      break;

                 case CS_ROW_RESULT:
                      fprintf( stdout, "CS_ROW_RESULT" );
                      fflush( stdout );
                      ct_cancel( ( CS_CONNECTION * )NULL,\
                        command, CS_CANCEL_ALL );
                      break;

                 default:
                      terror( "Unexpected result type\n" );
                 }
            }

       /* SEND A SELECT TO THE SERVER */

       ct_command( command, CS_LANG_CMD,\
          "SELECT * FROM sysprocesses", CS_NULLTERM, CS_UNUSED );
       ct_send( command );
       ct_results( command, &resultType );

       /*
        * NORMALLY, THE PROGRAM SHOULD PROCESS THE RESULTS OF
        * THE QUERY HERE. IN THIS CASE, WE ARE GOING TO CANCEL
        * THE RESULT SET.
        */

       ct_cancel( ( CS_CONNECTION * )NULL,\
         command, CS_CANCEL_ALL );

       /* CLEAN UP THE CONNECTION & TERMINATE */

       ct_cmd_drop( command );
       ct_close( connection, CS_UNUSED );
       ct_con_drop( connection );
       ct_exit( context, CS_UNUSED );
       cs_ctx_drop( context );

       exit( 0 );
}

/*
 * FATAL ERROR ROUTINE
 */
void terror( message )
char *message;
```

```
{
      fprintf( stderr, "\nTerminal Errorl %s\n", message );
      exit( 1 );
}

/*
 * CLIENT MESSAGE HANDLER
 */
CS_RETCODE CS_PUBLIC clientMessageHandler( context, connection,
errorMessage )
CS_CONTEXT *context;
CS_CONNECTION *connection;
CS_CLIENTMSG *errorMessage;
{
      fprintf( stderr, "\nOpen Client Message:\n" )
      fprintf( stderr,\
        "Message Number: LAYER = (%ld) ORIGIN = (%ld)",\
        CS_LAYER( errorMessage->msgnumber ),
        CS_ORIGIN( errorMessage->msgnumber ) );
      fprintf( stderr, "SEVERITY = (%ld) NUMBER = (%ld)\n",\
        CS_SEVERITY( errorMessage->msgnumber ),\
        CS_NUMBER( errorMessage->msgnumber ) );
      fprintf( stderr, "Message String: %s\n",\
       errorMessage->msgstring );

      if ( errorMessage->osstringlen > 0 ) {
            fprintf( stderr, "Operating System Error: %s\n",\
              errorMessage->osstring );
            }

      fflush( stderr );

      return( CS_SUCCEED );
}

/*
 * SERVER MESSAGE HANDLER
 */
CS_RETCODE CS_PUBLIC serverMessageHandler( context,\
      connection, serverMessage )
CS_CONTEXT *context;
CS_CONNECTION *connection;
CS_SERVERMSG *serverMessage;
{
      CS_COMMAND *command;
      CS_RETCODE retCode;

      fprintf( stderr, "\nServer Message: \n" );
      fprintf( stderr, "Message Number: %ld, Severity %ld, ",\
        serverMessage->msgnumber, serverMessage->severity );
      fprintf( stderr, "State %ld, Line %ld\n",\
        serverMessage->state, serverMessage->line );

      if ( serverMessage->svrnlen > 0 )
            fprintf( stderr, "Server %s\n", serverMessage->proc );
```

14.1.2   Environment variables

For the SYBASE software to function properly, it is necessary to make certain modifications to the user's operating environment. In the .cshrc or .profile file of the sybase user, the SYBASE environment variable must be set to point to the full path of the Sybase software directory. In the following *.cshrc* file (for UNIX C shell), this would be */opt/sybase*. The DSQUERY environment variable should be set to the name of the SQL Server as specified during the installation.

```
# @(#)cshrc 1.11 89/11/29 SMI
set noclobber
set filec
umask 022
set path=(/usr/lang /usr/openwin/bin /bin /usr/bin /usr/ucb /etc ~/bin/opt/
sybase/bin .)
if ( $?prompt ) then
          set history=32
endif
setenv DISPLAY bluto:0.0
set prompt="`hostname`:`pwd`:{`whoami`}\:"
# SYBASE environment
setenv SYBASE /opt/sybase
setenv DSQUERY elvee
stty intr \^C
stty erase \^H
stty kill \^U
stty susp \^Z
tset
alias ff 'find . -name \!* -print'
alias sql 'isql -Ugwa -Ppassword -S${DSQUERY}'
if ( $?prompt ) then
          set history=50
          set savehist=50
          alias cd 'cd \!*;set prompt="`hostname`:`pwd`:{`whoami`}\:"'
endif
setenv EDITOR vi
```

14.1.3   The *interfaces file*

The SQL Server and Open Server applications (such as OmniCONNECT and Replication Server) are identified by an entry in the *interfaces* file. The *interfaces* file contains information about where the server application resides on the network and is usually maintained in the $SYBASE directory, which is the *sybase* user's home directory. It lists the name and network address of every SQL Server and Open Server application to which a user might connect. The *interfaces* file is automatically created or appended during installation. There are entries in the *interfaces* file for SQL Servers, Backup Servers, SQL Monitor Servers, OmniCONNECT Servers, and other Open Server applications. User-written Open Server applications must be identified by an entry in the *interfaces* file.

How a client communicates with a server.   Client programs can connect to any server listed in the *interfaces* file. Let's examine the steps that ISQL will use to establish a connection with an SQL Server.

1. ISQL determines the name of the SQL Server by using a command line option or finding the value of the DSQUERY environment variable. If no server name is supplied from the command line or by DSQUERY, the software looks for an *interfaces* file entry with the default server name of SYBASE.

2. Find a matching entry for the server in the *interfaces* file. If no matching entry is found, an error message is written to the client's standard error.

3. Attempt to make a connection with the SQL Server, using the network address and port number listed in the *interfaces* file. Client applications use the Database-Library *dbopen()* or Client-Library *ct_connect()* function calls to set up communication with the network and log into the server.

File format. The System 10 and System 11 installation program *sybinit* is used to create entries in the *interfaces* file. The format of an entry in the *interfaces* file is

```
# comments here e.g. Server Name, Server Type, ...
servername      retry            delay
        serviceName      protocol       network    machine      port
```

The first line of an *interfaces* file entry contains the *servername, retries,* and *delay*. The servername is the name by which this server is known; this is the value specified in DSQUERY or by a command line argument. The client program will attempt to connect to the server *retry* times with a pause of *delay* between connection attempts.

The following lines contain network information for the server entry. Here *serviceName* describes the type of service that the entry defines; possible values are *query* and *master*. The *master* entry defines the service that the server program uses to listen for log-in requests from client applications. A *query* entry is used to define the service that a client uses to log into the server. The *query* entry is mapped to the client program's DSQUERY environment variable.

Pre-System 10 servers use a service entry called *console* to perform DUMP (DATABASE/TRAN) and LOAD (DATABASE/TRAN) commands to tape. The console entry is used to identify the console program. In System 10 and System 11 SQL Servers, the console program is replaced by the Backup Server.

The name of the network protocol is *protocol*. On UNIX machines this is usually represented by *tcp* in the *interfaces* entry. The *network* entry is not currently used; on most platforms *ether* is used as a placeholder. And *machine* is the network name of the machine that this server application is running on; *port* is the port number that this interface has been assigned. Port numbers are between 2000 and 65535 and must be unique.

There may be variations in the format of network information for different operating systems. For example, the OS/2 platform does not use an *interfaces* file, and SYBASE is not the default server. Microsoft Windows' clients use an SQL Server section in the *win.ini* file to define server applications.

Example of *interfaces* file.   The following *interfaces* file resides on a Sun SPARCstation running SunOS. It has entries for two SQL Servers, a Backup Server, and an SQL Server Monitor Server.

```
#
# System 10 Server running on IBM RS/6000
#
REPOMAN
     query       tcp       ibm-ether       repoman       2048
     master      tcp       ibm-ether       repoman       2048
#
# System 11 Server on SPARC 20 running SunOS
#
SWAPS
     query       tcp       ether           swaps         2048
     master      tcp       ether           swaps         2048
#
# System 11 Backup Server on SPARC 20
#
SYB_BACKUP
     query       tcp       ether           swaps         4096
     master      tcp       ether           swaps         4096
#
# SQL Monitor Server on SPARC 20
#
MONSERV
     query       tcp       ether           swaps         5120
     master      tcp       ether           swaps         5120
```

It is possible to set up multiple query entries in an *interfaces* file so that if *dbopen()* or *ct_connect()* fails to establish a connection with a server, an attempt is made to establish a connection with an alternate server:

```
#
# System 10 Server running on IBM RS/6000
#
REPOMAN
     query       tcp       ibm-ether       repoman       2048
     query       tcp       sun-ether       swaps         2048
     query       tcp       hp-ether        equity        2048
     master      tcp       ibm-ether       repoman       2048
SWAPS
     query       tcp       sun-ether       swaps         2048
     master      tcp       sun-ether       swaps         2048
EQUITIES
     query       tcp       hp-ether        equity        2048
     master      tcp       hp-ether        equity        2048
```

In this example, when a client application tries to connect to REPO-MAN, it is directed to port 2048 on the UNIX host called *repoman*. If REPOMAN is not available, the client tries to connect to the server at port 2048 on host *swaps*. Likewise, if the connection to SWAPS fails, the client will automatically attempt to connect to the third host, named *equities*.

14.1.4 Embedded SQL

Sybase offers two Embedded SQL precompilers; Embedded SQL/C and Embedded SQL/COBOL. Embedded SQL is a means of using SQL in an application program. The application programmer uses Embedded SQL statements in a host language (C or COBOL) application, then uses the Embedded SQL precompiler to resolve the Embedded SQL statements into Client-Library function calls.

Embedded SQL provides some advantages over a call-level interface:

- The programmer uses Transact-SQL with some extensions and added features that facilitate using it in an application. The programmer does not need to learn the intricacies of the call-level interface.

- It is an ANSI/ISO standard programming language.

- Embedded SQL requires less coding than a call-level approach to do the same amount of work.

- The precompiler has the ability to analyze the Embedded SQL calls and create ISQL scripts. These ISQL scripts are used to build stored procedures that are loaded into the database's back end.

- Programming conventions and syntax change very little across different host languages.

Following is a simple Embedded SQL/C program. Compare it to the CT-Library program provided in Sec. 14.1.1. The Embedded SQL calls are in uppercase and are preceded by the EXEC SQL keywords:

```
EXEC SQL INCLUDE SQLCA;  /* EMBEDDED SQL COMMUNICATION AREA */

void main( argc, argv )
int argc;
char **argv;
{
        /* DECLARING VARIABLES */

        EXEC SQL BEGIN DECLARE SECTION;
        char userName[32], password[32];
        EXEC SQL END DECLARE SECTION;

        /* INSTALL ERROR HANDLING ROUTINES */
```

```
      EXEC SQL WHENEVER SQLERROR PERFORM errorHandler();
      EXEC SQL WHENEVER NOT FOUND CONTINUE;

      strcpy( userName, argv[1] );
      strcpy( password, argv[2] );

      /* LOGIN TO THE DATABASE */

      EXEC SQL CONNECT :userName IDENTIFIED BY :password;

      /* ISSUE TRANSACT-SQL STATEMENTS */

      EXEC SQL USE pubs2;
      EXEC SQL SELECT * FROM titles;

      /* CLOSE ALL DATABASE CONNECTIONS */

      EXEC SQL DISCONNECT ALL;
}

void errorHandler()
{
      /*
       * DISPLAY ERROR CODE, MESSAGE AND LINE NUMBER
       * OF THE STATEMENT THAT CAUSED THE ERROR.
       */
      printf( "\nError code %d at source line %d\n %s\n",\
        sqlca.sqlcode, sqlca.sqllno, sqlca.sqlerrmc );
}
```

14.2   Client/Server Performance Issues

This section describes a variety of performance issues encountered in client/server configurations.

Reducing SYBASE network traffic. Reducing the number of packets communicated over the network is critical to making a client/server environment run efficiently. The speed and efficiency of the network can be a gating factor to a high-performance system. Many networks have outstanding performance, but it is never possible to match the performance of a stand-alone machine.

In many client/server environments, the number of packets transmitted across the network is more important than the size of each packet. Both small and large packets take approximately the same amount of time to transfer between machines. Significant savings can be realized by reducing the number of network transfers needed.

Section 13.4.6 provides some simple pointers that can be used to tune network performance. Pay particular attention to the server configuration parameters *default network packet size, max network packet size,* and *additional network memory.* Also, remember to use the *-A* command line parameter with ISQL and BCP to set the packet size for individual sessions.

A Transact-SQL extension to the Sybase cursor interface provides the capability to set the number of rows returned by the FETCH statement. This is a network optimization over the ANSI standard one-row fetch. The ANSI-89 standard specifies a FETCH of only one row at a time. To change the number of rows FETCH returns:

```
SET CURSOR ROWS 100 FOR mycursor
```

14.3 Distributed Databases

By using distributed-database technology such as Replication Server, a database can be strategically partitioned among multiple physical databases located on distinct database servers. From a user's point of view, there appears to be a single logical database (single system image). For example, assume that Bogus Bank's mortgage processing department is located in Boca Raton, Florida, and the savings and checking account departments are in New York, as illustrated in Fig. 14.2. These two departments use two distinct application programs, with minimal data crossover. Network and application performance can be improved by strategically locating database servers in two cities and adding a high-performance communications link between them.

Sybase SQL Server in conjunction with OmniCONNECT and Replication Server supports distributed-database queries. Distributed updates are also supported. Using two-phase commit functionality, applications can guarantee that commits or rollbacks issued against distributed databases are enforced as a single unit of work. Distributed

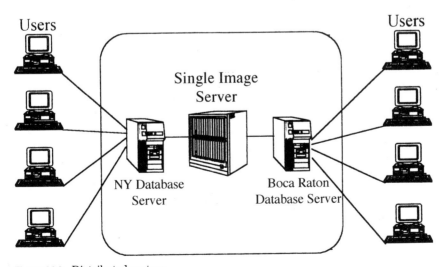

Figure 14.2 Distributed system.

transaction management and Replication Server are the subject of Chap. 16.

14.4 Monitoring the Network

This section provides an overview of how to monitor network traffic and utilization on systems based on UNIX and Windows NT.

UNIX. The *netstat* and *nfsstat* commands are commonly used to display information about network activity in a UNIX system. Command syntax varies among host operating systems, so check the UNIX *man* page for command options. On a Sun Solaris system, *netstat* is used to show the network status and report the contents of network-related data structures. When called with no options, *netstat* displays a list of active sockets for each protocol.

```
elvee:/home/gwa:{gwa}\: netstat
TCP
  Local Address      Remote Address        Swind Send-Q Rwind Recv-Q  State
  ----------------   ------------------    ----- ------ ----- ------ ------
  elvee.33742        sparky.6000            8760    0    8760    0  ESTABLISHED
  localhost.32773    localhost.33956       16384    0   16340    0  CLOSE_WAIT
  enterprise.login   hammer.1023            8760    0    8760    0  ESTABLISHED
  enterprise.sybase  146.125.130.240.1027   2880    0   10080    0  ESTABLISHED
  enterprise.login   screw.1023             8760    0    8760    0  ESTABLISHED
  enterprise.login   driver.1023            2880    0   10080    0  ESTABLISHED
  enterprise.login   flyer.1022             8760    0    8760    0  ESTABLISHED
  enterprise.46320   flyer.6000             8760    0    8760    0  ESTABLISHED
  enterprise.login   140.155.130.223.1023   2880    0   10080    0  ESTABLISHED
  enterprise.login   hammer.1021            8760    3    8760    0  ESTABLISHED
  enterprise.46531   hammer.6000            2880    0   10080    0  ESTABLISHED
  enterprise.telnet  elmo.1161              2880    0   10080    0  ESTABLISHED
```

When called with the *-i* option, *netstat* will report the state of the interfaces that are used for TCP/IP traffic. Information displayed in the report includes

```
elvee:/home/gwa:{gwa}\: netstat -i
Name Mtu  Net/Dest       Address    Ipkts    Ierrs  Opkts   Oerrs Collis Queue
lo0  8232 loopback       localhost  38368    0      38368   0     0      0
le0  1500 140.155.150.128 hammer    3609250  0      481991  1     2826   0
```

The *nfsstat* command is used to report on network file system statistics. The *-m* option is used to display statistics for each mounted file system including server name and address, mount flags, read/write sizes, and retransmission count.

```
elvee:/home/gwa:{gwa}\: nfsstat -m
/usr/data/error from hammer:/usr/data/error
 Flags: hard,intr,dynamic read size=8192, write size=8192, retrans=5
 Lookups:  srtt=1 (2ms), dev=1 (5ms), cur=0 (0ms)
 All:      srtt=1 (2ms), dev=3 (15ms), cur=1 (20ms)
```

```
/usr/data/archive from hammer:/usr/data/archive
Flags: hard,intr,dynamic read size=8192, write size=8192, retrans=5
Lookups:    srtt=3 (7ms), dev=3 (15ms), cur=1 (20ms)
All:        srtt=3 (7ms), dev=3 (15ms), cur=1 (20ms)

/usr/data from hammer:/usr/data
Flags: hard,intr,dynamic read size=8192, write size=8192, retrans=5
Lookups:    srtt=7 (17ms), dev=4 (20ms), cur=2 (40ms)
All:        srtt=7 (17ms), dev=4 (20ms), cur=2 (40ms)

/usr from hammer:/usr
Flags: hard,intr,dynamic read size=8192, write size=8192, retrans=5
Lookups:    srtt=7 (17ms), dev=3 (15ms), cur=2 (40ms)
Reads:      srtt=7 (17ms), dev=3 (15ms), cur=2 (40ms)
All:        srtt=7 (17ms), dev=3 (15ms), cur=2 (40ms)
```

Windows NT. The Windows NT Performance Monitor allows the user to monitor several aspects of network performance. Some of the categories that the administrator can view include (note that not all these categories are valid for all machines)

- NetBEUI and NetBEUI resources
- NWLink IPX and NWLink NetBIOS
- Server
- Redirector

Figure 14.3 displays server-level network throughput statistics including bytes received and sent per second and total bytes per second (bytes received plus bytes sent).

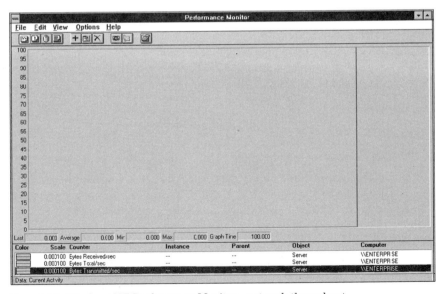

Figure 14.3 Windows NT Performance Monitor—network throughput.

The *sp_sysmon* procedure. The *sp_sysmon* system procedure can be used to monitor SQL Server network utilization and throughput. The output is shown here:

```
= = = = = = = = = = = = = = = = = = = = = = = = = = = =
Kernel Utilization
-----,-----------------
   Engine Busy Utilization:
      Engine 0                    0.2 %

   CPU Yields by Engine         per sec    per xact    count  % of total
   ------------------------     ----------  ----------  -------  ----------
                                   0.0         0.0        0        n/a

   Network Checks
      Non-Blocking                271.0     16254.0     16254      93.2 %
      Blocking                     19.7      1183.0      1183       6.8 %
   ------------------------     ----------  ----------  -------  ----------
   Total Network I/O Checks:     290.8     17437.0     17437
   Avg Net I/Os per Check         n/a          n/a  0.00046        n/a

   Disk I/O Checks
      Total Disk I/O Checks      290.8     17437.0     17437        n/a
      Checks Returning I/O         0.0         0.0         0       0.0 %
= = = = = = = = = = = = = = = = = = = = = = = = = = =
Network I/O Management
-------------------------     ----------  ----------  -------  ----------
   Total Network I/O Requests    0.1          8.0        8        n/a
      Network I/Os Delayed        0.0          0.0        0       0.0 %

   Total TDS Packets Received   per sec    per xact    count  % of total
   ------------------------     ----------  ----------  -------  ----------
   Engine 0                       0.1          6.0        6      100.0 %
   ------------------------     ----------  ----------  -------  ----------
   Total TDS Packets Rec'd        0.1          6.0        6

   Total Bytes Received         per sec    per xact    count  % of total
   ------------------------     ----------  ----------  -------  ----------
   Engine 0                      19.5       1168.0      1168     100.0 %
   ------------------------     ----------  ----------  -------  ----------
   Total Bytes Rec'd             19.5       1168.0      1168

   Avg Bytes Rec'd per Pcket    .n/a          n/a       194        n/a
   ------------------------     ----------  ----------  -------  ----------
   Total TDS Packets Sent       per sec    per xact    count  % of total
   ------------------------     ----------  ----------  -------  ----------
  ·Engine 0                       0.0          2.0        2      100.0 %
   ------------------------     ----------  ----------  -------  ----------
   Total TDS Packets Sent         0.0          2.0        2

   Total Bytes Sent             per sec    per xact    count  % of total
   ------------------------     ----------  ----------  -------  ----------
   Engine 0                       9.7        582.0       582     100.0 %
   ------------------------     ----------  ----------  -------  ----------
Total Bytes Sent                  9.7        582.0       582
   Avg Bytes Sent per Packet      n/a          n/a       291        n/a

= = = = = = = = = = End of Report = = = = = = = =
```

SQL Server Monitor. SQL Server Monitor provides some assistance with monitoring SQL Server network traffic. The Performance

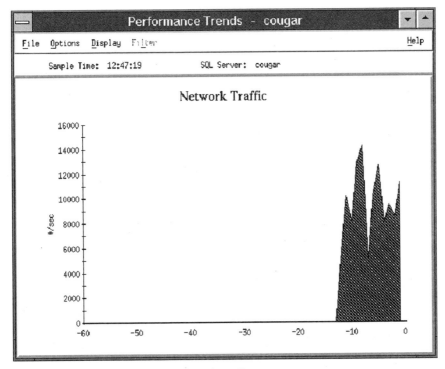

Figure 14.4 SQL Server Monitor—network traffic.

Summary window (see Fig. 8.5) is used to view data on network traffic including a display of bytes received and bytes sent. In addition, the network traffic window (see Fig. 14.4) is used to monitor network I/O.

14.5 Running Long-Running Jobs at the Server

Running overnight reports; performing exports, index, and statistics maintenance; and doing other long-running jobs on the database server can improve overall response time in client/server environments. Typically, the database server is a high-end machine with large amounts of disk storage and memory. By eliminating the transfer of packets over the network, performance can be dramatically improved. Further, other client applications will benefit from a reduction in network traffic, whether they are loading a word processor or performing ad hoc queries.

14.6 Tuning Open Client

In this section, we look at three factors that can affect the performance of Open Client applications:

- Transport stacks
- Variable-sized TDS packets
- TCP/IP packet batching

Transport stacks. When personal computers are used in a SYBASE environment, the recommendation is to choose a stack that supports *attention signals* (also known as *out-of-bound data*). This provides for the most efficient mechanism to cancel queries. This is essential for sites providing ad hoc query access to large databases.

Without attention signal capabilities (or the URGENT flag in the connection string), the DB-Library functions *dbcanquery()* and *dbcancel()* will cause SQL Server to send all rows back to the client DB-Library program as quickly as possible, so as to complete the query. This can be very expensive if the result set is large and, from the user's perspective, causes the application to appear as though it is hung. This also results in unnecessary network traffic.

With attention signal capabilities, Net-Library is able to send an out-of-sequence TDS packet requesting the SQL Server to physically throw away any remaining results providing instantaneous response.

Both variable-sized TDS packets and TCP/IP packet batching are discussed in Chap. 13. Additional recommendations are made in Sec. 13.4.6, "Tuning Performance," and Sec. 13.4.7, "The DBCC *tune* Interface."

Transaction Management

Part 3 provides a complete discussion of transaction management. Locking and concurrency issues are described in great detail. The discussion covers ANSI isolation levels and transaction modes and Sybase's compliance with the ANSI standards. The Sybase locking strategy is profiled including DML options, dirty reads, and configurable lock promotion. Also provided is a discussion of deadlocks, deadlock monitoring, and deadlock avoidance. Several undocumented SQL Server commands are described in the discussion. SYBASE locking strategies are compared with those of Oracle and Informix.

Chapter 16 covers topics such as database transactions and distributed transaction management, including distributed two-phase commit and transaction monitors. The X/Open distributed transaction processing (DTP) reference model is also described in this chapter. Transaction monitors such as IBM's CICS, Encina from Transarc, and Novell's Tuxedo are described. SYBASE XA compliance is also described. Part 3 closes with a discussion and overview of SYBASE Replication Server's capabilities.

Locking and Concurrency

As discussed in Chap. 1, locking preserves data integrity by preventing multiple updates to the same record or set of records simultaneously. Users or processes that are locked out from access must wait until the required data is freed. When this happens, the user's response time—and thus a perception of DBMS performance—suffers. For instance, table-level update locks, as a rule, result in poor performance. While locking, in itself, preserves data from corruption, it can limit the number of users simultaneously accessing the RDBMS.

15.1 Introduction

Before we proceed, let's define several terms commonly used in any locking discussion.

- *Row-level locking* (RLL). The smallest level of lock granularity in commercial databases is the *row* level. Row-level locking implies that the database can use a lock granularity of a single row. This means that multiple users can simultaneously update different rows on the same data or index page. Each user locks only the row on which the operation is performed, and does not interfere with other users in the same page.

- *Page locks.* The next level of lock granularity is the *page* level. Thus, when one user updates a row, the entire page is locked and other users are blocked from updating—and sometimes even reading—rows in that page. The SYBASE RDBMS can *escalate* locks from the page level to the table level and can release lower-level locks when their number exceeds the user-defined limit.

- *Table locks.* Table-level locking means that the database can lock an entire table at a time. This level is useful for locking a table for batch updates, locking out users for maintenance or reporting, etc.

- *Deadlocks.* A deadlock occurs when a transaction (T1) locks a record that another transaction (T2) needs, and T2 locks the record that T1 needs. Each program must wait until the other completes, which is impossible. Thus, a deadlock (sometimes known as a *deadly embrace*) has occurred.

- *Concurrency.* This is the process of managing simultaneous access to a database in a multiuser environment.

- *Dirty read.* This can result in the ability to read uncommitted data. It allows simultaneous access to a resource (e.g., a page) in a multiuser environment.

- *Blocking.* A blocking lock does just that—it blocks other transactions. For example, a transaction (T1) has a lock on a page that another transaction (T2) wants. T1 is said to be blocking T2.

- *Optimistic locking.* An optimistic locking strategy assumes that the index (used to locate the row) will change infrequently; it allows nonlocking access to the index.

- *Pessimistic locking.* A pessimistic locking strategy assumes that a transaction searching the index will modify the index. The transaction must acquire an address lock (see Sec. 15.3) for each step of the index search. Lock overhead is high, resulting in reduced concurrency and reduced performance. By default, SQL Server uses a pessimistic locking strategy.

Read consistency is an important concept in multiuser databases. Providing a consistent view of a database that may be constantly changing is a difficult task. The level at which a table is locked can greatly influence access to data. Data can be locked at three levels:

1. The entire table can be locked.

2. The page can be locked (page size becomes a factor here).

3. Individual rows can be locked.

The *granularity* of locks in an RDBMS refers to the amount of data locked at one time. The database server can lock as little as a single row of data or an entire database. By increasing the lock granularity, the amount of processing overhead required to obtain a lock becomes smaller. Large lock granularity can, however, degrade performance because users must wait until locks are released to access the data. Conversely, as lock granularity decreases, additional

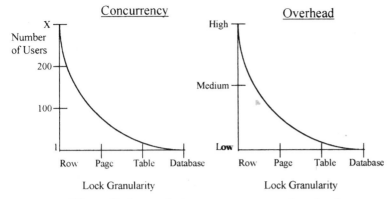

Figure 15.1   Effects of lock granularity on concurrency and overhead.

processing is required to maintain and coordinate the increased number of locks.

Page-level locking is generally better when large numbers of updates are being performed on a table. Although the next major release of SQL Server is expected to support row-level locking, SQL Server does not currently do so.

Concurrency is an attempt to maximize the number of simultaneous transactions or users that can be supported by a DBMS. Concurrency is also affected by the lock granularity. Obviously, if an entire database is locked for every transaction, the per-transaction overhead is very small, but in effect the system becomes a single user. Large lock granularity (e.g., table level) affects performance when more users must wait for locks to be released.

Using a row-level locking strategy, concurrency is at a maximum; however, so is lock overhead. The goal of the system administrator and system designers is to balance overhead and concurrency to achieve optimal system performance and reliability. Figure 15.1 illustrates the effects of lock granularity and the number of users on concurrency and overhead.

15.2   Locking Levels

Consistency of data requires that the system ensure that the operations performed by users in a multiuser environment are equivalent to the results that would be obtained if users ran their transactions serially. This means that simultaneous reads and writes do not interfere with each other. In a paper on locking written by James Gray, he defined the consistency levels outlined in Table 15.1. Note that Gray's locking levels do not correspond to ANSI transaction isolation levels.

TABLE 15.1   Consistency Levels Defined by James Gray

Consistency level	Description
Level 0	A transaction does not overwrite the dirty data of any other transaction.
Level 1	Level 0 locking plus: A transaction commits all its writes at once.
Level 2	Level 1 locking plus: A transaction does not read the dirty pages of other transactions. This is the SYBASE default locking level.
Level 3	Level 2 locking plus: Other transactions do not dirty any data read by the transaction before it commits.

15.2.1   ANSI isolation levels

The term *isolation level* is used to indicate how strictly transactions are isolated from one another. The ANSI standard defines four levels of isolation for SQL transactions based on the presence or absence of three phenomena, as defined below.

- *Level 1 (read committed).*   Isolation level 1 prevents *dirty reads.* A dirty read occurs when one transaction (T1) modifies a row and a second transaction (T2) reads that row before the first transaction has committed the change. If the first transaction rolls back the change, information read by the second transaction is invalidated. This is disallowed by Gray's consistency level 2. By default, SQL Server prevents dirty reads by locking the data used in T1 until the transaction is committed or rolled back.

- *Level 2 (repeatable reads).*   Isolation level 2 prevents *nonrepeatable reads.* Nonrepeatable reads occur when one transaction reads a row and a second transaction modifies that row. If the second transaction commits the change, subsequent reads by the first transaction will produce different results from the original read. This is disallowed by Gray's level 3.

- *Level 3 (serializable).*   Isolation level 3 prevents *phantom reads.* Phantom reads occur when one transaction reads a set of rows that satisfies a search condition and a second transaction modifies the data through an INSERT, UPDATE, or DELETE statement. If the first transaction repeats the query with the same search conditions, it obtains a different set of rows.

ANSI also specified transaction isolation level 0 (read *uncommitted*)—it permits dirty reads. Dirty reads, also known as *isolation level 0 queries,* do not have locks on readers and writers. When a transaction modifies data, other transactions are allowed to read the modified (dirty) data before the transaction modifying the data is committed.

TABLE 15.2   ANSI Isolation Levels

Isolation level	Dirty reads	Nonrepeatable reads	Phantom reads
Read uncommitted (dirty reads)	Yes	Yes	Yes
Read committed (cursor stability)	No	Yes	Yes
Repeatable reads	No	No	Yes
Serializable	No	No	No

Transactions reading dirty data may get an inaccurate view of the data. Later versions of System 10 (Version 10.0.3 and later) and the System 11 SQL Server support dirty reads.

Table 15.2 illustrates the transaction characteristics of the four ANSI isolation levels.

15.3   SYBASE Locking Strategy

This section provides an overview of the SYBASE locking strategy and describes Sybase's compliance with ANSI isolation levels. As discussed in Chap. 1, some servers permit manual locking, but in reality, automatic locking in a database management system is imperative. Locking is handled automatically by SQL Server with a few notable exceptions, described in this section.

Currently, SQL Server supports two primary levels of locking: *page* locks and *table* locks. Page locks are obviously less restrictive than table locks. Table locks may be more efficient when an entire table is being accessed. By default, after a statement has acquired 200 page locks, SQL Server will attempt to obtain a table lock. This can be tuned by the system administrator's using the *lock promotion threshold* configuration variables.

15.3.1   Page locks

Page-level locking is generally better when large numbers of updates are being performed on a table. SQL Server uses two types of page locks:

1. *Address locks* are applied on nonleaf index pages.

2. *Logical locks* are applied on leaf nonclustered index pages and on data pages.

Pre-System 11 versions of the SQL Server always apply exclusive address locks to a page. If a task is holding an address lock on a page, then no other task can access that page (even for read-only purposes). System 11 can apply *shared* or *exclusive* address locks to a page, resulting in improved concurrency. Shared-address locks allow other readers to access a page protected by an address lock. Address locks are held by a process when the process moves from one node of an index tree (see Chap. 5) to another.

Logical locks are used on leaf nonclustered index pages and on data pages. The following is a brief summary of the characteristics of different types of logical locks used by SYBASE:

- *Shared (S) lock.*   Multiple transactions can lock a shared page. No transaction can acquire an update lock on a page that has a shared lock on it.

- *Update (U) lock.*   An update lock will allow reads but will not allow other update or exclusive locks. An update lock is promoted to an exclusive lock when the page is ready to be modified. This is an internal lock used by the SQL Server kernel to help avoid deadlocks.

- *Exclusive (X) lock.*   One and only one transaction can have an exclusive lock on a page. When other transactions are blocked by an exclusive lock, they are placed in a *lock sleep* state until the exclusive lock releases.

Read operations generally acquire shared locks, and write operations acquire exclusive locks. If a process owns a shared lock on an object, no other process is able to obtain an exclusive lock on that object. Shared locks are normally released after the data page has been read. When a process has an exclusive lock on an object, no other process can obtain any type of lock on that object. Exclusive locks exist for the duration of a transaction. No other process can acquire an update or exclusive lock on an object having an update lock. Other processes can still acquire shared locks on the object having the update lock. SQL Server escalates an update lock to an exclusive lock when the page is ready to be modified. Figure 15.2 illustrates the effects of update transactions on *committed read* statements.

15.3.2 Table locks

Table-level locks are used to restrict access to an entire table, including all indexes on the table. The following table-level lock types are used by SQL Server:

- *Shared.*   A shared table lock is similar to a shared page lock. SQL Server uses shared table locks when a nonclustered index is being created.

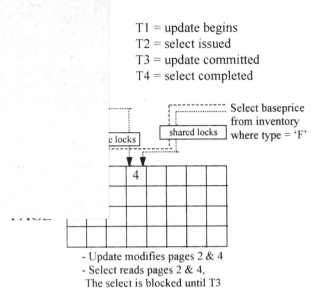

T1 = update begins
T2 = select issued
T3 = update committed
T4 = select completed

Select baseprice
from inventory
where type = 'F'

shared locks

e locks

4

- Update modifies pages 2 & 4
- Select reads pages 2 & 4,
The select is blocked until T3

Figure 15.2 SYBASE locking.

- *Exclusive.* Exclusive locks (like shared locks) can be acquired at the table and/or page level, on a data page, or index page. SQL Server applies exclusive table locks when the CREATE CLUS-TERED INDEX statement is executed. If no index is available, the UPDATE and DELETE statements will apply exclusive table locks. For this reason, the database designer must make sure that UPDATEs and DELETEs do not scan the table.

- *Intent.* An intent lock is used to prevent a transaction from obtaining a shared or exclusive lock on a table having page-level locks. SQL Server applies an intent lock to a table when a shared or an exclusive page lock is granted to a transaction.

15.3.3 Extent locks

An *extent* lock is a lock held on a group of eight database pages (an extent) while they are being allocated or deallocated. Extent locks are typically acquired by a CREATE or DROP command (e.g., CREATE TABLE) or when an INSERT operation requires new data or index pages.

15.3.4 Demand locks

A *demand* lock prevents any more shared locks from being set, so that a write transaction can proceed. SQL Server uses a demand lock to indicate that a transaction is next in line to lock a table or page.

Demand locks are used to avoid a situation where read transactions acquire overlapping shared locks on a table or page, so that a write transaction is blocked from acquiring an exclusive lock. This scenario is also referred to as a *live lock*.

15.3.5   Row-level locking

Although the next major release of SQL Server should support row-level locking, SQL Server does not currently support RLL. Eventually Sybase will provide row-level locking; however, at this point the best that Sybase has to offer is *max_rows_per_page*. The CREATE TABLE statement can be used to simulate RLL by limiting the number of rows stored on a page to one. Note that when a row is deleted or updated (out of place), the server needs to acquire locks on surrounding data pages to deallocate the page where the deleted row was located.

15.3.6   Transaction modes

SQL Server Release 10 and SQL Server Release 11 can operate in two different transaction modes:

- *Chained mode*—ANSI-compatible mode
- *Transact-SQL mode*—unchained mode

Transact-SQL mode, also known as unchained mode, requires explicit BEGIN TRANSACTION statements paired with a COMMIT TRANS-ACTION or ROLLBACK TRANSACTION statement to complete transactions. Transact-SQL mode is the default transaction mode for SQL Server.

Chained mode, or ANSI-compatible mode, implicitly begins a trans-action before any data retrieval or modification statement. These statements include DELETE, INSERT, SELECT, UPDATE, OPEN, and FETCH. Applications must still end transactions with COMMIT TRANSACTION or ROLLBACK TRANSACTION.

ANSI requires all SELECTS and data manipulation language (DML) statements to be executed inside a transaction. Applications can use a SET command to switch between chained mode and Transact-SQL mode. The syntax is as follows:

```
SET CHAINED {ON | OFF}
```

15.3.7   Isolation levels

SQL Server allows the user to set transaction isolation levels by using a *set* command. By default, SQL Server's transaction isolation level is 1. The default mode of operation is also referred to as the *cursor stability*. The syntax is

```
set transaction isolation level {0 | 1 | 3}
```

or

```
set transaction isolation level
  { read uncommitted | read committed | serializable }
```

The current isolation level can be determined by querying the value of the @@*isolation* global variable as follows:

```
1> select @@isolation
2> go
------------
      0
```

System procedures. Sybase-supplied system stored procedures always execute at isolation level 1, regardless of the session level. All Sybase system procedures explicitly set the isolation level to 1 at the start of the procedure. The scope of any isolation-level change is the life of the system procedure. When a system procedure completes, the isolation level is restored to the previous session level.

15.3.8 Dirty reads

As described earlier, several RDBMS products support a fast read mode without data integrity where the database system can scan the data as it currently exists on disk or in memory, regardless of whether the data has been committed. Even though dirty reads offer measurable performance advantages, their use has to be modified against the potential exposure to inaccurate data.

Dirty reads allow readers and writers to access the same data. This provides a faster response time and improved system throughput for queries *tolerant* of seeing dirty data.

In SYBASE, when transaction isolation level 0 is set, SQL Server allows dirty reads by not applying locks on pages or tables being read. Dirty reads are acceptable when approximate query results are acceptable. Use transaction isolation level 1 (the default) or higher for high-value transactions when incorrect results cannot be tolerated.

15.4 Parallel Lock Manager

The System 11 release also sports a new parallel lock manager (PLM). The PLM incorporates three main modifications to the System 10 code line:

1. Deferred deadlock search
2. Engine free-lock cache

3. Spinlock decomposition

A task initiates a *deadlock search* when it is placed in the sleep queue on a lock request. SQL Server Release 11 provides the ability to defer the deadlock check for a user-configurable amount of time. The *dead-lock checking period* server configuration variable is used to specify the minimum time in milliseconds before SQL Server initiates a deadlock search for a process waiting on a lock to be released. This is discussed further in Sec. 15.7.

When running in the SMP environment, each SQL Server will have its own cache of locking structures, as shown in Fig. 15.3. Lock structures are allocated from the *global free-lock list*. Access to the global free-lock list is controlled by the LOCK_FREELIST_SPIN spinlock. The size of each engine's *free-lock cache* (engine free-lock list) is configurable via the *max engine freelocks* configuration parameter. The size of the block of free locks transferred from the global free-lock list to the engine free-lock list is configurable using the *freelock transfer* configuration parameter.

The design of the System 11 parallel lock manager replaces the single spinlock used by System 10 to protect the lock manager data structures with multiple spinlocks. The primary benefits of the parallel lock manager are

- Reduced overhead for deadlock checking. Deadlock checking is expensive! In System 10 servers, deadlock checking is performed every time a task waits for a lock. If deadlock checking is deferred, a lock can be granted without deadlock checking's ever taking place.

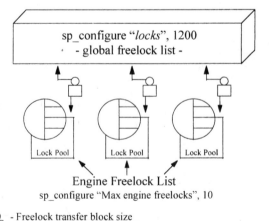

sp_configure "*locks*", 1200
- global freelock list -

Lock Pool   Lock Pool   Lock Pool

Engine Freelock List
sp_configure "Max engine freelocks", 10

○ - Freelock transfer block size
□ sp_configure "*freelock transfer*", 30

Figure 15.3 SQL Server lock pools.

- Improved scalability. The single spinlock used for lock manager structures is a scaling bottleneck in the System 10 dataserver.

15.4.1 Configurable lock promotion

Table locks can sometimes provide more efficient locking for large transactions or batch updates. As mentioned earlier, SQL Server Release 11 supports lock escalation from the page level to the table level. The default behavior of SYBASE is to escalate page-level locks to the table level after a statement has accumulated 200 page locks. System 11 allows the administrator to tune the lock escalation behavior by using several server configuration variables. The lock promotion threshold can be set at the serverwide level (by using server configuration variables) or at the table level by using the *sp_lockpromote* stored procedure. The configuration variables include

> *lock promotion LWM*
>
> *lock promotion HWM*
>
> *lock promotion PCT*

lock promotion PCT. The *lock promotion PCT* (percentage) parameter is used with the *lock promotion HWM* (high watermark) and *lock promotion LWM* (low watermark) parameters. This parameter sets the percentage of page locks permitted by a Transact-SQL command (if the number of locks is between *lock promotion LWM* and *lock promotion HWM*) before the server attempts to escalate the page locks to a table-level lock. The default is 100 percent. The lock promotion threshold for a table is computed internally based on the *lock promotion PCT* as

```
( PCT x table_size ) / 100
```

lock promotion LWM. This parameter specifies the number of page locks allowed during a single scan of a table or index before SQL Server attempts to promote page-level locks to a table lock. If the computed lock promotion threshold is less than the low watermark, then lock promotion will occur at the low watermark.

lock promotion HWM. The lock promotion high watermark sets the number of page locks allowed before SQL Server escalates the page locks to a table-level lock. The System 11 SQL Server behaves as System 10 does when the *lock promotion LWM* and *lock promotion HWM* parameters are left at the default values. System 10 escalates page locks to table locks when the number of page locks exceeds 200.

If the lock promotion threshold is greater than the high watermark, then lock promotion will occur at the high watermark.

Setting lock promotion thresholds.   The *sp_setpglockpromote* system stored procedure is used to set lock promotion thresholds for a database, table, or the current SQL Server. The syntax is

```
sp_setpglockpromote server, null, new_lwm, new_hwm, new_pct
```

or

```
sp_setpglockpromote
  { 'database' | 'table' }, objname, new_lwm, new_hwm, new_pct
```

for example,

```
sp_setpglockpromote server, null, 200, 200, 100
```

The first form of the procedure is used to set serverwide configuration variables, which can also be done with the *sp_configure* system procedure. A new server configuration file is written for each serverwide option that is changed.

The *new_lwm, new_hwm,* and *new_pct* parameters correspond to the new values for low watermark, high watermark, and (lock promotion) percent. Any of these parameters may be NULL, in which case the current value will be unaffected.

The second form of the statement is used to set lock promotion thresholds for a database or table. For example,

```
sp_setpglockpromote 'table', 'inventory', 200, 300, 60
```

A row is placed in the *sysattributes* table when *sp_setpglockpromote* is used on a database or table.

The *sp_dropglockpromote* procedure.   The *sp_dropglockpromote* procedure is used to remove lock promotion values from a table or database. The syntax is

```
sp_dropglockpromote { 'database' | 'table' }, objname
```

for example,

```
sp_dropglockpromote 'eei'
```

Serverwide configuration values are used when user-defined lock promotion values are removed from a table or database.

15.5   SELECT Syntax

SQL Server Release 11 provides several optional keywords that can be used in conjunction with the SELECT statement to influence the SYBASE locking strategy. Specifically, the keywords are *holdlock, shared,* and *at isolation.*

15.5.1   Keyword *holdlock*

Shared locks are normally released by a transaction after the data page has been read. The *holdlock* keyword is used with the SELECT statement to force SQL Server to hold shared locks until the completion of a transaction.

When transaction isolation level 3 is active, SQL Server automatically applies a HOLDLOCK to all SELECT operations in a transaction. If chained mode is also active, that isolation level remains in effect for all data retrieval and modification statements that implicitly begin a transaction. When SQL Server is operating in this manner, all shared locks will be held until the transaction is completed with a commit or rollback. The HOLDLOCK keyword will hold all read locks for the duration of the transaction, which has the effect of locking out all UPDATES and can cause serious concurrency problems. The NOHOLDLOCK keyword can be used to prevent SQL Server from holding shared locks during the execution of a SELECT statement regardless of the transaction isolation level that is currently in effect.

When SQL Server is operating in default mode (transaction isolation level 1), shared locks are released when the data page is no longer needed. The use of SELECT WITH HOLDLOCK should be avoided unless absolutely necessary. Also, be very careful when you use transaction isolation level 3. Applications that are ANSI-compliant should be tested for concurrency issues. The following is a simple example of the use of the HOLDLOCK keyword:

```
SELECT partNumber, partName FROM inventory HOLDLOCK
```

15.5.2   Keyword *shared*

The *shared* keyword is used to force SQL Server to apply shared locks instead of an update lock on a specified table or view. The *shared* keyword can only be used when the SELECT statement is part of a DECLARE CURSOR statement. For example,

```
DECLARE myCursor CURSOR
  FOR SELECT
        partNumber,
        partName
  FROM inventory SHARED
  WHERE type='F'
```

15.5.3 Keyword *at isolation*

The *at isolation* keyword is used with the SELECT statement to set
the isolation level of the query. If the *at isolation* keyword is omitted,
SQL Server uses the current isolation level of the SQL Server session.
The *at isolation* keyword is valid for individual queries or within a
DECLARE CURSOR statement. The syntax is

```
SELECT ...
   [at isolation {read committed | read uncommitted | serializable}]
```

or

```
SELECT ...
   [at isolation {0|1|3}]
```

For example,

```
DECLARE myCursor CURSOR
FOR SELECT
     partNumber,
     partName
FROM inventory
WHERE type = 'F'
AT ISOLATION serializable
```

15.6 Deadlocks and Lock Monitoring

Locking is associated with another well-known performance problem—deadlocks. As mentioned earlier, a deadlock occurs when a
transaction (T1) locks a record that another transaction (T2) needs
and T2 locks the record that T1 needs. Each program must wait until
the other completes, which is impossible. Thus, a deadlock (sometimes known as a *deadly embrace*) has occurred. The DBMS server
should automatically detect deadlocks and use appropriate algorithms to resolve them. As with global optimization, deadlock detection becomes much more complicated in a distributed environment.
The time criterion might not be sufficient, since network delays and
slow response time may be confused with a lock at a remote site. A
truly distributed RDBMS server should be capable of resolving "distributed" deadlocks, even though the majority of the available DBMS
implementations use some simple, timeout-based rules to resolve
deadlocks.

SQL Server automatically detects deadlocks and chooses the transaction which has accumulated the least amount of CPU time as the
deadlock victim. SQL Server terminates the process of the *victim* with
an error message. Application programmers should write error-han-
dling routines to check for the possibility of deadlocked transactions

(which return error message 1205). When deadlocks are encountered by an application, the application should resubmit the transaction. It may be a good idea to display an error message to the user and ask the user to resubmit the transaction.

The following SQL Server options can be used to troubleshoot application concurrency. Also see Sec. 8.2.3, "SQL Server Lock Activity."

15.6.1 The *print deadlock information* option

The *print deadlock information* server configuration option is used to print out (to the error log) deadlock chains and victims in simple language. This information can be used to determine which transactions are resulting in deadlocks and the probable causes of those deadlocks. An error log fragment is shown here:

```
Deadlock Id 7 detected. 1 deadlock chain(s) involved.
Process 13 was executing a FETCH CURSOR command in the procedure
  'pr_getloc'
Process 9 was executing an UPDATE command in the procedure 'pr_set_wrk
  flow'
Process 9 was waiting for an 'exclusive table' lock on the 'tb_workflow'
  table in database 5 but process 13 already had a 'shared intent' lock on it.
Process 13 was waiting for a 'shared page' lock on page 10512 of the
  'tb_workflow' table in database 5 but process 9 already had an 'exclusive
  page' lock on it.
Process 9 was chosen as the deadlock victim. End of deadlock information.
```

Because the server will incur extra overhead when this option is enabled, it should be used for troubleshooting purposes only. Pre-System 11 servers can achieve the same results by using the 1204 and 1205 server trace flags.

15.6.2 Obtaining Lock-Wait Information

The 1213 server trace flag is used to report time spent by SQL Server waiting for locks. When enabled, SQL Server reports lock-wait statistics on a server process ID (spid) and object ID (objid) basis:

dbcc traceon(1213)

dbcc traceoff(1213)

The *dbcc object_stats* keyword can be used to obtain lock-wait statistics for a specific object. The syntax is

```
dbcc object_stats( init_locks | locks, dbid, objid )
```

for example,

```
1> dbcc object_stats( locks, 5, 1637580872)
2> go
Objid = 1637580872, Name = <inventory>,
 SH_PAGE = 0 msec, UP_PAGE = 0 msec, EX_PAGE = 0 msec
```

The *init_locks* parameter is used to initialize the statistics to 0. The *locks* option is used to display lock statistics. The *dbid* and *objid* parameters are the database ID and object ID, respectively.

The *dbcc user_stats* keyword is used to display user lock-wait statistics. The syntax follows:

```
dbcc user_stats( init_locks | locks, spid )
```

for example,

```
1> dbcc user_stats( locks, 1 )
2> go
Spid = 1, SH_PAGE = 0 msec, UP_PAGE = 0 msec, EX_PAGE = 0 msec
```

The *init_locks* parameter is used to initialize the statistics to 0. The *locks* option is used to display lock statistics. The *spid* parameter is the server process ID of the SQL Server user.

15.6.3   The *sp_sysmon* procedure

The *sp_sysmon* system procedure can be used to look for blocking locks. It should be used routinely to identify the presence of a problem.

```
1> sp_sysmon
2> go
 .
 .
 ===========================================
Lock Management
----------

Lock Summary            per sec    per xact    count    % of total
-------------------     --------   ---------   ------   ----------
Total Lock Requests       0.2        14.0        14        n/a
Avg Lock Contention       0.0         0.0         0        0.0 %
Deadlock Percentage       0.0         0.0         0        0.0 %

Lock Detail             per sec    per xact    count    % of total
-------------------     --------   ---------   ------   ----------
 .
 .
 .
Shared Page
  Granted                 0.2        14.0        14      100.0 %
  Waited                  0.0         0.0         0        0.0 %
-------------------     --------   ---------   ------   ----------
Total SH-Page Requests    0.2        14.0        14      100.0 %
```

```
Exclusive Address
  Granted                      0.0         0.0        0 %
  Waited                       0.0         0.0        0 %
---------------------- ----------- ----------- -------- ------------
Total EX-Address Requests   %

Shared Address
  Granted                      0.0         0.0        0 %
  Waited                       0.0         0.0        0 %
---------------------- ----------- ----------- -------- ------------
Total SH-Address Requests   %

Last Page Locks on Heaps
                               0.0         0.0        0        n/a
---------------------- ----------- ----------- -------- ------------
Total Last Pg Locks          0.0         0.0        0       0.0 %

Deadlocks by Lock Type   per sec    per xact   count    % of total
---------------------- ----------- ----------- -------- ------------
                               0.0         0.0        0        n/a
Deadlock Detection
  Deadlock Searches          0.0         0.0        0        n/a

Lock Promotions
                               0.0         0.0        0        n/a

Parallel Lock Management Statistics Not Implemented Yet
= = = = = = = = = = = = = = = = = = = = = = = = = = = = = = = = = = = = = =
```

15.7 Avoiding Deadlocks

The possibility of encountering deadlocks in the SQL Server environment can be influenced by three areas of configuration and design.
The key factors are

1. Proper database design
2. Proper application design
3. Proper server configuration

Ensure that an index is used for all UPDATE and DELETE operations if the table is more than a few pages in size. If no index is available, the entire table will be locked for the duration of the transaction. Make sure that UPDATEs and DELETEs don't scan the table.

When transaction isolation level 3 is active, SQL Server automatically applies a HOLDLOCK to all SELECT operations in a transaction. If chained mode is also active, that isolation level remains in
effect for all data retrieval and modification statements that implicitly begin a transaction. When SQL Server is operating in this manner,
all shared locks will be held until the transaction is completed with a
commit or rollback. The HOLDLOCK keyword will hold all read locks
for the duration of the transaction; this has the effect of locking out
all UPDATES and can cause serious concurrency problems.

Keep transactions as short as possible and avoid user interaction with them whenever possible. An example of user interaction is a message box within a transaction asking, Are you sure? (Y/N). If the user decides to go to lunch at that moment, the transaction is pending and the affected resources remain locked.

Be aware of the effects of UPDATEs on tables with multiple indexes. The greatest area of I/O contention may be in the index pages and not the data pages. Remember, if the UPDATE causes the row to move, all index entries must also be updated (as a DELETE followed by an INSERT).

Well-designed applications will always access multiple tables within a transaction in the same order. The following transactions will increase the probability of deadlock because transaction A has locked a data page that transaction B needs (and vice versa).

Transaction A	*Transaction B*

```
begin tran                            begin tran
 insert inventory                      insert inventory_location(
  values( '1', 'HAMMER', 'F' )          values( '1', '000001', 100, 10.00 )
 insert inventory_location             insert inventory
  values( '1', '000001', 100, 10.00 )   values('1', 'HAMMER', 'F' )
 end tran                              end tran
```

Other simple application design tips include the avoidance of long-running transactions and the use of stored procedures to perform transactions. Stored procedures eliminate the need for client/server interaction within a transaction.

The *deadlock checking period* server configuration variable is used to specify the minimum time in milliseconds before SQL Server initiates a deadlock check for a process waiting on a lock to be released. This is a dynamic configuration variable; the default value is 500.

```
sp_configure 'deadlock checking period', 600
```

The *deadlock retries* variable specifies the number of times the server will retry a lock before declaring a deadlock and terminating one of the offending processes. This parameter works in conjunction with the deadlock checking period.

The maximum number of locks available to the SQL Server can be set with the *locks* parameter. This is the total number of locks available (serverwide) in the global free-lock list. SQL Server requires approximately 72 bytes of static memory for each configured lock.

15.8   Other Vendors' Locking Strategies

Well, almost everyone offers row-level locking with the notable exceptions being Microsoft (as of Version 6.0) and SYBASE. IBM,

Oracle, and Informix all offer row-level locking with their flagship DBMS products. IBM introduced row-level locking to DB2 with Version 3.

Sybase has maintained that row-level locking increases lock management overhead to an unacceptable level. Sybase has taken a significant amount of criticism from customers, competitors, application developers, and industry analysts. They still, however, have not delivered row-level locking with SQL Server.

15.8.1 Oracle

Oracle offers sophisticated concurrency control and row-level locking; however, as mentioned previously, this level of lock granularity does not come cheaply. Approximately 110 bytes of fixed overhead is used on an Oracle data page. At the top of the page is fixed overhead for the page header followed by row overhead, free space, and data storage. Row overhead is 2 bytes times the maximum number of rows ever on the data page. This means that if there were once 50 rows on the page and 45 rows are deleted, the row overhead on the page will remain at 100 bytes. The row overhead is not maintained dynamically. The Oracle page layout is represented in Fig. 15.4.

Free space on the page is reserved for row expansion. Free space is usually set to 10 percent, which amounts to approximately 170 bytes on a 2K data page. Free space is used for row expansion when variable-length data or NULL columns are updated. The concept behind free space is similar to using the SYBASE *fillfactor* facility. Page splitting occurs when there is no free space available on a data page for row expansion or insertion. Oracle calls the resulting page chains *row chains*.

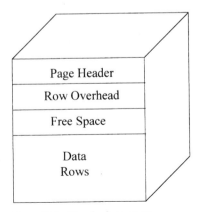

Figure 15.4 Oracle data page.

When a transaction needs to update a row, first it checks to see if any other transaction is locking the row. Then it writes a 23-byte transaction identifier into the free space of the data page which is used to logically lock the row. The locks are not held in a separate pool of shared memory, so essentially there is no memory overhead associated with the row-level lock.

At this point, the before image of the row is copied to another part of memory and is eventually written to the database as part of a *rollback segment*. A rollback segment is used to keep "undo" information for a transaction rollback or to support Oracle's consistency model. This processing typically involves a minimum of one physical I/O. Additionally, the data page header is updated with a new *system change number* (SCN), which is used for internal tracking purposes.

If a second and third transaction update rows on the same data page, first they need to check existing transaction entries for conflict. Next they dynamically allocate space in the data page for their transaction identifiers and copy out the before images of the affected data rows. Finally, the before images are written to a rollback segment and may eventually get logged (written to the *redo log* file). If there is no more free space in the data page or if the maximum number of transaction entries for that page is exceeded, the transaction is forced to wait for locks to be freed.

Obviously, the processing overhead for multiple row updates on multiple data pages is significant. When a commit is issued, the transaction entries are cleared from free space, the SCN on the page is updated, the entire transaction is logged, the dirty pages are written back to the database, and the rollback segment is marked *old*. If a query is running against the table at the time, all the rollback information is held until the query is completed.

15.8.2 Informix

Informix-OnLine also offers row-level locking. When a table is created, the administrator can specify whether the table will use row-level locks or page locks. SQL statements run by a user will use the locking mechanism specified for the table at creation.

To create an Informix-OnLine table with row-level locking, the user must specify the LOCK MODE ROW clause as follows:

```
CREATE TABLE inventory(
        partName        char(10),
        partNumber      char(6),
        partType        char(1)
        ) LOCK MODE ROW;
```

Similarly, the LOCK MODE PAGE clause is used to create a table with page-level locking. Page locking is the default method for locking.

```
CREATE TABLE inventory(
     partName        char(10),
     partNumber      char(6),
     partType        char(1)
     ) LOCK MODE PAGE;
```

After a table has been created, the lock mode can be changed by using the ALTER TABLE statement.

```
ALTER TABLE inventory LOCK MODE(ROW)
```

The LOCK TABLE statement can be used to lock an Informix-OnLine table in one of two modes: *shared* mode or *exclusive* mode.

```
LOCK TABLE inventory IN EXCLUSIVE MODE
```

The lock mode for a table is maintained in the *systables* system catalog table. The *systables* table can be queried to determine the lock level for a table as follows:

```
SELECT locklevel FROM systables
  WHERE tabname = 'mytable'
```

A *locklevel* of 'P' means the table has page-level locking, while a *locklevel* of 'R' means the table uses row-level locking.

Summary. The SYBASE SQL Server might benefit by taking notes from the Informix-OnLine implementation. I like the ability to specify the locking mode at table creation and by using the ALTER TABLE statement. This allows the administrator to control which tables will incur the overhead of row-level locking. The LOCK TABLE statement is also a welcome and usable capability for database and table maintenance.

16

Distributes Transaction Management

A truly distributed database management system should support distributed requests by providing data location and fragmentation transparency to the applications and end users. However, the transparency requirements are only the beginning of a long list of features that a distributed DBMS must have. One of the most important issues of the distributed DBMS is the integrity of updates applied to the distributed database. Distributed data integrity and consistency of databases are based on the previously mentioned fundamental concept of transactions. This means that a truly distributed DBMS is responsible for maintaining the database in either of the two consistent states—before the update transaction begins, and after the update transactions have executed successfully. Partially completed transactions should not be allowed.

Specifically, update data integrity is supported by the concept of the database transaction management.

16.1 Database Transactions

As applied to distributed data management, the *database transaction* can be defined as a sequence of one or more data manipulation statements that together form an atomic, logical unit of work. Either all statements in the transaction will execute successfully, or none of the statements will be executed. Formally, a database transaction should possess the ACID properties, defined as

- *Atomicity.* An entire transaction is either completed or aborted.

- *Consistency.* A transaction takes databases from one consistent state to another.

- *Isolation.* The affect of a transaction is transparent to other transactions, applications, and end users until the transaction is committed.

- *Durability.* The changes to recoverable resources made by a committed transaction are permanent.

It may also be useful to consider another transaction property—serialization—the importance of which becomes especially evident in a multiuser multiprogramming environment.

- *Serialization.* As long as a transaction in progress depends on certain information, this information is locked to prevent any other transaction from changing it.

In general, a transaction, or logical unit of work, is said to be *committed* when it completes all processing successfully. A database transaction is committed when all data manipulation statements have been executed successfully. In this case, all changes made by the transaction to recoverable data become permanent. Transactions can be committed implicitly, by successfully terminating, or explicitly, by issuing special commitment statements. If any of the data manipulation statements fail, the entire database transaction fails, and all partial changes to the database made before the data manipulation statement failure (if any) must be rolled back in order to bring the database to its before-transaction consistent state. In a relational database, a database transaction that consists of one or more SQL statements is committed when all SQL statements are completed successfully, and it is aborted if one of the SQL statements fails. SQL supports database transactions through two SQL transaction processing statements, COMMIT and ROLLBACK.

The ANSI/ISO SQL standard defines an SQL transaction model and the roles of the COMMIT and ROLLBACK statements. Most commercially available RDBMS products (for example, IBM's DB2) use this transaction model. Briefly, this transaction model specifies that an SQL transaction must automatically begin with the first SQL statement executed by a program or a user and must continue to execute the subsequent SQL statements until

- The COMMIT statement *explicitly* ends the transaction successfully, making the changes to the recoverable data (e.g., databases) permanent.

- The ROLLBACK statement *explicitly* aborts the transaction, backing out uncommitted database changes.

- A program executing the transaction terminates successfully (implicit COMMIT), making the database changes permanent.

- A program executing the transaction terminates abnormally (implicit ROLLBACK), backing out all partial, uncommitted changes to the database.

When the transaction processing environment is localized (not distributed), and the only recoverable resource in question is a database, the DBMS itself can handle database transaction processing.

Usually, the DBMS uses a sophisticated transaction logging mechanism. Before-the-change and after-the change images of the changed database records as well as COMMIT indications are written in reliable, nonvolatile, storage, before the database record itself is changed and written back to disk storage.

The picture changes drastically as the environment becomes distributed and additional resources (e.g., databases, files) come into play.

16.2   Distributed Transaction Management

To better illustrate the complexity of database transaction management in a distributed environment, consider a banking application.

Assume that the business requirements caused the *savingsAccount* table for all customers to be placed in the central office located in New York City, New York, while all checking account records reside at the checking processing center, located in Boca Raton, Florida. A money transfer (MT) transaction, which debits the savings account (in New York City) and credits the checking account (in Boca Raton), deals with two physically remote databases and resource managers (DBMSs). The MT transaction starts with the first SQL statement to subtract the required amount from the savings amount value, and proceeds to add this amount to the checking account. For example, the MT transaction might look like this:

```
begin work
    update ny.bankdb.dbo.savingsAccount
    set balance = balance - transferAmount
    where accountNumber = xxx
    update boca.bankdb.dbo.checkingAccount
    set balance = balance + transferAmount
    where accountNumber = xxx
commit work
```

If both these actions are successful, the transaction should commit the changes to the appropriate databases. If any one of the SQL statements fails, then the transaction should abort and the changes made before the point of failure should be rolled back. Clearly, neither debiting the savings account without crediting the checking account nor crediting the checking account without debiting the savings account, satisfies the requirements of a business or customer.

The DBMS at each of the processing sites can take care of the local COMMIT and /ROLLBACK processing. The issue here is the coordination between the actions taken by multiple participants, in this case, the local and remote DBMS resource managers. That's where the transaction manager services become extremely important. These transaction services can be performed by a distributed DBMS itself or by a separate transaction processing manager (TPM), which then also becomes a participant in the transactions it manages. In order to decide whether to make the changes to the distributed databases permanent (i.e., to treat the COMMIT request as global) or roll them back, the DDBMS or TPM must follow a special set of rules, called the *two-phase commit* protocol.

Logging both the prepare and commit phases of the two-phase commit protocols allows all participants to determine the same outcome of the global, distributed transaction. It is either committed, thus placing the distributed resources into a new consistent state, or rolled back, nullifying the effects of the transaction as if it never happened. One of the better-known examples of the two-phase commit implementation is the transaction management performed by IBM's CICS in coordination with such resource managers as DB2, VSAM, or IMS/VS.

SYBASE provides a programmable two-phase commit while some other RDBMSs supply automatic 2PC (Oracle System 7). SYBASE Open Client DB-Library (and CT-Library) provides a special two-phase commit library for application programs.

16.2.1 Two-Phase Commit Protocol

Two-phase commit (2PC) logic ensures data integrity when updates are performed in a distributed database environment. The two-phase commit protocol forces a database update to be a multistep process (as illustrated in Fig. 16.1): The two-phase commit protocol is the process by which a *global commit* request is performed. It works as follows:

1. When an application attempts to commit a multiple-participant transaction, one of the participants is first designated as the *coordinator* of the two-phase commit process.

2. In phase 1, which is called the *prepare phase,* the coordinator requests that all participants in a global transaction *prepare* to commit their local resources and signal their readiness back to the

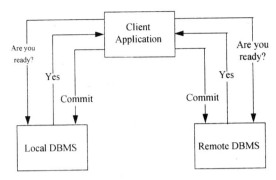

Figure 16.1 Two-phase commit protocol.

coordinator. Once the participant is prepared, its log file is marked accordingly, and this participant can no longer attempt to abort the transaction.

3. If all participants are ready to commit, the coordinator brings the transaction into phase 2, the *commit phase,* by broadcasting the COMMIT signal to all participants. At that point, all local resource managers commit their local recoverable resources.

4. If any of the transaction participants fails to prepare to commit, it notifies the coordinator. In this case, the coordinator broadcasts the ROLLBACK signal to all participants, and the entire global transaction is rolled back.

These are some of the characteristics of the two-phase commit protocol:

- The 2PC is used to implement tightly consistent distributed data.
- One transaction incurs the delay due to the synchronous effects of all servers.
- Transactions will fail if any part of the system is unavailable.
- The 2PC does not scale well; adding distributed components severely degrades system performance.
- The 2PC is appropriate when absolute consistency is required. This is necessary in high-value transactions, e.g., some banking and trading applications.
- Because of the high overhead involved with synchronization, a high-speed network is preferred.

The two-phase commit protocol (2PC) is an all-or-nothing approach that requires all components of the distributed network to be available.

If one site is unable to commit, the transaction is rolled back. This may not be practical or desirable from a business viewpoint. Two-phase commit protocol presents performance problems with the network traffic required during the transaction, thus affecting transaction throughput and making unrealistic assumptions about network reliability. Sybase has tried to minimize the necessity for two-phase commit by providing, as an alternative, the SYBASE Replication Server.

16.2.2 Distributed two-phase commit

Complex distributed transaction processing applications may involve several transactions in different systems to be executed in order to perform the required application function. One way to accomplish this is to use the structured approach of the master/slave tree (see Fig. 16.2). There, the initial request starts the front-end transaction (master of the entire tree), which in turn starts another, remote transaction (its slave), which initiates its slave, etc. This approach, while offering the least-complicated design, makes this distributed transaction's synchronization points involve all tree nodes. Unless the request for synchronization (either COMMIT or ROLLBACK) originates from the tree master, the synchronization is unlikely to succeed.

The tree master (transaction coordinator) must perform the following functions:

- Identify all participants involved in the transaction.
- Send PREPARE-TO-COMMIT (PTC) requests to all participants.
- Ensure that all participants successfully acknowledge the PTC request.

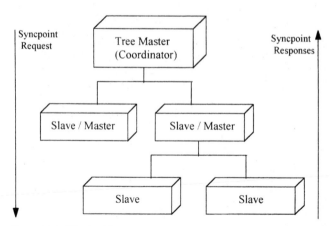

Figure 16.2 Master/slave tree.

- Log the fact that all participants are prepared.

- Send the COMMIT request to all participants.

- Ensure that all participants successfully acknowledge the COMMIT request.

- Log the fact that all participants have committed.

Logging of the commit phases is critical to transaction consistency and durability, i.e., implementation of a successful two-phase commit. Therefore, a transaction selected as the distributed transaction coordinator must be able to log the commit phases or interact with the transaction logging services provided by the transaction manager.

To support proper synchronization of the two-phase commit protocol, the transaction coordinator (tree master) should initiate the COMMIT process, and the synchronization signals should be propagated all the way down the tree. The COMMIT and ROLLBACK responses flow in the opposite direction, from the leaf nodes through the intermediate masters, to the tree master. The transactions should be designed in such way that if any of the transactions attempting to execute the COMMIT command (explicit or implicit) abends, that abend should be propagated to every other transaction in the tree and all transactions should back out their protected resources.

The two-phase commit protocol is just one of a long list of distributed data management issues. RDBMS distributed query optimization, distributed DBMS administration, concurrency and locking, heterogeneous and homogeneous DDBMS implementation, access control (security), and other issues are described in the next chapter.

16.2.3 Transaction monitors

Middleware is a run-time software layer that binds the client and the server applications into seamless but complex networked applications. The middleware glue facilitates the distribution of processing among multiple systems and interactions between dissimilar systems, and it provides the ability to share resources between individual interconnected systems, multiple specialized and heterogeneous nodes, and networks. Building applications requiring the coordinated and responsive resource sharing in the distributed environment is difficult, time-consuming, and error-prone. This is partly due to the fact that large production systems are often supplemented by new distributed systems. Another reason for the difficulty in building applications is the level of detail required by the programmer in constructing distributed network applications. The solution is the enabling software that constructs a stable, platform-independent application environment—middleware. Functionally, distributed transaction managers like IBM's

CICS are capable of providing that enabling layer not only in main-frame-based OLTP systems, but also in the new, distributed heterogeneous environment. Therefore, often TP managers are considered as a special class of middleware solutions, characterized by the ability to provide consistent application-to-application interface in a distributed on-line transaction processing (OLTP) environment. In addition to interface consistency, TP managers as middleware solutions can typically support transaction routing, execution of remote functions (e.g., function shipping), transparent access to remote data, and transaction integrity, security, manageability, and recoverability.

Although a detailed discussion of transaction managers is beyond the scope of this book, a list of available TP manager products may make the picture more complete. Several TP manager products are available today for use in distributed OLTP environments:

IBM's CICS. The ability to provide a common application environment, good portability, and a strong and mature mechanism for transaction and function routing across systems make CICS an extremely popular tool. The CICS family of products includes CICS/ESA, CICS/VM, CICS/400 for AS/400 midrange systems, CICS/2 for the OS/2 operating system, and CICS/6000 for AIX (IBM's version of UNIX). The last is ported to non-IBM UNIX environments—HP-UX from Hewlett-Packard and Solaris from Sun Microsystems—an indication that CICS has significant potential in the distributed computing environment arena, especially as a means to provide mainframe coexistence for the new OLTP applications. In addition, since IBM's distributed CICS products are based on Transarc's DCE services and the Encina Transaction Manager, the resulting relationship between DCE and CICS may ensure DCE's leading role as the technology of choice for network communications.

The CICS system is very strong in its API, intersystem communications facilities, server-to-host interoperability, security, interprocess communications between servers, and scheduling. On the downside, the historically centralized approach to transaction processing (taken by CICS) results in poor load balancing. CICS/6000 cannot distribute client requests to multiple replicated nodes, and it cannot manage all nodes from a centralized location—each of the nodes has to be managed independently.

Novell's Tuxedo. Tuxedo is a TP manager from Unix System Laboratories, a Novell company; the majority of Tuxedo installations are UNIX-based, although there is a version of Tuxedo that runs on IBM mainframes under the MVS/ESA operating system. Tuxedo is the least complex of these transaction managers, and it excels in performance, availability, and data-dependent routing. However, Tuxedo is not as strong as CICS in the areas of host connectivity and server-to-server IPC. A lack of integration with DCE affects Tuxedo's security capabilities.

Transarc's Encina. Encina is an advanced TP manager that employs transactional RPCs. Encina is ported to many UNIX environments committed to the OSF DCE, and in fact it provides underlying low-level TP services to the CICS/6000. Encina is excellent in multi-threaded application support, nested transactions, durable queues, and transaction suspend/resume processing. Encina provides a high degree of distributed system capabilities, and it supports both server replication and routing across nodes, which enhances its availability. In addition, Encina is well integrated with the DCE, which results in strong security and server-to-server communications. On the downside, Encina lacks flexible priority schedule capabilities; its host connectivity is based on APPC/LU6.2, which makes the programming relatively complex; and its Structured File System based file access is relatively slow.

16.3   Sybase and Distributed Transaction Management

Transaction management technology continues to evolve and improve to reflect such current computing trends as client/server computing, platform downsizing, increased modularity, and especially interfaces tailored to open systems. The user's view of open systems is gradually focusing on two major open-system benefits—interoperability and portability. These benefits become even more desirable as major governments and industries such as communications, financial services, transportation, manufacturing, retailing, and distribution rely on on-line transaction processing systems to manage critical strategic information in heterogeneous, multivendor, multiplatform, and multiple-operating-system environments. Centralized OLTP systems are moving to distributed client/server computing architectures exemplified by SYBASE. In fact, SYBASE was designed from the ground up as an OLTP client/server solution, which most definitely contributed to its success in the market.

Today, users and vendors alike have begun to realize that transaction management has become a unifying force that can glue all the various components of distributed transaction processing into a single, global system image. The need for a global, standards-based, cross-platform transaction manager has resulted in the emergence of a variety of approaches to transaction management.

In general, an enterprise OLTP environment can be characterized by

- Heterogeneous hardware and software platforms
- Distribution of work among multiple platforms (clients and servers)
- Large number of relatively short interactions
- Many users
- Large sharable databases

A transaction manager (TM) plays a critical role in such an environment by providing the following functions:

- Naming services
- Transaction security
- Sending and receiving of messages between clients and servers across a network
- Managing the flow and balancing the workload of transactions
- Interacting with resource managers (e.g., DBMS) using standardized, generic interfaces
- Defining and supporting global transactions that span multiple distributed systems
- Coordinating transaction recovery

16.3.1 X/Open DTP reference model

The standard interfaces employed by an OLTP transaction manager include X/Open's XA and TX interfaces for communication with resource managers and application programs.

X/Open has defined its common application environment through the X/Open Portability Guide (XPG). Its current issue (XPG4) incorporates the distributed transaction processing reference model (see Fig. 16.3).

The X/Open DTP reference model contains three software components:

- An application program (AP) that defines business actions that constitute the transaction.
- Resource managers (RMs) such as databases and file systems that provide access to shared resources. SYBASE SQL Server is an example of a resource manager.
- A transaction manager (TM), frequently called a *transaction processing monitor,* that assigns global identifiers to transactions, monitors their progress, manages the transaction integrity protocols, and manages recovery from failures.

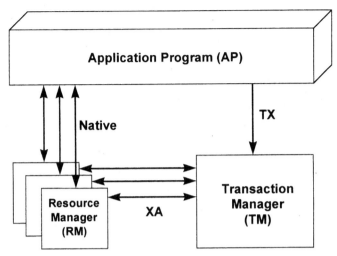

Figure 16.3 X/Open Distributed Transaction Processing reference model.

As part of that reference model, an interface between a transaction manager and resource managers such as database management and file system is defined through the XA specification, and it provides for transaction control by using such constructs as *transaction begin, transaction commit, transaction abort,* and *transaction end.* XA includes the concept of global and branch transactions. A global transaction accomplishes a unit of work as seen by an end user or an application. One global transaction may cause several branch transactions to occur, each performing a particular function (i.e., update a resource file, insert a record into a database, etc.), possibly in association with a particular resource manager. Branch transactions may be either loosely or tightly coupled, where tightly coupled transactions share isolation policies (locks) in order to guarantee that no deadlocks occur within a transaction.

Sybase XA compliance. To adhere to the X/Open DTP model, SYBASE SQL Server should be able to participate in global and branch transactions by communicating with a transaction manager via the XA API. To that end, Sybase has extended its Open Client Client-Library to include the XA API. With the XA API available for the interactions with a transaction manager, SYBASE SQL Server may participate in distributed transactions coordinated by such transaction managers as IBM's CICS, Transarc's Encina, AT&T GIS's Top-End, and USL/Novell's Tuxedo.

Sybase transaction management services. Note that the X/Open DTP model assumes multiple resource managers participating in a transaction, with a transaction manager being in control of the transaction. In the situation where a single resource manager, such as Sybase, accomplishes the transactional needs, then Sybase's SQL Server can provide the necessary transactional actions without the need for a TM. Sybase's suite of products provides the following transaction management functionality necessary for OLTP:

- Naming services allow clients to use a resource manager name or service name rather than a specific location. Sybase does it via an *interfaces* file, but plans to rely on DCE naming services (and Windows NT services) in the near future.

- Transaction-level security. SYBASE SQL Server provides log-in-based security.

- Transaction recovery. SYBASE SQL Server provides transaction logging and resource locking for the tight-consistency transaction model, and it supports homogeneous two-phase commits and rollbacks of atomic transactions.

- Sybase supports the loose-consistency transaction model, where asynchronous updates are guaranteed via the Replication Server for both homogeneous (SYBASE only) and heterogeneous DBMSs (DB2, Oracle, Ingres, etc.), with the assistance from the SYBASE OmniCONNECT Server.

16.4 SYBASE Replication Server

The SYBASE Replication Server provides features to satisfy the demands of sophisticated client/server distributed computing systems. The architectural requirements of these systems often demand widely distributed heterogeneous networks.

The SYBASE Replication Server addresses data distribution and high performance. Both are extremely important and traditionally represent the most difficult aspects of DDBMS and C. J. Date's rules.

There are several key architectural approaches to data placement in a distributed client/server environment. One is based on the implementation of a truly distributed database management system, while another is based on data replication. The former approach is quite complex and requires a distributed DBMS that complies with the 12 rules for a distributed database (first formulated by C. J. Date) that include, among others, an automatic global two-phase commit and a stable high-bandwidth communication network.

The alternative approach to a distributed database is based on data replication—placing necessary data copies at the locations where the data is needed the most. Replication is embraced by the majority of DBMS vendors today, with Sybase being the leader. Replication is the process of creating and maintaining replicas of the original version of data at distributed sites. Two main forms of replication are peer-to-peer and subscriber-publisher. In the first, data is geographically distributed among systems for considerations such as speed, security, business need, or convenience. Each system has an identical copy (replica) of the original data, and each system is allowed to modify its data and replicate it to other systems. Since the location of the original data is constantly changing, the management of this model is more complex than that of the subscriber-publisher model.

Subscriber-publisher replication is based on a well-known model: A publisher (the source of the original data) replicates the data (or its fragments) to the requesting subscribers on a periodic basis. Typically, the roles of subscriber and publisher do not reverse, although a subscriber can become a publisher to other subscribers. An example of this replication model is a situation in which a user (subscriber) maintains a local copy of data (replica) on the client system, with the original data source residing on the server; if the local data is changed by the subscriber, it will be reconciled with the server at a later time via a special process. A similar model can be implemented between servers placed at different geographical locations to maintain a "warm" backup site.

A strong business case can be made for using data replication in preference to a distributed DBMS, especially where the two-phase commit protocol is not appropriate. Let's review the characteristics of data replication and Sybase's implementation of this approach.

16.4.1 Site autonomy

C. J. Date's first rule defines the distributed DBMS (DDBMS) requirement for site autonomy. The rule states that in a distributed environment, the sites should be autonomous. To conform with this rule, the different DBMS locations are characterized by the following:

- The local database is processed by its own DBMS.
- The DBMS (at every site) handles the security, data integrity, data consistency, locking, and recovery for its own database.
- Local data access operations use only local resources.

SYBASE Replication Server is the first architecture that allows organizations to build DDBMSs that are reliable enough for enterprise client/server computing. Replication Server keeps copies of data up to date at multiple sites, providing client applications with access to local data instead of remote, centralized databases. The Replication

Server provides reliable data and transaction delivery despite network failures, and it automatically synchronizes data after failure.

Replication Server has an open architecture, allowing organizations to build a replicated data system from existing systems and applications. Systems can be expanded incrementally as the organization grows and business requirements change.

16.4.2 Replication transparency

C. J. Date's sixth rule requires a distributed database system to be capable of updating replicated, redundant data, transparently from applications and users. That is the key requirement that imposes a significant technical challenge to DBMS designers. The way in which Replication Server handles this problem is discussed later in this chapter.

16.4.3 Data replication versus two-phase commit

At the lowest level there are two technical approaches to data replication: tight consistency and loose consistency. Here are some characteristics of both along with some of the characteristics of the two-phase commit protocol.

Two-phase commit.   We have learned that the two-phase commit protocol is an all-or-nothing approach that requires all components of the distributed network to be available. If one site is unable to commit, the transaction is rolled back. Two-phase commit presents performance problems with the network traffic required during the transaction, thus affecting transaction throughput and making unrealistic assumptions about network reliability.

Tight consistency.   The tight-consistency model typically uses the two-phase commit protocol. The System 10 and System 11 tight-consistency transaction model is built by using the X/Open distributed transaction processing (DTP) model described earlier in this chapter.

X/Open DTP has three components:

- An *application program* defines transaction boundaries and the actions that constitute a transaction. An application program can be a stored procedure, a C language program, a PowerBuilder application, an ISQL session, etc.

- *Resource managers* provide access to shared resources. SQL Server and Open Server applications provide the functions of a resource manager.

- The *transaction monitor* is an overseer and coordinator that has to assign IDs to transactions, monitor their progress, coordinate multiple resource managers, and manage transaction completion and failure recovery (rollback). Examples of transaction managers include CICS/6000, Encina, Tuxedo, and Top-End.

X/Open defines the *XA interface* between a transaction manager and resource manager. X/Open also defines an interface between application programs and a transaction monitor, called the *TX interface* (see Fig. 16.4). To conform, a resource manager (in this case, the SQL Server) must provide support for transactions as defined by the OSI TP model. The 2PC protocol is used by transaction monitors and resource managers to support transaction completion and recovery. The XA interface is built on top of Client-Library and was described earlier in this chapter. X/Open does not define an interface between an application program and a resource manager; Sybase uses Client-Library as the *resource manager interface*. The XA interface provided in Systems 10 and 11 provides an XA-compliant interface to the SYBASE 2PC.

Some characteristics of the tight-consistency model include these:

- All copies of data are identical. Because the tight-consistency model uses 2PC, all copies of distributed data are identical, or else the transaction will fail.

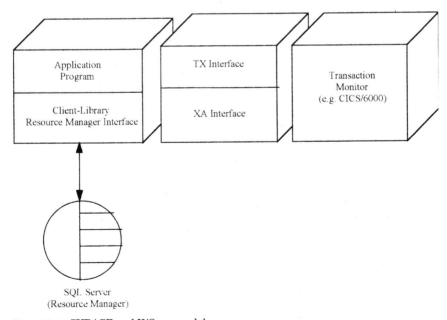

Figure 16.4 SYBASE and X/Open model.

- Replication is transparent to applications.
- There is high overhead for protocols.
- Fault tolerance and data availability may be reduced.

Loose-consistency replication.   Data that is replicated at a site is said to be *loosely consistent* with the primary version of the data. The replicated data lags the primary data by the time it takes the replication system to distribute updates from the primary. Replication Server uses a replicated data model to implement loose transaction consistency.

A replicated data system copies tables into multiple databases across several resource managers. Replication Server allows the resource manager to be a SYBASE SQL Server, an Oracle database, a DB2 database, etc. There is one primary copy of each data element (e.g., row or tuple) in a replicated data system. Tables in the replication system can contain both primary and replicated data at the same time.

The primary goal of data replication is system performance and data availability. A by-product is compliance with Date's first rule regarding site autonomy. Some characteristics of loose-consistency replication are as follows:

- There is always a primary copy of data—one site is designated the *owner* of the data.
- Primary tables and replicated tables are not always identical. There is a latency period involved in distributing updates to all sites in the replication system. Also, in the event of failure (network or some other component of the replication system), transactions will not be distributed until the failure is resolved.
- Data replication is not transparent to all applications, although it may be transparent to some applications—as decision support is.
- The loose-consistency transaction model provides high performance with low overhead for protocols.
- There is high data availability and resilience to failure. A replicated database is processed by its own DBMS. The DBMS at every site handles security, data integrity, data consistency, locking, and recovery for its own database. Local data access operations use only local resources.
- System failures may delay the propagation of data by minutes, hours, or days. During these situations users may be looking at data that is very old.

Tolerance for the loose-consistency model depends entirely on the application. Application designers must be able to distinguish between high-value and low-value transactions. Applications may be able to tolerate greater lag time for low-value transactions.

16.4.4   High availability

The SYBASE Replication Server has a store-and-forward capability to accommodate the fact that network connections and components do fail. Replication ensures that the information is updated one site at a time. There is no all-or-nothing requirement across the network. One Replication Server can manage multiple data nodes, but more Replication Servers can improve overall system performance and data availability. Store-and-forward asynchronous stored procedures also contribute to performance and data availability.

Replication Server has a switchover capability. The switchover capability can be used in a global trading application where transactions occur on virtually a 24-hour basis. At close of business in New York, the primary data site could be switched from New York to Tokyo and back. The switchover capability can also be used when the primary dataserver (usually a SYBASE SQL Server) goes down. Another site can become the primary, regardless of whether the remote dataserver is an SQL Server or some other data source. This provides a level of fault tolerance and allows updates to continue even if the primary data source fails.

16.4.5   Performance

Sybase's asynchronous store-and-forward replication architecture has significant performance benefits over 2PC. It also eliminates the requirement to first extract the updated rows from the primary-site database before sending them, as in other replication schemes. All this results in improved performance at the primary site. Further, replication ensures that reads are performed quickly since all data is local. The replicated database is local and is processed by its own DBMS.

16.4.6   The Sybase implementation—
SYBASE on-line asynchronous replication

SYBASE Replication Server provides continuous distribution of updates with row-level granularity. Continuous distribution of remote transactions is also provided. Primary sites retain control over their own data.

The Replication Server replicates transactions, not tables across servers in the network. Only rows that are affected by a transaction at the primary site are replicated to the secondary sites. Transaction replication maintains the referential integrity of all distributed information. Business rules, when enforced enterprisewide, ensure the quality and consistency of data.

The SYBASE replication process is initiated by a database event (transaction) at the primary data site. It is not scheduled to occur at a particular time interval for the database as a whole (table snapshots or bulk downloads). Due to the transaction replication approach, Replication Server can be used to replicate data on a near-real-time basis. Typical update latency can be between 8 and 15 s, although this may vary widely.

Replication system components.   A replicated data system may support many components. The replication system is an integration of dataserver (not necessarily SQL Server), Open Server, and network technology. The SYBASE Replication System incorporates the following components:

- *Network*—transport and physical layer.

- *Replication Server*—a process built on Open Server technology.

- *Replication Server system database (RSSD)*—the system catalog for the Replication Server. The RSSD must be maintained by a SYBASE SQL Server.

- *SYBASE SQL Server*—required to manage the RSSD.

- *Log Transfer Manager (LTM)*—another program built on Open Server technology.

- *Stable device*—a raw disk partition used as the Replication Servers store-and-forward queue.

- *Dataserver*—SQL Server or other data destination (such as Oracle or DB2).

- *Replication Server Manager (RSM)*—a graphical administration tool for managing the replication system.

- *Replication Server Manager agents*—RSM agents are Open Server applications used by the Replication Server Manager.

Figure 16.5 describes a simple Replication Server configuration.

Asynchronous stored procedures.   Sybase supports asynchronous stored procedures (ASPs) that can be used by remote sites to update data indirectly (see Fig. 16.6). Applications at the remote site issue updates via stored procedures. The stored procedure is picked up by the log transfer manager (LTM) and passed to the local Replication Server. The local Replication Server passes the stored procedure off to the Replication Server at the primary data site, which executes the

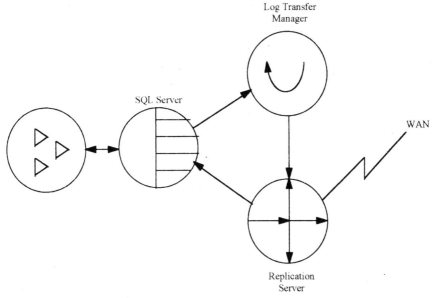

Figure 16.5   Replicated data system.

stored procedure. The LTM at the primary data site then replicates the data to all remote sites that subscribe to the affected data.

In the event of a network failure, the stored procedure is queued up (in the stable queue) and is processed when the failed component is brought back on line. Due to the asynchronous nature of the stored procedure, the user can continue to work on other tasks.

Selective subscription.   A *subscription* instructs Replication Server to replicate all or part of a table. Replicated copies of a table do not have to be complete copies of the primary table. Replication Server can replicate a row subset (fragment) or column subset (projection) of a table. Projections can save network and storage resources when the remote doesn't need all the columns in the primary table. The columns that comprise the primary key cannot be excluded at a site. A projection is constructed by creating a replication definition that includes only the columns that are required to be distributed to the remote site.

Heterogeneous systems.   Replication Server can support heterogeneous dataservers through an open interface. Any system for storing data can be used as a dataserver if it supports a set of basic transaction processing directives. These are requirements for heterogeneous dataservers:

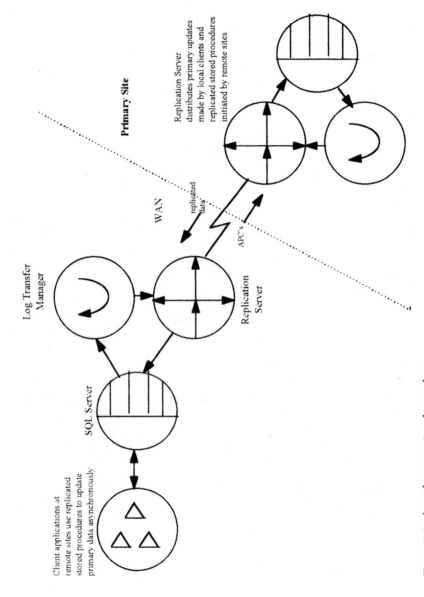

Client applications at
remote sites use replicated
stored procedures to update
primary data asynchronously

SQL Server

Log Transfer
Manager

Replication
Server

WAN

replicated
data

APC's

Primary Site

Replication Server
distributes primary updates
made by local clients and
replicated stored procedures
initiated by remote sites

Figure 16.6 Asynchronous stored procedures.

- *Client/server interface support.* This may be provided through the dataserver directly or through an Open Server Gateway. The SYBASE OmniSQL gateway can also be used to provide the client/server interface.

- *Log transfer manager support.* LTM support may be provided by Sybase or a third-party vendor (e.g., Platinum's log transfer manager for DB2).

- *Error handling.* Class definitions, mappings and processing actions must be written.

- *Function strings.* Function strings and function classes must be written to send transaction processing directives (UPDATE, INSERT, DELETE) to dataservers. Function strings are a set of commands to perform on foreign systems.

16.4.7   Replication Server application architecture

Replication Server is an extremely flexible product, and it can be implemented in several architectures. While an in-depth discussion of the various application architectures is beyond the scope of this book, here are some high-level details of Replication Server architecture. Replication Server can be configured to support

- Corporate rollup replicate—used for decision support

- Redundant primaries—used to maintain a "warm standby" for failover purposes

- Central primary and replicate database on local-area network

- Central primary and replicate database on wide-area network

- Central primary and remote update

- Central primary, remote update, and local changes

- Distributed partitioned primary

Decision support. SYBASE Replication Server can be used to maintain a *corporate rollup* database for decision support. Decision support applications can run against an up-to-date replicated database without disrupting the high-performance OLTP environment.

In Fig. 16.7, remote branch offices (located in Chicago, Los Angeles, and the Bahamas) support OLTP applications. Decision support applications run against an SQL Server located at corporate headquarters in New York. The Replication Server at corporate headquarters subscribes to all data located in the branch offices. A Replication Server located in each branch office replicates transactions to the

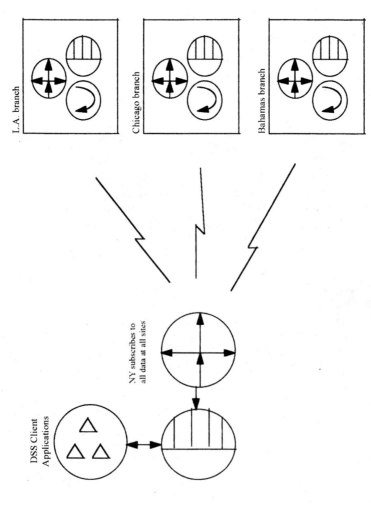

L.A. branch

Chicago branch

Bahamas branch

DSS Client
Applications

NY subscribes to
all data at all sites

Figure 16.7 Decision support on replicated data.

New York site. The New York database is a near-real-time consolidation of all corporate data.

Redundant primaries. A redundant primary application uses SYBASE Replication Server to maintain multiple primary databases. Client applications update one active primary database, and Replication Server maintains a standby primary database. Replication Server can be used to maintain multiple standby databases. If the active primary fails, clients can connect to the standby primary database. In addition to providing a warm backup facility, the redundant server can be used as a decision support database, thus offloading reports and report queries from the primary OLTP database server.

The *redundant primary* model can also be used to switch the primary database at designated times. This technique is often used to transfer primary responsibilities at given times of the day in global applications (such as trading). Primary responsibilities can be passed from a dataserver located in New York to a dataserver located in Tokyo, and back again.

Central primary and remote update. Updates are issued at the primary copy and are propagated to replicated tables in subscribing databases. Replicate sites may update their replicated data by using remote asynchronous transactions to the primary copy, which will then update the replicated copy.

Central primary, remote update, and local changes. Remote updates are asynchronously (using ASPs) sent to the primary database and are synchronously applied to a local pending copy. The primary Replication Server returns the data to the replicate Replication Server where function strings update the replicated table as well as delete the entry from the pending table.

Distributed partitioned primary. Primary copies are fragmented (by key) to any number of databases in the system. Only one primary copy still exists, but not in a single table on a single server. Each site owns its own data while subscribing to data at other sites. This configuration is useful to keep data geographically close to its source.

16.5 Microsoft's SQL Server

Leave it to Microsoft to provide fully integrated replication as a no-extra-cost feature. Microsoft has made asymmetric replication an integral part of its SQL Server database offering. SQL Server replication supports homogeneous replication, with support for heterogeneous targets (using ODBC) available in a future release. Similar to the SYBASE replication system, the Microsoft replication model states that a single server owns a replicated database object; this server is the owner of the data. Other database servers can *subscribe* to replicated database objects, using a publisher-subscriber model, but cannot modify them. The data published from a primary site table is referred to as an *article*; a replicated copy can be a row and/or column subset of the primary table. Articles can be grouped together to create *publications,* which can be replicated as a unit of work. Publications help to ensure data integrity constraints. A server that requests an article is referred to as a *subscriber.* Replication latency, and the number of transaction in a batch (batch size) can be specified when the replication system administrator defines a subscriber. These values are tuning parameters for the replication system.

Like the SYBASE log transfer manager, Microsoft's SQL Server reads data modifications from the transaction log. A *log reader* task runs continuously and captures log changes while they are still in memory. This method eliminates the need to reread any transactions from disk, resulting in reduced overhead. A scheduling and execution facility referred to as SQL Scheduler runs a distributed task for each subscriber database. SQL Scheduler can run continuously to minimize replication latency or in batch mode. Batch mode improves replication for large databases using narrow bandwidth networks.

Configuration and administration are possible using the Microsoft's SQL Enterprise Manager. Stored procedures are also available to provide manual configuration of SQL Server 6.0 replication. The SQL Server Performance Monitor is used to graphically display replication-related statistics.

4

Transact-SQL

Part 4 deals with issues of application development using SYBASE Transact-SQL. A general discussion covering SQL Server error handling and coding techniques is included. This part of the book is especially invaluable for SYBASE DBAs, system administrators, and developers. Practical rules, hints, and guidelines are given together with essential utilities and commands. Issues such as referential integrity, enforcement of business rules, and housekeeping tasks are also covered here.

17

Stored Procedures

This chapter includes a description of Sybase query processing and stored procedure programming techniques. Such topics as output parameters, transactions, save points, transaction modes, and isolation levels are covered. Included are a description and a step-by-step guide to creating system stored procedures. A key piece of information provided is a description of SQL Server error checking, stored procedure return codes, and severity levels.

Stored procedures are precompiled SQL statements that are stored on the SQL database server. They can accept command line arguments and can also return values to the calling program. Stored procedures offer several benefits:

- *Improved execution performance.* Because the SQL statements are already optimized and compiled, most of the query processing work has already been done when the stored procedure is executed.

- *Reduced network traffic.* A client can send two words across the network (i.e., *execute procedure_name*) rather than the hundreds of words that may be in the procedure.

- *Single point of code maintenance.* Stored procedures provide a single point of code maintenance (at the server, not the client workstations or application programs).

- *Security.* The authority to execute a stored procedure is independent of any permissions required to execute the specific statements that the procedure performs.

Frequently executed queries are likely candidates for stored procedures. Stored procedures can accept command line arguments and can also return values to the calling program.

The chapter closes with several tips regarding stored procedure development, use, and monitoring.

17.1   The Procedure Cache

The procedure cache has been discussed throughout much of this book. Let's cover a few final points before we continue the discussion of stored procedures.

Procedure cache size.   When SQL Server is started, it writes messages to the error log about the size of the procedure and data caches.

```
00:95/12/29 09:24:31.74 server Number of proc buffers allocated: 2258.
00:95/12/29 09:24:32:13 server Number of blocks left for proc headers:
2307.
00:95/12/29 09:24:32.13 server Memory allocated for the default data
cache: 17122 Kb
```

Proc buffers.   A *proc buffer* is a data structure used to manage compiled objects (e.g., a stored procedure, trigger, rule, default, or view) in the procedure cache. There are a total of 21 proc buffers on a 2K page. The number of proc buffers represents the maximum number of compiled objects that can reside in the procedure cache at one time. In our example, the number of proc buffers is 2258, requiring 108 2K pages.

Proc headers.   *Proc headers* indicate the number of pages dedicated to the procedure cache. In our example, 2307 2K pages have been allocated to the procedure cache.

How queries are processed.   Figure 17.1 provides a high-level overview of how SQL Server processes stored procedures and Transact-SQL queries. When stored procedures are created, the text of the stored procedure is stored in the *syscomments* table. A query tree (which is a normalized form of the query) is stored in the *sysprocedures* table. The query tree has already been parsed.

When a stored procedure is executed for the first time (after SQL Server has been booted), the query tree is read into memory from the *sysprocedures* table. It is then passed through the query optimizer, using the parameters provided to the procedure, and placed on the MRU side of the procedure cache. The access plan created on the first pass is used for all subsequent executions of this copy of the stored procedure.

Note that there may be more than one copy of the stored procedure in the procedure cache. The access plan created for each copy is not guaranteed to be the same. This is because the query optimizer creates an access plan for the procedure using the parameters passed to the procedure. When the values of the parameters provided to a

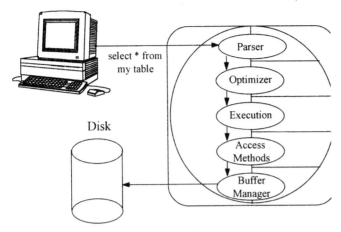

Figure 17.1   SQL Server query processing.

stored procedure vary widely, the procedure may benefit from a new access plan each time it is run. In this case, the developer should create the procedure using the WITH RECOMPILE option. This will slow down the process; however, the new plan may provide a faster route to the result set.

17.2   Stored Procedures

The standard way to run user-defined transactions in the SYBASE environment is to put the BEGIN TRAN ... COMMIT TRAN logic in a stored procedure. The stored procedure is then executed at the server by the client. With this method, the client only has to look for a rollback error and then reexecute the stored procedure.

Pre-System 10, SQL Server limits the size of stored-procedure code to 64K. System 10 eliminated that limitation by increasing the size of stored-procedure code to 16 Mbytes. This increase also applies to triggers, views, defaults, rules, and constraints. When a stored procedure is created, the text of the procedure is stored in the *syscomments* table. A normalized form of the procedure (called a *query tree*) is stored in the *sysprocedures* table.

Stored procedures are created by using the CREATE PROCEDURE command. The syntax is

```
create procedure [owner.]procedureName[;number]
  [[(]@parameterName datatype [(length) | (precision [, scale])
  [ = default][output]
  [, @parameterName datatype [(length) | (precision [, scale])
  [ = default][output]]...[)]]
  [with recompile]
  as
SQL statements
```

The *procedureName* option is used to specify a name for the stored procedure to be created. The *;number* parameter is an optional integer value used to group stored procedures of the same name so that they can be dropped as a group by using a single DROP PROCEDURE statement. For example, if a group of stored procedures is created as *pr_trades;1, pr_trades;2,* and *pr_trades;3,* then the entire group of procedures can be dropped with the command

```
drop procedure pr_trades
```

When stored procedures have been grouped, there is no way to drop an individual procedure in the group, e.g.,

```
drop procedure pr_trades;1
```

The *parameterName* option specifies the name of an argument to the procedure. The value of each parameter is supplied at run time. Parameter names must be preceded by the symbol @. The *datatype* placeholder provides the data type of the parameter (e.g., int, char, float). And *default* allows the creator of the procedure to define a default parameter value for the procedure. If a default is defined, a caller can execute the procedure without supplying a parameter. The *output* keyword indicates that the parameter is a return parameter. Its value can be returned to the caller who executed the stored procedure.

Stored procedures are generally faster than ad hoc queries because their execution plans are stored in the procedure cache, thus requiring less I/O. However, stored procedures can be slower when a search value cannot be determined until run time; i.e., a parameter is being passed to the stored procedure. This is due to the fact that the plan stored with the procedure may not be optimal for the search value(s) being passed to the procedure. The with recompile option tells SQL Server not to save a plan for the procedure. Each time the procedure is executed, it will be recompiled. This results in a decrease in performance and should only be done when the execution plan may be atypical.

And *SQL statements* represents the SQL statements that define the actions the stored procedure is to take, e.g.,

```
create procedure sp_usertables(
      @userName char(30) = null
      )
as
      select id, sysusers.name as owner,sysobjects.name
      from sysusers,sysobjects
      where sysobjects.uid = sysusers.uid and sysobjects.type = 'U'
      and sysusers.name like @userName
```

for example,

```
1> sp_usertables dbo
2> go
id              owner               name
----------      ---------------     --------------------------
  16003088      dbo                 team
 448004627      dbo                 trades
 880006166      dbo                 inventory
2041058307      dbo                 location
2137058649      dbo                 inventory_location
 223812938      dbo                 tranhist
```

Control-of-flow language can be used as part of the SQL statement or batch-used to build a stored procedure. These are some available constructs: *begin ... end, break, continue, declare, goto, if-else, return,* and *while*. Also special error handling techniques are available to the Transact-SQL programmer. The RAISERROR and PRINT statements, in combination with control-of-flow language, can direct error messages to the users of Transact-SQL applications. Programmers can also capture return values from stored procedures, pass parameters from a procedure to its caller, and get status information from global variables such as @@error.

17.2.1 Related commands

This section provides a brief description of several Transact-SQL commands and system procedures related to stored-procedure creation and maintenance. The Transact-SQL commands include

- *drop procedure*
- *print*
- *raiserror*

The system procedures covered here are

- *sp_recompile*
- *sp_addmessage*
- *sp_dropmessage*

Stored procedures are dropped from a database with the DROP PROCEDURE command. The syntax is

```
drop procedure [owner.]procedureName [, [owner.]procedureName]...
```

for example,

```
drop procedure pr_orders;1, pr_tradePrice, pr_listdevices
```

The *sp_recompile* system procedure causes each stored procedure and trigger that uses a named table to be recompiled the next time it is run. The *sp_recompile* procedure should be used after running the UPDATE STATISTICS command against a table to optimize the query plans for greater efficiency. The syntax is

```
sp_recompile tableName
```

for example,

```
1> update statistics inventory
2> go
1> sp_recompile inventory
2> go
```

The PRINT statement displays a user-defined message on the client's screen. The syntax for PRINT is

```
PRINT { format string | @localVariable | @@globalVariable } [, argu-
ments]
```

for example,

```
PRINT ''%1!' is not a valid action code', @opcode
PRINT @@servername, @@version
```

The *sp_addmessage* and *sp_dropmessage* system procedures are used to maintain user-defined messages in the *sysusermessages* table. The messages stored in *sysusermessages* are for use by stored-procedure *print* and *raiserror* calls. The syntax for *sp_addmessage* is

```
sp_addmessage messageNumber, messageText [, language]
```

for example,

```
sp_addmessage 20100, 'Failed to specify an action code'
```

User-defined messages are always assigned a message number greater than 19,999 because Sybase reserves the first 19,999 message numbers for internal use.

The *sp_dropmessage* system procedure drops user-defined messages from the *sysusermessages* table. The syntax for *sp_dropmessage* is

```
sp_dropmessage messageNumber
```

SQL Server allows the caller to drop messages that are in use by stored procedures. There is no "referential integrity" check performed by *sp_dropmessage,* so be careful when dropping user-defined messages.

The RAISERROR statement displays a user-defined message on the client's screen and sets a system flag to indicate that an error condition has occurred. It should be used to communicate errors to clients; do not rely on return codes from stored procedures to do this. The syntax of RAISERROR is

```
RAISERROR errorNumber [{formatString | @localVariable}] ], argumentList]
    [extendedValue = extendedValue [{, extendedValue = extendedValue}...]]
```

for example,

```
exec sp_addmessage 20200, "%1 IS NOT A VALID ACTION CODE!"
raiserror 20200, @opcode
```

The *errorNumber* is an integer having a value greater than 17,000. Error messages between 17,000 and 19,999 are used by SYBASE system procedures and are retrieved from the *master.dbo.sysmessages* table. User-defined messages (those having a value of 20,000 and over) are retrieved from the *sysusermessages* table located in the current database.

The *formatString* is a string of characters used to format the output string. A format string can optionally be declared in the local variable *@localVariable,* as illustrated in the following example.

```
create procedure pr_ytdsales(
        part# char(10) = null
        )
as
        declare @formatString char(255)

        select @formatString = '%1! is not a valid part number'

        if not exists (select * from inventory where partNumber = @part#)
        begin
                raiserror 20000, @formatString, @part#
                return -999
        end
        return 0
```

The *argumentList* is a series of variables or constants separated by commas to be displayed in the *formatString*. The *extendedValue* parameter is a string of characters used to return extended error data. This includes the names of the tables and columns involved with the error message. These errors include duplicate-key violations, referential integrity constraints, and rule violations.

17.2.2 Output parameters

When a CREATE PROCEDURE statement and an *execute* statement both declare a parameter using the *output* keyword, the stored procedure returns the value to the caller. The following procedure declares the *@value* parameter as an output parameter:

```
create procedure pr_inventoryValue(
    @part#              char(10) = null,
    @value              float = null output
    )
as
    if ( @part# = null )
    begin
            return -100
    end

    select @value = qtyOnHand*baseprice
    from inventory_location(index x0inventory_location prefetch 16 MRU)
    where partNumber = @part#

    if ( @@rowcount = 0 )
    begin
            return -100
    end

    return 0
go
```

Now, let's create a simple stored procedure that can be used to call the *pr_inventoryValue* procedure.

```
create procedure pr_valuation(
    @part# char(10) = null
    )
as
    declare        @retCode        int,
                   @value          float

    exec @retCode = pr_inventoryValue @part#, @value output

    print 'Part#: %1!, Value: %2!, Status: %3!', @part#, @value, @retCode
go
```

Here is the stored-procedure output; note that the *execute* statement includes the *output* keyword.

```
1> exec pr_valuation '1'
2> go
Part# 1 , Value: 550, Status: 0
(return status = 0)
```

17.2.3 Transactions and save points

A *save point* is a placeholder that the user puts inside a user-defined transaction. The user can later use the ROLLBACK TRAN or COMMIT TRAN command to roll back or commit any subsequent commands. Save points are inserted into a transaction by using the SAVE TRANSACTION command.

If a stored procedure defines a logical transaction which may be rolling back, it might be a good idea to include a save point of the same name as the stored procedure. Any rollback in the procedure should be to the save point, and not to the original BEGIN TRANS-ACTION statement. An example follows:

```
create procedure pr_priceChange(
      @part#          char(10) = null,
      @newPrice       float = null
      )
as
      save transaction pr_priceChange

      update inventory_location set baseprice = @newPrice
       where partNumber = @part#
       .
       .
      if (successful)
              return 0                 /* Processing OK */

      /* Processing not OK, rollback to the savepoint */

      rollback tran pr_priceChange

      return 1
```

Now, let's look at how this procedure might be called:

```
/* BEGINNING */
declare @status int
begin transaction price_change

update inventory set partName = 'EXPENSIVE HAMMER'
 where partNumber = @part#

update inventory_location set partName = 'EXPENSIVE HAMMER'
 where partNumber = @part#

/* Call a stored procedure to modify inventory price */

exec @status = pr_priceChange @part#, @newPrice

if ( @status = 0 )
        commit tran price_change
/* END */
```

This SQL batch calls the stored procedure that modifies the price of a part in the *inventory_location* table. The stored procedure issues a SAVE TRANSACTION command with the name of the stored procedure. By placing the SAVE TRAN here, the procedure can roll back its changes without affecting those of the original transaction.

17.2.4 Isolation levels

We learned in Chap. 15 that the ANSI standard defines three levels of isolation for SQL transactions. SQL Server allows the user to set transaction isolation levels by using a SET command. By default, SQL Server's transaction isolation level is 1. The syntax is

```
set transaction isolation level {0 | 1 | 3}
```

See Chap. 15 for more information on transaction modes and isolation levels.

17.2.5 Security issues

Stored procedures can also be used to enhance security. A user with permission to execute a stored procedure can do so without having permissions on the tables or views accessed by the stored procedure. Permission to execute stored procedures is independent of any access privileges that may exist on database objects referenced by the stored procedure.

By performing accesses exclusively through stored procedures, user privileges can be limited to *execute* privileges on the stored procedures. Because the procedure itself owns the privilege of updating base tables, the user does not need to be granted that privilege explicitly. If applications are designed such that data accesses are performed using direct SQL statements, users must be assigned direct update permissions to the database tables. These permissions will carry through to utilities such as ISQL, DWB (Data Workbench), and other data access tools, thereby permitting ad hoc updates to the data. A fringe benefit is that the use of stored procedures will ensure all updates are performed in a consistent manner.

Here is a stored procedure that can be used to SELECT data and perform single-row UPDATEs, DELETEs, and INSERTs on the bankbook table. The procedure presented here illustrates the capabilities of stored procedures.

```
USE testdb
GO
sp_addmessage 20100, "FAILED TO SPECIFY AN ACTION CODE"
GO
sp_addmessage 20105, "'%1!' CODE NOT PRESENT"
GO
sp_addmessage 20110, "'%1!' IS NOT A VALID ACTION CODE"
GO
CREATE PROCEDURE pr_buildlist
 @action char(6) = NULL,
 @cpt_id char(16) = NULL,
 @cpt_nm char(52) = NULL
AS
  /* CHECK TO SEE IF THE CALLER SPECIFIED AN ACTION CODE */
  IF ( @action = NULL )
  BEGIN
      RAISERROR 20100
      RETURN
  END

  /* IS THE ACTION A SELECT ? */
  IF ( @action = 'SELECT' ) OR ( @action = 'select' )
  BEGIN
```

```
    IF ( @cpt_id ! = NULL ) AND ( @cpt_nm ! = NULL )
    BEGIN
      SELECT cpt_id, cpt_nm FROM v1conpty WHERE
       cpt_id LIKE @cpt_id AND cpt_nm LIKE @cpt_nm
      RETURN
    END
   IF ( @cpt_id ! = NULL ) /* QUERY w/cpt_id, AVOID TABLE SCANS! */
   BEGIN
      SELECT cpt_id, cpt_nm FROM v1conpty WHERE
       cpt_id LIKE @cpt_id
      RETURN
   END
 IF (@cpt_nm ! = NULL) /* USER WANTS TO QUERY ON cpt_nm */
 BEGIN
      SELECT cpt_id, cpt_nm FROM v1conpty WHERE
       cpt_nm LIKE @cpt_nm
      RETURN
   END
END

IF ( @action = 'INSERT' ) OR ( @action = 'insert' )
BEGIN
   RAISERROR 20105, @action
   RETURN
END

IF ( @action = 'DELETE' ) OR ( @action = 'delete' )
BEGIN
   RAISERROR 20105, @action
   RETURN
 END

 IF ( @action = 'UPDATE' ) OR ( @action = 'update' )
 BEGIN
    RAISERROR 20105, @action
    RETURN
 END

 RAISERROR 20110, @action

 RETURN 0 /* HISTORY */
GO
```

For further security, stored-procedure execution can be restricted by the SQL commands that are programmed into it. For example, the System 11 SQL Server uses the *proc_role* function in system stored procedures where security is critical. The *proc_role* function checks to see if the invoking user has a specified role. And *proc_role* returns a 1 if the user has the specified role and returns 0 if the user does not have the role.

```
IF (proc_role("sa_role") = 0)
BEGIN
    PRINT "YOU ARE NOT AUTHORIZED TO USE THIS PROCEDURE"
    RETURN -1
END
```

Example.   Before we close this section, let's look at another stored-procedure example to reinforce some of what we have talked about to this point.

```
use eei
go
exec sp_addmessage 20100, 'Failed to specify an action code'
exec sp_addmessage 20105, 'Failed to provide a part number'
exec sp_addmessage 20110, 'Part number not found'
exec sp_addmessage 20115, '%1! is not a valid action code'
go
create procedure pr_inventory(
        @action        char(6) = null,
        @part#         char(10) = null
        )
as
        /* Check to see if the caller provided an action code */

        if ( @action = NULL )
        begin
                raiserror 20100
                return -100
        end

        /* select ? */

        if ( upper( @action ) = 'SELECT' )
        begin
                if ( @part# ! = NULL )
                begin
                        select partNumber,partName,type from inventory
                        where part# = @part#

                        if ( @@rowcount = 0 )
                        begin
                                raiserror 20110
                                return -100
                        end

                        return 0
                end
                else
                begin
                                raiserror 20105
                                return -100
                end
        end

        raiserror 20115, @action

        return -100
go
```

17.3   Creating System Procedures

System stored procedures are created in the *sybsystemprocs* database and can be run from any database. System procedure names must begin with '*sp_*'. System procedures are usually written by the system or database administrator. All system procedures must have a user ID of 1, which is the user ID of the database owner. The *dbo* in every SQL Server database has a user ID of 1.

Typically, system procedures will query the system tables. System procedures can be written to modify system tables but should not do so without very good cause. Database administrators should use extreme caution when writing system stored procedures that modify system tables. Whenever possible, write these procedures against a test database, not against a production database.

The steps below should be followed when system procedures are created that modify system tables:

1. Use the *sp_configure* system procedure to enable the *allow updates* engine configuration variable. When this option is enabled, any SQL Server user with permissions can modify the system tables. All system stored procedures created with this flag on will be able to update system tables even when the *allow updates* option is off.

2. Create the system procedure using the *create procedure* command.

3. Immediately following procedure creation, use the *sp_configure* system procedure to disallow updates to the system tables. It is a good idea to include these steps in a Transact-SQL script that can be used to create the procedure.

The following script illustrates the steps required to create a system procedure that updates the SQL Server catalog.

```
use master
go
exec sp_configure 'allow updates',1
go
reconfigure with override
go
use sybsystemprocs
go
if exists (select * from sysobjects where id =
 object_id('dbo.sp_newuser'))
begin
          print "Dropping old copy..."
          drop procedure sp_newuser
end
go
print 'Creating sp_newuser...'
go
CREATE PROCEDURE sp_newuser
      @loginame varchar(30), /* user's login name in syslogins */
      @uid int = 0, /* NEW PARAMETER — GWA */
      @name_in_db varchar(30) = NULL,/* user's name to add to current db */
      @grpname varchar(30) = NULL /* group to put new user in as */
   declare @suid int/* user's system id
   declare @grpid int  /* group id of group to put user in */
```

```
.
.
insert into sysusers(uid, suid, gid, name)
  values (@uid, @suid, @grpid, @name_in_db)
.
.
.
/* 17335, "New user added." */

exec sp_getmessage 17335, @msg output print @msg

return (0)
go
use master
go
exec sp_configure 'allow updates',0
go
reconfigure with override
go
```

17.4   SQL Server Error Checking

This section describes SQL Server error messages and severity levels. The intent is to provide some tips that can be used for communicating error codes and messages as well as coding techniques for stored procedures and triggers.

Every SQL statement executed in SYBASE generates an error message number which is stored in the global variable @@*error*. If no error is encountered during execution, the value of @@*error* will be 0. The error number contained in @@*error* can be used to obtain additional information about the error from the *master.dbo.sysmessages* table.

The *sysmessages* table resides in the *master* database and contains one row for each system error or warning that can be returned by the SQL Server. The structure of the *sysmessages* table is as follows:

```
create table sysmessages (
  error        int           not null,   /* unique error number */
  severity     smallint      not null,   /* severity level of error */
  dlevel       smallint      not null,   /* descriptive level of this
                                            message */
  description  varchar (255) not null,   /* explanation of the error */
  langid       smallint      null,       /* language */
  sqlstate     varchar (5)   null        /* unused */
  )
create clustered index sysmessages
  on sysmessages( error, dlevel ) on 'system'

create unique nonclustered index ncsysmessages
  on sysmessages( error, dlevel, langid ) on 'default'
```

For more information on the *sysmessages* table, refer to the SYBASE SQL Server System Administration Guide.

17.4.1 More global variables

Global variables are SQL Server system-supplied variables that are maintained by the *dataserver.* Global variables are distinguished from local variables by two @ signs preceding their names. Refer to Sec. 8.2.1 for more information.

The *@@error* variable is used to check the completion status of the most recently executed SQL statement. It contains 0 if the previous statement succeeded; otherwise, it contains the last number generated by the system. Every Transact-SQL statement resets *@@error,* including PRINT statements or IF tests; so the status check must immediately follow the statement whose success is in question (or the value of *@@error* should be saved to a local variable).

The *@@rowcount* variable contains the number of rows affected by the last command. It is set to 0 by any command which does not return rows, such as an IF statement. Again, if the value is not checked immediately following the statement, the value of *@@rowcount* should be saved to a local variable. For cursors, *@@rowcount* represents the cumulative number of rows returned from the cursor result set to the client, up to the last FETCH request.

The *@@sqlstatus* variable contains status information resulting from the last FETCH statement. It is only valid when used with database cursors. The *@@sqlstatus* variable may contain the values shown in Table 17.1.

SQL Server supports the nesting of transactions within other transactions. The *@@trancount* global variable contains the nesting level of transactions. Each BEGIN TRANSACTION in a batch increments the value of *@@trancount.* If *@@trancount* is queried in chained transaction mode, its value is never 0 since the query automatically initiates a transaction (ANSI implicit BEGIN TRAN).

The *@@transtate* variable contains the current state of a transaction after a statement executes. It does not get cleared for each statement. And *@@transtate* may contain the values shown in Table 17.2.

To obtain the best coverage of error instances in stored procedures, the developer should rely on a combination of RAISERROR and return codes. The caller of a stored procedure should always check the return status as follows:

TABLE 17.1 *@@sqlstatus* **Values**

Value	Description
0	The FETCH statement completed successfully.
1	The FETCH statement resulted in an error.
2	There is no more data in the result set.

TABLE 17.2   @@transtate Values

Value	Description
0	Transaction in progress.
1	Transaction succeeded; the transaction completed and committed its changes.
2	Statement aborted; the previous statement was aborted with no effect on the transaction.
3	Transaction aborted and rolled back any changes.

```
DECLARE @returnCode int
.
.
.
PUT THIS IN A LOOP FOR RE-EXECUTION...
SAVE TRANSACTION myprocedure
EXEC @returnCode = myprocedure
IF ( @returnCode < 0 )
BEGIN
    PRINT "myprocedure — error '%1!' occurred during execution",
      @returnCode
    ROLLBACK TRAN myprocedure
END
```

In the above example, the value of *@returnCode* is the value of the most serious error that occurred in the stored procedure. Errors that are of severity level 10 are ignored; SYBASE will return a 0 to indicate successful execution.

17.4.2   Stored-procedure return codes

SYBASE always returns a status for every execution of a stored procedure. Return codes are always an integer value. The values 0 and −1 through −99 are reserved by SYBASE. Table 17.3 represents the current values and meanings for Sybase reserved errors.

In the case of stored procedures, error severity levels 10 through 18 or return status values of −1 through −8 will not prevent stored procedures from executing to completion. Only a severity error of 19 and above or a return status less than −9 will cause an error in a stored-procedure run.

User-written stored procedures can use positive values or values less than −99 for return status numbers.

17.4.3   Severity levels

The severity level of an error provides information about the type of problem SQL Server has encountered. SYBASE ignores messages

TABLE 17.3 Stored-Procedure Return Codes

Return value	Meaning
0	Procedure executed without errors
−1	Missing object
−2	Data type error
−3	Process was chosen as a deadlock victim
−4	Permission error
−5	Syntax error
−6	Miscellaneous user error
−7	Resource error, such as insufficient space
−8	Nonfatal internal problem
−9	System limit reached
−10	Fatal internal inconsistency
−11	Fatal internal inconsistency
−12	Table or index corrupt
−13	Database corrupt
−14	Hardware error
−15−−99	Reserved by Sybase for future SQL Server use

that are of severity level 10. Fatal errors generate messages with severity levels of 19 and higher. When a fatal error occurs, the user's connection to SQL Server is broken and a message is recorded in the SQL Server error log. To continue, the user must reestablish a connection to SQL Server. The system administrator should monitor the error log for fatal error messages. The following text is a fragment from an SQL Server error log. Note the error number, severity, and description which are obtained from the *sysmessages* table.

```
00:95/11/03 14:50:40.60 server Error: 4409, Severity: 20, State: 1
00:95/11/03 14:50:40.61 server
        The columns in the query definition and the view definition do
        not match.             .

.
.
00:95/11/07 12:11:35.37 server Error: 8402, Severity: 21, State: 6
00:95/11/07 12:11:35.40 server
        Index row for object 336772307 (index id -1) was not found in
        database 8.
```

Table 17.4 lists SQL Server error severity levels and their descriptions.

The following code fragment illustrates how the *master.dbo.sysmessages* table can be queried to obtain information about error messages.

TABLE 17.4   Error Severity Levels and Descriptions

Severity level	Description
10	Status information. Messages of severity level 10 are informational messages and not errors. Level 10 messages are used to communicate additional information after certain commands have been executed.
11	Specified database object not found. SQL Server cannot find an object referenced by the SQL command. Common causes are typographical errors, incorrect owner name, or that the specified object has been dropped from the database.
12	Incorrect datatype encountered. This occurs when the user tries to enter a value of the wrong data type into a column or when incompatible data types are compared.
13	User transaction syntax error. Severity 13 indicates that something is wrong with the current user-defined transaction. Severity 13 can also indicate a deadlock, in which case the deadlock victim process is rolled back.
14	Insufficient permission to execute command. The user does not have the permissions necessary to successfully execute the command or access the database object.
15	Syntax error in SQL statements. Message indicates that the user has made a mistake in the syntax of a command.
16	Miscellaneous user error. User has made a nonfatal mistake that doesn't fit into the other categories. An example can be seen when a user attempts to insert or update a view created with the *check* option. The error occurs when a resultant row from the command does not qualify under the *check* option constraint.
17	Insufficient resources. SQL Server has run out of resources. The resource can be disk space, lock, or some other limit set by the system administrator.
18	Nonfatal internal error. These messages indicate an internal software bug (feature). The command will run to completion, and the user's connection to SQL Server is maintained. Users should be instructed to report these messages to the system administrator when they occur.
19	SQL Server fatal error in resource. A nonconfigurable limit in SQL Server has been exceeded.
20	SQL Server fatal error in current process. SQL Server has encountered a bug in a command.
21	SQL Server fatal error in database processes. SQL Server has encountered a bug that affects all processes in the current database.
22	SQL Server fatal error: table integrity suspect. The table or index specified in the message has been damaged by a software or hardware problem.
23	SQL Server fatal error: database integrity suspect. The integrity of the database is suspect due to damage caused by a software or hardware problem.
24	Hardware error or system table corruption. These messages indicate a media failure or corruption of *master..sysusages*.

```
DECLARE @errorMessage      int,
        @rowCount          int,
        @severity          smallint,
        @description       varchar(255)

SELECT * FROM aBusyTable

SELECT @errorMessage=@@error       /* Save the value of @@error */
SELECT @rowCount=@@rowcount        /* Save the value of @@rowcount */

IF ( @errorMessage !=0 )
BEGIN
        SELECT @severity=severity,@description=description
        FROM master..sysmessage
        WHERE error = @errorMessage

        /* Analyze the severity */

        IF ( @severity = 13 )
        BEGIN
            PRINT "SELECT - Error performing transaction or possible
            victim of deadlock"
            PRINT "Error: %1! - severity = %2!", @description, @severity
        END

        IF ( @severity > 19 )
        BEGIN
            PRINT "SELECT - Encountered serious internal or configuration
             error"
            PRINT "Report this message to the SA immediately!"
            PRINT "Error: %1! - severity = %2!", @description, @severity
        END
END
```

Note that the values of *@@error* and *@@rowcount* are reset after each
and every SQL statement is executed. For that reason it is necessary to
save the values of *@@error* and *@@rowcount* to local variables so that
any errors and row-count checking can be processed appropriately.

17.4.4   SQL-92 enhancements

The SQL-86 and SQL-89 standards did not cover the subject of error
handling in detail. The SQL standards specified that a status variable
(SQLCODE) should be used for status messages. A value of 0 means
successful completion, and a value of 100 indicates that no data was
affected by the statement. The standard also specifies that any negative value designates an error. With such a vague specification, it
becomes obvious that vendors would choose their own error designa-
tions for negative values. For example, a syntax error in SYBASE
maps to a -5 error code, while Informix uses -5 to indicate an operating system I/O error.

SQL-86 and SQL-89 also provide the WHENEVER statement for
use in embedded SQL application programs. Using the WHENEVER

statement, programmers can declare the action they want to take whenever a specific condition is encountered.

```
/* INSTALL ERROR HANDLING ROUTINES */

EXEC SQL WHENEVER SQLERROR PERFORM errorHandler();
EXEC SQL WHENEVER NOT FOUND CONTINUE;
```

The SQL-92 specification added two significant enhancements:*

1. The SQLSTATE variable
2. The diagnostics area

The SQLSTATE variable is a character string 5 bytes long. The first 2 bytes (called the *class code*) are used to indicate the primary condition code information. The last 3 bytes are used for the *subclass code* and reports additional information related to the *class code*.

The diagnostics area is an SQL managed data structure that applications can query to obtain information about SQL statement executions. The data structure includes elements such as server name, connection name, catalog/schema/table name, trigger name, and routine name.

The System 10 and System 11 precompilers support these SQL-92 enhancements.

17.5 Stored-Procedure Tips

For performance, maintainability, and ease of use, use stored procedures whenever possible. This section provides some useful pointers.

- Always use the *execute* keyword before system procedures. The *execute* keyword is used to run a system procedure or a user-defined stored procedure. It is only necessary to use *exec* if the stored-procedure call is not the first statement in the batch. It is, however, a good idea to get into the habit of using *exec* regularly. For example,

```
1> exec sp_newuser elvira
2> exec sp_newuser elena
3> exec sp_newuser ralph
4> exec sp_newuser rita
5> go
```

- Stored procedures should always use a return code, 0 for success and other values for failures. Avoid using error codes reserved by the SQL Server. Zero is reserved for success, and −1 through −99 are

---

*Jim Melton, "SQL Update," *Database Programming and Design,* April 1995.

reserved by Sybase for various error conditions. The user-written procedure can use positive values or values less than -99 for return status numbers, to inform the caller of user-defined error conditions.

- The *execute with recompile* option can be used to force SYBASE to create a new plan for a stored procedure prior to execution (e.g., exec pr_valuation '1' with recompile). Use the *create procedure with recompile* option to ensure that a new plan is compiled for a procedure every time it is called. Both of these options will affect performance, so use them only when necessary.

- Use the *raiserror* command to communicate errors to clients; do not rely exclusively on return codes from stored procedures.

- SQL Server system procedures use the *proc_role* function when security is critical. The *proc_role* function checks to see if the invoking user has a specified role. The *proc_role* returns a 1 if the user has the specified role and returns 0 if the user does not have the role.

```
IF (proc_role("sa_role") = 0)
BEGIN
        PRINT "YOU ARE NOT AUTHORIZED TO USE THIS PROCEDURE"
        RETURN -1
END
```

- Application developers should use a table to contain application-defined error numbers and messages. As of Version 4.9, including System 10 and System 11, the table *sysusermessages* should be used. These messages are for use by stored-procedure *print* and *raiserror* calls and by *sp_bindmsg*. The system procedures *sp_addmessage, sp_dropmessage,* and *sp_getmessage* are used to manage error messages.

- Stored-procedure parameters should be named explicitly when the procedure is executed. It may not be a good idea to rely on passing parameters by position rather than by name, for example,

```
exec pr_inv_deliver    @fromLocation = 'ProdLine001',
                       @toLocation = 'WareHouse002',
                       @part = '00646WH1S3',
                       @qty = 5000
```

instead of

```
exec pr_inv_deliver    'ProdLine001',
                       'WareHouse002',
                       '00646WH1S3',
                       5000
```

- Whenever possible, default values should be defined for all stored-procedure parameters. Parameter values should be verified by the stored procedure, and the procedure should raise a meaningful error message if the values are inappropriate.

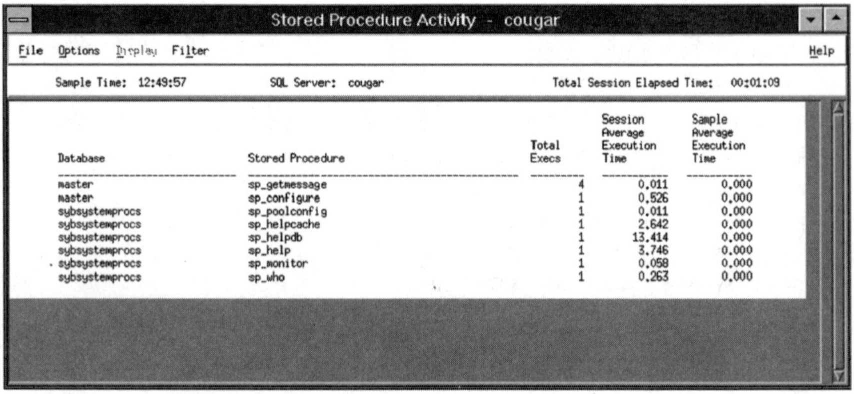

Figure 17.2   SQL Server Monitor—stored procedure activity.

Please refer to the SYBASE Transact-SQL *User's Guide* for more information.

17.6   Stored-Procedure Monitoring

Several tools are available for stored-procedure monitoring.

- SQL Server Monitor

- The *sp_sysmon* system procedure. The *sp_sysmon* system procedure can be used to obtain information regarding the procedure cache. Specifically, look at the *procedure cache management* section of the output.

- *DBCC MEMUSAGE*. As described in Sec. 7.1, SQL Server memory utilization can be determined by using the DBCC MEMUSAGE command. Information is displayed about total server memory, the actual size of the SQL Server code, number of page buffers, and procedure buffers available. Also listed are the top 20 users of procedure cache and buffer cache.

SQL Server monitoring.   The SQL Server Monitor Stored Procedure Activity window is used to monitor (you guessed it) stored-procedure activity. The output includes database and stored-procedure name, number of executions, and average execution time. The output is shown in Fig. 17.2.

18

Triggers

Triggers are similar to stored procedures and are associated with a particular table. They are automatically invoked by the server in response to a database event (whenever the table is the target of an INSERT, UPDATE, or DELETE operation). Triggers cannot be executed manually. As with stored procedures, the text of a trigger is stored in the *syscomments* system table. The execution plan for a trigger is maintained in the *sysprocedures* table.

The SQL statements that define the trigger are executed when the *triggering statement* (the INSERT, UPDATE, or DELETE) is completed. In the event of an error, the trigger can cause all actions performed by the trigger and the triggering statement to be rolled back. Only one trigger can be defined for each operation on a particular table. A table can have a maximum of three triggers—one each for INSERT, UPDATE, and DELETE. A single trigger can be defined for all operations associated with a table. Triggers can be quite complex, and as a result, they are more flexible than the declarative integrity constraints introduced with System 10.

The syntax of the CREATE TRIGGER statement is

```
CREATE TRIGGER [owner.]triggerName on [owner.]tableName
  for { insert, update, delete } as SQL_Statements
```

for example,

```
CREATE TRIGGER tr_account ON tb_account FOR INSERT,UPDATE, DELETE
AS
    SQL Statements
  .
  .
```

Triggers can be used to compare the before and after images of a row or rows during a transaction. Within the batch, SYBASE uses two virtual tables called the *inserted* and *deleted* tables. These tables are local to the trigger; i.e., a trigger can cause other triggers to fire, and that trigger will have access to its own set of *inserted* and *deleted* tables. The *inserted* table contains copies of rows that have been inserted into the target table as the result of an INSERT or DELETE operation. The *deleted* table contains copies of rows that have been removed from the target table by the effects of a DELETE or an UPDATE statement. An UPDATE statement is treated as a DELETE statement followed by an INSERT statement; therefore an UPDATE will cause a row to be placed into both tables (*inserted* and *deleted*). In this case the *deleted* table contains the before image of the row, and the *inserted* table the after image.

The *inserted* and *deleted* tables can be thought of as a view on the *syslogs* table which is not indexed. In most cases, declarative referential integrity offers better performance than triggers. This can be significant when a large number of referential integrity constraints are needed. This is because triggers must scan the *inserted* and *deleted* tables, a process which, without indexes, is inherently slow.

The IF UPDATE clause is used when a trigger is conditioned on the modification of data contained in specific columns of the table. Also note that the IF UPDATE condition can include a combination of the use of *and* and *or*. The syntax of the CREATE TRIGGER statement when used with the IF UPDATE clause is

```
CREATE TRIGGER [owner.]triggerName on [owner.]tableName
  for { insert, update } as
  [if update(columnName) [{and | or} update(columnName)]...]
    SQL_Statements
  [if update(columnName) [{and | or} update(columnName)]...]
    SQL_Statements]...
```

for example,

```
CREATE TRIGGER tu_account ON tb_account FOR UPDATE
AS
    if update( creditLimit )
    begin
        insert into tb_account_audit( suid, suserName, updateTime,
          newLimit )
          SELECT suid = suser_id(), suserName = suser_name(),
          updateTime = getdate(), creditLimit FROM inserted )
    end
```

Order of execution. A trigger fires after the data modification statement has completed and SQL Server has satisfied data type, rule, and referential integrity constraints. Declarative referential integrity is applied by SQL Server when a violation occurs, thus aborting the statement causing the violation. Any triggers that will be fired as a result of the statement are fired after all declarative referential integrity conditions have been satisfied.

Nested triggers. When the *allow nested triggers* server configuration variable is enabled, data modifications caused by triggers can cause other triggers to fire. By default, SQL Server allows nested triggers. To disable nested triggers, use the *sp_configure* system procedure:

```
sp_configure 'allow nested triggers', 0
```

18.1   Related Commands

- The DROP TRIGGER command is used to drop a trigger. When a table is dropped, any triggers associated with the table are automatically dropped.

- The SET *self_recursion* statement toggles self-recursion on or off. Self-recursion means that triggers can cause themselves to fire again.

- The ROLLBACK TRIGGER statement rolls back the work done in a trigger, including the data modification that caused the trigger to fire.

- The RAISERROR statement displays a user-defined message on the client's screen and sets a system flag to indicate that an error condition has occurred.

- The *sp_help* is used to display information about a trigger.

- The *sp_helptext* is used to display the text of a trigger. The text of the trigger is stored in the *syscomments* system table.

- The *sp_depends* procedure reports on the tables and views that are referenced by a trigger.

18.2   Transaction Processing

This section provides some tips and techniques for trigger processing, error detection, and error reporting.

Triggers always execute at transaction isolation level 1 or the transaction's isolation level—whichever is higher. There are several Transact-SQL commands designed to facilitate trigger programming. Specifically, the commands discussed in this section include

- ROLLBACK TRIGGER (with RAISERROR statement)

- ROLLBACK TRANSACTION
- RAISERROR. The RAISERROR statement is used (in conjunction with the PRINT statement) to display a user-defined message on the client's screen and to set a system flag to indicate that an error condition has occurred.

As we already know, the ROLLBACK TRANSACTION command is used to roll back a user-defined transaction to the last save point (established with the SAVE TRANSACTION command) or to the beginning of the transaction. Transaction save points were discussed in Sec. 17.2.3. The syntax of the ROLLBACK TRAN command is

```
ROLLBACK {tran[saction] | work}
  [transaction_name | savepoint_name]
```

for example,

```
ROLLBACK TRANSACTION price_change
```

The ROLLBACK TRIGGER statement rolls back the work performed by a trigger including the data modification that caused the trigger to be fired. This syntax also provides for an optional RAISERROR statement:

```
ROLLBACK TRIGGER [with raiserror_statement]
```

for example,

```
ROLLBACK TRIGGER with raiserror 20100
  "CANNOT DELETE TEAM, MUST TRADE PLAYERS FIRST"
```

For every SQL statement executed, an error message number is stored in the global variable @@error. If an error has not been encountered, the value of @@error is 0. The optional *raiserror* statement is used to print a user-defined error message and to set the @@error variable to indicate that an error condition has occurred. In the case of triggers where a status code cannot be returned, examination of the @@error global variable is the only means of interrogating (and handling) the error outside of the trigger. For this reason, good descriptive messages inside the trigger code are essential.

Because triggers work underneath another event, there is the problem of identifying whether an error status was caused by the primary UPDATE, DELETE, or INSERT operation (the triggering statement) or by the trigger. One method that can be used to simplify the problem employs the *raiserror* command.

The *raiserror* command (or *rollback trigger with raiserror*) stores the error number into the @@error global variable, which can be used to check the event. SYBASE requires that user-defined error numbers

TABLE 18.1   Application-Specific Error Codes

Message range	Usage
20,000 thru 29,999	Application-specific errors and messages
30,000 thru 39,999	Used for referential integrity constraints
> 99,999	Trigger messages—triggers should also use messages in the 20,000–39,999 range (e.g., 100,000 + 30,000 signifies that message number 30,000 was encountered by a trigger)

be greater than 20,000. An application can reserve a block of error numbers from 100,000 to 200,000, for example, to handle trigger error codes. (Table 18.1 provides some possible message number assignments.) Then SYBASE errors occurring in triggers can be captured and identified by the main process (usually a stored procedure) by subtracting 100,000 from the trigger error code.

Let's use an example to clarify the situation:

```
declare @errorMessage      int,
        @triggerError      int,
        @severity          int,
        @description       varchar(80)

/* This INSERT statement fires the insert/update trigger
   for the inventory table */

insert inventory( partNumber, partName, partType)
  values( '1', 'VERY EXPENSIVE HAMMER', 'F' )

select @errorMessage = @@error

if ( @errorMessage ! = 0 )
begin
        /* Let's see if the error occurred in the trigger */

        if ( @errorMessage > 100,000 )
        begin
          /* Error in trigger processing */

          select @triggerError = @errorMessage - 100,000

          /* Look up error in sysmessages to determine the
             severity level of the error condition */

          select @severity = severity, @description=description
            from master.dbo.sysmessages
            where error=@errorMessage

          print "INSERT trigger - error(s) occurred while processing
             change to inventory"
          print "Error status = %1!", @triggerError
          print "Error description:%1!", @description

          if ( @severity > 13 )
          begin
                rollback transaction
```

```
                return -100       /* Return code to indicate rollback */
        end
     end
     else
     begin
        /* Look up error in sysmessages to determine the
              severity level of the error condition */

        select @severity=severity, @description=description
           from master.dbo.sysmessages
           where error=@errorMessage

        print "INSERT — error(s) encountered inserting row into
          inventory"
        print "Error status = %1!", @errorMessage
        print "Error description:%1!", @description
end
```

The trigger for the *inventory* table should have error checking and good descriptive messages at critical points of failure:

```
/* insert and update trigger for prices table */
create trigger trprices on prices for insert, update
as
        .
        .
        .
        update invhist_temp
         set invhist_temp.price = inserted.price
         where invhist_temp.key = inserted.pkey

        select @errorMessage = @@error

        if ( @errorMessage ! = 0 )
        begin
           /* Look up error in sysmessages to determine the
                 severity level of the error condition */

           select @severity=severity, @description=description
            from master.dbo.sysmessages
            where error=@errorMessage

           /* If it is necessary to capture errors of level 13 or
                 greater, raiserror should be used */

           if ( @severity > 13 )
           begin
                 select @triggerError = @errorMessage + 100,000

                 rollback trigger with raiserror @triggerError
                    "trprices — error occurred in update of invhist_temp"
           end
        end
```

18.3   Triggers as Security Mechanisms

Triggers are traditionally used to provide procedural referential integrity and to cascade change requests within database tables. Triggers are automatic and are independent of application programs. An UPDATE trigger on a database table will function even if the UPDATE is issued by ISQL, SQL Server Manager, or a PowerBuilder application.

Triggers can be used to implement unique security requirements, such as restrictions on data access and modifications based on time of day. For example, the following trigger disallows UPDATEs to the *tb_stocks* table on Saturday and Sunday.

```
CREATE TRIGGER tr_stocks ON tb_stocks FOR insert, update
AS
       IF datename(dw, getdate()) IN ("Saturday", "Sunday")
       BEGIN
               ROLLBACK TRANSACTION
               PRINT "CANNOT TRADE STOCKS ON THE WEEKEND"
       END
       .
       .
       .
GO
```

Triggers can be used to maintain an audit trail of critical data modifications. A trigger can be used to record values before and after an update to provide a detailed audit trail of change activity. An example of trigger-based change auditing is provided in the next section.

18.4 Examples

In this section we look at some examples of triggers that do the following:

1. Manage denormalized data

2. Maintain foreign key integrity

3. Cascading deletes

4. Auditing changes to sensitive tables

Note that the following examples are used for illustrative purposes and are not presented as production quality code. The reader is encouraged to experiment with and expand on the foundation presented here.

Managing denormalized data. In this first example, we look at how triggers can be used to manage denormalized data. Consider the following schema:

```
create table inventory(
       partNumber      char(10)        not null,
       partName        char(40)        not null,
       type            char(1)not null
       )
create unique clustered index x0inventory
  on inventory(partNumber) with fillfactor = 75
```

```
create table location(
        location          char(6)          not null,
        locationName      char(30)         not null
        )
create unique clustered index x0location
 on location(location) with fillfactor = 75

create table inventory_location(
        partNumber        char(10)         not null,
        location          char(6)          not null,
        partName          char(40)         not null,
        qtyOnHand         int              not null,
        baseprice         float            not null
        )
create unique clustered index x0inventory_location
 on inventory_location(partNumber,location)
```

Note that the *partName* column is stored in the *inventory* and *inventory_location* tables. The trigger presented here is an UPDATE trigger created on the *inventory* table. Whenever the *inventory* table is the target of an UPDATE statement, the trigger is fired. The Transact-SQL *if update* clause is used to condition the triggers' execution on the modification of data contained in the *partName* column. Whenever the *inventory.partName* column is updated, the trigger synchronizes redundant data in the *inventory_location.partName* column.

```
CREATE TRIGGER tuinventory ON inventory FOR UPDATE
AS
        DECLARE         @rows                   int,
                        @errorMessage           int,
                        \#64>triggerError       int,
                        @severity               int,
                        @status                 int,
                        @description            varchar(255)

        DECLARE         @partNumber             char(10),
                        @partName char(40)

        SELECT @status = 0

        IF UPATE( partName )
        BEGIN
                DECLARE inventory_cursor CURSOR FOR
                  SELECT DISTINCT
                        partNumber,
                        partName
                  FROM inserted
                FOR READ ONLY

                OPEN inventory_cursor

                WHILE ( @status = 0 )
                BEGIN
                        FETCH inventory_cursor INTO
                          @partNumber,
                          @partName

                        SELECT @status = @@sqlstatus
```

```
            IF ( @status = 1 )
            BEGIN
                    PRINT "Cursor error occurred in tuinventory!"
                    BREAK
            END

            UPDATE inventory_location
              SET partName = @partName
              WHERE partNumber = @partNumber
        END

        CLOSE inventory_cursor
        DEALLOCATE CURSOR inventory_cursor
    END
GO
```

Foreign key integrity. Triggers can be used to prevent the deletion of primary keys when there are matching foreign keys. This type of constraint is commonly referred to as a *restrictive constraint*. These constraints can also be used to modify or delete all matching key information. Let's look at how triggers can be used to maintain foreign key integrity. We use the following for the rest of the examples in this section:

```
create table team(
        team            int             not null,
        name            char(30)        not null
        ) on 'default'
create unique clustered index x0team
  on team(team)

create table player(
        player          numeric(8,0)    not null,
        name            char(30)        not null,
        team            int             not null
        ) on 'default'
create unique clustered index x0player
  on player(player)

create table trades(
        player          numeric(8,0)    not null,
        oldTeam         int             not null,
        newTeam         int             not null,
        tradeDate       datetime        not null
        ) on 'default'
create unique nonclustered index x1trades
  on trades(player,tradeDate)
```

To illustrate the use of triggers to maintain foreign key integrity, assume that we cannot delete a team from the team table if there are players assigned to that team.

```
CREATE TRIGGER tdteam ON team FOR DELETE
AS
        DECLARE         @status         int,
                        @team           int

        SELECT @status = 0
```

```
DECLARE team_cursor CURSOR FOR
 SELECT
      team
 FROM deleted
FOR READ ONLY

OPEN team_cursor

WHILE ( @status = 0 )
BEGIN
      FETCH team_cursor INTO
       @team

      SELECT @status = @@sqlstatus

      IF ( @status = 1 )
      BEGIN
           PRINT "Cursor error occurred in tdteam!"
           BREAK
      END

      IF EXISTS ( SELECT * FROM player WHERE team = @team )
      BEGIN
           PRINT "Cannot delete team, must trade players first"
           ROLLBACK TRAN
           RETURN
      END

      CLOSE team_cursor

      DEALLOCATE CURSOR team_cursor
END
GO
```

Cascading deletes and updates. The DBA may wish to enforce referential integrity through cascading deletes and updates. When a primary key is deleted, all rows containing matching foreign keys are also deleted. A cascading constraint is more complex than a restrictive one. This is because automatic UPDATED and DELETES enable the user to change large amounts of data with a single UPDATE or DELETE.

The next case involves a cascading delete. When we delete a team, a trigger on the *team* table will delete any players (from the *players* table) who are assigned to that team.

```
CREATE TRIGGER tdteam ON team FOR DELETE
AS
      DECLARE          @status        int,
                       @team          int

      SELECT @status = 0

      DECLARE team_cursor CURSOR FOR
       SELECT
            team
       FROM deleted
      FOR READ ONLY

      OPEN team_cursor

      WHILE ( @status = 0 )
      BEGIN
```

```
            FETCH team_cursor INTO
             @team

            SELECT @status = @@sqlstatus

            IF ( @status = 1 )
            BEGIN
                 PRINT "Cursor error occurred in tdteam!"
                 BREAK
            END

            DELETE player WHERE team = @team
       END

       CLOSE team_cursor

       DEALLOCATE CURSOR team_cursor
GO
```

Auditing critical data.   Triggers can be used to maintain an audit trail of critical data modifications. A trigger can be used to record values before and after an update, to provide a detailed audit trail of change activity. The following is an example of trigger-based change auditing:

```
create table trades_audit(
       player        numeric(8,0)       not null,
       oldTeam       int                not null,
       newTeam       int                not null,
       tradeDate     datetime           not null,
       suser_name    varchar(30)        not null,
       eventTime     datetime           not null
       ) on 'default'
create unique nonclustered index x1trades
 on trades(player,tradeDate)

CREATE TRIGGER titrades ON trades FOR INSERT
AS
       DECLARE        @status            int,
                      @team              int

       SELECT @status = 0

       DECLARE trades_cursor CURSOR FOR
         SELECT
             player,
             oldTeam,
             newTeam,
             tradeDate
         FROM inserted
       FOR READ ONLY

       OPEN trades_cursor

       WHILE ( @status = 0 )
       BEGIN
             FETCH trades_cursor INTO
              @player,
              @oldTeam,
              @newTeam,
              @tradeDate
             SELECT @status = @@sqlstatus
```

```
        IF ( @status = 1 )
        BEGIN
                PRINT "Cursor error occurred in titrades!"
                BREAK
        END

        INSERT trades_audit(
                player,
                oldTeam,
                newTeam,
                tradeDate,
                suser_name,
                eventTime)
        VALUES(
                @player,
                @oldTeam,
                @newTeam,
                @tradeDate,
                suser_name(),
                getdate())
    END

    CLOSE trades_cursor

    DEALLOCATE CURSOR trades_cursor
GO
```

18.5   Triggers in Replication Server Environments

Triggers pose an interesting challenge when they are used in Replication Server environments. Because replication is done on a subscription basis (by using an SQL SELECT statement), an UPDATE on a primary server can result in an INSERT or a DELETE in a replicated database. If triggers are maintained on the replicated tables, this situation will cause the UPDATE trigger to fire at the primary site and the INSERT or DELETE trigger to fire at the replicated site. Consider the following scenario:

An account table is maintained on the primary database located at corporate headquarters in New York.

```
create table tbaccount(
        key         char(6)        not null,
        name        char(30)       not null,
        address     char(60)       not null,
        location    char(5)        not null)

create unique clustered index x1account on account(key)
```

The data is replicated with the following replication definition:

```
create replication definition account_repdef with primary at NY.database
        (key char(6), name char(30), address char(60), location char(5))
        primary key(key)
        searchable columns(location)
```

Branches in London, Hong Kong, and Tokyo subscribe to the data using a subscription definition similar to the following:

```
create subscription account for account_repdef with replicate at
  HK.database
        where location = 'HK'
```

If a row is modified in the New York (primary) database to fit the subscription issued in Tokyo, the following will occur:

1. The UPDATE trigger will fire on the New York database.
2. The log transfer manager (LTM) will scan the transaction log and see that this transaction now fits the Hong Kong subscription for data.
3. The row will be replicated to the Hong Kong database where it will cause the INSERT trigger to fire.

```
key:         'NY0001'
name:        'GEORGE ANDERSON'
address:     '1000 ANY STREET, NY'
location:    'NY'
update account set location='HK' where key='NY0001'
```

Use care when you are writing triggers on replicated database tables.

18.6 Summary and Tips

Here are some comments and essential tips for using triggers:

- Triggers are fired after SQL Server has processed the affected rows.
- A trigger fires only once per query, so care must be taken to allow for multiple rows being updated. For example, the statement

```
UPDATE inventory SET baseprice = baseprice * 1.05
```

will only cause the UPDATE trigger to fire once. It will not fire for each row in the table that is being updated. If triggers are used to enforce referential integrity, care must be taken to code the triggers to allow for multiple rows being updated.

- Triggers provide the programmer with the ability to perform several referential integrity (RI) checks in a single trigger. They also offer tremendous flexibility in the actions that can be taken when RI rules are violated.
- Triggers give the programmer the ability to code cascading DELETES and UPDATES.
- Transact-SQL statements are available to roll back the effects of the trigger or the entire transaction. These statements are ROLLBACK TRIGGER and ROLLBACK TRANSACTION.

- Triggers should never select data to the client; only assignment selects are allowed, for example,

      DECLARE @status int
      SELECT @status = 0

- Triggers can be used to maintain an audit trail of critical data changes. A table should be used for the audit trail with the following columns: server user ID, date and time, before value, and after value.

Cursors

A database cursor is a mechanism for accessing the results of an SQL SELECT statement, one row at a time. See Fig. 19.1. Normally, a SELECT operation will return all rows to the application in some order. In SYBASE versions prior to System 10, DB-Library provides a mechanism to process each row in a result set. The row buffering is, however, done by the client, not the server.

Beginning with System 10, Sybase provides full support for back-end database cursors. Rows are returned to the requesting client on demand rather than all at once. By using the cursor mechanism, applications can take action on each row rather than the entire set of

```
DECLARE mycursor CURSOR FOR
  SELECT team, captain, goalie
  FROM team FOR read only
```

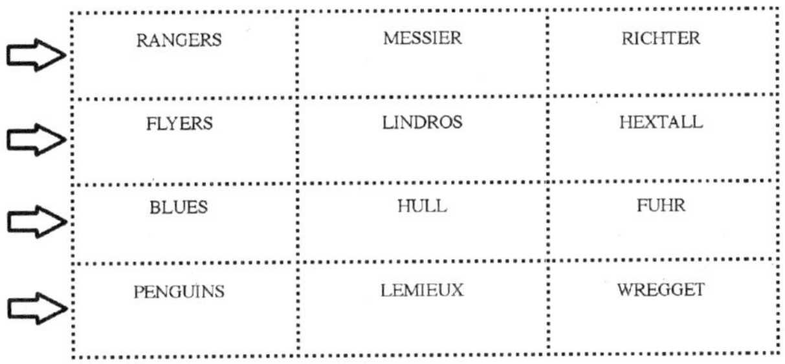

RANGERS	MESSIER	RICHTER
FLYERS	LINDROS	HEXTALL
BLUES	HULL	FUHR
PENGUINS	LEMIEUX	WREGGET

• Rows are returned to the requesting client on demand rather than all at once
• Applications can take action on each row rather than the entire set of rows returned by the SELECT statement
• Applications can do positioned UPDATEs and DELETEs

Figure 19.1 Database cursors.

rows returned by the SELECT. Applications can also do positioned UPDATEs and DELETEs. The new cursor commands are

CLOSE

DEALLOCATE CURSOR

DECLARE CURSOR

FETCH

OPEN

Database cursors are supported by SYBASE in the Embedded-SQL precompiler products, Open Client front ends, and Transact-SQL. Using Transact-SQL, cursors are available in stored procedures and triggers. Cursors are declarable as read-only or updatable which can help the server to choose an optimal execution path.

19.1   Transact-SQL Extensions

Sybase has built some important extensions into the Transact-SQL cursor implementation:

- Cursors are declarable as read-only or updateable (as specified by SQL-92).
- The client can set the number of rows returned by the FETCH statement, an optimization designed to reduce network traffic.
- ANSI closes the cursor with each commit. Using Transact-SQL, cursors can remain open across transactions.

The first extension to cursors allows the client to declare a cursor as read-only or updateable. The DECLARE CURSOR statement is used to define a cursor. The syntax is

```
DECLARE cursor_name CURSOR
  FOR select_statement
  [for {read only | update [of column_name_list]}]
```

for example,

```
DECLARE mycursor CURSOR
  FOR SELECT player, name, team
  FROM player
  FOR UPDATE OF name
```

The read-only and update capabilities have two main benefits:

1. To assist with program structure
2. To help the server choose an execution path

In general, cursors that are declared read-only use shared locks on each data page to avoid reading dirty data from an uncommitted transaction. Cursors that are declared updateable use update locks by default when scanning tables or views and exclusive locks on each page they change. The *shared* keyword is used to force SQL Server to apply shared locks instead of an update lock on a specified table or view. The *shared* keyword can be used only when the SELECT statement is part of a DECLARE CURSOR statement. For example,

```
DECLARE mycursor CURSOR
  FOR SELECT player, name, team
  FROM player SHARED
  FOR UPDATE OF name
```

Another Transact-SQL extension provides the capability to set the number of rows returned by the FETCH statement. This is a network optimization over the ANSI standard one-row fetch. The ANSI-89 standard specifies a FETCH of only one row at a time. To change the number of rows FETCH returns,

```
SET CURSOR ROWS 100 FOR mycursor
```

Finally, cursors can optionally remain open across transactions. ANSI closes the cursor with each commit, which can result in poor throughput and concurrency. By default, SQL Server does not change a cursor's state when a transaction ends through a commit or rollback. SQL Server provides a SET command to enforce ANSI-compliant behavior. The syntax is

```
SET close on endtran on
```

Additionally, when chained mode is set on, SQL Server begins a transaction when a cursor is opened and closes the cursor when the transaction is committed or rolled back.

19.2 Common SQL Statements

The CLOSE statement is used to deactivate a Transact-SQL cursor. The syntax is

```
CLOSE cursor_name
```

The DEALLOCATE CURSOR statement is used to make a cursor inaccessible, and it releases memory resources committed to the cursor. The syntax is

```
DEALLOCATE CURSOR cursor_name
```

TABLE 19.1   @@sqlstatus Values

Value	Description
0	The FETCH statement completed successfully.
1	The FETCH statement resulted in an error.
2	There is no more data in the result set.

The *FETCH* statement is used to return a row or set of rows from a cursor result set. The syntax is

```
FETCH cursor_name [INTO fetch_target_list]
```

for example,

```
DECLARE     @owner        char(30),
            @balance      float

FETCH mycursor INTO @owner, @balance
```

The *fetch_target_list* is a comma-separated list of parameters or local variables used to accept cursor results.

The *@@sqlstatus* global variable contains status information resulting from the last FETCH statement. It is only valid when used with database cursors. The *@@sqlstatus* variable may contain the values listed in Table 19.1.

For cursors, the *@@rowcount* global variable represents the cumulative number of rows returned from the cursor result set to the client, up to the last FETCH request.

The OPEN statement is used to open a cursor for processing. The syntax is

```
OPEN cursor_name
```

19.3   Advanced Features

This section provides a brief overview of the concepts of scrollable cursors and cursor locking.

19.3.1   Scrollable cursors

A limitation of the FETCH statement on a standard cursor is that the cursor can only navigate forward through the set of rows. This makes it necessary to close and reopen the cursor in order to fetch a given row for a second time. The SQL-92 DECLARE CURSOR syntax is

```
exec sql declare cursor_name [insensitive] [scroll] cursor for
    subselect
    {union subselect form}
    [order by result_column [asc|desc]
      {, result_column [asc|desc]}
    [for read only | for update of column_name {, of column_name}];
```

The new syntax elements are *insensitive* and *scroll*. When the *insensitive* keyword is used, the server should define a cursor that makes a temporary copy of the data to be used by the cursor. Requests to the cursor are serviced from the temporary table; therefore, modifications made to the base tables will not be reflected in the data returned by fetches made to this cursor. Cursors defined as insensitive do not allow modifications.

When the *scroll* keyword is used in the DECLARE statement, the cursor is said to be *scrollable*. The new capabilities of the FETCH statement can be used with scrollable cursors. The syntax of the FETCH statement is

```
exec sql fetch
    [{next|prior|first|last
    |{absolute|relative} value_spec} from]
    cursor_name into host_variable {, host_variable};
```

Section 19.6 provides a brief description of the cursor implementation in Microsoft SQL Server. This section is provided so that the reader can compare the Sybase implementation to that of a competitor.

19.3.2 Cursor locking

As described earlier, cursors that are declared read-only use shared locks on the data page that includes the current cursor position to avoid reading dirty data from an uncommitted transaction. Cursors that are declared updateable use update locks when scanning tables or views and exclusive locks on each page they change. If the FOR UPDATE clause is empty, tables and views referenced in the FROM clause of the SELECT statement receive update locks.

When the cursor position moves off a data page, SQL Server releases the shared locks on that page. For cursors that are not declared updateable, when a row is updated or deleted, SQL Server promotes its shared or update lock to an exclusive lock. Exclusive locks (acquired by the cursor) in a transaction are held until the end of the transaction.

The following describes the locking behavior of cursors at each isolation level.

At level 0 isolation:

- No shared locks are permitted on current page.

- A unique index is required for scan.

- Cursors are nonupdateable.
- The *for update* clause cannot be used.

At level 1 isolation, the default:

- If the cursor is nonupdateable, shared locks are applied to the current page.
- Update locks on the current page are promoted to exclusive locks when data is modified.
- An index lock is also acquired.
- Locks are maintained until the cursor moves to another page or closes.

At level 3 isolation:

- Shared or update locks are applied to any base table or index pages read in a transaction through the cursor.
- Locks are held until the transaction ends (provided the *close on endtran* option is set—ANSI mode) or the cursor closes.
- Locks are not released when the cursor moves to another page.

The *shared* keyword is used to force SQL Server to apply shared locks instead of an update lock on a specified table or view. The *shared* keyword can only be used when the SELECT statement is part of a DECLARE CURSOR statement.

The HOLDLOCK keyword can be used in conjunction with the SHARED keyword after each table or view name. The HOLDLOCK keyword must precede SHARED in the SELECT statement, e.g.,

```
DECLARE mycursor CURSOR
  FOR SELECT player, name, team
  FROM player HOLDLOCK SHARED
  WHERE team = 'MIAMI'
  FOR UPDATE OF name
```

19.4   A Cursor Example

Let's look at a small example application that uses a stored procedure to perform month-end processing for a brokerage firm. The following business requirements must be performed:

- If the balance in a customer account is greater than $1000, then interest is added to the account.
- If the balance is less than $1000, a service charge is deducted from the account.

- If the balance is greater than $50,000, a bonus is also given to the account.

Now let's write the procedure, using Transact-SQL without database cursors.

```
CREATE PROCEDURE pr_month_end(
     @interestRate    float,
     @serviceCharge   float,
     @bonus           float)
AS
     BEGIN TRANSACTION

     /*
      * First, add interest to accounts with a balance > $1,000
      */
     UPDATE account
      SET balance = balance + (@interestRate*balance)
      WHERE balance > 1,000

     /*
      * Add the bonus to accounts having a balance > $50,000
      */
     UPDATE account
      SET balance = balance+@bonus
      WHERE balance > 50,000

     /*
      * Deduct the service charge from the other accounts
      */
     UPDATE account
      SET balance = balance - @serviceCharge
      WHERE balance < 1,000

     COMMIT TRANSACTION

     RETURN 0
```

Note that this procedure performs a table scan for each UPDATE statement, resulting in three table scans. Now let's look at the same procedure implemented by using database cursors:

```
CREATE PROCEDURE pr_month_end(
     @interestRate    float,
     @serviceCharge   float,
     @bonus           float)
AS
     DECLARE           @updateFlag       int,
                       @balance          float

     DECLARE mycursor CURSOR
      FOR SELECT balance
      FROM account
      FOR UPDATE OF balance

     OPEN mycursor

     FETCH mycursor
```

```
    INTO @balance

    /*
     * @@sqlstatus = 1 — error on previous fetch
     * @@sqlstatus = 2 — reached end of result set
     */

WHILE ( @@sqlstatus != 2 )
BEGIN
        IF ( @@sqlstatus = 1 )
        BEGIN
                PRINT "Error occurred"
                RETURN -100
        END

        IF ( @balance < 1000 )
        BEGIN
                SELECT @balance = @balance -@serviceCharge
                SELECT @updateFlag = 1
        END
        ELSE IF ( @balance > 1000 )
        BEGIN
                SET balance = balance + (@interestRate*balance)
                IF ( @balance > 50000 )
                BEGIN
                        SELECT @balance = @balance + @bonus
                END
                SELECT @updateFlag = 1
        END
        ELSE
        BEGIN
                SELECT @updateFlag = 0
        END

        IF ( @updateFlag = 1 )
        BEGIN
                UPDATE account
                 SET balance = @balance
                 WHERE CURRENT OF mycursor
        END

        FETCH mycursor INTO @balance
END

CLOSE mycursor
DEALLOCATE CURSOR mycursor

RETURN 0
```

What are the benefits of using a cursor in this example?

- We avoided the multiple table scans experienced in the traditional Transact-SQL example.

- The cursor procedure used shorter transactions because each UPDATE commits as it is made.

- Each row was touched once and remained locks for less time. The result is greater concurrency and higher throughput.

19.5   Comments

Database cursors should be used for any SELECT statement that could be followed with an UPDATE. By design, SQL is a set-oriented language and was not conceived of as a row-oriented language. Most SQL DBMSs are extremely efficient when working in set-oriented mode. Row-by-row processing of data in the SQL Server should be accomplished through the use of cursors.

Cursors are not needed when the rows to be selected have the same uniform qualification criteria or when the same operation is performed on every row in the result set. For example, assume we want to increase the price of all items in an inventory table by 5 percent. Here a single UPDATE is much better than using a cursor to decide which rows to update, e.g.,

```
UPDATE inventory SET price = price * 1.05
UPDATE inventory SET price = price * 1.05 WHERE type = 'SOFTWARE'
```

SQL Server dynamically maintains tables and indexes. This means that during a cursor scan, UPDATEs by the *same* process can interfere with the scan. An example is a table with no clustered index where if a row changes size or nonclustered key data is updated, it migrates to the end of the table. To avoid these problems, the SQL Server uses unique indexes for scanning tables (hence the recommendation that each table have a unique clustered index).

Identity columns can be used to influence a cursor's selection of certain access paths for tables. Any index which includes the identity property column is implicitly available for a cursor's access path.

19.6   Microsoft Implementation

This section is provided so that the reader can compare the Sybase implementation to that of a competitor. Since the Microsoft-Sybase breakup, the two vendors are taking their products in different directions. With the introduction of Version 6.0, Microsoft SQL Server provides ANSI-SQL cursors and engine-based cursors. MS SQL Server cursors are fully scrollable.

MS SQL Server cursors provide the capability to navigate forward and backward through the result set. This eliminates the need to close and reopen the cursor in order to fetch a given row multiple times. Microsoft cursors can be used within a command batch, a stored procedure, and a trigger.

The Microsoft DECLARE syntax is ANSI-92 compliant including support for the *insensitive* and *scroll* keywords. The *scroll* keyword allows the PRIOR, FIRST, LAST, ABSOLUTE *n,* and RELATIVE *n* FETCH commands to be used. Cursors will automatically be declared insensitive if the SQL SELECT statement contains any of the following commands: DISTINCT, UNION, GROUP BY, and/or HAVING. In addition to being able to read data from a cursor, cursors can be used to perform positioned UPDATEs and DELETEs against the data contained in the cursor. UPDATES are not allowed when a cursor is defined as insensitive.

Like Sybase SQL Server, MS SQL Server uses global variables to monitor the status of a cursor. The global variables are *@@fetch_status* and *@@cursor_rows.* The *@@fetch_status* variable displays the status of the last FETCH command, and *@@cursor_rows* displays the number of rows in the cursor result set.

20

Housekeeping and Maintenance

Frequently when an application is first installed, performance is adequate and users are happy. Over time, performance may start to degrade, and users will wonder why. The inevitable questions and complaints will find their way to management and, in turn, trickle down to the application developers and DBAs. This chapter includes some tips and pointers to make sure that SQL Server is always running smoothly and efficiently.

The first part of the chapter is dedicated to a description of the new SQL Server housekeeper task. Immediately following is a discussion of clustered and nonclustered index maintenance. Some valuable scripts and techniques have been written for added value. Section 20.3 provides some pointers for monitoring and maintaining SQL Server Release 11 partitioned tables. A complete discussion of index statistics and stored-procedure plan maintenance is provided in Sec. 20.4. Finally, the chapter closes with some tips regarding an often overlooked part of system administration—log file maintenance.

The UNIX shell scripts contained in this chapter may be of special interest to the reader.

20.1 The Housekeeper

The *housekeeper* is an internal SQL Server Release 11.0 task that is responsible for buffer washing. The housekeeper improves CPU utilization by using SQL Server idle cycles to wash buffers. The housekeeper task can be seen in the output from the *sp_who* system procedure. See Fig. 20.1.

The housekeeper maximizes SQL Server efficiency by using the following algorithm to wash buffers:

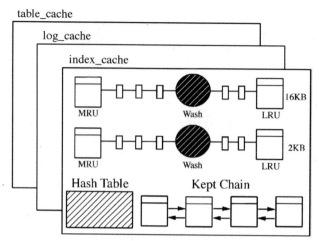

table_cache

log_cache

index_cache

Figure 20.1   SQL Server buffer washing.

1. Wait for SQL Server idle cycles.

2. Check the MRU and LRU queues.

3. Start washing dirty buffers from the wash marker, working toward the MRU side of the queue.

4. If all buffer pool wash markers are at the MRU, the checkpoint task is notified.

The housekeeper task runs as a low-priority thread, actually one priority lower than a user task. One benefit of the new architecture is the fact that if SQL Server is busy, the housekeeper task does not do any work. Because the housekeeper task waits for SQL Server idle cycles, buffer washing does not normally interfere with the execution of a transaction. In pre-Release 11.0 SQL Server, when the SQL Server needs to wash buffers other transactions are delayed.

The *buffer wash marker* is located in the MRU/LRU chain and is used to ensure that buffers on the LRU side of the chain are either clean or in the process of being written to disk. Any dirty buffer that crosses the marker causes an I/O to start on that buffer. The housekeeper washes buffers in batches to prevent flooding the system with an excessive number of writes. One buffer pool is cleaned at a time.

If there are enough idle cycles for the housekeeper to run and reach the MRU end of all active buffer pools in all configured named caches, the housekeeper will notify the checkpoint task to checkpoint the databases. Sybase calls this process a *free checkpoint*. As a result of free checkpoints, the time required for automatic recovery may be reduced.

In the event that a page in a database is repeatedly updated, the housekeeper may repeatedly write that page to disk unnecessarily. This can result in additional overhead and a reduction in system performance. The *housekeeper free write percent* configuration parameter specifies the maximum percentage by which the housekeeper task can increase database writes. The default value is 20 percent. Most sites will see optimal performance when using the default value. A value of 50 percent enables the housekeeper task to use 50 percent additional free writes. This parameter can be used to limit the activities of the housekeeper task. The percentage value is expressed as

$$\text{Value} = \frac{\text{actual number of writes} - \text{possible number of writes}}{\text{possible number of writes}}$$

The housekeeper process can be disabled by setting the *housekeeper free write percent* parameter to 0, using the *sp_configure* system procedure as follows:

```
sp_configure 'housekeeper free write percent', 0
```

As mentioned in Chap. 11, it is a good idea to disable the housekeeper task before you measure CPU utilization. Overall, the housekeeper should have the following effect on SQL Server CPU utilization:

- Because the housekeeper task waits for SQL Server idle cycles, the result should be lower CPU utilization during peak periods. Buffer washing will not occur during periods of high SQL Server utilization.

- The housekeeper task runs when there are SQL Server idle cycles. This should result in fewer overall SQL Server idle cycles.

Monitoring checkpoint activity.   The *sp_sysmon* system procedure is used to gauge the effect of housekeeper activity on checkpoint. Partial output from the procedure is shown here:

```
1> sp_sysmon
2> go
.
.
===========================================================
Recovery Management
-------------------

Checkpoints          per sec    per xact    count    % of total
-------------------  ---------- ----------  ------   ----------
                       15.2        9.8       576       85.2
===========================================================
.
.
```

20.2   Index Maintenance

When heap tables, clustered indexes, or nonclustered indexes are created, they exhibit optimal performance, especially when prefetching is being used. SQL Server allocates space contiguously when it creates databases and tables. Over time, the effects of fragmentation caused by DELETES and UPDATES result in an increased cost of I/O. The resulting page links can span extents, allocation units, and disk devices. Ideal performance for large I/Os when a table scan is performed can be defined as

$$I/Os = \frac{\text{number of pages in the table}}{\text{number of pages per I/O}}$$

I/O efficiency drops off as a result of fragmentation because page chains are no longer located in contiguous extents.

20.2.1   Clustered index

As we learned in Chap. 5, clustered indexes are dynamically reordered to maintain clustering. When there is not enough space on a data page for a new row, a new page is spliced into the page chain (known as *page splitting*). The CREATE INDEX ... with *fillfactor* command can be used to specify how full to make an index page, and data page if the index is clustered. This allows the DBA to reserve some free space to avoid the overhead of page splits. Unlike *max_rows_per_page,* *fillfactor* is only in effect during index creation. Pages can get full over time, requiring the DBA to rebuild indexes to maintain a free space reserve.

If I/O for range queries using a clustered index is exceeding expectations, the administrator should drop and recreate the clustered index. For clustered and nonclustered indexes that will continue to be the target of INSERTs and UPDATEs, the clustered index should be created by using *fillfactor* to slow fragmentation. Common sense dictates that this activity should occur during off-peak hours so as not to impact on-line applications.

Refer to Sec. 13.5 for information about creating indexes on tables concurrently.

20.2.2   Maintaining heap tables

Over time, as changes occur to SQL Server databases, I/O on heap tables can become extremely inefficient. Data modifications can result in a high number of partially filled pages which can lead to inefficient, large I/Os because page chains will not be stored on contiguous extents.

There are two ways to reclaim space in heap tables after DML operations have created empty space on pages or have caused excessive fragmentation:

1. Create and drop a clustered index on the heap table.
2. Use BCP to unload the table, use TRUNCATE TABLE to empty the table, and use BCP to load the data back into the table.

The following UNIX C shell script, named *rebuild.csh,* can be used to rebuild heap tables. It performs these operations:

- It uses BCP to unload data from the tables.

- It uses ISQL to pass a simple Transact-SQL script to the SQL Server. The SQL script is user-created and contains commands to drop the indexes for a table and to truncate the table.

- After the table has been truncated, BCP is used to reload the table's data.

- In the final step, a second Transact-SQL script is sent to the server to rebuild the table's index(es).

```
#!/bin/csh -f
#ident "@(#)rebuild.csh 1.1 - 24 Dec 1995 — 15:32:45"
#
# Author:      George W. Anderson
#
# Purpose:     Used to load and unload heap tables
#
# Parameters:  $1 = SQL Server name as found in $SYBASE/interfaces
#              $2 = SQL Server user ID
#              $3 = SQL Server password
#
#############################
# SET ENVIRONMENT VARIABLES #
#############################
set ERROR = $SYBASE/error
set WORKDIR = $SYBASE/bcp
set OUTPUT = $SYBASE/output
set SQL = $SYBASE/sql

cd $WORKDIR

echo "Start: 'date'"

foreach I (*.bcp)

    ####################
    # BCP OUT THE DATA #
    ####################

    echo "Unloading $i:r"
    $SYBASE/bin/bcp database.dbo.$i:r out $i:r.dat -S $1 -A2048 -U $2 -P $3 -c
    if ( $status ) then
            echo "Error BCPing data out of $i:r"
    endif
```

```
###################################################
# DROP INDEX & TRUNCATE TABLE PRIOR TO LOADING #
###################################################

echo "Truncate $i:r"
$SYBASE/bin/isql -U $2 -S $1 -P $3 -H 'hostname' -i $SQL/$i:r.sql
if ( $status ) then
        echo "Error truncating $i:r prior to load"
endif

##############################
# RELOAD THE DATA USING BCP #
##############################

echo "Loading $i:r"
$SYBASE/bin/bcp database.dbo.$i:r in $i:r.dat -S $1 -A2048 -U $2 -P $3\
 -b 5000 -c
if ( $status ) then
        echo "Error BCPing data into $i:r"
endif

###############################
# REBUILD THE TABLES INDEX(ES) #
###############################

echo "Rebuilding index(es) for $i:r"
$SYBASE/bin/isql -U $2 -S $1 -P $3 -H 'hostname' -i $SQL/$i:r.idx
if ( $status ) then
        echo "Error rebuilding index(es) for $i:r"
endif
end

echo "Finish: 'date'"

set WORKDIR = $SYBASE/bcp
set OUTPUT = $SYBASE/output
set SQL = $SYBASE/sql

cd $WORKDIR

echo "Start: 'date'"

foreach I (*.bcp)
```

Three files are required for each SQL Server table to be processed. The first file is named *<tablename>.bcp* and is located in the *$SYBASE/bcp* directory. The file does not need to have any contents; however, I usually type the table name into the file.

```
elvee:/opt/sybase/bcp:{sybase}\: ls -l
-rw-rw--     1 sybase database      8 Dec 24 19:11 team.bcp
-rw-rw--     1 sybase database      8 Dec 24 19:11 player.bcp
-rw-rw--     1 sybase database      8 Dec 24 19:11 trades.bcp
```

The second file is named *<tablename>.sql* and is located in the *$SYBASE/sql* directory. This file contains the Transact-SQL command necessary to drop the table's index(es) and truncate the table, e.g.,

```
use eei
go
drop index player.x1player
go
drop index player.x2player
go
truncate table player
go
```

The third file is named *<tablename>.idx* and is also located in the
$SYBASE/sql directory. This file contains the Transact-SQL com-
mands required to rebuild the table's index(es), e.g.,

```
use eei
go
create index x1player on player(playerName)
go
create index x2player on player(teamID)
go
```

20.3 Maintaining Partitioned Tables

To achieve optimal performance, it is necessary to establish regular
maintenance procedures for partitioned tables. The *sysusages* table
can be used to monitor space for a given partition. The *unreservedpgs*
column lists pages in extents that have not been allocated. This can
be used to monitor the space available to a given fragment to see if it
is filling up, e.g.,

```
1> select dbid,segmap,lstart,size,vstart,unreservedpgs
2> from master..sysusages
3> where dbid = db_id()
4> go
```

dbid	segmap	lstart	size	vstart	unreservedpgs
5	3	0	5120	50331648	4528
5	8	5120	1024	67108864	1016
5	8	6144	1024	83886080	1024
5	8	7168	1024	100663296	1024
5	4	8192	1024	117440512	1024

The *sysusages.segmap* column is the key to the segment map. The
row with *segmap* = 3 contains the *system* and *default* segments. The
row with *segmap* = 4 is for the *logsegment*. The rows with *segmap* = 8
correspond to a user-defined segment. In this example, the partitioned table resides on this segment. The *unreservedpgs* column contains the number of pages in extents that are not yet allocated. If the
fragments are not filling up equally, the administrator should use
BCP to copy the data out of the table, and back in. Section 13.8 provides pointers for using BCP on data in partitioned tables.

20.4   Statistics and Stored-Procedure Maintenance

Over time, as indexes are added to tables and other changes are made to tables that affect statistics, stored procedures and triggers will lose some of their efficiency. By recompiling stored procedures and triggers on a regular basis, queries can be optimized for greater efficiency.

The *sp_recompile* system stored procedure causes each stored procedure and trigger that uses a named table to be recompiled the next time it is run. The *sp_recompile* procedure should be used after the UPDATE STATISTICS command is run against a table to optimize the query plans for greater efficiency. The syntax is

```
sp_recompile tableName
```

for example,

```
sp_recompile team
```

SQL Server keeps statistics about the distribution of key values in each index. The statistics page has a 32-byte header, followed by index field key values. The index field key values are obtained by sampling the value of the index key at each nth position in the table. These statistics are used by the query optimizer to make decisions regarding which index or indexes to use for a query. Information maintained on the index statistics page is also used to estimate the number of rows in a table. This information is used by the *rowcnt* system function and the *sp_spaceused* system stored procedure.

Index statistics pages are maintained by running the UPDATE STATISTICS command; they are not dynamically updated by SQL Server. The UPDATE STATISTICS command should be run on a table after a significant number of updates have occurred to provide the query optimizer with current statistics from which to create optimal query plans. Query optimization is heavily dependent on the accuracy of the distribution statistics. Statistics are automatically updated if data is present in the table at the time of index creation. However, if data is not present in the table, the UPDATE STATISTICS command must be executed.

The UPDATE STATISTICS command should be performed as part of routine database maintenance. Automate the process by writing Transact-SQL scripts and running them from the UNIX *cron* daemon. Also, call the Transact-SQL scripts automatically as part of any job that makes significant UPDATEs to a database table.

The *sp_recompile* system procedure is used to cause stored procedures that access a particular table to be updated the next time they are run. The syntax of *sp_recompile* is

```
sp_recompile tableName
```

The *sp_recompile* command should be run after every UPDATE STA-
TISTICS command. The following code can be used to automate the
process of statistics and stored-procedure plan maintenance.

Example.   The following stored procedure, named *sp_updatestats,* can
be used to generate scripts for stored-procedure plan and statistics
page maintenance. The procedure reads the *sysobjects* table to find
the names of user-defined tables in the current database.

```
use sybsystemprocs
go
if exists (select * from sysobjects where id = object_id('dbo.sp_update-
stats'))
begin
        print 'Drop procedure sp_updatestats'
        drop procedure sp_updatestats
end
go
print 'Creating sp_updatestats'
go
        declare      @status           int,
                     @tableName        varchar(30),
                     @database         varchar(30)
  select @status = 0

  declare mycursor cursor for
        select name from sysobjects
          where type = 'U'
  for read only
  open mycursor

  select @database = db_name()

  print 'USE %1!', @database
  print 'GO'

  while ( @status = 0 )
  begin
        fetch mycursor into @tableName

        select @status = @@sqlstatus

        if ( @status = 1 )
        begin
                print 'Cursor Error'
                return -100
        end

        print 'UPDATE STATISTICS %1!', @tableName
        print 'EXEC sp_recompile %1!', @tableName
  end

  close mycursor
  deallocate cursor mycursor

  print 'GO'
go
```

Note that this can also be accomplished with a SELECT statement; however, the stored procedure formats the output nicely. Here is the SELECT syntax:

```
SELECT "UPDATE STATISTICS " + name FROM sysobjects
    WHERE type = 'U'
```

The next part of the process is to create an operating system text file which contains the SQL statements to be run in the target database. The host file is named *updatestats.sql:*

```
use eei
go
sp_updatestats
go
```

Now we can send the Transact-SQL commands to the SQL Server, using ISQL:

```
% isql -Ugwa -Selvee -iupdatestats.sql -Ppassword > eei.sql
password:
```

The resulting output will be similar to the following:

```
USE eei
GO
UPDATE STATISTICS team
EXEC sp_recompile team
UPDATE STATISTICS player
EXEC sp_recompile player
UPDATE STATISTICS trades
EXEC sp_recompile trades
GO
```

This script can now be used on a regular basis for stored-procedure and statistics maintenance. The following UNIX C shell script is used to create an SQL script using the *updatestats.sql* host file. The resulting SQL script is then sent to the SQL Server engine.

```
#!/bin/csh
#
# Author:      George W. Anderson
# Date:        01/07/96
# Description: Script used for statistics and stored procedure plan
#                  maintenance
#
cd $SYBASE/maintenance
$SYBASE/bin/isql -Ugwa -Selvee -iupdatestats.sql -Ppassword > eei.sql
$SYBASE/bin/isql -Ugwa -Selvee -ieei.sql -Ppassword > /dev/null
```

Finally, to automate the process, add an entry to the SYBASE user's *crontab* file. This *crontab* entry will cause the job to be executed every Sunday at 11:00 p.m.

```
% crontab -e
#ident "@(#)sybase       1.12 95/12/20 SMI"       /* Svr4.0 1.1.3.1 */
#
# maintenance procedures
#
0 23 * * 6 /opt/sybase/maintenance/eei.csh 1>/dev/null 2>&1
```

20.5   Log File Maintenance

An often overlooked part of system administration is the cleanup and
maintenance of server log files. Log files are generated by SQL
Server, the Backup Server, SQL Monitor Server, Replication Server,
log transfer managers, etc. If these files are left to their own devices,
they will continue to grow until the file system is filled to capacity.
The following UNIX C shell script, named *file_archive.csh,* can be
used to archive log files.

```
#!/bin/csh -f
#ident "@(#)file_archive.csh 1.1 - 24 Dec 1995 - 15:32:45"
#
# Author:     George W. Anderson
#
# Purpose:    Used to generation error logs.
#             Takes input from the ./file_list file
#
cd /usr/bin

if ( -w junkmail ) then
        rm junkmail
endif

echo "'date' - file_archive.csh running on 'hostname'" > junkmail
echo "'date' - file_archive.csh running on 'hostname'"

set flist = 'cat ./filelist'
foreach f ($flist)
        #
        # Build file names
        #
        set filenew = 'echo "/dev/null"'
        set file0 = 'echo $f".0"'
        set file1 = 'echo $f".1"'

echo "Processing file: $f" >> junkmail
echo "Processing file: $f"
#
# Copy $f.0 to $f.1
#
if ( -w "$file0" ) then
        set var = 'cp "$file0" "$file1"'
        set rc = $status
        if ( $rc != 0 ) then
                echo " Error processing $file0 to $file1..." >> junkmail
                echo " Error processing $file0 to $file1..."
        endif
endif
#
# Copy current file to $f.0
```

```
#
set var = 'cp "$f" "$file0"'
set rc = $status
if ( $rc ! = 0 ) then
        echo " Error processing $f to $file0..." >> junkmail
        echo " Error processing $f to $file0..."
endif
#
# Truncate current log file
#
set var = 'cp "$filenew" "$f"'
set rc = $status
if ( $rc ! = 0 ) then
        echo " Error processing $filenew to $f..." >> junkmail
        echo " Error processing $filenew to $f..."
endif
end
echo "<<< Done >>>" >> junkmail
echo "<<< Done >>>"

mail -s "File archive report" dba < junkmail
```

The *file_archive.csh* script receives its input from a file named *file_list,* which should be located in the same directory as the *file_archive.csh* script. This is a simple text file that contains the location of all files that *file_archive.csh* should archive, e.g.,

```
/opt/sybase/install/errorlog_elvee
/opt/sybase/install/backup.log
/opt/sybase/install/monitor_elvee.log
/opt/sybase/repserver/RS_elvee.log
/opt/sybase/repserver/LTM_inventory.log
```

The recommendation is to schedule the *file_archive.csh* script to run on a regular basis, e.g., once a month, using the UNIX *cron* facility or a job-scheduling package such as AutoSys from Platinum Technologies.

20.6   Patching a Database

It is sometimes necessary to *patch* a database to correct problems with database integrity. This is a very complex process and is not for the faint-hearted. There are minor (and sometimes major) differences in SYBASE versions and the command syntax required for them. This section is provided for informational purposes only. Never attempt to patch a database on your own; page patching is almost *never* required and should not be done without first consulting Sybase technical personnel.

With that disclaimer, the following information is included:

■ Identify the database objects that are frequently patched.

■ Identify the tools used to patch databases.

- Describe the tasks required in a patching session.
- Discuss situations where patching is required.

Index and data pages. Index and data pages may be patched for several reasons:

- Repair the page chain (the next and previous page values in the page headers are changed to repair a corrupt page chain).
- Time stamps in the page headers are changed to modify the order of recovery.
- Rows can be deleted to synchronize a table with its index.

Log records. Log records are commonly patched to

- Update the time stamps in log records to modify the order of recovery
- Change the log record type to *noop* (see App. L) to skip the record at recovery

Extents. Extents may be patched to correct the following problems:

- Allocation bit maps may be updated to correct the effects of errors in the 25*xx* range.
- The *objID* (object ID) for an extent can be cleared.

DBINFO area. The last checkpoint RID can be changed to point to the actual last checkpoint row in the transaction log. If the last checkpoint record in a database's DBINFO structure is incorrect, automatic recovery may fail. To correct this problem, the system administrator should locate the last checkpoint record and update the DBINFO structure to point there.

20.6.1 The patching process

This section describes the typical sequence of events prior to and during the patching process.

Typically, an error is detected in the SQL Server error log (e.g., 2540 error—table corrupt: page is allocated but not linked), indicating that there is a problem on pages in a database. At this point the system administrator should run any available diagnostics on objects reported in the error message. This is done to identify all the objects that may require patching to solve the problem.

Prior to patching a database, the administrator must have sole access to the database. This is done by placing the database in *single-user* mode. Back up the database prior to the patching process. If something goes awry during patching, it should be possible to restore the database to its previous state from the dump file.

At this point, the patching can be performed. When the patching has been completed, the administrator should rerun any available diagnostics on the object(s) reported in the initial error message. Assuming that the diagnostics run cleanly, the next step is to checkpoint the database; a manual checkpoint is necessary because patched changes are not logged. The final step is to back up the database. Because the patch commands are not logged, all transaction log dumps taken prior to the patching process are invalidated.

20.6.2 Data Workbench

Sybase Data Workbench is a little-known (and aged) tool used for DBMS administration, data entry, query composition and data manipulation, and report generation. Data Workbench is an APT Workbench client application. One of the features provided by Data Workbench is the page editor.

Page editor. The page editor is a low-level interface to data, index, and log pages of an SQL Server. The page editor can be used to change any portion of any page in the dataserver. To access the page editor:

- Set the PAGEDIT environment variable at the operating system level.

```
setenv PAGEDIT 1
```

- Use Data Workbench to log into the target SQL Server, using the *sa* log-in account.
- The page editor is accessed from the *dbo utilities* top-level menu option.

As input, the page editor accepts a database name and logical page number.

20.6.3 DBCC commands

There are several undocumented DBCC commands used for page patching. Several of those commands are described here.

The DBCC *delete_row* keyword is used to delete an index or data row by specifying a row number or an offset of the row on the page.

```
dbcc delete_row( dbid, page, delete_by_row, number )
```

The DBCC *extentzap* keyword is used to clear all extents matching the specified parameter values. The syntax is

```
dbcc extentzap (dbid, objid, indid, sort)
```

The DBCC *save_rebuild_log* keyword generates a new log containing a single checkpoint record while preserving old log extents by changing the object ID.

```
dbcc save_rebuild_log( databaseName )
```

The DBCC *rebuild_log* keyword generates a new log containing a single checkpoint record. The syntax is

```
dbcc rebuild_log( dbname, rebuild, all )
```

The DBCC *fix_al* makes an allocation bit map match corresponding page chains. The entries in Object Allocation Map (OAM) pages will also be corrected.

```
dbcc fix_al( databaseName )
```

The DBCC *report_al* keyword is the same as *fix_al,* except *report_al* is used to report the items that *fix_al* will actually change. This is a read-only command.

```
dbcc report_al( databaseName )
```

The DBCC *rebuildextents* keyword corrects all extents for a specified object. When necessary, OAM pages will also be updated for the object. The database must be in read-only mode for this command to run. The syntax is

```
dbcc rebuildextents( dbid, objid, indid )
```

20.7   Platinum Log Analyzer

The information contained in the transaction log can be used for tasks ranging from the recovery of lost data to performance analysis. Unfortunately, the *syslogs* table is not accessible through Transact-SQL. The Platinum Log Analyzer for Sybase is a product designed to read the *syslogs* table and present the information contained in it, in an easily readable format.

Log Analyzer for SQL Server is an Open Client program that reads not only transaction log pages in the SQL Server, but also actual table data pages. It bypasses normal SQL access methods to read pages directly, including their contents and status, and it presents the information in an easy-to-read format. Log Analyzer for SQL Server

- Reads the active SQL Server log and archived logs to identify indexes and tables altered by a transaction, hot spots, excessive index modifications, deadlocks, and poorly written transactions and to understand the actual sequence of events in the SQL Server.

- Regenerates data manipulation language (DML) statements from the active log and archived logs to reverse or replicate DELETE, INSERT, and UPDATE statements.

- Creates an audit report from the active log or archived logs to maintain a trail of data modification statements without incurring a performance impact.

- Provides the ability to browse data pages to determine the actual location of data stored in the SQL Server.

- Provides the ability to recover data from data pages and from damaged databases so the administrator can clear DBCC error messages without data loss.

- Allows the administrator to examine the impact of client applications on SQL Servers in a production environment so that client applications can be debugged.

- Provides the ability to determine how long a transaction took within the server. This information can be used to tune client applications, SQL Server indexing, and physical storage to improve performance in a production system instead of creating a complex test setup.

21

Conclusion

This chapter provides a brief overview of the prevailing trends in client/server computing and SYBASE directions in particular. Some of the technologies covered include data warehousing, DCE, future SQL Server enhancements such as parallelization, and the addition of new features such as governers and application queues. Also discussed are planned enhancements to SYBASE Open Server and Open Client products.

The chapter concludes with a description of other Sybase directions including DCE integration, wireless communications, multimedia enhancements, Optima C++, and the new Object Transport System.

21.1 Data Warehousing

We have entered an era when an entire market cycle can begin and end in 18 months, where competition is global, and where the window of opportunity is narrow. In this type of business climate, the advantage tips in favor of the company that can most quickly analyze important information—historic and geographic, and across business units and product lines. Information on how to respond to a product opportunity, a competitive threat, or a trade imbalance can all be *mined* from data contained in various information systems in departments within an organization.

Extracting quality information from a quagmire of data requires redefining the very concept of decision support. Overnight batch reports that no longer provide acceptable response time do not represent an adequate solution. Managers need to operate in discovery mode, constructing their queries on the fly. Even a simple question about pricing can lead to more detailed queries about operations:

- What products are selling well and in what geographic areas?
- What products did our competitors advertise?
- What advertisements performed well and in what geographic areas?
- What's the tolerance for a price differential between us and our competitors?

The ability to quickly ask follow-up questions allows a manager to better understand the business environment before making critical business decisions. The requirement for interactive access to information, coupled with the promise of rapid response, has become the focus of a type of application called *data warehousing*. Recent studies suggest that the market for data warehousing will grow to over $2 billion by 1997.

Sybase defines data warehousing as the ability to pull together information from a variety of sources, at regular intervals, to construct an integrated view of business activities. Source data may reside on different servers and may be stored in a variety of relational and legacy systems. To be valuable for decision making, this data must be *transformed* to a consistent view and distributed where needed.

To optimize the value of this information, rapid response to requests for information is mandatory. Information must be delivered quickly, for data warehouse applications are becoming less batch-oriented and more interactive. The end result is no longer a report or presentation, but a strategic decision upon which millions of dollars may be riding.

21.1.1 Warehouse WORKS

An effective data warehousing strategy must deal with the complexities of the modern enterprise. Data is generated everywhere and controlled by different databases, hardware, and software. Users constantly demand access to data that is customized to their needs. Data warehouse architecture must be flexible enough to evolve with changing user requirements and business conditions.

Sybase has developed Warehouse WORKS, a data warehousing framework designed specifically for client/server computing. It leverages the strengths of client/server interoperability, performance, and flexibility to quickly adapt to changes while offering the consistency and manageability of centralized systems.

Some of the basic steps required to build a data warehouse include these:

1. Assemble the data.
2. Transform the data.
3. Access the data.

Assembling data. As mentioned earlier, in many organizations, data can be found in relational and nonrelational formats on the mainframe, on client/server systems, and in departmental servers scattered throughout the enterprise. One of the goals of Warehouse WORKS is to automatically extract information from where it currently exists and migrate it to the data warehouse.

SYBASE Enterprise CONNECT supplies transparent access to a large number of data sources, both on the mainframe and across the enterprise. Some of the data sources supported by Enterprise CONNECT include IMS, VSAM, DB2, and IDMS on the mainframe; and Oracle, Informix, Rdb, and AS/400 in departmental servers and distributed sites. With Enterprise CONNECT, users can assemble data from many popular data sources and leverage the SYBASE architecture to support new products and data sources in the future.

Transforming data. For users to rely on information contained in the data warehouse, data from production systems must be analyzed and made consistent. Before it can be loaded into the warehouse, the data must be *cleansed* and validated, to filter out the effects of invalid data. When users access and deliver data to the warehouse, the following challenges may be encountered:

- Data formats are often inconsistent between business systems.
- The actual use of a data field in the production environment may not match the metadata specification for that data item.
- Data may need to be decoded.
- Data may have different meanings across business systems.
- Data identifiers (such as account number) may differ across systems.
- Data may need to be derived
- External data may need to be added.

As companies construct data warehouses that become critical to the decision-making process, the ability to automate the data transformation process becomes critical to success. Processes to ensure data quality must be developed and supported within the products and utilities used for data movement. Sybase's solution to data transformation involves data movement products within the Enterprise CONNECT architecture.

Within the Enterprise CONNECT architecture, both Replication Server and InfoPump contain scripting facilities to specify data transformations. Using Replication Server, production sites can replicate transactions to a central warehouse, where the schema reflects an integration of various data sources.

InfoPump, which is Sybase's bulk data movement facility, provides a visual basic language for scripting transformations. Using this scripting language, data administrators can extract data from various data sources and specify summarizations and aggregations. InfoPump also provides the ability to integrate a number of different data sources as well as handle differences in data types and naming conventions in each data source. InfoPump provides interfaces to products such as SQL Server, Oracle, and Lotus Notes, and it also works with Enterprise CONNECT to deliver a solution for products from other vendors.

Accessing data.   Timely access to information is crucial to obtaining retail value, and return on investment, from the data warehouse. The warehouse must provide fast, efficient data delivery for multiple users from any tool. Warehouses must support a variety of applications from large-scale reporting and data aggregation to high-speed access for complex ad hoc queries. To meet the performance objectives for the data warehouse, Sybase offers the following products:

- SYBASE MPP provides virtually unlimited scalability and parallel high-speed data maintenance operations.
- SYBASE SQL Server with IQ provides high-speed access for ad hoc queries.
- Sybase OmniCONNECT Server provides data access transparency.

21.1.2   SYBASE IQ

The SYBASE Interactive Query Accelerator (SYBASE IQ) uses new *Bit-Wise* indexing technology to deliver rapid response to user queries. Its unique design enables it to perform less work per query, resulting in performance gains from 10 to 100 times on the same hardware.

In an attempt to speed throughput, all the major RDBMS vendors have added parallel query capabilities that spread the work of a single query over a large number of processors. Parallel processing has reduced response times for large bulk processing operations where all the data must be scanned. These tasks include report generation and data maintenance. Also, the addition of more processors enables the system to be scaled up to maintain acceptable performance as the amount of data grows.

Parallel processing is less efficient for interactive applications, where only a small subset of the data is needed. Users typically ask a series of questions, drilling more deeply into the data with each successive query, seeking very specific information. Response times must be short enough that users can maintain their train of thought and complete their projects quickly.

The challenge of maintaining fast throughput is further complicated by additional users. Recent studies suggest that data warehouses can expect upward of 500 users. Simultaneous users lead to increased contention for processors and diminished scalability.

These interactive users need a new approach to query processing, an approach that

- Works smarter by not scanning all the data

- Provides truly interactive performance on uniprocessor as well as parallel systems for multiple users

- Offers the flexibility to deliver interactive performance on a fully relational schema without tuning

A number of nonrelational database products have used software solutions to address the unique need of the decision support marketplace. In many cases, their performance gains have come from the use of inverted list or bit-map indexes as opposed to B-tree indexes. Simply stated, instead of using a tree, bit maps represent the presence of a given value for a field as true or false for each record. See Fig. 21.1.

Traditional bit-map indexes address some of the limitations of B-tree indexes. Unlike B-tree indexes, bit-mapped indexes efficiently index low-cardinality data, are much smaller and easier to maintain, and can be evaluated concurrently.

Unfortunately, bit-map indexes also have disadvantages. Although efficient for low-cardinality data, bit-mapped indexes are not suitable for high-cardinality data because every unique value requires a separate index column. Bit-mapped indexes have also been limited in their

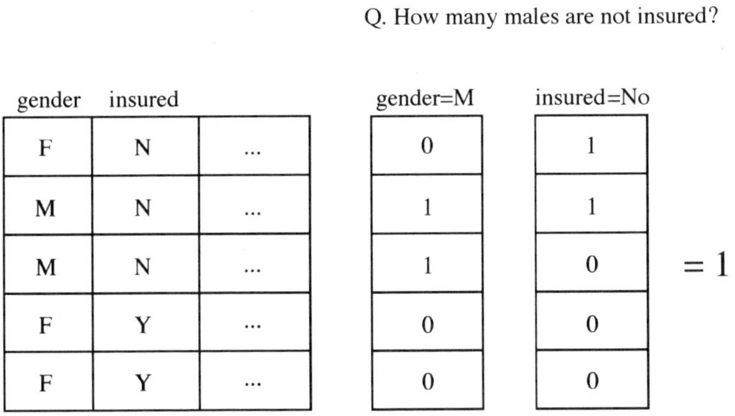

Q. How many males are not insured?

gender	insured		gender=M	insured=No	
F	N	...	0	1	
M	N	...	1	1	
M	N	...	1	0	= 1
F	Y	...	0	0	
F	Y	...	0	0	

Figure 21.1 Bit-map indexes.

ability to aggregate data, implement relational joins, and retrieve raw data values, such as names and addresses.

In approaching the problem of decision support query performance, Sybase has produced a unique, patented advancement to relational technology called *Bit-Wise* indexing, which forms the core of SYBASE IQ. Bit-Wise technology works smarter, not harder. The result is that even a highly ad hoc query sequence is accomplished with fast response times. The technologies incorporated into IQ include advanced indexing, preoptimized and ad hoc join strategies, and several other innovations that overcome the limitations of traditional bit maps.

Bit-Wise technology

- Handles all types of data, including data with a large number of distinct values

- Offers the ability to quickly aggregate as well as count data values

- Answers many queries without having to retrieve the raw data

- Preserves relational flexibility with any data design, without the need to preaggregate data

Figure 21.2 illustrates the high-level architecture of SYBASE IQ.

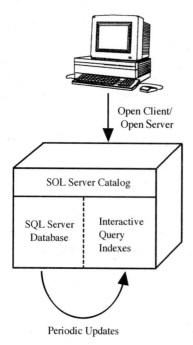

Figure 21.2 SYBASE IQ Architecture.

SYBASE IQ integrates Bit-Wise technology into Sybase's modular open architecture, enabling users to capitalize on all the strengths of traditional database technology while adding high-performance query resolution. The technology is an optional extension of the SYBASE SQL Server RDBMS. The appropriate technology—whether Bit-Wise indexes or the underlying RDBMS—is automatically invoked to furnish the optimal response. A built-in query manager identifies and transparently passes database updates to SQL Server and uses the IQ to resolve any decision support queries. The Bit-Wise indexes are then periodically updated as required.

IQ provides rapid performance while seamlessly integrating into existing environments. The technology processes standard SQL commands as it supports DB-Library, CT-Library, and ODBC client calls. An integrated catalog serves both the SQL Server and SYBASE IQ, enabling security and other services to be managed consistently throughout the SYBASE environment.

21.2   SQL Server: Future Trends

This section offers some insight into future directions for SYBASE SQL Server including

- Application queues
- Query governors
- Symmetric kernel
- Dynamic configuration
- Internal parallelization

Application queues.   Sybase may provide *application queues* in a future version of the SQL Server RDBMS. Application queues can be used to further divide SQL Server resources between OLTP and DSS applications. The implementation may include the following capabilities:

- Scheduling of priorities per thread or stored procedure
- Affinity threads and procedures (applications) to any engine
- Run-time engine on/off lining—can be tailored to load
- The ability to bind a client and server application into an application unit—implemented through CT-Library interface

Figure 21.3 illustrates how application queues might be implemented to segregate OLTP and DSS applications.

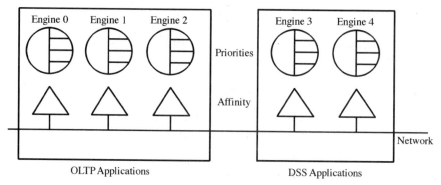

Figure 21.3 Application queues.

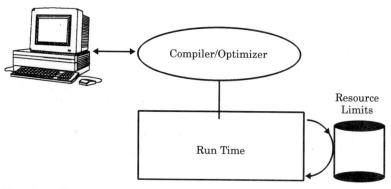

Figure 21.4 Query governors.

Query governors. Several RDBMS products provide a query governor facility which is used to prevent a database user from issuing impossibly complex and resource-consuming queries. A query governor facility might have the following characteristics:

- Management of resource consumption of queries
- Preexecution and run time: based on I/O cost, elapsed time, and number of rows affected
- Resource limits per server, database, or table
- Configurable time range specifications
- Scope of enforcement: query, query batch, transaction with the ability to specify action taken on violations

Figure 21.4 provides a high-level view of the architecture of a query governor facility.

Symmetric kernel. Sybase will continue to improve on the architecture of the SQL Server kernel. With the introduction of System 11, Sybase made two very significant changes to the kernel:

- Symmetric networking
- Symmetric lock management

The System 10 SQL Server kernel does not provide symmetric networking. SQL Server engines prior to System 11 perform all network I/O using engine 0. Multiple-network engine (MNE) extends network I/O capability to all SQL Server engines in the SMP environment. This improves server performance, scalability, and load balancing by distributing network I/O operations to each server engine on a per-connection basis. MNE also increases the number of connections that SQL Server can support. Typically, the number of connections supported by an operating system process is limited by the operating system itself. By routing all network I/Os to engine 0, the total number of simultaneous user connections is limited (say, to 4096). By making networking symmetric, each engine can handle the maximum number of connections.

Release 11.x. In a future release of the SQL Server RDBMS, Sybase should provide symmetric sleep and run queues, as shown in Fig. 21.5. This architecture will prevent engines from competing for work found in a single sleep and run queue. This is a logical extension of the work performed for Release 11.0. The reader is encouraged to compare the illustration to Fig. 11.2 which represents the current architecture of SQL Server.

Dynamic (run-time) configuration. As stated in Chaps. 1 and 7, for a database to be highly available, it must support dynamic configuration of parameters such as total server memory, size of internal memory pools and procedure caches, and number of available lock structures. If the RDBMS does not support dynamic configuration, the system administrator must schedule downtime to restart the server and must set new parameters. In distributed environments, especially those using Replication Server, this can be extremely difficult. Sybase must make SQL Server more dynamically configurable if SQL Server is to support very large, mission-critical applications.

Parallel SQL engine. While competitors Oracle, IBM, and Informix support varying degrees of internal parallelization, Sybase has not built parallelization into the SQL Server process. Sybase intends to provide the following levels of parallelization in future versions of SQL Server:

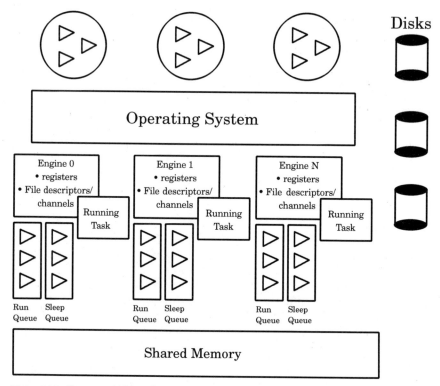

Figure 21.5 Symmetric kernel.

- Parallel access to partitioned and nonpartitioned data
- Internal SQL Server parallelization
- Shared disk and shared database

Figure 21.6 illustrates the targeted market segments for different release levels of the Sybase engines.

Parallel load. The following features will be provided with SQL Server Release 11.x:

- Parallel DBCC
- Parallel recovery
- Parallel sort operations for CREATE INDEX
- Parallel BCP which can copy data into the same table using slices (partitions)

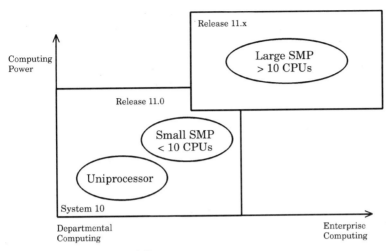

Figure 21.6 SYBASE scalability.

Parallel scans. The following parallel scan options will be built into ReleaseII.x.

- Parallel table scans
- Parallel index scans
- Parallel joins
- Parallel aggregates (both vector and scalar)
- Parallel sorts (ORDER BY and GROUP BY)
- Parallel SELECT INTO

21.3   Other Trends

Sybase, like all vendors, is constantly monitoring emerging technologies and planning how to incorporate them into the Sybase product line. Some of these technologies include

- Distributed computing environment
- Wireless communications
- Multimedia
- Object relational extensions

21.3.1   Distributed computing environment

The OSF's distributed computing environment (DCE) empowers both end users and software developers to take advantage of truly distributed open systems. The DCE provides the foundation that is needed to use and develop distributed applications in heterogeneous hardware and software environments.

Through its open Request for Technology (RFT) process, OSF has selected and integrated the best technologies available to date. The selected technologies were mostly derived from the DECorum proposal jointly submitted by Hewlett-Packard (HP), Apollo, IBM, DEC, Microsoft, Locus, and Transarc.

The resulting architecture (DCE) provides solutions to several fundamental questions facing the developers of distributed cooperative client/server environments. Among them are the client's and server's ability to locate each other across the network, the mechanism to share information between clients and server across the network, and the ability to synchronize processing among many distributed systems to achieve true cooperation.

DCE architecture. In general terms, the distributed computing environment is an integrated environment consisting of the following components:

- Distributed file system
- Directory service
- Remote procedure calls
- Threads services
- Time services

Distributed file system. Distributed file systems (DFSs) operate by allowing a user on one system that is connected to a network to access and modify data stored on files in another system. From a client/server architecture's point of view, the system on which the user is working is the *client,* while the system in which the data is stored is the *file server.*

When data is accessed from the file server, a copy of that data is stored, or *cached,* on the client system, so that the client can read and modify it. Modified data is then written back to the file server. An obvious problem arises when multiple clients attempt to access and modify the same data. One solution to this problem is to force the file server to keep track of clients and their cached data. DCE DFS uses a set of *tokens* to keep track of cached information. The tokens are allocated to a client by a server when the client caches the data based on the type of access the client requested. For data modification, a client must request a *write token* from the server. Once the write token is allocated, the server can inform other clients that the write token is issued. If other clients had the same data allocated and cached to them for read purposes, they will be notified that their data is no longer current, and the server can revoke their tokens.

DCE DFS provides the following advanced DFS features:

- *Access security and protection.* While original UNIX systems were notorious for their weak security, DCE DFS implements enforced security by supporting both user *authentication* (Kerberos system allows clients to exchange encrypted information with the authentication server, so that clients carry Kerberos tickets that in effect prove that a client is who he or she claims to be) and an *access control list* mechanism for awarding file access to authorized clients.

- *Data reliability.* While distributed systems theoretically allow elimination of the single point of failure, improperly designed distributed systems may force a single client to rely on a number of critical resources, loss of any one of which would result in the client's inability to continue processing. To prevent this problem, DCE DFS supports *replication* for all its network services. If one of the servers becomes unavailable, a client is automatically switched over to one of the replicated servers.

- *Data availability.* DCE DFS allows the system administrator to perform routine maintenance (such as data backup and file movement) on network resources without bringing the network or any of its servers down.

- *Performance.* DCE DFS is an efficient, extensible system. By caching file status information and data on a client system, DFS reduces the number of data requests from clients, thus reducing a server and network's workload.

- *Manageability.* DCE DFS uses distributed databases to keep track of file location, authentication, and access control lists used by both clients and servers. These databases are broken into separately administered and maintained domains that can be accessed by any client. In addition, these databases are self-configuring and easy to operate.

- *Standards conformance.* DCE DFS conforms with the IEEE POSIX 1003.1 file system semantics standard.

- *Interoperability with Network File System (NFS).* DCE DFS provides gateways that allow clients using NFS to interoperate with DCE DFS servers, thus providing a migration path from NFS to DCE DFS.

DCE DFS is based on the Andrew File System from Transarc Corporation. It differs from Sun's Network File System (NFS), a current de facto standard, in these two main categories:

- DFS uses global file space (all network users see the same paths to accessible files). Global file names ensure uniform file access from any network node via a *uniform name space*; in NFS, each network node has a different view of the file space.

- DFS provides integrated support for both local- and wide-area networks; NFS was designed primarily to operate in a local-area network environment.

Directory service. Computer networks, like people, require names and directories to describe, record, and find the characteristics of the various services and information they provide. Like a real mail system, an electronic mail system must be able to locate a user's mailbox in order to deliver the mail.

In a distributed computing environment, the mail delivery application will contact a directory or name services application to look up the user's name and location (address). In the DCE, anything that can be named and accessed individually (e.g., network services, electronic mailboxes, computers) is called an *object*. Each object has a corresponding listing (an *entry*) in the directory service. Each entry contains *attributes* that describe the object. Name entries are collected into lists called *directories*. In the DCE, directories can be organized into hierarchies in which a directory can contain other directories. An example of such a hierarchy is an international telephone listing that contains directories of individual countries.

The name and directory services are central to DCE. That is because all DCE objects are defined by their names, and applications and services gain access to objects by accessing an appropriate directory entry and retrieving its attributes. Thus, object characteristics are separated (decoupled) from the object itself, and, most importantly, the *location independence* of objects is ensured. Such an organization allows applications and services to access objects even if the object moves or changes several of its attributes. The DCE Directory Service is integrated with the other DCE components, including DCE DFS, and possesses the same advanced characteristics (security, reliability, availability, manageability, performance) as the DCE DFS.

The DCE Directory Service is designed to participate in the CCITT's and ISO's (International Standards Organization) Open Systems Interconnection (OSI) X.500 worldwide directory service. Local DCE users can be tied into X.500 directory service, and conversely users in other parts of the world are allowed to access local names via X.500. To implement this feature, DCE supplies naming gateways called *global directory agents,* or *GDAs.*

In a client/server DCE environment, a local client in one part of the DCE network (in one domain) that needs to look up the name of a remote client sends its request to a local GDA residing on a name server. The GDA on that server forwards the request to the worldwide X.500 service, which looks up a name and returns the result to the GDA, which in turn passes it back to its client.

To ensure portability and interoperability, and to isolate application programmers from the details of the underlying services, the OSF DCE uses a service-independent application programming interface (API). This API is based on the X/Open Directory Services (XDS) API specifications. Applications that use XDS can work with the DCE Directory Service and with X.500 without modifications.

Remote procedure calls. Remote procedure call (RPC) syntax, semantics, and presentation services represent the extension of high-level language subroutine calls. RPCs allow the actual code of the called procedure to reside and be executed on a physically remote processor in a manner transparent to the application. The RPC mechanism is the most critical aspect of the entire DCE architecture—it acts as the glue that holds all DCE components together.

The basis of the OSF DCE RPC is HP/Apollo's Network Computing System (NCS) Version 2.0 remote procedure call. DCE's RPCs are easy to use, are designed to be transparent to various network architectures, and support threads (described below).

Threads services. A typical network computing environment achieves its goals by linking all participating processors. Therefore, opportunities exist to implement a certain degree of parallel processing. Among many strategies in existence to implement the parallel processing code, the OSF selected the threads strategy for its distributed computing environment. The threads strategy uses subprocesses (threads) that exist and operate within a single instance of the executing program and its address space. The program itself can use special synchronization tools, such as semaphores, to control access to a common, modifiable resource shared by several users (e.g., memory variable).

Of course, there are many other methods of implementing parallel processing (i.e., shared memory among multiple programs, or use of explicit synchronization verbs to exchange messages among several programs). However, these methods usually involve resources external to the program. DEC's Concert Multithread Architecture (CMA) is the foundation of DCE's threads services. It offers portability and supports the POSIX 1003 application and system services interface specification.

Time services. The function of the time services component is to synchronize the clocks of all network nodes with the clock that controls the network as a whole. Due to its completeness and simplicity, OSF selected DEC's distributed time synchronization service.

The result—DCE client/server model. OSF DCE is designed to fit into the client/server paradigm. Therefore, DCE components must be present on the service requester, DCE client, and the service provider, DCE server (see Fig. 21.7). DCE is not simply a software package that can be installed on a server. In fact, DCE components are placed "between" applications and networking services on both the client and the server. Even though DCE is a multilayered architecture containing a number of basic services, the DCE client/server model hides actual details of these services from end users.

Essentially, DCE components represent an integral part of the distributed computing model being developed by such standards bodies as ISO (International Standards Organization).

DCE services are complementary to the services provided by Sybase's client/server products. Sybase's products provide higher-level distributed application building blocks than DCE; this allows Sybase to take advantage of the services DCE provides.

System 10 Client-Library provided support for running in a DCE threaded environment. This support to the XA Interface to the SQL Server is required since some of the transaction monitors run in a DCE threaded environment. Sybase also plans to use DCE threads in Server-Library (distributed with Open Server).

The DCE directory service will be made available to Open Client and Open Server applications. The DCE directory will be supported

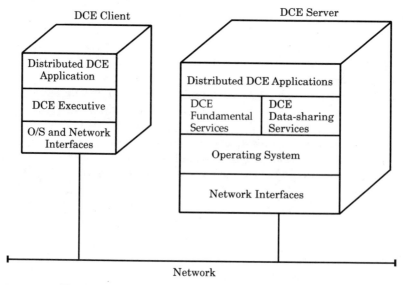

Figure 21.7 The DCE client/server model.

as a replacement for the *interfaces* files on platforms that provide DCE. This will allow new and existing Open Client and Open Server applications to take advantage of centralized DCE directory services.

DCE's Distributed Time Services will be made available through the existing CS-Library time services API. Applications using this API will automatically be provided access to this service in a DCE environment.

Open Client and Open Server will provide APIs to access the authentication and authorization services provided by DCE. This will allow Open Client and Open Server applications to be built that can take advantage of these services. Existing Open Client and Open Server applications will be able to take advantage of the DCE authentication service without changes. The integration with the authorization service will be transparent to existing applications.

The RPC service provided by DCE is a static binding model. All RPC return results must be defined at compilation time. This makes DCE RPCs unsuitable for providing access to database management systems where a single RPC may return a run-time-determined number of results. SYBASE's database RPC provides complete support for returning database results.

However, the use of DCE RPCs to communicate between client and server for other distributed application services is very powerful. To facilitate this use, Sybase will not exclude the use of DCE RPCs between clients built on Open Client and servers built on Open Server. This will allow application programs to use the appropriate mechanism for the distributed application being built.

21.3.2 Wireless communications

Sybase is closely following the progress of handheld devices that use wireless communication channels. These devices have the characteristic of being connected to a network for short periods of time. This characteristic makes client/server communication services that rely on reliable connection-oriented transport services inappropriate for this class of devices. Store-and-forward messaging technologies are being investigated as an answer to providing communication services to these devices.

SYBASE Replication Server already provides store-and-forward technology for data replication between servers. One possibility is to extend the Replication Server to provide support for client store-and-forward services. This would allow a client's wireless device to issue queries and pick up the results at some later time without maintaining a continuous transport connection.

21.3.3 Multimedia

The incorporation of multimedia data types such as image, graphics, video, and audio into SYBASE's client/server architecture is ongoing. System 10 Open Client and Open Server products have added support for variable-length long character and binary data types. These data types can be used by Open Client and Open Server applications to transfer BLOBs between clients and servers. However, this is only a small step toward multimedia support.

21.3.4 Object transport system

This section provides an overview of ObjectCONNECT for OLE and how it works. ObjectCONNECT can be used to create an OLE Automation-enabled application that accesses relational data stored in Sybase SQL Server or SQL Anywhere databases.

By treating relational data as objects, different OLE-enabled applications can access data stored in relational databases, without regard to how the data is actually stored and managed. Objects and the rows of data in relational database tables both store information about real-world entities, such as trades, employees, or sales. They differ in that objects consist of not only data but also information about the operations, called *methods,* that can be performed on the data.

Objects are, in some senses, self-contained programs. For example, a typical ObjectCONNECT object can retrieve data from a related object when it is asked to update an attribute that maps to a foreign key in its relational implementation. In the relational model, however, all the operations that can be performed on the data execute external to the data. One advantage of this method is that OLE-enabled applications that cannot access relational data directly have access to objects that map to relational data. In effect, ObjectCONNECT for OLE *publishes* the data to which different applications may *subscribe.*

ObjectCONNECT for OLE services. ObjectCONNECT for OLE is software that connects an OLE Automation-enabled application and a Sybase RDBMS. In an ObjectCONNECT for OLE environment, objects that map to relational data are created and made available to object-oriented applications at run time. These objects store data locally, making data access more efficient, and include the procedures that perform operations on the back-end data store, such as INSERTs, UPDATEs, DELETEs, and queries.

The services that make up ObjectCONNECT for OLE are

- Object and relation mapping methods
- The ObjectCONNECT for OLE Automation Server

- Repositories
- Repository manager tool
- Object services

Figure 21.8 illustrates the ObjectCONNECT for OLE services, which are layered on Client-Library for SQL Server access and on ODBC for SQL Anywhere access. An OLE Automation-enabled application sends a request through OLE to the ObjectCONNECT for OLE Automation Server. The server guarantees that the appropriate operations take place, based on mapping information stored in the repositories, which reside on the database server. Information stored in the database can thus be updated and retrieved as required.

A graphical management tool called the *repository manager* is used to map object interfaces to relational database tables. Applications built using development tools such as PowerBuilder or Visual Basic create objects from these interfaces. Interface information is stored in *repositories* on the database server. Because the information is stored

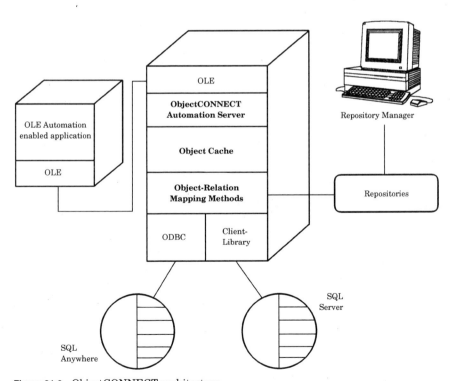

Figure 21.8   ObjectCONNECT architecture.

in repositories, applications do not need to know the physical implementation of the database.

12.3.5 PowerSoft Optima++

Optima++ is a rapid application development (RAD) tool that will enable developers to use the C++ language for building client/server and Internet applications. Optima++ will leverage the successful technology found in other PowerSoft products including PowerBuilder, Watcom C/C++, and SYBASE SQL Anywhere.

Optima++ will address the increasing demand for high-performance, component-based application development tools and will enable developers to create powerful and efficient C++ applications without a steep learning curve. Optima++ is based on a component-centric architecture that will allow developers to leverage OLE and native component technology to quickly build custom applications. A drag-and-drop programming approach will enable developers to use Optima++ to create native 32-bit C++ applications that use the new user interface controls and operating system features of Windows 95 and Windows NT. Applications can be deployed as a single executable program (EXE) or with dynamic link libraries (DLLs).

Based on Watcom C/C++ technology, Optima++ will deliver native 32-bit executables with highly optimized code. For client/server application development, Optima++ will include PowerBuilder technology, including the DataWindow, DataPipeline, and InfoMaker. As a key part of the Sybase web works architecture for the development and deployment of business applications on the Internet, Optima++ will enable users to develop Internet client and server applications as well as Sun Java applets, Microsoft OLE sweeper controls, and Netscape browser plug-ins.

21.4   System 11 Connectivity

The Sybase System 11 Connectivity release includes Open Client, Open Server, and Embedded SQL. This product suite provides a set of connectivity interfaces, tools, and products for connecting various client devices to servers of all types. Many types of data sources can be linked to client applications, including SQL Server, real-time data feeds, flat files, legacy mainframe applications, query tools, and non-Sybase databases. The most significant new feature of the System 11 release is the addition of distributed services support.

The distributed services functionality included with Release 11 consists of directory support and security services in Open Client and Open Server. Support for each distributed service is detailed in Tables 21.1 and 21.2.

TABLE 21.1   Directory Services

Operating system	Service
Windows 3.1	Banyan
Windows NT	Microsoft Registry
Windows 95	Microsoft Registry
Sun Solaris	DCE
HP UX	DCE
IBM AIX 4.1	DCE

TABLE 21.2   Security Services

Operating system	Service
Windows 3.1	LAN Manager
Windows NT	LAN Manager
Windows 95	LAN Manager
Sun Solaris	DCE
HP UX	DCE
IBM AIX 4.1	DCE

21.4.1   Open Client/Open Server

The following new features are supported in the System 11 Open Client software:

- Thread safe.   This enables the development of multithreaded Client-Library applications.

- Performance.   Client-Library performance should be better than or equal to that of DB-Library applications.

- Persistent binds.   Batch applications are accelerated by allowing binds to be reused many times.

Other enhancements to the System 11 Open Client/Open Server release include

- Configuration services
- Directory services
- Security services

Configuration services.   The Open Client/Open Server software must have specific services to function correctly. Configuration is the process of setting up a system to make this information available. Open Client and Open Server programs use configuration information to initialize the application and make a connection to a server.

The initialization process includes the following tasks:

1. Determine the SYBASE home directory.

2. Determine the character set and language used by the application.

3. Load the appropriate directory driver, security driver, and network (Net-Library) driver.

Clients and servers communicate via a connection. For a client to be able to connect to a server, the server application must be listening for the client's connection request. Establishing a connection to a server encompasses these tasks:

1. Determine the target server, using the DSQUERY environment variable.

2. Retrieve the target server's address from the *interfaces* file or from a directory service (such as DCE).

To listen for client connection requests, Open Server

1. Determines the name of the Open Server application using the DSLISTEN environment variable.

2. Retrieves the application's address from the *interfaces* file or from a directory service.

Directory services. Client-Library and Open Server (note the omission of DB-Library) can both use a directory service to maintain information about servers. A directory service manages the creation, modification, and retrieval of information about network entities. The advantage of using a directory service is that the system administrator does not need to maintain multiple *interfaces* files when a new server is added to the network, or when a server address is changed. Unix platforms can use the Cell Directory Services (CDS) provided by the distributed computing environment.

For Open Client and Open Server to use a directory service, the directory service must contain information about servers. To that end, Sybase provides a new utility called DSCP which is used to add or modify information in a directory service. A directory service identifies a server entry as a *directory object.* A directory object has a unique set of *attributes,* including

■ Server object version

- Server name
- Class of service—the default value is SQL Server
- Server status
- Transport address
- Security mechanisms

Open Client and Open Server software uses a *directory driver* to retrieve information from a directory service. A directory driver is a Sybase library which provides a generic interface to a directory service. Sybase provides a directory driver for each supported directory service.

Security services.   Client-Library and Open Server can use security services provided by third-party security software to authenticate users and to protect data transmitted between machines on the network. Sybase defines a security mechanism as external software that provides security services for a connection. Unix platforms can use the security mechanism provided by the distributed computing environment.

Sybase provides *security drivers* that enable Client-Library and Open Server to communicate with the security mechanism. Each Sybase security driver maps a generic interface to the security provider's interface. Each security mechanism provides a set of *security services*. These services are used for establishing a secure connection between a client and a server. Security services can be divided into two categories: authentication services and per-packet security services.

Object-oriented.   The System 10/11 Open Server and Open Client products can be used with C++ class libraries. Sybase is investigating the best way to provide object-oriented interfaces to these libraries.

21.4.2   Embedded SQL

Enhancements to the System 11 precompilers include

- Dynamic SQL—use of dynamic descriptors (SQLDA).
- Persistent binding for variables.
- Optional use of the Open Client/Open Server configuration file to handle the connection to the server, by specifying a precompiler option.
- Manipulation of text and image data types within Embedded SQL programs.
- Sybase extensions—support for the *deallocate cursor* statement and the *exit* statement. The *exit* statement closes Client-Library and deallocates all Embedded SQL resources allocated to programs.

Access method   A method used to move data between the main storage and peripheral devices (e.g., I/O devices such as tapes and disks). Access can be *sequential* (records are accessed one after another in the order they appear in the file), *random* (individual records can be referred to in any order), or *dynamic* (both sequential access and random access are allowed).

Ad hoc query   An unplanned query that is given to a data server. The contents of the query are not known when the database is designed and optimized.

Advanced Interactive eXecutive (AIX)   IBM's version of the Unix operating system.

Advanced Peer-to-Peer Networking (APPN)   Data communication support that routes data in a network between two or more APPC systems that are not directly attached.

Advanced Program-to-Program Communications (APPC)   Peer-level data communication support, based on SNA's logical unit type 6.2 protocols.

Affinity   A process in which a certain SQL Server task runs only on a certain engine, or a certain engine runs only on a certain CPU.

Alert   An error message sent to the central network control point (e.g., SSCP) at a host system.

American National Standard Code for Information Interchange (ASCII)   The code developed by ANSI for information exchange among data processing systems, data communications systems, and associated equipment. The ASCII character set consists of 7-bit characters plus 1 bit for parity check.

American National Standards Institute (ANSI)   An organization sponsored by the Computer and Business Equipment Manufacturers Association for establishing voluntary industry standards.

API   See Application programming interface.

APPC   See Advanced Program-to-Program Communications.

Application program   (1) A program written for or by a user that performs a user's work. (2) A program used to connect and communicate with stations on a network.

Application programming interface (API)   The formally defined programming language interface between a program (system control program, licensed program) and its user; in VTAM, SPI is the interface through which a program interacts with the access method.

Application requester (AR)   In DRDA, the source of a request sent to a remote relational database management system.

Application server (AS)   In DRDA, the target of a request from an AR.

APPN   See Advanced Peer-to-Peer Networking.

Architecture-neutral distribution format (ANDF)   A way to develop and distribute software independently from the hardware architecture platform the software is intended to run on.

AS/400   Application System/400, a family of IBM's midrange computers.

Asynchronous processing   A series of operations that are done separately from the job or transaction in which they were requested.

Asynchronous transmission   In data communication, a method of transmission in which sending and receiving of data are controlled by control characters rather than by a timing sequence.

Back-end program   In CICS, a program that is initiated by the front-end program in order to support an LU6.2 conversation.

Batch   In contrast with interactive, a group of jobs to be run on a computer sequentially, with little or no operator intervention.

BCP   The SYBASE Bulk Copy Program, used to copy data into and out of database tables.

Binary large object (BLOB)   Very large (possibly several gigabytes in size) binary representation of an image data type.

Binary synchronous communications (BSC)   A data communications line protocol that uses a standard set of transaction control characters and control line character sequences to send binary-coded data over a communication line. Contrast with synchronous data link control.

Bind   A request to activate a session between two logical units.

Blocked   A task that is blocked is prevented from executing because another task or activity stands in its way. For example, if one task holds an exclusive lock on some data, when another task tries to acquire a lock on the data, it is said to be blocked by the first task.

Boundary function   In SNA, (1) the capability of a subarea node to provide protocol support for adjacent peripheral nodes, such as transforming network addresses to local addresses, performing session sequence numbering, and providing session-level pacing support; and (2) a component that provides these capabilities.

Bridge A means (device) of connecting two similar environments at relatively low protocol levels (such as two LANs at the logical link level).

Buffer A portion of storage for temporarily holding input or output data.

Buffer replacement Algorithm to reuse buffers in the data cache.

Cache Memory area used to buffer recently used data.

Cache hit When the server finds required data in cache memory, it is called a cache hit.

Cache hit rate The percentage of time that data is found in the cache.

Cache miss When the server does not find required data in cache memory, it is called a cache miss.

Channel A path along which signals can be sent, e.g., System/390 data channels.

Channel-attached Descriptive of a device directly attached to the computer channel.

Check constraint A check constraint ensures that a data item is in the correct format. A check constraint is similar to a rule.

CICS (Customer Information Control System) A teleprocessing and transaction management system which runs as a VTAM application.

Client A system entity (combination of hardware and software components) which requests particular services to be done on its behalf from another entity—a server.

Cluster controller A channel-attached or link-attached device that can control the input/output operations of more than one device connected to it (e.g., IBM 3174).

Clustered index An index on a table in which the data rows are physically ordered by the order of the index.

Commit A process that causes the changes to the protected resources to become permanent. See also Sync point.

Communication controller Communication hardware that operates under the control of the network control program (NCP) and manages communication lines, cluster controllers, workstations, and routing of data through the network.

Complex instruction set computing (CISC) As opposed to RISC (reduced instruction set computing), a computer system architecture that utilizes a relatively large set of complex instructions where each instruction requires more than one CPU cycle to execute. Modern CISC designs incorporate some of the performance enhancements seen in RISC chips.

Composite index An index built using more than one column of the table.

Configuration block The first block of the *master* device. The "config block" is used to store SQL Server configuration information. System 10 and earlier versions of SQL Server use the configuration block to store serverwide configuration data. The System 11 SQL Server stores a small amount of information in the configuration block.

Configuration file   The System 11 SQL Server uses a configuration file to store configuration information. The configuration file is stored in the SYBASE home directory and can be modified by using a text editor.

Configurator   In SYBASE MPP, a tool used for up-front planning and ongoing management of the SYBASE MPP configuration.

Congestion   An overload condition caused by traffic in excess of the network's capabilities.

Control server   A component of SYBASE MPP that acts as a front-end request processor.

Conversation   The logical connection between a pair of transaction programs for serially sharing a session between two type 6.2 logical units. Conversations are delimited by brackets to gain exclusive use of a session.

CORBA (Common Object Request Broker Architecture)   An architecture developed by the Object Management Group (OMG) to provide portability and interoperability of objects over a network of heterogeneous systems. CORBA defines an object-oriented switching mechanism, Object Request Broker, for the messages passed between objects.

Correlated subquery   A subquery that refers to tables and columns from the outer query.

CS-Library   A library of routines that are useful to both client and server applications. All Client-Library programs will include at least one call to CS-Library. Client-Library is included with both the Open Client and Open Server products.

CT-Library   A call-level interface also used to write client applications. Client-Library is designed to accommodate cursors and other advanced features in the SYBASE System 10 and System 11 product line. Advanced programming features such as asynchronous programming and callback events are supported. Connection processing and error message handling have all been improved (over DB-Library).

Cursor   A database cursor is a mechanism for accessing the results of an SQL SELECT statement, one row at a time.

Database cursor   A mechanism for accessing the results of an SQL SELECT statement one row at a time. Using a cursor, applications can process each row individually rather than having to process the entire set of rows returned by the SELECT.

Database device   In SYBASE, a location device that is mapped to a raw disk partition or an operating system file.

Database management system (DBMS)   A software system that controls and manages the data to eliminate data redundancy and to ensure data integrity, consistency, and availability, among other features.

Database mirroring   DBMS capability to maintain a duplicate of the database and transaction log, each on separate devices.

Data cache A memory area used to hold copies of data and index pages.

Data channel A device that connects a processor and main storage with I/O control units.

Data definition language (DDL) A part of the structured query language (SQL) that consists of the commands responsible for the creation and deletion of database objects.

Data manipulation language (DML) A part of the structured query language (SQL) that consists of the operators responsible for the data manipulation (e.g., SELECT, DELETE, INSERT, UPDATE).

Data page A page of a database used to hold data from a table.

Data Server Interface (DSI) An Open Client connection from a Replication Server to a *dataserver* that maps to a connection.

Data stream A continuous stream of defined format data elements being transmitted, or intended to be transmitted.

DBCC The SYBASE Database Consistency Checker, used to ensure database integrity.

DB-Library A call-level interface used to write SYBASE client applications. DB-Library includes a bulk-copy library and a special two-phase commit library.

Default A value given to a column when no value is supplied.

Deferred update Deferred updates are used by SQL Server for processing SQL, which may have a cascading effect, thus causing rows to appear twice. A deferred update is performed by deleting and then inserting the data. SQL Server first logs the change before applying the change to the table.

Definite response A protocol that directs the receiver of the request to unconditionally return a positive or negative response to that request.

Demand lock A demand lock prevents any more shared locks from being set so that a write transaction can proceed. Demand locks are used to avoid a situation where read transactions acquire overlapping shared locks on a table or page, so that a write transaction is blocked from acquiring an exclusive lock.

Digital Network Architecture (DNA) A network architecture developed by Digital Equipment Corporation.

Direct memory access (DMA) A disk controller with direct memory access can bypass the computer's CPU to access the memory directly. When a controller does not have direct memory access, the CPU is responsible for reading and writing information.

Directory services Services for resolving user identifications of network components to network routing information.

Direct update A direct update, also referred to as an *update in place*, occurs when an update changes the data in a table directly, as opposed to a physical delete followed by an insert. Because of reduced overhead, direct updates are much faster than deferred updates.

Distributed computing environment (DCE)   The standards-based environment developed by the Open Software Foundation (OSF) that provides interoperability and portability across heterogeneous distributed systems.

Distributed data management (DDM)   An architecture that allows application programs or users on one system to access data stored on remote systems.

Distributed management environment (DME)   A standards-based computing environment proposed by the OSF that provides distributed management solution for the DCE.

Distributed Relational Database Architecture (DRDA)   A connection architecture developed by IBM to provide access to relational databases distributed across various (IBM) platforms.

Distributed request   An extension of the distributed-unit-of-work (DUW) method of accessing distributed relational data where a single SQL statement may reference data residing in different systems; distributed request support includes unions and joins across distributed DBMSs.

Distributed transaction processing (DTP)   A type of transaction processing that is characterized by synchronous communication between partners, accomplished via LU 6.2 protocols.

Distributed unit of work (DUW)   A method of accessing distributed relational data where each SQL statement may reference only one system location, but the unit of work may consist of several SQL statements that can read and write data from several distributed DBMSs.

Duplex   Simultaneous two-way independent data transmission in both directions.

Duplicate key   A key column which allows many copies of the same value in the column.

Engine   A process running an SQL Server that communicates with the other SQL Server processes via shared memory. An engine can be thought of as one CPU's worth of processing power. It does not represent a particular CPU.

Ethernet   LAN architecture that uses CSMA/CD for the media access control.

Event callback model   A presentation logic technique used in some graphical user interface (GUI) routines to handle events.

Event control block (ECB)   A control block used to represent the status of an event.

Event loop model   A presentation logic technique used in some graphical user interface routines to handle events.

Exception response   A protocol that directs the receiver to return a response only if the request is unacceptable or cannot be processed.

Exclusive lock   One and only one transaction can have an exclusive lock on a page, thus preventing other tasks from accessing the same data.

Exit routine   Special-purpose user-written routine.

Fiber distributed data interchange (FDDI) High-performance networking standard based on the token-passing technique used on fiber-optic cable.

fillfactor Variable used to set the percentage to which index and clustered data pages are filled during initial creation and loading.

Finite-state machine An architectural entity that can be placed in a limited number of defined states as a result of applying allowed input sequences.

Flow control The process of managing the rate at which data traffic passes through a network.

Formatted Data Object Content Architecture (FD:OCA) A collection of constructs designed to interchange formatted data.

Front-end program In CICS, a program that is responsible for starting an LU 6.2 conversation with the back-end program.

Function shipping A CICS facility that allows certain CICS functions, requested in one CICS system, to access resources on another, remote CICS system.

General data stream (GDS) Data and commands that are defined by length and identification bytes.

Graphical user interface (GUI) An interface used by display workstations to interface with end users, which provides a consistent API and a standard look and feel. Microsoft's Windows, OSF's Motif, Sun's Open Look, and OS/2 Presentation Manager are some of the most popular GUIs.

Group commit A group commit occurs when SQL Server consolidates several transactions into a single write to the transaction log.

Index covering Index covering occurs when SQL Server uses only a nonclustered index to return data for a query. A covered query does not need to read the actual data rows, therefore requiring a small percentage of the page I/O required for a table scan.

Index page A page of a database used to hold data from an index.

Infected A task that has received an unexpected signal or is in an unknown state is referred to as an *infected process*. SQL Server usually prints a stack trace to the error log when a task is infected.

Intent lock An intent lock is used to prevent a transaction from obtaining a shared or exclusive lock on a table having page-level locks. SQL Server applies an intent lock to a table when a shared or exclusive page lock is granted to a transaction.

Interclient definition language (IDL) A language used to define interfaces to interconnect clients and servers; examples include RPC IDL in OSF's DCE and ORB IDl in CORBA.

Internet Protocol (IP) A part of the TCP/IP protocol suite that performs data packet segmentation and routing.

Intersystem Communications In CICS, a way of providing communication between two CICS systems residing in different processors by using the ACF/VTAM access method. Contrast with CICS multiregion operations (MROs).

ISQL (Interactive Structured Query Language) SYBASE's command line interface to the SQL Server.

Join clause The part of a WHERE clause used to connect two tables using the key columns of the tables.

Layer An architectural grouping of related functions that are logically separated from the functions of the other layers.

Leaf index page The leaf level is the lowest level of an index. In a clustered index, the leaf pages are the actual data pages of the table.

Link connection The physical equipment that provides two-way communication between link stations.

Link station The combination of hardware and software that allows a node to attach to, and provide control for, a link.

Local-area network (LAN) The physical connection that allows information exchanges among devices (typically personal computers) located on the same premises.

Logical read SQL Server performs a logical read when it reads data found in the data cache rather than on database devices. A logical read is the result of a cache hit.

Logical unit (LU) A port through which an end user accesses an SNA network in order to communicate with another end user.

Logical unit of work (LUW) Work that is performed between the start of a transaction and COMMIT or ROLLBACK of the same transaction.

Log Transfer Manager (LTM) A component of SYBASE Replication Server that facilitates replication of changes throughout the replicated sites.

Loose consistency In SYBASE Replication Server, the data consistency protocol implemented via replication (contrast with tight consistency that is based on the two-phase commit protocol).

LU6.2 Logical unit type 6.2, a special type of logical unit that supports advanced program-to-program communication (APPC) between programs in a distributed processing environment. APPC/LU6.2 is characterized by peer-to-peer communication support, comprehensive end-to-end error processing, optimized data transmission flow, and a generic application programming interface.

Management services In SNA, one of the types of network services in the network control point and physical units (PUs) that provide functions for problem management, performance, accounting, configuration, and change management.

Mapped conversation In APPC, a type of conversation in which the data can be sent and received in a user-defined format, while the data transformation is performed by APPC/LU6.2.

Massively Parallel Processor (MPP) A computing architecture based on a distributed memory share-nothing approach.

Message unit A generic term for the unit of data processed by a communication system.

Metropolitan-area network (MAN)   A network using a city infrastructure to connect nodes within the geographic limits of a city.

Microsecond   One-millionth of a second.

Middleware   A generic term that defines a set of run-time software services designed to insulate clients and servers from the knowledge of environment-specific communications and data access mechanisms.

Millisecond   One-thousandth of a second.

Motif   A popular window manager selected by the Open Software Foundation for presentation management in its version of the open system environment.

Nanosecond   One-billionth of a second.

Native cursor   Cursor implemented in the database server.

Negative response   A response indicating that a request did not arrive successfully or was not processed successfully by the receiver.

NetView   An IBM product used to monitor, manage, and diagnose a network.

Network address   An address that identifies a link, a link station, or a network addressable unit.

Network affinity migration   The process of moving network I/O from one engine to another. SMP systems which support this migration allow SQL Server to distribute the network I/O load among all its engines.

Network File System (NFS)   Popular method of accessing remote file systems in a Unix system environment (developed by Sun Microsystems).

Network operating system (NOS)   A generic term for the operating-system-level software used to manage and control networks.

Node   An endpoint of a link, or a junction common to two or more links.

Nonclustered index   The leaf pages of a nonclustered index contain pointers to the data pages. Data rows are not physically ordered by a nonclustered index.

Nonleaf index pages   Nonleaf index pages are intermediate pages of an index that are not the lowest level of the index. These pages contain page pointers to the next level of the index.

Object   A named unit that consists of a set of characteristics that are encapsulated within the object and describe the object and data; certain characteristics of an object are inherited from its "parents" and can be inherited by its "children"; operations valid for the object are stored together with the object as its methods; in computer architecture, an object can be anything that exists in and occupies space in storage (e.g., programs, files, libraries) and on which operations can be performed.

Object Request Broker (ORB)   A key component of CORBA, an object-oriented message-switching mechanism designed to provide portability and interoperability of objects over a network of heterogeneous systems.

Open Look   A popular window manager that is used primarily by the members of Unix International (UI).

Open Network Computing (ONC)   Unix International's architecture for an open distributed computing environment.

Open Software Foundation (OSF)   Not-for-profit technology organization that intends to develop and promote an open computing environment by selecting technology solutions from its members.

Open systems interconnection (OSI)   A layered architecture that is designed to allow for interconnection between heterogeneous systems.

OS/2 (Operating System/2)   A multiprogramming, multitasking operating system, developed for the PS/2 family of personal computers.

Pacing   A technique by which a receiver controls the rate of transmission by the sender.

Packet   A data transmission information unit, consisting of a group of data and control characters.

Packet switching   The process of routing and transferring data by means of addressed packets.

Page   The smallest unit of allocation in an SQL Server database. Pages are 2K on most hardware platforms.

Page lock   A lock on a database page.

Paging   Moving parts of an application or process out to secondary storage (swap space). This provides a computer with limited memory with the ability to simulate a computer with more memory.

Parallel sessions   Two or more concurrently active sessions between two logical units using different pairs of network addresses.

Physical memory   The main memory of a computer.

Physical read   When SQL Server does not find data in the data cache, it must read the data from the appropriate database device. This is referred to as a physical read.

Pipelining   A fundamental implementation technique used in RISC architectures. Pipelining allows more than one instruction to be processed at the same time.

Positive response   A response indicating that a request has been successfully processed.

Prefix   The prefix of an index refers to the leading columns of a composite index built on multiple columns.

Presentation Manager (OS/2 PM)   An OS/2 component that provides graphical API.

Procedure cache   The procedure cache holds internal structures for rules, stored procedures, and triggers, i.e., anything that is compiled.

Process   In SYBASE, an execution environment scheduled onto physical CPUs by the operating system.

Protocol boundary   A synonym for the architecturally defined application program interface.

Queuing A store-and-forward communication mechanism often employed by messaging middleware.

RAS programs Reliability, availability, and serviceability programs that facilitate problem determination.

Reduced-instruction-set computing (RISC) As opposed to CISC (complex-instruction-set computing), a computer system architecture that utilizes a relatively small set of computer instructions where each instruction is "simple" enough to require one CPU cycle to execute.

Referential constraint A constraint that is added by coding the primary key in a parent table and one or more foreign keys in dependent tables. Declarative referential integrity is applied by SQL Server when a violation occurs, thus aborting the statement causing the violation.

Reformatting SQL Server creates an index on a worktable to improve the performance of a query.

Relational database (RDB) A database built to conform to the relational data model; includes the catalog and all the data described therein.

Remote data access (RDA) A proposed ANSI standard to access remote relational databases.

Remote procedure call (RPC) A connectionless method of communication between two programming systems where a requester (client) issues an RPC to execute a procedure on a remote system (server).

Remote request The form of SQL distributed processing where the application runs on a system different from the one housing the RDB. Contains a single SQL statement referencing data located at a single site.

Remote unit of work (RUW) The extension of the remote request form of SQL distributed processing where multiple SQL statements may reference data located at a single remote site.

Replication Server interface (RSI) An asynchronous interface from one Replication Server to another.

Replication Server Manager (RSM) A GUI-based administration tool for managing the Replication Server system.

Replication Server system database (RSSD) The SYBASE system catalog for the Replication Server.

Rollback The process of restoring protected resources to the state at the last commit point.

Rule A rule is a user-defined integrity constraint linked to a column or data type and enforced at data entry time.

Runnable A task, in the SQL Server run queue, that is not blocked and will run the next time it is assigned to an engine.

Running A task that is currently being run by an SQL Server engine.

Scale-up Scale-up means that the user gets comparable performance on a request as the size of the database increases.

Schema server   A component of the SYBASE MPP system used to control the global directory.

Search clause   Part of a WHERE clause used to restrict the values of columns within a table.

Seek time   The amount of time required to move the head of a disk drive from one track to another.

Self-join   Join of a table with itself.

Server   A system entity (combination of hardware and software components) which performs particular services on behalf of another entity—a client.

Session   A logical connection between two network addressable units that allows them to communicate.

Session-level pacing   In SNA, a flow control technique that permits the receiver to control the data transfer rate.

Shared lock   Multiple transactions can lock a shared page. No transaction can acquire an update lock on a page that has a shared lock on it.

Shared memory   Memory that is shared by several processes running on the same host computer.

***Showplan* output**   Output produced by SQL Server after a SET *showplan* has been issued.

Sleeping   State of a task (in the SQL Server sleep queue) waiting for some resource to become available.

Small computer system interconnect (SCSI)   A standard interface for connecting peripherals (e.g., disk drives and tape drives) to computer systems.

Speed-up   The same request takes less time on the same amount of data.

Spinlock   A synchronization mechanism for mutual exclusion provided by the SQL Server kernel. It controls access to data structures shared among SQL Server engines. If a spinlock is locked, other engines attempting to access it "spin," repetitively testing the lock until it becomes available.

Split server   A component of the SYBASE MPP system used primarily to process join requests in parallel systems.

SQL Debug   Sybase's source-level debugger for Transact-SQL code.

Stored procedure   An advanced design technique employed by Sybase to allow a collection of SQL statements and flow-control directives (e.g., IF, THEN, ELSE) to be parsed, verified, compiled, bound, and stored at the DBMS server; stored procedures are invoked by client applications in a fashion similar to RPC and provide a significant performance improvement over a traditional embedded SQL.

Structured Query Language (SQL)   A standard for nonnavigational data access and the definition language used in relational databases.

Subquery   A query that appears as part of another query's WHERE clause.

Subscription   In SYBASE Replication Server, a technique that allows all or parts of data tables to be replicated to the subscribers of that data; uses **subscription resolution engine (SRE)** to match primary data with the subscription for that data.

Swapping   Swapping occurs when entire processes are copied from memory to secondary storage (e.g., disk).

SYBASE Backup Server   A component of SYBASE System 10 and System 11 designed specifically to perform backup operations. It is built using Open Server technology.

SYBASE MPP   A component of SYBASE System 11 (formerly known as Navigation Server) that is designed to provide database scalability and performance by taking advantage of SMP and MPP computing architectures.

SYBASE OmniCONNECT Gateway   Sybase's gateway product (an Open Server application) designed to provide transparent access to distributed heterogeneous databases.

SYBASE Open Client   A programmable client component (a set of library routines and the corresponding APIs like DB-Library and CT-Library) of Sybase's suite of client/server products.

SYBASE Open Server   A programmable server component of Sybase's suite of client/server products.

SYBASE Replication Server   SYBASE System 10 and System 11 component that implements and manages database replication.

SYBASE SQL Server Monitor   SYBASE System 10 and System 11 tool used to monitor SYBASE SQL Server performance.

Symmetric multiprocessing (SMP)   A computer architecture where several tightly coupled CPUs share a common memory and common workload.

Synchronization level   In APPC, the specification indicating that the conversation allows no synchronization (SYNLEVEL = NONE), supports confirmation exchanges (SYNCLEVEL = CONFIRM), or full synchronization (SYNCLEVEL = SYNCPT).

Synchronous transmission   In data communication, a method of transmission where the sending and receiving of characters are controlled by timing signals.

Sync point   (1) A point in time when all protected resources accessed by an application are consistent. (2) An LU6.2 verb that causes all changes to protected resources to become permanent, and therefore the resources are consistent. See also Commit.

Systems network architecture (SNA)   The description of the logical structure, formats, protocols, and operational sequences for transmitting information through and controlling configuration and operation of networks.

Systems Network Architecture Distributed Services (SNADS)   An IBM architecture that defines a set of rules to receive, route, and send electronic mail across networks.

Table lock   A lock granted on an entire table.

Table scan   The process of reading every row in a table.

Task   In SYBASE, an execution environment within the SQL Server scheduled onto engines by the SQL Server. Tasks are also referred to as *server processes* and *server threads*.

Terminal   In data communication, a device capable of sending and receiving information.

Terminating   Descriptive of an SQL Server task that is being killed.

Threads   A unit of context management under the control of a single process that can be implemented within the server process or via operating system services.

Threshold Manager   A feature of SYBASE System 10/11 that monitors the amount of free space available on a particular database segment and executes a predefined stored procedure when a threshold is reached.

Timesharing option (TSO)   A feature of an operating system (i.e., MVS) that provides conversational timesharing of system resources from remote stations.

Top End   A transaction monitor developed by the NCR Corporation to provide transaction management in the open systems (Unix-based) distributed environment.

TPMC   Transactions per minute measured with the Transaction Processing Council's standard benchmark, TPC-C.

TPS   Transactions per second.

Transaction   In communications, a unit of processing and information exchange between a local and a remote program that accomplishes a particular action or result.

Transaction [Processing] Monitor/Transaction Manager (TPM)   Software system that provides control and management functions to support transaction execution, synchronization, integrity, consistency, atomicity, and durability.

Transaction Processing Council (TPC)   An organization created to define industry standard benchmarks.

Transaction program (TP)   In APPC, a program that uses APPC API to communicate with a partner transaction program on a remote system.

Transaction routing   In CICS, a facility that allows CICS transactions initiated on a local CICS system to be executed on a remote CICS system.

Transact-SQL   Sybase's proprietary programming and control language.

Transfer rate   The rate at which information moves from one place to another (e.g., from a disk drive to computer memory).

Transmission Control Protocol/Internet Protocol (TCP/IP)   Communication protocol popular because of its openness and easy interoperability features.

Triggers   In a DBMS, triggers can be viewed as a special type of stored procedure that have the ability to initiate (trigger) certain user-defined actions based on a particular data-related event. Triggers are often used to implement referential integrity constraints.

Tuxedo   A transaction monitor developed by AT&T to provide transaction management in the Unix distributed environment.

Two-phase commit (2PC)   A protocol that ensures the integrity and consistency of all protected resources affected by a distributed transaction.

Uniqueness constraint   Unique key constraints are used to ensure unique values in a column. Unique constraints are implemented as unique indexes by SQL Server.

Unit of work (UOW)   The amount of processing that is executed from the time the transaction is started to the time the transaction is ended.

Update in place   Also referred to as a *direct update*. Occurs when an update changes the data in a table directly, as opposed to a physical delete followed by an insert.

Verb   In APPC, an LU6.2 command, defined in the APPC API.

Virtual server architecture   In SYBASE, consists of two or more SQL Server processes running in parallel. Virtual SQL Server starts and coordinates these parallel SQL Server processes to present a single virtual SQL Server interface and functionality.

Virtual Telecommunications Access Method (VTAM)   An IBM licensed program that controls communication and data flow in an SNA network.

Visual Instruction Set (VIS)   Used by the Sun UltraSPARC to provide an array of on-chip multimedia, graphics, and imaging technologies.

VTAM application program   A program that (1) has identified itself to VTAM by opening an ACB and (2) can issue VTAM macroinstructions.

Wide-area network (WAN)   A network connecting node located across large geographic areas.

Workstation   A terminal or personal computer at which a user can run applications.

Worktable   A temporary table created by SQL Server to hold intermediate results while processing a query.

XA interfaces   X/Open's proposed standards for the portable application programming interfaces between transaction managers and resource managers (DBMSs).

X/Open   Not-for-profit organization founded to develop standards for interoperability between unlike systems. Its specifications for system interoperability and portability are listed in the *X/Open Portability Guide* (currently in its fourth issue—XPG4).

X Window System   A distributed presentation management system developed by MIT for Unix-based environments.

Yielding   An SQL Server task that is giving up the engine to allow another task to execute.

SQL Server System Specifications

System Specifications

Hardware	
Processor	32-bit and 64-bit implementations
RAM required for SQL Server	8–10 Mbytes
Minimum RAM per additional size)	50K (with default stack size and packet connection

Database statistics	
Databases per SQL Server	32,767
Default database size	2 Mbytes
Maximum database size	$(2^{31} - 1) * 2K$
Minimum database size	2 Mbytes (default)
Creation of clustered index	Free space needed in database is 1.1 × (size of table) + 10%
Maximum size of a database device	$2^{24} * 2K$
Maximum number of database devices per server	256
Maximum number of databases per server	2,147,483,647
Maximum number of devices or device pieces per database	128

Table statistics	
User objects per database	$2^{31} - 100$
Columns per table	250
Indexes per table	250 (one clustered)
Rows per table	Limited by available storage
Maximum size of a row	1962 bytes
Columns per composite index	16
Bytes per index key	256
Characters per database object name	30

Query statistics	
Maximum number of databases participating in one transaction	8[†]
Practical number of databases participated in one query	16[‡] (dependent on available memory)
Maximum number of tables participating in a query	16[§]
Maximum number of WHERE clauses referencing a table in a query	128

System statistics	
Number of buffers and procedure caches	Configurable [¶]
Minimum memory required per stored procedure	2K
Maximum number of parameters per stored procedure	255

[†]Includes the database where the transaction began, all databases changed during the transaction, and *tempdb* if it is used for results or worktables.

[‡]Includes database where the transaction began, all databases queried during the transaction, and *tempdb* if it is used for results or worktables.

[§]Includes all worktables, results tables, tables referenced by views (the view itself is not counted), correlations, and self-joins.

[¶]Limited by the amount of RAM and maximum size of the shared-memory segment.

System table	Contents
	System Tables that Occur in All Databases
sysalternates	One row for each SQL Server user mapped to a database
sysattributes	One row for each object attribute definition (new to System 11)
syscolumns	One row for each column in a table or view and for each parameter in a procedure
syscomments	One or more rows for each view, rule, default, trigger, and procedure giving SQL definition statement
sysconstraints	One row for each referential and check constraint associated with a table or column
sysdepends	One row for each procedure, view, or table that is referenced by a procedure, view, or trigger
sysindexes	One row for each clustered or nonclustered index, one row for each table with no indexes, and an additional row for each table containing text or image data
syskeys	One row for each primary, foreign, or common key; set by user (not maintained by SQL Server)
syslabels	(Secure SQL Server only) One row for each unique label in the database unless the *syslabels* table is in the *master* database. In the *master* database, the *syslabels* table contains one row for each unique label defined in all databases
syslogs	Transaction log
sysobjects	One row for each table, view, procedure, rule, trigger, default, log, and (in *tempdb*) temporary object
syspartitions	One row for each partition (page chain) of a partitioned table (new to System 11)
sysprocedures	One row for each view, rule, default, trigger, and procedure giving internal definition
sysprotects	User permissions information

System table	Contents
	System Tables that Occur in All Databases
sysreferences	One row for each referential integrity constraint declared on a table or column
sysroles	Maps of serverwide roles to local database groups
syssegments	One row for each segment (named collection of disk pieces)
systhresholds	One row for each threshold defined for the database
systypes	One row for each system-supplied and user-defined data type
sysusermessages	One row for each user-defined message
sysusers	One row for each user allowed in database
	System Tables that Occur in the *master* Database Only
syscharsets	One row for each character set or sort order
sysconfigures	One row for each user-settable configuration parameter
syscurconfigs	Information about configuration parameters currently being used by SQL Server
sysdatabases	One row for each database on SQL Server
sysdevices	One row for each tape dump device, disk dump device, disk for databases, and disk partition for databases
sysengines	One row for each SQL Server engine currently on line
syslanguages	One row for each language (except U.S. English) known to the SQL Server
syslocks	Information about active locks
sysloginroles	One row for each server log-in that possesses a system-defined role
syslogins	One row for each valid SQL Server user account
syslogshold	Information about the oldest active transaction and the Replication Server truncation point for each database (new to System 11)
sysmessages	One row for each system error or warning
sysprocesses	Information about SQL Server processes
sysremotelogins	One row for each remote user
syssrvroles	One row for each serverwide role
sysservers	One row for each remote SQL Server
sysusages	One row for each disk piece allocated to a database
	System Tables that Occur in the *sybsecurity* Database Only
sysaudits	One row for each audit record
sysauditoptions	One row for each global audit option

Appendix

D

System Stored Procedures

Procedure name	Description
sp_addalias	Maps one user to another in a database.
sp_addauditrecord	Allows user to enter user-defined audit records (comments) into the audit trail.
sp_addgroup	Adds a user group to a database.
sp_addlanguage	Defines an alternate language for the server and adds it to *master.dbo.syslanguages*.
sp_addlogin	Adds a new user account to SQL Server.
sp_addmessage	Adds user-defined messages to the *sysusermessages* table for use by store-procedure PRINT and RAISERROR calls and *sp_bindmsg*.
sp_addremotelogin	Authorizes a new remote server user by adding an entry to *master.dbo.sysremotelogins*.
sp_addsegment	Defines a database segment in the database device in the current database.
sp_addserver	Defines a remote server, or defines the name of the local server.
sp_addthreshold	Creates a free-space threshold to monitor the space remaining in a database segment. When free space on the segment falls below the specified levels, SQL Server executes the associated stored procedure.
sp_addtype	Creates a user-defined datatype.
sp_addumpdevice	Adds a dump device to SQL Server.
sp_adduser	Adds a new user to the current database.
sp_auditdatabase	Establishes auditing of different types of events within a database or of references to objects within that database from another database.
sp_auditlogin	Audits an SQL Server user's attempts to access tables and views; audits the text of a user's command batches; lists users on which auditing is enabled; gives the auditing status of the user; displays the status of table, view, or command text auditing.

537

Procedure name	Description
sp_auditobject	Establishes auditing of accesses to tables and views.
sp_auditoption	Enables and disables systemwide auditing and global audit options, and reports on the status of audit options.
sp_auditsproc	Audits the executions of stored procedures and triggers.
*sp_bindcache**	Binds a database, table, index, text, or image object to a data cache.
sp_bindefault	Binds a default to a column or user-defined data type.
sp_bindmsg	Binds a user-defined message to a referential integrity constraint or check constraint.
sp_bindrule	Binds a rule to a column or user-defined data type.
*sp_cacheconfig**	Creates, configures, reconfigures, and drops named data caches. Used to report information about named data caches.
*sp_cachestrategy**	Enables or disables large I/O (prefetching) and MRU cache replacement strategy for a table, index, text, or image object.
sp_changedbowner	Changes the owner of a database.
sp_changegroup	Changes a user's group.
*sp_checknames**	Checks the current database for names that contain characters not in the 7-bit ASCII set.
sp_checkreswords	Detects and displays identifiers that are Transact-SQL reserved words. Checks server names, user-defined data types, object names, column names, log-in names, and remote log-in names.
*sp_chgattribute**	Used to change the *max_rows_per_page* value for future space allocations of a table or index.
sp_clearstats	Initiates a new accounting period for all server users or for a selected user. Prints statistics for the previous accounting period by executing *sp_reportstats*.
sp_commonkey	Defines a common key—columns that are frequently joined—between two tables or views.
sp_configure	Displays or changes configuration variables.
sp_configurelogin	(Secure SQL Server only) Initializes the security-relevant information for a new SQL Server log-in.
sp_cursorinfo	Reports information about a specific cursor or all cursors which are active (declared by a user and allocated by SQL Server).
sp_dboption	Displays or changes database options.
sp_dbremap	Forces SQL Server to recognize changes made by alter database commands. Run this procedure only if instructed to do so by SQL Server messages.
sp_depends	Displays information about database object dependencies—the view(s), trigger(s), and procedure(s) that depend on the table or view specified, and the table(s) and view(s) that are depended on by the view, trigger, or procedure specified.

Procedure name	Description
sp_diskdefault	Sets a database device's status to *defaulton* or *defaultoff*. This indicates whether a database device can be used for database storage if the user does not specify a database device or specifies default within the *create database* or *alter database* commands.
sp_displaylogin	Displays information about a log-in account.
sp_dropalias	Removes the alias user name identity that had been established with *sp_addalias*.
sp_dropdevice	Drops an SQL Server database device or dump device.
*sp_dropglockpromote**	Removes lock promotion values from a table or database.
sp_dropgroup	Drops a user group from the database.
sp_dropkey	Removes from the *syskeys* table a key that had been defined by using *sp_primarykey*, *sp_foreignkey*, or *sp_commonkey*.
sp_droplanguage	Drops an alternate language from the server and removes its row from *master.dbo.syslanguages*.
sp_droplogin	Drops an SQL Server user account by deleting the user's entry in *master.dbo.syslogins*.
sp_dropmessage	Drops user-defined message from *sysusermessages*.
sp_dropremotelogin	Drops a remote user log-in.
sp_dropsegment	Drops a segment from a database or unmaps a segment from a particular database device.
sp_dropserver	Drops a server from the list of known servers.
sp_dropthreshold	Removes a free-space threshold from a segment.
sp_droptype	Drops a user-defined data type.
sp_dropuser	Drops a user from the current database.
sp_estspace	Estimates the amount of space required for a table and its indexes, and the time needed to create the index.
sp_extendsegment	Extends the range of a segment to another database device, or extends the current segment on the current database device.
sp_foreignkey	Defines a foreign key on a table or view in the current database.
sp_getmessage	Retrieves stored message strings from *sysmessages* and *sysusermessages* for PRINT and RAISERROR statements.
*sp_grantlogin**	Used to assign SQL Server roles or *default* permissions to Windows NT users and groups.
sp_help	Reports information about a database object (any object listed in *sysobjects*) and about SQL Server supplied or user-defined data types.
*sp_helppartition**	Lists the first page and the control page for each partition of a partitioned table.
*sp_helpcache**	Reports information about objects bound to a data cache or the amount of overhead required for a specified cache size.
sp_helpconstraint	Reports information about any integrity constraints specified for a table.

Procedure name	Description
sp_helpdb	Reports information about a particular database or about all databases.
sp_helpdevice	Reports information about a particular device or about all SQL Server database and dump devices.
sp_helpgroup	Reports information about a particular group or about all groups in the database.
sp_helpindex	Reports information about indexes created on a table.
sp_helpjoins	Lists the columns in two tables or views that are likely join candidates.
sp_helpkey	Reports information about a primary, foreign, or common key of a particular table or view, or about all keys in the current database.
sp_helplanguage	Reports information about a particular alternate language or about all languages.
sp_helplog	Reports the name of the device that contains the first page of the log.
sp_helpremotelogin	Reports information about a particular remote server's log-ins or about all remote servers' log-ins.
sp_helpprotect	Reports on permissions for database objects, users, or groups.
sp_helpsegment	Reports information about a particular segment or about all the segments in the current database.
sp_helpserver	Reports information about a particular remote server or about all remote servers.
sp_helpsort	Displays SQL Server's default sort order and character set.
sp_helptext	Prints the text of a system procedure, trigger, view, default, rule, or integrity check constraint.
sp_helpthreshold	Reports the segment, free-space value, status, and stored procedure associated with all thresholds in the current database or all thresholds for a particular segment.
sp_helpuser	Reports information about a particular user or about all users in the current database.
sp_indsuspect	Check user tables for indexes that have been marked as suspect during recovery following a sort order change.
sp_lock	Reports information about processes that currently hold locks.
sp_locklogin	Locks an SQL Server account so that the user cannot log in, or displays a list of all locked accounts.
sp_logdevice	Puts the system table *syslogs,* which contains the transaction log, on a separate database device.
*sp_loginconfig**	Reports the value of one or all integrated security parameters.
*sp_logininfo**	Reports all roles granted to Windows NT users and groups via *sp_grantlogin.*
*sp_logiosize**	Used to change the log I/O size used by the SQL Server to a different memory pool when performing I/O for the transaction log of the current database.

Procedure name	Description
sp_modifylogin	Modifies an SQL Server log-in's default database, default language, or full name.
sp_modifythreshold	Modifies a threshold by associating it with a different threshold procedure, level of free space, or segment. The sp_modifythreshold procedure can change the name of the stored procedure associated with the log segment's last-chance threshold, but cannot change that segment's amount of free space or the segment name.
sp_monitor	Displays statistics about SQL Server.
sp_password	Adds or changes a password for an SQL Server log-in account.
sp_placeobject	Puts future space allocations for a table or index on a particular segment.
sp_primarykey	Defines a primary key on a table or view.
sp_poolconfig*	Used to create, drop, resize, and report information about memory pools within named data caches.
sp_procqmode*	Displays the query processing mode of a stored procedure, view, or trigger.
sp_procxmode	Displays or changes the transaction modes associated with stored procedures.
sp_recompile	Causes each stored procedure and trigger that uses the named table to be recompiled the next time it runs.
sp_remap	Remaps a Release 4.8 or later stored procedure, trigger, rule, default, or view to be compatible with 10.0. Use sp_remap on objects that the Release 10.0 upgrade procedure failed to remap.
sp_remoteoption	Displays or changes remote log-in options.
sp_rename	Changes the name of a user-created object in the current database.
sp_renamedb	Changes the name of a database.
sp_reportstats	Reports statistics on system usage.
sp_revokelogin*	Used to revoke SQL Server roles and default permissions from Windows NT users and groups.
sp_role	Grants or revokes roles to an SQL Server log-in account.
sp_serveroption	Displays or changes remote server options.
sp_setlangalias	Assigns or changes the alias for an alternate language.
sp_spaceused	Displays the number of rows, number of data pages, and space used by one table or by all tables in the current database.
sp_syntax	Displays the syntax of Transact-SQL commands, system procedures, utilities, and DB-Library routines.
sp_thresholdaction	Default threshold procedure called when the log segment of a database reaches the last-chance threshold. This procedure is not supplied; it must be created by the user.
sp_trustlogin	(Secure SQL Server only) Modifies the security-relevant information for a secure SQL Server log-in account.
sp_unbindcache*	Used to unbind a database, table, index, text, or image object from a named data cache.

Procedure name	Description
*sp_unbindcache_all**	Used to unbind all objects that are bound to a named data cache.
sp_unbindefault	Unbinds a created default value from a column or from a user-defined data type.
sp_unbindmsg	Unbinds a user-defined message from a constraint.
sp_unbindrule	Unbinds a rule from a column or from a user-defined data type.
sp_volchanged	Notifies the Backup Server that the operator has performed the requested volume handling during a dump or load.
sp_who	Reports information about a particular user or about all current SQL Server users and processes.

*Introduced with SQL Server Release 11.

E

SYBASE Data Types

Data type	Synonyms	Range	Bytes of storage
tinyint		0 to 255	1
smallint		$2^{15} - 1$ (32,767) to -2^{15} (−32,768)	2
int	Integer	$2^{31} - 1$ (2,147,483,647) to -2^{31} (−2,147,483,648)	4
numeric(p, s)		$10^{38} - 1$ to -10^{38}	2 to 17
decimal(p, s)	dec	$10^{38} - 1$ to -10^{38}	2 to 17
float(precision)		Machine-dependent	4 or 8
double precision		Machine-dependent	8
real		Machine dependent	4
smallmoney		214,748.3647 to −214,748.3648	4
money		9,223,772,036,854,775,807 to −9,223,772,036,854,775,808	8
smalldatetime		January 1, 1900 to June 6, 2079	4
datetime		January 1, 1990 to December 31, 9999	8
char(n)	character	≤ 255 characters	*n*
varchar(n)	character varying, char varying	≤ 255 characters	Actual entry length
nchar(n)	national character, national char	≤ 255 characters	*n** @@nchar size
nvarchar(n)	nchar varying, national char varying, national character, varying	≤ 255 characters	@@nchar size* number of characters

Data type	Synonyms	Range	Bytes of storage
text(n)		$\leq 2^{31} - 1$ (2,147,483,647) bytes	0 or multiple of 2K (4K on Stratus)
binary(n)		≤ 255 bytes	*n*
varbinary		≤ 255 bytes	Actual entry length
image		$\leq 2^{31} - 1$ (2,147,483,647) bytes	0 or multiple of 2K (4K on Stratus)
bit		0 or 1	*1*

CT-Library API Calls

Function	Description
ct_bind	Binds server results to program variables
ct_br_column	Retrieves information about a column generated by a browse-mode SELECT
ct_bt_table	Returns information about browse-mode tables
ct_callback	Installs or retrieves a Client-Library callback routine
ct_cancel	Cancels a command or the results of a command
ct_capability	Sets or retrieves a client/server capability
ct_close	Closes a server connection
ct_cmd_alloc	Allocates a CS_COMMAND structure
ct_cmd_drop	Deallocates a CS_COMMAND structure
ct_cmd_props	Sets or retrieves command structure properties
ct_command	Initiates a language, package, RPC, message, or send-data command
ct_compute_info	Returns computed result information
ct_con_alloc	Allocates a CS_CONNECTION structure
ct_con_drop	Deallocates a CS_CONNECTION structure
ct_con_props	Sets or retrieves connection structure properties
ct_config	Sets or retrieves context properties
ct_connect	Connects to a server
ct_cursor	Initiates a cursor command
ct_data_info	Defines or retrieves a data I/O descriptor structure
ct_debug	Manages debug library operations
ct_describe	Returns a description of result data
ct_diag	Manages in-line error handling
ct_dynamic	Initiates a prepared dynamic SQL statement command

Function	Description
ct_dyndes	Performs operations on a dynamic SQL descriptor area
ct_exit	Exits Client-Library
ct_fetch	Fetches results data
ct_get_data	Reads a chunk of data from the server
ct_getformat	Returns the server user-defined format string associated with a results column
ct_getloginfo	Transfers TDS log-in response information from a CS_CONNECTION structure to a newly allocated CS_LOGINFO structure
ct_init	Initializes Client-Library
ct_keydata	Specifies or extracts the contents of a key column
ct_options	Sets or retrieves the values of server options
ct_param	Defines a command parameter
ct_poll	Polls connections for asynchronous operation completions and registered procedure notifications
ct_recvpassthru	Retrieves a TDS packet from a server
ct_remote_pwd	Defines or clears passwords to be used for server-to-server connections
ct_res_info	Returns result set information
ct_results	Sets up result data to be processed
ct_send	Sends a command to the server
ct_send_data	Sends a chunk of text or image data to the server
ct_sendpassthru	Sends a TDS packet to a server
ct_setloginfo	Transfers TDS log-in information from a CS_LOGINFO structure to a CS_CONNECTION structure
ct_wakeup	Calls a connection's completion callback

Command
allocdump(dbid | dbname, page)
allocmap(dbid, one_all, allocpg, bit_stat)
bhash(cname [, { print_bufs | no_print }, bucket_limit])
bufcount [(num_chains [, cache_name])]
buffer [(dbid | dbname [, objid | objname [, nbufs [, printopt = { 0 | 1 | 2 } [, buftype = { kept | hashed | nothashed | ioerr } [, cachename]]]]])
bytes(startaddress, length)
checkalloc [(dbname [, fix | nofix])]
checkcatalog [(dbname)]
checkdb [(dbname [, skip_ncindex])]
checktable({table_name | table_id} [, skip_ncindex])
dbinfo([dbname])
dbrecover(dbname)
dbrepair(dbname, option = { dropdb | fixindex | fixsysindex }, table, indexid)
dbtable(dbid)
delbuff(dbid | dbname, pageid [, flushdirty = { 0 | 1 | 2}[, lock = {0 | 1 | 2} [, cache_name]]])
delete_row (dbid | dbname, pageno, delete_type, row_num | offset) delete_type can be 'row' or 'offset'
des([dbid][, objid])
engine(online | offline)
engine(net, migrateon | migrateoff)
engine(net, {showall | show} [, engine_number])
extentchain(dbid, objid, indexid, sort, display [, order])
extentcheck(dbid, objid, indexid, sort = {0 | 1})
extentdump(dbid, page)

Command

---

extentzap(dbid, objid, indexid, sort)

findnotfullextents(dbid, objid, indexid, sort = {0|1})

fix_text({table_name | table_id})

gettrunc

help(dbcc_command)

ind(dbid, objid, printopt = { 0 | 1 | 2 })

indexalloc(tablename | tabid, indid, [full | optimized | fast], [fix | nofix])

listoam(dbid, objid, indid)

locateindexpgs(dbid, objid, page, indexid, level)

lock

log([dbid][,objid][,page][,row][,nrecords][,type]{−1..36}],printopt = {0|1})

logtransfer

memusage

monitor(action, group | all, [on | off])

newalloc [(dbname)]

page(dbid | dbname, pagenum [, printopt = {0|1|2} [, cache = {0|1} [, logical = {0|1} [, cachename | −1]]]])

pglinkage(dbid | dbname, start, number, printopt = {0|1|2}, target, order = {1|0})

procbuf(dbid, objid, nbufs, printopt = { 0 | 1 })

prtipage(dbid, objid, indexid, indexpage)

pss (suid, spid, printopt = { 1 | 0 })

rebuildextents(dbid, objid, indexid)

rebuild_log(dbname, rebuild, all)

reindex({ table_name | table_id })

report_al [(dbname)]

resource

save_rebuild_log(dbname)

showbucket(db_id, page, lookup_type)

showtext(cache_name, db_id | dbname, pageid, text | image)

tab(dbid, objid, printopt = { 0 | 1 | 2 })

tablealloc(tablename | tabid, [full | optimized | fast], [fix | nofix])

traceoff(tracenum [, tracenum...])

traceon(tracenum [, tracenum...])

tune(parameter_name, parameter_value [, table|index_name])

usedextents(dbid | dbname, type = { 0 | 1 }, display_opts = { 0 | 1 } [, bypiece = { 0 | 1 }])

Suggested Publications

- *SYBASE and Client/Server Computing,* by Alex Berson and George Anderson (McGraw-Hill, New York)
- *Client/Server Architecture,* by Alex Berson (McGraw-Hill, New York)
- *SQL Forum Journal,* Fremont, CA
- *Database Programming & Design*
- *Advanced Computer Architecture,* by Richard Y. Kain (Prentice-Hall, New York)
- *Microprocessor Architectures,* by Steve Heath (Butterworth-Heinemann, New York)
- *SYBASE System Administration Guide*
- *SYBASE System Administration Guide Supplement*
- *SYBASE SQL Server Reference Manual, vols. 1 and 2*
- *SYBASE SQL Server Troubleshooting Guide*

I

C. J. Date's Distributed Database Rules

In 1987, C. J. Date, one of the first designers of relational databases (together with Dr. E. F. Codd, the author of the relational theory), proposed 12 rules that a fully distributed database management system (DDBMS) should follow. These rules do not represent absolute requirements. They had been proposed only to bring some clarity to the ever-heated debates on DDBMS. However, C. J. Date's rules have become widely accepted as the working definition set and the criteria of a distributed database.

Rule 1: Local Autonomy

The first rule defines the DDBMS requirement for local autonomy. The rule states that in a truly distributed database environment, the sites (DBMS locations) should be autonomous, or independent of one another. This rule assumes that each site where a distributed database resides is characterized by the following:

- A local database is processed by its own database management system.
- The DBMS at every site handles the security, data integrity, data consistency, locking, and recovery for its own database.
- Local data access operations use only local resources (e.g., local DBMS).
- Even though each site is independent of other sites for local operations, all sites cooperate in accessing distributed data from multiple sites in one transaction.

Rule 2: No Reliance on a Central Site

Date's second rule is designed to complement the first rule. The second rule states that the truly distributed database system should not rely on a central site. It means that no one DBMS site (DBMS server) is more important and necessary than any other.

This rule dictates that a distributed DBMS environment not be built to rely on one (and only one) particular site. Otherwise, such an arrangement could cause this central site to become the bottleneck for the system throughput and performance. Also, one central site may become a single point of failure for the entire distributed system.

Date's second rule is sometimes misinterpreted to mean that a distributed DBMS should not have a central site even from the point of view of global control. On the contrary, even the example of a two-phase commit in a distributed transaction environment illustrates that there exists a need for a "central" coordinator to manage the distributed commit process. This "logical" central point may exist only for the duration of the distributed transaction, but exist it must.

Rule 3: Continuous Operations

The third rule specifies that the distributed database management system must never require downtime. The rule means that no planned database activity, including backing up and/or recovering databases, should require a distributed system shutdown.

Technically, continuous operations in the distributed database environment can be implemented by such DDBMS features as

- Support for full and incremental (the data that has changed since the last backup) *on-line* backup and archiving. In other words, each database server should be able to back up its databases on line, while processing other transactions.

- Support for fast (preferably, on-line) database recovery. One way of speeding the recovery is to keep a mirror image of the database available. Some database servers have a disk mirroring feature implemented in their hardware architecture. Some DBMSs implement software disk mirroring, thus providing DBMS fault resistance.

- Support for DBMS fault tolerance. Fault-tolerant DBMSs usually require fault-tolerant hardware.

Rule 4: Data Location Independence

This rule describes a highly desirable, even critical feature of a truly distributed database system. The rule defines a distributed environment where data is distributed among multiple sites, but users and applications are not aware of the fact that the data is distributed, and should not need to know where the data is.

Instead, a truly distributed DBMS that satisfies Date's fourth rule provides users and applications with a single image of the database, "local" to the user or application in its appearance and behavior. Therefore, the fourth rule is sometimes called the rule of *data location transparency*. In a client/server architecture, where a client application is typically remote to the DBMS server, support for the data location independence rule is extremely important.

That's where the data dictionary or directory plays a critical role. To implement data location transparency, designers of the distributed DBMS could use the following approach:

- Users and applications refer to data by its aliases.

- The distributed data dictionary or directory must maintain a table of data elements, their aliases, and their locations.

- The distributed DBMS must be able to automatically maintain and use this data dictionary, even when a particular data object has been moved from one location to another.

- In order for every user and application to perceive the distributed database as a single local database, the DDBMS must distribute (replicate) the data dictionary or directory to every site and maintain all replicas of the data dictionary or directory synchronized among all distributed system locations.

Many DBMS vendors today implement at least some degree of data location transparency by supporting remote requests and remote transactions that use different variations of the data dictionary or directory approach.

Rule 5: Data Fragmentation Independence

Date's fifth rule says that in a truly distributed database, a table that has been fragmented must appear as a single table to users and to applications. In other words, the fragmentation must be transparent to the users and applications.

Data fragmentation transparency is closely related to Date's fourth rule on data location transparency. However, if the data location transparency rule deals mostly with such objects as databases and tables, data fragmentation transparency applies when a single table is broken into several portions, each of which resides at a different site.

The difficulty of supporting data fragmentation transparency lies in the way the original table can be reconstructed from the fragments. A typical access to fragmented data may require the "logical" combination of data from two fragments into one unfragmented table.

When data from one table is distributed by fragmentation, data access to fragments may require conceptual table reconstruction. Depending on the type of fragmentation (vertical or horizontal), the operation that the application may request from the DDBMS can be a join of two tables. Horizontally fragmented tables may be reconstructed by using an SQL UNION operation.

Data fragmentation transparency requires the implementation of data location transparency in the context described above. But just using data dictionary or directory is not sufficient to implement data fragmentation transparency. Regardless of the type of data fragmentation, access to fragmented data may require data from multiple locations within a single transaction. The data access may be a distributed transaction or a distributed request. And that is in addition to the need to synchronize distributed database dictionaries!

Distributed transactions and distributed requests present several serious problems, among them the coordination of distributed updates, distributed data integrity, and consistency. Several DBMS products offer a degree of support for data fragmentation transparency. Among these products, Sybase's OmniSQL offers an interesting approach to data fragmentation.

Rule 6: Data Replication Independence

Date's sixth rule expands the data location and fragmentation transparency requirements into the data distribution method of replication. The rule requires a distributed database system to be capable of updating replicated, redundant data transparently from applications and users.

As the name implies, replicated data is a copy of data that exists elsewhere in the system (at other servers and even at some clients). Since the replicated data is one of the types of distributed data, Date's sixth rule requires the implementation of the data location transparency rule. But the data replication transparency rule has far-reaching implications.

As a result of adhering to Date's sixth rule, the DDBMS is becoming ever more complex and must perform increasingly involved, complicated tasks. Look at the task of adding records to the replicated table, for instance. Inserting rows will cause the DDBMS to enforce referential integrity constraints in a distributed environment, where multiple copies of the foreign keys must be checked against multiple copies of the primary key.

Another complicated issue is locking. Locking is the technique that a DBMS uses to support the consistency of data. While one transaction is updating a particular record or a group of records, the data being updated is held by an exclusive lock, i.e., is locked from updates (and sometimes also from read access in order to prevent the view of the inconsistent, "dirty" data) by any other transaction. In a distributed environment, where multiple replicas are to be updated, how should a DDBMS ensure that all copies of a given record are locked in every data location?

And when two or more applications wish to exercise exclusive control over the same resources, such as database records that are already locked by these or other applications, these applications are in a deadlock. The DDBMS must resolve the deadlock condition, even though the locked resources reside in multiple remote nodes. Global deadlock detection is a serious problem that the truly distributed database system should be capable of solving. Typically, a DDBMS detects and resolves deadlocks by keeping a timer and terminating a transaction that timed out waiting for a resource. In addition, some DDBMS products maintain a fixed, limited number of requests active at any given time in the system. Sometimes, a DDBMS employs a deadlock detection algorithm (e.g., terminate or interrupt shortest-running task, or terminate a task with fewer updates).

The complexity of the data replication synchronization forced database vendors to look for alternative solutions. In addition, the business requirements of many organizations make the synchronous nature of the two-phase commit protocol unacceptable for a number of applications. Instead, many business requirements give a higher priority to the need for a guaranteed delivery of data. Therefore, an alternative approach to data replication, suitable for the business applications where the integrity of the replicas can be supported on the asynchronous, guaranteed-delivery basis, attracted a lot of attention. This innovative approach is successfully pioneered by Sybase's Replication Server.

Rule 7: Distributed Query Processing

Date's seventh rule deals with the performance issues of the distributed database system. Performance becomes a major issue in *distributed* query processing. The seventh rule says that in a truly distributed database system, the optimization must take into account not only local but also global factors, including distributed nodes and network characteristics.

Rule 8: Distributed Transaction Management

Date's rule 8 is intended to provide data consistency, integrity, concurrency, and recovery in a distributed database system. Updating a distributed database introduces a new set of complicated problems.

Two-phase commit allows a COMMIT / ROLLBACK process to be implemented in a distributed environment (distributed COMMIT and distributed ROLLBACK). In essence, the two-phase commit protocol supports the atomicity, consistency, and durability of database transactions in a distributed environment. By supporting consistent rollback, the two-phase commit protocol also supports distributed database recovery from a transaction failure. However, the two-phase commit protocol requires a coordination of efforts between all participating parties during the PREPARE and COMMIT phases of the process. The synchronization task is assigned to a transaction coordinator. A distributed data manager (DDM), often acts as a coordinator.

In business, it is not always enough that the DDM can support the two-phase commit protocol. This support ideally should be intelligent and automatic, and it should guarantee that the proper actions (COMMIT and/or ROLLBACK) will take place automatically on all protected resources of a distributed transaction, without user or application intervention. Some DDBMS vendors support an automatic two-phase commit protocol, while others offer a set of commands and procedures that allows applications and users to implement a two-phase commit protocol manually.

The distributed commit is not the only problem that transaction management has to solve in a distributed environment. Among other issues are distributed locking, deadlock detection, local backup and global recovery, logging, administration, and security. Each one represents a complex DDBMS design problem in itself.

The difficulty of distributed transaction management and the large potential scope of the distributed transaction processing resulted in the emergence of the transaction management products developed by non-DBMS vendors. Indeed, if a distributed transaction involves resources other than DBMS-managed data, the distributed transaction manager is required to guarantee the integrity and synchronization of all protected resources. In addition, production-strength mainframe-based on-line transaction processing has demonstrated that the overall transaction processing management, availability, and robustness will benefit if the transaction management is separated from the DBMS code. Products such as IBM's family of CICS products, Encina from Transarc, and Top End from AT&T/NCR offer distributed transaction management solutions, running on a variety of hardware and software platforms and supporting a number of relational DBMSs via a set of standard interfaces such as the XA and ATMI standards from X/Open.

Hardware, software, networks, and DBMS independence. Satisfying the desire for database management systems to work interdependently across networks is complicated by the fact that computing environments are increasingly heterogeneous. The next four of Date's rules—rules 9, 10, 11, and 12—deal with the heterogeneous nature of distributed systems. These rules say that a truly distributed database system must not depend on underlying hardware platforms, operating systems, networks, and even individual database management systems. The aim of the last four rules is to support the goals of open systems by allowing the implementation of distributed database systems in practically any networking environment, including existing networks, databases, and equipment.

Rule 9: Hardware Independence

Date's ninth rule states that distributed database systems must be able to run on different hardware platforms with all systems able to participate as equal partners. This rule allows designers to build a distributed environment that can consist of the computer systems from different vendors and different hardware architectures. This rule is essential to developers of client/server computing systems. The rule actually reinforces the notion of client and server specialization. And it is easy to picture a distributed database (e.g., Oracle) in a client/server environment, where the client B1 is an Intel-based personal computer, server S1 is a RISC-based machine (e.g., IBM's RS/6000), server S2 is a symmetric multiprocessor (SMP) from Sun Microsystems, and server S3 is an IBM mainframe. This is not at all unusual. Therefore, many DDBMS vendors (e.g., Oracle, Sybase, Informix, Ingres) support Date's ninth rule by providing the DDBMS support for a wide variety of hardware platforms.

Rule 10: Operating System Independence

Date's rule 10 supplements and expands rule 9. The rule allows DDBMS designers to choose the hardware platform and at the same time not to be limited by a single operating system. Adherence to rule 9 by itself does not guarantee support for multiple operating systems. This rule can be supported by selecting a DDBMS solution designed according to international and industrywide standards, i.e., designed to operate in an open systems environment.

Today, the marketplace offers DDBMS solutions designed for a particular operating system (e.g., IBM's DB2 for MVS, DB2/6000 for AIX, DB2/2 for OS/2, Microsoft's Advanced SQL Server for Windows NT), as well as solutions for various implementations of the Unix operating system (e.g., Sybase, Informix, Ingres, Oracle). The client/server environment shown in Chapter 7 (Fig. 7.4) supports both rule 9 and rule 10. Indeed, the Oracle DBMS shown here runs under MS/DOS, Unix, and MVS.

Rule 11: Network Independence

Date's rule 11 supplements rules 9 and 10 by adding a requirement for the DDBMS not to depend on a particular network implementation and protocols. This rule is natural for any distributed network environment, especially a client/server environment. Adherence to the standards (OSI, ANSI, IEEE) allows many DDBMS vendors to support rule 11.

Rule 12: DBMS Independence

Date's rules, discussed up to this point, have been implicitly applied to distributed database systems where every node was supporting a "like," homogeneous DBMS. In other words, the intention of rules 1 through 11 appears to be to transform an existing database system (such as DB2, Oracle) to a truly distributed DBMS. In fact, most DDBMS implementations available today support some of Date's rules only in a homogeneous DBMS environment.

Date's rule 12 expands the horizons of homogeneous data access by specifying that a truly distributed database must be able to interoperate with different kinds of databases, regardless of whether the DBMSs are from the same vendor.

The variation of homogeneous data access that satisfies rule 12 is a distributed environment where not all databases are the same, but all support a common data model—the relational data model—via a common, standardized data access language—Structured Query Language. In fact, the data management middleware products like Microsoft's ODBC are designed specifically to satisfy Date's rule 12.

From the data management perspective, the implementation of a heterogeneous DRDBMS environment is not a simple task. The SQL standard is still emerging. Not every RDBMS vendor supports the currently available version of the SQL standard in full. Every RDBMS vendor implements its product differently, with different name lengths, different return codes, and proprietary SQL extensions.

The situation becomes even more complicated when legacy nonrelational data is brought into the picture. Indeed, the real world is much more complicated than a single, homogeneous, or strictly relational DBMS environment.

A business enterprise may adopt the MS DOS/Windows operating system and an Oracle DBMS for its client platform; Oracle and Sybase DBMSs for the Unix-based servers; DB2, IMS, IDMS, and VSAM for the mainframe MVS platform. In fact, the majority of data today usually resides in legacy databases and files (i.e., IMS, IDMS, VSAM). This is true for many IBM and compatible mainframe sites. The problem of implementing a distributed DBMS in such an environment is complicated by the fact that each local DBMS "speaks" its own data access language, and so the translation of an SQL query, e.g., to a hierarchical IMS data access is not a trivial task. Sometimes, it simply cannot be done without rewriting a query, or an entire application.

Driven by the real business need of heterogeneous data access, various middleware solutions from DBMS vendors are now emerging to address this issue. Almost every RDBMS vendor provides access to IBM's DB2 as well as to its own RDBMS (for example, by building DB2 mainframe gateways utilizing Advanced Program-to-Program Communications protocol). Providing access to heterogeneous distributed data further complicates distributed DBMS issues of data integrity, locking, administration, and security. Notwithstanding the difficulties of heterogeneous data access, however, it is easy to see that support of Date's rule 12 is a real business requirement for the truly distributed database system. The key to such a solution will be support for the industry data access standards (Remote Data Access from the ISO, SQL from ISO, SQL Access Group and ANSI, XA Interfaces from X/Open), and the maturity of various middleware solutions.

Sybase position.   Sybase provides interoperability with other database management systems via its suite of gateways and Open Server products. By acquiring Micro DecisionWare, Sybase has expanded its list of interoperable platforms and database management systems even further. In addition, Sybase goes beyond pure DBMS-to-DBMS interoperability by allowing access not only to the "foreign" DBMS, but also to a well-established OLTP environment—IBM CICS and, by extension, all CICS-accessible resources.

SQL Server Trace Flags

SQL Server can be started with several special-purpose trace flags. The administrator should only start SQL Server with a trace flag at the direction of Sybase technical support or an EBF letter. Use of these flags at any other time can cause serious problems.

These trace flags are an *undocumented* feature of SYBASE technology and may *not* be supported by Sybase technical support.

Trace flag	Description
−1	Turns off all previously enabled trace flags; System 11 only
200	Before image of query tree
201	After image of query tree
260	Prevent "done in proc" messages
302	Information on index selection
310	Information on join selection
315	Prints out join and SARG structures
317	Complete (voluminous) information on join selection
318	Forces reformatting
319	Prints information about reformatting
320	Turns off join-order heuristic
699	Turns off transaction logging for the SQL Server (only essential logging is performed)
1200	Prints out process ID and type of lock requested
1204	Prints out deadlock chains and victim in simple language
1205	Prints out stack traces of deadlocked PIDs; used in conjunction with trace flag 1204
1603	Uses only standard Unix calls for disk I/O

Trace flag	Description
1604	Traces memory initialization at start-up
1605	Turns off debug symbol table loading at start-up time
1606	Enables a debug engine to be put on line
1608	Does not automatically put engines on line
1610	Disables TCP/IP packet batching
1611	Locks shared memory into physical memory (NCR, DG, SGI, SCO Unix).
2512	Bypasses *syslogs* table when doing DBCC CHECKALLOC
3300	Displays each log record as it is processed by recovery (voluminous)
3304	Displays buffers as resource locks are released whenever an index split or shrink backout concludes
3307	Prints process ID waiting for a resource lock when in index split or shrink backout.
3402	Does an allocation upgrade during load DB recovery
3500	Does not do any checkpoints
3604	DBCC output to screen
3605	DBCC output to error log
3607	Does not recover any database, clear *tempdb,* or start-up checkpoint
3608	Recovers the *master* database only, does not clear *tempdb* or start up checkpoint
3609	Recovers all databases; does not clear *tempdb* or start up checkpoint
3620	Does not kill infected processes
3701	Allows dropping and creating of system indexes (use with caution)
4000	Crash server at next loop for recovery testing
4001	Displays log-in structures
4006	Dumps out buffer information after every command
4012	Boots without starting up a checkpoint process
4013	Places a record in the error log each time someone logs into SQL Server
4014	Checks allocation buffer pool in PSS for buffers still held
4020	Boots without recovery
5101	Engine 0 performs all network and disk I/O
5102	Prevents engine 0 from running nonaffinitied tasks
7810	Disables MNE when server boots (System 11)
8101	Disables chargeback accounting (VAX only)
8399	Enables descriptive names for groups (used with DBCC MONITOR interface)

ACB	Application control block or access (method) control block
AEI	Application-enabling interface
AFS	Andrew file system
AIX	Advanced Interactive eXecutive
ANDF	Architecture-neutral distribution format
ANSI	American National Standards Institute
API	Application programming interface
APPC	Advanced Program-to-Program Communications
APPN	Advanced Peer-to-Peer Networking
AR	Application Requester (in DRDA)
AS	Application Server (in DRDA)
AS/400	Application System/400
ATM	Asynchronous transfer mode
BCP	Bulk Copy Program
BIU	Basic information unit
BLOB	Binary large object
BSC	Binary synchronous communications
CCITT	Consultative Committee of International Telephone and Telegraph
CDDL	Copper distributed data link
CDRA	Character data representation architecture
CDS	Cell directory services
CICS	Customer Control Information System, a teleprocessing and transaction system which runs a VTAM application
CICS	Complex-instruction-set computing

CLI	Call-level interface
CMIP	Common management interface protocol
CNM	Communication network management
COM	Component Object Model (Microsoft), Common Object Model (Digital)
CORBA	Common Object Request Broker Architecture
COS	Class of service
CP	Control point
CSMA/CA	Carrier Sense Multiple Access/Collision Avoidance
CSMA/CD	Carrier Sense Multiple Access/Collision Detection
DB2	Database 2 (IBM)
DBCC	Database Consistency Checker
DBMS	Database management system
DCE	Distributed computing environment
DDF	Distributed data facility
DDL	Data definition language
DDM	Distributed data management
DFC	Data flow control (layer)
DFS	Distributed file system
DIA	Document interchange architecture
DLC	Data link control (layer)
DLL	Dynamic link library
DLR	Dynamic link routine
DME	Distributed management environment
DML	Data manipulation language
DNA	Digital Network Architecture
DS	Database server
DSI	Data Server Interface
DSOM	Distributed system object model
DTP	Distributed transaction processing
DUW	Distributed unit of work
EBCDIC	Extended Binary-Coded Decimal Interchange Code
ECB	Event control block
EHLLAPI	Emulator High-Level Language Application Programming Interface
FCS	Fiber channel standard
FDDI	Fiber distributed data interface
FD:OCA	Formatted Data Object Content Architecture

FMH	Function management header
FR	Frame relay
FSM	Finite-state machine
FTP	File transfer protocol
GDS	General data stream
GUI	Graphical user interface
ICCM	Interclient Communications Conventions Manual
ICF	Intercommunication function
IPC	Interprocess communication
ISC	Intersystem communication
ISDN	Integrated services digital network
ISQL	Interactive Structured Query Language (SYBASE)
ISV	Independent software vendor
LAN	Local-area network
LR	Logical record
LS	Link station
LU	Logical unit
LUW	Logical unit of work
LU6.2	Logical unit type 6.2
MAN	Metropolitan-area network
MAPI	Mail API
MAP/TOP	Manufacturing automation protocol/technical and office protocol
MCA	Microchannel adapter
MDA	Multidimensional analysis
MDI	Multiple-document interface
MFC	Microsoft foundation class
MIMD	Multiple-instruction multiple-data
MIPS	Millions of instructions per second
MLFLOPS	Millions of floating-point instructions per second
MNE	Multiple-network engine
MPP	Massively Parallel Processor
MRO	Multiregion operation
NAU	Network addressable unit
NCP	Network control program
NFS	Network file system
NLM	NetWare loadable module
NOS	Network operating system

ODBC	Open database connectivity
OLCP	On-line complex processing
OLE	Object linking and embedding
OLTP	On-line transaction processing
ONC	Open Network Computing
ORB	Object Request Broker
OSF	Open Software Foundation
OSI	Open systems interconnection
OS/2	(IBM) Operating System/2
PM	(OS/2) Presentation Manager
POSIX	Portable operating system interface
PROFS	Professional office system
PU	Physical unit
PWS	Programmable workstation
RAS	Reliability, availability, and serviceability (programs)
RDA	Remote data access
RDBMS	Relational database management system
RISC	Reduced-instruction-set computing
RPC	Remote procedure call
RPL	Remote program link
RSI	Replication Server interface
RSM	Replication Server Manager
RSSD	Replication Server system database
RUW	Remote unit of work
SAA	Systems Application Architecture (IBM)
SCSI	Small computer system interface
SDLC	Synchronous data link control
SIMD	Single-instruction multiple-data
SLU	Secondary logical unit
SMP	Symmetric multiprocessing
SMTP	Simple mail transfer protocol
SNA	System network architecture
SNADS	Systems Network Architecture Distributed Services
SNMP	Simple network management protocol
SOM	System object model
SQL	Structured Query Language
SRPI	Server-Requestor programming interface
SVID	Unix System V interface definitions

SVR4	Unix System V Release 4
TCOS	Technical Committee on Open Systems
TCP/IP	Transmission Control Protocol/Internet Protocol
TP	Transaction program
TPM	Transaction processing manager
TPS	Transactions per second
TSO	Timesharing option
UI	Unix International
UOW	Unit of work
VAN	Value-added network
VIM	Vendor independent messaging
VIS	Visual instruction set
VLDB	Very large database
VM/SP	Virtual machine/system product
VR	Virtual route
VTAM	Virtual Telecommunications Access Method
WAN	Wide-area network
WOSA	Windows Open Services architecture
XPG4	*X/Open Portability Guide,* issue 4
XRF	Extended recovery facility

L

Log Record Types

Log record type	Description
alloc	Allocate another page.
alloc extent—mark pages used	Reserve space for an object.
alloc for new page of split	Request made to get more space for a page split.
alter database	An ALTER DATABASE command was issued.
beginxact	Beginning of a transaction.
checkpoint	A checkpoint occurred in the database.
deallocate page	Used to mark a page for deallocation; page has been released to free space.
dealloc extent	Used to mark an extent for deallocation.
deferred insert text	Text is logged and optionally rolled back (e.g., for Replication Server).
delete	Delete a row in the table.
delete text log record	Text is logged and optionally rolled back.
direct change to *sysindexes*	Used to log a change to the *sysindexes* table—for performance reasons, this algorithm is different from the one for user pages.
direct insert text	Text inserted (WRITETEXT command).
dnoop	Flags a row to be deleted later.
endxact	End of a transaction.
extent	Allocate another extent (8 pages).
idelete	Delete from an index.
iinsert	Insert into an index.
indirect log insert	Indirect log insert.
inoop	Flag a row to be inserted later.
insert	Insert a row in the table.
insind	Indirect insert.

Log record type	Description
modify	When applied to a user table, an update in place; otherwise, used to indicate a change to an allocation page.
noop	Flag a row to be changed.
savexact	Used to indicate a save point in a transaction.
sort dealloc	The complement to *sort record*; sort pages are deallocated.
sort record	Pages used for sorts such as index builds.
split	Page or index page split.

Index

About the Author

George W. Anderson (Long Beach, New York) has more than 10 years of experience in information technology as an independent consultant. He specializes in distributed computing architecture and high-performance computing. He has implemented several large distributed client/server databases and is coauthor of *SYBASE and Client/Server Computing*, also published by McGraw-Hill.